7

Mennonites in Canada, 1920-1940

A People's Struggle for Survival

Frank H. Epp

Macmillan of Canada
A Division of Gage Publishing Limited
Toronto, Canada

Canadian Cataloguing in Publication Data

Epp, Frank H., date
    Mennonites in Canada, 1920-1940

Bibliography: p.
Includes index.
ISBN 0-7715-9708-8

1. Mennonites—Canada—History.   I. Title.

FC106.M45E66   289.7'71   C82-094222-7
BX8118.5.E663

Endpaper maps and charts by A. E. Hildebrand

The publishers gratefully acknowledge the assistance of
the Mennonite Historical Society of Canada and the
Multiculturalism Program, Government of Canada,
in making the publication possible.

Macmillan of Canada
A Division of Gage Publishing Limited

Printed in Canada

Contents

iii

List of Tables

vi

List of Charts

Author's Acknowledgements

THE WRITING of this first general history of all Mennonites in Canada was initiated in 1967, the year of Canada's centennial, with the modest goal of accomplishing the task with a single volume. However, the unfolding of a fascinating, sometimes complex, and occasionally powerful history could not easily be contained, and we now know that even this second volume will not be the last one.

History is the recollection and interpretation of a heritage. It is also a reminder of human indebtedness, in my case not only to those who made history and laid life's foundations for me and my generation but also to those, an ever-growing number, who helped to write this history, and without whom it would not have been possible.

Gratefully I acknowledge the financial support of the Social Sciences and Humanities Research Council, the Mennonite Historical Society of Canada and its funding sources (various Mennonite conferences and the Mennonite Central Committee (Canada)), the Dr. David Friesen Family Foundation, the P. W. Enns Family

Foundation, and Peter Redekop. The University of Waterloo and Conrad Grebel College provided computing grants.

I acknowledge also the special assistance of T. D. Regehr, well-known Canadian historian and, during this project, President of the Mennonite Historical Society of Canada, and of Lyle Friesen, a congenial research colleague for two years. Others who assisted were research assistants and special contributors, manuscript critics and proofreaders, historical society members, treasurers and fund-raisers, a cartographer and technical advisors, stenographers and computer clerks, and, last but not least, all the members of my immediate family, as well as the truly professional people at Macmillan of Canada. I name them all to thank them all: Miriam Jantzi Bauman, Pauline Bauman, Wesley Berg, Lorna Bergey, Glenn Brubacher, Marianne Coleman, Edward Dahl, Ernie Dick, Arthur Driedger, Leo Driedger, Abe Dueck, Adolf Ens, Helen Epp, Marlene Epp, Esther Epp-Thiessen, David Fransen, Leonard Freeman, J. W. Fretz, Bert Friesen, Louella Friesen, Ted Friesen, Douglas Gibson, Herbert Giesbrecht, Orland Gingerich, George Groening, A. E. Hildebrand, Anne Holloway, Martin Holmberg, William Janzen, Larry Kehler, Lawrence Klippenstein, Fred Lichti, Harry Loewen, Gerhard Lohrenz, Lloyd Mackey, Noah Martin, Vic Neglia, Ruth Peckover, G. I. Peters, Jake Peters, John Pope, Vern Ratzlaff, P. J. B. Reimer, Peter Rempel, Lorraine Roth, Rodney Sawatsky, Nelson Scheifele, Eleanor Sinclair, Sam Steiner, Ingrid Unruh, Paul Voegtlin, Linda Walker, Alson Weber, and Ruby Weber.

As well, there is an ongoing indebtedness to my readers and to future scholars, who, since every historical record has its imperfections, could assist me by sending me the kind of feedback which will help to improve future editions of this work.

Frank H. Epp
Conrad Grebel College
University of Waterloo
Ontario, Canada
June 30, 1982

Foreword

THE DOMINANT THEME of *Mennonites in Canada 1786 – 1920* (published in 1974) was the Mennonite search for a measure of separation from Canadian and other secular societies. In the present volume, the struggle to survive despite the failure to maintain the traditional physical or geographical separation becomes dominant.

In Canada, wartime passions and reforms made it impossible for the Mennonites to maintain the educational and cultural institutions which had enabled them to achieve a degree of physical separation from Canadian society. Consequently, in the 1920s, those Canadian Mennonites who still regarded such separation as essential for the preservation of their faith decided to leave Canada. At very considerable economic and social cost, they moved to Mexico or Paraguay when it became clear that provincial governments in Manitoba and Saskatchewan were determined to enforce educational "reforms" which were unacceptable to the Mennonites. They, however, were a minority, even among the Mennonites.

The majority of Canadian Mennonites tried to accommodate themselves to the new conditions of post-war Canada, but many had serious doubts about whether the distinctive features of their faith could survive and prosper without the safeguards of physical separation. Certainly, other safeguards and other institutions would have to be created to replace those destroyed by provincial reforms. Thus the Mennonite struggle to preserve some cherished nonconformist values against the onslaught of alien ideas and modes of life could be observed on many fronts. The disasters of the Great Depression of the 1930s further intensified the struggle for survival, adding economic concerns to those of culture and religion.

For other Mennonites, the struggle for survival in the 1920s and 1930s was even more desperate. During the war, Mennonite churches in Germany and Holland made old and venerable religious principles optional for their members, and many quickly flocked to the colours in the military defence of their fatherland. In Russia, where Mennonites had enjoyed exceptional privileges and achieved phenomenal successes, the war, revolution, and civil strife completely destroyed the social and economic viability of the Mennonite colonies. The colonists were faced with the harsh choice of immigration or forcible induction into an alien and hostile new reality under the Soviets. Survival, not separation, became the overriding concern of a people whose desperation rose to incredible intensity in these decades.

These experiences, while in some respects unique, had a great deal in common with the struggles of other peoples in all parts of the world. Certainly in Canada, Mennonites were only one of many minority groups who at times felt the survival of the things dear and precious to them was threatened. Each minority group tended to see itself as being alone, threatened by all the others. French-Canadian Catholics were often inclined to see all other Canadians as English Protestants, and certainly small groups such as Jehovah's Witnesses thought themselves a very small minority opposed by everyone else. In many Mennonite communities the *Englaender* (English) were all non-Mennonites, whether or not they knew any English. This history, therefore, reveals important aspects of Canadian history as well as specific details of Mennonite history.

It is well known that when war broke out again in 1939, the Canadian government was determined to avoid a crisis with the

French Canadians over the question of compulsory military service overseas. The French-Canadian objections to conscription were certainly not the same as those of the Mennonites to active military service, but the willingness of the Canadian government to accommodate both was rooted in a respect for minority groups unmatched by any other wartime government. The Mennonites are only one of many groups which make up the Canadian mosaic. Their struggles in the 1920s and 1930s are therefore relevant for anyone wishing to understand Canada better.

The writing of this volume, like Volume I, was sponsored by the Mennonite Historical Society of Canada. It was supported financially by the Social Science and Humanities Research Council, several Mennonite organizations, and private donors. Equally important, but less tangible, support has come from many interested readers and critics of the manuscript. This volume is intended to foster a better understanding not only of Canadian Mennonites, but also of the country in which, after struggling for years to survive, Mennonites have now found opportunities to participate actively and positively in virtually all aspects of community life.

T. D. Regehr
Professor of History
University of Saskatchewan
Saskatoon

Prologue

THE WORLD had survived the Great War (1914–1918), but peace did not bring with it a feeling of contentment or even a sense of security. On the contrary, in the words of Sir Robert Borden, Canada's wartime Prime Minister, "the world had drifted from its old anchorages and no man could with certainty prophesy what the outcome would be." The post-war international community was confronted by many problems, some of which the war had not solved and some of which the war had created. The war-to-end-all-wars did not end all wars. And before the twentieth century was half spent, the nuclear bombs of a second world-wide conflagration focused the survival question for the whole of humanity as never before.

The impact of the first total war just concluded was felt by the European states, their colonies, and other parts of the world, including the separated Mennonite world, for decades to come. The big revolution in Russia, which the war helped to precipitate, sent shock waves of its own around the globe, shaking old and new nations in ever-recurring quakes. Revolutions and counter-revolutions threatened the democracies with authoritarian forms of government, both of the left and of the right. Communism and fascism in turn stirred new rivalries, which the crumbling empires, the awakening colonies, and their distant allies could not escape.

Complicating the emergence of a secure international order were the world-wide economic dislocations of the 1930s, which accentuated political instabilities, class conflict, and extremist solutions. Slowly but surely, the world stage was set for more belligerency. And the international instruments created by the Peace of Versailles and the League of Nations were too weak, or their leaders too unwilling, to prevent the ensuing conflict.

The historical period framed by the two world wars was an age of displacement in every way. People by the tens of millions lost their homes and became refugees. The borders of nations and empires were adjusted as changing international realities required a massive redrawing of the maps. Old traditions and cultures were confronted and often swept aside by new political ideologies, social movements, and technologies. The advent of radio heralded the age of mass communication and the further invasion of minority cultures by the majorities.

These developments all had their international dimensions, but each national society mirrored the struggle for continuity in its own way. And within the nation-states themselves, smaller populations of all kinds were caught in the squeeze of contradictory forces at work. No groups, no matter how isolated or separated, could escape the big question of the century: the survival of humankind in general and of minorities and their values in particular. Canadianization, urbanization, and various reform movements were threatening the traditional cultures of ethnic and religious minorities alike.

In Canada, the problems of minority groups were complicated during this time by the country's own dilemmas, resulting partly from her own choices and partly from forces beyond her control. Should Canada be simply a British dominion or should she be a nation in her own right? If nationalism was the most logical direction, should that nationalism move Canada closer to, or further away from, the United States? Was international co-operation and interdependence the call of the hour or did the American idea of isolation hold the key to the Canadian future?

   Fundamental questions about basic political and economic directions remained unanswered, as Canada's internal confidence was
shaken repeatedly by many dashed hopes. The idea that the twentieth
century belonged to Canada was fast losing credibility for several
reasons. Canada's capacity to attract and keep immigrants was cast
into doubt by the large outflow to the United States and other
countries. The promises of the golden West were shattered when the
price of wheat fell temporarily from $2.32 per bushel in 1919 to 76
cents per bushel in 1921 and a low of less than 40 cents per bushel a
decade later. Low prices, moreover, were accompanied in the 1930s
by severe drought, dust storms, and great numbers of grasshoppers
throughout most of the prairie region. An accelerating move to the
cities was not only threatening rural values but also ushering in a new
class-consciousness, as had become evident in the Winnipeg strike.

   Intellectual leadership was not lacking during these critical times,
but achieving a popular consensus was quite another matter. There
was a turning away from the old political, social, economic, and
religious institutions and ideals which seemed unable to meet and
solve the problems of post-war Canada. None of the new ideas and
new movements, however, gained nation-wide majority support.
Clergymen spoke out boldly, but neither the convinced pacifists nor
the ardent nationalists were the leaders of majorities. Newspaper
editors, like the politicians, succumbed to parochialism in order to
survive or, as some believed, to follow the better course. Other
writers, as well as artists, commanded too little recognition and were
too poorly paid to have a national voice. And radio was preoccupied
with establishing itself as an institution, unsure whether to take its
cues from Britain or the United States.

   In this national and international situation the Mennonites tried to
find themselves and their future. Throughout their 400 years they
had sought to survive by separating themselves from the main
thoroughfares of the world and the power plays in the international
community. Yet separation and isolation were never complete or
entirely successful. The Mennonites were not spared the tribulations
of the wars and of the inter-war years. No place on earth, not in the
east and not in the west, not in the north and not in the south,
provided a seclusion sufficient to protect them from the storms of the
twentieth century, though many sought such a place of refuge with
diligence.

Thus, the Mennonites became a part of the struggle for survival in places and ways so diverse that they recorded a chapter quite unique in the history of the twentieth century. Canada was the setting and the focus for much of that history. The Mennonites found this country to be both a friend and an enemy in their struggle, one to which they fled with great eagerness and one which some left with equally great sadness. Perhaps it will surprise no one that a time of many troubles also gave rise to many different responses.

1. The Uncertain Future

*In the profound unsettlement of the first post-war years, the form
of the future was still largely hidden behind cloudy and angry
ambiguities; and all that seemed certain was that the old order had
been wrecked, the old conditions undermined, the old assumptions
contradicted* — DONALD CREIGHTON.[1]

THE GREAT WAR had changed irrevocably the order of
things and delivered an uncertain future not only for
Canada and the world but also for the Mennonite people.[2] Canada's
58,800 Mennonites[3] represented less than one per cent of that
country's population, but about 11 per cent of the total Mennonite
population around the world in 1921 (see Table 1). Canadian
Mennonites nevertheless became the focus of an intense struggle for
survival, both nationally and internationally, during the inter-war
period. From abroad came desperate calls for help from a beleaguered people facing the physical and spiritual calamities of the
Bolshevik revolution.[5] In Canada, the changing political, social, and
economic conditions represented external threats to the traditional
way of life. Internal weaknesses too, while not great enough to render
the Mennonites helpless, significantly impaired their ability to deal
effectively with the problems of the day.

Among the external and internal conditions essential to Mennonite
continuity some were more fundamental than others. Most of all,

1

TABLE 1[4]

SUMMARY OF WORLD MENNONITE MEMBERSHIP
(BY COUNTRY C.1920)

COUNTRY	NUMBER
Argentina	100
Belgian Congo	200
Canada	58,800
China	10,000
Danzig	5,000
France	4,000
Germany	9,000
India	20,000
Java/Sumatra	10,000
Netherlands	70,000
Poland	2,500
Switzerland	2,000
U.S.A.	202,500
U.S.S.R.	120,000
Total	514,100

Canadian Mennonites needed good land, much good land, for themselves and for their offspring in order to make a living but also to support a way of life. Yet the best lands available in Canada were already settled. Mennonites needed compact communities, but exclusive blocks of land available to them alone were gone forever in Canada, and settlement patterns generally militated against islands of separateness such as the Mennonites had once known.

Mennonites also needed tolerant laws, tolerant political leaders, and tolerant public opinion to support their way of life, but tolerance for Mennonite pacifists, many of them German-speaking, had been seriously undermined by the propaganda and the passions unleashed by the Great War with Germany. They needed to educate their own children in their own schools, but separate schools had fallen into disfavour, at least in the prairie provinces. They needed internal solidarity and a united front to withstand societal pressures and to maintain their nonconformist values, but the Mennonite community was everywhere divided and poorly prepared for the forces that increasingly demanded accommodation. On all of these fronts and others the times and circumstances were not the best.

While the total situation made for an uncertain future, the Mennonites were not without confidence and hope. Their religious roots were deep and their moral orientation remained strong. Some ethnic characteristics and cultural insularity contributed to cohesion and the desired separateness from unwanted influences. Their general reputation as good farmers and positive citizens, especially in Ontario, was in their favour, and some outsiders were willing to come to their defence. A very enduring linkage between them and the land had been established, and while the links could not easily be lengthened or multiplied the existing ones could not be broken.

The Need for Land

The availability of an abundance of land, preferably in parcels sufficiently large and compact to allow the formation of strong agricultural communities, was probably the most essential external condition for Mennonite continuity and the preservation of everything important to them. Such self-sufficient communities could sustain the Mennonite culture through the neighbourhood schools and nurture the Mennonite faith through the congregational fellowships. To be sure, not all Mennonites rated rural life equally high on the scale of values. While agriculture was considered essential by most, some only preferred it. Still others considered it marginal, and some business people and professionals had turned their backs on it. Generally speaking, however, there was a close correlation between Mennonite continuity and land-based community. It was as H. H. Ewert, the outstanding Mennonite educator of the day, said:

> The favourite occupation of Mennonites is farming. This suits their love for independence and their desire for leading a quiet life. City life they find too much exposed to all sorts of temptations.[6]

Mennonites, of course, were not alone in their rural base and outlook. In the 1921 census, about half of Canada's people — 50.5 per cent — were classed as rural, with rural people comprising 64 per cent of the population on the prairies.[7] Mennonites, on the other hand, were overwhelmingly rural. The most urbanized parts of their world were the Waterloo County area of Ontario and the West Reserve area of Manitoba. In both of these areas about 10 per cent of the population was urbanized, slightly more in Ontario and slightly less in Manitoba.[8] However, even the southern Manitoba Mennonite towns, like Altona and Winkler, here classed as urban,[9] really reflected the rural life and values of surrounding areas.

All of the Mennonite immigrants who had entered the country from 1786 to 1920, about 12,000 altogether, had done so as agriculturalists. Their ancestors had not all been farmers—there having been academics, professionals, craftsmen, and artisans among the sixteenth-century Anabaptist pioneers—but their repeated search for seclusion and security had always pointed in rural directions. Eventually, the Mennonite way of life had become identified as an agricultural way of life, first in various parts of Europe—the Netherlands represented a notable exception to this observation—and then in North America.[10]

The four movements of Mennonites into Canada (see Table 2) coincided with the settlement and agricultural development of the country. The first to arrive were approximately 2,000 Swiss-South German Mennonites (hereafter known as Swiss or SSG) who came to Upper Canada from Pennsylvania in the fifty years or so following the American Revolution. While they settled chiefly in the Niagara Peninsula and in the York and Waterloo counties,[12] small family groups did go farther afield so that by 1841 they were found in 30 townships, though 23 of these had fewer than 50 Mennonites each.[13] Second were the Amish, a Mennonite branch originating in Europe in the 1690s (hereafter frequently included with the Swiss), who arrived both from Europe directly and from Pennsylvania, attracted by an Upper Canada land grant designated the German Block in Wilmot township.[14] Beginning in 1824, these people too kept coming for about fifty years, though the total number did not exceed an average of about 15 a year.

As the Amish immigration was coming to an end, the Dutch-North German Mennonites (hereafter known as Dutch or DNG), began to arrive in Canada from Russia, where they had made their home since the end of the eighteenth century. They had moved to the land of the tsars from the Vistula Valley of Prussia, which had been their first permanent refuge from sixteenth-century persecution in the Netherlands. For 250 years they had lived in relative peace and

TABLE 2[11]

SUMMARY OF MENNONITE/AMISH MIGRATIONS TO CANADA
(1786–1920)

TIME PERIOD	ORIGIN	DESTINATION	NUMBER	CULTURE
1786–1836	Pennsylvania	Ontario	c. 2,000	SSG
1824–1874	Alsace Bavaria Pennsylvania	Ontario	c. 750	SSG
1874–1880	Russia	Manitoba	c. 7,000	DNG
1890–1920	U.S.A. Prussia Russia	Alberta British Columbia Manitoba Saskatchewan	c. 2,250	DNG/SSG
		Total	c. 12,000	

prosperity, but when the Prussian monarchs had increasingly seen fit to curtail religious liberty and economic opportunity, the Mennonites had responded positively to the invitation of Catherine the Great and her successors. The 10,000 original immigrants to Russia had increased to a population of nearly 60,000 by the 1870s. From 1874 to the close of the decade, about 7,000 immigrants transplanted the colony and village system from Russia to the East and West reserves of Manitoba, while another 11,000 chose Kansas and other midwestern American states. About 40,000 stayed in Russia.[15]

To these three basic migratory movements into Canada—the Swiss from Pennsylvania, the Amish from Alsace and Bavaria, and the Dutch from Russia—must be added a sequence of small immigrations in the three decades prior to 1920. These smaller movements involved an additional number of approximately 2,250 immigrants who arrived as individuals, family units, or small groups.[16]

Some came directly from Russia and Prussia. Most of them were people from the United States, once more seeking out the agricultural frontier. Some of these immigrants were of the Swiss Mennonite cultural family, descendants of the approximately 8,000 Swiss Mennonites who had arrived in America over a period of two centuries.[17] The majority were related to those 11,000 Dutch Mennonites who had made the American midwest their home following the emigration from Russia in the 1870s.[18]

A few of these American immigrants settled in Manitoba and British Columbia, but most took advantage of the homestead opportunities in the provinces of Alberta and Saskatchewan. At this point in time, Ontario Mennonites were exclusively of the Swiss variety including the Amish, and Manitoba and British Columbia Mennonites were exclusively of Dutch origin. Saskatchewan and Alberta represented a mixture, the Dutch being predominant in the former and the Swiss, at least for the time being, in the latter.

The land possessed by the immigrants—the farms of the German Land Company and the German Block in Ontario, the reserves in Manitoba and Saskatchewan, and homesteads in Alberta, British Columbia, and Saskatchewan—had been ploughed by them for the first time. Mennonite families were large and as the sons married, additional acreages were needed. This meant settlement farther afield already in the second generation. The Mennonite population had increased to 58,797 by 1921 (see Table 3), and the land areas under their control had likewise expanded.

The Ontario Mennonites had spread, however thinly, virtually throughout the province, although it was impossible to specify the exact location and compare the acreages held by them in the various districts. While 71 per cent of the 13,645 Mennonites and Amish in Ontario were concentrated in five electoral districts, which embraced the pioneer communities as they had expanded and consolidated through the years, 29 per cent or 4,097 were distributed in over 62 other districts (see Table 4).

This scattering, which had been characteristic of Mennonite settling in Ontario from the beginning,[21] meant the slow but sure absorption of many Mennonites into English Canada and into other religious denominations.[22] In the Niagara Peninsula this assimilation proceeded more rapidly and completely than in other places, according to Ivan Groh, as a consequence of the War of 1812.[23] British

TABLE 3[19]

MENNONITE POPULATION* IN CANADA, 1901 – 1921
(ACCORDING TO THE CANADIAN CENSUS)

PROVINCE	1901	1911	1921
British Columbia	11	189	172
Alberta	522	1,524	3,125
Saskatchewan	3,751	14,400	20,544
Manitoba	15,246	15,600	21,295
Ontario	12,208	12,828	13,645
Quebec	50	51	6
Nova Scotia	9	18	2
New Brunswick	———	1	4
Prince Edward Island	———	———	3
Newfoundland	———	———	———
Yukon and N.W.T.	———	———	1
Total	31,797	44,611	58,797

* Including non-member children and young people.

Upper Canada leaders as well as London statesmen "were embarrassed by the situation" because in the Peninsula "the Palatine Germans and other aliens outnumbered the British Anglicans ten — or perhaps twenty — to one." What was more serious was the way in which the Methodist circuit riders were outwitting the Family Compact and out-converting the Anglican bishops. Mennonites and Tunkers remained aloof, but to the extent that they were open to outside influence, the Methodists were winning out. The situation had to be changed.

> The Niagara Peninsula simply had to be made British. Bilingualism was a disgrace in a British colony. Germans in the Niagara Peninsula were almost as objectionable as French in Lower Canada. The English language, British institutions, and the Anglican church simply had to dominate. The inevitable and immediate reaction was to pretend the Palatine Germans and other aliens in the Niagara Peninsula did not exist. They were left out of all the text books. It worked in the Niagara Peninsula.[24]

TABLE 4[20]

ONTARIO MENNONITE POPULATION BY DOMINION ELECTORAL
DISTRICTS
(COMPARED TO THE TOTAL IN 1921)

DISTRICT	MENNONITES	TOTAL	DISTRICT	MENNONITES	TOTAL
Algoma East	66	40,618	Ontario South	108	31,074
Algoma West	2	33,676	Ottawa	3	93,740
Brant	3	20,085	Oxford North*	698	24,527
Brantford	12	33,292	Oxford South	1	22,235
Bruce North	329	20,872	Parkdale		
Bruce South	34	23,413	(Toronto City)	17	80,780
Dufferin	44	15,415	Parry Sound	1	27,022
Dundas	1	24,388	Peel	2	23,896
Elgin East	102	17,306	Perth North*	1,118	32,461
Elgin West	5	27,678	Perth South	217	18,382
Essex North	2	71,150	Peterboro West	5	29,318
Fort William &			Port Arthur &		
Rainy River	1	39,661	Kenora	2	43,300
Grenville	1	16,644	Prince Edward	1	16,806
Grey North	105	30,667	Renfrew North	1	23,956
Grey South	136	28,384	Simcoe East	15	37,122
Haldimand	170	21,287	Simcoe North	391	22,100
Halton	13	24,899	Simcoe South	11	24,810
Hamilton East	3	49,820	Timiskaming	1	51,568
Hamilton West	1	39,298	Toronto Centre	24	51,768
Hastings East	2	23,072	Toronto East	20	64,825
Hastings West	9	34,451	Toronto North	6	72,478
Huron North	10	23,540	Toronto South	2	37,596
Huron South	213	23,548	Toronto West	42	68,397
Kent	7	52,139	Waterloo North*	4,556	41,698
Kingston	1	24,104	Waterloo South*	2,574	33,568
Lambton East	52	25,801	Welland	422	66,668
Lambton West	21	32,888	Wellington North	453	19,833
Leeds	3	34,909	Wellington South	55	34,327
Lincoln	329	48,625	Wentworth	12	64,449
Middlesex East	5	27,994	York East	88	77,950
Middlesex West	13	25,033	York North	368	23,136
Muskoka	6	19,439	York South*	602	100,054
Norfolk	12	26,366	York West	30	70,681
Northumberland	5	30,512	Others (14)	-	456,743
Ontario North	81	15,420			
			Overall Totals	13,645	2,933,662

* Five districts containing 71 per cent of Ontario Mennonites.

Re-education of the people and "heavy immigration did the trick." Gradually, the Mennonites of Swiss extraction disappeared and "99 per cent of the descendants of the [Mennonite and other] pioneer Germans of the Niagara Peninsula" forgot their heritage.[25] What happened there was an indication of what could in time happen in the rest of Canada.

Manitoba was home for 21,295 Mennonites in 1921. About two-thirds (14,277) were in the Lisgar electoral district, which included the former West Reserve, and nearly another third (5,987) were in the Provencher and Springfield districts, which embraced the former East Reserve. The balance of 1,031 were already present in 12 other districts (see Table 5).

In Saskatchewan, likewise, the concentrations of Mennonites in the Saskatoon (8,631) and Prince Albert (3,393) districts accounted for earlier block settlements in the Saskatchewan Valley, while the 6,961 in the Swift Current district were essentially the inhabitants of the former Swift Current Reserve. An additional 1,559 Menno-

TABLE 5[26]

MANITOBA MENNONITE POPULATION BY ELECTORAL DISTRICTS
(COMPARED TO THE TOTAL IN 1921)

DISTRICT	MENNONITES	TOTAL
Brandon	9	40,183
Dauphin	32	35,482
Lisgar	14,277	29,921
Macdonald	37	23,824
Marquette	13	41,254
Neepawa	1	28,356
Nelson	68	19,806
Portage la Prairie	713	22,254
Provencher	4,117	29,308
Selkirk	33	55,395
Souris	1	26,410
Springfield	1,870	58,870
Winnipeg Centre	42	76,470
Winnipeg North	41	62,957
Winnipeg South	41	59,628
Total	21,295	610,118

nites, to make a total of 20,544 in the province, were scattered into 13 other districts (see Table 6).

Mennonite settlement in Alberta was different from that in the other three provinces already named in that no block settlements, such as characterized the founding of communities in Ontario, Manitoba, and Saskatchewan, were established in that province. On the contrary, the numerous small unattached settlements were a foreshadowing of the Mennonite scatterings of the future. In 1921, Alberta's 3,125 Mennonites were found in all 12 electoral districts, and not one of these districts had as many as one thousand in them (see Table 7). Similarly, in British Columbia, which had just barely been penetrated, the handful of 172 Mennonites was scattered over eleven districts (see Table 8).

TABLE 6[27]

SASKATCHEWAN MENNONITE POPULATION
BY ELECTORAL DISTRICTS
(COMPARED TO THE TOTAL IN 1921)

DISTRICT	MENNONITES	TOTAL
Assiniboia	66	34,789
Battleford	34	33,641
Humboldt	935	55,225
Kindersley	43	44,772
Last Mountain	19	50,055
Mackenzie	39	55,629
Maple Creek	113	56,064
Moose Jaw	3	50,403
North Battleford	233	47,381
Prince Albert	3,393	56,829
Qu'Appelle	1	34,836
Regina	32	49,977
Saltcoats	26	43,795
Saskatoon	8,631	55,151
Swift Current	6,961	53,275
Weyburn	15	35,688
Total	20,544	757,510

Within a few decades, the Alberta and British Columbia patterns would be modified somewhat, but several things were clear in 1920 with respect to agricultural settlement. The golden years of opportunity for rural conquest and agricultural expansion were, to a very considerable extent, a thing of the past. Consequently, the formation of solid, relatively compact and exclusive ethnic or religious communities had also become virtually impossible.[30] This situation, compounded as it was by a political mood and government policies which, quite understandably, favoured settlement opportunities for returning soldiers, had serious implications for the Mennonite future.

Canadian agricultural opportunities at the start of the 1920s were quite limited. Those who felt that settlement had been curtailed only on account of the war had to face other realities as well. To begin with, Canada's agricultural land was not unlimited. The horizons were distant and the prairies expansive, but not all that the eye could see was land suited for agriculture. On the contrary, according to

TABLE 7[28]

ALBERTA MENNONITE POPULATION BY ELECTORAL DISTRICTS
(COMPARED TO THE TOTAL IN 1921)

DISTRICT	MENNONITES	TOTAL
Battle River	43	49,173
Bow River	375	55,356
Calgary East	664	44,995
Calgary West	370	44,341
Edmonton East	8	56,548
Edmonton West	101	74,267
Lethbridge	782	37,699
Macleod	220	34,008
Medicine Hat	165	43,179
Red Deer	133	49,629
Strathcona	3	42,520
Victoria	261	56,739
Total	3,125	588,454

TABLE 8[29]

BRITISH COLUMBIA MENNONITE POPULATION BY ELECTORAL
DISTRICTS
(COMPARED TO THE TOTAL IN 1921)

DISTRICT	MENNONITES	TOTAL
Burrard	9	69,922
Cariboo	22	39,834
Kootenay East	1	19,137
Kootenay West	69	30,502
Nanaimo	1	48,010
New Westminster	13	45,982
Skeena	2	28,934
Vancouver Centre	12	60,879
Vancouver South	10	46,137
Victoria City	11	38,727
Yale	22	35,698
Others (2)	—	60,820
Total	172	524,582

estimates at that time, only about 10 per cent — 230 million acres — of Canada's land total was capable of supporting some form of agriculture. Moreover, grain crops could be grown on a mere 110 million acres, or 4.8 per cent of Canada, of which only 10 million acres were class one agricultural land.[31] In 1921, the existing farms covered nearly 141 million acres, half of which were unimproved land. The other half included both crop, fallow, and pasture lands.[32]

The extent to which the prairies had filled up in the great pre-war immigration and settlement push now became evident. In the first twenty years of the twentieth century the population of the prairies had increased nearly five times, from slightly over 400,000 in 1901 to slightly under 2,000,000 in 1921.[33] Anticipating another boom, land agents were holding blocks of good land along rail lines and near towns served by the railways in the hope that they could be sold in more profitable times.[34] However, the collapse of the wheat market, due to poor crops and low prices in the early post-war years, had the effect of curtailing for sale lands held for speculation by agents.[35]

And besides, war veterans were given the first opportunity under various soldier settlement schemes to obtain what lands were still available. The more fundamental reality, however, was that most of the good farm land was all occupied. In 1921, 50 million acres were under crop, only 12 million short of the all-time high.[36]

Conditions had changed. As one Canadian historian assessed the post-war situation, "there was very little of the 'last best west' left to go to."[37] There still was land, but the best, most accessible land had been taken. And for the Mennonites the available parcels were not laid out in sufficiently large or exclusive areas to create self-sustaining communities. While some would eagerly have accepted the further establishment of "German Blocks" or "Mennonite Reserves," most Mennonites knew that they had passed into history and could not be re-established again.

The Importance of Tolerance

Next to land, perhaps before land, Mennonites held certain other conditions essential to the survival of their way of life, their faith, and their culture. In 1920, the principle of nonresistance, popularly known as pacifism, was an indispensable part of their faith. To live that faith without too much difficulty, the Mennonites needed governmental recognition and legal protection of their desire to be exempted from military service. And, besides favourable laws, they needed empathetic political leaders and the goodwill of the people.

The refusal to bear arms in defence either of themselves or of the social order had been one of the distinguishing characteristics of the sixteenth-century Anabaptists,[38] of which the main surviving sub-group was later called Mennonites after an early leader, Menno Simons (d. 1561). These radical reformers took Jesus' admonitions not to resist evil quite literally. According to their understanding, Christian disciples were called to absorb wickedness through suffering love and to return evil with good. Christ's kingdom was to be advanced not by alienating or even killing the enemies but by loving them and turning them into friends. This conviction and the refusal to bear arms made the Mennonites unpopular at first, but in due course various countries, including Canada, guaranteed them exemption from military service.

In post-war Europe, the Mennonites in Germany, the Netherlands, and Switzerland no longer attached great significance to such guarantees. Over the centuries the doctrine of nonresistance had fallen into benign neglect and, as Mennonites increasingly had joined their compatriots in performing military duty, special concessions had become unnecessary. As one historian observed, "nonresistance as a doctrine and practice is a dead letter among most of the European Mennonites."[39]

In 1898, for instance, the Dutch Parliament had passed a new military service law which did away with earlier provisions for exemption or the hiring of substitutes, and the Mennonites had raised no objections. According to C. Henry Smith, Mennonite members in the States General at the time were in fact "the most outspoken in their opposition to any exemption clause for religious scruples."[40] In the church, there was some interest among church members in the Anabaptist position, but a return to the original faith remained the exception among the *Doopsgezinde* (Anabaptists) rather than the rule.[41] During the Great War, only one of the Mennonites called up for military duty in the Netherlands was known to have been a conscientious objector.[42]

Universal military conscription had also come to Switzerland and Germany in the nineteenth century, and while the Mennonites there tried to escape the full implications through noncombatant service, participation in the armed forces soon followed. During the Great War, one-third to one-half of all males in the German Mennonite congregations went to war and about 10 per cent of them were killed in action.[43]

The decline of nonresistance in Europe was not without its good explanations. In the first place, the religious convictions of the Mennonites in Switzerland, the Netherlands, and Germany were effectively weakened by the emigrations to east and west of those most committed to this religious principle. After their departure, there no longer existed groups large enough or persistent enough to resist the further erosion of the nonresistance principle. Secondly, the European Mennonites in their respective homelands were part of the national culture in all other ways. They lacked the element of foreignness, which tended to postpone their absorption into, and full participation in, the prevailing ethos. Whereas an "alien" culture protected those who had moved to Russia and North America for several more generations, for those who stayed in their native cultural environments there was no such protection. It remained to be seen whether the Mennonites of Canada, the U.S.A., or the U.S.S.R. would retain their nonresistant stance any longer in those countries than the Mennonites of Western Europe had retained theirs.

In 1920, however, the preservation of nonresistance as a doctrine, and the exemption from military service as a law, remained as high a priority for Mennonites in Canada as it had ever been. They were in fact, along with other North American Mennonites, "unconditionally opposed to war-participation."[44] And in some ways they had nothing to fear. The laws which late in the eighteenth century guaranteed recognition to Mennonites, Quakers, and Tunkers and late in the nineteenth century to Doukhobors, Hutterites, and Mennonites had been generalized — specific groups were no longer named — but the basic statutes had not been changed in their fundamental nature. And the Canadian government, during the war at least, had "shown a high regard for the tender consciences of Mennonites."[45]

What was worrisome, however, was that the popular and political support for such recognition had eroded and that this erosion had become evident in various governmental measures and administrative procedures during and after the war. The Mennonite press had been censored under provisions of the War Measures Act.[46] All conscientious objectors had lost the franchise under the Wartime Elections Act,[47] and there had been confusing interpretations and unfair applications of the Military Service Act.[48] Worst of all, the immigration into the country of all Mennonites, as well as Doukhobors and Hutterites, had been prohibited by a 1919 Order-in-Council following a great public outcry[49] which confused the identity of the three groups to the disadvantage of the Mennonites, who tended to be viewed somewhat more favourably than either the Doukhobors or the Hutterites.[50]

To be sure, the Mennonites had not lost all their friends. In the House of Commons, among the people, and even among the Royal North West Mounted Police there were vigorous defenders of the Mennonite people and of the law protecting them.[51] And, what turned out to be most fortuitous for them, the politician who succeeded Wilfrid Laurier as leader of the Liberal Party and Conservative leader Arthur Meighen as prime minister in 1921 was their friend. William Lyon Mackenzie King knew them, and they had known him ever since 1908 and his first election to the House of Commons for the riding of Waterloo North. Mennonites in other areas also made his acquaintance following his election in York North in 1921 and in Prince Albert in 1926. The mutual support and respect that developed served the Mennonites well, for King influenced or even dominated Canadian politics either as prime minister or as Opposition leader for the entire period of this history.[52]

Understanding and goodwill on the part of ruling authorities had been important to the Mennonites ever since the sixteenth century. Although the persecution that attended their beginnings sometimes strengthened the movement, the Mennonites soon learned that tolerance and friendship at the highest levels of government were quite important to their survival. Fortunately for them, they found such acceptance with many heads of state. Among those who most endeared themselves for the measures of freedom they afforded were William I (d.1584)[53] and William III (d.1702)[54] of Orange, both stadholders of the Netherlands; Frederick the Great of Prussia (d.1786);[55] Catherine II of Russia (d.1796);[56] George I (d.1727)[57] and George IV (d.1830)[58] of England. Several British governors, most notably William Penn[59] of Pennsylvania and John Graves Simcoe[60] and Sir Peregrine Maitland[61] of Upper Canada, were also known for the practical steps they took to make Mennonites feel welcome in their respective lands.

In Canada, the sympathies and benefactions of such leaders as Simcoe, Maitland, and Mackenzie King helped to open wide for them the doors of Canadian immigration and to create the essential climate of public acceptance. Not only were such leaders responsible for favourable provisions in the law, but they helped to moderate and guide the popular mood in more positive directions when there were attempts to undermine or overrule the law. Be that as it may, the historic relationship between benevolent rulers and the Mennonites had generally profited both parties. During Canada's pioneering years, for instance, concessions were made to the Mennonites in order that the state might gain from them the service of agricultural pioneering in particular and the domestication of the land in general. The problem confronting the Mennonites in 1920 was that their earlier bargaining power had largely vanished. The country, having received from them what it had hoped to gain, could now presumably get along without them. The granting of special privilege was no longer necessary to attract immigrants, as settlers or as workers.

Prime Minister King promised to remove discriminatory immigration restrictions, and he succeeded in other ways in creating a more favourable climate for minority groups. But he could not restore the educational and cultural autonomies, which had been irretrievably lost during the Great War. Patriotic fervour among the populace and the rhetoric of politicians had made essential and irreversible the "Canadianization" of hundreds of thousands of foreign immigrants who had made Western Canada their home in the late nineteenth and early twentieth centuries.[62] Even if it had been in the prime minister's power to recreate an earlier situation, it is unlikely that he would have disregarded the strong sentiment to the contrary that swept the land.[63]

Canadianization meant many things, but above all it meant the anglicization and integration of the many ethnic conclaves strung across the prairies. Its foremost instrument of promotion was the public school.[64] This use of the elementary school to foster a particular national identity hit the Dutch Mennonites in Western Canada hard, for one of the conditions of their entry into Canada in the 1870s, according to their understanding, had been complete freedom in matters of education. Educational autonomy had lessened gradually, as the provincial governments, exercising their constitutional prerogatives in matters of education, had set about establishing comprehensive nondenominational public school systems.[65]

The Mennonites in Western Canada had viewed these developments with some concern, but those who considered the church-directed elementary school indispensable to their survival did not really feel threatened until the patriotic heat of wartime caused first Manitoba and then Saskatchewan to pass adverse legislation. The new laws made it compulsory for children to attend either public schools where English was the language of instruction or private schools which could pass government inspection. Most were considered substandard and failed the test. The result was that at least 10 per cent of the Mennonites then in the country were having second thoughts about Canada as an abiding dwelling place.[66] A country which could not allow them their own schools was not for them.

Emigration to another country, which would once again offer the desired autonomy in school matters, was one option under serious consideration. Accepting the public school and the socialization of the young in the Canadian context without much question was another option, allowed by those who felt that the home and church should and would make up for any deficiencies in the public system. A third option was pursued by those who thought that the public schools might be acceptable if they were staffed with empathetic teachers who could supplement the regular curriculum with daily ethnic and religious additives, such as the German language, Bible stories, and appropriate music.[67]

Those who found this last option most appealing believed they could combine the best of both worlds: the tax base and curriculum of the public system and the input of Mennonite ethnic and religious values by Mennonite teachers. For the training of such teachers three special schools had been founded: in Manitoba the Mennonite Collegiate Institute at Gretna and the nearby Mennonite Educational Institute at Altona, and in Saskatchewan the German-English Academy at Rosthern. This approach, however, was no answer for those who had rejected the state schools, on the one hand, or for those who lived on the fringes of Mennonite culture and religion, on the other hand. For the latter group, the acceptance of the public school was taken for granted.

The Swiss in Ontario shared with the Dutch Mennonites in the west the struggle to survive in the midst of strong influences to integrate and assimilate. However, the focus of their struggle was not so much the public school or the German language as it was the general encroachment of "worldly culture" upon their communities. They were much more exposed to outside influences because of settlement patterns, because of their presence in the country for more than 100 years, because of the language transition already accomplished in many areas, and because Ontario was more urbanized than were the prairie provinces. It was precisely the greater exposure which provoked the greater concern and reaction.

Before 1920, three basic directions had already been charted among them by nineteenth-century schisms: namely, the acceptance of newness and adaptation; the stubborn resistance to accommodation; and the middle-of-the-road position, which emphasized both, keeping the best that tradition had to offer and allowing adjustments which were believed to be necessary and useful but not threatening to the faith. The New Mennonites, since 1883 known as Mennonite

Brethren in Christ, the Old Order Mennonites, and the Old Mennonites represented these various options, respectively. The latter
two positions were alive also among the Amish, among whom an Old
Order Amish faction was also clearly identified.

Confronted by outside influences on an unprecedented scale, the
Ontario Mennonites and Amish were now moving farther in the
directions already chosen in order to maintain themselves. Some
accepted the cultural traits of their Anglo-Saxon neighbours readily,
others resisted any accommodation with great determination. Still
others would try very hard to remain progressive in some ways and
conservative in other ways. Whatever the direction, none of the
groups was free from anxiety, in spite of the fact that all were
convinced that their way was better than all the others.

The Lack of Solidarity

The divergent Mennonite responses to the societal pressures were
part of the overall Mennonite problem of survival. There was no
unified approach because the Mennonites lacked solidarity on almost
every social question, except perhaps military service and the importance of land, and even there the consensus showed early signs of
trouble ahead. Moreover, the fragmentations resulting from varying approaches were many times augmented by the geographical
scattering already referred to, and by the structural separation of the
58,800 Mennonites into no fewer than 18 autonomous and independent congregational families, 8 of them among the Swiss, 9 among
the Dutch, and one of them mixed, being both Swiss and Dutch (see
Chart 1, Table 9, and Appendix I).

There was, of course, a good explanation for this apparent fragmentation of the Mennonite society. The localized congregational
community had been the ideal from the time of Anabaptist beginnings in the 1520s. The Anabaptists rejected the Roman Catholic
view, also accepted by the Reformers, that the church was synonymous with civil society as a whole. Rather, they believed the church
was an intimate, disciplined community of voluntarily committed
believers, who had been baptized not as infants but upon personal
confessions of faith after reaching maturity. For them the Kingdom
of God proceeded not from hierarchical institutions but from small
groups of disciples.[69]

TABLE 9[68]

MENNONITE CONGREGATIONAL FAMILIES IN CANADA

NO.	NAME	DATE[1]	PROVINCE	TYPE[2]	ORIGIN[3]	UNITS OR CENTRES[4]	MEMBERSHIP[5]
1.	Old Mennonite Church						
	Mennonite Conference of Ontario	1820	Ontario	C	SSG	25	1638
	Alta., Sask. Mennonite Conference	1907	Alta., Sask.	C	SSG	6	273
2.	Amish Mennonite Churches[6]	1824	Ontario	B	SSG	5	1379
3.	Reformed Mennonite Churches[6]	1825	Ontario	B	SSG	6	300
4.	Kleine Gemeinden[6]	1873	Manitoba	B	DNG	6	629
5.	Mennonite Brethren in Christ						
	Ontario District	1874	Ontario	C	SSG	25	1435
	Northwest District	1908	Alta., Sask.	C	SSG	21	349
6.	Chortitzer Mennonite Church	1874	Manitoba	B	DNG	12	955
7.	Reinlaender Mennonite Churches[6]						
	West Reserve Area	1875	Manitoba	B	DNG	8	1893
	Hague-Osler Area	1895	Saskatchewan	B	DNG	4	1135
	Swift Current Area	1905	Saskatchewan	B	DNG	4	880
8.	Church of God in Christ, Mennonite	1881	Man., Alta.	C	DNG, SSG	4	346
9.	Old Order Mennonite Churches[6]						
	Waterloo Area	1889	Ontario	B	SSG	5	370
	Markham Area	1889	Ontario	B	SSG	4	95
	Niagara Area	1889	Ontario	B	SSG	4	38
10.	Old Order Amish Churches[6]	1891	Ontario	B	SSG	2	120

11.	Sommerfelder Mennonite Churches[6]						
	West Reserve Area	1892	Manitoba	B	DNG	11	2692
	Herbert Area	1900	Saskatchewan	B	DNG	3	483
12.	Krimmer Mennonite Brethren Churches[6]	1899	Sask., Alta.	C	DNG	3	115
13.	Bruderthaler Mennonite Churches[6]	1897	Man., Sask.	C	DNG	3	250
14.	Beachy Amish Churches[6],[7]	1903	Ontario	B	SSG	2	313
15.	Bergthaler(S) Mennonite Churches[8]						
	Hague-Osler Area	1902	Saskatchewan	B	DNG	3	483
	Carrot River Area	1908	Saskatchewan	B	DNG	1	65
16.	Conference of Mennonites in Central Canada	1903	Man., Sask., Alta.	C	DNG	21	2022
17.	Mennonite Brethren Churches, Northern Dist.	1910	Man., Sask.	C	DNG	20	1553
18.	David Martin Old Order Mennonite Church	1917	Ontario	B	SSG	1	50

Notes:

[1] First date of the body in question is used; in some cases individual congregations precede this date, as in the case of the Mennonite Conference of Ontario, whose first congregation was formally established in 1801; the Mennonite Brethren, whose first Canadian congregation appeared in 1888; or the Conference of Mennonites in Central Canada, whose Bergthaler Church was established in 1874. See Table 29 for founding dates of congregations.

[2] C—Conference-oriented; B—Bishop-oriented.

[3] SSG—Swiss-South German; DNG—Dutch-North German.

[4] Meeting places and/or congregational groups or congregations.

[5] Baptized persons only. Figure given is the one available closest to 1920.

[6] Use of plurals indicates more than one congregation, each with a bishop or leading minister.

[7] Beachy was a name that came into use in the late 1920s.

[8] Bergthaler(S) meaning Bergthaler(Saskatchewan), as distinct from the Bergthaler in Manitoba and the Bergthaler in Alberta, the latter groups both members of the Conference of Mennonites in Central Canada.

CHART 1

MENNONITE GROUPS IN CANADA IN 1920

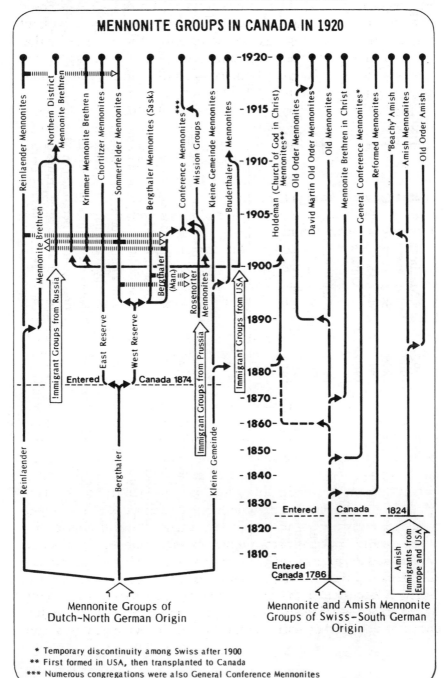

MENNONITE GROUPS IN CANADA IN 1920

* Temporary discontinuity among Swiss after 1900
** First formed in USA, then transplanted to Canada
*** Numerous congregations were also General Conference Mennonites

These companies of believers or congregations were not only small, but relatively independent and autonomous. Since their leaders—a bishop or elder, ministers, and deacons—were chosen from the ranks of the believers and since they served without remuneration, the congregations were self-sufficient also in that sense. If and when the geographic area of a community or the numbers became too large, additional self-sufficient and autonomous congregational communities would be formed.

Still another characteristic of the original Anabaptists contributed to ongoing divisions among the Mennonites, namely their lack of a centrally recognized authority other than the Scriptures. Some common confessions of faith had been fashioned, as at Schleitheim and Dordrecht, but since all believers were "priests," free to read and interpret the Scriptures for themselves, there were frequent differences of opinion, some of which could be accommodated only by divisions in the community.

The theology, organization, and discipline of the Anabaptists laid the foundation for their ongoing fragmentation. Severe persecution, periodic migrations, and diverse settlement patterns reinforced and perpetuated such fragmentation. Frequent personality clashes among leaders, the inability to resolve conflicts amicably, and divisive renewal movements of all kinds internally and externally influenced, confirmed the so-called "Anabaptist sickness" as a permanent condition.

The local congregation was a fundamental fact of the Mennonite landscape in 1920, but it was possible also to speak of congregational families, which united in various ways and to various degrees like-minded groupings of congregations. The very nature of the congregational principle and the uniqueness of each of these congregational families make broad and neat categorizations somewhat problematic. Yet, at the risk of oversimplification, one can identify two kinds of Mennonite congregational families in existence in 1920. The first of these types was traditional and included those congregational units whose essential linkage was through a common congregational membership and the ministry of one bishop plus a number of subordinate ministers and deacons. The second kind of congregational family, largely a late-nineteenth- or early-twentieth-century development, linked local congregational communities through so-called conferences. The general evolution of the Mennonite movement was from the first type to the second, and vestiges of the former could often be found in the context of the latter. Both types were strongly represented on the Canadian Mennonite scene.

The words "bishop-oriented" and "conference-oriented" will be used to identify the two congregational families, mainly because bishop and conference were the important identity symbols in the common understanding and not because of any intention, at this point at least, to characterize the respective structures as either authoritarian or democratic. Some of the bishops were authoritarian, to be sure, but others were quite humble and subservient. Others acted as little more than articulators of a common, usually unwritten, consensus or guardians of a rather stable tradition. Some of the conference moderators, on the other hand, were really super-bishops with immense powers until constitutional revisions progressively reduced their roles, mostly by limiting their terms.

The use of the word bishop requires some explanation, because another translation of the word *Aeltester*, from which it is derived, was in use, namely elder. Both terms, bishop and elder, were employed, sometimes interchangeably, though the former connoted a more authoritative role. Among the Swiss, the Mennonite Brethren in Christ employed the term presiding elder, and the more progressive of the Dutch groups preferred elder over bishop as well.

The conference-oriented congregational family usually began in its evolution where the bishop-oriented congregational family left off. At first, the decision-makers in a conference might be only the members of the ministry, namely the bishops, ministers, and deacons, as they had been traditionally in the bishop-oriented congregational family. At a later stage, elected representatives constituted the decision-making body. These elected people tended to be members of the ministry until the election of some lay delegates was encouraged or even required. At first, such lay delegates were only men, but later, usually much later, women were also included.

Both types of congregational families took on several forms. The bishop-oriented congregational family could involve a single meeting-place or numerous units with numerous meeting-places within a limited geographic area. These units could be tied in very closely to a centre or they could be semi-independent with their own membership lists, local ministers, and some local decision-making. The latter condition existed wherever numbers, distance, local initiative and/or the bishop's encouragement allowed it to happen. A bishop-oriented congregational family, with numerous semi-autonomous units, would begin to develop the characteristics of a conference whenever representatives of the local groups came together for central decision-making.

Generally speaking, bishop-oriented congregational families were a single congregation, however many might be its local units, while conference-oriented congregational families were a collection of autonomous congregations. The former were limited in their geographic scope to areas no larger than was practical for the bishop to traverse with the prevailing modes of transportation. The conferences, on the other hand, embraced provinces, the country, or even the continent. The bishop-oriented congregations tended to be identified as "conservative" in the sense of resisting innovation and the conference-oriented ones as "progressive" in the sense of being more open to change. But again it would be misleading to attach one or other of the two labels, as defined, to the various congregational families because conservatism and progressivism were matters of definition and degree, and all the Mennonite congregational families could in fact be found somewhere along a continuum, most characterized by diverse mixtures of conservatism and progressivism. Other features further distinguished the two groups, but these will appear at later points in the narrative. Both kinds of congregational families were found among both the Swiss and the Dutch Mennonites.

The three main Swiss Mennonite congregational families in Ontario were, to use the popular names for purposes of characterization, the Old Mennonites, the New Mennonites, and the Old Order Mennonites. In 1920 the Old Mennonites in Ontario were represented by the Mennonite Conference of Ontario, which had been meeting for about a century, but whose delegate body still included bishops, ministers, and deacons only.[70] Its counterpart in Western Canada was the Alberta-Saskatchewan Mennonite Conference, founded in 1907 to serve the new congregational communities, one in Saskatchewan and five in Alberta.[71] The North American body embracing these two Canadian Old Mennonite conferences was the Mennonite General Conference organized in 1898.[72] This body, with its 16 district conferences and more than 25,000 members, was the largest of the North American congregational families, and occasional reference will be made to this larger body because of its influence on the two Canadian districts.

Equal in numerical strength to the Old Mennonites in Ontario were the more "progressive" New Mennonites, or Mennonite Brethren in Christ, as they were officially known after 1883. Like the Old Mennonites, the Mennonite Brethren in Christ were represented by two Canadian conferences, one in Ontario and one in the Northwest (meaning Alberta-Saskatchewan) and were linked to their counterpart American districts in a North American conference.[73] The New Mennonites distinguished themselves from the Old Mennonites chiefly in their willingness to neglect Mennonite organizational, doctrinal, ethical, and cultural traditions for the sake of a missionary outreach.

Completely opposite the New Mennonites in their cultural outlook were bishop-oriented Swiss congregational families who were very zealous about the heritage. The largest of these were the Old Order Mennonite churches, which were confirmed in 1889 when a number of bishops concluded that the Old Mennonites were adopting too many of the ways of the New Mennonites.[74] The David Martin Old Order Mennonite group, an ultra-conservative offshoot from the main body, emerged a generation later.[75] A similar traditionalist orientation held for the Reformed Mennonites, whose origins dated back to 1812 in the United States but whose strength in Ontario was beginning to wane.[76]

The Swiss Amish, like their Mennonite counterparts, included "progressive" and "conservative" streams. Representing the latter were the Old Order Amish, also known as House Amish because of their refusal to go along with the building of church buildings in the 1880s.[77] Between the "progressive" Amish and the Old Order Amish there were several congregations with a middle position, who, like the Old Order Amish, were a minority movement. All were bishop-oriented in their organization. The more progressive majority Amish were calling themselves Amish Mennonites and taking the first steps leading to the formation of a conference.[78]

In 1920 the congregational families of the Dutch tradition still included the original three groups that had come to Manitoba in the 1870s, but some offshoots and modifications now existed as well. The Kleine Gemeinde, which had arisen in 1812 in Russia as a conservative protest[79] and which had been transplanted to Manitoba, became the population base for two other new Canadian groups. One of these was the Church of God in Christ Mennonite, members of which were also known as Holdemaner after John Holdeman, the Swiss Mennonite evangelist who had come from the U.S.A. to revive them. The Holdemaner were the first group to include both the Dutch and Swiss Mennonites, as both migrated to Alberta from Manitoba, Kansas, Oklahoma, and Oregon to form a single community, and as the Canadian Holdemaner joined their American counterparts in a North American conference in 1921.[80]

The Holdeman schismatics from the Kleine Gemeinde remained rural and conservative while eliminating the bishop and adopting revivalism. But another Kleine Gemeinde offshoot, begun by the American evangelists of the Bruderthaler Mennonites, represented town culture and readiness to make cultural adaptations in the evangelical context. Later, the Bruderthaler of Manitoba were joined in Canada by Bruderthaler immigrants from the U.S.A. who settled in Saskatchewan. All were part of a North American Bruderthaler Conference.[81]

The Reinlaender made up a second immigrant congregational family from Russia. Originally concentrated in the West Reserve in Manitoba, this group had expanded to become three separate bishop-oriented congregational families with the establishment of two additional reserves in Saskatchewan, one north of Saskatoon and the other south of Swift Current.[82]

A third immigrant congregational family, the Bergthaler Mennonite Church,[83] had been transplanted from Russia as a single colony. By 1920 it had undergone several permutations. In the East Reserve, the Bergthaler, who had declined to follow others to the West Reserve, had quickly become an autonomous congregational family called Chortitzer Mennonite Church,[84] after the village of their bishop, Gerhard Wiebe. In the West Reserve, they had divided into Bergthaler and Sommerfelder Mennonite Churches over education issues, with the majority Sommerfelder, named after the village of their new bishop, opting for the more conservative course.[85] Those Bergthaler who were moving on to Saskatchewan retained that name, though they were in their orientation really Sommerfelder.

Thus, the Saskatchewan Bergthaler had to be differentiated from the Manitoba Bergthaler, not only because of their different outlook but also because they were independent of each other in organization.

A third group carrying the Bergthaler name was represented by the settlers who had moved from Manitoba to Didsbury, Alberta. The Saskatchewan Sommerfelder, like the Saskatchewan Reinlaender, founded independent bishop-oriented congregations in their respective regions, while retaining a loose association with their Manitoba counterparts.

The Manitoba Bergthaler congregation, still bishop-oriented, had joined together with the Saskatchewan Rosenorter church, a bishop-oriented congregational family from Prussia,[86] to form the Conference of Mennonites in Central Canada. Other congregations in Saskatchewan, recently immigrated from the U.S.A., and the Bergthaler in Alberta likewise joined that Conference after its founding in 1903.[87] The Conference's Saskatchewan congregations, mostly of Prussian and American origin, also joined the American-based General Conference Mennonite Church of North America.[88] This was true also of the Bergthaler congregation at Didsbury, Alberta.

Since not all congregations of the Canadian Conference joined the American-based General Conference, they will hereafter be known not as General Conference Mennonites, this being the common though not quite accurate term, but simply as Conference Mennonites or as the Canadian Conference. The Rosenorter, for instance, joined the General Conference; the Bergthaler in Manitoba did not. The General Conference Mennonite Church, dating back to 1860, was the second-largest North American congregational family and included in the U.S.A. both Swiss and Dutch traditions. The Conference of Mennonites in Central Canada would, with the immigration of the 1920s, become the largest of the conference-oriented congregational families in Canada.

Destined to become the second largest, though in 1920 it was still very small, was the Mennonite Brethren conference-oriented congregational family. The Mennonite Brethren traced their beginning in 1860 to a renewal movement which swept the South Russian colonies.[89] In Canada they were first organized as the Northern District of the General Conference of Mennonite Brethren Churches of North America and included among their members converts from the Reinlaender and Sommerfelder in Manitoba and immigrants from the U.S.A. and Russia in Saskatchewan. The North American body of Mennonite Brethren was becoming the third-largest North

American congregational family. The Krimmer Mennonite Brethren, a conference originating in the "Krim" or Crimea of Russia, had two congregations in Saskatchewan. Both were transplanted from the U.S.A.[90]

Diversity Within a Corporate Personality

As already indicated, the various bishop- and conference-oriented congregational families represented a great diversity of approaches and styles, but in spite of that diversity, there also existed a commonality, a corporate Mennonite personality, which identified and separated Mennonites from other Christian denominational groups. Its characteristics included a degree of social withdrawal tempered by a general readiness to assist needy strangers, a wariness of the state modified by a strong sense of obedience in most matters, a refusal to swear an oath of loyalty while regularly and sincerely praying for those in authority, great familiarity with the land and agricultural processes, a love of family and children, and at least some degree of ethnic culture. The German language remained the first or the second language for most. Almost all spoke a dialect, either Pennsylvania German as among the Swiss or Low German as among the Dutch.

Also belonging to this corporate personality was a deep religious devotion. At the heart of Mennonite faith were a voluntary confession leading to baptism, a disciplined community, though interpretation of community and application of discipline fluctuated widely, a lifestyle guided by the Sermon on the Mount, and a commitment to nonresistance as taught and exemplified by Jesus of Nazareth. Mennonite ordinances were few and the forms of worship generally simple. There was among all Mennonites a sense of obligation to other people, though the understanding of that obligation differed.

The differences among Mennonites arose from the multifarious applications of that faith and those values, which had been of such great importance to them since their beginnings. In 1920 most groups adhered basically to the same doctrines, but they did so with different emphases, varying degrees of zeal, divergent understandings of the role of cultural forms, variant liturgies and symbols, and distinctive notions of what it meant to be in the world but not of it. Thus, as a minority religious group the Mennonites demonstrated that the minority syndrome has no ending; that is to say, every minority has other minorities in it, just as every part of the human body or the universe is constituted of even smaller parts.

All Mennonites were conservative compared to the rest of society, when it came to preserving religious and cultural forms, but none were quite so consistent in their rural lifestyle and determined to avoid modernistic influences in their congregations as were the Old Order Mennonites and the Old Order Amish. They demonstrated best of all that all forms of outside influence could successfully be resisted and that alternative societies could function with a great degree of self-respect.

All Mennonites practised some form of discipline to check doctrinal error and moral deviance among their members, but none were so particular, consistent, and legalistic about it as were the Reformed Mennonites, the Kleine Gemeinde, and the David Martin Old Order Mennonites. This did not necessarily mean an authoritarian congregational culture or the heavy hand of discipline on children and young people. What it did mean was group discipline for those who had voluntarily confessed the faith, joined such a group, and submitted to its norms as well as to the discipline.

All Mennonites could be characterized as the quiet in the land. All resisted noise, spectacle, and showmanship. All had a sense of the humble and exemplary life, but few succeeded better in remaining unnoticed than did the Amish Mennonites. They were "conservative" enough to be "quiet" but not so stubborn or extreme in their conservatism as to draw attention to themselves. Quietly they went about their task of tilling the soil, raising their families, and being the kindest and gentlest Mennonites of all to their neighbours, including the Catholics, with whom their leaders had positive relationships, more so than any other Mennonites.

All Mennonites still saw the best prototypes of the Kingdom of God in small, voluntary communities of believers, but none exemplified this smallness as much as did the Krimmer and the Bruderthaler, the former in the rural setting and the latter at least partly as urbanizers. Actually, the Bruderthaler exemplified how fine Mennonite distinctions could be drawn, for few in number as they were in their Canadian congregations, they were of several kinds. At Steinbach in Manitoba they emerged because of the urbanizing thrust, which separated them from the Kleine Gemeinde heritage, and because of the desire nonetheless to remain Mennonite with an acceptable evangelical piety. At Dalmeny in Saskatchewan, on the other hand, the Bruderthaler were rural immigrants from Minnesota, the North American birthplace of this conservative evangelical group. The Dalmeny group, being rural, thus tended to be more "retentionist," while the Steinbach group, being urban, was more "accommodationist." For both groups, this represented a reversal of roles, since in the immigration of the 1870s those going to Minnesota had been more liberal than those going to Manitoba. And, as if to say that cellular breakdown knows no end, the Dalmeny group had become two Bruderthaler groups to accommodate differences of opinion on the form of baptism.

Few Mennonites were incapable of some sense of compromise, adjustment, and tolerance. But few were so diligent in steering a middle course as were the Old Mennonites. For several generations they occupied the delicate middle ground between the New Mennonites and the Old Order Mennonites, hoping to avoid losing too many to the former by being sufficiently progressive, while making it possible to gain some of the latter by being sufficiently conservative. Actually, most Mennonites were middle-of-the-roaders, viewed either subjectively or objectively, for most felt themselves to be somewhere in between the extremes, and in every separate collection of Mennonites some actually were. Among the Amish the minority middle order, "Beachy" Amish, stood between those more progressive and those more conservative.

Whenever there was borrowing and adjustment, most Mennonites arrived at a new synthesis in the context of some mode of conservatism. Few groups combined in their congregational life the conservatism of the rural, nonconformist way of life and the conservatism of evangelical piety as well as did the Holdeman people. Their preachers were revivalists who wore beards, at the time a sure sign of conservatism.

All Mennonite congregations experienced internal divisiveness due to the clashing of so-called conservative and progressive forces around them and among them, but few were caught in between as painfully as were the Sommerfelder of Manitoba and their cousins the Bergthaler of Saskatchewan. They were torn, on the one hand, by the isolationist mentality of the Reinlaender and, on the other hand, by the "accommodationist" mentality of the Manitoba Bergthaler or

the Saskatchewan Rosenorter. Like all Mennonites, the Sommerfelder were ready to confront society and state on some matters and to
pay the price of such confrontation, but no Mennonites, including
most Sommerfelder, were so determined and so ready to sacrifice
material advantage as were the Reinlaender and Chortitzer in matters
of education.

All Mennonites believed in conversion and the new birth, though
few used the born-again vocabulary as much in their liturgy, their
preaching, and their teaching as did the Mennonite Brethren, and
some hardly used the language at all. All Mennonites had a tradition
of evangelical passion, of biblical literalism, and of saving souls, but
no group borrowed these images from North American evangelical
fundamentalism as heavily as did the Mennonite Brethren in Christ.

All Mennonites were troubled, to a greater or less degree, by
disunity in the congregations or in the wider Mennonite family, but
few worked so hard at building bridges and tying together the many
isolated and fragmented Mennonite communities as did the Conference of Mennonites in Central Canada, which embraced such distant
groups as the Rosenorter from Prussia, who had settled in Saskatchewan in the 1890s, and the Bergthaler from Russia, who had settled in
Manitoba in the 1870s.

A common problem facing all the Mennonites was the survival of
so many small and widely scattered congregational communities,
surrounded as they were by other communities with different cultures and values and by Canadian society at large. But there was little
Mennonite solidarity even in the individual settlements. Almost
every Mennonite community was thoroughly fragmented by Mennonite congregationalism.[91] United, the Mennonites might have had
less reason to fear the onslaught of external culture via the public
school, social influences generally, and the mass media. But standing
against those pressures as a divided people was quite another matter.

A good omen of what could be expected as a result of Mennonite
scattering was suggested by the recently established settlements in the
Grande Prairie district of Alberta's Peace River country and at
Vanderhoof in British Columbia's Nechako Valley. Both communities had received Mennonite immigrants from the U.S.A. during
the Great War. Both had made strong settlement starts. Both faced
early extinction.

At its peak the Krimmer Mennonite Brethren community north-west of Grande Prairie had 60 members, some of whom were converts from among the local populace.[92] Soon after their arrival from Kansas in 1917 the Krimmer realized that they could have a future only if they expanded their population base either through more immigration of Mennonites or through the evangelism of non-Mennonites. The brave homesteaders and evangelizers showed early signs of strength, but the end of the community could be foreseen almost from the beginning. Isolation from other Mennonites, intermarriage and integration with the local evangelical community, and the militaristic and nationalistic attitudes assumed by the district's populace contributed to the extinction of the congregation.

The community west of Vanderhoof and east of Engen was begun in April of 1918 and reached a peak of about 100 before it disintegrated before the end of 1920.[93] Consisting largely of Mennonite Brethren from various points in the U.S.A., chiefly Minnesota, as well as southern Manitoba, the settlement was motivated to a very high degree by the desire to escape military conscription. The settlers established themselves on both sides of the Nechako River and were connected only by a ferry.

The community soon discovered that isolation from other Mennonites and geographic scattering even in the new settlement represented distinct obstacles to survival. Roads were bad, making the two Model T Fords practically useless. Additionally, markets for agricultural products were far away, local job opportunities were scarce, and communications with the outside world were almost nonexistent. Drownings and influenza took their toll, and the end could be foreseen when Elder Heinrich Voth, the leader, died of heart failure. One by one the settlers returned to their former homes in the interests of material and spiritual survival.

As has already been pointed out, the common Mennonite problem — new pressures from the state and society — did not predicate a common Mennonite response. On the contrary, the Mennonites in Canada — and in other countries as well — were reacting in diverse ways to their dilemmas. Basically, and speaking generally, the Mennonite response pointed in one of two directions: one allowed certain kinds and degrees of accommodation; the other was characterized by certain kinds and degrees of isolation, resistance, and withdrawal. Neither of these positions was absolute, except in extreme manifestations. Most Mennonites found themselves somewhere between the two extremes. Those accommodating themselves to state and society were not without selective resistance; and those resisting state and society were not entirely free from selective accommodation.[94]

Accommodation was of several kinds and degrees. It could have reference only to cultural habits, or to language, or to urbanization, or to professionalization, or to acceptance of evangelical Protestant forms and structures, or to ideological acculturation to the point of dropping pacifism as a basic tenet. Resistance to accommodation, or deliberate withdrawal and isolation, likewise manifested itself in divergent ways and variant degrees. Some Mennonites, depending on their location in the world, wanted to resist every aspect of americanization, anglicization, or russification; others were quite selective and limited in their resistance.

Generally speaking, the Mennonites in Canada had devised two approaches to, and two distinct models for coping with, Canadian society, the vast Canadian geography, and the possibilities of scattering and absorption. The one formula emphasized the Mennonite colony, the rural life, the most solid communities possible, strong reliance on tradition, ethnic peculiarities, the German language, and well-understood congregational norms interpreted by the bishops. The other formula stressed the Mennonite conference and other institutions, as a means of linking the congregations and home mission stations in the cities.

Except in their extreme manifestations, these two formulas — the Mennonite colony and the Mennonite conference — were not mutually exclusive. As the Canadian Mennonite community developed, both could often be seen existing side by side. Both still had in common a primary attachment to the land. Both were concerned with keeping the Mennonite community intact. The emphasis placed on the one formula or the other would vary from group to group, from time to time, and from situation to situation. As the 1920s began, both formulae had their champions. Some sought salvation for the Mennonites in the restoration of the Mennonite colonies, some in the expansion of the Mennonite conferences.

The basic orientation determined the response to a whole range of issues which the Mennonites faced in the years just ahead: whether or not to accept the public school as a vehicle for educating the children; whether or not to establish supplemental private schools; whether to remain farmers or to become business people and to enter the professions; whether or not to consider a future in the cities; whether to insist on German culture and language or to succumb to anglicization; whether or not to make a determined effort to maintain the traditional identity; whether to adopt new technologies and modernization generally or whether to resist; whether or not to participate in political processes; whether to build communities along the lines of the co-operative movement or to accept capitalistic competition as the norm; whether or not, or to what degree, to accept innovations in church life, new styles of liturgy, and new forms of ministry; whether to win the young through careful nurture and education or to adopt revivalistic styles and the methods of evangelism.

The International Connections

The Mennonites in Canada were scattered in their settlements, fragmented in their organizations, and separated in their approach to problems, but they were not completely isolated and parochial. They were not totally islands unto themselves, nor were they without any international connections. Indeed, for people as separatist and withdrawal-oriented as they were, the Mennonites were remarkably international in their experience and cosmopolitan in their outlook. Not only were Canadian Mennonites as a whole being affected by international upheavals, but they themselves were touching the world's distant places, either as lonely missionaries or as delegates planning further migrations or as relatives of desperate co-religionists in the U.S.S.R.

The American Mennonites were in many ways closest to the Canadian Mennonites, but there were also some important exceptions, especially with respect to the Dutch. The pronounced differences between those who had chosen Manitoba for their home and those who had settled in the American midwest after the 1870s migration, coupled with the different socio-political realities of their respective environments, resulted in different degrees and forms of cultural adaptation.[95] The Dutch in the U.S.A. had begun to give up the German language; their counterparts in Canada had no such intentions.[96] The Americans were also swifter to accept many of the values and cultural traits of the American environment.[97] There were other differences as well. While the American Mennonites were

already building colleges, the Canadian Mennonites were still resisting or only cautiously accepting the high school.

The situation was considerably different for those Dutch who had
migrated to Canada from the U.S.A., who were tied into conferences
whose base was the U.S.A., or who in other ways were quite
dependent on American sources for their ongoing nurture and
activity. The congregations of the Bruderthaler, the Krimmer, the
Holdemaner, and the Brueder were all tied into American-based
conferences organizationally in a primary sense, the Brueder
through a Northern District Conference. The same was true of
certain congregations of the Conference of Mennonites in Central
Canada, the Saskatchewan Rosenorter, for instance, to name the
largest of such groups, who were tied into the General Conference
Mennonite Church of North America. For all of the above groups
the U.S. connection represented a tie-in with foreign missions,
Sunday school materials, other publication efforts and educational
resources, as well as leadership and additional financial resources.

The connection between American and Canadian Mennonites was
strongest for the Swiss, be they of the New, Old, or Old Order
Mennonite and Amish varieties. They kept moving across the
international border as though it were not there, reinforcing each
other in their common life and in their search to maintain purity of
doctrine and a nonconformist lifestyle.[98] Leadership and literature in
many forms originating in the U.S.A. was supportive of the Swiss in
Canada.[99] Together they faced the threats to their faith. Together
they also addressed their national leaders on the spirit of militarism
and compulsory military service in the immediate post-war era. That
message of the Old Mennonites read, in part:

> The experience of the past few years has brought about a
> change in the minds of many with reference to maintaining a
> large army and making military training compulsory and uni-
> versal. This, according to our faith, would require of us serv-
> ice which, we believe, would involve the violation of a princi-
> ple of the Gospel of Christ whose teachings we regard as our
> rule of life and conduct.[100]

This common witness of the word was reinforced by the common
deed. Partly to appease the critical public sentiment, which arose
during the war years out of their refusal to take up arms, the

Mennonites in the U.S.A., joined by some from Canada, became actively involved in relief work abroad. Volunteer workers went to give aid in Western Europe (Germany and France) and in the Near East (Syria and Turkey), and large amounts of money were raised to alleviate famine conditions in China and India.

The main arena for relief, however, for all North American Mennonites was Russia, where 120,000 Mennonites were suffering the effects of revolution, civil war, disease, and famine.[101] In 1920 a delegation from that country arrived in the U.S.A. and Canada to interpret the needs. As a minimum, its members wanted immediate and direct famine relief, as a maximum a new homeland. The immediate result was the organization that same year of all the relief committees that had emerged in the U.S.A. during the war into a Mennonite Central Committee.[102] Food, clothing, and tractors, sent over in large quantities in co-operation with the American Relief Administration, saved many people from starvation.

So great, however, were the disruptions of the Russian Revolution that thousands of Mennonites were coming to the conclusion that a better future must await them elsewhere, preferably in Canada. Almost any other place would be better than Soviet Russia, perhaps even Australia, New Zealand, or South Africa, and soon some would be leaving the country via the North Sea, the Black Sea, or overland through China or India.[103]

At that time there were Mennonite congregations already in two of these countries. Though the missions in India and China were started from North America, the Russian Mennonites had also become quite conscious of Asia. Not only had they been subjected to Asian influences in their settlements in the Ukraine and in the Caucasus, but these settlements had expanded to Asiatic Russia. Besides, and perhaps most importantly, missionaries from Russia had been going to Java and Sumatra for half a century and to India for three decades.[104]

The notion of Class Epp—a radical millennialist of the 1880s— that Christ could meet his people in the East as well as in the West had never been lost, though Epp himself had been discredited and his particular fanaticism rejected.[105] To be sure, Mennonites in Russia, eyeing a better future, usually looked north and west, but some saw their salvation to the east and to the south. The delegation that came seeking relief soon targeted Canada as the most desirable place to go and pursued that possibility, in spite of the 1919 Order-in-Council barring immigration which stared them in the face.[106]

Some Mennonites had already been separated from their Russian homeland by that time owing to the provisions of the Treaty of Versailles. A small group of churches located in Russian Poland were severed from the Soviet state when Poland once again became a nation on the basis of pre-partition boundaries. The reconstitution of Poland from its Russian, Prussian, and Austrian parts had other effects on the Mennonite community. A large number of German Mennonites, for instance, were lost by Germany, partly because they were now in Poland and partly because they were in the newly created Free City of Danzig, which alone included 5,000 Mennonites within its borders.[107]

Germany also lost Mennonites on its western flank, where the transfer of Alsace-Lorraine to France doubled the Mennonite population in that country. Thus, Germany lost half her Mennonite people to France, Poland, and Danzig. But in an effort to maintain these co-religionists in the German fellowship, the German Mennonite Conference adopted "Conference of German-Speaking Mennonites" as its name.[108] The reasoning behind the name-change was that even though the German national borders had to be reduced, this need not happen to the ecclesiastical and cultural boundaries of the Mennonites.

The Conference name-change foreshadowed or reflected the new German internationalism, which would assert itself in the inter-war period. Much restricted by geography, the greater Germany would appeal to a cultural pan-Germanism in order to embrace Germans all over the world, including Canada, where some Mennonites were a ready target. Like the German Mennonites, the defeated German nation could not and would not easily forget the fragmentation resulting from the loss of territory and people.

In Europe, only the Netherlands and Switzerland provided relative stability for the Mennonite people, the former because its borders remained unchanged, the latter because it had managed to maintain its neutrality. This was a fortunate circumstance because once again the *Doopsgezinde* (Anabaptists) in the Netherlands would be called upon to exercise their traditional role of extending relief and aid to their brothers and sisters in distress. And the *Taufgesinnten* (Anabaptists) in Switzerland, who had provided the cradle for the movement, would become the hosts for the first world gathering of Mennonites on the occasion of the 400th anniversary of the movement's founding. This too was a timely role because such a Conference sought to help Mennonites everywhere, not only in their physical distress but also in their spiritual need. In Europe the faith had fared almost as poorly as the people and the territories. As one historian observed:

> It is a regrettable fact that European Mennonites had, except in Russia, practically dropped the principle of non-resistance. . . [and also in Russia there was] this flagrant violation of the principle of non-resistance. [109]

There was, therefore, no place on earth where Mennonites in 1920 were not confronted by questions of survival, for either internal or external reasons. The Mennonite body was sorely threatened only in some places. The Mennonite soul, however, was everywhere endangered by outside influences or by internal reorientations, or by both.

As previously suggested, Canada became a focal point in the ensuing struggle. For their own good reasons some Mennonites in Canada felt compelled to leave the country. Others, for equally good reasons, were determined to find in it their promised land. Among those who stayed, some sought stubbornly to resist societal encroachments; others were ready to accept the world and to accommodate themselves to it; the majority tried to find a setting for survival somewhere in the middle. The stage was set for restless Mennonites everywhere to move simultaneously in numerous directions in search of their uncertain future, hoping to make it more secure for themselves and for their children.

FOOTNOTES

1   Donald Creighton, *Dominion of the North: A History of Canada* (Toronto: Macmillan of Canada, 1957), p. 455.

2   Speakers at the 1919 Conference in Hepburn of the Northern District of Mennonite Brethren Churches reflected this general sense of uncertainty. Nikolai Janz spoke about "this modern time" in which everything is becoming "so dark." Jakob Ewert described the times as "gruesome." See *Verhandlungen* (NK), 1919.

3   Population figure based on *Census of Canada, 1921*, 5 vols. (Ottawa:

King's Printer, 1925), 1:568. Exact figure of 58,797 includes Hutterites.

4   Statistics for Europe and North America include nonbaptized family members. This is not the case for Africa, Asia, and Latin America for the following reasons: it is less likely for family members to be part of the Mennonite congregation (most converts being first generation), and the unavailability of statistics. The author recognizes the conceptual discrepancy arising from these different applications of "Mennonite," the "ethnic" definition being allowed in the former case. But this dualism is a reflection of Mennonite realities at this point in history. Argentina: an estimated figure, for 1920, recognizing organization of mission in 1919 and establishment of Conference in 1923; see "Argentina," *Mennonite Encyclopedia,* 1:154; T.K. Hershey, "History, Growth, and Activities of the Mennonite Church in the Argentine," *Mennonite Year-Book and Directory, 1923,* pp. 21–22, counts 67 members and 40 applicants for membership in two congregations. Belgian Congo: 1923 statistic; A. Neuenschwander, "Congo Inland Mission," *Mennonite Encyclopedia,* 1:690. Canada: *Census of Canada, 1921,* 1:568; the baptized membership would be about 21,800, calculated on the basis of comparing 1911 census with 1912 membership figures, the former being about 2.7 times greater (not 2.4 as stated in Frank H. Epp, *Mennonites in Canada, 1786–1920: The History of a Separate People* (Toronto: Macmillan of Canada, 1974), p. 321 [hereafter referred to as Frank H. Epp, *Mennonites in Canada 1786–1920*]) than the latter. China, India, Java/Sumatra: H.S. Bender, "Asia," *Mennonite Encyclopedia,* 1:176–77. Danzig, France, Germany, Netherlands, Poland, and Switzerland: based on Ernst H. Correll, *Das Schweizerische Taeufermennonitentum* (Tuebingen: J.C.B. Mohr, 1925), p. 23. Russia: Cornelius Krahn, "Russia," *Mennonite Encyclopedia,* 4:388. United States of America: based on 1925 report by H.J. Krehbiel in *Bericht ueber die 400 Jaehrige Jubilaeumsfeier der Mennoniten oder Taufgesinnten,* p. 11. Compare with P.M. Friesen, *Alt-Evangelische Mennonitische Brudershaft in Russland (1789–1910)* (Halbstadt: Raduga, 1911), pp. 774–76.

5   See Frank H. Epp, *Mennonite Exodus: The Rescue and Resettlement of the Russian Mennonites Since the Communist Revolution* (Altona: D.W. Friesen & Sons, 1962); John B. Toews, *Lost Fatherland: The Story of the Mennonite Emigration from Soviet Russia, 1921–1927* (Scottdale, Pa.: Herald Press, 1967); *idem,* ed., *Selected Documents: The Mennonites in Russia from 1917–1930* (Winnipeg: Christian Press, 1975); Gerhard P. Schroeder, *Miracles of Grace and Judgment* (Lodi, Cal.: By the Author, 1974).

6   H.H. Ewert, "The Mennonites," an address given under the auspices of the Historical and Scientific Society of Manitoba, 18 April 1932. CGC, XV-31.2, "1910–H.H. Ewert."

7   *Census of Canada, 1921*, 1:346.

8   *Ibid.*

9   The 1921 census does not classify Altona as an urban centre since it was not yet incorporated. However, because its population was very similar to that of Winkler, it may be considered urban for all practical purposes.

10   The exception was found in Europe where many of the Mennonites of Amsterdam, Danzig, Elbing, and other cities had been involved in commerce and the professions for generations. See Horst Penner, *Die Ost- und Westpreussischen Mennnoniten in ihrem Religioesen und Sozialen Leben in ihren Kulturellen und Wirtschaftlichen Leistungen* (Weierhof: Mennonitischer Geschichtsverein, 1978).

11   *Ibid.*, pp. 56–63, 80–81, 200, 306–18.

12   Frank H. Epp, *Mennonites in Canada, 1786–1920*, pp. 56–63. See also CGC, Ivan Groh, "United Empire Loyalists and Mennonite Pioneers of the Niagara Peninsula"; CGC, Ivan Groh, "The Swiss-Palatine-German-Pennsylvania-'Dutch' Pioneers of the Niagara Peninsula."

13   Frank H. Epp, *ibid.*, p. 72.

14   *Ibid.*, pp. 80–81.

15   *Ibid.*, pp. 183–206.

16   *Ibid.*, p. 303–31. Little has been written about this immigration compared to others, but the following memoirs are useful: *Memoirs of Ernest A. Jeschke* (Goshen, Ind.: Marlin Jeschke, 1966) tells the story of a family leaving Poland and settling in Volhynia, then a province in Russia, in 1875, then migrating to North Dakota in 1909 and to Saskatchewan in 1912; Jacob Klaassen, "Memories and Notations About My Life: 1867–1948" covers migration from Prussia to Oklahoma in the 1870s and to Saskatchewan during the Great War; *Personal Diary of Peter Neufeld: 1917–18* (Surrey, B.C.: J.V. Neufeld, 1980) tells the story of movement from Manitoba and the U.S.A. to Vanderhoof, B.C., during the Great War.

17   Frank H. Epp, "The Migrations of the Mennonites," in Paul N. Kraybill, ed., *Mennonite World Handbook* (Lombard, Ill.: Mennonite World Conference, 1978), pp. 10–19.

18   *Ibid.*, p. 12; see also C. Henry Smith, *The Coming of the Russian Mennonites: An Episode in the Settling of the Last Frontier, 1874–1884* (Berne, Ind.: Mennonite Book Concern, 1927).

19   *Census of Canada, 1921*, 1:568–69.

20   *Ibid.*, 1:588–97.

21   Frank H. Epp, *Mennonites in Canada 1786–1920*, p. 72.

22   *Ibid.*, p. 234; see also Chapter 10 of this present volume.

23   CGC, Ivan Groh, "The Swiss-Palatine-German-Pennsylvania-'Dutch' Pioneers of the Niagara Peninsula," pp. 44–45.

24   *Ibid.*, p. 45.

25   *Ibid.*

26   *Census of Canada, 1921*, 1:597–98.
27   *Ibid.*, 1:599–600.
28   *Ibid.*, 1:600–1.
29   *Census of Canada, 1921*, 1:602–3.
30   The Hutterites were an exception, because they bought blocks of land, not because they were granted such blocks. Their solid, relatively compact, and exclusive colonies in Canada, except for the original ones, were all formed after 1920. See, for instance, John Ryan, *The Agricultural Economy of Manitoba Hutterite Colonies* (Toronto: McClelland & Stewart, 1977).
31   Government of Canada, Department of Agriculture, Eugene F. Whelan in an address to the Rural Ontario Municipal Association, 6 February 1979.
32   M.C. Urquhart and K.A.H. Buckley (eds.), *Historical Statistics of Canada* (Toronto: Macmillan, 1965), p. 352.
33   M.C. Urquhart and K.A.H. Buckley, p. 14. See also Robert England, *The Colonization of Western Canada* (London: P.S. King & Son, 1936), p. 71.
34   James B. Hedges, *Building the Canadian West: The Land and Colonization Policies of the Canadian Pacific Railway* (New York: Macmillan, 1939), p. 351. The federal Department of Natural Resources estimated land held by speculators to be about twice that actually occupied.
35   J. Bartlet Brebner, *Canada: A Modern History* (Ann Arbor: University of Michigan Press, 1960), pp. 427–29.
36   M.C. Urquhart and K.A.H. Buckley, p. 352.
37   J.M.S. Careless, *Canada: A Story of Challenge* (Toronto: Macmillan of Canada, 1963), p. 357.
38   Guy Franklin Hershberger, *War, Peace and Nonresistance* (Scottdale, Pa.: Herald Press, 1946).
39   C. Henry Smith, "Mennonites and Culture," *Mennonite Quarterly Review*, 12 (April 1938):78.
40   C. Henry Smith, *The Story of the Mennonites* (Berne, Ind.: Mennonite Book Concern, 1941), p. 231.
41   *Ibid.*, pp. 239–43.
42   Guy F. Hershberger, "Nonresistance," *Mennonite Encyclopedia*, 3:897–906.
43   Ernst Crous, "Nonresistance in Germany," *Mennonite Encyclopedia*, 3:907.
44   Smith, "Mennonites and Culture," p. 78.
45   *Ibid.*
46   Frank H. Epp, *Mennonites in Canada 1786–1920*, pp. 392–94.
47   Canada, Statutes, 7–8 George V, ch. 39, sec. 154(f).
48   Frank H. Epp, *Mennonites in Canada 1786–1920*, pp. 374–86; George H. Reimer, "Canadian Mennonites and World War I" (paper submitted to the Manitoba Historical Society, 1972), pp.

27-35; Adolf Ens, "Mennonite Relations with Governments: Western Canada, 1870-1925" (Ph.D. dissertation, University of Ottawa, 1979), pp. 296-301.

49   Canada, Privy Council Office, P.C. 1204. This Order-in-Council was published in *Canada Gazette* 52 (14 June 1919):3824.

50   A.M. Willms, "The Brethren Known as Hutterites," *The Canadian Journal of Economics and Political Science* 24 (August 1958):391-405.

51   PAC, RG 18, Vol. 1939, File 48, Letter from Sgt. A.B. Perry, Regina, to Lieut. Colonel Starnes, Winnipeg, 11 April 1919.

52   The most comprehensive works on the Mackenzie King era are R. MacGregor Dawson and H. Blair Neatby, *William Lyon Mackenzie King: A Political Biography*, 3 vols. (Toronto: University of Toronto Press, 1958-1976) and J.W. Pickersgill and D.F. Forster, *The Mackenzie King Record*, 4 vols. (Toronto: University of Toronto Press, 1960-1970).

53   Christian Neff and N. van der Zijpp, "William I of Orange," *Mennonite Encyclopedia*, 4:956-57.

54   N. van der Zijpp, "William III of Orange," *Mennonite Encyclopedia*, 4:957; Frank H. Epp, *Mennonites in Canada 1786-1920*, pp. 37, 98.

55   H.G. Mannhardt, "Frederick II," *Mennonite Encyclopedia*, 2:383-84.

56   Christian Neff, "Catherine II," *Mennonite Encyclopedia*, 1:532.

57   Christian Hege, "George I," *Mennonite Encyclopedia*, 2:475-76.

58   Orland Gingerich, *The Amish of Canada* (Waterloo, Ont.: Conrad Press, 1972), pp. 28-29.

59   Wilbur J. Bender, *Nonresistance in Colonial Pennsylvania* (Scottdale, Pa.: Herald Press, 1949), p. 5.

60   Frank H. Epp, *Mennonites in Canada 1786-1920*, pp. 99-100.

61   Orland Gingerich, pp. 28-29, 127.

62   R. MacGregor Dawson and H. Blair Neatby, Vol. 3: *The Price of Unity, 1932-1939*, by H. Blair Neatby. The Introduction has an excellent though brief discussion of King's style of leadership and the limits or constraints of power under which he operated.

63   Donald Avery, *"Dangerous Foreigners": European Immigrant Worker and Labour Radicalism in Canada, 1896-1932* (Toronto: McClelland & Stewart, 1979), pp. 65-89; John Herd Thompson, *The Harvests of War: The Prairie West, 1914-1918* (Toronto: McClelland & Stewart, 1978), pp. 73-94. See also James S. Woodsworth, *Strangers Within Our Gates* (Toronto: University of Toronto Press, 1972), and Marilyn Barber, "Canadianization Through the Schools of the Prairie Provinces Before World War I: The Attitudes and Aims of the English-speaking Majority," in *Ethnic Canadians: Culture and Education*, ed. Martin Kovacs (Regina: Canadian Plains Studies Centre, 1978), pp. 281-94.

64   John Herd Thompson, p. 43.
65   Frank H. Epp, *Mennonites in Canada 1786–1920*, pp. 333–58.
66   This estimate of 10 per cent is based on the number who actually left during the 1920s.
67   Frank H. Epp, "Educational Institutions and Cultural Retention in Canada: The Mennonite Experience" (paper presented to the Canadian Historical Association, University of Western Ontario, June 1978).
68   Sources include *Conference Journal, 1920*, Proceedings of Ontario Conference of the Mennonite Brethren in Christ; *Conference Journal, 1920*, Proceedings of the Northwest Conference of the Mennonite Brethren in Christ; *Mennonite Year-Book and Directory, 1920* (Scottdale: Mennonite Publishing House, 1920), pp. 39, 48, 49, 53, 74, 76, 79; Frank H. Epp, "Directory of Mennonite Congregations," CGC, XV-31.2; Frank H. Epp, *Mennonites in Canada 1786–1920*, pp. 321, 323; [Benjamin Ewert], "Statistik der Mennoniten-Gemeinden," *Der Mitarbeiter* 12 (February 1918):8; Adolf Ens, "Mennonite Relations with Governments, Western Canada: 1870–1925" (Ph.D dissertation, University of Ottawa, 1978), pp. 270–71.
69   For more discussion of this subject, see, for example, William R. Estep, *The Anabaptist Story*, rev. ed. (Grand Rapids: William B. Eerdmans, 1975); Walter Klaassen, *Anabaptism: Neither Catholic nor Protestant* (Waterloo, Ont.: Conrad Press, 1973); Franklin H. Littell, *The Anabaptist View of the Church* (Boston: Starr King Press, 1958).
70   For Mennonite Conference of Ontario history, see L.J. Burkholder, *A Brief History of the Mennonites in Ontario* (Markham, Ont.: Mennonite Conference of Ontario, 1935).
71   Ezra Stauffer, *History of the Alberta-Saskatchewan Mennonite Conference* (Ryley, Alta.: Alberta-Saskatchewan Mennonite Conference, 1960), pp. 1–39; Frank H. Epp, *Mennonites in Canada 1786–1920*, pp. 303–10, 322–23.
72   J. C. Wenger, *The Mennonite Church in America* (Scottdale, Pa.: Herald Press, 1966), pp. 234–37.
73   For Mennonite Brethren in Christ history, see Everek R. Storms, *History of The United Missionary Church* (Elkhart, Ind.: Bethel Publishing Company, 1958).
74   See L.J. Burkholder, pp. 197–200.
75   CGC, VIII-2.1.1, Isaac G. Martin, "The Story of Waterloo-Markham Mennonite Conference," c. 1953.
76   Daniel Musser, *The Reformed Mennonite Church: Its Rise, Progress, with its Principles and Doctrines*, 2nd ed. (Lancaster, Pa.: Inquirer Printing and Publishing Co., 1978); Wilmer J. Eshelman, "History of the Reformed Mennonite Church," *Lancaster County Historical Society* 49 (1945): 85–116; C. Henry Smith and Harold S.

Bender, "Reformed Mennonite Church," *Mennonite Encyclopedia*, 4:267–70.

77   Orland Gingerich, pp. 78–79, 169–71.

78   *Ibid.*, pp. 96–99.

79   P.J.B. Reimer, ed., *The Sesquicentennial Jubilee: Evangelical Mennonite Conference, 1812–1962* (Steinbach, Man.: Evangelical Mennonite Conference, 1962).

80   Clarence Hiebert, *The Holdeman People: The Church of God in Christ Mennonite, 1859–1869* (South Pasadena, Calif.: William Carey Library, 1973).

81   H. F. Epp, "Evangelical Mennonite Brethren," *Mennonite Encyclopedia*, 2:262–64.

82   Calvin Wall Redekop, *The Old Colony Mennonites: Dilemma of Ethnic Minority Life* (Baltimore: Johns Hopkins Press, 1969); Harry Leonard Sawatzky, *They Sought a Country: Mennonite Colonization in Mexico* (Berkeley: University of California Press, 1971).

83   H.J. Gerbrandt, *Adventure in Faith: The Background in Europe and the Development in Canada of the Bergthaler Mennonite Church of Manitoba* (Altona: D.W. Friesen & Sons for the Bergthaler Mennonite Church of Manitoba, 1970).

84   CGC, Hist. Mss. 13.53, Peter Peters, "History of Chortitzer Church in Canada."

85   Menno Hildebrand, "The Sommerfelder Mennonites of Manitoba," *The Canadian Mennonite* 18 (27 November 1970): 6–7, 15–17. See also E.K. Francis, *In Search of Utopia: The Mennonites of Manitoba* (Altona, Man.: D.W. Friesen & Sons, 1955), p. 171; H.J. Gerbrandt, pp. 92–3.

86   J.G. Rempel, *Die Rosenorter Gemeinde in Wort und Bild* (Rosthern, Sask.: D.H. Epp, 1950).

87   J.G. Rempel, *Fuenfzig Jahre Konferenzbestrebungen, 1902–1952*, 2 vols. (n.p. [1952]), 1:46, 70, 91, 114.

88   Samuel Floyd Pannabecker, *Open Doors: A History of the General Conference Mennonite Church* (Newton, Kans.: Faith and Life Press, 1975), pp. 151–67.

89   John A. Toews, *A History of the Mennonite Brethren Church: Pilgrims and Pioneers* (Fresno, Calif.: Board of Christian Literature, General Conference of Mennonite Brethren Churches, 1975).

90   Harold S. Bender, "Krimmer Mennonite Brethren," *Mennonite Encyclopedia*, 3:242–45, and Toews, *History of the Mennonite Brethren Church*, pp. 176–93.

91   See Frank H. Epp, *Mennonites in Canada 1786–1920*, p. 317, with special reference, for illustrative purposes, to Aberdeen, Langham, and Waldheim.

92   Frank H. Epp, "The true north (2): The Church that disappeared, whose influence lives on," *Mennonite Reporter* 4 (19 March 1974):11.

93   CGC, XV-31.2, "1910–Vanderhoof": J.V. Neufeld, "The Men-
      nonite Settlement near Vanderhoof in Nechako Valley, British
      Columbia, 1918"; *Personal Diary of Peter Neufeld, 1917–1918*
      (Surrey, B.C.: J.V. Neufeld, 1980).

94   For a similar analysis of social change among Mennonites, see Leo
      Driedger, "The Anabaptist Identification Ladder: Plain-Urbane
      Continuity in Diversity," *Mennonite Quarterly Review* 51 (October
      1977): 278–91.

95   Rodney J. Sawatsky, "Domesticated Sectarianism: Mennonites in
      the U.S. and Canada in Comparative Perspective," *Canadian
      Journal of Sociology* 3 (Spring 1978):233–44.

96   Harold S. Bender, "Language Problem," *Mennonite Encyclopedia*,
      3:291.

97   See, for example, James H. Juhnke, *A People of Two Kingdoms: The
      Political Acculturation of the Kansas Mennonites* (Newton, Kans.:
      Faith and Life Press, 1975).

98   J. C. Wenger and Harold S. Bender, "Nonconformity," *Menno-
      nite Encyclopedia*, 3:896.

99   Gospel Herald and *Christian Monitor*, two of the periodicals
      published by the Mennonite Publishing House of Scottdale,
      enjoyed wide readership among Swiss Mennonites in Canada and
      the editorship of the latter was located in Canada for most of its years
      of publication. For a history of the Old Mennonite publishing
      firm, see John A. Hostetter, *God Uses Ink: The Heritage and
      Mission of the Mennonite Publishing House After Fifty Years* (Scott-
      dale, Pa.: Herald Press, 1958).

100   S. G. Shetler and J. S. Hartzler, "Our Position on Peace,"
      Mennonite Year-Book and Directory, 1920, p. 21.

101   John D. Unruh, *In the Name of Christ: A History of the Mennonite
      Central Committee and Its Service, 1920–1951* (Scottdale, Pa.:
      Herald Press, 1952), pp. 11–40. See also P.C. Hiebert and Orie
      O. Miller, eds., *Feeding the Hungry: Russia Famine 1919–1925*
      (Scottdale, Pa.: Mennonite Central Committee, 1929).

102   Guy F. Hershberger, "Historical Background to the Formation of
      the Mennonite Central Committee," *Mennonite Quarterly Review*
      44 (July 1970): 213–44; Hiebert and Miller, pp. 27–54.

103   Harold S. Bender, "Asia," *Mennonite Encyclopedia* 1:177. For the
      story of one group's escape from Siberia to Manchuria, see Abram
      Friesen and Abram J. Loewen, *Die Flucht ueber den Amur* (Stein-
      bach, Man.: Echo-Verlag, 1946). See also Chapter 4 of this present
      volume.

104   Gerhard Lohrenz, "The Mennonites of Russia and the Great
      Commission," in Cornelius J. Dyck, ed., *A Legacy of Faith*
      (Newton, Kans.: 1962):171–91.

105   Fred Richard Belk, *The Great Trek of the Russian Mennonites to
      Central Asia 1880–1884* (Scottdale, Pa.: Herald Press, 1976).

106 See Chapter 4.
107 H. G. Mannhardt and Harold S. Bender, "Danzig, Free City of," *Mennonite Encyclopedia*, 2:7.
108 Heinold Fast, *Die Vereinigung der Deutschen Mennonitengemeinden, 1886–1961* (Weierhof: Vereinigung der Deutschen Mennonitengemeinden, 1961), pp. 28–30.
109 John Horsch, "Post-War Conditions Among European Mennonites," *Mennonite Year-Book and Directory, 1922* (Scottdale, Pa.: Mennonite Publishing House, 1922), p. 22.

2. Reaffirmation of the Fundamentals

Many a firm believer in the atonement of Jesus' blood has been swallowed up in modernism because he gave heed to some broad religious call, which was nothing better than socialism — OSCAR BURKHOLDER.[1]

"Fundamentalism" is not necessarily, and in fact not generally, synonymous with the fundamentals — VERNON SMUCKER.[2]

O NE RESPONSE to the societal pressures which were threatening the Mennonite faith and way of life was to bolster that faith and to reinforce that way of life from within. While some Mennonites emphasized selective accommodation to society and others deliberate segregation from society as survival strategies, still others chose to cope with unwanted external influences primarily by strengthening the internal resources through teaching, preaching, and the production of literature. To this end, various organizational initiatives had been undertaken, schools and conferences had been founded, and publishing ventures had been established in earlier decades.

The varying approaches to survival were not mutually exclusive. Both accommodation and segregation were rarely ends in themselves, but rather means to the desired ends. In the minds of their respective advocates, the adoption of some things new or the isolation from all things new contributed to the strengthening of the faith. And those who promoted Mennonite institutions and organizations

48

must have known instinctively that those institutions represented a degree of accommodation as well as a degree of segregation. At one and the same time, they represented an adjustment to a society which was obsessed with organizations and institution-building, and a protection from that society through institutions uniquely Mennonite.

In the 1920s the issue was not so much the proliferation of institutions but the filling of those already part of the Mennonite scene with the right content, in other words with the true faith. And while this involved elements of both accommodation and segregation, the central thrust was neither of these two but rather the accentuation of that which had always come first, the centralities of Christian doctrine. To achieve this purpose, leaders of the century-old Mennonite Conference of Ontario sought a return to those things which were basic for the church. A statement on Christian Fundamentals, prepared in part by Bishop S. F. Coffman of Ontario and endorsed by the 1921 sessions of the Mennonite General Conference, provided the springboard for that "return," which, however, was accomplished only with divisive results.

The reaffirmation of the fundamentals meant not only strengthening Mennonite peculiarities such as the doctrine of nonresistance, directly tested by the war, and the practice of nonconformity, increasingly under siege, but also Christian theology and ethics in general, as historically taught by the Mennonites. This reaffirmation, however, could no longer happen only with reference to Anabaptism; it also had to take into consideration the religious winds which were blowing contemporaneously across the Canadian and American landscapes, because Mennonites were being influenced as much by their environment as by their heritage.

That Mennonites were not immune to the coming and going of religious movements had already been amply demonstrated in both Europe and North America in the nineteenth century. Most of the religious battles among them in the century just past had to do with degrees of adjustment or degrees of resistance to religious and secular movements confronting them from without. In Canada, the "migration" of the New Mennonites in the direction of revivalism and the objection of the Old Order Mennonites to every new fad, religious and otherwise, were already a matter of record. The Old Mennonites, anxiously seeking a reasonable middle course between the two extremes, were being pulled in both directions, as they sought to rediscover and reaffirm the centralities of the faith.

It was precisely in that middle ground where the struggle here reported was most intense and this explains why the Old Mennonites of North America in general and the Mennonite Conference of Ontario in particular are centre-stage in this chapter. It is also true that the Mennonite General Conference was the largest of the Mennonite bodies in North America, though not in Canada and not in Ontario. However, whatever their numbers, wherever they were, they, the Old Mennonites, of all Mennonites, were most pulled in two directions. The normal tension between progressive and conservative forces in their midst was now complicated and accentuated by, or overlaid with, another set of forces. These were sometimes perceived to be allies and sometimes enemies in the struggle.

The effort to achieve a restatement of the faith coincided with, and to a certain extent perhaps was prompted by, a parallel movement in North American Protestantism known as fundamentalism. A certain borrowing therefrom was inevitable, not least of all because of the common language in use. Only a few people would learn to differentiate between the Mennonite fundamentals being espoused by the Old Mennonite Church and the Christian fundamentalist movement as such, or among the various literalist approaches to the Bible being advanced. To the promoters and to the laity the language and the meanings tended to be the same or, if not exactly the same, very similar and quite interchangeable.

Fundamentalism was basically an American movement, as was its counterpart, the modernist social gospel. However, both theological streams had Canadian parallels, which served to reinforce the influences from the south. On the one hand were the efforts within Canada towards reform in society and towards ecumenical association of the churches, the latter culminating in the formation in 1925 of the United Church of Canada.[3] On the other hand were the promotions of personal salvation and piety, such as came from the flamboyant fundamentalist, and schismatic, Baptist preacher T. T. Shields in Toronto.[4]

In Canada the fundamentalist movement had a strong anchor in the Niagara Bible Conference, incorporated by that name under the laws of Canada in 1893.[5] Indeed, in its 25-year history the institution had already exercised leadership throughout the continent as "the mother of the very influential North American prophecy and Bible conference movement [and] a major force in shaping conservative Protestant theology into what soon was called fundamentalism."[6] The Conference helped to popularize a general preoccupation with the end times, the verbal inspiration of the Bible, faith missions, and revivalism.

For a variety of reasons the fundamentalist movement exerted the greater influence among Mennonites, but the social gospel stream did not go unnoticed. The American-based General Conference Mennonite Church, for instance, had become a member of the Federal Council of Churches, one of fundamentalism's main targets, at its founding in 1908 and remained in it for a decade.[7] There were other connections to the non-fundamentalist side. In Ontario numerous "assimilated Mennonites" ended up as members of the newly formed United Church of Canada, having previously become Methodists or members of the Evangelical Association, two of the denominational tributaries flowing into the ecumenical body.[8]

Moreover, one of the favourite German gospel hymnbooks, especially among the Dutch Mennonites in both the U.S.A. and Canada, turned out to be *Evangeliumslieder* (Gospel Songs), translated and edited by none other than Walter Rauschenbusch, one of the giants of the social gospel movement, who was much misunderstood and wrongly maligned. As with Rauschenbusch, so also with the Mennonites the evangelical faith had compelling social dimensions. The love of one's fellow human beings was inseparably linked to a professed love of God. In the words of Menno Simons:

> For true evangelical faith is of such a nature that it cannot lie
> dormant, but manifests itself in all righteousness and works of
> love; . . . it clothes the naked; it feeds the hungry; it comforts
> the sorrowful; it shelters the destitute; . . . it serves those that
> harm it; . . . it binds up that which is wounded; . . . it has
> become all things to all men.[9]

However, the impediments to a Mennonite embracing the social gospel movement were also great, above all because it implied political involvement of some kind at some level, an activity at that time quite foreign to Mennonites. Only a small minority at that time voted in national or even civic elections, though the election to public office of some individuals has been previously noted.[10] Besides, in both Canada and the U.S.A. the influence of the social gospel accented the citizenship obligations of the Christian, and for many social gospel advocates, though not for all, this led directly to support of the war effort. Indeed, it was the militarism of the Federal Council in the U.S.A. which prompted the General Conference to withdraw from membership in that body.[11] The social gospel, requiring social and political involvement, often produced different modes of involvement. For some it reinforced pacifism, for others militarism.

Similarly in Canada, diverse ideological and organizational alliances sprang from the social gospel and, from the Mennonite perspective, led its proponents and followers in strange directions. The Mennonites could have accepted the temperance and prohibitionist movements, or even joined them, as some of them did.[12] The cause of the Lord's Day Alliance was also to their liking. Mennonites kept not only the Sabbath but numerous additional Christian holidays. However, unions for workers and suffrage for women appeared unnecessary, if not dangerous, while militarism as a religious duty and Canadianization as the deliberate assimilation of minority groups[13] were totally unacceptable. Most problematic also was the social gospel's link to modernism and generally also its language. For most Mennonites the word "fundamentalism" sounded much better than "modernism."

Fundamentalism in America

Before examining the precise impact of the fundamentalist movement upon the Mennonite churches, the manner in which it gained entry into their ranks, and the degree to which the churches in Canada were affected, brief attention must be given to a general review of the nature of the fundamentalist-modernist controversy and its major issues. Fundamentalism and modernism emerged and evolved essentially as different religious responses to the rapidly changing social conditions in the latter part of the nineteenth century. The depression and shock resulting from the civil war had been followed by the disruption of rural traditions and the disorientation resulting from rapid urbanization and industrialization.

In the midst of these great changes was planted the message of progress. Astonishing advances in the fields of science, medicine, and technology gave rise to a growing wave of optimism and with it the hope that, through judicious use and application of this new knowledge, the world could be made a better and more peaceful place for mankind. Theories of progress, expounded variously by Darwin, Marx, and others, exploded upon the world in the latter part of the century with enormous implications in many areas of life.[14]

Increasingly, all disciplines became subject to exacting scientific methods and analysis. It was not long before the Bible and its teachings were affected by the intellectual climate of the times. The message of Scripture was reassessed in relation to the new scientific findings and along with the insights provided by recent discoveries in biology, psychology, and sociology. The new textual scrutiny of the Bible, called "higher criticism," tended to emphasize the ethical aspects of Scripture over the doctrinal teachings.[15] Reflecting the positive scientific mood of the times, the new ethic stressed the need for, and the possibility of, the transformation of the social environment and not only the rebirth of the individual. The advocates of such social gospel views were called progressives, modernists, or liberals.

Set over against them were those traditionalists and conservatives who believed that the new theories threatened the very fundamentals of the Christian religion. Though the spokesmen for fundamentalism rarely attained a well-defined solidarity, they still managed to counter effectively the "modern apostasy" along lines described as both apologetic and apocalyptic. Apologetics had reference to doctrine and the defence of the faith. Apocalyptics had to do with the unfolding of history and the end times. Essentially, it was the union of two nineteenth-century theological systems, the so-called Princeton theology and Plymouth Brethren dispensationalism, that gave fundamentalism a definable form.[16]

Princeton theology, emanating from the seminary bearing the same name, was committed to the defence of an "inerrant and infallible" Scripture, a phrase that was to become the fulcrum of the fundamentalist movement. A basic tenet of the school's belief was that divine inspiration rested in some external authority and that this authority was an inerrant Bible. A perfect God, so these theologians declared, would not have revealed himself through a fallible work. Consequently, they argued that not only was the Bible verbally inspired, but it was also inerrant in its every "reference, statistic, and quotation when first written down on the original autographs."[17] In the popular translation of this teaching, it was usually forgotten that inerrancy was claimed only for the original autographs. Indeed, what was understood was that the King James Bible was inerrant and infallible, and such understanding was only one short step removed from implying that the fundamentalist interpreters themselves were beyond challenge and criticism.

The fundamentalists also challenged the overly optimistic liberal spirit with respect to human development and social evolution. Helpful to this end were the doctrines of dispensationalism. Dispensationalist teaching had originated with the Plymouth Brethren in England and Ireland a century earlier and become a popular doctrine within American Protestant circles by the 1870s.[18] As already indicated, the Niagara Bible Conference was a strong Canadian source of such teaching. According to the dispensationalists, history was divided into periods or dispensations, usually seven in number. In each age, God had his followers, though the qualities of the faithful differed from period to period and certain divine expectations did not apply to them until the dawn of the millennium, a 1,000-year period referred to in the Book of Revelation.[19]

In this way, the ethical teachings of the Kingdom, which spelled out the social obligations of the church, could be omitted from fundamentalist dogma since, it was conveniently argued, they were not applicable in the present age. The overriding concern of the church in the present time should be to preach and to save souls for the future. Christian energies should be channelled not towards action for social reform but rather towards the salvation of individuals.[20]

The dispensationalist neglect of social betterment was consistent with an intensely pessimistic view of the world's future and with a belief in the imminent and direct intervention of God in the affairs of the world. Thus, in sharp contrast to the optimism of the American creed and the fresh theological articulations of the liberals, modernists, and progressives, the dispensationalists and fundamentalists insisted that society was doomed, while at the same time enthusiastically championing the possibility of man's personal salvation.

Although incipient fundamentalism was evident in Canada during the 1800s, not least of all in the emergence of the Mennonite

Brethren in Christ denomination, it maintained a relatively low profile prior to the turn of the century. Its character was tempered by the steady conservative influence of Moody Bible Institute in Chicago, which school had attracted not only such young Mennonite men as John F. Funk, the outstanding American Mennonite publisher prior to the twentieth century, but also S.F. Coffman, the outstanding Old Mennonite bishop in Canada in the first half of the twentieth century and leader in the Ontario Mennonite Bible School, and later William J. Bestvater of the Herbert Bible School in Saskatchewan.[21] Moody and his followers defended the faith against the inroads of heresy not through open polemics with the modernists, but rather through the medium of Bible conferences, revival meetings, pamphlets, and periodicals which strengthened the faithful. In other words, the conservative and fundamentalist stance of Moody Bible Institute and its graduates had a moderating quality about it because of its restrained rhetoric and tempered tone.

A radical shift in the complexion of fundamentalist leadership, and subsequently a change in the entire tenor of the movement, occurred early in the twentieth century. From that point on, every "modernist heresy" was answered with all the authoritativeness and straightforwardness of direct quotations from Scripture, even if this meant taking passages out of their biblical context. The Great War played a crucial role in converting a relatively sedate fundamentalism into an aggressive, offensive-minded movement, dedicated to the annihilation of the modernist foe. The scale of the carnage and destruction produced by the war, without precedent in human history, appeared to verify fundamentalist convictions that any attempts at world reform and peace were in vain.[22] Moreover, the war supplied the fundamentalists with an increasingly militant language that could be used against the religious enemy.[23]

And through an interesting twist of logic, the fundamentalists endeavoured to link the modernists—at least those modernists who were also pacifists—with the German foe and indeed with all the enemies of America.[24] The cries of the modernists for peace and reform, the fundamentalists contended, had undermined morale and left the West unprepared for the treacheries of the German empire. Subsequently, the fundamentalist critique of social reform programs became even more vehement, and proponents of pacifism and overseas relief were quickly accused of harbouring pro-German and pro-

Bolshevik sympathies. Common were the claims that modernism and evolution had brought together the following:

> the Reds of Russia, the university professors of Germany, England, and America, the IWWs [Industrial Workers of the World, also known as "Wobblies"], and every bum from the "down and out" sections of every city in America.[25]

Fundamentalism Among Old Mennonites

The simple but forceful and self-assured character of the fundamentalist message exercised a powerful attraction upon the minds of a large segment of the American populace, including the Old Mennonites. Offering simple answers to a complex set of questions, fundamentalism provided a measure of security to a people just emerging from their long history of isolation. Here was a religion that was conservative in its theology, straightforward and biblicist in its claims, traditional and rural in its appeal, one that reaffirmed the authority of church leaders.

Mennonites had much in common with the fundamentalists and, because they lacked full awareness of crucial differences, it was hardly surprising that some Mennonites found common cause with the fundamentalist position. Fundamentalism allowed them to remain true to the biblicism of their Anabaptist traditions and at the same time to step outside of that tradition into a wider Christian identity. The appeal was irresistible, especially where the implications for the Mennonites of following fundamentalism were not fully understood.

Historic Anabaptism and North American fundamentalism none the less represented two different "forms of faith," which, according to J.B. Toews, clashed with each other.[26] The one form was that of "an existential Christianity" and the other that of a "creedal theological system." The two forms represented different approaches to essential elements of the faith in a number of areas, including the Scriptures, conversion, discipleship, and the church, as well as missions and evangelism.

The devotion to the Bible as the Word of God for the Anabaptists was "not the end of a chain of logic" but much more "an exercise of faith" that manifested itself in obedience to the teaching and life of

Jesus. Hence, a shift from Anabaptism to fundamentalism meant shifting "the centre of faith" from a relationship of obedience to a creedal polemic and proof-texting which focus "on the inerrancy of the Scriptures in the original autographs which are non-existent." In other words, fundamentalism substituted for true faith and gradual guidance into all truth by the Holy Spirit "a system of logic for the absolute trustworthiness of the Bible."

Further, Anabaptism understood conversion "as a transformation of life" verified "in a life of discipleship," which included nonresistance, non-swearing of the oath, and the pursuit of peace. Fundamentalism, on the other hand, exalted only the *work* of the cross, meaning grace, and neglected the *way* of the cross, meaning disciplined and abstemious living. Fundamentalism was aggressive, unusually self-assertive, militant, militaristic, and also individualistic. Whereas for Anabaptism the Christian life was lived in the context of the congregation, fundamentalism was highly individualistic and the experience of the church as a community tended to be absent.

For the time being, the differences between the "two forms" were obvious to the dissenters, but less so to those leaders in the Old Mennonite Church whose passion was a return to the fundamentals. They were fighting, as it were, a two-front war: the trends towards new modes of living, arising from modernity, and the threat of new modes of thinking, arising from modernism. In this struggle, fundamentalism was an obvious ally, though Mennonites wanted a Mennonite variety of fundamentalism.

Mennonite fundamentalism suffered from the absence of a definitively worded contemporary theology. That such a confession had not yet been formulated was due to the agrarian Mennonite background, the satisfied reliance on such historic documents as the Dordrecht Confession, and the interest in publishing being relatively recent. The printed word and written self-expression had only begun to play an important role through the pioneer publishing efforts of John F. Funk, first at Chicago, then at Elkhart, Indiana.

Funk's *Herald of Truth* (1864–1908),[27] as the first Mennonite periodical in America, was eventually replaced by the more official, and for this topic crucial, *Gospel Herald* (1908–), published at Scottdale, Pennsylvania, by the Mennonite General Conference.[28] It was the *Gospel Herald*, as well as the earlier German-language

Herold der Wahrheit (1864–1901),[29] a twin-publication of *Herald of Truth*, which gave to the church its foremost articulators of the fundamentals during this period. The first of them was John Horsch (1867–1941), born in Austria and partially educated in Germany, whose emigration to America to escape military service gave Funk his much-needed German editor in 1887. Thus began a 55-year career for Horsch in editorial work and historical and theological writing which was most influential in the 1920s.[30]

The second was Daniel Kauffman (1865–1944). As editor for 39 years of the *Gospel Herald* (1908–1943), frequent moderator of the church and omnipresent committeeman—at one time he was a member of 22 committees and boards—and a speaker in much demand, Daniel Kauffman moulded the life and thought of the church as no other individual during that time.[31] Both Horsch and Kauffman fashioned the official policy and polity of the Old Mennonite Church in the mould of their own conservative, authoritarian, and also very decisive preferences. Through them the church was transformed to correspond closely to classic fundamentalist sentiments.

The view of Scriptures embodied in the Princeton theology was widely disseminated throughout the church by Daniel Kauffman. During his long association with the *Gospel Herald*, that periodical was filled with editorials and articles endorsing fundamentalist thought.[32] His *Bible Doctrine*, an interpretative work prepared in response to a conference request, confidently asserted that the Bible was "inspired from cover to cover; that every part is alike inspired, and that the words of Scriptures express inerrantly, the truths God wished to declare."[33] Both the periodical and the book were widely read in Canada.

Along with Kauffman, Horsch contributed much of the material propounding similar thinking. The study of early Mennonite history was Horsch's consuming passion, but even here his predisposition coloured his interpretation of the origins. His examination of the Anabaptist progenitors appeared to be prompted more by a desire to affirm their religious orthodoxy in the light of contemporary faith than to uncover objectively the essence of their teachings. Accordingly, the early Anabaptists were pictured more as theologically sound twentieth-century conservatives than as radical sixteenth-century dissenters.[34]

Horsch possessed a genuine dread of the new, popular, religious liberalism. He sincerely believed that modernism threatened the very foundations of true Christianity, and he marshalled his best forces to combat the admission of heresy into Mennonite ranks. *The Mennonite Church and Modernism*, published in 1924, was one such effort aimed at exposing and discrediting the liberal elements resident within the Mennonite Church.[35] Indicted most heavily were educators such as Vernon Smucker, John E. Hartzler, and Noah E. Byers, faculty members at Goshen College. They were accused of spiritual unorthodoxy with regard to such items as the authority of Scripture, the divinity of Christ, and the authority of the bishops. The charges were not supported with credible evidence, but they typified Horsch's ready inclination to denounce those men and institutions that were not, in his opinion, sufficiently anti-modernist and not solidly fundamentalist.

The adoption of "Eighteen Fundamentals" at the 1921 Mennonite General Conference reflected the widespread adoption of fundamentalist language within the Church. While there was some objection to the addition of yet another confession of faith to the "canon," the "Fundamentals" were accepted as a "restatement of [the Dort (*sic*) Confession] in the light of present religious contentions and teachings."[36] What this meant was that historical Mennonitism was now firmly related to, if not identified with, contemporary fundamentalism.

A brief survey of the articles quickly demonstrates the degree to which the fundamentalist ideas had penetrated Mennonite ranks.[37] Article I affirmed "the plenary and verbal inspiration of the Bible as the Word of God . . . inerrant in the original writings . . .". Article III announced "that the Genesis account of the Creation is an historic fact and literally true." Article X, with probable reference to the advocates of the social gospel, admonished the church "to keep herself aloof from all movements which seek the reformation of society independent of the merits of the death of Christ and the experience of the new birth." Article XIV, sounding the familiar pre-millennial warning bell, observed that "the latter days will be characterized by general lawlessness and departure from the faith; . . . further, that present conditions indicate that we are now living in these perilous times." Articles XV – XVIII predicted "the bodily resurrection" of all men, after passing through an "intermediate state" and an ultimate destiny in either heaven or hell. Significantly, only a passing reference was made in the "Eighteen Fundamentals" to the principle of nonresistance.

The inflammatory and judgmental spirit accompanying the fundamentalist-modernist dispute made a reasonable approach to conciliatory discussion virtually impossible, especially when emotions ran high on both sides, and persons or institutions often emerged as the focal points of the debate. Within the Old Mennonite Church, Goshen College assumed a central role in the protracted religious wranglings.[38] A minority faculty group, led by Smucker and Byers, and drawing its support mainly from the younger, relatively well educated constituency, challenged the majority, represented by the older, less erudite leadership, more attuned to fundamentalist ways of thought. Suspect theological opinions on various issues, ranging from the deity of Christ to the plenary inspiration of the Bible, were most often cited as the root cause of the college's internal turmoil. Compounding the difficulties was the fact that the conflict was, to a large extent, generational and related as much to varying approaches to historic Anabaptism as to the theological movements of the day. O.B. Gerig, a spokesman for the younger group, confirmed this much when he explained that "a small section of the Mennonite Church, mostly the younger generation, has come to see the really noble sentiments and ideals of their historic faith."[39]

For six years, from 1918 to 1924, the Goshen controversy ground on. In the end, the conservative faction, headed by the perennial leaders, Horsch and Kauffman, excised what they considered to be "liberal" elements from the college's faculty. The latter, disillusioned and frustrated by the experience, left the Old Church to accept positions at Bethel College or Bluffton College, schools of constituencies within the more tolerant General Conference Mennonite Church.[40] But these individuals did not give up their cause.

Very promptly, they founded the monthly *Christian Exponent* as an alternative voice,[41] contending that " 'fundamentalism' is not necessarily, and in fact not generally, synonymous with the fundamentals."[42] They cautioned against an uncritical acceptance of fundamentalism and urged that those elements which were incongruous with the tradition be promptly discarded. They were also repelled by the acrimonious language and the intolerant spirit which were common to fundamentalist rhetoric. In response to Horsch's brash offensive mounted in *The Mennonite Church and Modernism*, Vernon Smucker replied:

> The methods and motives [of Horsch] must be utterly abhorrent to anyone who is a true Christian and who desires to see fair play and knows the facts in the case.[43]

The forced faculty resignations at Goshen College signalled a decisive victory for the conservative forces. Curriculum revisions subsequently introduced at the college reflected the institution's new alliances. The denominational Mennonite Board of Education, to which the college was ultimately responsible, declared that it would tolerate no compromise on "religious essentials," which were interpreted to include areas such as dress and nonconformity.[44] Pronouncements endorsing the verbal and plenary inspiration of the Scriptures were made, along with outspoken criticism of institutions that were deemed "unsound." Additionally, the Board recommended that "the first and fundamental work of the church was to evangelize the world rather than to reform the world."[45]

One specific area of contention between the leaders and the young educators was the doctrine of nonresistance. This principle, though somewhat brittle in its application and often not understood in any comprehensive manner by its adherents, remained a basic and indispensable position. But not all who deemed the doctrine important interpreted it in the same way. For some, nonresistance was a personal ethic. Others saw it as a relevant social and political ethic. Evangelist John S. Coffman, for instance, had felt a kinship with political and humanitarian peace movements, which he regarded as Christian, if not in identity, then in terms of direction.[46]

Now, however, the Mennonite stance on peace and nonresistance was modified by the absorption of mainstream American religious values. Embracing fundamentalism, the Old Church was compelled to reinterpret one of its historic fundamentals. It thus found itself opposing "modern pacifism" because of its link to the social gospel and urging believers to do their utmost to avoid "the so-called peace movement."[47] This position on war and the peace movements, though widely accepted, suffered from an ironic inconsistency that was readily recognized by its detractors. On the one hand, the Mennonites had energetically campaigned for the military exemption of their members during the war. At the same time, they denounced all social peace programs, proclaiming them to be unchristian. It became incumbent upon them somehow to reconcile the contradiction within their platform and provide themselves with historical and biblical legitimacy.

This task was undertaken and accomplished by Horsch, who submitted a revised critique of nonresistance which was to become the official Mennonite position. Horsch's formulation was ingenious for its simplicity. According to its premise, biblical nonresistance was "based on the Gospel which teaches that righteousness is the fruit of the new birth." Hence, nonresistance was only the fruit, not the root, of the gospel. It followed on Christian conversion, which was an essential prerequisite. This was fundamentally distinct from modern pacifism, which substituted mere social betterment for biblical regeneration.[48]

The inevitable conclusion of his position was that Christians were preferably nonresistant but not necessarily nonresistant, this virtue being a fruit of the gospel. But equally important was the fact that only Christians, as defined by him, could be nonresistant or pacifist. Hence, all other forms of peace concern or opposition to war were unacceptable because they were not properly grounded. Horsch's interpretation was warmly received by the majority of the church leaders. His dichotomy permitted them to retain their ties with fundamentalist orientations, while at the same time allowing them to remain true to their historic faith as they perceived it.

A second problematic situation involved the doctrine of nonconformity. Since the sixteenth century, the Mennonites had held the notion that they were to be separate from, and nonconformed to, the world. Thus, they believed that their way of living was not to be guided by the standards and modes of the surrounding society but by the biblical imperatives of such passages as the Sermon on the Mount in particular. In North America this doctrine of separation had been reinforced by the continued use of the German language in an English-language culture and by geographic isolation in the context of a rural and agricultural way of life.

Early in the twentieth century, however, the Old Mennonites in North America had abandoned the German language to a very large extent and thus severed one form of cultural separation. The result was much greater social intercourse with the outside world, and a new fear that such association would lead to the loss of their unique identity. In other words, the loss of traditional social controls threatened the preservation of the old way of life. The German language and other symbols of separation having been lost, simplicity in clothing styles became for conservative Mennonites the final citadel "which must be held at all cost."[49]

Fundamentalism in Ontario

Canadian developments in many ways paralleled the American experience. In Ontario the leaders of the church grappled with many of the same issues confronting their southern colleagues and, in almost every instance, the outcome was the same. This was not surprising, because both areas of the church were served by the same periodicals, and the international border was not one that made a big difference in the Old Church. Fundamentalism, as defined and endorsed by the 1921 Conference session, and as disseminated to many Canadian homes through the medium of the *Gospel Herald*, became the approved theology of the Mennonite Conference of Ontario. Basic fundamentalist motifs, such as biblical infallibility, millennialism, and personal salvation, made their way to the people and experienced a warm reception.[50] Naturally, fundamentalism had its practical applications as well. Mennonites were admonished from the pulpit or at evangelistic meetings to remain aloof from sinful worldly amusements, life insurance companies, secret societies, sports, radio, and secular music.[51] "For fifty years," one Ontario minister claimed, "this book [Daniel Kauffman's *Bible Doctrines*] was of great influence" especially with respect to fundamentalism and nonconformity.[52]

An effective blend of traditional Mennonite piety and contemporary fundamentalist conservatism was thus established. The synthesis worked, not in small part because of the positive impression made by the leaders upon their followers. Strong personalities such as S.F. Coffman, Oscar Burkholder, and later C.F. Derstine were convinced that the tenets of fundamentalism and Mennonitism were compatible. Their absolute confidence was transmitted to, and observed by, the people who responded to firm leadership as they faced the changing forces of the twentieth century. Fundamentalist-inspired precepts provided this direction. In the words of Paul Martin:

> ... Mennonites showed their greatest interest in the Funda-mentalists. I believe it was at this stage that we learned to use the Bible in very legalistic and prescriptive ways.[53]

S.F. Coffman, bishop of the Lincoln County area Old Mennonite Churches, is considered by many to have been Ontario's most influential voice in the first half of the twentieth century.[54] He was a moderate who consistently held that a policy of patience and restraint was the wisest approach to the religious developments overtaking Ontario and the wider church. His first love lay in preparing exegeses on such books of the Bible as Acts or Corinthians or in elaborating on the significance and symbolism of the tabernacle in the Old Testament. Had Coffman's talents as a co-ordinator, committee person, and mediator been less exceptional, he likely would have devoted his working life to biblical research. However, both the Mennonite Conference of Ontario and the Mennonite General Conference recognized Coffman's abilities, and as a result, the bishop was recruited for a myriad of church-related assignments. He represented the conferences on history, peace, literature, music, fundamentals, and Sunday School committees. During the Great War he also served as official liaison between the Ontario Menno-nites and Ottawa.

Coffman's gentle disposition precluded his involvement in public disputes with those with whom he disagreed. Quiet counsel and reasoned dialogue were to him preferable, and more scriptural, than outright verbal battle. Coffman had, like his mentor John F. Funk, achieved an effective fusion of Anabaptism and the theology of Moody Bible Institute, and his reputation for orthodoxy and depend-ability resulted in his being named to a select committee appointed to study, and then prepare a statement on, the Mennonite doctrinal position. The culmination of this work was the adoption of the aforementioned "Eighteen Fundamentals" which were intended "to safeguard our people from the inroads of false doctrines which assail the Word of God and threaten the foundation of our faith...."[55]

Coffman was at first reluctant to accept the assignment, not because he objected to affirming the fundamental truths, but because he considered the church to be adequately served by the Dordrecht Confession formulated in 1632. The Ontario leader questioned the need for another doctrinal statement and worried whether such might not prove injurious to church unity. He also wondered whether the committee was only to delineate the church's position on disputed doctrine or whether it was to compile a comprehensive statement on the church's faith.[56] In the end, Coffman suppressed his reservations and submitted to the responsibility. The Conference was fortunate that he did so, for throughout the course of the project, Coffman distinguished himself as a champion of tolerance and charity. He reminded his fellow members that even the Dordrecht Confession had shown some flexibility on non-essential matters, and he recommended that

> the same sincerity must be observed by us concerning the foundations of our faith. The same charity concerning our individual opinion regarding some of the teachings of Christ and the apostles, among which are some things hard to understand.[57]

Coffman's thoughts on the subject of the Bible and its inspiration were unequivocal. "Any position on the authenticity of the records of the Bible but that of simple faith is unsatisfactory," he testified. "Every record of events must be true."[58] The inspiration of the Scriptures held a fascination for the Vineland bishop, and he inserted a number of articles on the topic in his "Bible Study" column, featured regularly in the *Christian Monitor*.[59] Partly as a result of Coffman's leadership, the Mennonite Conference maintained a strong belief in the Bible as reliable and undisputed authority and pre-millennialism as the basis of human hope. The annual meeting in Vineland in June 1924 drew attention to the "tide of unbelief that is sweeping over the world, preventing the salvation of multitudes, and destroying the faith of some." The recommended antidote to the religious malaise was to be found in a "prayerful, obedient application of the Word."[60]

Other well-known and influential Ontario leaders concurred with Coffman on the Bible's infallibility. One such person was Oscar Burkholder, who had been ordained to the pastorate of Cressman Church in Breslau early in 1913.[61] Burkholder embodied many of those attributes that one might have expected to find in a Mennonite leader of his time. He was totally self-assured, stern, dogmatic, and not infrequently given to making authoritarian pronouncements. The Breslau minister served in a number of different roles during his long association with the Old Mennonite Church. He spent 36 years as an instructor at the Ontario Mennonite Bible School in Kitchener (1917 – 1954). He was also a prolific writer. During his lifetime, he authored three books[62] and contributed many forceful articles to the *Gospel Herald*, the *Christian Monitor*, the *Christian Ministry*, and the *Sword and Trumpet*.[63] As if these activities, not to mention the demands of his home congregation, were not enough to consume Burkholder's energies, he was also extremely active as an itinerant evangelist. Between 1910 and 1949, Burkholder conducted over 180 religious rallies, most of which were held outside Ontario.[64]

The classroom, the printed page, and evangelistic meetings proved ideal vehicles through which Burkholder could channel his message and spiritual insights. Never one to dodge issues, particularly if these related to the contemporary religious scene, the Breslau pastor left no doubts with his audience as to his position on any number of subjects. For example, Burkholder confessed that Christian conduct was not always plainly defined in the Holy Writ, but "where we approach the realms of doctrine and stated truth there can be no two ways or attitudes that are right."[65] He stood absolutely convinced that ultimate truth and salvation were the exclusive property of fundamentalist Christianity. Other religious systems were acknowledged, but in Christianity was found "the only right religion" capable of dispelling "the darkness that is hanging over this sin-sick world."[66]

He maintained that an inerrant Bible constituted the foundation of the genuine church. Scripture acted as the Christian's indispensable guide to righteous living and as the "higher authority to decide whether a certain doctrine or teaching is true or untrue."[67] This latter role was of vital importance to Burkholder for he and other believers were surrounded by well-dressed seducers who gave the appearance of being morally upright but who inwardly were "as ravenous as wild beasts."[68] The seducers, who generally were identified to be misguided intellectuals, were revealed by their scientific, philosophical, and religious opinions to be opposed to biblical fundamentals. What these tamperers with the sacred biblical truths needed, Burkholder contended, was the illuminating "light of the Scriptures."

The crusader's preoccupation with religious deceivers and false prophets was very closely tied to his pre-millennialist theology. He concluded that the world had entered into its final stage, proof of which was demonstrated by the rampant signs of apostasy and unbelief proliferating everywhere. So provoked was Burkholder by the insidious modern-day deceptions that he was compelled to write *The Predicted Departure from the Faith*. The purpose of this popular treatise was "to present a message on the signs of apostasy and the responsibility connected with backsliding from Christian experience"[69] and to focus attention on the special problems created by the "terrific pressure brought to bear upon believers in these last days."[70] Burkholder spared few words in getting to the heart of the matter:

> Sunday school teachers will deliberately and boldly declare
> that they do not believe the Genesis account of the Creation,
> and claim kinship with a monkey instead of an omnipotent
> God; . . . when mothers will switch on the radio for the bed-
> time stories for their children, rather than tell them the stories
> of truth from the Bible.[71]

Burkholder was an avowed opponent of modernism, a phenomenon which he termed "nothing better than socialism."[72] He was also deeply distrustful of humanitarian and social reform movements, including pacifist organizations.[73] In this instance he was joined by others, such as Manasseh Hallman, who insisted that "modernist and fundamentalist cannot work together"[74] and S.F. Coffman, whose credentials as a dedicated pacifist were beyond reproach. Coffman had carried on lengthy negotiations with Ottawa to assure his church of official nonresistant privileges. Yet, in his capacity as secretary for the provincial Peace Problems Committee, he warned his fellows to "keep aloof from other peace movements, of a humanitarian principle, or political affiliation."[75]

Further evidence that fundamentalism had taken root in the Mennonite Conference of Ontario presented itself through the Bible conferences and conventions held in the province.[76] The thirteenth session of the Mennonite General Conference, meeting in Waterloo during the summer of 1923, selected as its theme "The Fundamentals of Christianity." The convention attracted several thousand people and, according to an official report, "one of the impressive features of these "Fundamentals" meetings was the unity that prevailed regarding the truths of the Bible which we regard as fundamental to the Christian faith."[77] A roster of prominent fundamentalist speakers was assembled and the subjects addressed ranged from "The Inspiration of the Scriptures" to "Modernism" to "The Second Coming of Christ."[78]

Several years later, at a locally sponsored Bible conference conducted near New Hamburg, the familiar fundamentalist concerns continued to appear. The subjects introduced by Oscar Burkholder and Alberta's Norman Stauffer included "Eight Signs of Modernism," "Evils of the Tongue," and "Worldly Organizations and the Christian."[79] All of these subjects led to fundamentalist-type pronouncements, including a 1924 Conference resolution which asked their members to reconfirm their faith in God and in Jesus:

> Whereas the world is abounding with false doctrines [that] are undermining the faith and attacking the foundation of the church, be it resolved, that the members of the Ontario Mennonite Conference declare themselves to believe that the Christ, Son of God, is the foundation upon which the church is built.[80]

Educational developments in Ontario lagged behind those found in the American Mennonite community. The absence in the province of a church-supported college was in one sense a blessing, since the area was spared the kind of bitter friction that enveloped Goshen. Even so, and despite its geographic separation from the Indiana campus, Ontario could not escape the shock waves released by that struggle. Through S.F. Coffman, who served as chairman of a literature committee assigned to scrutinize, appraise, and recommend texts for use in the Bible, science, and history departments at the Goshen and Hesston colleges, and through the occasional student, the province was kept closely informed of the situation at Goshen.[81] The bishop's choice of competent and trustworthy authorities, to whom questionable books could be referred for evaluation, said much for his personal leanings. James Gray, R.A. Torrey, and B. Riley, all of them fundamentalist giants, were included in Coffman's list.[82]

Coffman discovered himself to be in a delicate, sometimes ambiguous, spot with respect to the school controversy. On the one hand, he agreed with many points made by the dissenting faculty members, some of whom were his close friends. On the other hand, Coffman felt constrained to support the conservative leadership, principally because he felt this would best serve the interests of church unity.

Closer to home, Coffman took a leading hand in the development of the Ontario Mennonite Bible School.[83] Established in 1907, the Kitchener school made valuable contributions to its constituency, both for the Bible-steeped students it returned to the home congregations and because it offered educational services in a largely rural district located far from the Old Mennonite educational centres. The school provided an accessible alternative to the more sophisticated American institutions. It had low entrance requirements and winter and evening courses which suited the constituency and its students. Attendance at the school was a way of making up for what was missing in the public schools. Coffman many times expressed regrets that the Bible, "the standard book of the world," had been omitted from the public classroom.[84] Some years later, Oscar Burkholder expanded on this same theme:

> For, while true education is to be desired, and its usefulness, as a servant of the believer, is accepted almost without question, the modern educational system, influenced, governed, and practically controlled by those who openly believe and teach evolution, is so far removed from the biblical position and teaching that no loyal follower of Christ can truthfully and conscientiously support it.[85]

The subject material taught at the Bible School throughout its 62-year history was constantly revised, but the emphasis on biblical studies, using the Bible as the primary text, remained unchanged. Coffman adhered to the notion that "to know the material of the sources of Christian life and experience" was of greater worth "than the teachings of subject material supported by selected texts."[86]

Fundamentalism and Divisiveness

Fundamentalism, as manifested in the doctrinal and educational spheres, did not precipitate a divisive internal reaction in Ontario as it had in the U.S.A. The situation was different, however, with respect to the issue of nonconformity. As the once-steady resistance to the world weakened in the face of persistent social pressures, and as Mennonite business, educational, and religious habits increasingly resembled those practised outside their group, nonconformity came to be legalistically equated with a prescribed manner of dress. Indeed, nonconformity became the single most-discussed topic in Ontario. The principal speaker at an annual conference held in Vineland was moved to declare that, like nonresistance during the last war, "the test today is nonconformity."[87]

Modern fashions had long been a source of concern to the Mennonite Conference of Ontario. Already in 1864 leaders had voiced alarm over the steady encroachment of the fashion monster into their own ranks. That year, the conference resolved that "we [Mennonites] witness against pride and the fashions of the world, etc. which has made too much inroad into the church."[88] In 1901, the conference again addressed itself to the subject of dress. Delegates agreed at this time to "use [their] influence to bring about more simplicity in the form of dress."[89] Four years later it was resolved that "we do more teaching on the subject of modest apparel."[90] Still, no specific pronouncements defining what could, and could not, be worn were introduced.

By the 1920s, the Ontario conference had definitely decided to promote the use of a uniform dress standard, meaning "the wearing of the bonnet by our sisters, and the regulation [plain] coat by the brethren."[91] This swing to dogmatic conservatism likely reflected the influence of Oscar Burkholder, who used Bible and nonconformity conferences to publicize his viewpoint.[92] Burkholder favoured the maintenance of a mandatory dress code, believing that if this was the announced will of the church, it should be observed by its members. The Breslau evangelist approvingly quoted Griffith Thomas as saying, "If the church said that all men should wear yellow pants, then all men should wear yellow pants."[93]

Women were most affected by the dress regulations. It was expected that they would wear the prescribed head covering to church and whenever they were out in public. Men were urged to adopt the black plaincoat, but except for bishops, ministers, and deacons, few did so. Women were understandably resentful of a standard that was applied more stringently to them than to the men. The latter were hard-pressed to justify this discrepancy. They frequently resorted to the argument that nonconformity meant "obedience to the wishes of the church."[94] Women were reminded that the church leaders knew what was best for their flock and should be obeyed. But these explanations fell short of assuaging the restless spirit and, in Toronto and Kitchener, discontent soon spilled out into the open.

An explanation of conference operations will contribute to a better understanding of the ensuing events. The "Constitution and Discipline," as adopted in 1909, governed the affairs of the Mennonite Conference of Ontario.[95] It specified that the membership of the conference included all bishops, ministers, and deacons. The conference met twice a year. The agenda of the public sessions included reports from the congregations, the executive committee, and other standing or ad hoc committees which were few in number. Submitted "Questions" approved for discussion in an advance private session constituted an important, though sanitized, part of the proceedings. At the annual session, the conference elected an executive committee consisting of a moderator, a secretary, and three other members, all of them bishops. Thus, the bishops were the strong persons in the conference and generally carried an authoritarian image. Of interest in this connection is their mutual characterization. Said one about the other at the latter's death:

> There was never any question about his orthodoxy. He was
> conservative — never liberal, — nor an ultra-conservative. He
> was dogmatic — but not "bulldogmatic." He was firm but
> resilient. Every message he preached rang true to the Book.
> He knew how to walk on the narrow road. He was no Phari-
> see — : he would add to the Scriptures. Neverthless, he was no
> Sadducee who would subtract from their pages.[96]

Within the congregations, the leading church officers were of course the bishops, who were chosen from among the ministers by the unanimous voice of the congregations in a given bishop district or by lot if two or more candidates had been nominated. The lot was a unique process for choosing, supposedly with divine approval and without human politics, the right person from among presumably equally qualified candidates.

The bishops performed the ordinary duties of the ministry, baptized and received into church fellowship "penitent believers," conducted communion and foot-washing services, solemnized marriages, and "excommunicated [with the counsel of the church] the disobedient." An all-important function and obligation was "the general oversight of the church" which meant many things, depending somewhat on the personality of the bishop and the needs, wishes, and tolerances of the congregations in a given district, as well as the needs of the times. An inescapable duty was the implementation of the instructions of the conference.

The bishops were assisted by ministers and deacons, who came to their positions in one of two ways. They were chosen "by the voice of the church" or, if necessary, by lot and ordained by the bishops. The choosing could also be initiated "by the ministry," which in practical terms could mean the bishop, and ordained with the consent of the congregation. The ordination of bishops or ministers required "the permission of the Conference in regular session or the advice of the executive committee" and the ordination of deacons the consent of the ministers' meeting of a given district.

Ministers were preachers and pastors and they could, "under the direction and oversight of the bishop, perform the duties usually performed by bishops." Deacons had "oversight of the poor" and special responsibility in removing difficulties and effecting reconciliation "when troubles or disagreements arise among the members." Ministers and deacons, like bishops, could "be relieved from the active duties" with the consent of the conference if they had proven themselves incapable, unqualified, or unsound.

The primacy of bishops, ministers, and deacons in the conference and the primacy of the bishops among their servant colleagues meant, in effect, a form of "centralized government" which had its very strong advocates. Centralization was a reflection of God the creator who "laid down both positive and negative laws" and of Jesus who "laid down regulations, rules, and laws by which the church should be governed." From the practical point of view the church had to stand up for authority at a time when due to modernism, bolshevism, and anarchism "no one is inclined to submit to authority."[97]

All of this was in the context of a "discipline" which specified the faith of the church and the duties of its members. The faith embraced the 18 articles, certain ordinances—baptism, communion, feet-washing, the devotional head covering, the salutation of the holy kiss, anointing of the sick with oil, and Christian marriage—and an ethical code. The latter specified civil obedience, respect and intercession for rulers, and refusal of activity involving the use of "the force of law or the administration of the oath." Other requirements were stated as follows:

> Believers should abstain from flagrant sins, ungodly conversation, extravagance in habits or living, excesses, fleshly and worldly lusts, the use of liquor and tobacco; renounce pride, vanities and worldliness in dress and associations; separate themselves from the world in questionable methods of business, in politics,and in carnal and worldly amusements, refrain from carnal warfare and shall not fellowship with secret societies or like organizations.[98]

Open resistance to the conference's dress policy first became visible in the early spring of 1922. Not surprisingly the setting was Toronto, where the most urban of the churches was located. Nelson Martin, superintendent of the recently founded Toronto mission, notified S.F. Coffman, the responsible bishop, on March 22 that a state of tension had seized the congregation.[99] The problem, according to Martin, was that many of the members believed the Old Mennonite Church to be antiquated in its message and appeal. The dress regulations, reflecting the church's traditional rural background, acted as an impediment to the church's work in an urban environment.

Martin volunteered several reasons for dropping the dress standards. For one thing, exceptions related to the manner of clothing had been made in other localities and similarly should be forthcoming in Toronto.[100] More to the point, the Toronto mission worker complained that the conspicuous bonnets created an unnecessary fuss, for "members in the cities were constantly subjected to criticism and misunderstanding."[101] Martin concluded that the Mennonite dress code worked against the church's future success. Unless certain changes were instituted, he would resign from his position.

The disclosure of events in Toronto caught Coffman quite off guard. The Old Mennonite bishop confided to a friend that he believed Martin had assumed "a very radical stand" that was "contrary to the teachings and practices of the Church."[102] His own response to the crisis was to meet with the mission group and to present a thoughtful defence of the "bonnet practice." Coffman defended his position with a series of arguments.[103] The wearing of the bonnet, he declared, was in no way the product of coercion, since all who had joined the Old Mennonite Church had done so voluntarily and in full awareness of the accompanying commitments. The congregation was also reminded that the practice of the church accorded with that of Jesus, who upheld the laws of the strict religionists among whom he found himself and who himself lived and taught the principle of self-denial and separation from the world.

Coffman also explained that nonconformity as represented by the bonnet, rather than attracting ridicule, actually served as a witness and an important symbol of identity. "If we neglect these principles," he maintained, "and discontinue the practice of them, our testimony would be lost and we would have nothing to offer them that has not been, and is not being offered by other societies." In conclusion, Coffman begged patience and understanding until that "time when there would be a natural transition in the customs of the church." Despite the bishop's conciliatory manner, Martin remained unswayed. His frustration at the lack of change in the conference position led him to resign his post in the summer of 1923.

The Toronto mission dispute was but a preview of the larger crisis that was to embroil Kitchener's historic First Mennonite Church, since the days of Bishop Benjamin Eby, a century earlier, one of the leading congregations in the conference. Such was the magnitude of this confrontation that not only did it precipitate a schism within the local congregation but it also threatened the unity of the entire Mennonite Conference of Ontario. The immediate dispute was again occasioned by the dress code. In its larger application, the conflict exposed the greater issue of congregational autonomy versus the authority of the conference and the bishop.

As in the case of the Toronto mission, the urban setting within which First Church found itself seemed to foster a more relaxed attitude towards the dress code. The urban liberalism was generally regarded as insubordination by the rural churches that dominated the conference, but by 1922 most members of the Kitchener congregation agreed that, within sensible bounds, individual freedom should be granted in the selection of a wardrobe, including headwear. These members were supported by their pastor, U.K. Weber, though not by the responsible bishops in the area. Weber directed a letter to S.F. Coffman in late March, criticizing the existing dress legislation and warning that "we are at the parting of the ways [meaning in the conference], for we must choose between the attitude taken by those in authority and by those of our young people."[104] S.F. Coffman was at that time on the Conference Executive Committee and the only bishop outside the Waterloo area.

Weber correctly sensed that his younger church members had almost lost patience with the dress regulations thrust upon them. Immediate remedial action was needed, the pastor advised, if a large defection from the congregation was to be averted. An appeal was made for Coffman to exercise aggressive and insightful leadership as a positive response to the younger people:

> What we need at the present time in our church is men who have a real vision of the needs of tomorrow, not [just] a blind following of tradition, suppressing of our young people, but adjusting ourselves to meet and solve their problems.[105]

Coffman, however, rejected the plea for instant action. He stiffened at the threat of schism suggested by Weber and warned that any attempt to force the conference's hand would only create additional, and perhaps more serious, troubles. The reference to a possible secession was no empty prediction on Weber's part. As an outspoken and somewhat emotional individual, Weber already had sharp critics and even some enemies.[106] Personality differences thus aggravated disagreements over the nonconformity issue. The dispute was formally brought out into the open in 1922, when a deputation representing the majority dissident faction notified the conference of their grievances.[107] The conference responded with a resolution that called for "reasonable and faithful compliance" or failing that "the proper discipline," as follows:

> . . . we . . . recognize the need of proper regulation of the apparel of the members of the church according to the apostolic teachings and practices. . . [we] recognize the need and practice of leniency on the part of conference towards our members, and regret the liberties assumed by some who have exceeded the advice and counsels of the church, therefore be it resolved that we earnestly appeal to all of our members in our various congregations to maintain the standards and practices repeatedly confirmed by our Annual Conference . . . expecting that there shall be a reasonable and faithful compliance with this request, or expect the proper discipline by the officers of the church, through the councils and decisions of the church.[108]

An Investigating Committee was appointed by the conference to inquire into the difficulties in the Kitchener congregation. The Committee, which elected S.F. Coffman as chairman, met four times within the space of eight days from June 20 to June 27, 1922.[109] The first was an informal meeting "to outline the nature and scope of work to be done." The second and third were preliminary meetings with representatives of the Kitchener congregation and with the chairman of the petitioners, respectively. The single regular meeting of the Committee was held on June 27. At that meeting a Committee of Petitioners, seven in number, presented twelve "charges. . . bearing on the conditions existing" but only after protesting "the fact that the privilege of representation on your committee was not granted."

The subsequent findings report of the Investigating Committee revealed considerable misunderstanding and poor communication among bishops, ministers, and members, some of it undoubtedly due to a structural flaw. Considerable "confusion" had arisen from the fact that the bishops of Waterloo County had failed to define their bishop districts. In other words, First Church was not within the particular district of one bishop but within the general area being supervised by two bishops, Jonas Snider and Manasseh Hallman, whose home congregations were Waterloo and Mannheim, respectively. A third area bishop was Abraham Gingerich at Floradale.

While ill-defined responsibilities, misunderstandings, and confused communications had exacerbated a problem and prevented a resolution, the real problems were differences of position on the wearing of the bonnet by the women, but even there the Committee found no absolute break with tradition because obedience had never been so complete or discipline so rigid that exceptions to the standard hadn't existed and been allowed. The Committee reported:

> that for more than 40 years there have been sisters in our
> congregations who have at times worn other than bonnets
> approved by the church and that they have been patiently dealt
> with. But, in no instance have we found a reversal of the cus-
> toms and practices of the church regarding the principle of
> separation from the world in the matter of dress.[110]

It was clear that, in the past, disobedience had been tolerated, quite probably because occasional, or regular but few, dissenters were not really a threat to the authority or standards of the conference. Besides, they were psychologically, if not sociologically, ostracized by the majority, and this was punishment or discipline sufficient. In any event, a review of the tradition made clear that the problem at first was not new and not recent and U.K. Weber could not be held "wholly responsible for conditions in the congregation at Kitchener," and yet it was precisely the minister's support of the growing number of dissenters which made the movement so dangerous. The causes of difficulties, the Investigating Committee acknowledged, were due to "a manifest desire on the part of many for the removal of conference regulations regarding the matter of dress, and a consequent questioning" of church authority. Members, parents, and "the spiritual oversight and leadership of the church" had not all been fully devoted "to the cause of maintaining the church's standards."

The recommendations for the resolution of the problem called for a defining of the bishop district, a general acknowledgement of failure and full forgiveness, a pledge of loyalty to the standards, a program of Christian service for the young people, and a special session of the conference to deal with the report. The special non-public session took place on December 21 and approved the findings and recommendations clause by clause, with only occasional dissent of one or two votes, in 23 separate motions duly made, seconded, and passed.[111]

In February 1923, the Investigating Committee, accompanied by Bishop Jonas Snider, met with the pastor and congregation of the troubled First Church to communicate the conclusions. The conference representative indicated that all of the involved parties stood guilty of a "general failure and offence" and requested a solemn pledge of loyalty to the church and her standards.[112] Most of the original dissenters, however, did not really believe themselves to be guilty of a "general failure." When asked to demonstrate their solidarity with conference policy by standing, many, especially the young women, remained seated.[113] The time had come when discussion alone failed to bridge the enlarging rift.

The deteriorating conditions at the First Church finally forced the conference to act. The 1923 session passed a motion calling for the forfeiture of communion rights and church council privileges for those people who "deliberately transgress the doctrine of Christ and decisions of Conference."[114] Ministers were instructed to deal quickly with recalcitrant members as the situation warranted. The actions proved ineffective in untangling the situation at First Church, though, since its pastor openly sympathized with the critics of the conference. The conference meeting in 1924 therefore adopted stiffer measures to ensure the obedience and conformity of all members to its decisions. A strongly worded statement declared that:

> Since the Ontario Mennonite Conference has decided in for-
> mer resolutions that simplicity in apparel, both in principle
> and practice, is a scriptural teaching . . . we resolve that all
> conference members be dealt with by the Bishops, and that all
> disobedient lay members be dealt with by the pastors under the
> Bishop's instruction, according to the provisions made by said
> former resolutions, and that this resolution be carried into
> effect before next communion in each congregation.[115]

The lines were now drawn. Bishop Snider, under pressure from an impatient conference, was planted squarely on a collision course with Weber and his party. The showdown came on August 3, when Weber refused to bar from a communion service those women who no longer wore head coverings in public, including places of work and, most importantly, the place of worship. Snider himself had no option but to revoke Weber's ministerial authority.[116] After the silencing of their minister by the bishop, whose action was in effect forced by the recent conference legislation, the dissenters believed they had no alternative but to secede and form their own congrega- tion. On August 19, 1924, they announced their intention of establishing an independent congregation,[117] which later became the Stirling Avenue Mennonite Church, located just a block away from the mother congregation. The conference, reacting to the develop- ment, recorded the following "as a matter of record":

> We deeply regret the circumstances . . . we earnestly pray for
> reconciliation and restoration of lost fellowship.[118]

The conference and the Kitchener congregation, as represented by its bishop, had been unable to accommodate the dissenters by liberal- izing the doctrine and practice of nonconformity, but the reasons for this apparent stubbornness were several. Indeed, there was even an element of political realism in the conference position. A crucial consideration was the fact that the conference was not only losing members but also gaining them because of its conservative stance. The gains for the Old Mennonites were from the Old Order Mennonites, where an even greater conservatism was pushing away those who felt the time had come to accept the telephone and the automobile.[119]

There was movement in this regard throughout Old Order country, in Haldimand, Lincoln, and York counties, but most significantly, in Woolwich Township of Waterloo County. There, the Old Mennonite congregations at St. Jacobs and Floradale had already registered significant membership gains. And in Elmira former dissenters from the Old Order became the core of a new Old Mennonite congregation formed with the help of the Floradale congregation in the very year that Stirling left First Church in Kitchener. Thus, there were gains as well as losses, and the most important gain of all was the satisfaction that the fundamentals of faith and practice were not being sacrificed just to accommodate impatient modernizers.

The new Stirling church with over 100 members — membership of First dropped from 293 to 175 — meant newness and modernization in a number of ways. Musical instruments were immediately introduced and a "meeting-house," more in the cathedral style, was erected on the hill "above" First. More significantly, the subsequent relations of Stirling with the U.S.-based General Conference Mennonite Church through its Eastern district, meaning mostly Pennsylvania, meant the return to Ontario of that other group of New Mennonites which had existed in Ontario in the nineteenth century and then disappeared in favour of a more evangelical form of New Mennonite, namely the Mennonite Brethren in Christ. Pennsylvania was distant, however, and Stirling, physically connected to the cemetery grounds of its former church home, remained tied to Ontario roots symbolically and otherwise.

The entire Kitchener incident promoted an even greater swing to conservatism among the surviving members at First Mennonite. This was evident in their choice of a new pastor, C.F. Derstine, an occasional visiting preacher from Pennsylvania and well-known for his fundamentalist inclinations. It was further reinforced by S.F. Coffman's support of the conservatives and his refusal to condone the actions of the Stirling group. His stance made an open split difficult to avoid, but it also prevented a more major rupture at the conference level, such as had occurred twice in the previous century.

Derstine, for his part, became a popularizer of the fundamentals as a frequent evangelist inside and outside his denomination. Using the medium of the monthly *Christian Monitor*, which he edited from 1923 to 1929, together with his preaching, he waged an unrelenting assault against the religious heresy that he felt was eroding true orthodoxy.[120] In his characteristically bold fashion, he sketched the perilous dangers inherent in all modernist teachings:

> The liberalist theology of the present day will close our churches, empty our pulpits, close our Sunday schools, silence our prayers, make Godless our family hearths, silence the lips of sacred song, put a question mark before the future, and plunge man into an abyss of unbelief and infidelity that can hardly be imagined by us today.[121]

The new Kitchener pastor blamed modernism for a host of society's ills, ranging from all shades of moral turpitude to the extremes of murder itself.[122] The need of the hour, he proclaimed, was a warm, passionate preaching of the Gospel, "which would serve as an absolute antidote to the modernistic theories which are working such havoc in the Christian Church."[123] Derstine himself was such a preacher, consistently attracting large audiences to an uncounted number of Bible conferences and evangelistic meetings, both inside and outside the Mennonite church. In Kitchener, Derstine's appeal to the larger community was reminiscent of Benjamin Eby, the popular preacher of Ebytown and first bishop of the region's Mennonite churches.

Derstine underlined the importance of evangelizing in preparation for the end times, calling it the "chief task of the Christian church."[124] He maintained that "the passion of every Christian should be to win men to Christ, to save men from their sins, to save men from the judgement of God, to save them from their doom."[125] Derstine's interest in eschatology manifested itself in his writing and in his preaching. His preoccupation with this subject made him a major force in propagating pre-millennialist theory not only in Ontario but throughout the United States. And yet, he remained a defender also of Mennonite principles. In 1925, in his first address to the conference, he reviewed 400 years of Mennonite history which was summed up as follows:

> Mennonitism has developed from the gospel principles of evangelical Christianity. . . . It stands for a church separated from the state and from the world, for the peace principles of Christ, for faith in God and in the brotherhood, for a spiritual social life, in a negative sense, holding aloof from sinful amusements, life insurance, secret societies, and swearing of oaths. Mennonitism advocates the simple life, a sound non-commercialized ministry, obedience to every doctrine and ordinance, the permanency and sacredness of the marriage vow, a practical church discipline. Mennonitism looks upon works as an evidence of faith in the Lord Jesus Christ and not as a means of salvation.[126]

The Kitchener schism was symptomatic and symbolic of both Mennonitism and North American Protestantism, which in many places was torn asunder by the controversies of the day. Perhaps the Stirling split would have been a province-wide experience had the nineteenth century not bequeathed to the twentieth century other options for conservatism. On the one hand, the Old Order Mennonites embodied the extremes of cultural conservatism, too extreme even for the nonconformity school of First Mennonite. On the other hand, the New Mennonites of the nineteenth century, now known as the Mennonite Brethren in Christ, represented the extremes of theological fundamentalism.

The Old Mennonites, caught between these two forms of conservatism, were moderates by comparison. But so fine did even the moderates define the faith and its practice that differentiations over detail, and the emotions generated thereby, could not survive personality clashes and inadequate procedures for conflict resolution. Even the wisdom and patience of a Coffman, capable of many compromises, was insufficient to bridge the gaps.

Fundamentalism and Fundamentals Elsewhere

Unwavering confidence in "old-time" Christianity was also the standard in Old Mennonite congregations located in Western Canada.[127] E.S. Hallman, bishop of the Alberta-Saskatchewan Con-

ference District, compared the challenges facing his church in its
confrontation with the world with those encountered by the first-
century apostles Peter and Paul.[128] Hallman observed that his
conference's mission prospects were made doubly difficult because
"some of the Protestant churches have drifted into modernism, the
greatest menace to the Church. . . ."[129] He remained convinced that
the gospel is "the only agency needed to win and save the northwest
with its different religions in this cosmopolitan race."[130]

Generally speaking, the same forces that assailed the Old Mennonite Church in the U.S.A., in Ontario, and in the Alberta-
Saskatchewan conference were at work also amongst the Amish,
though in a different way. Because of their more pronounced cultural
conservatism, and an even greater appetite for quietistic ruralism,
the Amish noticed and integrated outside influences more slowly than
did the Mennonites. Emphasizing a practical Christianity and discipleship, they were "disinterested in the scholarly debate or doctrinal
correctness, which characterized the fundamentalists." While the
Amish missed the fundamentalist controversy itself, they "absorbed a
fundamentalist mood and dogmatism. . . [which] became the 'bed
partner' of revivalism and did much to transform and direct the
theological framework towards evangelical, conservative Old
Mennonitism."[131]

Within the more progressive Amish body, the spirit of awakening
at this time was calling for adjustments along organizational, rather
than theological, lines. The Great War and later developments
convinced the leaders of this group that changes were necessary.
Accordingly, after a previous attempt had failed, the Ontario Amish
Mennonite Conference was organized in 1923.[132] Thereafter, and
though still harbouring a small measure of suspicion of modern
innovations, the Amish conference followed the Old Mennonite lead
in its adoption and support of institutions such as Bible conferences,
revival meetings, winter Bible Schools, and mission projects. In
most things seemingly about a generation behind the Old Mennonites, the Amish Mennonites represented important exceptions to
that conclusion. From among them came some of the first missionary
couples to leave Canadian soil, the Amos Schwartzentrubers and the
Nelson Litwillers to Argentina, in 1924 and 1925, respectively. The
very first had been sent out in 1901 by the Mennonite Brethren in
Christ Conference.[133]

The founding of an Amish Mennonite Conference was prompted in part by the earlier emergence of a Sunday School Conference, which "tended to be the avenue through which progressive laymen expressed their views and propagated new ideas." In that process, they became involved in a "power struggle" with the "ordained leadership" which "tended to be more conservative. . . the champion of the status quo and. . . the block to progress."[134] The conference was founded in part to check innovation and, ironically, to bring progress under control. Although a trial conference session had been held in 1918, five years had elapsed before another session, leading to annual meetings, was held.

In 1925 a constitution for the newly organized Amish Mennonite Conference was adopted to help "advance the cause of Christ and promote the unity and general welfare of the church."[135] Members of the conference were all the "elders (bishops), ministers, and deacons," and, in the absence of any of these, one delegate "from their brethren" for each 100 members or fraction thereof. In this provision, too, they were ahead of the Old Mennonites, who had not yet made provision for lay delegates. A year later, the conference adopted "rules and discipline" which prescribed guidelines for the faith and life of the church, including the choice of leaders.[136] They specified that in the selection of deacons, ministers, and elders the lot should "be used to decide whom the Lord had chosen" if the congregation itself was not unanimous.

The discipline also specified the conference's teaching on ordinances and the related symbolisms. Water baptism by pouring was identified as the initiating rite into "the visible church." The "partaking of the bread and the fruit of the vine" was recommended for frequent observance "to keep the suffering and death of our Lord vividly before our minds." The "washing of the saints' feet" was seen as a "true symbol of humility." A "special devotional head covering" was prescribed for "all women professing godliness. . . during worship (or engaged in teaching, prayer, or prophesying)." "Salutation with the holy kiss" was enjoined as "a symbol of Christian love." The anointing with oil "in cases of extreme illness" was practised as "a symbol of God's grace in healing power." Marriage was taught as "divinely instituted for the propagation, purity, and happiness of the human race." There could be no marriage "between a believer and an unbeliever, nor between members of different denominations."

Obligations to government were binding so long as they did not conflict with "the teaching of Christ and His apostles." "Carnal warfare" was opposed, as was the swearing of oaths. Nonconformity to the world meant opposition to "intemperance, unholy conversation, fashionable attire, covetousness, worldly amusements, Sunday desecration, and pride." Life insurance was viewed as wrong because it made "merchandise of human lives." Membership in secret societies was held to be unacceptable because they "are generally oath bound" and because they were "detrimental to Christian churches and antagonistic to the spirit of Christ." "Liberal support" of home and foreign missions was encouraged.

The Swiss Mennonites and the Amish were not the only groups in North America forced to re-evaluate and readjust their patterns of thought and work during the turbulent early decades of this century, but the experience of the Dutch Mennonites in Western Canada was somewhat different. In the congregations of the Conference of Mennonites in Central Canada, for instance, the fundamentalist-modernist debate did not attain crisis proportions until several decades later. This was partly due to the preoccupation with other problems by its leaders, notably David Toews. As bishop of a large church himself and moderator of the conference, Toews had neither the time nor the energy to spend on matters unrelated to the issues at hand, which included the survival of the German-English Academy. Besides, he had always been more predisposed to a practical Christianity and action than to abstract theological debate. This and other factors prevented the fundamentalist-modernist dispute from becoming a prominent feature in this area until later, when it struck with the same divisive impact experienced in the east in the 1920s.

The theological position of the Mennonite Brethren churches, as yet only a small number in the west, likewise anticipated future directions. A strong emphasis on doctrine, biblical orthodoxy, clear-cut conversions, strict discipline, and pre-millennialism, which had characterized the denomination since its founding 60 years earlier,[137] was now reflected in the first of the Mennonite Bible Schools founded in Western Canada. The Herbert school, established in 1913 by J.F. Harms from Kansas and reopened in 1921, after a two-year closing, by William J. Bestvater, a former Winnipeg city missionary, was modelled in part after the American Bible Schools. The denomination's historian at least assumed that both Bestvater and Harms "appear to have been inspired to establish schools in their own brotherhood by the pattern and program at the Moody Bible Institute."[138]

Bestvater's specific goals in reopening the school were to provide "sound biblical training" and to establish and strengthen youth "in fundamental principles and doctrines." Since suitable texts in German were not available, Bestvater wrote his own *Glaubenslehre* (doctrine) and *Bibelkunde* (Bible introduction), based on his own training.[139] This included dispensational and eschatalogical teaching at the Light and Hope Bible Institute and correspondence courses like "the Scofield Bible Courses [and] Bible Conferences [with] men like A.C. Gaebelein, William Evans, A.C. Dixon, William B. Riley, Harris Gregg, and others,"[140] all of them of the fundamentalist mould. The dependence on such theological sources was a harbinger of things to come in the Mennonite Bible School movement in the prairies, especially among the Brethren.

The Anabaptist sickness, which historically caused the Mennonite people as a whole to resolve their problems by further fragmentation, was not helped by the fundamentalist-modernist controversy. On the contrary, it spawned divisive debate and created centres of conflict for decades to come. The language of fundamentalism and modernism, in any event, became convenient handles for many of the battles that ensued between cultural conservatives and progressives, between rural and urban Mennonites, between strict and less strict ethical codes, between isolation and accommodation, between those opposing and those promoting higher education, between doctrinal simplicity and theological sophistication, between denominational separatism and ecumenicity. Hardly a Mennonite denomination and hardly a Mennonite congregation remained untouched in the decades to come as the struggle for the survival of the faith and of the Mennonite people in the Canadian environment evolved.

Relatively untouched at this time by North American theological controversy were the bishop-oriented congregations of Mennonites in Manitoba and Saskatchewan, going back to the immigration from Russia of the 1870s. Their struggles related more to the assimilationist pressures from the provincial governments and society in general than to the theological schools of thought sweeping the continent. Rather than engage in a prolonged battle and open confrontation, these Mennonites firmly made their point and then quietly prepared to escape worldly influence by emigrating to other countries more tolerant of minorities and their religion-based way of life.

FOOTNOTES

1   Oscar Burkholder, *The Predicted Departure from the Faith* (Scott-dale, Pa.: Mennonite Publishing House, 1930), p. 95.

2   Vernon Smucker, " 'Fundamentalism' and the 'Fundamentals,' " *Christian Exponent* 1 (23 May 1924):165.

3   See John Webster Grant, *The Canadian Experience of Church Union* (Richmond: John Knox Press, 1967); Claris Edwin Silcox, *Church Union in Canada: Its Causes and Consequences* (New York: Institute of Social and Religious Research, 1933).

4   John Webster Grant, *The Church in the Canadian Era* (Toronto: McGraw-Hill Ryerson, 1972), pp. 113–33; H.H. Walsh, *The Christian Church in Canada* (Toronto: Ryerson Press, 1956), pp. 318–20.

5   Walter Unger, "Earnestly Contending for the Faith: The Role of the Niagara Bible Conference in the Emergence of American Funda-mentalism, 1875–1900" (Ph.D. dissertation, Simon Fraser University, 1982).

6   CGC, XV-31.2, "1920–Fundamentalism," Walter Unger, "Predicting the End: It Started at Niagara," n.d.

7   Don E. Smucker, "Federal Council of the Churches of Christ in America," *Mennonite Encyclopedia*, 2:318–19; Samuel Floyd Pan-nabecker, *Open Doors: The History of the General Conference Menno-nite Church* (Newton, Kans.: Faith and Life Press, 1975), p. 384.

8   See Frank H. Epp, *Mennonites in Canada, 1786–1920: The History of a Separate People* (Toronto: Macmillan of Canada, 1974), pp. 144–45. The Vineland United Church, for example, has strong Mennonite roots, as is attested to by the cemetery and membership lists.

9   *The Complete Writings of Menno Simons*, ed. J.C. Wenger, trans. Leonard Verduin (Scottdale, Pa.: Herald Press, 1956), p. 307.

10   For several examples, see Frank H. Epp, *Mennonites in Canada 1786–1920*, pp. 107–8, 311, 326–27.

11   Don E. Smucker, p. 319.

12   C.F. Derstine, the Kitchener pastor to appear later in this history, was involved in both the temperance and the alliance movement. The Ontario Conference of Mennonite Brethren in Christ called "atten-tion of our women to the importance of the Women's Christian Temperance Union whose object is . . . the standard of total absti-nence . . . the complete extinction of the liquor traffic." *Conference Journal*, 1928, pp. 41–42.

13   A prominent social gospeller whose concern for immigrant groups went deeper than that of most people, J.S. Woodsworth was also convinced that aliens must be assimilated, for both their own good and Canada's. See J.S. Woodsworth, *Strangers Within Our Gates* (Toronto: University of Toronto Press, 1972).

14   See Richard Hofstaedter, *Social Darwinism in American Thought* (Boston: Beacon Press, 1955).

15 Richard C. Wolf, Introduction to *The Origins of Fundamentalism: Toward a Historical Interpretation*, by Ernest R. Sandeen (Philadelphia: Fortress Press, 1968), p. v.

16 Ernest R. Sandeen, *The Origins of Fundamentalism: Toward a Historical Perspective* (Philadelphia: Fortress Press, 1968), p. 3.

17 *Ibid.*, p. 13.

18 See F. Roy Coad, *A History of the Brethren Movement: Its Origins, its Worldwide Development and its Significance for the Present Day* (Grand Rapids: William B. Eerdmans, 1968); C. Norman Kraus, *Dispensationalism in America: Its Rise and Development* (Richmond: John Knox Press, 1958).

19 The Revelation of John 20:4, 6.

20 See reference to *"Weltverbesserung"* or social betterment as a false Christian task at 1920 session of Conference of Mennonites in Central Canada in J.G. Rempel, *Fuenfzig Jahre Konferenzbestrebungen*, I, p. 135.

21 The appreciation the Mennonites had for Moody was acknowledged by Funk, who in 1927 testified that they owed "D.L. Moody a vote of thanks for the influences that he has brought to bear upon the interest of the Mennonite Church." Quoted in William Ward Dean, "John Funk and the Mennonite Awakening" (Ph.D. dissertation, State University of Iowa, 1955), p. 62.

22 Norman F. Furniss, *The Fundamentalist Controversy, 1918–1931* (Hamden, Conn.: Archon Books, 1963), pp. 23–24.

23 A.Z. Conrad, quoted in Furniss, p. 36.

24 Rodney Sawatsky, "The Influence of Fundamentalism on Mennonite Nonresistance" (M.A. thesis, University of Minnesota, 1973), pp. 63–64.

25 Quoted in *ibid.*, pp. 61–62.

26 J.B. Toews, "Influences on Mennonite Brethren Theology," a paper presented to Symposium sponsored by the Center for Mennonite Brethren Studies in Canada, 21–22 November 1980. Toews writes this paper with hindsight and with special reference to the Mennonite Brethren denomination, but his analysis is applicable and useful here. While Toews contrasts Fundamentalism with the historic Mennonite Brethren faith, he makes that faith synonymous with Anabaptism and our own juxtaposition seems appropriate.

27 Helen Kolb Gates et al., *Bless the Lord O My Soul: A Biography of Bishop John Fretz, 1835–1930*, ed. J.C. Wenger (Scottdale, Pa.: Herald Press, 1964), pp. 52, 68–70.

28 John A. Hostettler, *God Uses Ink: The Heritage and Mission of the Mennonite Publishing House After Fifty Years* (Scottdale, Pa.: Herald Press, 1958), pp. 134–37.

29 Harold S. Bender, "Herold der Wahrheit," *Mennonite Encyclopedia*, II, p. 711.

30 See Harold S. Bender, ed., *John Horsch Memorial Papers* (Scottdale, Pa.: Mennonite Publishing House, 1947).

31   A standard introductory treatment on Mennonite History offered the following assessment of Kauffman: "In the long span, 1905–43, more than any other man, 'D.K.,' as his friends knew him, served as the chief leader and the major voice of the Old Mennonite Church." Cornelius J. Dyck, ed., *An Introduction to Mennonite History* (Scottdale, Pa.: Herald Press, 1967), p. 173. See also Daniel Kauffman, *Fifty Years in the Mennonite Church, 1890–1940* (Scottdale, Pa.: Mennonite Publishing House, 1941).

32   For some examples of Kauffman's editorials in the *Gospel Herald*, see "Modernism vs. Fundamentalism," 17 (22 May 1924):145; "Why Do They Do It?" 18 (27 August 1925):433; "Are You a Fundamentalist?" 18 (28 January 1926):897; "Liberalism's Bid for the Mennonite Church" 22 (23 May 1929):161–62.

33   Daniel Kauffman, ed., *Bible Doctrine* (Scottdale, Pa.: Mennonite Publishing House, 1914), p. 108.

34   See Walter Klaassen, *Anabaptism: Neither Catholic Nor Protestant* (Waterloo, Ont.: Conrad Press, 1973). For Horsch's own views, consult John Horsch, "The Faith of the Swiss Brethren," *Mennonite Quarterly Review* 4 (October 1930):241–66; 5 (January 1931):7–27; (April 1931):128–47; (October 1931):245–59.

35   John Horsch, *The Mennonite Church and Modernism* (Scottdale, Pa.: Mennonite Publishing House, 1924).

36   S.F. Coffman, ed., *Mennonite Church Polity: A Statement of Practices in Church Government* (Scottdale, Pa.: Mennonite Publishing House, 1944), p. 67.

37   The articles were published in *ibid.*, pp. 68–75.

38   The crucial role of church college education, as perceived at the time by Old Mennonites, is reflected in the following: "Extracts from the Report of the 11th Mennonite General Conference . . . 1909," *Mennonite Year-Book and Directory*, 1920, pp. 14–22; D.H. Bender, "Education in the Mennonite Church," *Mennonite Year-Book and Directory*, 1920, p. 102; I.R. Detweiler, "Education and the Denominational College," *Mennonite Year-Book and Directory*, 1921, pp. 13–16.

39   O.B. Gerig, "Mennonite Ideals and Modern Life," *Christian Exponent* 2 (30 January 1925):38.

40   See C. Henry Smith and E.J. Hirschler, eds., *The Story of Bluffton College* (Bluffton, Ohio: Bluffton College, 1925), and Bluffton College Faculty, *Bluffton College: An Adventure in Faith, 1900–1950* (n.p., [1950]).

41   Harold S. Bender, "Christian Exponent," *Mennonite Encyclopedia*, I, p. 581. See also Sawatsky, pp. 98–102.

42   Vernon Smucker, " 'Fundamentalism' and the 'Fundamentals,' " *Christian Exponent* 1 (23 May 1924):165.

43   Vernon Smucker to H.S. Bender, as quoted in Rodney Sawatsky, "History and Ideology: American Mennonite Identity Definition

Through History" (Ph.D. dissertation, Princeton University, 1977), pp. 177–78.

44   CGC, Hist. Mss. 1.1.1.2.3(5), Daniel Kauffman, Report on recommendations of executive committee re Goshen College, 13 July 1922.

45   *Ibid.*

46   Rodney Sawatsky, "Influence of Fundamentalism," p. 126.

47   J.H. Mosemann, "The Modern Peace Movement," *Gospel Herald* 18 (28 January 1926):898.

48   Quoted in Guy F. Herschberger, "John Horsch, a Proponent of Biblical Nonresistance," *Mennonite Quarterly Review* 21 (July 1947):157. See John Horsch, *Die Biblische Lehre von der Wehrlosigkeit* (Scottdale, Pa.: Mennonite Publishing House, 1920), pp. 74–81.

49   Melvin Gingerich, *Mennonite Attire Through Four Centuries* (Breinigsville, Pa.: Pennsylvania German Society, 1970), p. 148.

50   Paul Martin says: "At least three major issues emerged because of *outside* influence: the inspiration of Scripture, the millennial question, and an individualistic approach to personal salvation." See "Factors of Influence and Change in the Mennonite Conference of Ontario: 1900–80" (research paper, Associated Mennonite Biblical Seminaries, 1979), p. 8.

51   C.F. Derstine, "The Development of Mennonitism in the Last Four Centuries," as reported in *Calendar of Appointments, 1925–26*, p. [13].

52   Martin, p. 6.

53   *Ibid.*, p. 11.

54   John S. Weber, "A History of Samuel Frederick Coffman, 1872–1954: The Mennonite Churchman" (M.A. research paper, University of Waterloo, 1975), p. 102. For biographies of S.F. Coffman, Oscar Burkholder, and C.F. Derstine (as well as J.B. Martin), see Urie Bender, *Four Earthen Vessels* (Scottdale, Pa.: Herald Press, 1982).

55   "A Statement of Christian Fundamentals Adopted by Mennonite General Conference, August 25, 1921." A copy of this statement was appended to *Mennonite Year-Book and Directory*, 1925 (Scottdale, Pa.: Mennonite Publishing House, 1925). See Appendix I.

56   CGC, Hist. Mss. 1.1.1.2.4 (5), S.F. Coffman to Noah Mack, 12 May 1921.

57   *Ibid.*

58   S.F. Coffman, "The Whale," *Christian Monitor* 9 (January 1917):15.

59   Some of these include "Education With the Bible," *Christian Monitor* 9 (May 1917):[142–43]; "Bible Study," *Christian Monitor* 9 (September 1917):272–73; "The Bible and Modern Thought," *Christian Monitor* 10 (November 1918):719, 734.

60   *Calendar of Appointments*, 1924 – 25, p. [15].
61   CGC, Hist. Mss. 7 – 14, Norma J. Shantz, "Oscar Burkholder, Minister and Bishop, 1886 – 1956," 1969.
62   *True Life Stories* (Scottdale, Pa.: Mennonite Publishing House, 1929); *The Predicted Departure from the Faith* (Scottdale, Pa.: Mennonite Publishing House, 1930); *True Stories from Life* (Scottdale, Pa.: Herald Press, 1942).
63   See, for example, "The Infallibility of the Word," *Gospel Herald* 22 (17 October 1929):600 – 1; "The Meaning of Feet Washing," *Gospel Herald* 22 (18 April 1929):67 – 69; "Duties of the Pastor," *Christian Ministry* 4:3 (1951):129 – 34; "The Doctrine of Separation," *Sword and Trumpet* 17:2 – 19:3 (1949 – 1951).
64   CGC, Hist. Mss. 7 – 14, Norma J. Shantz, "Oscar Burkholder, Minister and Bishop, 1886 – 1956," 1969, p. 13.
65   Oscar Burkholder, *Predicted Departure*, p. 74.
66   *Ibid.*, p. 70.
67   *Ibid.*, p. 77.
68   *Ibid.*, p. 27.
69   Advertisement, in *Mennonite Year-Book and Directory*, 1931 (Scottdale, Pa.: Mennonite Publishing House, 1931), back cover.
70   Oscar Burkholder, *Predicted Departure*, p. 5.
71   *Ibid.*, p. 44.
72   *Ibid.*, p. 95.
73   *Ibid.*, p. 99.
74   *Calendar of Appointments*, 1925 – 26, p. [11].
75   CGC, Hist. Mss. 1.1.3.1.6(2), S.F. Coffman, "The Church and Particular Doctrines" (a report on the work of the Peace Problems Committee), 27 January 1932.
76   *Mennonite Year-Book and Directory*, 1928, pp. 20 – 1.
77   "Mennonite General Conference," in *Mennonite Year-Book and Directory*, 1924 (Scottdale, Pa.: Mennonite Publishing House, 1924), p. 27.
78   A program from this conference is found in CGC, III-12.3.1, *First Mennonite Kitchener, #1 Programs, Clippings, Photos*; Programs.
79   "New Hamburg, Ont.," *Gospel Herald* 20 (18 August 1927):453.
80   *Calendar of Appointments*, 1924 – 25, p. [15].
81   John S. Weber, p. 108.
82   CGC, Hist. Mss. 1.1.1.2.3(5), J.B. Smith to members of Literature Committee, 28 January 1920.
83   See Clarence Fretz, "A History of Winter Bible Schools in the Mennonite Church," *Mennonite Quarterly Review* 16 (April 1942):59 – 60. See also Newton Gingrich, *History of the Ontario Mennonite Bible School* (n.p., n.d.). The student yearbooks of the school.
84   S.F. Coffman, "Bible Study," *Christian Monitor* 9 (September 1917):272 – 73.

85 Oscar Burkholder, *Predicted Departure*, p. 57.
86 OMBS *Clarion* (Kitchener, Ont.: n.p., 1939), p. 5. This was the annual yearbook printed by the Ontario Mennonite Bible School.
87 *Calendar of Appointments*, 1921–22, p. [15].
88 CGC, II-1.A.1, *A Manual of Conference Resolutions of the Mennonite Church of the Canada Conference District* (n.p., 1904), p. 6.
89 *Ibid.*
90 Oscar Burkholder, S.F. Coffman, and Gilbert Bergey, comps., *Resolutions: Ontario Mennonite Conference, 1847–1928* (n.p., 1929), p. [5].
91 *Calendar of Appointments*, 1918–19, p. 13; 1922–23, p. [15]; 1923–24, p. [15], 1924–25, p. [15].
92 Melvin Gingerich, *Mennonite Attire*, p. 150.
93 Norma Shantz, p. 10.
94 C.F. Derstine, "Twenty-one Reasons," *Christian Monitor* 20 (February 1928):44. In the same article Derstine advised that those in leadership should be listened to since they "watch for your souls."
95 CGC, II-1.A.1, "Constitution and Discipline of the Mennonite Conference of Ontario," adopted at Vineland, Ontario, 27 May 1909.
96 C.F. Derstine, "Bishop Jonas Snider," *Mennonite Year-Book and Directory*, 1945, pp. 22–3.
97 D.H. Bender, "Our Form of Church Government," *Mennonite Year-Book and Directory*, 1924, pp. 17–19.
98 "Constitution and Discipline," p. 11.
99 CGC, Hist. Mss. 1.1.1.2.6(1), "Toronto File," Nelson Martin to S.F.Coffman, 22 March 1922.
100 CGC, Hist. Mss. 1.1.1.2.6, "Toronto File," S.F.Coffman to Ab. S. Snyder, 12 June 1922.
101 *Ibid.*
102 CGC, Hist. Mss. 1.1.1.2.6, "Toronto File," S.F.Coffman to C.F.Derstine, 27 March 1922.
103 CGC, Hist. Mss. 1.1.1.2.6, "Toronto File," S.F. Coffman to Ab. S. Snyder, 12 June 1922.
104 CGC, Hist. Mss. 1.1.1.2.6 (1), "Toronto File," U.K. Weber to S.F. Coffman, 27 March 1922.
105 *Ibid.*
106 CGC, Interview between Lyle Friesen and Elvan Shantz, 20 October 1977.
107 The seven members of this delegation included: Allan Cressman, Moses Shantz, Titus Shantz, Allan Shantz, William Backert, Melvin Shuh (president), and E.B. Betzner (secretary). CGC, XV-31.2, "1920-Stirling Church," Minutes of Committee of Group of Members of First Mennonite Church, 27 June 1922.
108 *Calendar of Appointments*, 1922–23, p. [15]. CGC, II-2.A.1, Minute Book 2, Mennonite Conference of Ontario, 1–2 June 1922.

109   CGC, "1920–Stirling Church," "Report by the Investigating Committee Appointed by Conference to Inquire into the Difficulties in the Kitchener Congregation," n.d.

110   *Ibid.*

111   Minutes of Special Session of the Ontario Mennonite Conference, 21 December 1922.

112   *Ibid.*, "Report of the Representative of Conference Appointed at the Special Conference to present the Findings and Recommendations of the Committee on Investigation of the Affairs of the Kitchener Congregation to the Congregation at Kitchener and the Bishops Concerned," n.d. See also CGC, II-2.A.1, Minute Book 2, Mennonite Conference of Ontario, 1–2 June 1922.

113   *Ibid.*

114   *Calendar of Appointments*, 1923–24, p. [15]. CGC, II-2.A.1, Minute Book 2, Mennonite Conference of Ontario, 5–6 June 1924.

115   *Calendar of Appointments*, 1924–25, p. [15].

116   J. Boyd Cressman, "History of the First Mennonite Church, Kitchener, Ontario," *Mennonite Quarterly Review* 13 (October 1939):277.

117   CGC, XV-31.2, Stirling Avenue–1920, "Minutes of the Second Meeting held in the First Mennonite Church, Aug. 19, 1924 to Discuss the Recent Action of the Conference Authorities."

118   *Calendar of Appointments*, 1925–26, p. [15].

119   Interview with Leonard Freeman, 6 February 1981.

120   The *Christian Monitor*, described as a monthly magazine for the "Home and Christian Worker," was published by the Mennonite Publishing House from 1909 to 1954. It enjoyed an extensive circulation within the Ontario Mennonite Church.

121   C.F. Derstine, "A Modernist Walks Out," *Christian Monitor* 17 (July 1925):201.

122   Derstine concluded, regarding a sensational murder committed in Chicago: "This [the murder] is the modern university doctrine of evolution in its maturity." "An Appalling Crime at the Door of a Modern University," *Christian Monitor* 16 (August 1924):617.

123   C.F. Derstine, "The Need of the Hour in the Mennonite Church," *Christian Monitor* 19 (December 1927):360.

124   C.F. Derstine, "The Chief Task of the Christian Church," *Christian Monitor* 20 (July 1928):200.

125   *Ibid.*

126   *Calendar of Appointments*, 1925–26, p. [13].

127   "Calgary, Alta.," *Gospel Herald*, 20 (10 November 1927):713.

128   E.S. Hallman, "Winning the North-West," in *Mennonite Year-Book and Directory*, 1924 (Scottdale, Pa.: Mennonite Publishing House, 1924), p. 16.

129   *Ibid.*, pp. 16–17.

130   *Ibid.*, p. 16.
131   Fred M. Lichti, "Outside Influences, Fundamentalism, and the Amish Mennonite Conference of Ontario" (research paper, Conrad Grebel College, University of Waterloo, 1975), pp. 5, 21 – 22.
132   Orland Gingerich, *The Amish of Canada* (Waterloo, Ont.: Conrad Press, 1972), pp. 98 – 100.
133   J.A. Huffman, *History of the Mennonite Brethren in Christ Church* (New Carlisle, Ohio: The Bethel Publishing Company, 1920), p. 188.
134   Orland Gingerich, p. 93.
135   *Ibid.*, p. 215 ff.
136   *Ibid.*, p. 218 ff.
137   John A. Toews, *A History of the Mennonite Brethren Church* (Fresno, Cal.: Board of Christian Literature, General Conference of Mennonite Brethren Churches, 1975), pp. 361 – 79.
138   *Ibid.*, pp. 160, 458.
139   *Ibid.*, p. 259.
140   CMBS, William J. Bestvater Box, Anna Redekop, "Wilhelm J. Bestvater: A Biography," 1975, p. 12.

3. Emigration to Latin America

These children will live to condemn us for not giving them the same opportunity for development as Canadian citizens as is afforded to our own children. . . . It is the duty of the state to see that this is done — J.T.M. ANDERSON.[1]

First of all, we desire and request complete freedom of religion, so that we may perform our churchly practices in accordance with our faith and teach our children religion and the German language — JOHANN P. WALL.[2]

F OR SOME Mennonites the defence of their fundamental institutions, rather than a reaffirmation of fundamental doctrines or basic lifestyles, had the highest priority. Thus, some of the Dutch Mennonites in Western Canada were stubbornly resisting an enforced conformity to the public school system,[3] while the Swiss Mennonites in Ontario were promoting Christian nonconformity with reference to the culture in general.[4] The battle to preserve the private elementary school dated back at least to 1890, but in the 1920s it was at its critical point, and the Mennonites were losing. The nationalistic passions of the Great War had subsided, but they had not been replaced by greater tolerance of nonconformist minorities in Manitoba and Saskatchewan. Some Mennonites could not surrender educational control over their children, and thus by 1922 they were packing their bags and once more migrating, this time to new lands of promise in Latin America.

Only a minority of Dutch Mennonites took this drastic measure, though the concern to preserve schools controlled by the church rather than the state was shared as well by most of those who stayed. Those not migrating early in the 1920s were also troubled, but they chose to respond in different ways to the unwanted encroachment of public pressures on their way of life. Some decided in the 1920s to stay in Canada, but later in the 1920s, or late in the 1940s, or even as late as the 1960s, followed their brethren to the isolated agricultural and cultural frontiers of the Spanish-speaking world as every new generation faced the survival question anew. And some simply sought the desired isolation within Canada.

The majority tried to make the best of the necessary compromise with governments, some unwillingly and some rather willingly. Those who reluctantly accepted the system did not do so without criticism. The 1921 session at Herbert of the Conference of Mennonites in Central Canada sent a message to the Manitoba and Saskatchewan governments deploring "the spirit of materialism and militarism" in the schools and requesting that such educational influence be curbed.[5] For itself, the conference recommended greater support for its own schools, active in the preparation of teachers strong in the faith, who could supplement the public school curriculum with instruction in Religion and German.

For the willing, the public school system was not without its advantages. For them, making the best of the situation meant using the public schools also for their special Mennonite educational goals. This could be done without too much difficulty, because many of the public school districts were in fact Mennonite school districts by virtue of the exclusive or predominating Mennonite population. Such school districts could elect Mennonite trustees, who could hire Mennonite teachers who were sympathetic to Mennonite values and who were ready, willing, and able to support a curriculum generally sympathetic to Mennonite values and supplemented by general instruction in the German language and Bible stories during the final hour of the week. This special instruction was possible because of the so-called Laurier-Greenway compromise of 1897 under which the Manitoba government's decision to withdraw tax support for private schools remained in force, but by which this limited bilingual and religious instruction was permitted in the public schools.

Indeed, the Mennonite Collegiate Institute at Gretna, the rival Mennonite Educational Institute at Altona, and the German-English Academy at Rosthern had been founded precisely for the purpose of

preparing teachers for such tasks.[6] This approach of selective accommodation, rather than determined isolation to the point of emigration, became one of the Mennonite survival strategies in educational
and other contexts. Escaping the system was one way. Joining and
"exploiting" or changing, or attempting to change, the system was
another way.

Private vs. Public Schools

In practice the two options were not that distinct, especially in
Manitoba, where changing provincial conditions had resulted in
changing Mennonite responses in the Mennonite school districts,
now numbering more than 100.[7] Throughout the years, there had
been a shifting of the schools from private to public status and vice
versa. Following the settlement of the immigrants in the 1870s, all
or most of their schools had been registered under the Protestant
board, giving them a denominational and public status. As the
Mennonites had become fully aware of the implications of this
registration and of their acceptance of public funds, they insisted, for
the most part, on private status for their schools, which they could
always get by forfeiting government grants.

After the passage of the Manitoba Public Schools Act in 1890,
which abolished tax-supported denominational schools, the government established public district schools wherever they were acceptable. With the help of H.H. Ewert, who at one and the same time was
the principal of the Mennonite Collegiate Institute and government
inspector, meaning also promoter, of public schools, the number of
Mennonite districts accepting public status had gone up from 8 to 42
by 1903, when Ewert lost his position as inspector[8] and the province
lost one of its most passionate promoters of education among his own
people. In Ewert's words:

> The school has to be if our people are to be saved from
> destruction.[9]

Ewert's dismissal by the Conservative government, the Gretna
school's subsequent loss of normal school status, and the compulsory
flying of the Union Jack demanded by the provincial government in
1907 had the effect of undoing Ewert's success. Even Ewert, for

whom the flag was a military symbol going back to his native Prussia,[10] now had second thoughts about the public school option, and numerous Mennonite districts reverted back to private status again. Under A.A. Weidenhammer, the German-speaking inspector, who later anglicized his name to Willows, the trend was once again reversed.

During the Great War provincial governments in Western Canada sought to use the schools to inculcate patriotic sentiments and to foster Canadian nationalism. The use of languages other than English for instruction was very severely restricted, the qualifications required to teach school were raised and more vigorously enforced, and patriotic exercises in the schools — flag-raisings, pictures of the reigning monarch in all classrooms, the singing of the national anthem and other patriotic songs, and the reading of patriotic literature — were made mandatory in all public schools. This was followed by legislation making attendance at accredited schools compulsory for all children.[11] In 1916, when Manitoba passed its compulsory school attendance legislation, over 60 schools in districts with exclusive or majority Mennonite population were public, this being an all-time high.

The wartime legislation, however, caused many Mennonites who had gone along with the public system to reconsider their position. The loss of bilingual instruction, the emphasis on Canadianization, and the popular designation of public schools as national schools were all causes for concern. At the end of the war, only 30 schools in Mennonite districts in Manitoba remained public.[12]

Most adamant and consistent in their opposition to Manitoba public schools were the Reinlaender in the West Reserve area and the Chortitzer in the East Reserve area. The other groups — the Bergthaler, Bruderthaler, Brueder, Holdemaner, Kleine Gemeinde people, and Sommerfelder — vacillated to varying degrees, but in the end, and under considerable pressure from the authorities, they acquiesced and accepted the public school rather than remain disobedient or emigrate. There were exceptions, of course. A goodly number of Sommerfelder on the West Reserve felt like their cousins, the Chortitzer, on the East Reserve.[13] Indeed, when the crunch came, the Sommerfelder bishop followed the examples of the Reinlaender and Chortitzer bishops and led his followers, a minority, out of the country.

In Saskatchewan, about 90 school districts could be called Mennonite districts. Two-thirds of them had been in the public column
since the founding of the province in 1905 and one-third in the
private column. The latter were in the Reinlaender communities of
the former reserve areas, Hague-Osler and Swift Current. It was the
Reinlaender who were most consistent — from the provincial point of
view, recalcitrant — in their opposition to public schools. While the
Sommerfelder and Saskatchewan Bergthaler (not to be confused in
their identity and position with the Manitoba Bergthaler) were
sympathetic with the Reinlaender position, they were not sufficiently
strong in conviction, concentration, and leadership to follow the
Reinlaender route. That is, they did not refuse to co-operate with the
public school system, though minorities in their groups eventually
chose to emigrate. Fully accepting the public option were the
Rosenorter, the founders of the German-English Academy at Rosthern, other conference congregations, as well as the Brueder,
Bruderthaler, Krimmer, and Old Mennonites who had settled in the
province.

As already stated, Reinlaender and Chortitzer, representing a total
population of about 12,000,[14] remained steadfast in their resistance.
To allow their children to be educated by the state was for them too
great a compromise. Indeed, they would not have chosen to leave
Russia and settle in Manitoba in the 1870s if the Canadian government had not guaranteed to the Mennonites in advance that they
could conduct their own private schools. To their great dismay, they
later discovered that the British North America Act had granted the
educational jurisdiction not to the Dominion but to the provinces and
that consequently there could be no special privileges which the
provinces did not see fit to grant.[15] As will later be seen, appeals to the
authorities, including the highest courts in Manitoba, Canada, and
London, were of no avail to the Mennonites. Their claim to complete
freedom in matters of education, like the earlier claim of Catholics to
public support of denominational schools, was not recognized.[16]

It is important to remember that the Mennonites were not the only
ethnic or religious minority group with concerns about provincial
education policies. In all fairness to them and to the governments
they confronted, the general nature of the question must not be
overlooked. The German-speaking Mennonites were part of a general social, hence educational, problem confronting the provincial
authorities. In the last decades of the nineteenth century and the first

decades of the twentieth century, hundreds of thousands of non-anglo immigrants had entered the country and been sent on to settle in Western Canada, often in colonies representing particular religions, cultures, and languages. The 1921 census revealed that 41 per cent of the people in the prairie provinces either had been born in a place other than Canada or the British Isles or possessed at least one parent who had.[17] Many immigrant groups clung to their traditional ways, and cultivated a strong sense of ethnicity. Among the Ukrainians, for example, 90 per cent still identified Ukrainian as their mother tongue.[18]

Not surprisingly, the authorities were concerned. How could they build a cohesive society out of so many ethnic islands? Notions of Canada as a social mosaic were already being expressed,[19] but even if multiculturalism had been an official Canadian policy, it is doubtful whether any governing authority would have accepted the status quo as normative. From the perspective of the general social order, Canadianization made sense, even before the Great War brought the assimilationist pressures of anglo-conformity to a peak.[20]

The best vehicle for the necessary Canadianization was perceived to be the public school,[21] though other institutions such as the press and the churches also had a role to play. Even social gospel advocates like J.S. Woodsworth, in general more tolerant of minorities than most, looked to the public school "to break down the walls" which separated the cultures from each other. He greatly deplored the existing bilingual school system in Manitoba and praised the great work "that has been accomplished . . . by our National Schools."[22] In Saskatchewan, the educational leader who later became premier, J.T.M. Anderson, articulated best this educational philosophy:

> The children in the public schools of to-day will be the fathers
> and mothers of the next generation, and it is essential that the
> former be given an insight into our Canadian life and ideals,
> so that they in turn may impart these to their offspring. . . .
> Unless we gird ourselves to this task with energy and determi-
> nation, imbued with a spirit of tolerance, the future of our
> Canadian citizenship will fail to reach that high level of intelli-
> gence which has ever characterized Anglo-Saxon civilization
> throughout the world.[23]

As we have seen, these sentiments translated themselves into public policy and into provincial laws governing the public schools.

The schools were spoken of as the melting pot for "the fusion of [the] races," the "blast furnaces" which were "developing the new Canadian."[24] As a consequence, the school curricula had little place for a study of ethnic groups, for appreciating cultural diversity, and for advancing pluralism as a positive concept. Children were taught to shed their ethnicity as if it were a mere "outer skin one could unzip and leave behind like a cocoon." No child could escape learning what was "proper."[25] And what was proper was the English language, English styles, English values, and English institutions, even English music. Such songs as "Rule Britannia," "In Days of Yore," and "God Save the King" were sung every morning after Bible reading and the Lord's Prayer. In the words of one ethnic child, later recorded:

> For the ethnic child of my father's and my generation, school could be, and often was, a painful place. Everything valued by one's parents, everything that made up one's after-school life, was feared, misunderstood, occasionally ridiculed, and always subtly undermined. Everything associated with the most significant landmarks of human existence, everything that was most sacred, most poignant, most satisfying — all of that was somehow second- or third-rate.[26]

Mennonites objecting to the public school did so for similar reasons. Sacred to them were such things as their religion and culture in general, the agricultural way of life, the German language, and pacifism in particular. As they saw it, the public school pointed to Anglo-Canadianism rather than German Mennonitism, to urbanization rather than the rural life, to militarism rather than pacifism, to ostentation rather than the simple lifestyle they and their ancestors in the faith had always advocated. The public school also pointed in the direction of other unwanted "worldly" influences and, what was worst of all, social integration and ultimate assimilation. From that perspective they had no choice but to resist the public school.[27] Their "great dissatisfaction" did not go unnoticed by public officials and was reported, among others, by the Royal North West Mounted Police.[28]

The passing of the School Attendance Act and an amendment to the Public Schools Act in Manitoba, followed by similar legislation in Saskatchewan and Alberta, signified a dramatic shift in events for the

Mennonites, at least in the former two provinces. A confrontation between the province of Alberta and its Mennonites did not materialize, mainly because of settlement patterns and attitudes.[29] Mennonites, like most other minority groups, were scattered much more thinly throughout the province. There were no reserves or other concentrated settlements. Besides, there were no Chortitzer, Sommerfelder, or Reinlaender in Alberta to resist the public school. And that in turn could be due to the fact that Alberta's settlement and education policies had been quite clear from the beginning.[30]

In Manitoba, bilingual schools were abolished and were replaced by government-supervised district schools offering instruction in English only and demanding the compulsory attendance of all school-age children, unless it could be demonstrated that satisfactory education was being provided in private schools. The changes were certainly not aimed primarily at the Mennonites, who constituted but one minority among many. However, the plight confronting them was worsened by other developments that coincided with the school legislation. Specifically, the Great War and the emergence of a violent reaction against everything German created a climate extremely antagonistic towards the sectarian pacifists. The entrance into the country from the U.S.A. of hundreds of Hutterites and Mennonites, the return of the veterans, and labour unrest all contributed to a social and political climate already unfavourable.[31] The Reinlaender and others ignored the new legislation and continued to operate their private schools as before, making no changes or improvements. Education Minister Thornton noted the resistance:

> A campaign was inaugurated to destroy our public school system in the rural districts. Meetings were held urging the ratepayers to give up the government grants and run the schools as private schools.[32]

The Crushing of Mennonite Resistance

Two years lapsed before the Manitoba government launched a campaign to crush such Mennonite resistance. Legislation was passed establishing provincial school districts in unresponsive areas. An official trustee for those districts claiming, or attempting to claim, private status was appointed. In 1919, twelve new districts were imposed in the Chortitzer districts of the East Reserve area.[33] Next to experience first-hand the iron grasp of the government were the Reinlaender. By February 1920, ten new school districts were carved into the heart of the stronghold of Mennonite resistance in the West Reserve area.[34]

Mennonite reaction to the government policy was one of shock and dismay. The *Privilegium* (charter of privileges or promises), in which they had placed so much confidence, and the federal government, which had granted it, had failed them. The issues were now clear. Either one conformed to the approved official program or one elected to continue a struggle against a much stronger opponent. The Reinlaender and Chortitzer, supported by some Sommerfelder, grimly determined to counter the government's assault upon the private schools with their own tactic of passive resistance. Parents refused to submit the names of their children during the annual school census. They boycotted the district schools. They steadfastly declined to assist the authorities, so that in some instances the latter were obliged to resort to expropriating school sites when resident landowners refused to sell land for that purpose. When government patience finally wore thin, fines were levied against those parents who deliberately violated the School Attendance Act.

An equally determined offensive marked Saskatchewan's clash with its Reinlaender dissenters.[35] Actually, it was Saskatchewan that led the way in forcibly creating provincial school districts in resisting Mennonite localities. In 1918, three such districts had been established in the Swift Current reserve, and five in the Hague-Osler area.[36] Parents were fined for not sending their children to district schools when these became available. The Reinlaender were deeply distraught over what they believed to be an infringement of their legal rights and served notice that they would continue to defy governmental demands. In reply, the province turned 56 Reinlaender cases over to the courts and charged the defendants with violation of the law.

Subsequent years witnessed a virtual epidemic of prosecutions as the province bore relentlessly ahead with its program of educational reform and conformity. Little official compassion was shown for the beleaguered Reinlaender, despite the call from some sectors of the public that a greater effort should be made to appreciate the religious

TABLE 10[38]

SCHOOL ATTENDANCE PROSECUTIONS
OF SASKATCHEWAN MENNONITES: 1920–1925

YEAR	NUMBER OF PROSECUTIONS
1920	1,131
1921	1,804
1922	837
1923–25	1,604

tenets and convictions motivating the protesters.[37] The government, however, was in no mood to temper its prosecution policy and in 1921 alone, 1,804 court judgments were delivered against the Reinlaender (Table 10), forcing them to pay a total of $13,150 in fines. Included in these prosecutions was the Hague trial in March 1921, when 60 Mennonites were fined and one individual was sentenced to 30 days in the Prince Albert jail.[39]

The legal basis for such action in both Saskatchewan and Manitoba was the inadequacy of the private school system and, in the light of that, the Mennonite refusal to co-operate with the public system. Measured by provincial educational standards, though not necessarily by provincially supported public schools, the private schools were probably inferior. On the one hand, some school inspectors claimed that many teachers, recruited from among the village farm folk, could not teach English even if they wanted to. Knowledge of the alternative High German language was also inadequate. Most teachers had no professional qualifications whatsoever. On the other hand, other inspectors who regularly visited the private schools, as well as public schools, had more favourable reports.

In Saskatchewan, the tone for much of the criticism was set by E.H. Oliver of St. Andrews College, University of Saskatchewan, whose reports were later discovered to be based on hearsay.[40] Clearly, some schools were inadequate, poorly equipped and furnished, with backless seats, poor lighting and heating, inadequate blackboards, and a paucity of maps, charts, and pictures. And the curriculum was frequently quite limited, with the primary emphasis on prayers, singing, Bible stories, and reading in the mornings and arithmetic and writing for three hours in the afternoons.[41] As Harold W. Foght, an American specialist appointed to survey education in Saskatchewan, wrote about the Reinlaender and their schools:

> In this atmosphere the Mennonite children spend six or more months each year — the boys from 6 to 14 years and the girls from 6 to 12, grinding through this limited school fare: German Fibel (primer), Catechism, New Testament and Old Testament. . . . Much time is devoted to prayer and hymn singing, and some to ciphering and writing. The Mennonite child has little conception of the geography of the land in which he lives. His only history is that of the Mennonite church. As for the ideals, the aspirations and the future of the Canadian people, they are largely meaningless to him; for while he lives in Canada he is not of Canada.[42]

The Mennonites may be *"morally* entitled to private schools" was the reluctant admission of J.T.M. Anderson, the Saskatchewan inspector of schools, *"but,"* he added in exasperation, *"not to inefficient private schools in which no English is taught"* (emphasis original).[43] But Anderson, like Foght and Oliver, was prejudiced to begin with and depended on second-hand accounts to make his judgements.[44]

Though fault could be found with the Mennonite private schools, it did not necessarily follow that all was well in the public schools. The unwieldiness of bilingual instruction and the inadequate knowledge of English acquired by students in French, Ukrainian, and Polish districts in particular,[45] the poor quality of teaching, and the lack of standardization within the public schools in Manitoba and Saskatchewan had led to the important changes in school legislation in the respective provinces. But even after this the public schools, particularly in rural communities, left much to be desired. In his exhaustive survey of the Saskatchewan government, Foght criticized everything from the low level of teacher training to the narrow curriculum to the neglect of hygiene to the dearth of proper teaching aids.[46] Clearly, the public schools were also in need of much improvement.

Some public schools in Mennonite districts, on the other hand, were of superior quality. The elementary schools had been brought "up to the highest standard," said H.H. Ewert, in accordance with the principle that "whatever is undertaken must be done thoroughly."[47] Scarcely a school was without a teacher's residence, thus encouraging married teachers to remain in the profession. Most teachers were bilingual or even trilingual and trained also in religious values, thus ensuring that "the Mennonite children get a broader education." The objective was

> not only to educate worthy members of their church . . . [but also to] equip them for a conscientious discharge of the duties of citizenship.[48]

The private Mennonite schools were not that broad in their objectives and in their curriculum, but neither were they as narrow and inferior as the critics often suggested. From the perspective of the Reinlaender and Chortitzer, the judgements of inadequacy rendered on their schools were much too harsh, mainly because their own philosophy of education was poorly understood. These groups viewed the schools as supplemental institutions to, rather than as substitutes for, the learning in the home. In their opinion, the children learned most of what they needed to know for the chosen way of life from their mothers and fathers, in the kitchen, in the garden, in the barn, and in the fields. And that part of the education was thorough and effective. The schools were there to provide only what was needed in addition, namely an essential amount of reading, writing, arithmetic, Bible stories, and language. Physical education and other extras of the public school were not only unnecessary but harmful, inasmuch as school marches were akin to the military drill and school sports programs drew the children away from their homes and communities. And whatever professional qualifications the teachers lacked were made up for by the qualities of character and the genuine love for children so characteristic of their communities.[49]

The position of the Reinlaender and Chortitzer was either not heard or not understood. The governments pressed ahead and the people suffered the consequences. Repeated fines pushed many of them to the brink of economic ruin. When the Reinlaender refused to pay the fines, the authorities sometimes seized their personal chattels or livestock and auctioned them off.[50] It was against the background of tremendous financial strain that Reinlaender Johann F. Peters found himself compelled to address Saskatchewan Premier Martin:

> If we send our children to public schools, we violate God's commands in not holding to that which we promised our God and Saviour at holy baptism. If we do not send them, we offend against your laws. Does Mr. Martin want us to transgress against God's commands in order to keep his?. . . Oh how difficult it is to be a true Mennonite. . . . And we came here precisely because of the freedom which the government promised us in full.[51]

The Mennonite *Privilegium* letter of 1873, written by John Lowe, furnished the base from which all Mennonites who resisted public schools argued the legality of their cause. Little did they know, for it had not been explicitly explained to them, that not Lowe's letter but the revisions of it made legal in an Order-in-Council constituted the federal guarantees. The Order was in harmony with the B.N.A. Act, the *Privilegium* letter was not. The respective readings of the pertinent section of the Order-in-Council and the Lowe letter were as follows:

> That the Mennonites will have the fullest privileges of exercising their religious principles, and educating their children in schools, *as provided by law* [emphasis added], without any kind of molestation or restriction whatever.[52]

> The fullest privilege of exercising their religious principles *is by law afforded* [emphasis added] the Mennonites, without any kind of molestation or restriction whatever, and the same privilege extends to the education of their children in schools.[53]

The result of the two versions was much confusion. In each instance that representations were made to the government, the Mennonites were informed that their argument was invalid since the province, rather than the Dominion, had been granted jurisdiction over educational affairs by the B.N.A. Act. In an unusual undertaking, and certainly not something which the Reinlaender or Chortitzer themselves would have attempted, lawyers for the Mennonites finally tested the legitimacy of their position by appealing a court decision that favoured the Crown.

The legal proceedings were initiated by the Manitoba Sommer-felder, with the encouragement of lawyers, in July 1919, just after a provincial court had ruled that nine parents of the Houston School District had violated the School Attendance Act. The cases of John Hildebrand and Dietrich Doerksen, two of the defendants, were presented to the Manitoba Court of Appeal.[54] At this hearing, the prosecution argued that, by virtue of the B.N.A. Act's delineation of powers, the provinces possessed autonomy with respect to educational matters. It also dismissed as an insufficient claim the original letter from John Lowe to the Mennonites, contending that the document had been found to be legally in error.

The judge presiding over the case ruled in the government's favour. He noted that a corrected version of the Lowe "guarantee" had been included in the 1873 Order-in-Council, clearing the way for the immigration of 7,000 Mennonites from Russia. He explained that the Mennonites were entitled to "the unhampered and unrestricted privilege of educating their children in the schools provided by the laws of the country in which they proposed to settle."[55] It did not, in his opinion, permit them to retain an independent school system outside the reach of provincial law as was implied in the Lowe letter.

The Sommerfelder made one final attempt to obtain legal sanction for their claim by taking their case to the Supreme Court of Canada. The Court in turn referred it to the Judicial Committee of the Privy Council in London. In July 1920 the Privy Council ruled against the Mennonites.[56]

Meanwhile, efforts other than legal action and passive resistance were made in an attempt to deflect the governments from their commitment to educational integration. At least seven petitions were directed to the provincial authorities by different groups at different times (Table 11). The first two of these were submitted to the Manitoba officials during the war. It is noteworthy that they were the only briefs specifically mentioning the question of language.[58] Later on, the public reaction against all things German made appeals on that basis counterproductive.

The five petitions addressed to the provincial governments beginning in 1919, four in Manitoba and one in Saskatchewan, differed in tone and some detail but essentially agreed with one another on the main points. All of the documents referred to the agreement reached

TABLE 11[57]

MENNONITE SCHOOL PETITIONS TO THE GOVERNMENTS OF
MANITOBA AND SASKATCHEWAN, 1916 – 22

GROUP	DATE	PRESENTED TO
Manitoba: Bergthaler-Sommerfelder	7 Jan. 1916	Hon. V. Winkler
All Manitoba groups except Reinlaender	15 Feb. 1916	Manitoba Gov't
Manitoba: Reinlaender	Feb. 1919	Manitoba Legislature
Chortitzer-Kleine Gemeinde	21 Oct. 1919	Manitoba Gov't
Chortitzer	13 Jan. 1920	Manitoba Gov't
Chortitzer-Sommerfelder	14 Oct. 1921	Manitoba Gov't
Swift Current Reinlaender	7 Jan. 1922	Sask. Gov't

between the Dominion and the Mennonites in 1873, and all indicated that the Mennonites expected the country to honour its original promise. Similarly, the petitions emphasized the importance of providing the children with sound instruction in schools supervised by the Mennonites, rather than by the province. The Chortitzer Church petition was representative of the concerns of all the resisting Mennonites when it testified:

> As a matter of conscience, your petitioners cannot delegate to others the all-important responsibility of educating their children, convinced as they are that instruction in other schools would result in weakening and even loss of faith, and would be generally detrimental to the moral and spiritual welfare of the children.[59]

Despite a clear offer by the Chortitzer in January 1920 to improve their private schools, the Manitoba government remained unmoved.[60] In setting a patriotic standard for accredited schools, it had, in effect, made all Mennonite private schools, no matter how strong pedagogically, unacceptable.

An appeal 15 months later to the Manitoba Legislature on the basis of "British tolerance and British fair play" likewise fell on deaf ears.[61] Where, asked the representatives of the Chortitzer and

Sommerfelder communities, could "British men with a British mind" be found to champion tolerance and to end the persecution which was being inflicted on "a quiet and peace-loving people who want to do good without expecting returns." And the British Empire "is not likely to go to pieces" if permission was granted to teach the mother tongue a few hours a day.

By now, every possible alternative had been exhausted by the Mennonites and their only recourse was to obey the law or carry through on their announced threats to emigrate. Migration sentiments had already been voiced among the Reinlaender at Hague. Similar pronouncements issued out of the Chortitzer and Sommerfelder camps. The Bergthalers of Manitoba, however, indicated that they would not participate in any emigration venture. They, along with the Kleine Gemeinde (with some exceptions in the Morris area), Brueder Gemeinde, and the Bruderthalers, demonstrated that they were basically prepared to accept the public schools and make the most of opportunities within the system.

The Search for a New Country

The decision by the resisting Mennonites to leave their prosperous farms and villages, which had quite literally transformed the wild prairie regions into productive agricultural centres, was an agonizing one. The risks involved were exceptionally high, for in exchange for a secure existence in Canada they were about to accept a future fraught with uncertainty. It was, however, a venture they were prepared to make for the sake of their way of life. They had done it before in leaving Prussia after 1789 and Russia after 1873, and they could do it again.

The uncompromising course of action which the conservative Mennonites agreed to pursue set them apart from other ethnic groups in Canada. To be sure, the large and vocal Francophone and Ukrainian communities protested the school legislation vigorously through newspaper editorials, petitions, and special visits with government officials. Yet eventually these groups resigned themselves to the system and sought other ways of preserving their language, the former by sending their children to some of the Catholic private schools, the latter by establishing bursas or boarding houses for students attending public institutions.[62]

TABLE 12[65]

REINLAENDER LAND-SEEKING DELEGATIONS, 1919–21

DATE	DESTINATION	GROUPS REPRESENTED
4 Aug. – 24 Nov. 1919	Brazil, Argentina	Manitoba, Hague, Swift Current
15 Jan. – 29 Jan. 1920	Mississippi	Manitoba, Hague, Swift Current
12 Apr. – 29 Apr. 1920	Mississippi	Manitoba, Hague
14 May – 25 May 1920	Mississippi	
19 Aug. 1920	Quebec	Manitoba, Swift Current
8 Sept. – 9 Oct. 1920	Mexico	Hague
9 Oct. – Dec. 1920	Paraguay	Hague
11 Nov. – 31 Dec. 1920	Mexico	Hague, Swift Current
24 Jan. – 12 Mar. 1921	Mexico	Manitoba, Hague, Swift Current
5 Apr. – 9 May 1921	Mexico	Manitoba, Hague, Swift Current
July 1921	Mexico	Manitoba, Swift Current
12 Aug. – 10 Sept. 1921	Mexico	Manitoba, Swift Current

Some groups, such as the Icelanders in Manitoba, had used English as the main language of instruction in their schools since their arrival in the 1870s[63] and were therefore not very concerned about compulsory attendance at English schools. A number of Polish immigrants returned to their homeland after the war, but their disillusionment with Canada was influenced more by the general wartime hostility directed towards them than by the school legislation in particular.[64] Moreover, only a few Poles left Canada. Thus, in their decision to emigrate to avoid English public schools, the conservative Mennonite groups were unique.

The Reinlaender led the way in the search for a land willing to absorb a large group of agricultural pacifists requiring complete freedom of religion, language, and education (Table 12). The first possibility suggested was Argentina.[66] Undoubtedly, the inaccessibility and isolation of that country appealed to the Reinlaender, as did perhaps the knowledge that large groups of Germans were already living there and that Canadian Mennonite foreign missionaries were preparing to enter that country.[67]

A fund-raising drive was launched to subsidize a proposed exploratory expedition. By August 4, 1919, a six-man delegation representing the Reinlaender in both provinces was set to depart. The men returned on November 24, without Johann J. Wall from Hague, who had died in September and been buried en route in Brazil.[68] The written confirmation of his passing and the details of his suffering during a week-long illness reached his distraught family two months after his burial at Curitiba.[69] Equally sorrowful and disappointing was the news delivered in person soon after by the returning delegates that Argentina had rejected the request for special privileges.[70]

By this time American land speculators had heard of the imminent Mennonite migration and besieged the Reinlaender with offers of land in Alabama, Florida, and Louisiana. The Reinlaender, however, opted to pursue settlement possibilities in Mississippi. In mid-January 1920, the five-man party, again representing all the Reinlaender groups, left for a study tour of Mississippi. The delegates were granted an interview with Governor Russell, at which time they presented the terms under which they would consent to locate in the southern state. The Reinlaender demands conformed almost exactly to the privileges awarded them by Canada in 1873. Russell himself appeared genuinely interested at the prospect of obtaining a sizeable body of proven farmers. He subsequently assured the Reinlaender in writing that, in the event of a move to Mississippi, they would be accorded complete freedom with respect to religion, education, and language. In addition, the Mennonites would be allowed to affirm rather than swear, and they would be permitted to administer their own benevolent societies.[71] This was indeed heartening news.

Consequently, a second delegation was dispatched in April 1920 to inquire into the question of military exemptions. A meeting was arranged with U.S. Attorney-General A. Mitchell Palmer, who informed the Reinlaender that the federal statutes contained no provision for absolute exemption from military service. However, there was provision for exemption in a noncombatant capacity.[72] This was less than the Reinlaender had expected, but it was still sufficient to cause them to decide formally on emigration to Mississippi.[73]

A third deputation departed on May 14 to negotiate the purchase of 125,000 acres of land. On its return, the entire Reinlaender constituency was canvassed to assess the total amount of land required. Each prospective buyer was obligated to advance a $2-per-acre down payment, the cumulative sum of which was deposited in a Winkler bank.[74] In June, a fourth delegation prepared to journey south with instructions to consummate the proposed deal. Then troubles began anew. Without explanation the delegates were denied admission into the United States. The Reinlaender interpreted this mysterious turn of events as divine intervention and scrapped all their Mississippi-related plans.[75]

The mystery arises from the fact that no satisfactory explanation of the denial was forthcoming. United States immigration officials in Winnipeg had refused entry to the Mennonites, but the Bureau of Immigration in Washington claimed no knowledge of that action. What the Commissioner-General could not deny was that a very considerable resistance, initiated by groups like the American Legion, had been building up against the proposed immigration.[76] Thus, though others, particularly real estate agents and certain governmental leaders, eagerly encouraged the Mennonite immigrants, the Mississippi scheme was abandoned. Similar efforts in states like Alabama, Arkansas, Colorado, Florida, and South Carolina likewise did not materialize.[77]

Twice within a year, Reinlaender emigration schemes had collapsed. The people were becoming restless. The leaders were acutely aware of the debilitating effect these failures were having on morale, and they therefore redoubled their efforts to find a solution. In desperation, they directed yet another plea to the Manitoba government wondering whether there was

> any place in Manitoba, where none other can live, in which we could found a colony, apart from the world, where we could bring up our children, unhindered by common laws, in the true faith of our forefathers?[78]

There was no such place, the government replied, quite probably thinking not of the availability of isolated land, of which there was plenty, especially in the inter-lake area, but of the nonavailability of a tolerant government. But scarcely had the Reinlaender again been rebuffed by Manitoba than they received news that Quebec desired colonists to develop its Abitibi and Gaspé regions. Initial conversations with Quebec officials led the Mennonites to believe they would be granted the sought-after privileges, including the right to private schools.[79] Therefore, on August 19, 1920, a delegation representing the Manitoba and Swift Current colonies conferred with Premier Taschereau. Members of the delegation outlined their demands to the premier, who, at least to them, appeared favourably disposed.[80] However, subsequent negotiations proved their optimism to be premature.[81] Yet another migration attempt had foundered.

Every setback added to the discontent circulating within the Reinlaender constituency. Parents continued to defy the school attendance orders, but it was doubtful whether their resolve could long persist in face of the heavy fines imposed upon them. The leaders argued, with some justification, that the prosecutions should be suspended in light of the expressed Reinlaender intention to leave the country. They petitioned the provincial authorities, in September 1920, for a two-year moratorium on the enforcement of the school attendance law so that they could concentrate on putting their affairs in order.[82] Their plea went unheeded.

The flagging spirits were suddenly rejuvenated by the return from Mexico of a delegation sponsored by the Hague colony. While others had been busy in Quebec, Hague had assembled one deputation to investigate Mexico and another to pursue opportunities in Paraguay. The first group returned with a positive report, prompting the Manitoba and Swift Current districts to abandon the Quebec scheme and redirect their energies to Mexico.[83]

A second expedition was immediately organized. Passport irregularities scuttled the planned participation of the Manitoba Reinlaender, leaving the Saskatchewan delegates alone responsible for assessing the situation in Mexico. They were so encouraging that a third delegation, this time fully representative of all the Reinlaender, left for Mexico on January 24.[84] A short scouting trip through select areas of the country was followed by a conference with President Obregon on February 20, 1921.[85] Eight days later, the elusive *Privilegium*, addressed to the representatives of the Reinlaender Church, was approved and signed by the President and his Minister of Agriculture.

Included among the guarantees were: complete exemption from military service, the unrestricted right to religious principles, and the authority to conduct schools "without the government in any manner obstructing you."[86] For Mexico, the admission of these "industrious farmers" bore the prospect of upgrading agriculture and stimulating "the present sluggish demand for implements, tools, and agricultural machinery and supplies in general."[87] The Reinlaender had achieved their goal, and their only reservation with respect to the *Privilegium* arose from the fact that the guarantees did not, at least not yet, have the force of congressional law.

The returning delegates were very realistic about material hardships in the prospective new homeland. At least Cornelius Rempel, the senior delegate, in addressing the Reinlaender brotherhood meeting was very modest in his promotion of the new homeland. The Mexicans, he said, had a very limited and simple way of making a living, and Mennonites too would not duplicate the wealth and surplus achieved in a rich and blessed Canada. To illustrate, he cited the situations of a typical Mexican household:

> If a farmer there has a wooden plow and two oxen, in order to plant a few acres of corn and beans, he is satisfied and he can feed his family. . . . If the woman mashes corn patties in the morning—often there are no table or chairs—and then adds beans and pepper sauce as a spread, then the meal is ready.[88]

Poverty, however, was not an insurmountable problem, said Rempel, given the fact that freedom for school and church was assured and that the diet was sufficient to maintain the health of old and young people alike. And, while social conditions were not the best either, the situation would not be different than formerly in Russia, where every village had a night watchman to guard against break-ins and theft.[89]

It was clear that a very difficult choice confronted the Reinlaender. On the one hand was their Canadian homeland with its well-developed villages and promise of continuous material prosperity but with the lack of educational autonomy and cultural isolation. On the other hand was Mexico, the new land of promise once again guaranteeing special privilege, full educational and cultural autonomy, but not a congenial social environment or a very prosperous agriculture.

Emigration to Mexico

Leadership was needed to help the community to decide, and that leadership came from the bishops, whose position in the congregations gave them unusual influence. In theory they were humble servants of the Lord and of the people, and in almost every sense they were also that in practice. They served without remuneration and with a great sense of responsibility. They took their calling and their ordination very seriously and expected their families to do the same. Their burdens were, or were perceived to be, enormous. Bishop Johann Friesen's life, for instance, was full of "manifold tribulations, [with] almost unbearable daily tasks" as described by his successor, whose own difficulties were equal to "a brook of tears." To his children Friesen wrote about his burdened life:

> you have known no other father than one in the form of a poor servant, always under pressure and much affliction with rarely a friendly face. [90]

From them he expected that they would always be obedient, that they would abstain from all worldliness, and that they would not burden his office with careless living. Of himself he expected the impossible, but that precisely was his dilemma, his internal punishment, for he found in himself none of the virtues which Paul required. As it was written:

> A bishop then must be blameless, the husband of one wife, vigilant, sober, of good behaviour, given to hospitality, apt to teach; not given to wine, no striker, not greedy of filthy lucre; but patient, not a brawler, or covetous; one that ruleth well his own house, having his children in subjection with all gravity. . . . [91]

In other words, the spirit, language, and outward form of the bishop was one of humility in the extreme — for pride was the greatest sin — but an exemplary life of humble service combined with longevity of tenure somehow translated itself into enormous power, which commanded the obedience of the followers. The "vital statistics" of some bishops were most impressive (see Table 13), but they could not be made known in the bishop's lifetime lest the heavenly reward be lost. However, every bishop kept careful record, and that record was an essential part of a bishop's obituary.

In any event, at this crucial time it was the bishops, especially Johann Friesen in Manitoba, who challenged the people to accept anew the tribulations required of all people of God who wanted to be faithful to their baptismal vows. Suffering, it was said, was necessary for the testing and refinement of the church — "as gold is proven in the fire"[93] — for the glory of God, as evidence of the church's loyalty, and as a witness to the world.

The entire Scriptures, as understood by the Reinlaender, confirmed the truth that people desiring to live a godly life had to expect persecution. The Old Testament prophets predicted tribulation and

TABLE 13[92]

SERVICE RECORD OF FOUR REINLAENDER BISHOPS

NAME	Johann Wiebe	Johann Friesen	Jacob Wiens	Isaak M. Dyck
DATES	1837–1906	1869–1935	1855–1932	1889–1969
PLACE OF SERVICE	Russia Manitoba	Manitoba Mexico	Manitoba Saskatchewan Mexico	Manitoba Mexico
YEARS AS MINISTER*	5	10	12	21
YEARS AS BISHOP	35	23	32	36
SERMONS†	1,544	1,816	1,577	3,000
BAPTISMS‡	2,228	1,713	1,396	4,988
WEDDINGS	294	229	184	300
FUNERALS	660	582	370	1,175

* Reference here is to ministerial years prior to ordination as bishop.
† Not including those given at baptisms, funerals, and weddings.
‡ Reference is to number of persons baptized, not number of events, as in weddings and funerals.

the New Testament illustrated it. The Book of Hebrews, especially, was a chronicle of martyrdom and of witnesses, who by their testimony and by their death conquered kingdoms. A survey of church history likewise made clear that the "true children of God and followers of Jesus have been born to suffer, to endure, and to be persecuted."[94] The same was true of "the beautiful *Maertyrerbuch*" (*Martyr's Mirror*) which was "read far too little in our dark and godless times and unknown in many of our homes and families."[95]

Thus, the appeal to the Scriptures and their teachings was augmented with an appeal to the faith, life, and death of the ancestors, whose example deserved emulation. Their faith, which they "sealed with their blood," should be "our faith." The commandments of God, which were the rules for life of the forefathers, should be the contemporary guideline as well.

There is only one difference between them and us, namely that they persevered in the heavy persecutions and through the hor-

rors of martyrdom. We, however, have not sacrificed our
blood in our battle against sin.[96]

The history of the immediate past was appealed to as a further
source of strength. The departure from Russia, the "beloved homeland and fatherland" of their fathers, bishops, and ministers, was an
act of faith, love, and hope. They were warned by those who stayed
behind that deprivation and starvation awaited them in North America. But God cared for them "as a loving father cares for his children"
and not a single person died of hunger. On the contrary, the people
soon became well-to-do and it was those who stayed behind who
within a short time were facing starvation.[97] The decision to leave
Russia had been a very difficult one for Bishop Johann Wiebe. The
fields of beautiful high grass and rich, waving wheat fields had been
a great temptation, but the voice from above had been clear:

> If the church is to be kept faithful to the pure teaching of the
> gospel, she will have to live once again among heathen
> people.[98]

In this case, faithfulness required emigration to Mexico, because
the prospects in Canada were not good. The government wanted to
use the public schools to make "hundred per cent Canadians" out of
everybody, including the Mennonites, and "the foundation of these
schools was the motto: one king, one God, one navy, one flag, one all-
British empire."[99] But it was not only the compulsion in school
matters, but the problem of worldliness in general. Conformity was
everywhere evident, especially with respect to automobiles and an
indescribable emphasis on pretty clothes.[100] If the church was to
escape absorption into the world, it had to escape that world. The
church was in turmoil because those who had become unfaithful ("*die
Abgefallenen*") did their best to frustrate the emigration movement.

It was, therefore, necessary to ascertain "who was remaining loyal
to the confession given at baptism and joining the church in the
emigration to Mexico."[101] Announcement was made that all those
willing should indicate their intention and register anew with the
bishop; otherwise it would be concluded that membership in the
Reinlaender church had been forfeited in favour of some other
church. Quite understandably, this made it very difficult for those
who decided not to emigrate. They were obliged to leave their church

and were condemned as being disloyal to their baptismal vows. While some none the less refused to reregister, others found it easier to indicate a willingness to emigrate but then not take any further action, or, having emigrated, to return. As it was written in Mexico many years later:

> How many of those who registered, whose names to this very day are in the church book as emigrants, . . . changed their minds, moved back, and are now sitting in the lap of the world.[102]

The way was now cleared for the final stages of the long-discussed migration. During September 1921, the Manitoba and Swift Current colonies each purchased tracts of land, adjacent to each other, in Chihuahua, consisting of 155,000 acres and 74,125 acres, respectively.[103] The purchase price was $8.25 per acre.[104] Severe problems and considerable friction accompanied the liquidation of Reinlaender holdings in Canada. Prior to the completion of the Mexican land scheme, a financial nightmare arose in connection with the attempted sale of 107,000 acres near Swift Current for five million dollars.[105] The deal with Florida entrepreneurs had miscarried, largely because the American promoters were unable to sustain their end of the bargain. However, Canadian lawyers demanded remuneration from the Reinlaender for their role in attracting a serious buyer and arranging a purchase. The case was submitted to the courts, whereupon the Mennonites were required to forfeit 10,200 acres of land in lieu of a settlement of $222,000 and court costs.

The entire protracted affair was extremely embarrassing for the Reinlaender, who viewed the final resolution as yet further evidence of persecution against them. Their bitterness becomes more understandable in light of the fact that the Court of King's Bench, the Saskatchewan Court of Appeal, and the Supreme Court of Canada all supported the Mennonites. The Privy Council in London reversed their judgments. There were other such disappointments. The Mennonites were also taken advantage of in Mexico. The land purchased at more than eight dollars per acre was said to be worth but thirty centavos or fifteen cents per acre.[106]

Additional problems arose for the Reinlaender. Depressed land prices caused by the first post-war recession eroded morale and

[Handwritten annotations in margins:]

Total Paid:
229,125 × 8.25
= 1,890,281.20

Total Actual Cost:
229,125 × .15
= 34,368.75

Difference:
1,855,912.4

Overpaid by:
↳ "

Thus Paid
54 times
the necessary
amount
(53.999997)

Total Land Bought
155,000
+ 74,125
229,125 total

deterred the more undecided members from joining the migration. As well, heated debates were held over whether all the Reinlaender land should be disposed of in one communal block, or whether the sale of farms should be left to private initiative. Despite pronounced resistance to their proposal, the leaders pressed ahead with their plan to effect a single sale. Only when it became apparent that such a transaction could not be completed were the Reinlaender permitted to dispose of their property in an individual manner.[107]

On March 1, 1922, the first chartered trainload of Reinlaender emigrants left Plum Coulee en route to Mexico. A second train followed the next day, and an eyewitness chronicled the emotional departure:

> Thursday, March 2, 1922, was a beautiful clear day. . . .
> Before departure time hundreds of people gathered around the
> station and hundreds of farewells were said. The locomotive
> was shunting railroad cars, . . . and animated conversations
> and quiet weeping were punctuated by the loud grumblings of
> coupled boxcars. Finally all twenty-seven freight cars and
> three passenger cars had been connected in proper order. . . .
> At 12:20 a.m. all were ready, the signal was given, and slowly
> the train pulled out of the little town of Haskett. . . . [108]

Of all the Reinlaender, those from Manitoba showed by far the most enthusiasm for the emigration. Between the peak years 1922 and 1926, 3,200 villagers from the province (about 64 per cent of the total Manitoba Reinlaender group) participated in the move.[109] Trains carrying the first groups of Reinlaender from the Swift Current area left about a week after the initial Manitoba departure. About 1,200 (one-third) of that district's Reinlaender eventually made their way to Mexico.[110]

The story at Hague unfolded apart from the others. This colony had indignantly withdrawn its participation in a united group migration after a financial dispute had flared up during the Mexico negotiations.[111] The Hague Reinlaender subsequently purchased 35,000 acres in the state of Durango, where the first settlement was established in 1924. Deflated land prices delayed the early departure of the Hague public school resisters and generally diminished the colony's support for migration. Altogether, 950 persons, representing one-fourth of the colony's population, decided to move to Mexico.[112]

TABLE 14[113]

CHORTITZER-SOMMERFELDER-BERGTHALER(S)
LAND-SEEKING DELEGATIONS

DATE	DESTINATION	GROUPS REPRESENTED
Feb. 1919	Brazil, Argentina, Uruguay	Self-appointed
11 Feb. – 2 Sept. 1921	Mexico, Paraguay	Chortitzer, Sommerfelder, Saskatchewan Bergthaler
Feb. 1921	Mexico	Saskatchewan Bergthaler
Oct. – Nov. 1921	Mexico	Sommerfelder, Chortitzer
Early Summer, 1922	Mexico	Sommerfelder

Emigration to Paraguay

Concurrent, but separate from the Reinlaender, the Chortitzer of Manitoba, the Sommerfelder of Manitoba and Saskatchewan, and the Bergthaler (Saskatchewan) groups conducted their own search for another home (Table 14). A self-appointed delegation of three visited several South American countries in 1919, but the mission boasted little success. Still, a connection had been made with Paraguayan officials who hinted that their government might be receptive to acquiring a group of farmers such as the Mennonites. Back home, the respective groups agreed to pursue the slim lead.

An official Chortitzer-Sommerfelder-Bergthaler(S) delegation, selected in September 1920, was instructed to locate and assess potential settlement sites in Paraguay and interview the authorities regarding the necessary privileges.[114] Irregularities in citizenship papers delayed the party until February 11, 1921. By this time, the second Reinlaender delegation had returned from Mexico, and consequently it was decided by the Sommerfelder to investigate both countries.

The Paraguay delegation was gone more than six months, and during this time it enlisted the aid of Samuel McRoberts, a New York financier, who had access to powerful officials in the Paraguayan government, including President Manuel Gondra. Gondra eagerly wished to stimulate economic and agricultural growth within his country. He also desired to assert Paraguay's hegemony over the vast territory of land known as the Gran Chaco lying west of the

Paraguay River. Populating the area with foreign nationals, Gondra surmised, was one method by which this might be accomplished.[115]

An interview between the president and the Mennonite delegates was arranged for April 4, 1921, by McRoberts. Discussions focused on the all-important consideration of special concessions, and both parties arrived at a common agreement. Before the end of July, a document outlining special status for the Mennonites was ratified by the Senate and Congress of Paraguay.[116] The *Privilegium* resembled the charter obtained by the Reinlaender from Mexico, with one major difference. The official written assurances from Paraguay carried with them the strength not only of presidential decree but also of congressional law.

Meanwhile, the delegation had set out on a four-week tour of the Chaco. Seasonally, the weather was at its best, but even so, the "green hell" must have vividly impressed and challenged the sensibilities of the visitors. The regional climate was semi-tropical, itself a feature that would require enormous physical adjustments by the Menno- nites. Patches of open grasslands, possessing few fresh-water wells, alternated with scrubby woodland. Various Indian tribes called the area their home and, until the arrival of the Mennonites, appeared to be the only people capable of carving a living out of this primitive wilderness. On balance, it did not appear to be a region that would easily lend itself to European-type settlement. Yet the report which the delegates prepared for the churches back home spoke quite optimistically:

> We are of the opinion that the land in general is well adapted
> for agriculture, stock-raising, fruit growing, and the raising
> of vegetables. We believe that grain, such as wheat, etc. can be
> grown at certain times of the year. . . . We believe that this
> land, blessed with its various advantages and its mild climate,
> would be well adapted to colonization if the necessary railway
> connection with the port on the river is established. . . [117]

En route home, the Manitoba delegates stopped in Mexico, where they were promised similar concessions to those awarded earlier to the Reinlaender. Their interest in Mexico was minimal, however, mainly because a *Privilegium*, given by the president only, lacked the guarantee of permanence. They looked for a *Privilegium* grounded in the statutes or entrenched in the constitution.

A West Reserve Sommerfelder group, headed by Bishop Abra-

TABLE 15[119]

MANITOBA AND SASKATCHEWAN MENNONITE IMMIGRANTS TO LATIN AMERICA, 1922–30

GROUP	ORIGIN	DATES	APPROX. NUMBER	DESTINATION
A. MEXICO				
Reinlaender	Swift Current	1922–26	1,200	Chihuahua
Reinlaender	Manitoba (W.R.)	1922–26	3,200	Chihuahua
Reinlaender	Hague	1924–25	950	Durango
Sommerfelder	Manitoba (W.R.) Herbert, Sask.	1922–25	600	Chihuahua
Total to Mexico			5,950	
B. PARAGUAY				
Chortitzer	Manitoba (E.R.)	1926–30	1,201	Chaco
Sommerfelder	Manitoba (W.R.)	1926–30	357	Chaco
Bergthaler	Rosthern, Sask.	1926–27	227	Chaco
Total to Paraguay			1,785	
Total to Latin America			7,735	

ham Doerksen, had in the meantime, however, become persuaded that Mexico was a more attractive homeland than Paraguay. Accordingly, a three-man delegation journeyed to Mexico in October 1921, carrying with it a ten-point request for special privileges. The ensuing negotiations were favourable and in the early summer of 1922, 12,000 acres of land were purchased in Chihuahua just to the north of the Manitoba and Swift Current settlements.[118] Sommerfelder migration to the site began later that year in October and involved 600 people over the next few years. Thus 5,950 Canadian Mennonites made Mexico their home (Table 15). In the fall of 1922 the Kleine Gemeinde, representing "about 300 Canadian and 150 American families," took an option on 150,000 acres of Santa Clara ranch land, but the immigration of this group did not materialize in the 1920s.[120]

The prospect of settling in Mexico elicited little excitement among the majority of Chortitzer and Sommerfelder considering emigration. Some regarded the social and political climate of the country as too unstable to accommodate nonresistant settlers. Many harboured suspicions as to the legality of the Mexican *Privilegium*, which bore the signatures of only the president and one of his ministers. Others simply wished to enter a territory where they could remain "unmolested." Thus it came about that the Chortitzer, accompanied by some Sommerfelder and Saskatchewan Bergthaler, removed themselves, beginning in 1926, to the most inaccessible refuge they could find — the Chaco of Paraguay.

McRoberts continued to assist them in their transfer to Paraguay. Under his direction, two companies were formed to facilitate the liquidation of assets in Canada and to secure land for the settlers in the Chaco.[121] The Corporación Paraguaya supervised the events in South America, while the Intercontinental Company co-ordinated the disposal of the Canadian properties. Enormous sums of money changed hands during the course of the proceedings, not always to the advantage of the Mennonites. In the sale of the Chaco lands, for instance, the Corporación Paraguaya netted a clear profit of $486,576.54.[122]

During the latter half of the decade, 1926 – 30, 1,785 Chortitzer, Sommerfelder, and Saskatchewan Bergthaler Mennonites left Canada for Paraguay.[123] This total fell considerably short of the number predicted by the leaders and organizers at the outset of the operation. The border war between Paraguay and Bolivia, the extreme hardships of settlement, and the deaths of many children, as well as depressed land prices, caused many to rethink their position and to become reconciled to the public school. An attempt had been made to organize the three emigrating groups into a single congregation, a not unlikely prospect since they did have common roots in the Bergthaler group of Russia, but the most that could be achieved at this time was a representative administrative committee to lead the emigration. At their destination in the Menno Colony of the Chaco, a single congregation of Sommerfelder and Chortitzer, led by the Chortitzer bishop, Martin Friesen, gradually came into being. The Bergthaler(S), though part of the same colony, formed their own group.

The consequences of the Canadian exodus were felt immediately (Table 16) among those staying behind in Canada. The departure of

TABLE 16[124]

SUMMARY OF LATIN AMERICAN SETTLEMENTS

LOCATION	DATE OF FOUNDING	CANADIAN SOURCE	CONGREGATION	BISHOP
		A. MEXICO		
Chihuahua	Mar. 1922	Manitoba (W.R.)	Reinlaender	Isaak M. Dyck
Chihuahua	Mar. 1922	Swift Current	Reinlaender	Abraham Wiebe
Durango	1924	Hague-Osler	Reinlaender	Jacob Wiens
Chihuahua	Nov. 1922	Manitoba (W.R.)	Sommerfelder	Abraham Doerks
		B. PARAGUAY		
Chaco	Nov. 1926	Manitoba (E.R.)	Chortitzer	Martin C. Friese
		Manitoba (W.R.)	Sommerfelder	
		Saskatchewan	Bergthaler	Aron Zacharias

Reinlaender, Chortitzer, Sommerfelder, and Bergthaler(S) stunned the reserves in Manitoba and Saskatchewan and permanently altered the socio-religious complexion of these areas. Those least given to compromise had left. Those ready for some accommodation to society and the educational system remained. Although large numbers of Reinlaender had stayed behind, congregations by that name ceased to exist, because the leadership had left, taking the all-important church registers with them. In due course, the people remaining in the Hague-Osler and West Reserve areas reorganized under a different name, but in the Swift Current area the remnant drifted towards the Sommerfelder or into the camps of other Mennonite groups who viewed them as a home mission field.

Several Reinlaender villages ceased to exist as a result of the migration, and the open field system, which had fallen into disuse among all but the Reinlaender, also disappeared. Blumengart, Eichenfeld, and Kronstal in the West Reserve lost all their residents. Other centres, such as Reinland, Rosengart, and Blumenort, never fully recovered from their population losses.[125] In some villages, fears were expressed that the vacant Reinlaender farms would be occupied by non-Mennonites. It was no secret that the outgoing Reinlaender favoured the sale of their land to people other than

Mennonites.[126] One A.P. Elias of Winkler voiced the concerns of many when he anxiously informed the government that:

> Some of them [Reinlaender] are moving to Mexico and are selling their land to any kind of people and we who like to stay here want to keep it as it was given to us. We want only Mennonites here. Please let us know what to do in this matter.[127]

No serious attempt was made by government officials to dissuade the Mennonites from leaving the country, probably on the assumption that the exodus would not happen.[128] In the end, it was expected, the Reinlaender would adjust to the new situation and accept the public schools. As one writer observed: "The gasoline filling station has already crept into the *darpen* or villages, which a few years ago were 'diehard' old Mennonite centers."[129] When the exodus did occur, it was assumed that the emigrants would return. Premier Martin of Saskatchewan likely typified the indifferent official opinion when he remarked:

> I am fairly sure personally that it will only be a short time until people who have gone to Mexico will be coming back and telling the Saskatchewan people the truth about conditions there. If this occurs, I have no fears that any considerable number of Saskatchewan people will go to Mexico.[130]

The Premier was both right and wrong. He was right in assuming that not everybody would go. He was wrong in miscalculating how deeply those who chose to leave felt about the issues and what price they were ready to pay for their convictions. Those leaving felt that they had been betrayed by governments, while they had kept their end of the bargain which had brought them to Canada in the first place. They had agreed to be the pioneer agriculturalists which Canada desperately needed at the time. They and their children and children's children had not turned their back on the land and drifted to the cities as so many other immigrants had done.[131] They had become an economic asset rather than a liability, and they wondered why the governments did not recognize this and allow them the essential cultural latitude. The answer was clear. The needs and priorities had changed. Cultural assimilation of new immigrant groups had become more important than their agricultural pioneering. The Mennonites had lost their former power to bargain for special privileges.

The departing Mennonites, for their part, did not overlook writing a letter to Ottawa to thank the governments of Canada and Britain for every consideration they had received in nearly fifty years of sojourn in Manitoba and Saskatchewan. They were grateful for original land grants, for loans, and for the general goodwill extended to them, and they wanted it to be understood that they were leaving because they felt a church could not survive if the word of God was absent from the schools. They also hoped that their departure would lead to greater tolerance in the future.[132]

The emigrating Mennonites lacked sympathy not only among certain political leaders, but also with public opinion and the press generally, though with exceptions. Journalist Gerald M. Brown of the *Saskatoon Phoenix* was convinced that it would be "difficult indeed to replace the sturdy, honest, and hard-working farmers who are leaving their Canadian homes in disgust and disappointment."[133] The distant-from-the-scene Victoria papers, however, reflected very much the wartime sentiment that Mennonites were undesirable citizens. The *Victoria Daily Times* was ready to see "200,000 Mennonites" leave the country without any "pang of regret" because

> Canada will be much better off in the long run without that
> type of citizenry whose tenets constitute the taking of all it can
> get without giving anything in return.[134]

The *Manitoba Free Press*, which through the years had sought to interpret fairly the Mennonites to the public,[135] especially with reference to their schools, could not side with them in the early 1920s. The legality, or rather the illegality, of their claims to educational autonomy had been determined by the Manitoba Court of Appeal and by the Supreme Court of Canada. The Mennonites were therefore without a claim which the state could recognize as legitimate. In the words of the editorial writers:

> The Old Coloniers are therefore reduced to establishing their
> case for particular treatment by an appeal based upon an
> assumption that it is a fundamental natural right of any sect,
> group, or nationality to set up a state within the state and arro-

gate to itself one of the state's prime functions, that of seeing
that children are suitably educated to discharge the duties of
citizenship. This is a point upon which the democratic state
cannot compromise.[136]

In Paraguay, as in Mexico, new chapters in the history of Mennonite pioneering were now being written. Whether the sacrifices
required by the new frontier would be rewarded with the survival of
those values for which the undertaking had been made in the first
place remained to be seen. Meanwhile, the places left vacant in
Canada, and the new countries being opened up, became a place of
potential refuge for émigrés of the Russian Revolution. Soon it
became clear that those departing Canada might be contributing to
the survival not only of themselves but also of those in Russia in need
of a new homeland, in Canada perhaps but quite possibly also in
Latin America. It so happened that, throughout the decade, Mennonites from Russia would be knocking on doors in both North and
South America.

In Paraguay there was a double welcome. Not only did the new
colony in the Chaco open wide its primitive homes to destitute people
with no other place to go, but the Paraguayan president himself made
them feel completely welcome and completely free. President José P.
Guggiari regarded the Mennonite "enterprise with great sympathy"
and gave assurances that laws and national authorities would protect
Mennonite properties and give "maximum guaranty for your persons, possessions, and work." Concerning the Mennonite value
system, he said:

> The first Mennonites who arrived in this Republic were pre-
> ceded by the just fame of honorable traditions. I hope that the
> colonists will show themselves worthy of such traditions,
> maintaining in all their purity their customs, their religion,
> and their culture.[137]

In Mexico the reverse was true. After two years of residence in the
country the Mennonites had not endeared themselves to the authorities and the people. As a consequence, Mennonites in the U.S.A.
negotiating for the admission of at least 50,000 from Russia were
told to forget about their plans. On December 26, 1924, the

president of Mexico admitted to the Governor of the State of Chihuahua that the state and its people had never really welcomed the Mennonites and that their "clannish spirit" and unwillingness "to become Mexican citizens" had been a disappointment:

> It was thought at first that they would be an educational asset to the nation, as there is no doubt they are good farmers and up-to-date in their methods, but they give no employment to and avoid intercourse with Mexicans, and choose for colonization purposes lands far from centers of population, thus maintaining a state of almost complete isolation and comparative independence of the federal and state governments, which is resented. In short, it is presumed that the same qualities which make the Mennonites unpopular in Canada and the United States are responsible for the objection to colonization by them in Mexico.[138]

Thus, the removal to Latin America of thousands of Mennonites was a mixed blessing from the beginning, accompanied by hope and promise but also fraught with economic, cultural, and national dangers, only some of which had been anticipated. But for the time being the dangers were greatest, not in the Americas but in faraway Russia, where tens of thousands were anxious to escape the new Soviet regime.

FOOTNOTES

1   J.T.M. Anderson, *The Education of the New Canadian* (Toronto: J.M. Dent & Sons, 1918), p. 78. Anderson's specific point was that either the private schools among these people should be raised to a proper standard or public schools should be established.

2   "Eingabe der Delegaten von Saskatchewan an die mexikanische Regierung," *Der Mitarbeiter* 14 (February 1921):12. Johann P. Wall was the leader of the delegation.

3   A good deal has been written on the Mennonite School Question. The following are particularly noteworthy: John Jacob Bergen, "The Manitoba Mennonites and their Schools from 1873 – 1924" (M.Ed. term paper, University of Manitoba, 1950); John Jacob Bergen, "A Historical Study of Education in the Municipality of Rhineland" (M.Ed. thesis, University of Manitoba, 1959); Adolf Ens, "Mennonite Relations with Governments: Western Canada, 1870 – 1925"

(Ph.D. dissertation, University of Ottawa, 1979), pp. 172–277; Frank H. Epp, *Mennonites in Canada, 1786–1920: The History of a Separate People* (Toronto: Macmillan of Canada, 1974), pp. 333–62; E.K. Francis, *In Search of Utopia* (Altona: D.W. Friesen & Sons, 1955), pp. 161–86; E.K. Francis, "The Mennonite School Problem in Manitoba, 1874–1919," *Mennonite Quarterly Review* 27 (July 1953): 204–37; Abraham Friesen, "Emigration in Mennonite History with Special Reference to the Conservative Mennonite Emigration from Canada to Mexico and South America after World War I" (M.A. thesis, University of Manitoba, 1960); I.I. Friesen, "The Mennonites of Western Canada with Special Reference to Education" (M.Ed. thesis, University of Saskatchewan, 1934); Cornelius J. Jaenen, "The Manitoba School Question: An Ethnic Interpretation," in M.L. Kovacs (ed.), *Ethnic Canadians: Culture and Education* (Regina, 1978), pp. 317–31; William Janzen, "The Limits of Liberty in Canada: The Experience of the Mennonites, Hutterites, and Doukhobors" (Ph.D. dissertation, Carleton University, 1981), pp. 197–267; W.L. Morton, "Manitoba Schools and Canadian Nationality, 1890–1923," in David C. Jones, et al., *Shaping the Schools of the Canadian West* (Calgary, Alta.: Detselig Enterprises Limited, 1979), pp. 3–13; "The West: The Schools and the Clash of Culture, 1880–1920," in F. Henry Johnson, *A Brief History of Canadian Education* (Toronto: McGraw-Hill Company of Canada, 1968), pp. 93–102; Andrew Willows, "A History of Mennonites, Particularly in Manitoba" (M.A. thesis, University of Manitoba, 1924).

4   The Swiss were not preoccupied totally with their own affairs. In 1920 the Old Mennonite Conference of Ontario felt "it expedient to use our influence on behalf of the misunderstandings between a certain branch of the Russian Mennonite church and the government, to adjust the difficulties. . . ." *Calendar of Appointments*, 1920–21, p. [15].

5   J.G. Rempel, p. 144.

6   Frank H. Epp, *Mennonites in Canada 1786–1920*, pp. 333–58.

7   See *ibid.*, p. 340, and Adolf Ens, pp. 268–69. Figures are approximate for later years, due to the fact that some Mennonite districts were only partially Mennonite, making inclusion or exclusion a relative matter.

8   Frank H. Epp, *Mennonites in Canada 1786–1920*, pp. 342–43.

9   Quoted in *Die Mennoniten Gemeinden in der Gretna-Altona Umgebung in Manitoba* (n.p., 1963), p. 9.

10   Adolf Ens, pp. 184–85.

11   Where there were not properly accredited schools, non-public or otherwise, the Manitoba and Saskatchewan governments were empowered to establish schools, if necessary over the objections of the

local populace. In Alberta, public schools had to be established through local initiatives, thus making isolated settlements in the Peace River district attractive, as long as no locally initiated public schools were established. Children living in districts where there were no public schools were exempt from the compulsory school attendance act.

12   *Ibid.*, p. 269.

13   For a detailed explication of the positions of the various groups at different times, see *ibid*.

14   "Statistik der Mennoniten-Gemeinden," *Der Mitarbeiter* 12 (February 1918):8.

15   Frank H. Epp, *Mennonites in Canada 1786–1920*, pp. 192–93.

16   See Lovell Clark, ed., *The Manitoba School Question: Majority Rule or Minority Rights?* (Toronto: Copp Clark, 1968), pp. 98–181.

17   The percentage is obtained from information supplied by Tables 36 and 45 in *Census of Canada, 1921* (Ottawa, King's Printer, 1925), 2:241, 257.

18   Ninety-seven per cent claimed a Slavic language as mother tongue. Percentages obtained from information supplied by Table 81 in *ibid.*, pp. 588–93.

19   George S. Tomkins, "Canadian Education and Cultural Diversity: Historical and Contemporary Implications," in *Multiculturalism and Education: A Report on the Proceedings of the Western Regional Conference, 1978*, p. 58. See also John Murray Gibbon, *Canadian Mosaic: The Making of a Northern Nation* (London: J.M. Dent & Sons, 1938), and *idem*, "European Seeds in the Canadian Garden," *Proceedings and Transactions of the Royal Society of Canada* 17 (1923), 3rd series, section 2, pp. 119–29.

20   George S. Tomkins, p. 58.

21   John Herd Thompson, *The Harvests of War: The Prairie West, 1914–18* (Toronto: McClelland & Stewart, 1978), pp. 87–88; Donald Avery, *Dangerous Foreigners* (Toronto: McClelland & Stewart, 1979), p. 8.

22   J.S. Woodsworth, *Strangers Within Our Gates* (Toronto: The Missionary Society of the Methodist Church of Canada, 1909), p. 281.

23   J.T.M. Anderson, pp. 238–40.

24   George Chipman, quoted in Neil Sutherland, *Children in English-Canadian Society* (Toronto: University of Toronto Press, 1976), p. 211.

25   Sonia Cipywynk, "Multiculturalism and the Child in Western Canada: Then and Now," in *Multiculturalism and Education*, p. 33.

26   *Ibid.*, p. 32.

27   Isaak M. Dyck, *Die Auswanderung der Reinlaender Mennoniten Gemeinde von Canada nach Mexiko* (Cuauhtemoc, Mexiko: Imprenta Colonial, 1971), pp. 43–44.

28   PAC, RG. 18, Vol. 585, File 682, "Secret and Confidential" report to the Commissioner, RNWMP, Regina from Superintendent, Commanding Manitoba District, Winnipeg, December 10, 1919.

29   See Marilyn Barber, "Canadianization Through the Schools of the Prairie Provinces Before World War I: The Attitudes and Aims of the English-speaking Majority," in *Ethnic Canadians: Culture and Education*, ed. Martin L. Kovacs (Regina: Canadian Plains Research Center, 1978), pp. 228–90.

30   W.A. Mackintosh and W.L.G. Joerg, gen. eds., *Canadian Frontiers of Settlement* (Toronto: Macmillan of Canada, 1934–1936), Vol. 8: *Pioneering in the Prairie Provinces: The Social Side of the Settlement Process*, by C.A. Dawson and Eva R. Younge, pp. 170–72; Howard Palmer, "Response to Foreign Immigration: Nativism and Ethnic Tolerance in Alberta, 1880–1920" (M.A. thesis, University of Alberta, 1971), p. 151; Joanne Levy, "In Search of Isolation: The Holdeman Mennonites of Linden, Alberta and Their School," *Canadian Ethnic Studies* XI:I (1979):115–30.

31   An editorial in the 3 August 1920 edition of the *Manitoba Free Press* summarized the public opinion that had been building for some time: "This is a land of freedom. . . . But we do not want a perverted sense of that principle to lead to isolated sections and divisions of the population. We want to be one people with a sense of national unity and with each section of the country interested in the progress and welfare of the rest of the country." In Swift Current a mass meeting convened in 1918 articulated its sentiments much more bluntly. The meeting resolved that "the children of these people [Mennonites] must be educated up to our standards of British and Canadian citizenship, so that they may, in the future, voluntarily relinquish their claims to an unjust exemption." *Canadian Annual Review*, 1918, p. 427.

32   PAM, MG 14, B 36, #45, Dr. R.S. Thornton, *Address to the Legislature of Manitoba, January 30th, 1920* (Winnipeg: Legislation Assembly of Manitoba, n.d.), p. 12.

33   Adolf Ens, p. 217.

34   *Ibid.*, p. 222.

35   I.I. Friesen, p. 140, contended that the action taken against the Saskatchewan Mennonites more closely resembled "persecution than it did prosecution."

36   Adolf Ens, pp. 227–29.

37   A.J. Sumner of Saskatoon criticized the government for its handling of the Mennonites. He contended that "the reason that negotiations failed was primarily due to lack of sympathy and failure to appreciate the deadly earnestness of these people by your colleagues and officials. There has been no change of attitude upon the part of the Mennonites, they are still endeavouring to carry out the tenets of

their faith and creed, in identically the same way as when they were invited to the Dominion, which privileges they were told they could always enjoy." SAB, W. M. Martin Papers, A.J. Sumner to Premier Martin, 9 December 1921.

38   In 1920, a total of 1,131 prosecutions against the Mennonites netted the courts $7,834 in fines. SAB, S.J. Latta Papers, SAB, M5, 6(2).

39   I.I. Friesen, p. 138.

40   Kurt Tischler, *The German Canadians in Saskatchewan with Particular Reference to the Language Problem, 1900–1930* (M.A. thesis, University of Saskatchewan, 1977), p. 95.

41   Harold J. Foght, *A Survey of Education in the Province of Saskatchewan* (Regina: King's Printer, 1918), p. 147; Anderson, p. 75; Bergen, "Manitoba Mennonites and Their Schools," pp. 44–45.

42   Foght, p. 174. Robert England, *The Central European Immigrant in Canada* (Toronto: Macmillan of Canada, 1929), p. 52, had a similar analysis.

43   J.T.M. Anderson, p. 223.

44   Interview with T.D. Regehr, 25 July 1981.

45   C.B. Sissons, *Bi-lingual Schools in Canada* (Toronto: J.M. Dent & Sons, 1917), p. 145.

46   See Harold Foght.

47   CGC, XV-31.2, "1910–H.H. Ewert," H.H. Ewert, "The Mennonites," an address given under the auspices of the Historical and Scientific Society of Manitoba, 18 April 1932, pp. 11–12.

48   *Ibid.*

49   CGC, XV-31.2, "1920–Mexico," David Harder, "Von Kanada nach Mexico," n.d.

50   Adolf Ens, p. 237.

51   SAB, W.M. Martin Papers, Johann F. Peters to Premier Martin, 13 April 1920.

52   PAC, RG. 2, *Order-in-Council* I, 957, 13 August 1873.

53   PAC, RG. 76, Vol. 173, 58764, John M. Lowe to David Klassen et al., 23 July 1873.

54   A full account of the case is documented in "Rex vs. Hildebrand, August 12, 1919," *Western Weekly Reports* (Calgary: Burroughs & Company, 1919), pp. 286–90. See also Adolf Ens, pp. 239–47, and Abraham Friesen, pp. 59–62.

55   Quoted in Adolf Ens, p. 241.

56   Adolf Ens, p. 247.

57   Table prepared by Adolf Ens, p. 272. The respective petitions may be found in *Der Mitarbeiter* 10 (January 1916):2–3; *Der Mitarbeiter* 10 (March 1916):4–6 and (April 1916):1–2; CMCA, XIX-A, Microfilm 66; J.H. Doerksen, *Geschichte und Wichtige Dokumente der Mennoniten von Russland, Canada, Paraguay und Mexico* (n.p., 1923), pp. 95–96; I.I. Friesen, appendix 17; Doerksen, pp. 107–9; SAB, M5,6.

58   Adolf Ens, p. 274.

59   Quoted in I.I. Friesen, p. 126.

60   The Chortitzer petition submitted in January radiated a truly concil-
      iatory spirit, but it is doubtful whether there was readiness to accept
      the flag and patriotic exercises. It read in part: "Your Petitioners are
      convinced that the aims of the Government can be accomplished . . .
      by retaining teachers of the Mennonite faith, but requiring these
      teachers to qualify for Normal School certificates, and by bringing
      into effect high standards of education and more efficient instruction
      in English. In short, it is proposed to bring these private schools up
      to public school standards in every respect within the shortest
      possible time." Quoted in *ibid.*

61   "Memorandum to the Members of the Manitoba Legislature from
      the Sommerfeld Community, Altona, Man., Chortitz Community,
      Niverville, Man.," March 1921.

62   See J. Skwarok, *The Ukrainian Settlers in Canada and Their Schools*
      (Edmonton: n.p., 1958), and Michael H. Marunchuk, *The
      Ukrainian Canadians: A History* (Winnipeg and Ottawa: Ukrainian
      Free Academy of Sciences, 1970).

63   Roy H. Ruth, *Educational Echoes: A History of Education of the
      Icelandic-Canadians in Manitoba* (Winnipeg: n.p., 1964), p. 21.

64   Howard Palmer, *Land of the Second Chance: A History of Ethnic
      Groups in Southern Alberta* (Lethbridge: Lethbridge Herald, 1972),
      p. 66.

65   Table prepared by Adolf Ens, pp. 331–32.

66   Abraham Friesen, p. 71; Harry Leonard Sawatzky, *They Sought a
      Country: Mennonite Colonization in Mexico* (Berkeley, Cal.: Univer-
      sity of California Press, 1971), p. 27.

67   See J.W. Shank et al., *The Gospel under the Southern Cross* (Scottdale,
      Pa.: Mennonite Publishing House, 1943). Within a few years the
      first Canadian Mennonite foreign missionaries would leave for
      Argentina. Orland Gingerich, *The Amish of Canada* (Waterloo,
      Ont.: Conrad Press, 1972), pp. 100–1.

68   PAC, RG. 18, vol. 585, File 682. Report from Saskatoon Detach-
      ment, Royal North West Mounted Police, Re: Rev. John P. Wall of
      Hochfeld and Rev. Johann J. Wall of Neuanlage, October 5, 1919.
      See also "Rev. J.J. Wall Died Recently in Argentine," *Saskatoon
      Daily Star*, 4 October 1919.

69   The full text of the letter, graphically describing his illness, suffer-
      ing, death, and burial, is contained in Isaak M. Dyck, *Die Auswan-
      derung der Reinlaender Mennoniten Gemeinde von Canada nach
      Mexiko* (Cuauhtemoc, Mexiko: Imprenta Colonial, 1971), pp. 59–
      66.

70   Abraham Friesen, pp. 70–71; Harry Leonard Sawatzky, p. 32.

71   NARS, RG. 85, File 54623/130, Governor Lee M. Russell to
      Julius Wiebe et al., 6 February 1920. For more detail on the

Mississippi affair, see Ens, pp. 330–37, and Abraham Friesen, pp. 74–75, 82–86, 102–3.

72   Adolf Ens, pp. 333–34. Abraham Friesen, pp. 75–76, 78, suggests that Palmer first informed the delegates that their people would be granted total military exemption, only later indicating that such a guarantee would not be forthcoming.

73   Isaak Dyck, p. 68; Adolf Ens, p. 333; Abraham Friesen, pp. 76–78.

74   Isaak Dyck, p. 68; Adolf Ens, p. 334; Harry Leonard Sawatzky, p. 34.

75   David Harder, himself a participant in the events, remarked of the border episode: "We could not find out why the border was closed to us; we were compelled to accept it as guidance from God who wanted to spare us unforeseen hardships. Very likely the offer of freedom was the hoax of a land speculator." Quoted in Cornelius Krahn, "Old Colony Mennonites," *Mennonite Encyclopedia*, 4:40.

76   See Adolf Ens, pp. 335–36, and NARS, RG. 85, File 54623/130.

77   Protests against Mennonite "undesirables" are on file in NARS, RG. 85, File 54623/130.

78   Harry Leonard Sawatzky, p. 35; Abraham Friesen, p. 78.

79   CGC, XV-31.2, "1920–Quebec," J.C.E. Lavoie, Public Works, Chief Architect's Office, to Jacob Friesen, Swift Current, 29 May 1920, assured the latter that the Reinlaender would "enjoy perfect freedom from speech and faith" in Quebec. Further, Lavoie testified that Quebec's school laws gave "all the powers regarding education to the parents." See also "Mennonite Delegates See Quebec Premier," *Manitoba Free Press*, 20 August 1920, p. 1; "Mennonites Submit Demands to Quebec," *Manitoba Free Press*, 21 August 1920, p. 2.

80   "Mennonites Received by Taschereau," *Regina Leader*, 20 August 1920, p. 1.

81   Isaak Dyck, p. 67; Harry Leonard Sawatzky, p. 35; Walter Schmiedehaus, *Ein Feste Burg ist Unser Gott: Der Wanderweg eines Christlichen Siedlervolkes* (Cuauhtemoc, Mexico: G.J. Rempel, 1948), p. 71.

82   Harry Leonard Sawatzky, p. 37; Abraham Friesen, p. 89.

83   Harry Leonard Sawatzky, p. 36–37; Adolf Ens, p. 341.

84   For a first-hand account of this delegation's experiences, see Johan M. Loeppky, *Ein Reisebericht von Canada nach Mexiko im Jahre 1921* (n.p., n.d.).

85   "Eingabe der Delegaten von Saskatchewan an die mexikanische Regierung," *Der Mitarbeiter* 14 (February 1921):12.

86   A complete reproduction of the privileges is given in Abraham Friesen, pp. 97–98; Sawatzky, pp. 39–40; Schmiedehaus, pp. 81–82; and Calvin Wall Redekop, *The Old Colony Mennonites: Dilemmas of Ethnic Minority Life* (Baltimore: Johns Hopkins Press, 1969), p. 251.

87   NARS, RG. 59, State Decimal File, Mexico, 1910-1929, 812.5541-812.5561M52.
88   Isaak M. Dyck, *Die Auswanderung der Reinlaender Mennoniten Gemeinde von Canada nach Mexiko* (Cuauhtemoc, Mexiko: Imprenta Colonial, 1971), p. 79.
89   *Ibid.*, p. 80.
90   *Ibid.*, p. 169.
91   1 Timothy 3:2-4, KJV.
92   Isaak Dyck, pp. 173-76.
93   *Ibid.*, p. 3.
94   *Ibid.*, p. 2.
95   *Ibid.*
96   *Ibid.*, p. 4.
97   *Ibid.*, p. 8.
98   *Ibid.*, p. 26.
99   *Ibid.*, p. 43.
100 *Ibid.*, p. 51.
101 *Ibid.*, p. 85.
102 *Ibid.*
103 Adolf Ens, p. 342.
104 Walter Schmiedehaus, p. 83. It was obvious the Reinlaender overpaid dearly for their Mexican properties. For their agriculturally superior Canadian holdings, many were receiving only $4/acre more than what they were paying for the relatively unproductive land.
105 Accounts of the Swift Current land fiasco are found in Harry Leonard Sawatzky, pp. 41-42; Abraham Friesen, p. 103; and Adolf Ens, pp. 342-43.
106 As reported by the Embassy of the U.S.A. in Mexico. NARS, RG.59, State Decimal File, Mexico, 1910-1929, 812.5541-812.5561M52, George T. Summerlin to Secretary of State, 4 October 1923. One hundred centavos equal one peso. In 1925 the Mexican peso equalled approximately fifty cents. Franz Pick and René Sédillot, *All the Monies of the World* (New York: Pick Publishing, 1971), p. 397.
107 Harry Leonard Sawatzky, pp. 46-48.
108 Jacob Peters, quoted in Peter D. Zacharias, *Reinland: An Experience in Community* (Altona, Man.: Reinland Centennial Committee, 1976), p. 201.
109 Conflicting figures have been cited with reference to the migration to Latin America. The numbers quoted in the present work rely on the statistical index compiled by Adolf Ens, p. 354.
110 *Ibid.*
111 For details, see Harry Leonard Sawatzky, pp. 43-44.
112 Adolf Ens, p. 354.
113 *Ibid.*, p. 346.

114　Paraguay was wooing immigrants. Not only Mennonites but Chinese, Japanese, Germans, and Russians were prospective colonists. NARS, Secretary of State Decimal File, 1910 – 1929, Box 8470, 834.51/132 – 834.543017.

115　See PAC, RG. 25, G.I., Vol. 1472, File 416 – 26c, Department of External Affairs, "Settlement of Canadian Mennonites in the Chaco," August 1932.

116　A copy of the document is reproduced in Abraham Friesen, pp. 117 – 19, and Walter Quiring, *Russlanddeutsche Suchen eine Heimat* (Karlsruhe: Heinrich Schneider, 1938), pp. 51 – 52.

117　Quoted in Walter Quiring, "The Canadian Mennonite Immigration into the Paraguayan Chaco, 1926 – 27," *Mennonite Quarterly Review* 8 (January 1934):35.

118　Harry Leonard Sawatzky, p. 51; Adolf Ens, p. 351.

119　Adolf Ens, p. 354.

120　NARS, RG.59, State Decimal File, Mexico, 1910 – 1929, 812.5541 – 812.5561M52, John W. Dye, "Mennonites take an option on 150,000 acres of ranch land in Chihuahua, Mexico," 20 September 1922.

121　Some writers, such as J. Winfield Fretz, *Pilgrims in Paraguay* (Scottdale, Pa.: Herald Press, 1953), p. 13, have attributed philanthropic motives to McRoberts's efforts to aid the Mennonites. Canadian officials, and the Mennonites themselves, were cognizant of baser impulses underlying McRoberts's work. This was indicated in a missive addressed to F. C. Blair, Dept. of Immigration and Colonization, from Bruce Walker, Director, Publicity and Information Bureau, on 17 January 1922. "Mr. McRoberts . . . has appeared amongst the Mennonites in this neighbourhood and explains as his reason (so I am told by the Mennonite Bishop) for interesting himself in their lands, that his wife and daughter have become greatly impressed with the Mennonite view of Scripture and . . . urged him to help the persecuted Mennonites in Manitoba. . . . The Bishop of course informs me that he was unaware of any persecutions . . . has an impression that the financial transaction is not entirely without interest to their kind patron." PAC, DCI. File 58764, Vol. 8.

122　CGC, XV-31.2, "1920 – Paraguay," "The Canadian Mennonite Emigrations: The Paraguayan Experience" (n.a., n.d.).

123　Various contradictory figures have been quoted in regard to the number of Mennonites entering Paraguay. Some of these include: a) "Report of Conditions of Mennonites in Paraguay," *Gospel Herald* 22 (16 May 1929):147 reports 1,743 souls left Canada for Paraguay; b) a Canadian government report (PAC, RG. 25, G.I., Vol. 1472, File 416 – 26c) lists the figure at 1,876; c) *Mennonitische Post* 1 (21 July 1977):2 reports the total as 1,742; d) Quiring,

"The Canadian Mennonite Immigration," p. 37, indicates 1,765 Mennonites settled in Paraguay. The total of 1,785 quoted in the present text again relies on Adolf Ens, p. 354. In the year from 1926 to 1927 the Chortitzer church membership dropped from 1,232 to 819 and the population from 2,930 to 1,939. Archives of Chortitzer Mennonite Conference, Chortitzer Mennonite Church, Register A, p. 394.

124 Adolf Ens, p. 354.

125 Peter D. Zacharias, p. 202.

126 It is alleged that, by selling their lands to non-Mennonites, the Reinlaender would force those who had remained behind to follow them to Mexico. Harry Leonard Sawatzky, pp. 47–48.

127 PAC, RG. 6, 58764, Vol. 9, A.P. Elias to Department of Immigration and Colonization, 12 October 1923.

128 W. J. Egan, the Deputy Minister in the Department of Immigration, related in a letter to David Toews on 26 June 1925 that "the Department has done everything possible to facilitate the entry of Mennonites for settlement on the land in Canada, and I am disappointed to hear of their movement [to Mexico]." He asked whether an additional large-scale exodus was pending. PAC, RG. 6, 58764, Vol. 9. Negative or indifferent Canadian attitudes are also documented in NARS, RG.85, 54623/130. In the words of one immigration inspector: "The writer in conversation with civil officers has been told repeatedly that the continued presence in Canada of this sect was detrimental to the interests of the country and that every pressure would be brought to bear to influence them to leave Canada."

129 Robert England, p. 54. The automobile was a symbol of *Gleichstellung* (accommodation) with the world. The Reinlaender had a rule forbidding members the use of the automobile. See Harder, p.8.

130 PAC, RG. 6, 58764, Vol. 9, Premier Martin to A.W. Golzen, 25 October 1922.

131 Donald Avery, pp. 9, 25.

132 The entire letter is reproduced in Walter Quiring, *Russlanddeutsche*, pp. 65–66.

133 Gerald M. Brown, "Progressive Mennonites Get in Step," *Saskatoon Phoenix* (28 June 1924):13.

134 "The Mennonites," *Victoria Daily Times*, 9 October 1922; see also "Mennonite Dreamers," *Victoria Daily Colonist*, 14 May 1920.

135 See Adolf Ens, "The Mennonites as Reflected by the *Manitoba Free Press*, 1910–1929" (research paper, University of Ottawa, 1973).

136 "The Plea of the Mennonites," *Manitoba Free Press*, 18 May 1920. See also "The Threatened Mennonite Exodus," *Manitoba Free Press*, 11 May 1920.

137 NARS, RG. 59, Secretary of State Decimal File, Paraguay, 1910–

1929, 834.51/132–834.543017, President José P. Guggiari to Mennonnite settlers, c. 29 September 1928.

138   NARS, RG. 59, State Decimal File, Mexico, 1910–1929, 812.5541–812.556 IM52, Thomas McNelly, American Consulate, Chihuahua, Mexico, to Department of State, 31 December 1924.

4. Immigration from Russia

*Even these peaceful Mennonite settlers who up till now have
remained aloof from all history-making events are caught up in the
general upheaval. They no longer enjoy the peace which dominated
their steppe for so long. They are no longer permitted to live in
seclusion from the world —* DIETRICH NEUFELD.[1]

*For the Mennonites there is only one sure way out: emigration,
meaning the return to the former homeland Holland and to the
relatives in America —* B.B. JANZ.[2]

WHILE 7,000 MENNONITES were leaving Canada for
Latin America in order to preserve their way of life,
thousands of their distant cousins in the U.S.S.R. were hoping to
enter Canada, also in order to ensure a better future for themselves
and for their children. Uprooted in every way by the Bolshevik
revolution, the Makhno reign of terror, and the ensuing civil war
between the Red and the White armies,[3] 20,000 of the Mennonites
in Russia—about one-sixth of the total—seized the opportunity to
make Canada their home. Their migration, beginning in 1923 and
continuing until the changing Canadian attitudes and policies closed
the door, represented the largest organized voluntary mass movement of Mennonites in history and helped to change permanently the
character of Mennonitism in both Russia and Canada.

This immigration was a mammoth undertaking for the Mennonite community in Canada, which was being reduced to nearly
50,000 by the exodus to Latin America, and required extraordinary
commitment, perseverance, and overall co-ordination. Obstacles to

the venture presented themselves on both continents with depressing regularity and constantly threatened to bring about the total collapse of the scheme. That so many people managed to leave the Soviet Union was a success attributable largely to the courageous and untiring work of David Toews in Canada and B.B. Janz in the U.S.S.R. Equally important, though perhaps not as prominent, in the migration drama were A.A. Friesen and B.H. Unruh. As deputies for the Russian Mennonites, the former in Canada and the latter in Germany, both men took on the difficult tasks of representation, mediation, and persuasion with unflagging determination. All of them, of course, were dependent on the willingness of governments and the readiness of transportation companies to serve their cause.

In this respect, a most critical intercession was made by S.F. Coffman of the Swiss Mennonites in Ontario, who during the war had accomplished for his people in the East what David Toews had done in the West. Coffman personified the good name and character of the pioneer Mennonite community in Canada, whose reputation had commended to the authorities the widest possible concessions in the first Mennonite migration from Russia in the 1870s and without whose positive image Canada would surely have been less eager for more of the same. If the troubles associated with the Dutch Mennonites in the West served to justify the 1919 Canadian ban on all Mennonite immigration,[4] the esteem in which the Swiss Mennonites were held in the East, especially in the mind of Prime Minister Mackenzie King, was an important factor in having that ban removed.

Mennonites and Russia

Those 40,000 Mennonites who in the 1870s had chosen to remain in Russia had enjoyed a half-century of unprecedented prosperity and expansion of their communities and institutions. With the pioneer years largely behind them, they had proceeded to develop rapidly their vigorous economy, based as it was on a diversified agriculture, flour milling, and the manufacture of farm equipment. Their population had tripled to 120,000, and the number of settlements, including the original four mother colonies, had increased to over 50, with a total of approximately 440 villages and some 2,300,000 acres of land. The holdings of 384 owners of large estates—a true Mennonite elite—brought the acreage held by Russian Mennonites to more than three million.[5]

With their help, the Ukraine had become the breadbasket for much of Russia, and more, because grain and flour for export in large quantities regularly left Black Sea ports for foreign destinations. A gold medal won for his flour by a Mennonite miller at the world fair in Paris symbolized the high achievements resulting from over a century of hard work devoted to agricultural excellence on the part of all the Mennonite people.[6]

They had introduced improved strains of dairy cattle, notably the famed German cow, and the so-called "colonist horse," which replaced the slow ox as draft power. Also, they had developed new techniques of tilling the soil, including use of the black and green fallow, use of better seed grains, rotation of crops, some use of manure as fertilizer, and extensive practices of tree planting, for both fruit and shelter. According to V.E. Postvikov, the Mennonite farming system was "higher in quality" than that which held sway among both Russian landowners and peasants.[7]

Their industrial endeavours, almost as impressive as agriculture, provided Russia with six per cent of its farm implements and large quantities of brick and tile.[8] The farm machinery, both tools and implements, introduced by the Mennonites included the multi-share plough, the reaper, a threshing machine, improved harrows, the winnowing machine, the row seeder, the straw cutter, a special type of hay rake, several types of wagons, and many others.[9]

Among both agriculturalists and industrialists there were some very wealthy people. Millionaires were not uncommon. This wealth and a strong economy supported a network of educational and other institutions, contributing to the culture and welfare of the total Mennonite community. In 1920 the school system embraced 400 elementary schools, 13 high schools, 4 girls' schools, 2 teachers' colleges, and 3 business schools.[10] University education was also quite common. Some 300 students were attending colleges, seminaries, and universities when the war came. One-sixth of them studied abroad, mostly in Germany and Switzerland. Among the graduates were medical doctors for the Mennonite hospitals and other welfare institutions.

Thus, driven by a concept of progress and a spirit of industry that were foreign to much of the indigenous Russian population, the Mennonites had established an economic and cultural "commonwealth" unmatched by other minorities around them or by the Russian populace at large. As is common among prosperous societies, the Mennonites were not much aware of their privileged position and the extent to which wealth was derived from land, freely given or easily purchased, as well as from servile labour in an abundant supply. Instead, they remembered their own erstwhile poverty and how hard they had worked, and consequently how much God had blessed them. Others could and would become prosperous too if only they applied themselves as the Mennonites had done. Thus, the idiosyncrasies of faith and culture, which set the Mennonites apart from the Russian peasants from the beginnings of settlement late in the eighteenth century, had been augmented in time by other differences based on the superior income, education, and social status of the Mennonites.[11] As David G. Rempel, using Russian scholarly sources as a basis for his assessment, has pointed out:

> of great value [were] a number of character traits among many of the colonists, such as sobriety, industriousness, thrift, generally high moral standards, religious and ethical beliefs and other values, plus higher levels of education, qualities in which the peasant was often deficient.[12]

The relationship of the Mennonites to their property and to the Russian people was permanently changed by the political upheaval, which catapulted the Bolsheviks into power in 1917 and which shook Russia and indeed the entire world. The privileged status of the Mennonites, which was formerly perceived to be an advantage, now became a definite liability. And it wasn't that there had been no warning, some handwriting on the wall which at least some leaders had clearly read. Premonitions of danger had arisen already during tsarist rule, and the emigration of the 1870s happened because some leaders sensed for their people a problematic future in Russia. The war with Japan in 1904 – 5 and the mini-revolution of that year were strong signals to that effect. In the first years of the Great War, discriminatory measures affecting language and land ownership had been applied against the country's German-speaking people, especially on the western side, a clear signal of the changing times.

In the 1917 interlude between the fall of the tsar in February and the Bolshevik seizure of power in October, the Mennonites generally had come to the conclusion that the future would be different from the past and that very considerable thought and deliberate action had to be taken with respect to that future.[13] The Mennonite debate on how best to secure the future began with attendance at a congress of German-speaking colonists, on the assumption that there were common interests to be represented to the provisional government headed by Kerensky.

More significant was the 1917 meeting of the General Conference of Mennonite Congregations in Russia. The agenda was modified to include not only the traditional devotional content but also the new socio-economic, educational, and political problems facing the Mennonite people. This in turn led to a reorganization of the Conference as well as the founding of the All-Russian Mennonite Congress, a civic organization, actually a Mennonite parliament, mandated to deal "with all non-religious internal problems and to represent the Mennonites in all external relations."[14]

The founding Congress held in Ohrloff, Molotschna, on August 14–18, 1917, was attended by 198 delegates representative of the various settlements, groups, and interests. Mennonite professionals — lawyers, engineers, teachers, and theologians — were prominent in the Congress, as were the educated class generally. At least 150 of the delegates had high school education and 30 had university training. Among the Congress leaders were Benjamin H. Unruh and Jacob H. Janzen, both of whom were university-educated teachers, whose leadership gifts brought them into the forefront again and again.

The Congress discussed the crucial issues of the day, including land reform and the relationship between Christianity and socialism, in all of which a keen awareness of the issues confronting Russia and the Mennonite people was expressed.[15] Some of those present represented the view that the Kingdom of God was to be realized on earth, but that Christianity did not represent any particular economic order, the agrarian question being one to be resolved by the professionals. Others explained that while socialism and Christianity could not be equated, socialism stood closer to the Christian faith than did capitalism. The Congress recommended the creation of a state land bank in order to facilitate land distribution to the poor and to the landless. Such a land bank would include state and church lands, as well as private lands acquired for appropriate compensation. An upper limit for private land ownership was agreed to in principle and reflected at least some Mennonite understanding of the crucial need for reform in Russia. As John B. Toews has written:

> Concern with the plight of the landless peasant (both Russian and Mennonite) generated amazingly socialistic debates on the redivision and nationalization of land even though over half of those present were landowners.[16]

The Congress further agreed to create a *Mennozentrum* (Menno Centre), a bureau with sufficient staff to implement the decisions of the Congress. Such policy decisions and organizational initiatives held great promise, but all were short-lived as the revolution engulfed all of Russia and as the Bolsheviks seized power in October. Then it became painfully obvious that all the talk about reform in Russia represented an effort which was too small and came too late.

After the revolution, the colonies were stripped of their former semi-autonomous status and brought under the supervision of regional soviets. These soviets consisted of representatives from the poorer, landless classes — individuals who, not surprisingly, used their new-found positions of authority and the revolutionary slogans of liberty and equality to better their own material conditions at the expense of the Mennonites.

In the early months of 1918, some Mennonite villages were overwhelmed by lawless military bands, generally not answerable to any higher authority. These bandits unleashed a ten-week nightmare of terror, looting, raping, and even killing.[17] The immense wealth locked into the Mennonite settlements, and the unfortunate history of Mennonite neglect, if not exploitation, of the Russian peasant, made them immediate and quite understandable targets of such aggression. In many ways they had been model farmers, and the peasants had learned many things from them. However, economic disparity bred jealousy and hostility. It was also true that Russian gentlemen farmers encouraged animosity towards the German elements in the hope of themselves escaping peasant wrath, at least for a while.[18] As Dietrich Neufeld wrote in *A Russian Dance of Death*:

> With increasing frequency, we are forced to realize that the Russian peasant is not kindly disposed towards our Mennonite settlers.[19]

The year saw the fortunes of the Mennonites in the Ukraine alternately rise and fall as successive units of German troops, White Army insurgents, Red Army forces, and dissolute robber bands battled for control of the region. Altogether, between 1918 and 1920, there were more than a dozen changes of regime in various parts of the Ukraine. After the signing of the Treaty of Brest Litovsk in 1918 and the German occupation of territories surrendered under that treaty, German soldiers brought order and security to the Mennonite colonies, for them a welcome respite. One local newspaper, the *Volksfreund*, expressed its gratitude to the liberators as it cried, "Thanks be to God that He has saved us from these robbers through Germany's and Austria's military might."[20] Reprisals were quickly taken against any remaining Bolshevik sympathizers, and some Mennonites assisted the Germans in the identification and arrest of such people.

In retrospect, the enthusiastic support given to the German occupation army was a political mistake, for the effects of this partisanship would follow the Mennonites into World War II and beyond. Seen against the anarchistic backdrop of the preceding years, however, the German-Mennonite alliance made sense. The Mennonites, like the other German colonists, abhorred and were repelled by violent insurrection, disorder, and theft. To them, the German troops appeared as if sent by providence, and in the crises of the moment there could be little reflection on the future implications of such association. All that mattered at the time was that they enjoyed the protection of authorities who spoke their language, who entrusted them with local power, who instilled in them a powerful sense of German cultural identity, and who equipped some of them with weapons useful in self-defence.[21]

Subsequently, all those suspected of having collaborated with the German enemy had to pay for their actions. They were branded as counter-revolutionaries, and their leaders were victimized by ruthless marauding peasant bands, such as those organized by the notorious Nestor Makhno.[22] At Makhno's hands, German colonists throughout the Ukraine, including the Mennonites, were subjected to a savage reign of terror during two successive winters. Once again they experienced indiscriminate torture and murder, rape and plunder.

In desperate response to the senseless savageries inflicted upon

them, some Mennonites, following the advice of, and with equipment provided by, the departing German troops, hastily assembled a
Home Defence (*Selbstschutz*) despite their historic refusal to bear
arms.[23] Yet, how could the men remain fully nonresistant, in the face
of cruel danger to the women and children they held so dear? The
existence of the paramilitary organization, however, compounded
the miseries of the Mennonites, for the conclusion was inescapable
that the Mennonites were open enemies of the Bolshevik state. The
Mennonites paid dearly for their resistance. At least 647 of their
people perished as a direct result of the brutal civil war that
crisscrossed the Mennonite domain.[24] In his analysis of the effects of
the Home Defence, one historian wrote:

> Caught up in the irrationalities of the movement few could
> foresee that bloodshed on both sides would be a much higher
> price to pay than the simple acceptance of the role of the suf-
> fering church. In the end the Home Defence contributed to
> more death than it prevented.[25]

This conclusion, of course, cannot be verified, and certainly not
all historians agree that the bandits would not have committed the
most outrageous acts had they had a free hand.[26] Be that as it may, the
Mennonites were stunned by the cataclysm engulfing them. Events
of the previous years had conditioned most of them to accept the
inevitability of change with respect to their privileged special status.
No one, though, could have predicted the utter economic, cultural,
and social ruin that their colonies would have to undergo, as well as,
and perhaps more significantly, the anti-Christian political ideology
to which they would be subjected.

Working for Survival

For the time being, however, most Mennonites did not have time to
dwell on the longer-term significance of the recent events. The needs
of the moment were too great for that. In addition to the famine
conditions and other deprivations caused by the civil strife, the
Mennonites were struck by an epidemic of typhus. Cold weather, a
chronic absence of wood for heating, an acute shortage of food,
insufficient blankets, and ragged clothing all worked to lower the

resistance of Mennonites to the dreaded disease. Eventually, typhus killed several times more Mennonites than were felled by bandits.[27]

In response to the dire exigency in which they found themselves, a *Studienkommission* (Study Commission) was created in the Molotschna colony in December of 1919 and dispatched abroad.[28] Its primary purpose was to inform the Mennonites in Europe and North America of the desperate plight of their people in Russia and to secure material aid for the sick and the starving. As well, the members of the Study Commission were to investigate immigration and settlement possibilities in other lands, for already a growing number within the Mennonite community were convinced that Russia held no future for them. The members of the Study Commission included the aforementioned A.A. Friesen and B.H. Unruh, both of them university- or seminary-educated teachers, and C.H. Warkentin, a merchant. J.J. Esau, an industrialist, was also chosen but he withdrew from the assignment for personal reasons. Friesen and Unruh were the leaders of the commission, the former as chairman, the latter as secretary.

The physical welfare of their people was a matter of urgent concern to these men and, accordingly, they first solicited help in Western Europe. In spite of the fact that post-war Europe itself was preoccupied with the ravages of war and its own reconstruction, the Study Commission met with some success. B.H. Unruh returned to Germany after his North American tour to concentrate on soliciting European aid for the Mennonites in Russia. His frequent appeals to governments to provide both financial assistance and opportunities for resettlement proved disappointing, but he was instrumental in encouraging the German and Dutch Mennonites to organize major relief efforts.[29]

When the commission arrived in the U.S.A. in June, Friesen, Unruh, and Warkentin soon discovered that the American Mennonites were not completely uninformed of the tragic state of affairs unfolding in Russia. Relief work in Western Europe and in the Middle East had made them aware of the devastations of war.[30] However, with the comprehensive information imparted by the delegates, a greater sense of urgency and mission emerged. A general meeting of all American Mennonite relief organizations, held on July 27, 1920, at Elkhart, Indiana, concurred that it was desirable to create a central committee for a co-ordinated relief action and volunteers were recruited immediately. The permanent organization of this new Mennonite Central Committee (MCC)[31] was completed on September 27, the very day that its first three workers, destined for Russia, arrived in Constantinople. They included Clayton Kratz, whose subsequent disappearance in Russia remains a mystery to this day, and Orie O. Miller, who later became MCC's longtime executive secretary.[32]

The initial attempts of the Mennonite Central Committee to alleviate suffering in Russia were rebuffed by Soviet officials who refused to grant entrance visas for the proposed action. Months of tedious work by Alvin J. Miller, an MCC representative working from Moscow with the American Relief Commission, seemed to yield no positive results. And all the time, the situation in the colonies was deteriorating. In one of his dispatches to the West, B.B. Janz reported the situation as follows:

> A time of dying is now beginning for us Mennonites. . . . In Russia there are few that are living, many that are vegetating, and the vast hungry South is dying. What a smell from the cadavers will rise towards heaven by May![33]

Finally, in October of 1921, an agreement was concluded by which the Mennonite Central Committee, affiliated with the American Relief Administration, was admitted for relief work in the Crimea and in the provinces of Taurida and Ekaterinoslav. In March of the following year, the first field kitchens distributed food to the famished settlers. During that winter alone, the Mennonites in North America sent approximately two million dollars' worth of aid in the form of food and clothing to Russia. When the more immediate problem of famine had been alleviated, the MCC also provided seed grain and tractors to aid in the reconstruction process.[34]

While the Study Commission abroad continued to promote relief and to prepare a new homeland, hopefully in North America, the Mennonites in Russia instituted measures for their own improvement and economic rehabilitation. What they needed above all else was a representative Mennonite civic organization, embracing all the colonies in a given area, something like the short-lived All-Russian Mennonite Congress, with its Menno Centre, founded just prior to the revolution. After months of work with the Soviets, both in the

Ukraine and in Moscow, a charter was granted to the Union of Citizens of Dutch Ancestry, hereafter known as the Union, formally organized on April 25, 1922.[35] Significantly, at that same time the Mennonites in Canada were establishing the Canadian Mennonite Board of Colonization, the organization which was to become the chief source of hope outside the country, but more of that later.

The name of the Union reflected attempts begun already during the war to achieve a more positive identity for the Mennonites. Now it was important that it be known that they were not German and that not only were they a privileged religious minority, but also Soviet citizens who happened to be of Dutch lineage. This so-called *Hollanderei* of the Mennonites did not meet with full internal approval,[36] but the Dutch connection, however remote, served the purposes of survival during and after the Great War and, as will later be seen, after World War II as well.

The leadership of the Union fell to B.B. Janz, the quiet but forceful school teacher from Tiege in the Molotschna.[37] Janz combined the rare qualities of keen political acumen, persistence bordering on outright stubbornness, and a genuine commitment to his people. In him, the Mennonites of the Ukraine discovered their needed spokesman.[38] For the next four years Janz used the Union as the umbrella vehicle for unceasing work on behalf of every Mennonite cause relating to the problem of survival. These causes included preventing the induction of draft-age Mennonite men into the Red Army, re-establishing the Mennonite economy, and negotiating visas for those wishing to leave Russia. Fortunately, the charter of the Union, liberally interpreted, permitted this broad range of activities. Early in his work Janz was convinced that the best solution for the Russian Mennonites was emigration.[39]

In this position he was supported by the Union itself, even though the organization's stated main purpose was economic renewal. Janz made no particular effort to keep his potentially controversial position secret. He had spoken about emigration to the central executive committee of the Ukrainian Communist Party and would soon press the case also in Moscow. But would Moscow willingly agree to the departure of those citizens who had only recently been some of its most prized agriculturalists and who were now needed to rebuild a desperately impoverished agrarian economy?

Janz responded to this delicate situation by resorting to a simple but ingenious tactic. The civil war had produced a Mennonite refugee problem and increased the number of landless, all of whom now constituted an "unproductive" element. By allowing these people to leave, Janz argued, the detrimental effects of the famine could be better mitigated and conditions would be created that would be more conducive to the future livelihood of the settlements.[40] Evidently the government accepted the logic of Janz's argument, for already in 1922 permission was granted for the Mennonites to leave, at that time for Paraguay.[41] But their destitute financial state, together with disinterest in Paraguay as a permanent homeland, caused them to decide against such a movement.

Janz was encouraged by the government's initial willingness to endorse an emigration scheme, and he continued to negotiate for the release of all those Mennonites who wished to leave the country. Incredibly, he had, by the end of 1922, won authorization for the emigration of up to 20,000 Mennonites. The government, it seemed, concurred with the notion that the removal of the surplus population would put an end to the restlessness existing within the colonies. Accordingly, it removed the legal obstacles which hitherto had prevented the possibility of such a large-scale movement. Now everything depended upon the North Americans to implement the speedy removal of thousands who were waiting in Russia.

Following the successful organization of the MCC in the United States to bring relief to Russia, the Study Commission had redoubled its search for land that would be suitable for the settlement of a large contingent of Russian Mennonites. Again, American Mennonites were expected to be of some assistance in this effort and for this purpose the Mennonite Executive Committee for Colonization (MECC) was founded in November 1920.[42] This central committee for colonization was intended to function parallel to the central committee for relief and to operate in a similar pattern, namely with the full support of the entire Mennonite constituency. In actuality, the colonization committee never gained a great deal of momentum, chiefly because of the surge of anti-immigrant sentiment throughout the States. In 1921, the United States government unveiled an immigration quota system, which decisively dashed any possibility of a mass movement to that country.[43]

Undoubtedly discouraged by this turn of events, A.A. Friesen, together with others, undertook an exploratory trip to Mexico during the winter of 1920–21. They were impressed with the liberal concessions the Mexican government was willing to grant. Mexico, it must be remembered, was at that time one of the prospective homes of Mennonites planning to leave Canada, and in general a new settlement frontier much-touted by American real estate agents. On balance, however, the political instability of that country, along with the questionable hospitality of the local populace, outweighed the probable advantages.[44] In any event, Mexico could not be embraced as a future homeland until the possibilities in Canada had been fully explored.

The Mennonites in Canada, especially those in the west, were well-informed of the disastrous developments in Russia through letters and newspaper accounts. They too were anxious to respond to human need. A project to gather and forward relief monies was organized in the summer of 1920 by Gerhard Ens and David Toews. Ens, a former Saskatchewan legislator, had himself been born in Russia and as an immigrant in 1890 he had played a leading role in pioneer Saskatchewan settlement.[45] Thus, Ens was interested as much in solving the Russian Mennonite problem through resettlement to Canada as through relief in Russia.

During the war David Toews had become known, because of his crucial role with governments, as the "Mennonite Bishop of Canada." In actual fact only the bishop of the Rosenorter congregation, he was, however, the moderator of the Conference of Mennonites in Central Canada and a founder of the German-English Academy in Rosthern. He had left Russia as a boy in the early 1880s after he and his family had participated in the famous trek of the excessively chiliastic Claas Epp into central Asiatic Russia, from which they had returned quite disappointed and disillusioned but with greater insight concerning the various possible destinies—to them they were discouraging—of Mennonites in Russia.[46] A decade later, Toews had left his parental Kansas farm home for Manitoba, having been recruited by H.H. Ewert to teach Mennonite children in a public school. Thereafter, the Rosthern area of the Saskatchewan Valley became his permanent home. He married a girl from a Prussian Mennonite family, taught school, and became a leader in the church. The insights and dedication as well as the leadership gifts of this cosmopolitan man would soon be required, in a way he himself had not imagined, to facilitate the survival of the Russian Mennonites.[47]

Meanwhile, the relief efforts of Toews and Ens were given a boost when in August the Study Commission was finally allowed to cross the border into Canada at Portal, North Dakota. Since the Canadian immigration ban of 1919 was still in effect, even Mennonite visitors, especially would-be immigrants, had difficulty entering the country. Arrangements were immediately undertaken for the delegates to consult the communities surrounding Rosthern and Herbert in Saskatchewan and the Mennonite reserves in southern Manitoba for the sake of promoting the interests of the Canadian Relief Committee, which was formally created on October 18.[48]

A Government and a Railway

Canada's settlement possibilities appealed to the Study Commission. The country was large and, so it seemed, only sparsely populated. Its soil and climate were in many places well-suited to agricultural practices with which the Mennonites were familiar, and, not to be overlooked, there were communities of Mennonites already well-established in Canada. The only problem, and it was a major one, was that the federal government had declared itself opposed to accepting immigrants from central and eastern Europe. Mennonites were specifically named in the post-war prohibition of 1919. The publicity being given to those Mennonites determined to leave for Latin America because Canada had disappointed them didn't help matters either. In other words, when the goodwill of politicians and people was most needed it was in short supply.

The prevailing policy was directly opposite the rather liberal pre-war practice, which placed few restrictions on the races and nationalities to be allowed into the country. Settlers were needed to stock and cultivate the spacious western interior and also to provide a cheap and readily accessible labour supply for the developing resource, transportation, and manufacturing industries.[49] Hundreds of thousands of immigrants had entered the country before the advent of the war. After 1918, Canadian authorities showed little interest in resuming the flow. Their disinterest was the product of several factors. For one thing, soldiers returning home from Europe had not all been able to find work, and it was generally believed that veterans should have the first opportunity to fill the available lands and jobs. In addition, destitute immigrants from previous years, unsuccessful at establishing themselves on farms, had migrated to the cities, where they were greeted by outright racial discrimination and unemployment rather than the hoped-for financial security.

The resentment felt by many Canadians towards Germany and her allies was understandable, given the recent international situation. Thus, an Order-in-Council barring enemy aliens such as Germans, Austrians, Hungarians, Bulgarians, and Turks was not surprising.[50] Less easy to explain, though no less real in fact, were the discriminatory measures invoked by the government against persons of central- and east-European origin in general. Continental Europeans had been welcomed before the war because they served the country's economic self-interest. But when Canada's economy slumped, as it did just prior to and again after the war, their usefulness suffered a corresponding drop.

Business and organized labour, industry, religious and patriotic organizations, and racial purists exploited the situation, protesting that the "sheep-skin peasants" were in fact a liability to Canada's progressive growth. Critics heaped blame on the foreign immigrants for a host of the country's social and political ills. Connections were made linking the immigrants to social and civil unrest, crime, disease, undesirable social customs, and a general diminution of Canadian standards of living.[51]

Ottawa was cognizant of the ground swell of nativist sentiment and took swift steps to regulate and curb the admission of unwanted immigrants. Amendments were made to the Immigration and Naturalization Act in 1919 subjecting immigrants to a literacy test, stricter medical examination, and an evaluation as to their political and social acceptability.[52] Then a monetary qualification was introduced requiring each male immigrant to possess $250 upon his arrival in Canada.[53] Immigrants were also expected to have with them a valid passport and to have made a continuous journey to Canada from their country of origin.

In 1923 additional revisions, this time designed to ensure ethnic selectivity, were appended to the immigration laws. Thereafter, immigration was restricted to bona fide agriculturalists, labourers, and domestics, all of whom were classified according to a system of preferred and nonpreferred countries. Under the terms of Order-in-Council PC 183, preferred status was given to white immigrants coming from the British Commonwealth or the United States.[54] Less valued were northern Europeans, who in turn were followed by the nonpreferred central and eastern Europeans. Jews, Blacks, and Orientals occupied the lowest rungs of the immigration scale.

Not everyone in Canada applauded this closing of the immigration door, including business groups whose economic well-being depended largely upon an inexpensive and undemanding labour pool. Mining companies, resource industries, and transportation firms led the way in insisting that the government relax its immigration policies.[55] They argued that non-English immigrants had a reputation for physical endurance and dependability and often were the only ones willing to accept the strenuous work, low pay, and northern isolation characteristic of most mining and lumbering operations.

The two transcontinental railways, Canadian Pacific and the new Canadian National, likewise needed an accessible supply of labourers for track maintenance and construction. An even more crucial consideration for them was the millions of acres of unused land in the west. Immigrants were still required to fill empty territories and to create and sustain future demands for railway services.

The hope in government circles had been that the reduction of continental immigrants could be balanced by increased immigration from Britain or the U.S. When such migration patterns failed to materialize, the railways and the resource extraction interests redoubled their efforts to bring about a change in immigration policy. Their efforts were rewarded in September 1925 when the so-called Railways Agreement was concluded.[56] The Agreement permitted the railway companies to recruit immigrants from countries previously designated as nonpreferred. It also authorized them to certify that prospective immigrants met Canada's requirements as these related to occupation and guaranteed employment. Between 1925 and 1930, about 185,000 continental Europeans were brought to Canada under these provisions.[57]

In 1921, however, the public mood, together with existing federal legislation, presented formidable barriers to a large-scale Mennonite movement into Canada. The greatest single obstacle to the migration was found in the 1919 Order-in-Council which specifically forbade Mennonite immigration to Canada. This prohibitory regulation reflected the special problems the war had created for the Mennonites. Some people considered the nonresistant Mennonites unpatriotic and charged them with shirking their obligations as citizens. Others confused all Mennonites with Hutterites and Doukhobors, whose social and economic practices, the public image of which did not always conform to reality, many Canadians found objectionable.

On a number of occasions, Mennonites, acting independently, had appealed to the government to remove the restrictive immigration legislation.[58] Each time the requests were rejected. A.A. Friesen insisted that the Mennonites continue their struggle. At his suggestion a meeting was held at Herbert, Saskatchewan, in early June 1921 to discuss this matter. Out of the meeting came a decision to send a delegation to Ottawa to argue the Mennonite cause personally.[59]

In July a five-man delegation representing Mennonites from Russia, western Canada, and Ontario arrived in the capital to plead for the admission of some 100,000 Mennonites.[60] Prime Minister Arthur Meighen was out of town and so, in his absence, the men met with Sir George Foster, the acting prime minister. They informed him of the cruel circumstances prevailing in Russia and of their hopes of rescuing their unfortunate co-religionists.[61] The delegation was careful to impress upon Foster the progressive attributes of the Russian Mennonites, assuring him they had willingly conformed to Russia's education and language laws and would do likewise in Canada. The Russian Mennonites, it was asserted, were valuable agriculturalists who, on coming to Canada, would be sheltered by their own people and therefore would not exacerbate the socio-economic problems in the cities.

The delegates rightly perceived that the key to assisting their overseas comrades lay in convincing the authorities of the law-abiding nature of the prospective immigrants, especially with respect to allowing their children to attend public schools.[62] Foster himself disclosed that the main objection of the government to a Mennonite migration stemmed from their reputation as a culturally aloof people.[63] The Reinlaender, he reminded the visitors, had been a thorn in the side of the provincial governments and he was afraid the Russian Mennonites would prove likewise. It was to counter just such an image that S.F. Coffman and T.M. Reesor, representatives of the more positively regarded Ontario Swiss Mennonites, had been invited to participate in the expedition. But despite their presence, the Conservative government offered little hope that the immigration law would be changed. A federal election was imminent and the government was reluctant to introduce new policies that might jeopardize its chances of re-election.

Before leaving Ottawa, the delegates consulted with Opposition leader Mackenzie King, leader of the Liberal Party.[64] This interview proved more promising, since King assured the Mennonite guests that, should his party form the next government, the prohibitory Order-in-Council would be lifted. Not wishing to leave any avenue unexplored, the delegation proceeded on to Toronto, where they presented themselves to provincial political leaders and representatives of several influential newspapers.[65] During these meetings they described the terrible plight of the Russian Mennonites, the intention to bring them over to Canada, and the readiness of the Mennonite immigrants to adapt themselves to Canada's customs. H.H. Ewert, reporting on the delegation's activities, later observed that "a form of propaganda for the Mennonites had been initiated."[66]

Renewed attempts to effect the repeal of the discriminatory immigration ruling followed soon after the Liberal election victory in December 1921. David Toews, realizing that the situation was becoming ever more desperate in Russia, recalled King's promise and in February 1922, A.A. Friesen told S.F. Coffman that some people were starving in the colonies and others were barely surviving:

> Many of our brethren are living on surrogates, as roots,
> cowhides, and bread of any kind [are] not obtainable. The rest
> of the cattle and horses are being butchered for meat. The
> prospects for spring sowing are hopeless unless help from the
> outside will be brought.[67]

Coffman had expressed reluctance to approach Ottawa again so soon, believing that the newly formed cabinet should be given more time to familiarize itself with the duties of office.[68] The compelling tone of Friesen's letter dispelled his reserve, however, and on Coffman's initiative, a second delegation was sent to Ottawa in March. Five Mennonite representatives met with King and other leading government personnel, reviewing with them many of the same points made during the last meeting.[69] King held true to his promise made earlier and had the immigration ban rescinded.[70]

One final legal question remained. Disclosure of a possible Mennonite movement into Canada had raised the question as to whether any unusual concessions had been offered to the Mennonites. The government's public denial raised fears in the Mennonite community, which now sought to clarify the military status of any newcomers. A delegation, led by David Toews, hastened to Ottawa in April 1923, where assurance was given that the existing laws relating to military exemptions would apply equally to the newcomers as they did to the Mennonites already residing in Canada. The government was thus able to confirm to the public that no exceptions had been made for the Mennonites, while the latter were comforted by the knowledge that their right to military exemption was enshrined in the law.[71]

The first giant obstacle to the migration had been bridged, though other formidable problems remained. A permanent immigration administration had to be assembled, chartered transportation facilities and credits had to be arranged, and support funds had to be collected from the various churches. On May 17, 1922, a second major advance was made with the establishment of the Canadian Mennonite Board of Colonization, hereafter referred to as the Board.[72]

Previous meetings had confirmed a genuine desire to organize an immigration committee representing as many Canadian Mennonite churches as possible. However, the discussions revealed a discouraging degree of political fracture within the Mennonite camp.[73] Tensions had developed early between the two leading western Mennonite spokesmen, Ewert and Toews. Their competitive instincts in turn contributed to an intense rivalry over which province, Manitoba or Saskatchewan, should function as the administrative centre of the operation. The May meeting, convened at the home of H.H. Ewert in Gretna, was intended to transform verbal commitments into real substance and a viable organization. Though David Toews himself wasn't present, Ewert, overcoming his earlier reservations, or being unusually gracious, nominated Toews as chairman of the Board, to which everyone agreed and which action also established Rosthern as the location of the office.

Finances were also discussed at the Gretna meeting. Obviously, huge sums of money were required for a mass migration. While transportation costs came first, settlement would require the larger amounts and for the moment these amounts represented the greater concern. The problem was where to find and how to collect these in the shortest possible time. Ewert suggested that one or more Canadian families should assume responsibility for one immigrant family and that thereby sufficient capital would be raised to purchase one of the villages being vacated by the emigrating Reinlaender or Chortitzer. This village could then be mortgaged for the purchase of another, which in turn could be mortgaged for a third.[74]

Toews later objected to Ewert's plan. He simply did not think the mortgages would generate enough cash, particularly since many properties were already burdened with debts. Instead, he endorsed a proposal worked out earlier by Gerhard Ens in co-operation with Rosthern lawyer A.C. March. The plan called for the incorporation of a shareholder's society under the name of Mennonite Colonization Association of North America Limited (MCANA).[75] The idea was to raise ten million dollars by selling shares of $100 to 100,000 Mennonites in the United States and Canada. No commission would be allowed for the selling of the shares. Thirty dollars of each share was to be paid immediately by the shareholder, the balance to be borrowed and subject to call at any time. Beneficiaries of the plan were required to repay the principal with interest not exceeding five per cent. In the end, the Toews plan won the greater support within the Board, and on July 26, 1922, the Association received its charter from the government.[76] The selling of the shares, however, was quite another matter. It never happened. A legal mechanism to secure funds had been provided, but not the monetary motivation for what essentially was a commercial scheme.

The Mennonites had provided themselves with an organization to administer the Canadian end of the immigration project, and a legal instrument for the securing of settlement funds, but there still remained the task of negotiating with a transportation company the willingness to transfer, on a credit basis, the passengers from Russia to Canada. The Canadian Pacific Railway showed early interest, having had its eye on a scheme involving the Mennonites in Russia already in the early years of the war. Created in the 1870s for the purpose of linking the new province of British Columbia with the rest of Canada, the CPR had since that time been heavily involved in the settling of the west. The railway's interest in colonization was a natural one — only through agricultural occupation of the land could it hope for profitable traffic—but the huge federal land grant of 25,000,000 acres meant direct involvement in settlement on a grand scale.[77] Under the energetic leadership of Colonel J.S. Dennis, who headed the company's Department of Colonization and Development for a time, the CPR spent more on immigration and settlement of the prairies than the federal government from 1905 to 1930.[78]

Colonel J.S. Dennis, not to be confused with John Stoughton Dennis, whose surveying crew had helped to precipitate the Red River Rebellion in 1869, was not unfamiliar with the Mennonites. He had first met them in 1874 when, as a young man working on the International, he had witnessed the arrival of an earlier group of Russian Mennonite immigrants. There had been more encounters later when Dennis had held the Regina-based position of Deputy Minister of Public Works for the Northwest Territories. Over the years the colonel had become impressed with the pioneering skills and adaptability of the Mennonites.

In the first year of the Great War, the CPR had taken note of the possibility of a mass Mennonite immigration from Russia.[79] Colonel Dennis, then assistant to President Thomas Shaughnessy, drew attention to the Russian government's decrees affecting adversely the "Austrian, Hungarian, German or Turkish subjects" in the empire and endangering particularly the possessions of those nearest the western borders.[80] After further investigation through the office of the High Commission in London, Dennis confirmed to Shaughnessy that "about six hundred thousand families of these people or some three million souls in all. . . recognized as the best farmers in Russia. . . are being expelled owing to their religious scruples about bearing arms or taking life in any form."[81] Clearly, the authorities were misinformed. There were not three million with "religious scruples about bearing arms" but at most 120,000. There were not even three million "Germans" but at most two million. The danger was not so much expulsion as dispossession. And the reasons were not religion but language, economics, and politics.

The accuracy of the information did not improve much with a direct report from A.M. Evalenko, publisher in New York of the Russian-American magazine and former immigration commissioner for the Santa Fe Railway Company. Evalenko was sent to Petrograd by the CPR and returned confirming the "enforced emigration" of "two million Russian Mennonites."[82] He indicated his willingness to act as agent in Russia for the CPR in bringing these people to Canada in return for commission on the sale of lands to the Mennonites in Canada, who, it was assumed, would be "in possession of sufficient capital to make a splendid start in the West."[83]

> Roughly estimated the lands of all the Mennonites in Russia are valued at about seven hundred million dollars, and this is the amount of money which they may possess after the land will be sold to the Russian peasants.[84]

The proposal of Evalenko was recommended in March of 1916 to the CPR president by Dennis, along with the practical suggestion that, given the wartime conditions in Europe, immigrants be brought across the Pacific from Vladivostok to Vancouver.[85] Evalenko was eager to proceed because he and his colleague, the agent working in Canada, would share equally five per cent of the commission, while another three per cent would be paid by him "to some officials in Russia."[86] The proposal had already been approved by the Minister of the Interior, the Minister of Agriculture, the Minister of Ways and Communications, and the President of the Peasants Bank. The State Councillor had been authorized "to enter into a contract" with Mr. Evalenko, following "special legislation of the Duma" to confirm the same, which "would be done at once."[87]

Thus, it was not surprising that Dennis welcomed delegations to his office in 1921 and 1922 and that he proved to be highly sympathetic to their representations. The first meeting with Gerhard Ens, who was an old acquaintance, A.A. Friesen, and H.H. Ewert came after their conference with government officials in Ottawa. Colonel Dennis indicated that his company stood ready to advance credits and offer transportation facilities for the resettlement of the Russian Mennonites, provided the Canadian Mennonites would guarantee repayment.[88] His pledge, however, was not conclusive, for he still had to convince his superiors to grant a contract on credit. In this, he was aided by the Mennonite reputation for paying their debts.[89] On June 20, 1922, Dennis informed David Toews that the CPR was willing to grant transportation credits to an initial party of 3,000 Mennonites.[90] Thus, good progress towards opening up at least the possibility of a migration was made also in the area of transportation.

Preparing the Way in Canada

Toews next turned to the imposing task of persuading the Mennonites in Canada to accept the obligations attending the contract. This
challenge was as formidable as had been the task of convincing the
federal government and the railway. Luckily for the Mennonites
waiting in Russia, Toews was one of those rare individuals who stood
his ground during the worst adversity and whose character thrived
on courageous action.[91]

It was apparent from the outset that winning approval of the
Mennonite constituency for the immigration would not be an easy
matter. At the July 1922 session of the Conference of Mennonites in
Central Canada, even before he had received the contract outlining
the particulars of the agreement, Toews inquired of the delegates
whether he should sign the proposed document.[92] His question was
greeted by nervous silence. Three times he repeated his request and
three times the delegates did not respond. Finally, Toews announced
that, given the indecision in the conference, his own church would
assume the contractual responsibilities until others were prepared to
co-operate. As reluctant as the conference was, all other Mennonite
groups in Canada at the time were even more unwilling to assume any
responsibility.

The antagonism towards Toews and the work he represented
intensified after the arrival of the contract in the second week of July.
The terms outlined in the document were not nearly as favourable as
expected and served to promote additional discord.[93] Collectively,
and ambiguously, made out between "The Mennonite Church of
Canada and the CPR Co.," the particulars of the contract were a tall
order.[94] At a total cost of approximately $400,000 to "the Mennonite
Church of Canada," the CPR stood ready to dispatch two ships, with a
combined capacity of 2,642, to the Black Sea.

It was the Board's responsibility to fill the ships with passengers
but should the Board, for any reason and to any extent, fail to do so, it
would still be obligated to provide a forfeit payment for each
vacancy. The terms of payment stipulated that 25 per cent of the total
cost had to be paid ten days after the account was rendered. The
second 25 per cent was due after three months, and the balance within
six months, together with an interest rate of six per cent per annum.

Toews found himself in a dilemma. On the one hand, the huge

debt associated with the movement, the responsibility of producing the right number of passengers at the right time and place in Russia, the poverty of many people in Canada and their resistance to receiving the immigrants, and plain common sense all suggested that he should abandon the scheme. On the other hand, Toews recognized that the fate of many Mennonites in Russia rested with bold action in Canada. He also realized that the terms of the contract, difficult as they were, represented the best terms available. His vacillation ended when he received word from the CPR that the Soviet authorities had granted passports to 3,000 people. The imperative for immediate action was reinforced in a wire received from B.B. Janz which disclosed that 2,774 Mennonites were gathered in Odessa, a port on the Black Sea, ready to leave.[95] Toews felt compelled to act and, despite considerable misgivings, he affixed his signature to the contentious contract on July 21. Toews admitted, while signing the document, that

> I did this hoping that the CPR would not carry out the contract as it read. When I came to Montreal, I told Colonel Dennis that the contract had been signed, but that we knew we could not carry it out as it read.[96]

Time-consuming negotiations in Russia and Canada had now finally set the stage for the actual commencement of the migration. In Russia, B.B. Janz had won legal approval for the emigration of 20,000 Mennonites from Russia, and an initial party of some 750 families was ready to leave. In Canada, David Toews, battling against tremendous odds, had cleared the way for the admission into the country of the first large contingent. The CPR was ready, Colonel Dennis having informed the federal government on July 6 that "we intend sending our ship forward to the Black Sea the moment we are advised of the signing of the contract at Rosthern, Saskatchewan."[97] Similarly, the Board had applied to the government for official authorization for the pending immigration,[98] even before formally endorsing the contract, since it was its declared aim to receive the immigrants before the advent of the fall harvest.

The Board was notified that its project enjoyed the full support of the government, providing three conditions were met: first, that the admitted Mennonites would be given shelter and support by their co-religionists in Canada; second, that the immigrants would be placed on the land as farmers; and third, that none of the immigrants would become a public charge.[99] It was also understood that the Mennonite immigrants would be subject to the immigration regulations applicable to all others. F.C. Blair, Secretary of the Department of Immigration and Colonization, later confirmed that "the Department desires to cooperate with your Association in every reasonable way with a view to assisting you in getting started the movement of settlers you have in view."[100]

The optimism thus generated was short-lived. A combination of bureaucratic delays, international disputes, and an intensifying crisis situation in Russia delivered a cruel blow to the hopes of the immigration leaders and marked 1922 as the year of bitter disappointments and opportunity irrevocably lost. The first premonition of impending trouble reached B.B. Janz in early September, when he learned that only 3,000 settlers could be transported from Russia that year. A profound mood of despair and virtual panic seized the chairman of the Union.[101] Many prospective emigrants had sold almost all of their personal possessions and had liquidated their property at deflated prices on the understanding that they would shortly be departing from Russia. Now, with the coming of winter, and only a poor harvest to sustain them, the people faced a critical situation. Furthermore, their visas, which had been obtained at the expense of tremendous effort and not a little luck, were due to expire soon.

Other unexpected developments further jeopardized all movement for that year. Responding to rumours that a dreaded cholera epidemic had broken out in southern Russia, Colonel Dennis met with Board officials in Saskatoon on September 5.[102] The decision was made to contact the CPR agent in Moscow, A.R. Owen, to investigate the veracity of the report. Their worst fears were confirmed when Owen replied that all of the southern Russian ports had been quarantined because of the cholera outbreak. In addition to this misfortune, there had been renewed hostilities along the Turkish-Greek border, which seriously interfered with any traffic moving through the Dardanelles. Colonel Dennis had no choice but to inform the Canadian government, on September 22, that the departure of the CPR ships had been cancelled and that the migration would have to wait until the spring.[103]

Then, just as suddenly, an alternative presented itself. Working behind the scenes, Colonel Dennis and his advisors calculated that a move was still possible in 1922, providing the immigrants could be rerouted through the Latvian port of Libau lying on the Baltic Sea.[104] There were difficulties connected with this scheme, not the least of which was the expense required for the long journey from the southern Ukraine to the Baltic. The Board, already strapped for funds, was unable to produce the additional cash. In the end, the Mennonites in Russia themselves managed to finance the northern trip.[105] Thus, at the beginning of November, the prospects seemed good that at least an initial party of 3,000 could still be brought to Canada in 1922.

This was not to be. On November 21, the planned movement was abandoned, ostensibly for medical reasons.[106] Canadian immigration policy specified that all immigrants had to meet specified medical standards. This in itself constituted no problem except that the Soviets, in retaliation for Canada's refusal earlier that year to grant visas to visiting Soviet officials, declared that the Canadian medical inspectors would be prohibited from entering their country, thus preventing inspection on Russian soil. By the terms of the Anglo-Russian Trade Agreement, Canada and the Soviet Union both consented to a mutual recognition of passports issued to persons travelling in the interests of trade. A clause, however, provided that any person could be refused entry to either country if such a person was not acceptable to the country to which he was going. Suspicious of the political sympathies of a small group of Russians, Canada declined to issue them visas, which in turn produced the Russian reaction.

It was decided, therefore, to verify the health of the immigrants after they had left the U.S.S.R. and arrived at Libau. The Soviets then further complicated matters by refusing to re-accept people who, having crossed the border into Latvia, might be rejected. The immigrants who would be disqualified by the medical officials would thus be consigned to a state of international limbo, unable to proceed to Canada or to return to their former homes, an unwelcome prospect in any event.[107] In view of these circumstances, Colonel Dennis relayed to the immigration officials his decision to "regretfully abandon the movement until much more satisfactory arrangements are entered into."[108]

The buoyant hopes and high expectations of July had by the year's end given way to a dark mood of growing despondency and resignation. A golden opportunity for beginning a mass Mennonite exodus from Russia had passed into history, first because of the time necessary to complete arrangements in and from Canada, and secondly, because of the unforeseen developments in Russia. Fortunately, the people knew of biblical parallels which sustained their faith and prevented them from giving up. As B.B. Janz said:

> Apparently the way, like that of the children of Israel, shall not be the closest one, but will once again be fought through a desert of difficulties. [109]

As if the parties involved had not encountered enough troubles, they were now forced to contend with mounting Mennonite opposition in Canada to the policies and practices of the Board. From the beginning, some had objected to the involvement of Canadian Mennonites in the rescue of the Russian brethren. An official protest was registered in July 1921 just prior to the sending of the first delegation to Ottawa. [110] The protest declared that the Waldheim-Rosthern district was categorically opposed both to the advance of money for the purposes of financing a migration and to the dispatching of an Ottawa delegation.

A large anti-Board protest meeting by leaders of the Mennonite Brethren conference took place on August 12, 1922, in Hepburn, Saskatchewan. [111] The temper of this gathering surfaced in an expansive letter subsequently forwarded to the CPR officials in Montreal. The communiqué reported that the churches represented at the Hepburn conference, namely, the Mennonite Brethren Churches of Brotherfield, Waldheim, Hepburn, Ebenezer, Neu Hoffnung, and Aberdeen, the two Bruderthaler Langham Churches at Langham, and the two Krimmer Churches, Salem and Immanuel, "refuse to be parties to the contract between the Mennonite Church of Canada and the Canadian Pacific Railway as already signed by the Rev. David Toews" and that the named churches would "assume no responsibility whatsoever in any form or contract entered into by other branches of the Mennonite Church of Canada." [112]

Reports critical of the Board's handling of the migration proceedings likewise surfaced in the United States. The most outspoken opposition appeared in the Mennonite periodicals.[113] The history of the Mennonites reveals much internal squabbling, but seldom has the disunity of these people been more graphically demonstrated than in the absorbing spectacle of Mennonite agitation against other Mennonites in the Mennonite press, concerning the proposed rescue of their people from Russia. *Vorwärts*, published at Hillsboro, *Der Herald*, published at Newton, and *Die Mennonitsche Rundschau*, published at Scottdale and later in Winnipeg for different reasons and at various times between 1922 and 1930, printed articles heavily prejudiced against the Board. Unsubstantiated allegations were published to cast aspersions on Toews and other Board officials as to the amount of financial remuneration being received, the huge debt they had irresponsibly incurred, and the religious orthodoxy of certain Board members.[114]

Toews steadfastly refused to relinquish his ground, despite the widespread antagonism to his work. His response to the critics was praiseworthy for its restraint and reasonableness:

> We are glad we signed the contract and kept it intact, in spite of all the attacks that we had to undergo. If it is poor judgement that was shown on our part I am in a way sorry, but I would rather show poor judgement in the way I did, than to show the soundest of judgement in the eyes of the world at large and fail to do our duty towards our suffering brethren.[115]

Why did so many people react so vehemently against an organization presumably dedicated to such a noble enterprise? Some opposition, undoubtedly, was connected to the matter of finances. The first post-war recession was just beginning to be felt in Western Canada. Many people, with some justification, feared the consequences of the material sacrifices that would shortly be asked of them. Their anxieties were fanned by the ambiguities with respect to the contract with the CPR. "The Mennonite Church of Canada" as a party to that contract was a new concept. A body by that name didn't really exist. There were Mennonite churches, a plethora of Mennonite churches, but not one that looked like the one referred to in the CPR contract. Was every Mennonite congregation in Canada meant? Would every Mennonite be held equally responsible for the accumulating debts? Despite repeated assurances from Toews and Colonel Dennis that the Board—and the Board only to the extent of its assets—and not individuals, churches, or conferences, would be held responsible, the doubts persisted.

Other criticisms targeted the Board's single non-Mennonite participant.[116] Gerhard Ens, a member of the Swedenborgian Church, was suspected of participating in the project for reasons of personal monetary gain. It was well known that good money had been made in the past by agents of immigration and settlement schemes. Why should the present be any different? Indeed, some opposition, especially in the U.S.A., was due to the fact that not every land agent could get in on the prospective action. Ens's position with respect to nonresistance was also questioned. Reaction against his involvement was such that he resigned from his work in 1923. His resignation was reluctantly received by Toews, because Ens, with all his experience and contacts in governmental, financial, and legal circles, had been invaluable through the years and was especially so now. As far as Toews was concerned, Ens had served his people well and though he had joined the Swedenborgians he was in many ways still a Mennonite.

Perhaps the heart of the antipathy directed towards the projected migration lay in the fundamental parting of the ways in the 1870s that divided the Mennonites in Russia and their cousins in Western Canada. Both those who left Russia at the time and those who stayed believed the other party to be in error and themselves to be right. Since then, a considerable spread had developed between the economic and the cultural sophistication of the two groups and this gave rise to misunderstandings, suspicions, and acrimony.

Of a more serious nature were the reactions sparked by the sketchy reports received in Canada of the formation of the Home Defence (*Selbstschutz*) during the Russian civil upheaval. Some suggested that the principle of nonresistance had been abandoned. Others worried over the religious purity of the Russian Mennonites in general. One such person speculated that the Molotschna Colony was infested with modernism and that its real need was for missionaries.[117] In all, it appears that the enmity and resentment precipitated by the 1870s migration, which for so long had remained latent, now exploded with special force.

It was an uncomfortable time for Toews and the Board. Whenever possible, he responded to the critics, either in person or through the press. He knew that the public grasp of the complexities of the proposed immigration was incomplete, often inaccurate, and badly distorted by hostile press. This deep conviction that the movement was right, and that his critics were wrong, strengthened his resolve to get the movement under way. Even a futile attempt to raise funds in the United States during the winter of 1922–23 failed to shake the Canadian leader's determination.[118]

The situation in 1923 remained deadlocked because of the Russian government's refusal to admit Canadian doctors into the country and the uncertainties this created for those emigrants who later would be disqualified from proceeding to Canada. A breakthrough came in April when B.H. Unruh obtained from the German government permission to transfer for temporary care any immigrants rejected at Libau to a holding camp at Lechfeld. In this former prisoner-of-war camp they would become the responsibility of German Mennonite Aid.[119] The Board quickly agreed to finance the transportation costs from Libau to Lechfeld, and thus the way was opened for the movement of Mennonite emigrants from Russia.

The numerous postponements had produced a restive spirit within the settlements. This disquietude was especially acute in Chortitza, a district that threatened to withdraw from the Union and to arrange for emigration independently. As in Canada, few of the rank-and-file Mennonites appreciated the awesome complexity of the task thrust upon David Toews and B.B. Janz and their colleagues. It was also true that the leaders were occasionally beset by doubts about immigration. When in the winter of 1922–23 J.P. Klassen, representing the impatient Chortitzer, stopped in Kharkov to pick up from B.B. Janz the Chortitza lists and to deliver them to Moscow directly, both Janz and Philip Cornies, vice-chairman of the Union, sought to dissuade him. Janz had just received a dispatch from B.H. Unruh suggesting considerable help from Germany in the restoration of the colonies, and both Janz and Cornies were excited about the reconstruction. Both begged him not to proceed, and according to a Klassen memoir, Cornies said:

> Think of our mission here in Russia, our Mennonite ideals,
> the beautiful villages, the productive land. What a wonderful
> future will be ours with help from Germany. No, our obliga-
> tions are and remain in Russia.[120]

Klassen would not change his mind, and, lists in hand, he went to A.R. Owen's office in Moscow, where Owen reported that the CPR was ready to proceed, if the Mennonites were ready. Those in Chortitza were, Klassen confirmed, and thus immigration planning proceeded. The complaints of the people were silenced in May, when it was learned that the migration was about to begin. J.P. Klassen, representing Chortitza, and B.B. Janz, representing the Molotschna, hastened to Moscow to complete the final arrangements. They were offered the full co-operation of the authorities and by mid-June all the details were in order.

The Immigration Under Way

On June 22, 1923, the first group of 738 persons left Chortitza en route to the Russian border town of Sebezh. They bumped along the rails for five days in boxcars, the interiors of which they themselves had modified to suit their purposes. On crossing the border, every immigrant was subjected to a thorough delousing and disinfection process lasting several days. Thereafter, they were brought by train alongside a designated ship, where they were inspected by Canadian medical officials. Today, it seems incongruous that a people as dedicated to personal cleanliness standards as are the Mennonites were subjected to the most meticulous disinfection routine. The demand was irksome to many Mennonites and led many in North America to protest that the medical examinations were too exacting. However, sound reasons rested behind the Canadian medical policies. In the decade preceding World War I, it was discovered that typhus was transmitted by lice embedded in clothing and woollen blankets. Their bedding was not free of lice and hence Mennonites were prime candidates for the disease.[121]

The results of the medical inspections were most distressing and brought further anguish to the movement. An unusually high proportion of the travellers failed to pass the tests in Libau. Initially, there was no reason to predict such a discouraging development. After examining the first immigrants, one doctor reported: "I have no doubt that if the balance which is coming forward is like this first party, they will prove to be good citizens for Canada."[122] His early confidence was unwarranted.

Evidently the ravages of civil strife and the ensuing hygienic decay in the colonies had taken a greater toll than was at first estimated. Close scrutiny of other groups passing through Libau disclosed a high incidence of trachoma, an extremely contagious eye disease. All suspected cases were re-examined twice to verify the presence of the malady. As a consequence, almost 13 per cent of that year's 3,000 immigrants were prevented from continuing on to Canada. Of the 389 detained, 378 were suffering from trachoma.[123]

Canadian officials expressed amazement and disbelief that the Mennonites should have taken so few medical precautions when selecting the emigrants. One inspector concluded that "great carelessness has been shown on the part of some people in Russia in allowing these people to come forward."[124] Yet it is implausible to imagine now, as it must have been then, that the Mennonites, who placed such a precious value on the family, would voluntarily have left loved ones behind because of sickness or physical defects. For many, the disruption caused by the detention of one or more family members was often a greater hardship than had been life back in the Ukraine.

Immigration leaders immediately challenged the detention policies of the Canadian officials. B.B. Janz contended that the government should exhibit a greater degree of understanding and tolerance, given the problems facing the Mennonites in Russia. David Toews, likewise communicating his displeasure to the immigration officials, bluntly charged that the Mennonites had been deceived.[125] Whereas the Board had previously been told that physically defective immigrants would be treated with flexibility, it now observed that the law was rigorously applied and enforced without exception.[126]

Contrary to the claims of the Mennonites, it does not appear that the medical inspectors unjustly exercised their prerogatives. T.B. Williams reported that he and his colleagues did what they could to allow as many as possible to pass the tests. Willams personally re-examined all suspected cases twice before giving a final decision, so as to eliminate the possibility of certifying as trachoma a case that was merely conjunctivitis. For their part, the Mennonites seem never to have appreciated the debilitating nature of trachoma and the ease with which it could be contracted. At the turn of the century and continuing up to the present, trachoma remains a major cause of blindness in North and sub-Saharan Africa, the Middle East and Asia, and northern India. The evidence would indicate that trachoma was introduced into the Mennonite settlements during the turbulence of the Russian civil war.

As time went on, medical inspectors were admitted into Russia and examinations of prospective immigrants took place in the colonies. By that time, Mennonite doctors in the Molotschna were "treating" trachoma patients to ensure that those affected would pass. The treatment consisted of flipping back the eyelids and removing the pus, etc. The operation was performed without the benefit of anesthesia and was extremely painful. It so exhausted children that they would need several days of sleep to recover, and sleep itself was a reason for medical leniency on the part of the examiners.[127] Since examinations could be repeated en route, escaping a negative medical verdict and visa refusal in Russia did not necessarily guarantee immediate admission to Canada.

Toews was disturbed not only by the forced separation of families, but also by the inflated financial burden caused by the unanticipated number of rejects.[128] More money was required from an already strained constituency to meet the expanded transportation costs to Lechfeld, to purchase basic food and clothing supplies for the refugees, and to support the required relief workers. The German government held the German Mennonite Aid responsible for the care of the detainees, but the Aid looked to the Board to cover most of the costs.

In an effort to ease the excessive pressure, Toews repeatedly, but unsuccessfully, inquired whether it would be possible to send all those detained to Canada, where they could receive treatment and where the strain imposed upon the ruptured families would be diminished. The government replied that, for reasons of health and politics, it could not accede to Toews's request.[129] For the duration of the migration, therefore, the problem of detained Mennonites persisted. Toews nevertheless continued to notify officials of complaints of irregular examinations and unjustified confinements and renewed his efforts to arrange for medical treatment in Canada.

A reception committee, appointed by the Board in the Rosthern area, had prepared for the billeting of the immigrants in eleven districts, avoiding those communities where the greatest opposition had appeared.[130] Even after the first ship had docked at Quebec City, the critics were warning people not to receive immigrants in their homes lest they become party to the contract. However, the critics were losing out. On July 21, when the first trainload was expected, a sense of responsibility, mixed with curiosity, took hold in the area. All roads led to Rosthern that day as people drove up in their Studebakers, Chevrolets, and Model T Fords—450 of them according to one account—as well as in their buggies, hayracks, and grain wagons. A Saskatoon journalist reported the emotional reception:

> A great hush fell upon the assembled thousands and to the ears of the Canadians came a soft, slow chant. . . a musical expression of the great tragedy and heartbreak. . . . Then the Canadian Mennonites took up the song, and the tone increased in volume, growing deeper and fuller, until the melody was pouring forth from several thousand throats. [131]

The needs of the immigrants put the hospitality of their hosts to the test, because days, often weeks, and even months of free lodging and housing had to be supplied, and, if possible, employment, the payment for which was intended to help pay the transportation debt. However, the willingness to help increased, and in due course most of the Mennonite communities on the prairies were involved in the reception. [132] H.T. Klaassen correctly assessed this contribution when he wrote in the history of Eigenheim "that without the help of the Canadian brotherhood the whole work of bringing over the destitute brethren would not have been possible." [133]

The newcomers themselves strove not to be a burden, and when their hopes of early settlement on land did not materialize, they accepted whatever jobs were available, however arduous or menial. They also proceeded to organize themselves immediately in order to attend to their own needs and to speak with a common voice. [134] The Central Mennonite Immigrant Committee had small beginnings but soon it was tied into all immigrant groups, which, no matter how small, appointed district representatives. Under the auspices of the committee, D.H. Epp founded Der Immigrantenbote, a newspaper to serve the immigrants beginning in January of 1924.

Much-needed support for the work of the Board and for the admission of more immigrants now came also from the public press. In his full-page Saskatoon Phoenix feature on the "progressive Mennonites," Gerald M. Brown lauded the "eager and willing" people who survived the "first winter without appeal to charity."[135] Though many of the immigrants were "pitifully incompetent" when it came to manual labour, having been university students, teachers, and "scions of wealthy families," they readily performed farm chores and accepted other odd jobs in order to provide for their families and to pay their debts:

> . . . day after day, with the mercury sinking in its tube, they labored away . . . there were no loafers, no drones; every man sought work, and, in most cases found it . . . and ten thousand more hard-earned dollars found their way into the coffers of the Canadian Pacific Railway.[136]

These people, said the *Phoenix*, were not "parasites" but "useful citizens." When formerly wealthy men like Heinrich Suderman, who owned 9,000 acres in Russia, accepted work as a section hand on the railroad or when a white-haired man of sixty like Isaak Zacharias, who was worth half a million before the revolution, became a farm labourer, then Canada could be certain that it was accepting good people who could "adjust themselves to the new order of circumstances." Besides, they were "enthusiastic supporters" of the Canadian educational system, eager to learn the English language:

> not only the children but their parents are anxious to learn English, and in consequence 25 night schools were established in the three western provinces, and each class has been filled to capacity with men and women since its inception.[137]

Notwithstanding the indebtedness of the Board and the disruptive impact produced by the Lechfeld situation, the relative success of 1923 brought fresh pressure upon the Board to obtain another contract. In February, David Toews and others met with CPR officials in Montreal to discuss the possibilities. President Beatty indicated he was prepared to make certain adjustments to the outstanding accounts, providing the terms of payment were so arranged that no transportation debt would remain unliquidated for a period longer than two years.[138]

In April, the second formal agreement was concluded between the Board and the CPR.[139] For the first time, the contract permitted the transport of both credit and paying passengers. This new dimension reflected the shift that had occurred in Russia. Janz was cognizant of the depleted financial reserves in Canada and successfully won governmental sanction for the emigration of individuals with means to pay their way quite apart from the movement of groups of people without any means. Individual visas involved greater expense than did group passports and assumed a certain degree of personal solvency, but some cash passengers helped the CPR to look more kindly on the movement of others on credit.

In Russia it appeared that those of lesser means were now being neglected. Destitute Mennonites who, according to the earlier agreement forged between the Union and the Soviet authorities, ought to have left the country were unable to do so. Wealthier Mennonites, who had not planned to leave their homes, were suddenly given the opportunity to reverse their decision.[140] The restiveness pervading the Ukrainian settlements coincided with agitation in the central provinces and in Siberia of other Mennonites who wanted to be included in the emigration lists. Their demands were legitimized and strengthened by the worsening local conditions compared to the slight economic improvement that had worked its way into the Ukraine.

The Board and the CPR had their own problems. Exactly how many immigrants could they process in 1924? Twice the figures were revised, first downward and then upward. At the year's end, the bolder course had successfully been concluded and 5,048 additional immigrants had been brought to Canada. Most of them located in Western Canada, especially Manitoba, but some 1,500 were stopped in Ontario and received by the Swiss Mennonites. A.A. Friesen justified to the immigration department his agency's decision to divert such a sizeable group to the eastern province, where it was feared they would not become agriculturalists in accordance with the agreement. "The Old Mennonites," he explained, "have been in sympathy with our work from the beginning. Last year we did not bring any immigrants to Ontario because we had ample room in the West."[141]

The Swiss Mennonites were ready to make an outstanding contribution to the success of the immigration[142] in spite of the fact that doubts about the undertaking had also arisen in Ontario. The repeated setbacks and delays had prompted many to question the capabilities of the Board. S.F. Coffman had been asked to throw his support behind American interests who wished to direct the refugees to Mexico. There was even talk of Ontario conducting its own relief and rescue mission through the auspices of the Non-Resistant Relief Organization.[143] But Coffman announced that the Ontario Mennonites were committed to work in partnership with the Rosthern organization. The promised support was translated into concrete action in 1924. In response to the Board's distress call, they offered their time, money, and homes to the needy immigrants.

For the 1924 movement, David Toews appealed to S.F. Coffman to arrange for the hosting of at least 2,500 people in Ontario. The 1923 immigration had taxed the resources in Saskatchewan, and the following spring most of the immigrants were still not on their own land. Besides, crop prospects on the prairies were not very good that year. It seemed like an impossible request to Coffman, and it wasn't because he didn't empathize with the movement or feel keenly for the plight of the Mennonites in and from Russia. On the contrary, he had already caused his conference to provide funds in 1921.[144] In that year Russian relief approached $4,000, one-third of all the amounts given for foreign causes, and in 1922 the amount exceeded $7,000, more than one-third of the total conference giving for that year.[145] Additionally, the Mennonite Conference of Ontario had acted immediately to authorize his participation in the Canadian Mennonite Board of Colonization upon its founding and in the delegation to Ottawa seeking removal of the immigration ban.[146]

In response to David Toews's plea, Coffman agreed to try for housing for 1,000, but so generous was the response from the New Mennonites, Old Mennonites, Old Order Mennonites, Amish Mennonites, and Old Order Amish that 1,340 persons were received and assigned to the various homes and districts (see Table 17). Reporting on the arrival of the first train on July 19, 1924, the local newspaper noted how complete was the involvement:

> Practically every Mennonite in the county was in Waterloo
> and their rigs and autos were crammed to capacity with
> humans while baggage was tied on in every conceivable
> place.[148]

Against almost insurmountable odds, almost 8,000 Mennonites had been transplanted to Canada by the end of 1924. Unfortunately,

TABLE 17[147]

SUMMARY OF IMMIGRANTS RECEIVED IN ONTARIO IN 1924
(BY POST OFFICE DISTRICT AND NUMBERS OF IMMIGRANTS)

Alma R.2	5	Kitchener	41	St. Agatha	6
Ayr	1	Kitchener R.2	15	St. Agatha R.1	2
Ayr R.1	4	Kitchener R.3	16	St. Jacobs	19
Ayr R.2	9	Kitchener R.4	32	St. Jacobs R.1	29
				Selkirk	7
Baden	28	Linwood	4	Shakespeare	9
Baden R.2	22			Shakespeare R.1	4
Beamsville	1	Millbank	7		
Blair R.1	7	Millbank R.1	18	Tavistock	14
Breslau	22	Milverton	18	Tavistock R.1	43
Breslau R.1	20	Milverton R.1	15		
Breslau R.2	9			Vineland	13
Bridgeport	4	New Dundee	48	Vineland Station	39
Bright R.1	15	New Dundee R.1	5		
Bright R.4	6	New Hamburg	18	Wallenstein	25
Brunner	1	New Hamburg R.1	11	Wallenstein R.1	9
		New Hamburg R.2	19	Wallenstein R.2	16
Conestoga	19	New Hamburg R.3	7	Waterloo	127
Crosshill	2			Waterloo R.1	29
		Petersburg	40	Waterloo R.2	25
Drayton	5	Petersburg R.1	13	Waterloo R.3	16
		Petersburg R.2	63	Wellesley	25
Elmira	35	Plattsville	10	Wellesley R.1	20
Elmira R.1	10	Plattsville R.1	3	Wellesley R.2	25
Elmira R.2	17	Plattsville R.2	5	West Montrose	2
Elmira R.3	8	Preston	44	West Montrose R.1	1
Elmira R.4	5	Preston R.1	8		
Hawkesville	7	Rainham	1	Zurich	17
Haysville	7	Roseville	8		
Heidelberg	6			Unknown	47
Hespeler	27				

Total Number of Immigrants: 1,340

the Board's depressed financial status, coupled with the poverty of the Mennonites still in Russia, discouraged the prospect of any further movement. A two-year transportation bill of over $825,000 had accumulated, of which only $183,000 had been repaid.[149] The CPR had shown commendable charity to the Mennonites in the past, but since it was a business company it began to press with persistence for greater punctuality in meeting the payments.

In an effort to forestall imminent collapse of the immigration movement, the Board issued an urgent financial appeal to the Mennonites in the United States. But the desired American response never materialized. At one point, the Mennonite Colonization Board (MCB), an American counterpart to the Canadian Board and successor to the Mennonite Executive Committee for Colonization, had endorsed the Canadian program. The American body even recommended that a policy of close co-operation be followed between the two organizations and that an emergency fund-raising campaign be launched in the United States.[150] The organization, however, never made good its assurances and actually served to undermine the stability of the Board.

From 1923 to 1926, the MCB aggressively promoted Mexico as the best destination for the beleaguered Russian Mennonites, and it met with some success. Over 500 Mennonites from Russia made Mexico their home, at least temporarily. Although the MCB was not the only American organization to which the Board appealed for funds, its response to the plea reveals much about the priorities of American Mennonites at the time. During the time that it made available $6,850 to the Board, 28 constituent churches pledged $56,000 for the Mexico settlement project.[151]

The American Mennonites advanced several sensible reasons for their preference of Mexico over Canada. They referred to the strict medical examinations demanded by Canada, the cold climate prevailing in the western prairies, and the presence in Mexico of other Mennonites. But they failed to explain satisfactorily the lack of unanimity between the Mennonite organizations in the two North American countries. Thus, the cool indifference, if not outright hostility, displayed by the American Mennonites to the Board remains one of the real puzzles of the entire rescue venture. Late in 1925, when a large migration to Mexico had proven to be impractical, the American committee redirected its resources to Canada. The support was welcomed, but at that juncture the help offered was too little coming too late. The best years for emigration from Russia and immigration to Canada were rapidly coming to a close.

The Board had meanwhile negotiated another contract with the CPR for the year 1925. Even though the terms of earlier contracts had not been met, the company agreed to extend its assistance in yet another contract. It insisted, however, that the Board incorporate and that $100,000 of the debt be covered by October 1. Both conditions were met, allowing 3,772 immigrants to come to Canada in 1925. They were joined by an additional 5,940 refugees the following year. The 1926 movement was unusually large—it was in fact the peak year—owing to the inclusion of nearly 3,500 cash passengers. That year's contingent included also the B.B. Janz family. Janz had officially laid down his duties as chairman of the Union in March 1926. Despite his justifiable fears that he would not be allowed to leave the country, the family managed the trip without incident, the cost being borne entirely by the CPR.[152]

The shrewd Janz had rightly gauged that time was fast running out for the Mennonites in Russia. The New Economic Policy, a reprieve from collectivization, was about to make way for the first Five-Year Plan. The Soviet Union's new leader, Josef Stalin, was implementing policies which sharply curtailed political, economic, and religious freedoms. The government's attitude towards emigration of its citizens likewise stiffened. After 1926, few Mennonites were allowed to leave the country. Only 847 arrived in 1927 and 511 in 1928 (Table 18).[153]

TABLE 18[153]

CASH AND CREDIT PASSENGERS
(BY YEAR OF IMMIGRATION)

YEAR	CREDIT PASSENGERS	CASH PASSENGERS	TOTALS
1923	2,759	—	2,759
1924	3,894	1,154	5,048
1925	2,171	1,601	3,772
1926	2,479	3,461	5,940
1927	340	507	847
1928	408	103	511
1929	1,009	10	1,019
1930	294	11	305
Totals	13,354	6,847	20,201

The Soviet door was closing and, unknown to most, the day of opportunity for entering Canada was also nearing an end. The successful settlement of the immigrants and a buoyant economy were essential to the ongoing admission of many more immigrants. The Board did what it could to put the people on land, but the Canadian door was closing anyway. Even the Canadian National Railways, jealous of the CPR's success and anxious to get a share of the action with the help of a rival Mennonite organization, could do nothing to reverse or slow the trend. The years of greatest opportunity for the rescue and resettlement of the Russian Mennonites has passed into history.

FOOTNOTES

1   Dietrich Neufeld, *A Russian Dance of Death: Revolution and Civil War in the Ukraine*, translated and edited by Al Reimer (Winnipeg: Hyperion Press, 1977), p. 11.

2   Quoted in John B. Toews, ed., *Selected Documents: The Mennonites in Russia from 1917 to 1930* (Winnipeg: Christian Press, 1975), p. 299.

3   See Frank H. Epp, *Mennonite Exodus: The Rescue and Resettlement of the Russian Mennonites Since the Communist Revolution* (Altona, Man.: D.W. Friesen & Sons for the Canadian Mennonite Relief and Immigration Council, 1962), pp. 28–38, and John B. Toews, *Lost Fatherland: The Story of the Mennonite Emigration from Russia, 1921–1927* (Scottdale, Pa.: Herald Press, 1967), pp. 21–50.

4   P.C. 1204, *Canada Gazette*, 14 June 1919, p. 3824.

5   Cornelius Krahn, "Russia," *Mennonite Encyclopedia*, 4:386–87.

6   CGC, XV-31.2, "1910-Agriculture;" David G. Rempel, "Mennonite Agriculture and Model Farming as Issues of Economic Study and Political Controversy, 1870–1917," an unpublished essay.

7   Quoted in Rempel, p. 55.

8   Cornelius Krahn, p. 389.

9   David G. Rempel, pp. 50–51.

10   C.J. Dyck, ed., *An Introduction to Mennonite History* (Scottdale, Pa.: Herald Press, 1981), pp. 178–79.

11   For an expanded discussion of the subject, see James Urry, "The Transformation and Polarization of the Mennonites in Russia, 1789–1914" (paper presented to the 1977 Conference on Russian Mennonite History, Winnipeg, November 1977), and "The Closed and the Open: Social and Religious Change Amongst the Mennonites of Russia (1789–1889)," 3 vols. (Ph.D. dissertation, Oxford University, 1975).

12   David G. Rempel, p. 53.
13   Frank H. Epp, *Mennonite Exodus*, p. 39 ff.
14   *Ibid.*, p. 40.
15   *Protokoll des Allgemeinen Kongresses in Ohrloff, Taurien, vom 14.-18. August, 1917*, in John B. Toews, pp. 449–78, 480.
16   John B. Toews, p. 395.
17   For several eyewitness accounts of the violent events, see Dietrich Neufeld, *Ein Tagebuch aus dem Reiche des Totentanzer* (Emden: By the Author, 1921), or *A Russian Dance of Death: Revolution and Civil War in the Ukraine*, translated and edited by Al Reimer (Winnipeg: Hyperion Press, 1977); Gerhard P. Schroeder, *Miracles of Grace and Judgment* (Lodi, Cal.: By the Author, 1974); Johann J. Nickel, *Thy Kingdom Come: The Diary of Johann J. Nickel of Rosenhof, 1918–1919*, translated by John P. Nickel (Saskatoon: By the Author, 1978).
18   David G. Rempel, pp. 81–82.
19   Dietrich Neufeld, *A Russian Dance of Death*, p. 9.
20   Quoted in John B. Toews, "The Halbstadt Volost 1918–22: A Case Study of the Mennonite Encounter with Early Bolshevism," *Mennonite Quarterly Review* 48 (October 1974):492.
21   Adam Giesinger, *From Catherine to Khrushchev: The Story of Russia's Germans* (Winnipeg: By the Author, 1974), pp. 261–63.
22   See Victor Peters, *Nestor Makhno: The Life of an Anarchist* (Winnipeg: Echo Books, 1970), p. 37 ff.
23   Cf. J.P. Epp, "The Mennonite Selbstschutz in the Ukraine: An Eye Witness Account," *Mennonite Life* 26 (July 1971):138–42; Lyle Friesen, "The Mennonite Selbstschutz in its Historical Perspective" (research paper, Conrad Grebel College, 1973); John B. Toews, "The Origins and Activities of the Mennonite *Selbstschutz* in the Ukraine (1918–1919)," *Mennonite Quarterly Review* 46 (January 1972):5–40; George C. Thielman, "The Mennonite Selbstschutz in the Ukraine during the Revolution," *The New Review* 10 (March 1970):50–60.
24   Adolf Ehrt, *Das Mennonitentum in Russland* (Berlin: Julius Beltz, 1932), p. 117.
25   John B. Toews, "The Halbstadt Volost 1918–22," p. 39.
26   See, for example, Gerhard P. Schroeder, *Miracles of Grace and Judgement*, pp. 37–79.
27   According to J.G. Rempel, "Typhus," *Mennonite Encyclopedia*, 4:760, 1,500 people died in the Chortitza settlement alone.
28   Frank H. Epp, *Mennonite Exodus*, pp. 44–72.
29   Benjamin Heinrich Unruh, *Fuegung und Fuehrung im Mennonitischen Welthilfswerk, 1920–1933* (Karlsruhe: Heinrich Schneider, 1966), p. 13. For more information on Unruh's work, see Toews, *Lost Fatherland*, pp. 118–29.
30   Vernon Smucker, "Our Relief Activities," *Mennonite Year-Book and Directory*, 1922, pp. 24–30.

31 For accounts of the founding of the Mennonite Central Committee, see John D. Unruh, *In the Name of Christ: A History of the Mennonite Central Committee and its Service, 1920-1951* (Scottdale, Pa.: Herald Press, 1952), pp. 14–16; Guy F. Hershberger, "Historical Background to the Formation of the Mennonite Central Committee," *Mennonite Quarterly Review* 44 (July 1970):213–44.

32 Paul Erb, *Orie O. Miller: The Story of a Man and an Era* (Scottdale, Pa.: Herald Press, 1969).

33 Quoted in Toews, *Lost Fatherland*, p. 91.

34 P.C. Hiebert and Orie O. Miller, *Feeding the Hungry: Russia Famine 1919-1925* (Scottdale, Pa.: Mennonite Central Committee, 1929), and D.M. Hofer, *Die Hungersnot in Russland und Unsere Reise um die Welt* (Chicago: KMB Publishing House, 1924); a detailed diary of early relief work in Russia is contained in "Relief Work," *Mennonite Year-Book and Directory*, 1921, pp. 4–11; further excellent reporting on the early work of the MCC is contained in Orie Miller, "Our Relief Work," *Mennonite Year-Book and Directory*, 1923, pp. 33–37; Levi Mumaw, "Secretary's Report," *Mennonite Year-Book and Directory*, 1923, pp. 37–38; Levi Mumaw, "Our Future Relief Work," *Mennonite Year-Book and Directory*, 1923, pp. 38–39; Orie O. Miller, "Russia—One of the War's Sad Tragedies," *Mennonite Year-Book and Directory*, 1922, pp. 17–21.

35 For B.B. Janz's chronicle of the founding of the Union and its protracted negotiations to obtain a charter, see John B. Toews, ed., *The Mennonites in Russia, 1917-1930: Selected Documents* (Winnipeg: Christian Press, 1975), pp. 89–113.

36 Walter Quiring, "Unsere 'Hollanderei'—ein geschichtlicher Irrtum?" *Der Bote* 12 (20 March 1935):1–2.

37 John B. Toews, "B.B. Janz and the Mennonite Emigration," *Mennonite Life* 23 (July 1968):111–13.

38 The work of Janz is more fully presented in John B. Toews, "B.B. Janz and the Mennonite Emigration," *Mennonite Life* 23 (July 1968):111–14. See also John B. Toews, *With Courage to Spare: The Life of B.B. Janz (1877-1964)* (Hillsboro, Kans.: Board of Christian Literature, General Conference of Mennonite Brethren Churches, 1978).

39 John B. Toews, *With Courage to Spare*, p. 28.

40 *Ibid.*, pp. 28–29, 32–33.

41 John B. Toews, *Lost Fatherland*, pp. 93–94.

42 Frank H. Epp, *Mennonite Exodus*, p. 69.

43 *Ibid.*

44 A.A. Friesen, "Alt-Mexico als Siedlungsgebiet fuer Mennoniten," *Vorwaerts* 19 (18 February 1921):9.

45 Frank H. Epp, *Mennonite Exodus*, p. 60.

46 Fred Richard Belk, *The Great Trek of the Russian Mennonites to Central Asia, 1880-1884* (Scottdale, Pa.: Herald Press, 1976).

47   Frank H. Epp, *Mennonite Exodus*, pp. 81–92. See also CMCA, XXII-A-1, Vol. 1184, File 139, B.J. Schellenberg, "Aeltester David Toews: Sein Leben und Wirken," n.d.

48   Esther Ruth Epp, *The Origins of Mennonite Central Committee (Canada)* (M.A. thesis, University of Manitoba, 1980), pp. 24–5; according to the treasurer's report from 27 July 1920 to 26 December 1924, the Canadian Central Committee had contributed $57,101.86 to a total amount of $647,657.74, *Mennonite Year-Book and Directory*, 1925, p. 31.

49   Donald Avery, *"Dangerous Foreigners": European Immigrant Workers and Labour Radicalism in Canada, 1896–1932* (Toronto: McClelland & Stewart, 1979), p. 16.

50   P.C. 1203, *Canada Gazette*, 14 June 1919, p. 3825.

51   Donald Avery, pp. 90–115.

52   Act to Amend the Immigration Act, 1919, 9–10 George V, ch. 25.

53   P.C. 2930, *Canada Gazette*, 4 December 1920, pp. 2180–81.

54   P.C. 183, *Canada Gazette*, 24 March 1923, p. 4106.

55   Donald Avery, pp. 93–101.

56   *Ibid.*, p. 100.

57   *Ibid.*, p. 101.

58   During the summer of 1920 both Gerhard Ens and Peter Janzen, the latter a member of the Nebraska State Senate, hosting the Studienkommission at Janzen's Nebraska home, had asked J.A. Calder, Minister of Immigration and Colonization, to have the prohibitory Order-in-Council rescinded. CMCA, XXII-A-1, Vol. 1270, File 602. In November, H.A. Neufeld sought permission for the entry to Canada of a small group of Mennonites born in Russia but living in Germany. His request, like those of Ens and Janzen, was turned down. PAC, Immigration Branch, RG. 76, Vol. 174, File 58764, Part 6.

59   Frank H. Epp, *Mennonite Exodus*, p. 72.

60   The delegation party included A.A. Friesen of Russia, Gretna's H.H. Ewert, H.A. Neufeld of Herbert, T.M. Reesor of Markham, and Vineland's S.F. Coffman. PAC, Immigration Branch, RG. 76, Vol. 196, File 79160, Part I, Petition presented to the Department of Immigration and Colonization, 19 July 1921.

61   H. H. Ewert, "Bericht ueber die Reise der Deputation nach Ottawa," *Der Mitarbeiter* 14 (September 1921):71, 75–76.

62   PAC, Immigration Branch, RG. 76, Vol. 196, File 79160, Part I, Petition presented to the Department of Immigration and Colonization, 19 July 1921.

63   H.H. Ewert, p. 71.

64   *Ibid.*, p. 75.

65   *Ibid.*

66   The German words were: "Eine Art Propaganda zu Gunsten der Mennoniten ist eingeleitet worden." *Ibid.*, p. 75.

67   CGC, XV-1.2. A.A. Friesen to S.F. Coffman, 7 February 1922.

68   John S. Weber, "History of S.F. Coffman 1872–1954: The Mennonite Churchman" (M.A. research paper, University of Waterloo,
1975), p. 77.

69   The delegates this time included A.A. Friesen, H.H. Ewert,
Gerhard Ens, Sam Goudie, and S.F. Coffman. CMCA, XXII-A,
Vol. 1270, File 602, "A Statement and Petition of the Mennonites of
Ontario and Western Canada," n.d.

70   According to E.K. Francis, *In Search of Utopia: The Mennonites of
Manitoba* (Altona, Man.: D.W. Friesen & Sons, 1955), p. 203, the
government did not publish the Order in the *Canada Gazette* because
it did not want to arouse public antagonism. A copy of the Order is
found in CMCA, XXII-A, Vol. 1270, File 602.

71   Henry Paetkau, "Particular or National Interests? Jewish and Mennonite Immigration to Canada after World War I" (paper presented
to Canadian Historical Association, June 1979), pp. 14–15.

72   "Protokoll, der Ersten Sitzung der Canadian Mennonite Board of
Colonization," *Der Mitarbeiter* 15 (June 1922):45–46. See also
Frank H. Epp, *Mennonite Exodus*, pp. 72–76.

73   CMCA, XXII-A-1, Vol. 1184, File 139, David Toews, "Erinnerungen aus der Zeit der Russlandhilfe und Immigrationsarbeit,"
n.d., p. 12.

74   *Ibid.*, pp. 10–11; Schellenberg, pp. 44–45.

75   CMCA, XXII-A-1, Vol. 1389, File 1532, "The Mennonite Colonization Association of North America, Limited: Prospectus," n.d.

76   *Canada Gazette*, 12 August 1922, pp. 650–51.

77   James B. Hedges, *Building the Canadian West: The Land and Colonization Policies of the Canadian Pacific Railway* (New York: Macmillan, 1939), p. 2.

78   Peter L. Neufeld, "Colonel J.S. Dennis: Catalyst of Prairie Development," *The Western Producer* 12 April 1973, p. C6. See also
Frank H. Epp, *Mennonite Exodus*, pp. 107–9.

79   CPR, RG. 2, (105187).

80   *Ibid.*, Col. J.S. Dennis to Sir Thomas Shaughnessy, 31 December
1914; *ibid.*, "Decisions and Orders of the Russian Government
Regarding Mennonites in Russia."

81   *Ibid.*, J.S. Dennis to Thomas Shaughnessy, 31 August 1915.

82   *Ibid.*, A.M. Evalenko to J.S. Dennis, 7 August 1915.

83   *Ibid.*, J.S. Dennis to Thomas Shaughnessy, 31 December 1914.

84   *Ibid.*, "Position of Mennonites Affected by This Act and Conditions
Under Which They Are To Be Moved," n.d.

85   *Ibid.*, J.S. Dennis to Thomas Shaughnessy, 13 March 1916.

86   *Ibid.*, A.M. Evalenko to J.S. Dennis, 7 August 1915.

87   *Ibid.*, J.S. Dennis to Thomas Shaughnessy, 13 March 1916.

88   H.H. Ewert, "Bemuehungen der Delegation in Bezug auf den
Transport der mennonitischen Auswanderer von Russland nach
Canada," *Der Mitarbeiter* 15 (April 1922):28–9.

89   A federal government loan of $100,000, granted to the Mennonite

pioneers in Manitoba in 1875, had been repaid by 1892. See Frank H. Epp, *Mennonites in Canada, 1786-1920: The History of a Separate People* (Toronto: Macmillan of Canada, 1974), p. 226.

90   CMCA, XXII-A-1, Vol. 1271, File 608, J.S. Dennis to David Toews, 20 June 1922.

91   Such was the eulogy awarded Toews at his funeral in Rosthern on 28 February 1947. J.J. Thiessen, "I Remember David Toews (1870-1947): the Good Samaritan of his time," *The Canadian Mennonite* 15 (13 June 1967), p. 31.

92   David Toews, "Erinnerungen," p. 12.

93   *Ibid.*, p. 13.

94   CMCA, XXII-A-1, Vol. 1271, File 607, "Memorandum of Agreement," 21 July 1922.

95   CMCA, XXII-A-1, Vol. 1270, File 602, David Toews, article for publication, 20 July 1922.

96   Quoted in Frank H. Epp, *Mennonite Exodus*, p. 115.

97   PAC, Immigration Branch, RG. 76, Vol. 196, File 79160, Part I, Colonel Dennis to the Department of Immigration, 6 July 1922.

98   *Ibid.*

99   David Toews, "Immigration from Russia in the Past and in the Future," in *Official Minutes and Reports of the Twenty-fourth Session of the General Conference of the Mennonite Church of N.A., 1926*, pp. 296-99.

100   PAC, Immigration Branch, RG. 76, Vol. 196, File 79160, Part I, F.C. Blair to Gerhard Ens, 21 September 1922.

101   John B. Toews, *Lost Fatherland*, p. 98.

102   CMCA, XXII-A-1, Vol. 1307, File 848, David Toews to B.B. Janz, 29 September 1922.

103   CMCA, XXII-A-1, Vol. 1270, File 604, Chronology of events from 31 March 1922 to 12 September 1923.

104   CMCA, XXII-A-1, Vol. 1270, File 602, J.S. Dennis to David Toews, 29 September 1922.

105   CMCA, XXII-A-1, Vol. 1270, File 602, J.S. Dennis to David Toews, 30 October 1922.

106   PAC, Immigration Branch, RG. 76, Vol. 196, File 79160, Part I, J.S. Dennis to F.C. Blair, 21 November 1922.

107   John B. Toews, *Lost Fatherland*, pp. 104-6.

108   PAC, Immigration Branch, RG. 76, Vol. 196, File 79160, Part I, J.S. Dennis to F.C. Blair, 21 November 1922.

109   Quoted in John B. Toews, *Lost Fatherland*, p. 100.

110   David Toews, "Erinnerungen," p. 6.

111   *Ibid.*, pp. 16-17.

112   CMCA, XXII-A-1, Vol. 1178, File 108, P.J. Friesen and F.J. Baerg to J.S. Dennis, 15 August 1922. The Steinbach Chortitzer Church dispatched a similar letter to Dennis.

113   CMCA, XXII-A, Vol. 1178, File 108, "Press Controversy." See,

for example, "Ein Wort zur Aufklaerung," *Der Vorwaerts*, 8 December 1922.

114 See Frank H. Epp, *Mennonite Exodus*, pp. 125–31.

115 CMCA, XXII-A-1, Vol. 1174, File 75, David Toews to C.E. Krehbiel, 5 May 1923.

116 David Toews, "Erinnerungen," pp. 8, 21.

117 David Toews, "Erinnerungen," p. 19.

118 When one of the Board members advised cancelling the contract with the CPR upon hearing of Toews's unsuccessful fund-raising attempt, the latter replied: "Nein, ich glaube wir muessen den Kontrakt aufrecht erhalten. Wenn die Bewegung nicht in Fluss kommen kann, dann wollen wir uns wenigstens nicht beschuldigen muessen." David Toews, "Erinnerungen," p. 21.

119 Benjamin Heinrich Unruh, pp. 18–19.

120 The quote is contained, and the whole incident reported, in J.P. Klassen, "So kam es zur Auswanderung," CGC, XV.31.2, "1920-Immigration." Klassen later was located at Bluffton College in Ohio as a teacher of art. Cornies remained true to his conviction that he should stay in Russia, but was subsequently exiled to Siberia by the Soviets. For another personal account of "small events" that led to emigration, see H.H. Kornelsen, "Vor 43 Jahren," *Mennonitische Rundschau* 89 (9 February 1966):14, 15; (16 February 1966):6, 14; (23 February 1966):14–16.

121 Cf. William H. McNeill, *Plagues & Peoples* (Garden City, N.Y.: Doubleday, 1976), pp. 148–56.

122 PAC, Immigration Branch, RG. 76, Vol. 196, File 79160, Part I, C. Moguin to T.B. Williams, 6 July 1923.

123 PAC, Immigration Branch, RG. 76, Vol. 196, File 79160, Part I, W.R. Little to Mr. Black, 20 September 1923.

124 PAC, Immigration Branch, RG. 76, Vol. 196, File 79160, Part I, T.B. Williams to F.C. Blair, 23 July 1923.

125 CMCA, XXII-A-1, Vol. 1271, File 608, David Toews to J.S. Dennis, 8 August and 3 October 1923. See also Vol. 1270, File 604.

126 PAC, Immigration Branch, RG. 76, Vol. 196, File 79160, Part I, T.B. Williams to F.C. Blair, 11 July 1923.

127 Interview with T.D. Regehr, 25 July 1981.

128 PAC, Immigration Branch, RG. 76, Vol. 196, File 79160, Part I, T.B. Williams to F.C. Blair, 23 July 1923. One immigration official observed that "it looks as though there is going to be considerable trouble and expense for somebody in connection with the rejected people if they are even permitted to reach Germany."

129 See, for example, CMCA, XXII-A-1, Vol. 1270, File 604, W.J. Black to David Toews, 8 October 1923.

130 Frank H. Epp, *Mennonite Exodus*, p. 145.

131 Gerald M. Brown in *Saskatoon Phoenix* (July 1923).

132   Frank H. Epp, *Mennonite Exodus*, pp. 146–47.
133   H.T. Klaassen, *Birth and Growth of Eigenheim Mennonite Church, 1892–1974*, p. 41.
134   Frank H. Epp, pp. 204–12.
135   Gerald M. Brown, "Progressive Mennonites Get in Step," *Saskatoon Phoenix* (28 June 1924):13.
136   *Ibid.*
137   *Ibid.*
138   Frank H. Epp, *Mennonite Exodus*, p. 151.
139   CMCA, XXII-A-1, Vol. 1271, File 607, "Memorandum of Agreement," 5 April 1924.
140   John B. Toews, *Lost Fatherland*, p. 147–49.
141   PAC, Immigration Branch, RG. 76, Vol. 196, File 79160, Part II, A.A. Friesen to S.J. Egan, 24 September 1924.
142   For a discussion of their co-operation, see John S. Weber, pp. 73–100.
143   *Ibid.*, pp. 82–87.
144   *Calendar of Appointments*, 1921–22, p. [23].
145   *Calendar of Appointments*, 1922–23, p. [14].
146   *Ibid.*, p. [19].
147   CGC, XV-1.1, "Billeting List for Russian Mennonite Immigration," 1924.
148   "Unexpectedly Large Quota of Mennonites for County," *Kitchener-Waterloo Daily Record* (21 July 1924).
149   Frank H. Epp, *Mennonite Exodus*, p. 153.
150   *Ibid.*, pp. 158–61.
151   Frank H. Epp, *Mennonite Exodus*, p. 164.
152   GAI, 1743, Box 46, File 520, T.O.F. Herzer to S.G. Porter, Manager, Dept. of Material Resources, CPR, Calgary, 14 March 1928.
153   Jacob H. Janzen, *David Toews: Vorsitzender der Kolonisationsbehoerde der Mennoniten in Canada* (Rosthern, Sask.: D.H. Epp, 1939), p. 18.

5. Community-Building: Settlements

Our future here in Canada very definitely lies on the land and not in the city, in the final analysis, on new land, our only prospect for settling in closed communities, . . . this being our strong desire — J.H. JANZEN.[1]

A BETTER future for 20,000 immigrants required not only their successful transfer to Canada but also their permanent settlement, preferably in compact Mennonite communities, on agricultural land. Appropriate parcels of land had to be found, their purchase and equipping, mostly on credit, had to be negotiated, and new ways of farming had to be learned.[2] In the process, old Mennonite communities were strengthened, a host of new ones were founded in the five western provinces, and the whole landscape of Canadian Mennonitism was changed. Compact and closed settlements, however, were for the most part a thing of the past.

Placement of the immigrants on land was a requirement of the government as well as the express wish of most of the Mennonite people, at least until the settlement options narrowed to homesteading in the northern wilderness. There was among the immigrants yet little deviation from "*Farmer-Mennonitentum*,"[3] a Mennonite way of life which was rooted in the soil, although some important exceptions should be noted.[4] Attracted to the towns and cities were a certain

187

number of skilled and unskilled labourers and the professional people, including a small contingent of teachers and an even smaller number of doctors, who quickly sought Canadian certification by attending the appropriate schools in the cities. There were also a few families of commercial and industrial background, who located in urban environments as soon as the time was opportune. Other early city-dwellers were immigrant girls, whose employment as domestics in affluent urban homes brought much-needed cash to the family coffers back on the farm.[5]

Working for hourly wages or monthly salaries was a necessity for hundreds of the first immigrants, males as well as females, whose settlement on their own land was held up for nearly a year. Such work was sought and found on other people's farms during harvest time for five dollars per day, on the railroads for up to three dollars per day plus board, in lumber or mining camps at 35 dollars per month plus room and board, in construction at five dollars per 13-hour day, in ditchdigging at two dollars per 10-hour day, and in city factories at 15–25 cents an hour, the latter especially in Ontario.[6]

It was in Ontario where early attempts to urbanize were sharply rebuked, both by Canadian society and by the Mennonite leaders. That such attempts were made should not surprise us, given the state of agricultural opportunities and given the urbanity which the immigrants had achieved in their Russian homeland, notwithstanding the basic rural context of their existence. Prosperity and educational endeavours had given them a cultural sophistication and a manner of life more akin to town dwellers than to village peasants.[7]

Not surprisingly, the immigrants arriving in the Waterloo County area were attracted to such towns as Waterloo, New Hamburg, and Hespeler with their furniture and clothing factories. These towns and their workers could not receive them wholeheartedly.[8] On the contrary, the labour organizations and politicians made an issue of "the foreign element," as the anxious battle for jobs soon replaced the welcome which had greeted the immigrants upon their arrival. People were in no mood to let in "Germans," against whom Canada had fought in the war and whose admission to Canada was on condition that they would work on the farm, not in factories and shops. Nor were they willing to see them achieve an early prosperity at the expense of the Canadians.[9]

Leaders in the immigrant community did not wish to jeopardize Canadian goodwill and the immigration movement as such. They took note of the repeated warnings of the authorities "not to bring any more of our brethren into the cities."[10] And they repeatedly encouraged the immigrants, with only partial success, to seek agricultural opportunities either in western Canada or in the more rural parts of Ontario or, failing acquisition of their own land for one reason or another, to get jobs where this would cause less resentment.[11]

One form of "urbanization" which was not controversial was the establishment of the so-called Chicken and Garden Village on the northeast outskirts of Winnipeg, namely in the newly established municipality of North Kildonan. Some Mennonite people from rural Manitoba had settled in Winnipeg as early as 1907. The Mennonite Brethren Church had established a mission with 22 members in 1913,[12] and ministers of the Mennonite Conference had also made Winnipeg a regular preaching outpost for urbanizing Mennonites.[13] This small contingent grew rather rapidly because Winnipeg, of all the Canadian cities, got the larger portion of immigrant students, labourers, professionals, and domestics, the latter requiring the establishment of two girls' homes by the mid-1920s.[14]

The emergence of the rural-urban garden village called North Kildonan was at this time a separate development, which, however, in later years contributed much to make Greater Winnipeg the largest urban Mennonite community anywhere in the world.[15] Meanwhile, this new "subdivision," with its five-acre and one-acre lots, characterized by chicken barns and vegetable gardens, became a significant bridge for urbanizing agriculturalists, at first only few in number but reaching 100 families within a decade.[16]

The immigrants, however, were called to be not labourers or even urban gardeners but farmers, the proper Mennonite vocation in Canada. As we have seen, the agricultural precedent was a strong one. Both the Swiss from Pennsylvania and the Amish from Europe had distinguished themselves in Ontario. They were a people committed to community life as well as to "stewardship of the soil."[17] They didn't "misuse the soil" but rather "they farmed it as though they would live on it forever... using just enough of nature's resources for their own need... then replanting and replacing these resources for the common good."[18] And of the departing Mennonites in western Canada it was said by even the most severe critics of their non-assimilationist way of life:

> The Mennonites are very successful farmers. They have beautiful gardens. . . . The work is well organized and farming is carried on as a business.[19]

The departure of such excellent farmers to Mexico and Paraguay represented "a serious economic loss" since they had "been an important factor in the development of the country's resources."[20] Only by replacing these pioneers with "other farmers equally experienced and industrious" could some of this loss of Canada's "best farmers" be tolerated. The immigrants arriving in the 1920s were the right people to replace the emigrants. Their agricultural genius, too, was a matter of record, though there was much learning to be done. Not only did ministers, teachers, craftsmen, estate owners who were really "gentlemen farmers," and accountants have to learn farming again but also they had to do so in the context of the Canadian situation.[21]

Settlement Organization and Processes

Canadian agricultural opportunities in the 1920s, however, did not quite measure up to their expectations. To begin with, Canada's agricultural land was not unlimited. The prairies had filled up and the best lands had been taken,[22] though large blocks of land were being held for private sale in more profitable times.[23] The wheat economy was unstable.[24] Yet none of these adversities excused the immigrants from seeking their future on the land.

In the end, the agricultural communities of the immigrants took on many forms in several settings: there were grain farms, cattle farms, pig and poultry farms, "pulpwood farms," vegetable farms, fruit farms, tobacco farms, and, mostly, mixed farms. There were large farms and small farms. Some were destined to produce considerable wealth, others guaranteed for their owners perpetual poverty. The settings were villages in former reserve areas, the open prairies, irrigation districts, bushlands, homestead lands, and gardenlands as in the lower mainland of British Columbia and the Great Lakes regions of Ontario (Niagara Peninsula and at several points along the north shore of Lake Erie). When the settlement and resettlement process was complete, 272 settlement districts, with a total of 6,127 households or family units, had been established in Canada's five western provinces (see Table 19).

Assuming overall responsibility in this settlement process was the Canadian Mennonite Board of Colonization, which had brought the immigrants to Canada. The Board was anxious and impatient in this matter from the beginning, because the liquidation of the *Reiseschuld* (transportation debt) and the accommodation of still more immigrants depended on the immediate settlement of those arriving.[26] Immigrant interests and obligations were represented by the Central Mennonite Immigrant Committee, an organization formed at Rosthern in 1924. This central immigrant committee developed provincial chapters, and district contact persons or representatives were elected or appointed in all settlement districts as these were established.[27]

The actual agent for finding properties, bringing vendor and buyer together, and concluding a sale on terms satisfactory to both parties was the Canada Colonization Association (CCA) and its Mennonite affiliate, the Mennonite Land Settlement Board (MLSB).[28] The CCA, at this time an agency of the Canadian Pacific Railway, had its beginnings as a post-war citizens' movement, known as the Western Canada Colonization Association. Its emergence was prompted by the conviction that Western development was

TABLE 19[25]

IMMIGRANT SETTLEMENT DISTRICTS IN FIVE PROVINCES

PROVINCE	DISTRICTS	HOUSEHOLDS
Ontario	17	972
Manitoba	89	2,081
Saskatchewan	108	1,645
Alberta	43	948
British Columbia	15	481
Totals	272	6,127

not complete, there being an excess of land and railway mileage for the existing population, and that a special effort would be required to bring prospective settlers and available land together, inasmuch as it was now often a question of settling not the best land in the most desirable locations but only the second or third best. The idea was a good one, but the organization lacked the necessary strength to pursue it.[29]

For one year the Canadian Pacific Railway, the Canadian National Railways, and the federal government assumed control of the Association and underwrote the costs. When the federal government surrendered its 50 per cent share to form its own settlement branch, the CPR and the CNR assumed joint responsibility, but only for a year. The CNR withdrew to establish its own settlement association, and in that withdrawal was planted the seeds of a later competition, as the two railroads and their agencies worked on the immigration and settlement causes with different sectors of the Mennonite community.[30]

It was Col. J.S. Dennis, who had played such an important role in persuading the CPR in 1922 to contract for the transportation of Mennonite immigrants, who now urged the railway to assume sole responsibility for the Canada Colonization Association as a desirable long-term business venture even though risks and subsidies were involved in the short term. He reasoned that there were 60 million acres of unoccupied lands along existing railway lines, 25 million acres of which were fit for immediate colonization and production by immigrant families. Since much of this land was in the private hands of absentee landowners, a special agency was needed to bring the vendor and the colonist together. He calculated the economic values as follows: a family of five represented an annual worth of $1,583 to the mercantile and industrial life of Canada and $716 in railway transportation.[31]

On the strength of the Dennis arguments, the CPR agreed in 1924 to operate the Canada Colonization Association on its own. The headquarters were maintained in Winnipeg and there were branch offices in Saskatoon and Calgary. Additionally, there were about a dozen full-time district representatives, and some 200 agents, most of them working part time and on a commission basis.[32]

The CCA soon discovered that immigrants responded best to

agencies at least partly of their own making. Thus, the Mennonites were encouraged to do what the Baptists and Lutherans had already done, namely to devise a denominational settlement agency. The Mennonite Land Settlement Board (MLSB) which came into being had nine members: three chosen by the central immigrant committee, three by the Canadian Mennonite Board of Colonization, and three by the Canadian Colonization Association. A.A. Friesen, the delegate from Russia, who had already invested so much of his life in the immigration, became the manager.[33]

The operations of the MLSB were handled according to precedents already set by the CCA with similar agencies. Regional MLSB offices, as adjuncts of CCA offices, were established in CPR buildings located in such cities as Calgary, Lethbridge, Saskatoon, and Winnipeg. Mennonite agents were recruited whose duty it was to inspect lands for sale and, if suitable, to negotiate their purchase on behalf of interested immigrants. A commission of $2^1/_2$ per cent on the purchase price financed the MLSB operations.[34] This financing was done through the CCA, which advanced money for the MLSB against the commissions being collected.[35]

In other words, the MLSB was totally dependent on the CCA and appeared to exist only for the sake of a better Mennonite connection and to enable the Board to be somewhat responsible for immigrant settlement policy. Settlement operations were not really handicapped by the largely symbolic role of the MLSB, given the back-up leadership role of the CCA. However, the existence of the structure, really quite impotent, frustrated those who were involved, and the ambiguity of the situation was undoubtedly one of the reasons why Manager Friesen resigned within a few years. The nine-member Board rarely met. There was no executive. There was little interprovincial co-operation. Accounts were not paid by the MLSB, and the contracts were not sent to the MLSB for approval.[36]

In due course, an effort was made to make the operations of the MLSB more real by creating an executive with provincial subcommittees, but the manager of the CCA was a member of the new MLSB executive, and thus nothing really changed. By the end of the decade it was freely admitted that the control of the MLSB was in CCA hands, and the only objection to that state of affairs was that the MLSB should have been allowed to surrender the control voluntarily.[37] A.A. Friesen, at least, resisted the loss of control. On one occasion he told T.O.F. Herzer, the CCA manager, in no uncertain terms:

> Our Land Settlement staff is quite capable of handling the settlement work in Saskatchewan and does not need any supervision or advice from Winnipeg.[38]

As already indicated, the settlement cause did not really suffer as a result of the state of affairs, because the MLSB-CCA partnership achieved what had been intended, namely an effective settlement operation. The CCA provided knowledge, management, logistics, financing, a network of representatives, and impressive real estate listings. The MLSB provided determined and reliable clients, formal and informal advice, and for the CCA some of its best agents. Of Jacob Gerbrandt, a CCA-MLSB district representative located in Lethbridge, it was said that "a great deal of good work has been accomplished by him in that part of Alberta."[39]

Indeed, so effective was the CCA-MLSB combination that it suggested opportunities for others. Thus it happened that a "Herbert Board" emerged for a brief period as a rival settlement agency for the Rosthern Board.[40] The differences could be negotiated away, because the congregationally based group at Herbert apparently had wanted only to speed up the settlement process, which it accomplished with the successful location of eight families on 2,000 acres of land at Monitor and 12 families on leased land north of Herbert.[41] Much more serious was the founding of a "Winnipeg Board" known as Mennonite Immigration Aid.

Mennonite Immigration Aid arose in 1926 — a federal charter was obtained on June 5 — under the direction of Gerhard Hiebert, a Winnipeg physician, who became president; Heinrich Vogt, a Winnipeg lawyer formerly from Altona; Abram Janzen, a retired farmer from Gretna; John J. Priesz, an Altona insurance agent; and Abram Buhr of Morse, Saskatchewan, who moved to Winnipeg and became the Aid's chief executive officer.[42] The Aid had both immigration and settlement in mind and before too long was approaching officials of the Canadian National Railways in order to become "a CNR Organization the same as the Board [Canadian Mennonite Board of Colonization] is a CPR one."[43]

This was, of course, a misconception, a weakness, which, translated into the working assumptions of the Aid organization, was a serious handicap throughout the time of its existence. When Mennonite Immigration Aid was compared to the Mennonite Land Settlement Board, the analogy had some validity. Compared to the Canadian Mennonite Board of Colonization, however, there was little similarity. The Board was firmly rooted in several Mennonite conferences of Canada and was motivated not by business but by compassion. The Aid was set up by individuals, none of whom had either the stature of a David Toews or that kind of a connection with the church. The business motivation was seen in the first steamship contract signed with the CNR—commissions, such as the Board had not even dreamt of, were part of the deal—and in some of the first business transactions, which involved stipends and railway passes for Aid principals.[44]

The CNR had regretted for some time that all the trans-Atlantic Mennonite business had gone to the CPR, and notice had also been taken that legitimate CNR settlement business had likewise passed into the hands of the CCA of the CPR. In November of 1926 it was learned that the CCA had settled 630 families along CNR lines in the years 1924 to 1926.[45] Not to be overlooked in the whole scheme of things was the hope of the CNR to settle its trans-Atlantic passengers on its own Canadian lands.

Aware of the possibilities, the CNR had expressed its desire to do business with the old Board and for that purpose had entered into discussions with the CPR/CCA, on the one hand, and Board officials, on the other hand. David Toews was entirely open because he saw the possibility of increasing the flow of immigrants and at the same time avoiding the confusion and competition which a new agency would bring. And T.O.F. Herzer of the CCA was also inclined to co-operate with the CNR to avoid competition in the settlement process.[46] After due consideration, however, CPR officials ruled out the possibility of co-operation because the Board was so heavily indebted that it would not be doing justice to their own interest "to agree to the Old Board accepting financial responsibility to another organization."[47]

At that point, the CNR had reluctantly talked to Mennonite Immigration Aid and, to make that option more acceptable, had insisted that some people get out of Aid and that others be brought in.

The removal of H. Vogt, because of his links to other transportation companies and his business reputation, was accomplished in due course,[48] but the support of "reliable and outstanding leaders among the Mennonite people at such principal points as Altona, Gretna, Winkler, Steinbach, Herbert, Rosthern, etc." was not accomplished, though a long list of names was submitted.[49] In the end, all the business of Aid was done by a four-member "Joint Mennonite Committee," consisting of two officials from Aid, Hiebert and Buhr, and two officials appointed by the CNR.[50]

It wasn't that Aid was without tacit Mennonite support, at least from those who for one reason or another had been unhappy with the Board or Bishop David Toews from the beginning, including some people at Herbert. Indeed, it was at Herbert on July 6, 1926, soon after Aid's incorporation, where it received its greatest boost. In a resolution, the Northern [Canadian] District Conference of the Mennonite Brethren Church of North America "wished the new board success and blessing," promising the same hospitality to its immigrants as to those of the Rosthern Board but withholding "any material obligations with regard to the new board."[51]

Actually, all the material support in the world would have made little difference because, for reasons beyond either Board's control, the immigration, and consequently later also the settlement movement, was coming to an end. More than two years after Aid and the CNR signed a contract, only 123 passengers had been delivered to Canada,[52] with the result that the CNR was constantly reviewing the relationship and discovering that "the amount of Mennonite business . . . did not justify our expenditures."[53] Settlement work fared little better, because the initiative gained by the CPR in sticking with the CCA had really paid off in a steady operation with the longest listings and the most reliable agents.

Meanwhile, the competition produced much confusion reaching all the way to the Mennonite settlements in Russia,[54] but not all the effects were negative. Two of the best land inspectors to work on behalf of immigrants, J.J. Hildebrand and Arthur H. Unruh, were in the employ of the CNR settlement association. They were also great believers in homestead settlement, and thus they helped to sharpen the debate among the immigrants, as will be seen, as to which setting offered the best future — the large well-equipped farms on the open prairie, which brought great indebtedness, or the northern wilderness, which allowed settlement without many resources and, more importantly, compact communities with little outside interference.[55]

There was one other positive effect of the unwanted competition. Challenged by a rival organization, the Mennonite Land Settlement Board concluded that the time had come to promote itself more vigorously as "a settlement mechanism for the protection of Mennonite immigrants." Listing the members of the executive committee, as well as the members of the provincial subcommittees, the MLSB reminded all immigrants of its contacts in all three provinces and of its performance. Already in November 1926, 1200 families had been settled on over 300,000 acres of land.[56]

Homesteads and Villages

When it came to selecting lands for settlement, there was an immediate divergence in points of view between the immigrants and their hosts. Members of the Canadian Mennonite Board of Colonization were more in favour of the so-called wilderness lands, owned either by the government or by the railways. There were several reasons for this position.[57] Most important was the factor of financial indebtedness. The Board was concerned that the *Reiseschuld* not be preempted by other debts.

The total debt burden of the immigrants could be minimized, so the Board reasoned, if the purchase of improved lands and fully equipped farms could be avoided. And, while the cash income from the homesteads would be minimal, a good percentage of that income could be applied to the transportation debt, relatively small compared to the investments required for developed and well-stocked farms.

Another argument pointing in the direction of the homesteads was community-building. The wilderness lands still allowed for a degree of compact settlement. Such settlements were also relatively closed to the outside world, thus allowing more time for adjustment to the new environment. They would also require a greater degree of working together, and neighbours would help each other in the difficult tasks of pioneering.

The first CPR plan called for the settlement of at least 40 families in the so-called Battleford Block, adjacent to or interspersed with "old-timer" Mennonite settlers, who had already shown some interest in the area.[58] The homesteading frontier, however, was not beckoning. To be sure, the offer of 160 acres of free land in exchange for a minimal registration fee and its development over a minimal three-year period was attractive enough. But the clearing of land was difficult, and available homestead lands now tended to be distant from railways. Besides, the failure rate since the 1872 Dominion Lands Act had started the homestead program was most discouraging.[59]

Taking up the challenge of the wilderness made little sense, however, in light of the fact that improved lands appeared to be available within a short distance from their earliest and main point of disembarkation, namely Rosthern. Immediately to the south, in lands once known as the Hague-Osler reserve, the emigration to Mexico was under way. Also, one immigrant leader had inspected Doukhobor lands at Kamsack and Verigin to the east which were being vacated partly to make possible a general Doukhobor emigration to Russia.[60] Negotiations with the latter group soon fell through because Peter Verigin wanted $500,000 in cash.[61]

The former Mennonite reserve lands held some promise, however. They reminded the immigrants of their homeland, and they also required the formation of community organization, so much a part of their identity. From the Board side, the main positive feature of this prospect was that additional homes near by would be in readiness to offer hospitality to more immigrants arriving from Russia.[62] Hence, the emigration was viewed as providential, and various options had been taken on their lands in 1922.[63]

When the first immigrants arrived in 1923 these desired options could not immediately be exercised for a variety of reasons. The emigrants did not leave all at once. Indeed, their leaving stretched through the 1920s, as did the arriving of the immigrants. Additionally, those who left sold some land to those who stayed. The perennial need for Mennonites to acquire more land for marrying sons applied here as it had applied elsewhere. The bigger obstacle, however, lay in the need of those emigrating to have cash for their land to enable them to buy new acreages in Latin America. In search of such resources, contacts were made with prospective financial middlemen. Early in 1924, for instance, Board officials were ready to sign a contract with a Chicago financier, by which he would agree to finance the purchase of 50,000 acres of Old Colony lands, equipment, and stock.[64]

The Chicago financier was expected to agree quickly so that spring plantings could be planned without delay. However, no quick acceptance of the proposal was forthcoming and besides, the departure of the emigrants was also being delayed, so that particular plan and other similar scheming failed to materialize.[65] Thus, the purchase of the lands was held up until several years later. And then only with the help of a London financier were Hague lands purchased at a cost of about $20 per acre at 6 to 7 per cent. In due course, 93 families settled in the villages of Gruenfeld, Hague, Hochfeld, Neuanlage, and Schoenwiese.[66]

Actually, the first village lands to fall into immigrant hands were in southern Manitoba where the choicest of properties were located. The "Mennonite lands" there were described by land agents as "the best improved farmlands in Canada, with first-class buildings" and near excellent railway service.[67] Some farmers leaving for Mexico had sold for $75 to $100 per acre, though an average conservative value, without farm implements and stock, would have been about $65. This was favourably compared to the block of land south of Swift Current which had brought $44 per acre, there being "absolutely no comparison in the two blocks," the Manitoba block being "admittedly far superior" in every respect. In short:

> ...the proposition is the most attractive all around...in fact
> the last of its kind available, and without the possibility of a
> recurrence.[68]

It was not surprising, therefore, that these lands were coveted by the immigrants, and in the end about 191 families settled in the villages of Blumenfeld, Blumenort, Chortitz, Gnadenthal, Gnadenfeld, Hochfeld, Osterwick, Reinland, Reinfeld, Rosenort, Rosengart, and Schoenwiese. The relationship began with the rental of village lands in 1923.[69] It appears that purchases were then made without the help of the Board or other outside middlemen.

In the former East Reserve area in Manitoba a complete replacement of the emigrants with immigrants was achieved on 44,000 acres of land with the help of American financiers. These financiers incorporated in Canada the Intercontinental Company Limited and bought the land for $900,000. The company persuaded American Mennonites and Amish to purchase $100,000 worth of second-mortgage farm lien bonds through its agent Alvin J. Miller, the former director of American Mennonite Relief in Moscow. The company then proceeded to sell the land in the Arnaud-Grunthal-Niverville-Steinbach area on long-term credit at an average price of $32.50 an acre, negotiated with the help of the CCA-MLSB, to 300 families.[70] About 100 of these families made a few of the surviving villages — Chortitz, Gruenthal, and Kleefeld — in the former East Reserve area their home.

Big Farms and Mennonite Terms

While the villages were preferred settlement opportunities, those being vacated could not possibly accommodate all the newcomers. Thus, very soon the CCA-MLSB agents took a close look at a surprising number of very large farm operations for sale in all three prairie provinces. Established in the late 1800s the farms were going out of style, and their owners were anxious to sell their holdings, preferably intact, to owners who would possess them either individually or communally. The impetus to consider this possibility came from W.T. Badger, manager of the Canada Colonization Association, who reminded the MLSB after the deal with the Doukhobors fell through that such "big deals have always resulted in disappointment." As an alternative, Badger drew the Board's attention "to the colonizing of some of the large farms that are available in blocks of from 4,000 to 10,000 acres."[71]

The large farms were owned by real estate, insurance, feed, and mortgage companies, by banks, brokers, and community organizations, as well as by private individuals.[72] Many of the farms were foreign-owned. The Bean farm at Springstein, for instance, was registered in the name of F.A. Bean Canadian Properties of Minneapolis. The Big Four farm at Flaxcombe was owned by the Hon.E.J. Strutt of London, England. And the buyers of a farm at Meadows had to deal with Mr. Paley of Cape Town in South Africa.[73] Another owner of several sections was E.C. Rohrer, a St. Louis stock and bond dealer, who was one of the first to use tractors for all field operations, working them 24 hours a day for breaking, seeding, and summer fallow work. Some pulled up to five binders at one time. Another large landowner was already using an airplane for transportation in the 1920s.[74]

Among the private foreign owners was also H.L. Emmert, a rich

American banker, farmer, and realtor of Pennsylvania Dutch descent. Emmert lost a fortune in the Chicago fire, which motivated him to invest whatever he had left—his estate was valued at $33 million at the time of his death—in Canadian land. He owned thousands of acres of land around the towns of Arnaud, Fannystelle, Glenlea, Morris, Oak Bluff, Selkirk, Sperling, Springstein, St. Elizabeth, Starbuck, Union Point, and Winnipeg. Being terminally ill in 1922, he had deeded this land to a college in Iowa, which in turn set up the H.L. Emmert Land Agency to dispose of the properties in the most profitable way.[75]

One of the persons working for the Emmert foundation was Roy Erb, the son of Benjamin Franklin Erb, a Swiss Mennonite from Preston who had sold his business in 1893 in order to take up farming at Arnaud.[76] There had been other Swiss Mennonites in the region. A small group, chiefly from Johnson County, Iowa, made the St. Elizabeth area their home around 1912. While they conducted a Sunday school in the local schoolhouse, they never organized into a congregation and within a decade the settlement was extinct.[77]

The CCA and the MLSB took a hard look at these farms and suggested that they be sold not to individuals but to groups of Mennonite families. But communal land ownership was not that strong in the Mennonite tradition, at least not in the sense practised by the Anabaptist cousins, the Hutterites, who allowed no private ownership in their colonies. To be sure, the commonwealth in Russia had originated with blocks of land deeded to the Mennonites as a collective society, and the village settlements were characterized by numerous communal features, including the common pasture. But the family *Hoefe* (yards) and adjoining lands were individually held.

The large farms, however, were too large for individual purchase and too attractive to turn down without further consideration even with the requirement of communal ownership, operation, and living, at least initially. Most represented huge parcels of land, up to 5,000 acres and more, and came fully equipped. An agent's description of the Green Briar farms at Lucky Lake in Saskatchewan included the following (composite of four Green Briar farm units):

> 2880 acres, all but about 100 acres under cultivation, 61 horses, cows; one 5-room house, two 6-room houses, 1 7-room house, with cellars, bunk-houses, cisterns; wells; barns

for 14, 16, 20 and 30 horses; machinery sheds, garages, blacksmith shop, granaries, chicken houses, hog houses; 29 sets of work harnesses, 9 binders, 7 drills, 6 three-furrow disk plows, 7 drag harrows and carts, 1 six-horse disk, 3 six-horse cultivators, 11 wagons, 3 sets of sleighs, 2 fanning mills, 2 grain pickers, 1 tractor, 1 14-inch gang plow, 1 threshing machine outfit, 1 blacksmith outfit, 1 sleeping car, 1 cook car, 1 land packer, 1 Ford car. Total cost $156,000.[78]

The movement onto the large farms began with the purchase of one such farm at Harris, Saskatchewan, by 20 families, with the help of Theodore Nickel, a prosperous farmer at Waldheim. The 5,588-acre farm was owned by Wilson Bros. and was equipped with machinery, 100 head of horses, and a number of cattle and was priced at $270,000.[79] The terms of sale were formalized on behalf of the CCA by the MLSB and its lawyer in what became known as the "Mennonite Contract."[80] The "Mennonite terms" allowed for purchase of the land with buildings, equipment, and stock without cash. Payments were spread over a maximum of 15 years and were based on a half-crop payment plan. The interest on the principal was at six per cent per annum. In the event of a crop failure, the payments, with the exception of taxes and insurance, could be postponed one year.

The terms allowed the vendor to appoint his own manager for a given number of years, but they also obligated him to make additional investments prior to sale if the farm was not fully operational. The contract further required the vendor to construct additional buildings, if needed, to accommodate individual families at the time of the anticipated break-up into average individual allotments of a half-section per family. This was expected to happen in three years. Once precedents had been set and a standard contract fashioned, the purchase of such farms with or without the help of the MLSB proceeded rapidly (Table 20).

The first crop year, 1925, was a good one, permitting substantial payments not only on the land but on the *Reiseschuld* as well. The fine beginnings reduced communal conflicts to a minimum and laid the foundations for an acceptable division of the properties as soon as the families were ready for it. Good crops in the initial years made communal life acceptable, but it also speeded the desire for separate and individual family farm units. Not infrequently, the break-up was accompanied by the enlargement of the community through the acquisition of additional properties.

TABLE 20[81]

EARLY PURCHASES OF LARGE FARMS
IN PRAIRIE PROVINCES

(list limited to groups of four families or more and approximately first two years
of settlement; dashes indicate information not available)

PLACE	FARM	ACREAGE	PRICE PER ACRE ($)	FAMILIES
		A. MANITOBA		
Arnaud	Emmert	6,788	40	21
Arnaud	Emmert	640	55	4
Arnaud	Greiner	1,420	65/67	11
Arnaud	Lyman	10,720	60	44
Brunkild	–	960	50	4
Cloverleaf	Carter	2,300	–	4
Crystal City	Fyfe	1,600	45	6
Crystal City	McKittrick	1,920	45	6
Culross	National Trust	1,622	52.50/65	7
Dominion City	Lawrence	1,280	42	6
Dominion City	Linklater	500	50	5
Dominion City	Sharpe	1,380	32	6
Dominion City	Saunders	1,500	42	9
Dufrost	Emmert	1,700	40	8
Dufrost	Emmert	640	47	4
Elm Creek	Anderson	720	55	4
Elm Creek	Gryte	960	50	5
Headingly	Dr. Hiebert	1,100	70	4
High Bluff	Aikius	1,523	51	5
La Salle	Stewart	2,000	65/75	9
Lasalle	Emmert	4,956	50	19
Lower Fort Garry	–	780	60	4
McDonald	Stewart	2,000	68	6
Meadows	Strutt	9,200	–	32
Morris	Schuhman	800	50	4
Newton	McMillan	2,251	65/68	11
Newton	Sandager	2,000	50	6
Niverville	Leistikow	2,542	54	8
Osborne	Meagher and Bereman	4,428	62.50	14
Springstein	Bean	2,940	60	9
St. Adolphe	–	1,155	–	6

Table 20 continued

PLACE	FARM	ACREAGE	PRICE PER ACRE ($)	FAMILIES
A. MANITOBA continued				
St. Anne	–	800	37	7
Starbuck	Leistikow	1,200	65	7
Westbourne	Bank of Nova Scotia	1,200	50	12
Westbourne	Campbell	640	47	4
Westbourne	McMillan	1,500	40	5
Westbourne	Schroeder	1,700	55	6
Whitewater	Webb-Jones	3,000	40	9
Whitewater	Wilson	3,600	40	12
B. SASKATCHEWAN				
Bredenbury	Bean	1,600	18	4
Colonsay	Chesley	3,620	50	12
Dundurn	Meilicke	2,685	52.50	10
Dundurn	Schwager	2,080	50	15
Fiske	Burns	3,040	50	9
Flaxcombe	Big Four	8,480	50	36
Hanley	Rowse	1,600	50	5
Hanley	Sheldon	9,120	50	37
Harris	Wilson	5,586	50	25
Herschel	Lamborn	3,200	50	10
Holdfast	Ennis	3,020	45	10
Jansen	Johnson	960	45	5
Milden	Dugan	5,424	54.25	16
Swift Current	Sykes	2,720	32.50	7
C. ALBERTA				
Acme	F. Williams	800	50	4
Hussar	O. Finkbein	1,280	45	4
Hussar	O. Finkbein	1,225	35	4
Namaka	Lane	12,265	43	36
Olds	P. Burns	3,680	31	11
Provost	Blair	2,080	45	6
Sedalia	Sedalia	1,280	30	4
Sterling	Lethbridge Northern	–	–	10
Wembley	Adair	3,250	18	15
Wembley	J. Carrel	870	22	4

A most interesting and successful big farm settlement was the Lane farm at Namaka, Alberta. The George Lane tract comprised 12,265 acres, extending from the CPR station at Namaka to the Bow River, a distance of eight miles and adjoining the Blackfoot Indian Reserve on the west side. The CCA accepted an offer to colonize the land on a rental basis and by 1926, 36 immigrant families had been placed on it. In 1927, the Lane Company was ready to have the lease applied to a sale and thus the land was purchased in three separate parcels, each with 12 families, for a total price of $527,578. Payments of $75,600, $30,000, and $31,500 were made in the first three years, respectively, after which separate contracts were drawn up for the individual families already residing each on a half-section. The only misfortunes besetting the group were extremely heavy hail losses in some years and conflict with "a clique . . . who sought to boss the farm without regard for the proper authority," but who left in a body to go to another farm elsewhere, after they were voted out of power.[82]

Not surprisingly, there often were problems to be worked out.[83] The 36-family group at Big Four could never agree with the manager and foreman appointed by the vendor. At the Strutt farm, the farm group insisted that the operating expenses of $45,000 incurred by the manager for a crop value of about $100,000 were altogether too high. At the Fyfe farm, six families living in a single dwelling ended up "squabbling among themselves." At the Taylor farm, two brothers, one of whom had owned about 6,000 acres in Russia, would not agree to the operation of the farm by the vendor, even though the signed contract had specified that arrangement. At the Britton farm, lack of weed control, owing to the vendor's not supplying the necessary mower, led to foreclosure. At the Blain farm, there was disagreement over the maintenance of buildings, fences, and equipment.

Adjustments in the contracts had to be made sometimes for reasons quite beyond the control of either the buyer or the vendor, such as crop failures. At Chinook an immigrant had agreed to pay $33,600 for a farm with equipment. He had a 75 per cent crop failure due to hail in the first year and a 100 per cent loss in the second year. A 65 per cent loss in the third year was only partially covered by insurance policies held by both the vendor and the buyer.[84]

Some contracts were broken. One vendor at Rivers, Manitoba, the Imperial Life Assurance Co., requested four families on 1,280 acres to leave the farm, "which they did, giving up possession peaceably." The reasons were "partly their own fault, partly intrigue of the farm manager, and partly the disappointment of the vendor in not getting peasants for his farm."[85] By 1929, 47 families with 16 contracts, accounting for 16,371 acres valued at nearly $700,000, had surrendered their contracts.[86] Cancellations were usually the result of early crops not being adequate to meet the obligations. Some farms had been priced too high at $50, $60, and $75 an acre. According to one study of land values, $40 an acre was a good average price for farms, including buildings, equipment, and livestock.[87]

Inadequate management and farming methods also accounted for some failures. Some immigrants resisted mixed farming, and others were reluctant to adopt different methods. In the words of one observer, there was a goodly number of immigrants who "were conservative to the bones" and who turned back all the advice of agricultural experts.[88] The breakdown of communal covenants was another factor. According to MLSB Manager A.A. Friesen, "Our farmers were too individualistically oriented to operate a communal establishment for any length of time."[89] Others were no match for "the business acumen of the vendors."[90] Affected families had to make new starts elsewhere.

There were also many happy vendors, pleased with the deal they had made.[91] The Sheldon group, for instance, was expected to harvest a 100,000-bushel crop in the first year, a crop larger than any previous ones. On the McMillan farm the vendor, a president of the Milk Producers' Association, dispensed with the services of his own expert when he discovered how well the "Mennonite group had done with the cows." The Lamborn group paid off $40,000 of a $160,000 indebtedness in the first year. At Namaka, the 36 families had quickly put the land "in better shape . . . than it ever was." When all was said and done the successes were greater than the problems, because

> The purchasers farm the land in the majority of cases better than it has ever been farmed, this is because they . . . do not tackle more than they are able to farm properly.[92]

Brush Land and Dry Land

The developed lands, as a potential place of immigrant settlement on the prairies, were not unlimited and, in due course, other possibilities were looked at, among them the so-called Battleford Block, which had been rejected earlier. The Block was part of the Northern reserve, a vast area, partly prairie and partly wooded, and was owned by the Canadian Pacific Railway. At the time of the building of the CPR, the federal government had granted to the railroad company a belt of land along the track 24 miles wide on either side. To the extent that mountains or muskeg made the land unfit for settlement as in the Canadian Shield, additional blocks were granted on the prairies. Thus, the CPR obtained four large reserves of land far removed from the main track. One of these, the Northern reserve, included the Battleford, Carrot River, and North Saskatchewan River area.[93]

Now the CPR was anxious to make quarter sections available to about 100 families on "brush land terms"[94] and, as a special incentive, offered free use of the land for four years.[95] The price per acre ranged from $8 to $15, depending on the usefulness of the land for agriculture, but the payment thereof could be spread over 34 years at seven per cent interest. Minimum capital needed to make a start was $500, though this could be less if family groups shared equipment and implements.[96] And they responded, not 100 families immediately, but nearly half that number. Among the pioneers was A.A. Friesen, who resigned his position with the MLSB to take up land near Rabbit Lake. The bushland farmers built their dwellings with logs and mud-plaster and shelters for their animals with poles and straw. At the same time they proceeded to clear the land and plant their crops.

The soil was fertile, and when frosts did not interfere with a normal growing season, bumper crops of 40 bushels per acre could be expected. Meanwhile, however, the settlers faced difficult years as they cleared and broke the land, put up log buildings, and dug wells up to 100 feet deep in order to obtain fresh water.[97] As A.A. Friesen recounted many years later:

> The first years were arduous and extremely difficult. We were all very poor, and could not foresee what the eventual outcome would be, and whether or not we would ever become prosperous.[98]

Most of the Manitoba (see Table 21) and Saskatchewan (see Table 22) immigrants had settled on the big farms, but the bushlands of the Battleford Block had also made farming possible for a significant

TABLE 21[99]

IMMIGRANT SETTLEMENTS IN MANITOBA

NO.	DISTRICT	HOUSEHOLDS	NO.	DISTRICT	HOUSEHOLDS
1.	Altona	47	33.	Hochfeld	19
2.	Arnaud, Dominion City	85	34.	Holmfield	15
3.	Alexander	25	35.	Holland	3
4.	Austin, Sidney	5	36.	Kirkella	13
5.	Blumenfeld, Eichenfeld	9	37.	Killarney	10
6.	Barkfield	18	38.	Kleefeld	4
7.	Blumenort	25	39.	Lena	29
8.	Beausejour, Brokenhead,		40.	LaSalle, Domain	34
	Lowland	9	41.	Lowe Farm	8
9.	Burwalde	15	42.	Margaret, Dunrea	16
10.	Brookdale, Moorepark	13	43.	Minnedosa	5
11.	Brandon	9	44.	Manitou	59
12.	Boissevain	32	45.	McCreary	8
13.	Clearwater,		46.	McAuley	23
	Crystal City	16	47.	Morden	49
14.	Chortitz		48.	Marquette	14
	(West Reserve)	14	49.	Meadows	7
15.	Chortitz		50.	Melita, Elva, Pierson	14
	(East Reserve)	53	51.	Myrtle, Kronsgart	14
16.	Carman	8	52.	Morris	16
17.	Culross, Elm Creek,		53.	Mather	9
	Fannystelle	31	54.	Neuenburg	6
18.	Carrol, Hayfield	5	55.	Neuhorst	2
19.	Elgin	3	56.	Ninga	3
20.	Elie	11	57.	Niverville	72
21.	Foxwarren	25	58.	Newton Siding	26
22.	Fork River,		59.	North Kildonan	79
	Winnipegosis	36	60.	Osterwick	9
23.	Grande Pointe,		61.	Osborne	11
	Lorette	7	62.	Oak Bluff	13
24.	Gretna	4	63.	Oak Lake, Griswold,	
25.	Graysville	3		Henton	35
26.	Gnadenthal	34	64.	Portage la Prairie	11
27.	Gruenthal	43	65.	Pigeon Lake	19
28.	Glenlea, St. Adolphe	24	66.	Plum Coulee	11
29.	Gradenfeld	17	67.	Reinland	17
30.	Gimli, Winnipeg Beach	2	68.	Reinfeld	13
31.	Headingly	9	69.	Rivers	13
32.	Horndean	9	70.	Rapid City	11

Table 21 continued

NO.	DISTRICT	HOUSEHOLDS	NO.	DISTRICT	HOUSEHOLDS
71.	Rosenort	12	81.	Swan River	3
72.	Rosenfeld	13	82.	Spencer	13
73.	Rosengart	21	83.	Stonewall, Balmoral	10
74.	St. Elizabeth	31	84.	Starbuck	16
75.	Springstein	25	85.	St. Rose du Lac	3
76.	Schoenwiese	11	86.	Whitewater,	
77.	St. Anne	17		Mountainside	48
78.	Steinbach	61	87.	Winkler	124
79.	Sperling	18	88.	Winnipeg	280
80.	Stuartburn, Gardenton	8			

number of immigrant families. And the same was true of irrigation lands in Alberta. The agricultural potential of southern Alberta for sugar-beet growing had been noted and tested for some time. And in 1925 the $1½ million plant of the Canadian Sugar Factories was in operation for the first time.[101] Adequate quantities of water brought in by irrigation canals was one essential condition to be met. Another one, equally important but more difficult to guarantee, was the supply of the right kind of farm labour, namely "continental labourers,"[102] meaning families with a number of workers, including women and children, who could provide the hand labour required for thinning, weeding, and topping.

Once again, Mennonites seemed to be the desired people. However, they were not coming into a settlement vacuum. The landowners of the area were "English-speaking people, very conservative, and not very anxious to receive foreign settlers." They were also reluctant to plant beets, "viewing them as a risky innovation."[103] The feeling was widespread. The MacLeod Board of Trade, for instance, had also gone on record against "this class" who take "from the right kind of settler the best of our lands."[104]

Thus, the new settlement at Coaldale became a testing ground for the immigrants, in both economic and social terms. Here they had to learn, and demonstrate the profitability of, sugar-beet farming on irrigation land. Where many had failed and abandoned sugar-beet

TABLE 22[100]

IMMIGRANT SETTLEMENTS IN SASKATCHEWAN

NO.	DISTRICT	HOUSEHOLDS	NO.	DISTRICT	HOUSEHOLDS
1.	Aberdeen	27	40.	Guernsey	16
2.	Annaheim	2	41.	Gilroy	12
3.	Abernathy	1	42.	Glenbush	70
4.	Big River	2	43.	Gull Lake	19
5.	Beechy	38	44.	Glidden, Madison,	
6.	Beverley	2		Kindersley	15
7.	Blumenhof	23	45.	Gouldtown	13
8.	Borden, Great Deer	14	46.	Schoenwiese	20
9.	Braddock	4	47.	Gruenfeld	16
10.	Balgonie	1	48.	Hochfeld	18
11.	Brocking	10	49.	Hague	15
12.	Bournemouth	24	50.	Neuanlage	24
13.	North Battleford	3	51.	Humboldt	4
14.	Biggar	5	52.	Hanley	32
15.	Carrot River	12	53.	Hepburn & Mennon	47
16.	Carnduff	2	54.	Herschel	45
17.	Colonsay	12	55.	Herbert	66
18.	Cactus Lake	1	56.	Harris, Ardath	9
19.	Central Butte	6	57.	Indian Head	6
20.	Cabri	10	58.	Jansen	8
21.	Canwood	2	59.	Kelstern	5
22.	Carmel & Hillsley	3	60.	Leader	2
23.	Capasin	7	61.	Leinan	6
24.	Clair	2	62.	Lorenze	8
25.	Duff	2	63.	Laird	56
26.	Dalmeny	22	64.	Langham	25
27.	Drake	57	65.	Lost River	19
28.	Davidson	3	66.	Luseland	1
29.	Dundurn	54	67.	Lanigan	9
30.	Eyebrow, Tugaske	15	68.	Maxstone	1
31.	Eyebrow "A"	3	69.	Main Centre	23
32.	Evesham & Hacklin	6	70.	Mayfair	30
33.	Eastbrook	11	71.	Mullingar	27
34.	Elbow	12	72.	Moose Jaw	6
35.	Fleming	6	73.	McMahon	14
36.	Fiske	16	74.	Meadow Lake	5
37.	Flowing Well	6	75.	Neville	3
38.	Foam Lake	4	76.	Nokomis	4
39.	Fairholme	33	77.	Osage	2

Table 22 continued

NO.	DISTRICT	HOUSEHOLDS	NO.	DISTRICT	HOUSEHOLDS
78.	Parkerview	28	93.	Speers	10
79.	Pikes Peak	1	94.	Superb	11
80.	Parry	2	95.	Sonningdale	11
81.	Rosthern	93	96.	Schoenfeld	4
82.	Rush Lake	11	97.	St. Boswells	5
83.	Ruddell	2	98.	Swan Plain	1
84.	Rabbit Lake	45	99.	Tompkins, Stone,	
85.	Regina	13		Carmichael	4
86.	Rosetown	5	100.	Truax	14
87.	Sheho	10	101.	Tessier	2
88.	Scottsburg &		102.	Viscount & Young	3
	Neidpath	4	103.	Waldheim	47
89.	Saskatoon	50	104.	Wymark	13
90.	Swift Current	17	105.	Watrous	38
91.	Swift Current		106.	Wishart	5
	(Syke's Farm)	17	107.	Wingard	3
92.	Springwater	10	108.	Wilkie	2

farming as a lost cause, they had to prove that it could be done. At Coaldale, also, the immigrants discovered that peaceful coexistence with their new Canadian neighbours would require effort by both parties. Fortunately for the Mennonites, they had strong leadership in the aforementioned CCA-MLSB representative, Jacob Gerbrandt, and from 1926 on in B.B.Janz.[105]

Area farmers were "converted" to growing sugar beets when the chairman of the newly created Irrigation Farms Colonization Board turned over his land together with horses, stock, and equipment to four families, including the enterprising Klaas Enns.[106] Enns was given the opportunity to purchase a farm, valued at $53,000, without down payment or written contract. The only condition required of Enns was that he sell 150 acres' worth of beets annually under the name of the vendor until the farm was paid for. Enns accepted the offer and, together with three of his brothers and their families, settled on the land in 1926. They, and others who followed, soon proved themselves. In the words of a CPR official:

> We have demonstrated in the Coaldale district the possibilities
> of developing irrigable land by the aid of Mennonites and the
> sugar-beet industry. Our experience is showing a way to the
> successful development of all the irrigable areas in Southern
> Alberta, the Eastern Section included. [107]

Very soon, the authorities developed schemes to bring in more
immigrants by providing 80-acre parcels of land at $40 to $60 per
acre and $400 worth of building material to be paid for from the
annual proceeds of 10 acres of crop. These settlement provisions,
known as sugar-beet contracts, became normative for land purchased
from the CPR as well as from private landowners.

The CPR prided itself on the "excellent colony established on a
good foundation."[108] But good prospects could not hide the difficult
struggles of the sugar-beet growers. They had arrived penniless,
without previous experience in irrigation and beet-growing, and
more often than not the lands they were taking over were run down
and badly infested with weeds.[109] They had to be taught sugar-beet
farming and that it was wise "to get beets out of the ground even in
snow and not to wait until snow was gone, lest the ground [and the
beets!] be frozen hard."[110]

In spite of their handicaps and problems, they were successful in
evoking jealousies among their neighbours sufficient to create what
was called "the Mennonite situation at Coaldale." A public Coaldale
meeting, sponsored by the United Farmers of Alberta, brought the
question out into the open. According to Janz, never one to mince
words or to avoid colourful speech, the meeting had to do with
"Hogs and Mennonites," how to import a new breed of the former
and how to export or deport the latter. Actually, the concern was only
to prevent further expansion of the settlement.[111]

The immediate occasion was community discontent over the
teaching of German and Religion in the small local schoolhouse on
Saturdays, for which the school trustees had given official approval.
The centre of opposition was the local congregation of the newly
formed United Church of Canada, which, needing larger facilities,
had made a deal with the local school trustees. The congregation
began to meet in the big schoolhouse and subsequently turned its own
smaller building over to the trustees, who needed additional classroom space to accommodate the children of the immigrants. The

Mennonites then sought and obtained permission from the school trustees to conduct their own Sunday worship service in the smaller building and special Saturday school classes in German and Religion. Resenting this latter use of *their* building, the United congregation announced a prohibition, which the local police then enforced.[112]

All of this had to be justified, of course, and so word spread through the community that the Mennonites were responsible for veterans and renters leaving the community because they could not compete with the newcomers. And more of the exploiting immigrants were on their way. A statistic of four families just arrived became 29 families, instead of 29 persons, and rumour had it that 60 more families were destined for Coaldale.[113]

The UFA meeting gave public expression to the resentment. Both the CPR and the Mennonites were criticized for bringing in people with tuberculosis, children thus infecting other children. They were blamed for a nearly tenfold increase in land prices compared to the prices 15 years earlier, and for the slave-like use of their women and children. Other people wanted land too, it was argued, but they could not obtain it because it was being kept for the Mennonites. They were even granted an acre of land for a cemetery before the soldiers were satisfied. What was the worst, though, was that these people wanted to enjoy all the privileges of a good country but do nothing to defend it. At that point, B.B. Janz rose to his feet and gave a defence of "war service," which, he said, had involved 11,000 men from a population of approximately 100,000 in Russia:

> Following the war it had been statisically confirmed that the percentage of Mennonites who died in action was larger than that of the Russian soldiers actively engaged. The Mennonites are not afraid to suffer or to die in fulfilling their duty.[114]

The events served to give an outlet to community feeling but also provided the Mennonites with an opportunity to explain themselves, something which they did thereafter in an ongoing way through their own committee and B.B. Janz, the provincial immigrant leader, and with the help of Jacob Gerbrandt, the CCA-MLSB representative stationed in Lethbridge. They also wasted no opportunity to express publicly their gratitude for their new homeland, as will later be seen. Their best long-term public relations lay in their contributions to the local economy, though local jealousies arising from immigrant prosperity were not easily set aside. A booming high-quality sugar-beet industry — in three years sugar content increased from 14.5 per cent to 18 per cent, and manufactured sugar increased from 75,000 bags to 100,000 bags[115] — in the end benefited the whole community. More importantly, irrigation farming in what was known as the Eastern Section was much encouraged as a result of the Coaldale experiment. Settlement there thus far had not been an unmitigated success, and in 1924 the Canada Colonization Association was confronted by mass abandonment of the land. To prevent this, interest and water rental accruals were written off, the contract price of dry land was reduced from $25 to $10 per acre, and some irrigable land, valued at $50 per acre, was reclassified as non-irrigable owing to seepage or the accumulation of alkali.[116]

For the settlement, or resettlement, of the so-called Eastern Section irrigation lands in the West Duchess, Rosemary, Countess, and Gem districts, the Canada Colonization Association devised the 100-family settlement scheme, of which immigrants took full advantage. The scheme called for settling individual families on quarter sections, of which at least 120 acres would be irrigable, and advancing them an average of $1,000 worth of equipment, feed, and lumber, on the assumption that the settlers themselves would have sufficient cash for household equipment plus a necessary 25 per cent down payment on four cows. The farms would each have a building, and the purchase price of about $5,000 would be paid on a sharecrop basis. A three-year farming program, worked out in advance and carefully supervised by competent men responsible to the CCA and the CPR's Department of Natural Resources, guided the settlers from unnecessary error and ensured reasonable profits from the outset.[117]

Peace River and Reesor

Another Alberta frontier was the Peace River country in the north. The completion of a Canadian National Railways branch line into Grande Prairie set the stage for settlement into the Central Peace River district by 1930 of 35,000 settlers, 630 of them Mennonites.[118] The attraction of the Peace River area was high-lighted by the 1926 bumper wheat crop, and the award a Peace River farmer won for his prize-winning wheat at the 1926 Chicago

International Fair.[119] Farmers had threshed as much as 60 bushels per acre, this being Marquis wheat. The land was remarkably free of wild oats, and there were no other noxious weeds "except a few small patches of 'twitch.' "[120]

The immigrants were not the first Mennonites to enter the Grande Prairie region, though their coming represented the more permanent presence. The Bear Lake district, northwest of Grande Prairie, had in 1917 and 1918 attracted a small community from the U.S.A., seeking refuge in the remote Canadian hinterland from American military conscription.[121]

Immigrant groups made brave starts at Crooked Creek, southeast of Grande Prairie, and westward at La Glace and Lymburn, bringing to 43 the number of settlement districts in Alberta (Table 23). Both the quantity and the quality of the land gift was generous. Homesteaders paid a $10 registration fee, not for a quarter section, but for 320 acres of very fertile farmland capable of enormous crop yields if the growing season was not cut short by frosts.[123]

The wider interest in the Peace River area coincided with the formation of Mennonite Immigration Aid in association with the CNR and with the emigration from Manitoba to the Paraguayan Chaco, and so, not surprisingly, there were those who felt that the isolation of Canada's northland might be a better settlement option than the troublesome Chaco, where those arriving now had "many boils all over their bodies."[124]

Among those lobbying for a turnaround, on the part both of governmental authorities and of the Mennonites, was C.W. Reimer, an unusual individual who was, according to his letterhead, "a dealer in high grade sewing machines and repairing of all kinds." A man of many interests and experiences, Reimer had already led a land-seeking delegation to Nicaragua in 1916.[125] He also spoke French and "during the many days of big-game hunting with half-breeds our conversation was in French only." He had also been on a 600-mile canoe trip with a sailor looking for land in western Canada.[126]

Reimer claimed to be working in the interests of both "our people" and "our powerful empire." After all, was it not a service to the government to keep noncombatant Mennonites and their millions of dollars, plus the taxes they would pay, in Canada? Dollars the "empire" had to have because without money the "empire" could not make use of its brave soldiers.[127] Besides, the "peace-loving, dili-

TABLE 23[122]

IMMIGRANT SETTLEMENTS IN ALBERTA

NO.	DISTRICT	HOUSEHOLDS	NO.	DISTRICT	HOUSEHOLDS
1.	Acme	12	23.	La Glace	35
2.	Beaverlodge	16	24.	Lymburn	23
3.	Blue Ridge	7	25.	Monitor	4
4.	Coaldale	255	26.	Munson & Drumheller	7
5.	Crowfoot	17	27.	MacLeod	5
6.	Chinook	4	28.	New-Brigden,	
7.	Carstairs	20		Sedalia, & Naco	25
8.	Castor	14	29.	Namaka	38
9.	Coronation & Lake		30.	Olds	9
	Thelma	7	31.	Provost	15
10.	Calgary	30	32.	Paradise Valley	2
11.	Countess	28	33.	Peoria	1
12.	Didsbury (Burns		34.	Pincher Sta.	2
	Ranch)	17	35.	Rosemary	81
13.	Didsbury (Town)	7	36.	Rimbey	1
14.	Duchess & Brooks	15	37.	Sunny Slope	15
15.	Edmonton	1	38.	Swalwell	14
16.	Grassy Lake, Tabor, &		39.	Springridge	10
	Purple Springs	20	40.	Tofield	51
17.	Gem	48	41.	Vauxhall	25
18.	Glenwoodville	12	42.	Wembley	35
19.	Hussar I	1	43.	Willow Creek,	
20.	Hussar II	5		Rosedale, & East	
21.	Irma	5		Coulee	1
22.	Lacombe	8			

gent, industrious, and quiet farmer" helped to build the "empire" as much as the soldier. Canadian history was witness to the fact that there were ways other "than mere guns" to build an "empire." After all:

When the British soldiers had fought and brought victory on the Plains of Abraham, [they] were conquered by the French girls that they married, who changed them all to French, except their names. . . . [128]

Apparently, C.W. Reimer was not a man for the CNR, to which organization he made his boldest suggestions. He was brushed aside with the railway's claim that it was not in the business of transporting people from one province to another. However, only two weeks later, the Canadian National Settlement Association was co-operating with another group whose interests would have precisely that effect, namely the transporting of hundreds, perhaps thousands, of Mennonites from Manitoba to Alberta. It was too late to stop the movement to Paraguay, but there were others in southern Manitoba, not of the immigrants, who took a great interest in the prospects of the Peace River district. While there were a number of individuals and groups who embarked on inspection tours,[129] none brought as much attention as the 1927 early summer delegation sponsored in part by some congregations in Manitoba and the newly organized Mennonite Immigration Aid.[130]

The interests of the delegation were very similar to those that had prompted thousands to establish a new home in Latin America, namely an exclusive block of land — about 15 townships of homestead land — and special concessions in education. There was a difference, however, in the latter matter. Those looking to the north were prepared to run their schools under certain government rules and regulations and under the supervision of a government inspector.[131]

There was no fear of pioneering once again, but the hopes of the delegation were not realized, with respect to either education or appropriate parcels of land.[132] As they made a thorough investigation of vast areas beginning with territory north of Lesser Slave Lake and moving on to Peace River Town — an overland trip to Fort Vermilion did not materialize — then to areas both east and west of Grande Prairie, and including also stretches along the Peace in British Columbia, they could not find exactly what they wanted. Everywhere they found reasonably successful pioneers, but none of these could show them the paradise they were hoping to find.[133] Nowhere did they find an area to their liking because one of the following essential ingredients was always lacking: a large exclusive land area or reasonably good soil or open prairie with only a minimum of bushland or reasonable prices.

The Gundy Ranch along the Peace in British Columbia at first looked the most attractive. There were over 30,000 acres, 1,000 of them already under cultivation, available at $20 an acre. Reluctantly,

J.J. Hildebrand, the field secretary of Mennonite Immigration Aid and leader of the delegation, concluded that "the buyers after a year of hard work would be deeper in debt than at the beginning."[134] The railway was 90 miles distant, and the earnings would not be sufficient to cover land costs, production costs, and taxes. The disappointment was great, and he and others could not easily forget Peace River country — until the dream was realized, at least partially, in the 1930s. Hildebrand also looked longingly at land occupied by Indians:

> The Indians have their reserve of land, but as they do not engage in farming, the question was raised whether these Indians could be given a reserve of land in some other place, and their present reserve be divided into homesteads. In case the rest of the land should be taken up, then it would be time to raise that question officially.[135]

Holdeman Mennonites were the next group to establish themselves in the Peace River district.[136] For them, the move to Crooked Creek in the late 1920s was the beginning of a steady, ever-expanding colonization in the Central Peace River area. Fifteen families signed up for 22 quarter sections, including 1,400 acres under cultivation, at $18 per acre, to be paid on a half-crop share basis at three per cent interest in the first year, four per cent in the second year, and six per cent thereafter.[137] The main sources of the Holdeman settlers were the communities at Swalwell and Linden, Alberta. Other sources were Manitoba, Kansas, and Oregon. This mixing of settlers, including those of both Swiss and Dutch ethnic origins, in every new community established by the Holdeman people contributed to the relative strength of the congregations, which, because of their isolation and closedness, were constantly in danger of losing that vitality. The Holdeman settlers also experienced all the troubles of pioneering. According to their own chronicles:

> Many homesteaders' possessions consisted of a saw, hammer, axe and a grub-hoe. Some of them even had a team of horses, a walking plow, harrows, and a cow or two. . . . In the early years of the settlement, the market and the doctor, being 45 miles away, took 3 to 4 days to make the return trip with horses. These horses were also the source of farm power. On Sunday many people would walk to church services and let the horses have a rest.[138]

A fascination similar to the attraction of the Peace River country in the west was in the east focused on northern Ontario, more precisely "the great clay belt on the Hudson Bay slope" which, when cleared, "will be one of the largest farm districts of the world."[139] The clay land, it was said, was very productive, and the Experimental Farm at Kapuskasing, 70 miles west of Cochrane, had proven this by successfully growing oats, peas, barley, clover and timothy, potatoes, turnips, mangels, sunflowers, strawberries, raspberries, and many kinds of vegetables. Additionally, the north was cattle country, though an abundance of wolves made sheep-raising quite hazardous, one wolf being known to have killed as many as 18 sheep in one attack! Bees did well in the north, gathering as much honey as 16 pounds per day per hive![140]

The new land of milk and honey did not require a large investment because plots of land were available on homestead terms. As an inducement to northern settlement, the provincial government offered homestead sites of 75 acres at 50 cents an acre. The property could be registered for only ten dollars and the buyer was given three years to pay off the balance. An immediate cash return lay in the cutting of pulpwood. The Spence Falls Pulp and Power Company was spending five million dollars to enlarge its pulp mill in Kapuskasing in order to serve the growing American demand.

Being pressured by both the CPR and Mennonite leaders to leave the cities so as not to create ill will among workers in a tight labour market, those immigrants who had remained in Ontario agreed to investigate the possibility of establishing a colony, accompanied by a CNR Land Settlement official, and by Thomas Reesor, a Swiss lay leader from Pickering who had done so much for the immigrants since the arrival of the Ontario group in July 1924. Following Reesor's advice, they agreed to start a settlement, provided a railway siding could be built to facilitate, primarily, the marketing of freight. Jacob H. Janzen, a prominent immigrant leader, who viewed virgin lands as the best settlement prospect all along, encouraged them:

> Here masses of our people can, through industry and perseverance, establish their own homes in which they will actually be their own masters, and do not have to sell themselves into the hands of others through the accumulation of great debts.[141]

More compelling yet than the promise of cheap land was the chance to build, with a minimum of outside interference, a community in the tradition of the commonwealth in Russia. The government stood prepared to award significant concessions to the settlers agreeing to reserve homesteads bordering the immediate community for exclusive Mennonite use in the future. "This is very good," one settler explained, "for it permits the possibility of closed settlements and the exclusion of other nationalities. In time, a colony could be built here after our own wishes."[142]

The creation of a community of this kind could only become a reality after difficult years of pioneering struggle and privations. People recognized the extreme nature of the sacrifices required for northern living, and in June 1925 only seven families showed themselves ready to challenge the wilderness. The pioneers selected timbered land in Eilber and Barker townships on both sides of the CNR line, 103 miles east of Cochrane. The nearest town was Mattice, located seven miles to the east. Hearst, 23 miles to the west, served as the regional headquarters. The stopping-off point was the newly built railway siding, which appropriately was named after Thomas Reesor.

The establishment of the Reesor settlement was one of the most difficult undertaken anywhere in Canada by the immigrants. There were no roads, not even trails, and all the supplies—bags of potatoes and flour, as well as building supplies like doors, window glass, and roofing—had to be carried by the people on their backs from the railway siding to their lots up to two miles away "because pack horses cannot pass through the brush on account of the muskeg."[143] Besides, maintaining horses and livestock was a very expensive proposition, feed costing about 35 dollars per ton and a team of horses as much as 500 dollars.

And yet progress was made because the settlers were not easily discouraged and they possessed other "pioneering qualities of a very high nature."[144] Although few of the settlers had any previous experience in bush work, they quickly became "remarkably proficient with the axe," and the buildings which they erected of logs were a "credit to old experienced axe men."[145] Pulpwood was plentiful and one man in a long day could cut up to two cords at four dollars a cord net. Some settlers were ingenious and skilled enough to manufacture their own tools, including a stump puller.

The CNR tried to be accommodating—though Thomas Reesor's request for a Caterpillar was rejected—by allowing more trains to stop and by building an immigrant shed at the siding, which doubled as a place of meeting and worship. And the provincial government assisted in the provision of a school and a teacher. After an inspection tour, Arthur H. Unruh was most optimistic about the permanence of the settlement and about its ongoing vitality.[146]

There were facts to support his optimism. By the fall of 1928 there were 226 persons on 55 homesteads in the settlement. There were 10 teams of horses, 17 cows and 1 bull, and 10 goats, including an essential male. A total of 35 acres had been cleared, the stumps had been pulled, and one farmer alone had planted 300 strawberry plants, 250 raspberry bushes, 20 gooseberry bushes, and 50 currant bushes, plus two apple trees.[147]

For both Unruh and Hildebrand, as well as Mennonite Immigration Aid and the CNR Land Settlement officials, Reesor was a badly needed boost for their cause. Soon they were promoting Reesor as a place where the immigrants could be their own bosses, free of debt, and "more contented and better off than the majority of the Mennonites who have taken up improved, equipped farms at high prices."[148] To the editor of the *Mennonitische Rundschau* Unruh wrote that he did "not notice the discouraged and embittered spirit which, I regret to say, is so frequent amongst the newly settled Russian Mennonites."[149]

For J.J. Hildebrand the prospects were even better.[150] He saw the possibility of a vast colony for hundreds of families emerging north of Mile 103, and all that was needed was an 18-mile railway spur to bring in settlers' effects and to haul out cordwood.[151] However, the CNR was not quite persuaded. Its own superintendent of land settlement viewed Hildebrand's reporting as "more favourable than the circumstances of the settlers justify" because much of the land was low and swampy.[152]

As the matter became a public debate in the press, officials of the Rosthern Board and their supporters entered into the fray. "Many of the newcomers were cheated," said D. Paetkau, "and are now bitterly disappointed."[153] H.B. Janz visited the settlement and wrote about economic hardships, especially for large families lacking able-bodied men.[154] One "J.P.F." passed on the criticism received from two girls who had told him:

I am not going back. I do not like it there. Six days of the
week we look like men. We have to dress ourselves like men
for the work in the bush. Only on Sundays we are able to dress
ourselves like girls.[155]

The pessimists too were justified in their thinking. The transition
from cutting pulpwood to agriculture was proving to be very
difficult. Some poorly motivated settlers had been attracted by the
glowing promotions and were only a burden to the hard-working
ones already there. The CNR was not sufficiently supportive. One of
its biggest mistakes was to withdraw the railway pass from Jacob H.
Janzen, the colony's spiritual advisor, and, as one of the great
believers in Reesor, a strong encouragement to the brave pioneers.
When he stayed away, the families started having second thoughts,
especially when they heard of the expanding possibilities in southern
Ontario.[156]

Gardens, Orchards, and Dairies

Elsewhere in Ontario three regions attracted immigrants, sufficiently strongly, in terms of appeal and numbers, to develop permanent settlements, although there was a great deal of moving to and fro
from community to community, from factory to farm and back
again, and between Ontario and the west as the immigrants pursued
the best opportunities for themselves on the basis of reports and
rumours. It was not until the depression of the prairie economy in the
1930s that Ontario became fully accepted and popular as a place of
permanent settlement.[157]

The Waterloo County region, especially the urban environs of
Hespeler, New Hamburg, Kitchener, and Waterloo, did retain or
regain a goodly number of immigrant labourers, in spite of local
opposition. Some immigrants started their own businesses or purchased farms ranging from 5 acres to 100 acres at prices from $50 to
$200 per acre as soon as their reputation and credit had been
established and the necessary down payments could be made. Vegetable crops, corn, chickens, beef cattle, and dairy cattle were the
sources of income.[158]

The Essex County region and Pelee Island in Lake Erie, the
southernmost parts of Ontario, attracted immigrant families en
masse — 31 families in the spring of 1925 alone — because of earning

possibilities in factories in Windsor and other towns and because of the great demand for labour on vegetable and tobacco farms best provided by families. The island settlement looked so promising that the CPR colonization department soon took an option on half of the island's arable land in order to establish a larger colony for the Mennonites.[159] For the Mennonites the isolation represented by the island had considerable appeal.

Both on the island and on the mainland the farm owners frequently found themselves without an adequate source of reliable farm workers. Thus, the American owners of Pelee Island land welcomed Mennonite sharecroppers, who earned enough from the wheat, vegetable, and tobacco farms to pay their *Reiseschuld* in the first year. The same was true in the Leamington and Harrow areas, where more than 50 families purchased farms ranging from 25 to 100 acres at prices from $100 an acre to $1,000 an acre, while others were renting or sharecropping. The raising of tobacco presented a problem, but so pressing were economic considerations that those who abhorred tobacco-growing accepted it as a necessity of life.[160]

The Vineland-Beamsville area, where Swiss Mennonites had also hosted immigrants and introduced them to work in orchards and factories, became the gateway to a very substantial Mennonite penetration of the peninsula in later years. Here also the cash and credit earned enabled the gradual purchase by groups of families of sizeable orchards. The communal approach reminded the immigrants of their native villages in Russia, and names like Memrik, Schoensee, and Steinbach were applied to the jointly held properties. In the peninsula, as on the prairies, the communal approach was of short duration, mostly because the individual immigrant families soon discovered that they could make it on their own.[161] When the settlements throughout Ontario had stabilized, there were 972 households in 17 districts (Table 24).

The beginnings of larger-scale and permanent Mennonite settlement in British Columbia occurred in February 1928, when the Crain and Eckert Company, owning 700 acres of land between the Vedder River and Vedder Mountain in the Yarrow area of the Fraser River Valley, began to sell the land in approximately 10-acre lots at $150 per acre.[163] Purchasers were paying $200 down and the balance $20 per acre yearly at six per cent interest. Initially, the families had some income from working in the hop gardens about four miles away

TABLE 24[162]

IMMIGRANT SETTLEMENTS IN ONTARIO

NO.	DISTRICT	HOUSEHOLDS	NO.	DISTRICT	HOUSEHOLDS
1.	Baden	12	10.	Pelee Island	22
2.	Dunnville	22	11.	Port Rowan	36
3.	Gormley	4	12.	Reesor	57
4.	Hamilton	5	13.	Toronto	29
5.	Hanover	3	14.	Vineland	123
6.	Hespeler	13	15.	Virgil	119
7.	Kitchener	177	16.	Waterloo	62
8.	Leamington	230	17.	Windsor	20
9.	New Hamburg	38			

or in sawmills, logging camps, and brickyards. At the same time, they began to cultivate their plots of land, experimenting alternately with sugar beets, green beans, rhubarb, and strawberries, but eventually settling on raspberries as the most promising crop. In two years, 46 families had made their home in the Eckert block and an additional 20 families on adjoining half-acre plots.[164] In addition to the economic opportunities, the settlers found the climate very agreeable.[165] The available land at Yarrow was soon exhausted and so Eckert directed others to the Stamersley Valley at Agassiz, where he assisted in the acquisition of land from his own holdings, from the Soldiers' Settlement Board, and otherwise.[166] Twenty-two families made Agassiz their home, and, on the assumption it was permanent, they built a church in 1930. However, land prices turned out to have been too high for what the farms could produce, and within five years the Agassiz settlement was no more.[167]

Another attractive piece of land was a 746-acre tract of land in the South Sumas District near Yarrow, owned by the Northern Construction Company. This was selling in 20-acre units at $115 per acre. A down payment of five per cent was required with the balance payable in 20 years at seven per cent. A committee of Yarrow settlers undertook the responsibility of settling the block.[168]

In the Abbotsford area, settlement began on sections of land cleared of timber but not of stumps.[169] In 1932, the Abbotsford Lumber Company had completed logging operations on a large tract of land west of Abbotsford between the U.S. border and the Matsqui Valley. The area had been divided into 20-, 30-, and 40-acre lots, which were selling at auction beginning at $10 per acre, with 25 per cent down. What could not be sold by auction was turned over to a local real estate agent for ongoing sale. Stumps covered the area, but between and among the stumps cattle could be raised and strawberries could be grown, thus providing food and income while the huge stumps were blasted one by one from their deep underground anchors and the fields were cleared. The opportunity attracted Mennonites from Agassiz and Yarrow as well as from the prairies, and before long Abbotsford-Clearbrook was challenging Yarrow as the most attractive centre.[170]

Besides berry-growing, dairy farming presented itself as a distinct agricultural opportunity in the Fraser Valley. After an inspection tour, CCA-MLSB representative A.W. Klassen reported that one farmer with 32 inferior cows, some of them giving as little as 5 pounds per day and none over 40 pounds, was none the less grossing $30 a day from these cows. Another, milking over 70 cows a day, showed a daily profit of $50 from retail milk sales. The demand for table cream, milk, and butterfat led Klassen to conclude "that a good dairy man in any part of this district within reach of Vancouver can do exceptionally well."[171] Dairy farming and berry-growing, supplemented by work in hop gardens and lumber camps, became the economic base for ever-expanding settlements, 15 in all, including one on Vancouver Island (Table 25).

TABLE 25[172]

IMMIGRANT SETTLEMENTS IN BRITISH COLUMBIA

NO.	DISTRICT	HOUSEHOLDS	NO.	DISTRICT	HOUSEHOLDS
1.	Abbotsford	120	8.	Cranbrook	1
2.	Agassiz	10	9.	Hutchison	1
3.	Armstrong	6	10.	Oliver	6
4.	Arrowhead	4	11.	Red Rock	1
5.	Black Creek	29	12.	Renata	2
6.	Coglan – Langley		13.	Sardis	82
	Prairie	18	14.	Vancouver	40
7.	Cottonwood	1	15.	Yarrow	160

Also in British Columbia, the immigrants pursued the dream of a large, compact, and reasonably exclusive settlement. A 7,000-acre fertile plot of reclaimed, but inadequately drained, marshland in the Pitt Meadows area held some promise in this regard, but the several attempts made to build a strong settlement faltered because drainage and transportation problems were never satisfactorily solved.[173] Some isolated areas of Vancouver Island held a similar appeal, and a small but permanent settlement took root on the east coast at Black Creek, south of Campbell River, where employment in pulp mills and logging camps provided cash while small plots of land were cleared for dairying and berry crops.[174]

The successful placement on land of so many immigrants was cause for rejoicing, but almost everywhere the settlers faced all the hardships of pioneering on new land, many difficult adjustments and many tears. As a leader of the Gem settlement recalled:

> So they came to Gem: landless, homeless, moneyless, saddled with debt, strangers to language and culture, "peculiar" in religious beliefs, quaint, and poor in dress, desiring a home of their own and a means of making a livelihood for themselves and their families.[175]

Hard work was the order of the day, but so was the co-operative effort. The break-up of the communal farms did not mean the end of community. On the contrary, the interdependence of neighbours became the greater reality as the individual households struggled not so much to compete with each other on a single farm as to help each other out on their respective individual farms in order to provide all that was necessary to keep the families fed, clothed, sheltered, and healthy.[176]

Fostering the communal spirit were the local immigrant committees, the provincial immigrant organizations, and the inter-provincial Central Immigrant Committee. But quite probably no other community experience contributed as much to the essential sustenance of the settlers as did the local congregation, which, since the days of Anabaptist beginnings, had provided the social fellowship and the spiritual faith for a people who, wherever they went, could not live by bread alone.

FOOTNOTES

1 J.H. Janzen, "Siedlungsmoeglichkeiten in Ontario," *Der Bote* 2 (25 November 1925): 2.

2 CMCA, XXII-A-1, Vol. 1176, File 89, "Bericht der Siedlungs-behoerde ueber die Provinz Saskatchewan, auf der Sitzung des Zentralen Mennonitischen Immigrantenkomitees, am 3ten und 4ten Juli 1929 in Rosthern, Sask." See also Isaak Klassen, *Dem Herrn die Ehre: Schoenwieser Mennoniten-Gemeinde von Manitoba, 1924 – 1968* (Winnipeg: First Mennonite Church, 1969), p. 60.

3 Isaak Klassen, p. 116.

4 John Friesen, "Manitoba Mennonites in the Rural-Urban Shift," *Mennonite Life* 23 (October 1968): 152 – 58.

5 Frank H. Epp, *Mennonite Exodus* (Altona: D.W. Friesen & Sons, 1962), pp. 185 – 86.

6 *Ibid.*, pp. 184 – 85. Herbert Enns of Waterloo remembers his father working in a button factory for 15 cents an hour. Those in furniture or rubber-product factories got a little more, up to 38 cents an hour before the 1920s ended.

7 David G. Rempel, "The Mennonite Commonwealth in Russia: A Sketch of its Founding and Endurance, 1789 – 1919," *Mennonite Quarterly Review* 48 (January 1974): 42 – 43.

8 Hank Unruh, *Of Days Gone By: History of the St. Elizabeth District* (St. Elizabeth, Man.: St. Elizabeth Mennonite Community Centennial Reunion Committee, 1970), p. 91.

9 Henry Paetkau, "A Struggle for Survival: The Russian Mennonite Immigrants in Ontario, 1924 – 1939" (M.A. thesis, University of Waterloo, 1977), pp. 41 – 43.

10 "Das Problem der Anhaufung von Immigranten, welche von den Farmen nach Kitchener gehen, soll vor dem Immigrationsminister gebracht werden," *Der Bote* 5 (11 January 1928):2; "Protokoll einer ausserordentlichen Sitzung des Kitchener-Waterlooer Immigrantenkomitees am 23. Januar 1928," *Der Bote* 5 (8 February 1928): 2.

11 D.E., "Ein wohlgemeintes Wort an die mennonitischen Arbeiter in den Fabriken Ontarios," *Der Bote* 3 (22 September 1926): 1. See also Henry Paetkau, pp. 44 – 46.

12 J.A. Toews, *A History of the Mennonite Brethren Church* (Fresno, Cal.: Board of Christian Literature, General Conference of Mennonite Brethren Churches, 1975), p. 162.

13 J.G. Rempel, *Fuenfzig Jahre Konferenzbestrebungen, 1902 – 1952* Vol. 1 (n.p., n.d.), p. 141.

14 H.S. Bender, "Girls' Homes," *Mennonite Encyclopedia*, 2:521 – 22. See also "Die Mennoniten in aller Welt," *Mennonitische Volkswarte* 1 (January 1935):9.

15 Leo Driedger, "Canadian Mennonite Urbanism: Ethnic Villagers or Metropolitan Remnant?" *Mennonite Quarterly Review* 49 (July 1975): 226.

16   *Fiftieth Anniversary of the Mennonite Settlement in North Kildonan*
      (Winnipeg: Anniversary Book Committee of the Mennonite
      Churches, 1978), pp. 13-40.

17   See John A. Hostetter in Foreword to *The Amish of Canada*, by
      Orland Gingerich (Waterloo: Conrad Press, 1972), p. 10.

18   CBC-TV on "The Plain People," 18 March 1973.

19   Robert England, *The Central European Immigrant in Canada*
      (Toronto: Macmillan of Canada, 1929), pp. 73-76.

20   GAI, 1743, Box 44, File 506, Arturo J. Brainiff, Mexico, "An
      Equitable Plan for the Resettlement of Mennonite Lands in Can-
      ada."

21   Isaak Klassen, pp. 4-5.

22   Robert England, *The Colonization of Western Canada* (London: P.S.
      King & Son, 1936), p. 70.

23   James B. Hedges, *Building the Canadian West: The Land and Coloni-
      zation Policies of the Canadian Pacific Railway* (New York: Macmil-
      lan, 1939), p. 351. The federal Department of Natural Resources
      estimated land held by speculators to be about twice that actually
      occupied.

24   Vernon C. Fowke, *The National Policy and the Wheat Economy*
      (Toronto: University of Toronto Press, 1957), p. 285.

25   CMCA, XXII-A-1, Vol. 1170, File 55, "Liste der Dis-
      triktmaenner des mennonitischen Immigrantengruppen in Mani-
      toba," 18 October 1937; ". . . in Saskatchewan," 18 October 1937;
      ". . . in Alberta," 22 July 1937. See Epp, pp. 305-6, for data on
      Ontario and British Columbia.

26   Frank H. Epp, *Mennonite Exodus*, pp. 183-202.

27   *Ibid.*, pp. 203-17.

28   *Ibid.*, pp. 188-89.

29   GAI, 1743, Box 82, File 646, "Address by Col. J.S. Dennis on the
      Occasion of the Opening of the New Premises for the Canada
      Colonization Association," 6 June 1927.

30   PAC, RG. 30, Canadian National Railways Records Related to
      Mennonite Immigration Aid.

31   GAI, 1743, Box 82, File 646, "Address by Col. J.S. Dennis."

32   *Ibid.*

33   David Toews, "Bekanntmachung," *Der Bote* 1 (13 August 1924): 4;
      Epp, pp. 188-89.

34   GAI, 1743, Box 82, File 644, Minutes of Executive Committee,
      Canada Colonization Association, 16 June 1925.

35   GAI, 1743, Box 82, File 643, Minutes of Board of Directors, 16
      December 1924.

36   GAI, 1743, Box 121, File 1165, "Memorandum Covering Pro-
      posed Reorganization, Mennonite Land Settlement Board."

37   GAI, 1743, Box 121, File 1164, W.R. Dick, Calgary, to T.O.F.
      Herzer, Winnipeg, 20 May 1930.

38 CMCA, XXII-A-1, Vol. 1170, File 47, A.A. Friesen to T.O.F. Herzer, 25 February 1926.

39 GAI, 1743, Box 113, File 1055, "Memorandum."

40 According to David Toews, some people at Herbert held the view that immigration work had begun there rather than in Rosthern, because the delegation from Russia had been helped across the border at Portal and because its first meetings had been conducted at Herbert. CMCA, XX-II-A, Vol. 1184, File 139, David Toews, "Erinnerungen aus der Zeit der Russlandhilfe und Immigrationsarbeit von David Toews," p. 2.

41 GAI, 1743, Box 82, File 644, Manager's Report to CCA Executive Committee, 2 June 1925. See also CMCA, XXII-A-1, Vol. 1289, File 743, Minutes of Mennonite Land Settlement Board, 4 June 1925.

42 PAC, RG. 30, Vol. 5632, File 5163-6.

43 PAC, RG. 30, Vol. 5632, File 5163-6, Arthur H. Unruh to F.J. Freer on "Annual Meeting of Mennonites at Rosthern, Saskatchewan," 10 December 1929.

44 PAC, RG. 30, Vol. 5632, File 5163-6.

45 PAC, RG. 30, Vol. 5632, File 5163-6, "Memo of Discussion with T.O.F. Herzer," 10 November 1926.

46 PAC, RG. 30, Vol. 5632, File 5163-6, F.J. Freer, "Memorandum of a meeting re: Mennonite Immigration," 12 April 1927.

47 PAC, RG. 30, Vol. 5632, File 5163-6, Memo re: "Mennonite Situation," 13 July 1926.

48 PAC, RG. 30, Vol. 5632, File 5163-6, Letter to Mennonite Immigration Aid, 13 August 1927. A close relative of H. Vogt informed the author on 16 March 1981 that he, Vogt, was always "into something," that with him "there was always an angle," and that he was debarred for a time.

49 PAC, RG. 30, Vol. 5632, File 5163-6, Dan M. Johnson to Mennonite Immigration Aid, 26 November 1926.

50 PAC, RG. 30, Vol. 5632, File 5163-6, "Memorandum of Agreement between Mennonite Immigration Aid and Canadian National Railways," 2 February 1927.

51 PAC, RG. 30, Vol. 5632, File 5163-6, J.J. Hildebrand, "Report on My trip to Herbert, Sask.," 7 July 1927.

52 PAC, RG. 30, Vol. 5632, File 5163-5, "Summary of Business Under Mennonite Agreement to March 20, 1929."

53 PAC, RG. 30, Vol. 5632, File 5163-6, J.S. McGowan to W.J. Black, 3 November 1928.

54 David Toews, "Wanderungen: Eine Erklaerung," *Mennonitische Rundschau* 50 (2 November 1927): 4; PAC, RG. 30, Vol. 5632, File 5163-6, F.J. Freer to David Toews, 21 September 1927; Arthur H. Unruh to F.J. Freer on "Annual Meeting of Mennonites at Rosthern, Saskatchewan," 10 December 1929.

55   The author bases the assessment of Unruh and Hildebrand on an examination of the records and the excellent reports filed by these men based as they were on thorough field work.

56   "Die Siedlungsbehoerde (Mennonnite Land Settlement Board)," *Der Bote* 3 (24 November 1926): 10.

57   CMCA, XXII-A-1, Vol. 1286, File 722, A.A. Friesen to W.T. Badger, Canadian Colonization Association, Winnipeg, 5 November 1923.

58   In the correspondence, reference is made to "Old Colony Mennonites," but Colony, here and in subsequent paragraphs, refers to Mennonites of the older settlements, namely the non-immigrant community, and not, as could be assumed, to those conservative Mennonites more commonly referred to as Old Colony, of whom so many had gone to Mexico in the 1920s. See GAI, 1743, Box 44, File 506, Colonel J.S. Dennis correspondence from September to November of 1924; GAI, 1743, Box 44, File 506, W.J. Gerow, CPR Land Agent, to P.L. Naismith, Manager, Department of Natural Resources, 4 January 1926.

59   Frank H. Epp, *Mennonite Exodus*, pp. 187–88.

60   GAI, 1743, Box 44, File 506, W.J. Gerow to P.L. Naismith, 4 September 1923.

61   CMCA, XXII-A-1, Vol. 1286, File 722, A.A. Friesen to W.T. Badger, 21 June 1924.

62   *Ibid.*, 14 November 1923.

63   Frank H. Epp, *Mennonite Exodus*, p. 186.

64   CMCA, XXII-A-1, Vol. 1176, File 89, David Toews and A.A. Friesen to F.J. Webster, Chicago, 21 January 1924.

65   See, for example, 27 May 1924 Board proposal to Morris Ginsburgh of Winnipeg to mediate the purchase of 40,000 acres at $32 an acre. CMCA, XXII-A-1, Vol. 1288, File 725.

66   CMCA, XXII-A-1, Vol. 1170, File 55, "Liste der Distriktmaenner der mennonitischen Immigrantengruppen von Saskatchewan," 18 October 1937.

67   GAI, 1743, Box 44, File 506, "Mennonite Lands," n.d.

68   *Ibid.*

69   Peter D. Zacharias, *Reinland: An Experience in Community* (Altona: Reinland Centennial Committee, 1976), pp. 222–25.

70   GAI, 1743, Box 82, File 646, T.O.F. Herzer, "Report to the Directors of CCA," 21 June 1926; Frank H. Epp, *Mennonite Exodus*, pp. 196–97.

71   CMCA, XXII-A-1, Vol. 1286, File 722, W.T. Badger to Canadian Mennonite Board of Colonization, 23 June 1924.

72   CMCA, XXII-A-1, Vol. 1289, File 743, examples included the following: A.J. Hansen & Co., Prince Albert, an investor in farm mortgages; J.H. Speers & Co., Saskatoon, a feed and seed company; E.H. Crandell, Calgary, a real estate company; R.M. Buchanan Co

Ltd., a broker; Eriksdale Settlers' Committee, Eriksdale, a community organization. A number of the large American landowners are listed in Unruh, p. 17.

73   GAI, 1743, Box 82, File 643, "Memorandum re: Mennonite Settlement Since the Inception of the Mennonite Land Settlement Board, August 1924," n.d.

74   *Ibid.*, p. 17.

75   Hank Unruh, pp. 13, 17–18. See also J.P. Dyck, *Das 25-Jaehrige Jubilaeum der Springsteiner Mennonitengemeinde, 1938–1963* (Springstein, Man., 1963).

76   [Peter R. Harder]. *Arnaud Through the Years* (1974), p. 163.

77   L.J. Burkholder, *A Brief History of the Mennonites in Ontario* (Markham, Ont.: Mennonite Conference of Ontario, 1935), p. 135.

78   CMCA, XXII-A-1, Vol. 1286, File 722, A.E. Love, Canadian Colonization Association, to Mennonite Land Settlement Board, 17 November 1924.

79   CMCA, XXII-A-1, Vol. 1288, File 725, newspaper clipping is from *Saskatoon Phoenix*, entitled "Wilson Bros. Dispose Of Harris Holdings For About $270,000."

80   Frank H. Epp, *Mennonite Exodus*, pp. 189–190.

81   GAI, 1743, Box 82, File 643, "Memorandum re: Mennonite Settlement Since the Inception of the Mennonite Land Settlement Board, August 1924," n.d.; GAI, 1743, Box 125, File 1224, "List of Settled Families in the Province of Alberta in 1926."

82   GAI, 1743, Box 164, File 1667, "Mennonite Settlement at Namaka."

83   GAI, 1743, Box 82, File 643, "Memorandum re: Mennonite Settlement Since the Inception of the Mennonite Land Settlement Board, August 1924," n.d.

84   GAI, 1743, Box 121, File 1172, "Memorandum: Foster-Schmidt, Chinook," 25 August 1930.

85   GAI, 1743, Box 82, File 646, T.O.F. Herzer, "To the Directors, CCA," 18 May 1926.

86   CMCA, XXII-A-1, Vol. 1176, File 89, "Bericht der Siedlungsbehoerde ueber die Provinz Saskatchewan, auf der Sitzung des Zentralen Mennonitischen Immigrantenkomitees, am 3ten und 4ten Juli 1929 in Rosthern, Sask."

87   CMCA, XXII-A-1, Vol. 1176, File 89, "Bericht ueber die Taetigkeit der Siedlungsbehoerde in der ersten Haelfte des Jahres, 1929." A 1925 dispatch lists prices for unequipped farms in Manitoba ranging from $53/acre for 1200 acres purchased by 5 families in Starbuck area to $75/acre for a 720-acre farm in St. Agatha area. See CMCA, XXII-A-1, Vol. 1290, File 744, Winnipeg Office of Canada Colonization Association to A.A. Friesen, Rosthern, Sask., 5 March 1925.

88   CMCA, XXII-A-1, Vol. 1176, File 89, "Bericht ueber die Tae
      tigkeit der Siedlungsbehoerde in der ersten Haelfte des Jahres
      1929." Still further evidence of such resistance on the part of som
      to learn new ways is provided in CMCA, XXII-A, Vol. 1176, Fil
      89, Minutes of Mennonite Land Settlement Board, 22 Februar
      1928.

89   Quoted in Lawrence Klippenstein, "A.A. Friesen," in *Mennonit*
      Memories: Settling in Western Canada, ed. Lawrence Klippenstei
      and Julius G. Toews (Winnipeg: Centennial Publications, 1977)
      p. 200.

90   Isaak Klassen, p. 27.

91   GAI, 1743, Box 82, File 643, "Memorandum re: Mennonit
      Settlement Since the Inception of the Mennonite Land Settlemen
      Board, August 1924," n.d.

92   GAI, 1743, Box 113, File 1058, W.R. Dick to Manager, Roya
      Bank of Canada, Gleichen, 2 March 1927.

93   James B. Hedges, *Building the Canadian West: The Land an*
      Colonization Policies of the Canadian Pacific Railway (New York
      Macmillan, 1939), pp. 34–46.

94   GAI, 1743, Box 44, File 506, W.J. Gerow to P.L. Naismith, 1
      June 1926.

95   GAI, 1743, Box 44, File 506, minutes of 71st meeting of th
      Advisory Committee of the Department of Natural Resources an
      the Department of Colonization and Development, 14 Januar
      1926.

96   GAI, 1743, Box 44, File 506, T.O.F. Herzer to Frank Schultz
      Winnipeg, 3 January 1926.

97   CGC, XV.31–2, "1920-Rabbit Lake." The "Diary of Theodor
      and Katharine Klassen" contains much detail on settlement prob
      lems in the brushlands area.

98   Quoted in Lawrence Klippenstein, pp. 200–1.

99   CMCA, XXII-A-1, Vol. 1170, File 55, "Liste der Di
      triktmaenner der mennonitischen Immigrantengruppen in Man
      toba," 18 October 1937.

100   *Ibid.*

101   GAI, 1743, Box 46, File 520, "Progress of Sugar Production i
      Southern Alberta," 14 April 1928.

102   GAI, 1743, Box 85, File 689, James Colley, Assistant Superir
      tendent of Colonization, CPR, "Memo re: Mennonite Settlement i
      the Coaldale District," 14 October 1926.

103   *Ibid.*

104   "Fear Influx from Central Europe to Southern Alberta," *Letl.*
      bridge Herald, 4 September 1927.

105   GAI, 1743, Box 46, File 520, T.O.F. Herzer to S.G. Porter
      Manager, Dept. of Material Resources, CPR, Calgary, 14 Marc
      1928.

106 An expanded account of Coaldale's beginning is found in Aron Sawatzky, "The Mennonites of Alberta and Their Assimilation" (M.A. thesis, University of Alberta, 1964), pp. 105–6.

107 GAI, 1743, Box 45, File 515, James Colley memo, 1 September 1926.

108 GAI, 1743, Box 45, File 515, James Colley memo, 23 August 1926.

109 GAI, 1743, Box 121, File 1172, J. Gerbrandt, "Mennonite Settlement at Coaldale," n.d.

110 GAI, 1743, Box 45, File 515, J. Gerbrandt to S.G. Porter, 12 November 1927, and S.G. Porter to J. Gerbrandt, 30 November 1927.

111 GAI, 1743, Box 46, File 520, B.B. Janz to T.O.F. Herzer, 16 March 1928.

112 *Ibid.*, 10 March 1928.

113 *Ibid.*

114 GAI, 1743, Box 46, File 520, B.B. Janz to T.O.F. Herzer, 16 March 1928. In one sense, the Janz claim was somewhat exaggerated, at least in terms of how it could have been understood by his audience. While there were about 12,000, not 11,000, enlisted in state service, no more than half of these were in war-related medical services, the balance being in the forestry service. See Guy F. Hershberger, "Nonresistance," *Mennonite Encyclopedia*, 3:901.

115 GAI, 1743, Box 46, File 520, "Progress of Sugar Production in Southern Alberta," 14 April 1928.

116 GAI, 1743, Box 36, File 436. Minutes, Advisory Committee of the Department of Natural Resources and the Department of Colonization and Development, 31 May, 1924.

117 CMCA, XXII-A-1, Vol. 1287, File 723, Committee Report on "100-Family Scheme," Brooks, Alberta, 20 September 1928.

118 Even without fertilizers, the land in the Peace River area is capable of oat yields of 110 bushels to the acre and barley yields of 60 to 70 bushels per acre. Frank H. Epp, "The True North: Land of Milk and Honey Not Without Its Bitterness," *Mennonite Reporter* 4 (29 April 1974): 9.

119 GAI, 1743, Box 121, File 1164, A. Klassen, "Reisebericht," 9 September 1927.

120 PAC, RG. 30, Vol. 5631, File 5163–1, J.J. Hildebrand, "Homestead Lands," June 1927.

121 Frank H. Epp, "The True North: The Church That Disappeared, Whose Influence Lives On," *Mennonite Reporter* 4 (18 March 1974): 11.

122 CMCA, XXII-A-1, Vol. 1170, File 55, "Liste der Distriktmaenner der mennonitischen Immigrantengruppen in Alberta," 22 July 1937.

123 Robert England, p. 178.

124 PAC, RG. 30, Vol. 5631, File 5163 – 1, C.W. Reimer, Steinbach, to Dan M. Johnson, CNR, 30 April 1927.

125 C.W. Reimer, "Unsere Landbesichtigungsreise nach Nicaragua," *Steinbach Post* 3 (22 November 1916):1; 3 (29 November 1916):2; 3 (6 December 1916):1; 3 (13 December 1916):1; 3 (20 December 1916):3, 6; 3 (27 December 1916):6.

126 PAC, RG. 30, Vol. 5631, File 5163 – 1, C.W. Reimer to Dan M. Johnson, 30 April 1927.

127 *Ibid.*

128 *Ibid.*

129 PAC, RG. 30, Vol. 5631, File 5163 – 1, Peter Buhr, Altona, to J.J. Hildebrand, Winnipeg, 14 July 1927, and N.S. McGuire, CNR Department of Colonization, to F.J. Freer, Winnipeg, 28 July 1927; GAI, 1743, Box 113, File 1053, G. Sawatzky, Calgary, to P. Thiessen, Saskatoon, 18 May 1927; PAC, RG. 30, Vol. 5631, File 5163 – 3, "Memorandum to Mr. Freer re: P.K. Derksen," 22 February 1929. See also CMCA, XXXI-24, Vol. 674, "A Petition of the Mennonite termed 'Sommerfelder Gemeinde' to the Dominion Government" based on 4 August 1926 meeting.

130 PAC, RG. 30, Vol. 5631, File 5163 – 1, A. Buhr, Mennonite Immigration Aid, Winnipeg, to F.J. Freer, 13 May 1927. One of the settlers was a Swiss Mennonite from Ontario.

131 PAC, RG. 30, Vol. 5631, File 5163 – 1, J.J. Hildebrand, "Report on My Trip with the Delegation of the Bergthaler Congregation."

132 "Mennonites Seeking Alberta Farm Lands," *Manitoba Free Press*, 26 May 1927; PAC, RG. 30, Vol. 5631, File 5163 – 1, J.J. Hildebrand, "Homestead Lands," June 1927. See German version of this article in *Mennonitische Rundschau* 50 (22 June 1927):7 and 50 (29 June 1927):7. Also printed in *Steinbach Post* 14 (22 June 1927):1 and (6 July 1927):5. Related articles are Klaas H. Friesen "Auf der Reise nach dem Peace River Tal," *Mennonitische Rundschau* 50 (13 July 1927):5; J.J. Hildebrand, "Schulfrage," *Mennonitische Rundschau* 50 (29 June 1927):2.

133 PAC, RG. 30, Vol. 5631, File 5163 – 1, J.J. Hildebrand, "Report on My Trips to the Mennonite Settlements East and West of the Red River, later part of April and first part of May 1927."

134 PAC, RG. 30, Vol. 5631, File 5163 – 1, J.J. Hildebrand "Homestead Lands," June 1927.

135 *Ibid.*

136 Frank H. Epp, "The True North: The Holdeman People Form Strong Communities," *Mennonite Reporter* 4 (13 May 1974):9 Sawatzky, p. 108.

137 GAI, 1743, Box 82, File 646, Minutes of CCA Executive Committee, 4 March 1926.

138 *History of the Congregations of the Church of God in Christ, Mennonite* (Ste. Anne, Man.: Gospel Publishers, 1975), pp. 215 – 1

139 PAC, RG. 30, Vol. 5631, File 5163 – 4, Thomas Reesor, "Narrative of My Experience in Starting the Mennonite Settlement at Mattice," 25 May 1927.

140 *Ibid.*

141 Henry Paetkau, "A Struggle for Survival: The Russian Mennonite Immigrants in Ontario, 1924 – 1939" (M.A. thesis, University of Waterloo, 1977), p. 48.

142 *Ibid.*, p. 48 – 49.

143 PAC, RG. 30, Vol. 5631, File 5163 – 4, J.J. Hildebrand, "Mennonite Homestead Colony, Mattice, Ontario," 2 September 1927.

144 PAC, RG. 30, Vol. 5894, File 19, F.J. Freer, "Report on Mennonite Settlement at Reesor," 2 February 1928.

145 *Ibid.*

146 PAC, RG. 30, Vol. 5631, File 5163 – 4, Arthur H. Unruh to F.J. Freer, 20 June 1928.

147 PAC, RG. 30, Vol. 5631, File 5163 – 4, Heinrich G. Enns to A.H. Unruh, 18 October 1928.

148 PAC, RG. 30, Vol. 5631, File 5163 – 4, F.J. Freer to W.J. Black, 15 December 1927. See also A.H. Unruh, "The Mennonite Settlement at Reesor," 2 February 1928, and A.H. Unruh to Heinrich G. Enns, 16 December 1927.

149 PAC, RG. 30, Vol. 5631, File 5163 – 4, A.H. Unruh to Herman Neufeld, 21 December 1927.

150 J.J. Hildebrand, "Die Neue Ansiedlung," *Mennonitische Rundschau* 50 (14 September 1927):4 – 5.

151 PAC, RG. 30, Vol. 5631, File 5163 – 4, J.J. Hildebrand, "Report of J.J. Hildebrand Second Trip to Mile 103," 19 October 1927.

152 PAC, RG. 30, Vol. 5631, File 5163 – 4, F.J. Freer to W.J. Black, 20 September 1927.

153 D. Paetkau, "Aus dem Leserkreise: Zur Steuer der Wahrheit," *Mennonitische Rundschau* 51 (18 January 1928): 8.

154 H. B. Janz, "Wie ich North Ontario fand," *Der Bote* 4 (30 November 1927): 1.

155 J.P.F., "Wanderungen: Noch einmal Nord, Ontario," *Mennonitische Rundschau* 50 (21 December 1927): 8.

156 PAC, RG. 30, Vol. 5631, File 5163 – 4, J.H. Janzen to A. Buhr, 7 April 1927; File 5163 – 4, H.G. Enns to A.H. Unruh, 12 December 1927.

157 Henry Paetkau, pp. 57 – 79.

158 Jacob H. Janzen, "Siedlungsmoeglichkeiten in Ontario," *Der Bote* 2 (2 December 1925): 1.

159 "CPR is Promoting Colony of Mennonites Pelee Island Centre," Toronto *Star* (2 February 1929):1, 2.

160 Henry Paetkau, p. 59; Jacob H. Janzen, "Siedlungsmoeglichkeiten in Ontario," *Der Bote* 2 (25 November 1925): 2 – 4.

161 Henry Paetkau, pp. 67 – 74.

162   Frank H. Epp, *Mennonite Exodus*, p. 306.

163   CGC, XV-31.2, "1930-British Columbia," J.C. Krause, "Wie einmal angefangen;" *ibid.*, "Protokoll der Provinzialen Vertret versammlung der mennonitischen Siedler in British Columbie abgehalten in Yarrow und Sardis, 9-10 November 1934."

164   GAI, 1743, Box 116, File 1102, P. Thiessen, "The Yarr Settlement," 25 April 1930. See also P. Thiessen, "Etwas uel British Columbien."

165   GAI, 1743, Box 116, File 1102, T.O.F. Herzer, to H Loughran, Assistant Superintendent of Colonization, CPR, V: couver, B.C., 1 November 1928.

166   John Jacob Krahn, "A History of Mennonites in British Columb (M.A. thesis, University of British Columbia, 1955), pp. 25-:

167   CGC, XV-31.2, "1930-British Columbia," Abe Stobbe, "1 Agassiz Settlement," February 1975.

168   GAI, 1743, Box 116, File 1102, P. Thiessen, "South Sur District," 25 April 1930.

169   H.J. Willms, *Die Sued-Abbotsford Ansiedlung, Abbotsford, B.* *Historischer Bericht* (n.p., [1955]), p.7.

170   CGC, XV-31.2, "1930-British Columbia," Abe Stobbe, "1 Story of God's Dealings with the South Abbotsford Churc October 1975; *ibid.*, "Autobiography of Abraham J. Stobbe Abbotsford, B.C.," 19 May 1976.

171   GAI, 1743, Box 116, File 1102, A.W. Klassen, "Memorandur 18 June 1928.

172   Frank H. Epp, *Mennonite Exodus*, p. 305.

173   CMCA, XXII-A-1, Vol. 1292, File 756, G. Sawatzky, ": Besiedlung des Landes in Pitt Meadows in B.C.," n.d.

174   John Jacob Krahn, pp. 33-34.

175   J.P. Doerksen, ed., [*Gem*] *Mennonite Brethren Church, 192 1979* (Gem, Alta.: Gem Mennonite Brethren Church, 1979), 10.

176   J.P. Doerksen, p. 16; Hank Unruh, pp. 106-7.

6. *Community-Building: Congregations*

The greatest and most beautiful thing about church membership is the mutual sharing, caring and being cared for. It should be that way in the church that members of the same body serve each other, promote each other's welfare, that they feel and suffer along with the pains of individual members — DANIEL LOEWEN.[1]

An integration with the established local Mennonite churches was out of the question. The common desire to worship God with one's own people and their distinct peculiarities became more and more pronounced — HERBERT P. ENNS.[2]

THE WIDELY scattered settlements of the immigrants, and indeed of all Canadian Mennonites, reinforced their traditional dependence on the *Gemeinde*, the local congregation, as the ongoing source of that faith and culture without which they saw no meaningful future for themselves or for their children. In the 1920s, as four centuries earlier, the congregations stood at the centre of Mennonite identity, activity, and history, not only because so many new ones were established at this time, but also because they represented to the people the spiritual salvation and social security to be found nowhere else.[3] Where there was no local congregation there was no Mennonite community.

In the congregation, the Mennonites found their identity, their social status in the community, and their fellowship. Since they shunned secret societies, and all kinds and places of worldly amusements, the church and its activities was also the centre of their social life.[4] The face-to-face primary relationships cultivated in the congregational community and the mutual caring contributed to group solidarity, which was a strong resource in time of need and effective resistance against the encroachments of modern culture.[5] For Mennonites, brotherhood and intimate caring for one another were of the essence of church life. As Robert Friedman has written:

> . . . the real dynamite in the age of the Reformation . . . was this that one cannot find salvation without caring for his brother. . . . This interdependence of men gives life and salvation a new meaning.[6]

Every Mennonite congregation was a relatively complete social institution, with a clearly identified leadership and a well-defined membership. The expectations and roles of both the leaders and the members were understood on the basis of traditional teaching and practice. The ministers, led by an elder or bishop, a leading minister, or a pastor, were the preachers and teachers of the Word. They met the spiritual need and gave moral direction. The deacons had the special task of attending to any physical needs, such as extreme poverty or family deprivation arising from illness or death, which individuals or families were unable to handle alone. Most family events—weddings, funerals, anniversaries—were also congregational events, which had a bonding effect in the community and which gave a sense of belonging to individuals and their families.

The place of the congregation in the life of every Mennonite was understood without a written constitution, or so it had been in the past, but the times were changing. Immigration and new settlement patterns represented breaks in continuity, which meant that a common understanding had to be arrived at in a new way. The preparation and acceptance of a congregational constitution was the way in which many immigrant congregations established the basis for their new life together. The typical document outlined the foundations of the congregation, the conditions of membership, the duties of membership, the discipline, the election and duties of the leaders and, quite possibly, also conference affiliation.[7] It began with a scriptural motto, such as "Bear one another's burdens, and so fulfi the law of Christ," found in the Epistle to the Galatians.[8] The "doctrines and truths of the Bible" were established as the foundation for faith and the guide for the Christian life of the church members The constitution might commit the local congregation to work hand in hand with the appropriate Canadian and North American conferences.

The essential conditions of membership were identified as baptism upon confession of faith (the form of baptism might be specified), the evidence of a Christian lifestyle, commitment to nonresistance, and perhaps also the refusal to swear an oath. Voting privileges might be spelled out to include both sexes or only men. While traditionally the brotherhood meeting included only the men, a transition was under way and some congregations already included the women. The importance of women also having the vote was defended and explained at one session of the Conference of Mennonites in Central Canada by one immigrant elder who acknowledged that his position might seem strange to some.[9] He argued that there were many single women, widows or single persons otherwise, who were heads of their households and actively involved in the work of the congregation and of the kingdom of God. There was no basis in Scripture "for keeping our sisters from participating in the election of church workers." Besides, it was the women in many families who were the source of religious life, who understood the needs of the congregations better than the men, and whose knowledge and assessment of people equipped them better to elect church workers than many men.[10]

The membership responsibilities specified in a constitution included attendance at the worship services as regularly as possible, advancement of the spiritual life through prayer and work, and attendance at the service of holy communion, which could be held as often as the congregation desired. The constitution would probably specify whether or not members of other congregations could be admitted to the communion. Some congregations were very restrictive, limiting participation to particular membership, modes of faith, and forms of baptism. Others were so liberal as to allow "visitors" to participate even in congregational discussions.

A constitution also specified procedures for the discipline of wayward members, usually a two-step process according to an interpretation of Matthew 18:15–17. The first step involved loving admonition by the elder or a minister, quite possibly in the presence of other ministers or members. When this admonition failed in the desired effect, the case was brought for decision to the entire congregation, which could vote for excommunication. In practice, some congregations resorted to this ultimate step very reluctantly and only rarely, while others considered strict disciplinary measures an essential mark of congregational spirituality and a necessary feature of congregational integrity.

Churchly communities of like-minded people were, of course, not the only institutional anchor of the Mennonites in the turbulent twenties. Not to be overlooked were the families themselves, usually larger than the average Canadian family, and in economic, social, and religious ways — many practised their own worship service in the home — more self-sufficient than most. Indeed, congregations had the character of extended families, partly because blood relatives tended to congregate in specific geographic localities and partly because the two institutions were in the Christian typology analogous and in the daily functioning of Mennonite society quite interdependent.

If the congregation was undergirded, on the one hand, by that smaller social entity known as the family, it was also strengthened, on the other hand, by the larger Mennonite world known as the conference. Measured by later standards, none of the Canadian conferences had yet attained institutional maturity, but they were growing in importance. They existed only partly for their own sake and mostly for the purpose of providing the congregations with those connections and resources which helped them, if they were weak, to survive, and, if they survived, to become strong.

In the two decades of this history, 1920 to 1940, the number of Mennonite congregational units in Canada increased from 191 to 387 (Table 26). While a total of 258 new ones were formed, 62 were dissolved for a variety of reasons, but mostly due to emigration to Latin America and to resettlement within Canada. The increase likewise resulted from a number of factors to be elaborated on later, but they included the formation of new Mennonite groups, the natural increase and expansion of the communities, as, for instance, in the case of the Bergthaler, Chortitzer, Rosenorter, and Sommerfelder, and the mission activity in Ontario and Alberta by such groups as the Old Mennonites and the New Mennonites (Table 27, p. 269).

The Different Cultural Groups

The greatest single factor contributing to the near-doubling of Mennonite congregations in Canada was the coming of the immi-

TABLE 26[11]

A SUMMARY OF CONGREGATIONS, 1920–1940

OVINCE	EXISTING IN 1920	FOUNDED BY IMMIGRANTS	FOUNDED BY OTHERS	DISSOLVED	EXISTING IN 1940
itario	88	19	17	14	110
anitoba	34	66	26	18	108
katchewan	49	48	22	12	107
berta	18	29	15	15	47
itish olumbia	2	14	2	3	15
tals	191	176	82	62	387

grants, who established 176 centres of worship or congregational units, only 39 of which did not endure, mostly because of the temporary nature of some settlements. This impressive number was, of course, largely due to the large number of immigrants, over 20,000, but that factor was multiplied by the numerous small and scattered settlements, and by the Mennonite proclivity to diversity, usually requiring in a given community more congregations than was necessary from the standpoint of numbers alone.

If there was one thing that the Mennonites did not possess, it was uniformity in the way they exercised their religion. Since the days of Anabaptist beginnings in the 1500s, the Christian community had been defined as autonomous and nonconformist rather than dependent and conformist, narrowly rather than broadly, in terms of smallness rather than bigness, and on the basis of a neighbourhood rather than in terms of a nation or an empire. The tradition of the intimate congregation had arisen from the biblical doctrine of the believer's church, as defined by the Anabaptists, and from their reaction to the massive national and imperial ecclesia. It had been frequently reinforced by the migrations and scatterings and the equally frequent internal divisions, which kept most Mennonite congregations from achieving memberships much above one hundred.[12] Narrowness and smallness made for the quality of intimacy and local solidarity so essential to the survival of minorities, but

they also prevented the various congregational families from forming a united front in the face of dangers threatening from the
outside.[13]

The 18 congregational families previously identified (see Table 9
Chapter 1) were sufficiently different from each other to justify, a
least to themselves, a separate identity, but so were the individua
congregations within those groups. Each congregation had its own
personality or, to use the language of the immigrants, its own
uniqueness (*Eigenart*), its own way of doing things. Consequently
the congregations represented a cultural mosaic as richly patterned as
the quilts designed by Mennonite women or the fields laid out by
Mennonite men. Like the quilts and the fields, the congregations al.
resembled each other, but none of them were exactly the same. In the
1920s, this mosaic was enhanced by Mennonite multiculturalism,
which the immigrants helped to expand, and by Mennonite denominationalism, which the immigrants failed, even though they tried
here and there, to heal.

Speaking broadly in terms of their cultures, the Canadian Mennonites at this point in time could be divided into four groups. The
immigrants of the 1920s were one group, which here will be referred
to as *Russlaender*, to differentiate them from another group, the
immigrants of the 1870s, which will be referred to as *Kanadier*,
more precisely early Kanadier, for reasons that will become clear. A
third group, which can be referred to as late Kanadier, were the
broad (not numerically, but in terms of definition) grouping of
Dutch Mennonites, who had arrived from America, Prussia, and
Russia between 1890 and 1920. The late Kanadier were closer to the
Russlaender than to the early Kanadier in their cultural orientation.
For that reason they might best be referred to not as late Kanadier but
as early Russlaender, except for the fact that they weren't all from
Russia. The fourth cultural group was represented by the Swiss, both
Mennonites and Amish. When the Russlaender arrived in Canada,
the only Mennonites to be found in Ontario were the Swiss.

The geographic scattering of the Russlaender into numerous new
areas lessened somewhat their need to come to terms with the
Kanadier and the Swiss, but where their settlements were in the same
districts there was, with very few exceptions, no easy coming
together of the various elements in single congregations. There were
language differences, of course, but even where they were minimal,

as with the Russlaender and the Kanadier, the gulf between the two cultures was too large to bridge.

From the beginning, the two groups identified each other as "Russlaender" and "Kanadier," and that was probably the first injury to the relationship. The usage on both sides carried pejorative meanings. The designations were born not exactly out of profound respect, and, besides, they were only partially accurate. The Russlaender were Russians only in the sense of Russia being their country of immediate origin and of their most recent citizenship. In terms of ethnic origin, the Russlaender were Dutch. In terms of culture they had become thoroughly germanized, even though they had learned to speak, and in some cases love, the Russian language. Whatever emotion had tied them to Russia had been largely dissipated by the Bolshevik takeover of their homeland.

The Kanadier, on the other hand, were far from being Canadian. To be sure, they had chosen Canada quite deliberately in the 1870s, and as citizens they prayed for those in authority, especially their majesties. But the general understanding of Canadianism, which in those days included patriotism and anglo-conformity, escaped them. Indeed, Canadianism was far enough removed from their hearts to allow many of them to exchange Canada for Mexico and Paraguay. Paradoxically, the Russlaender became Canadian in their hearts sooner than the Kanadier, though the latter had a 50-year start. The Canadianization of the Russlaender was held up only by their reluctance to accept English as a primary language. Thus, the Kanadier and Russlaender names were not altogether appropriate, yet they were sufficiently useful to become general and to find their way unavoidably into the history books.

The differences between the Kanadier and the Russlaender can easily be made too simple and too general, since the Russlaender were not a homogeneous community and the Kanadier were even less so. As has already been spelled out, there were important differences between the early and the late Kanadier and also within these two broad groupings. But, speaking generally, for the early Kanadier especially, the Russlaender were too proud, too aggressive, too enthusiastic about higher education, too anxious to exercise leadership, too ready to compromise with the state, too ready to move to the cities, and too unappreciative of the pioneering done by the Kanadier. As far as the Russlaender were concerned, the Kanadier were too withdrawn, too simple-minded, too uncultured, too weak in their High German because of their excessive dependence on Low German, too afraid of schools and education, and too satisfied to follow traditions, social or liturgical, generation after generation without modification and change.[14]

Another important difference lay in the attitudes towards the American Mennonites. The early Kanadier felt little commonality with the Mennonites south of the border. In leaving Russia in the 1870s, the two groups destined for the U.S.A. and Canada had operated with different assumptions concerning the most appropriate environment for themselves and their children. In choosing America and its open plains in the midwest, on the one hand, and Canada and the closed Manitoba reserves, on the other hand, they had determined different destinies for their communities. Only those minorities among the Kanadier who were nurtured by American Mennonite evangelists and home mission workers were pleased with the American connection. The majority feared Americanization, especially at the hand of other Mennonites, even more than they feared Canadianization.

The Russlaender, on the other hand, raised no fundamental objection to fraternization with the Americans, at least not yet. Some immigrants made their way immediately to the American Mennonite colleges, notably Bethel, Bluffton, and Tabor, and before long two Russlaender leaders in Canada, Jacob H. Janzen and A.H. Unruh had been awarded honorary doctorates by Bethel College. Clearly the Russlaender could not appreciate the haste with which the Americans had surrendered the German language, but the common acceptance of much formal education, private and public, reflected their kindred minds. If the Russlaender of the 1920s had migrated in the 1870s, most of them undoubtedly would have chosen America rather than Canada.

There was also no easy coming together of the Russlaender with the Swiss, for a variety of reasons. While the respective German dialects overlapped sufficiently for the two groups to understand each other if they tried hard enough, the communication gap was considerable none the less. Good intentions on both sides could not conceal the deep cultural differences separating the two groups. The two Mennonite families had developed somewhat differently during the preceding centuries and since both groups tended to define their way of life in terms of cultural minutiae, little things were of considerable consequence. This was the case especially since the two cultures were suddenly brought into unavoidable proximity with each other, often in the context of family life under one roof.[15]

Various behavioural peculiarities emerged to trouble the cohabitating groups. The Swiss hosts were uneasy over what they believed to be the overly liberal tendencies of their Russlaender guests. They criticized the women for the unseemly practice of wearing flowers or small black bows in their hair. Simple prayer veils or bonnets, the Swiss maintained, were the appropriate dress accoutrements of the Christian woman. The immigrants earned further rebuke for their custom of placing crosses on their tombstones. This, it was argued, bordered too closely on the Catholic tradition. For their part, the Russlaender found their hosts to be generally pleasant, if rather plain in a cultural sense. They were amused by the Pennsylvania Dutch dialect, which they enjoyed mimicking, and which if done in disrespect caused unnecessary offence.

The Russlaender presented a paradoxical image.[16] They were, on the one hand, penniless and poor for the most part, still suffering emotionally from the uprootings of revolution and civil war, consequently submissive, cognizant of their dependence, and willing to learn. On the other hand, they were still very much what the years of prosperity and co-operation with the tsarist state had made them. They were culturally sophisticated, for the most part better educated, progressive in their outlook, and quite aggressive in their style, all of which suggested *Hochmut* (high-mindedness or pride) or even arrogance.

Noah M. Bearinger, one of the organizers of the Swiss hospitality, recalled an immigrant teacher saying to his host: "We have not come here to work; we are guests." To which the host replied, "Guests do not stay around so long."[17] And, as their hosts perceived them, they were not only high-minded but also liberal and to some extent heretical. It would take some time for the Russlaender to explain that wartime service in the medical corps had not meant the surrender of nonresistance and that self-defence, though recognized by a minority as necessary, had, at least in retrospect, been acknowledged by the majority as wrong.[18]

Despite the cultural variations, the overall relations between the respective Mennonite groups remained more cordial than strained. The Swiss were deeply impressed with the piety of their Russlaender cousins. Bible readings, audible prayers, and enthusiastic singing, all of which were commonplace among the immigrants, likewise left a favourable impression upon the Swiss. Bishop E.S. Hallman observed that "the Christian family life seems very noticeable, and the young people and the parents seem to be a unit in Christian life activities."[19] The accommodation of the immigrants in the Swiss homes was intended to be temporary in duration, pending the permanent settlement of the newcomers. But it lasted long enough — in some cases over six months — to allow for the blossoming of lasting friendships. One host family testified:

> We shed tears when we learned we had to take a family right into our living quarters, but we shed more tears when the time came for this family to leave.[20]

The question arises, why did the longevity of association in the families not lead to an even minimal acceptance by the Russlaender of Swiss congregational life? Apart from the occasional membership resulting from intermarriage, the Russlaender steered clear of the Swiss congregations, even though they politely accompanied their hosts to Sunday morning worship while they were guests. The immigrants felt a strong need for their own religious gatherings, not only for reasons of essential social contact with people of their own kind, but also for the purposes of gathering new strength for their daily life and of interpreting their past experience. To achieve this, they had to find or form congregations of their own kind. The movement to Western Canada from the Waterloo-Kitchener area had as much to do with the more congenial social environment of the Russlaender as it did with the greater economic opportunities, as these were perceived. As one observer wrote:

> To worship God with one's own people, outweighed all other considerations at that point. . . .[21]

Whenever and wherever services were arranged, the attendance was strong and facilities were crowded with people both sitting and standing. There was much thanksgiving for the rescue from the land of terror and much pleading for the blessing of God in the new land.[22] It was in that context of intimate reflection and projection that the Russlaender needed most to be among themselves, to speak their own language, to sing their own hymns, and to hear their kind of sermons. According to one memoir:

> At first they worshipped in the churches of their hosts. However, the new language, even the Pennsylvania-Dutch dialect, presented great difficulties to them. A longing to listen again to a German sermon and to have an opportunity to share one's experiences became more and more evident.[23]

Those Swiss congregations with which the Russlaender might have had the greatest cultural and theological affinity, namely the Old Mennonites and the New Mennonites, had switched to the English language a generation or more ago,[24] though High German was still understood and sometimes used. Those congregations which were still using High German, namely the Old Order Mennonites, the Old Order Amish, and the Amish Mennonites, used preaching and singing styles quite foreign to the newcomers. The Swiss mixing of High German with the Pennsylvania Dutch dialect was symptomatic of the deep cultural differences. The Mennonites from Russia were trying to get away from their equivalent dialect, Low German, considering it to have less cultural value. The purity of High German, not the perpetuation of Low German, had become their linguistic passion. Bringing everyday social dialects into the school — or church! — was the farthest thing from their self-understanding.

Differences Among the Russlaender

How the Russlaender related, or did not relate, to each of these cultures in their congregational life is significant, but equally significant is the problem of integration internal to the Russlaender themselves. The Russlaender were not all of the same kind either. In one immigrant community the writing of a simple constitution turned out to be "a formidable problem" because the 23 families involved represented almost as many different congregations in their Russian homeland. The churches in these communities all had their own peculiarities. Each had its own method of conducting the worship service, its own division of church offices, and its own church rules.[25] As one minister later recalled, after his congregation of great initial diversity had survived its first 25 years:

> They came from the various regions and localities in Russia. There were people from the Crimea, from Molotschna, from the Old Colony (Chortitza), from Orenburg, from Samara, and also from Asiatic Russia. Even if we don't easily admit that we are dependent on traditions and habits, we do know that circumstances, conditions, and customs, the educational situation, indeed the climate and soil conditions determine the character of man . . . and as these were different in different places in Russia so also the people were different in their attitudes and characteristics.[26]

As significant as they were, the differences among the Russlaender arising from the habits of their respective regions were overshadowed by the differences arising from their denominationalism. The Russlaender represented three distinct congregational families, in other words, three distinct religious cultures, again speaking somewhat broadly. They were commonly known as *Kirchengemeinde* (they will be known hereafter as Conference churches if only for the reason that they joined the Conference of Mennonites in Central Canada), *Bruedergemeinden* (Mennonite Brethren churches), and *Allianzgemeinden* (Alliance churches).[27]

These three congregational types — Conference churches, Brethren churches, and Alliance churches — were brought to Canada by the immigrants, though in a sense they already existed in North America. Parallels for all of them were already present, and this fact prevented even greater proliferation of Mennonite congregational families. The Conference congregations found their North American church home in the Conference of Mennonites in Central Canada[28] and, for the most part, also in the related General Conference Mennonite Church of North America,[29] while the Brethren groups related to the General Conference of Mennonite Brethren Churches in North America, either directly or through the Northern District of that Conference.[30]

The closest North American body for the Alliance churches was a group whose popular designation was Bruderthaler Conference after the founding Bruderthaler congregation at Mountain Lake. Established in 1889 as the Conference of United Mennonite Brethren in North America, the group, which 30 years later had one Canadian congregation in Steinbach, Manitoba, and two at Langham, Saskatchewan, had changed its name and then was known as the Defenseless Mennonite Brethren in Christ of North America.[32] Yet another change before 1940 named that group the Evangelical Mennonite Brethren Conference. The people themselves, however, were known as Bruderthaler, at least for the time being.

The first Bruderthaler congregations at Mountain Lake, Minnesota, and Henderson, Nebraska, in the U.S.A. had arisen from impulses similar to those giving birth to the Alliance in Russia, namely to achieve a spirituality and a discipline greater than that which existed in the Conference churches but to allow for greater flexibility than the Brethren churches practised in such matters as baptism.[33] Founders of the Alliance were deeply troubled that the pursuit of greater spirituality among Mennonites seemed always to lead to hostility and separation rather than to mutuality and union.

While the *Allianz* was, so to speak, another *kleine Gemeinde*, a small remnant carrying a minority idea, that body represented the larger vision of the more inclusive Mennonite or Christian communion and for that reason it also carried considerable influence. It was a rare occurrence when Mennonites remembered in their respective congregations and denominations that the congregation of the Lord was more than just one's own people or one's own church. When it happened, the source of such an idea would most likely be the Alliance or the Bruderthaler. Jacob P. Schultz of the Langham Bruderthaler put it this way:

> We are remembering, of course, that we as an individual congregation and as a Conference are only a fraction of the body of Jesus Christ of which he is the head.[34]

Among Mennonites in general and the Russlaender in particular the fractions were still all-important, for reasons both positive and negative. On the plus side was the original concept, still strong, of the congregation as the best expression of the kingdom of God. On the minus side were measures of intolerance, stubbornness, and pride, which prevented full mutual acceptance[35] of the respective groups. The recognition of this fact was partly responsible for the emergence in Russia of the Alliance as a bridge between the two main groups, the Conference churches and the Brethren churches, which had stood in ecclesiastical competition ever since a revivalistic movement, protesting the lack of spirituality among Mennonites generally, had given birth in the 1860s to the Brethren.

Having found many things wrong with the Conference churches the Brethren churches, in their search for a new spirituality, had adopted a new liturgical style which included more public prayer by more people, gospel songs, and a manner of preaching which frequently climaxed in a revivalistic call, inviting the people to repent and be converted. Most significant of all, at least in terms of relationships between the two groups, was the adoption of the immersionist form of baptism, "a fitting spiritual symbol...to emphasize their distinctiveness."[36] Not only was it the preferred form, to Brethren church leaders it was the only acceptable form there being no other that befitted a true born-again child of God

For the Brethren, immersion and conversion went hand in hand and conversion was all-important. Reacting strongly to the style of the Conference churches, which had an educational approach and catechism classes to induce faith and to prepare the young people for baptism and church membership, the Brethren introduced evangelism and the cataclysmic emotional experience as the essence of conversion. For them, immersion symbolized the radical change the old self dying and being buried and the new self rising to a new life in Christ.

As time went on, the differences between the two groups had become less pronounced, at least so it seemed. In Russia the problem of war, revolution, civil war, famine, reconstruction, and emigration had prompted various forms of co-operative undertaking. And in Canada the problems of pioneer settlement resulted in both groups working together closely in settlement matters. In quite a few communities there were even joint worship services for a while, in few cases for a number of years.

Some Brethren churches had learned to acknowledge, however reluctantly, styles of spirituality other than those of the revival or the prayer meeting, and some Conference churches had learned to sing gospel songs and to accept Bible study and prayer meetings as desirable, if not essential, part of congregational life. By and large the Conference churches also had no quarrel with the insistence of the Brethren on the faith of members being very personal and the experience of the new birth being very real. But most of the Conference church ministers would also have argued that the new birth and personal faith could be arrived at just as well via education and the catechism as through the evangelistic meeting and the altar call.

It was less the essence than the form of things that often turned out to be a stumbling block and a barrier between the two groups, and baptismal form proved to be even more than a stumbling block. It was, very literally, a gulf to be bridged, because, very simply and bluntly put, it was the *Flusz* (river) and the *Flusztaufe* (river baptism) which separated the two groups. In the beginning there was revivalistic enthusiasm, the search for distinctive symbols, and new biblical articulation, resulting in some renewal on both sides, but in the end there was an ecclesiastical and political position so ruinous that families, villages, and congregations, having felt its divisive force, could not be repaired for decades or even generations.[37]

If on any other occasion members of the two groups happened to meet together — weddings, funerals, Sunday worship, Bible conferences, evangelistic campaigns, prayer meetings, or mission gatherings — they would definitely separate on the day of Pentecost, one traditional day of baptism and communion. The Conference churches initiated their new members kneeling at the church altar through a baptismal form called sprinkling or pouring, while the Brethren churches met at the nearest river, natural lake, or artificial pond to completely immerse their new converts. If the respective forms of baptism symbolized to themselves everything that was right about the two church groups, to each other and to outsiders they also signified everything that was wrong. The Alliance churches represented the compromise position on baptism. Though the preferred form was immersion, they did not insist on the rebaptism of those who had been baptized by another form but who wished to join the Alliance or simply to have communion there.[38]

Ontario and Manitoba

The spirit of the Alliance was clearly present among the immigrants who made Ontario their home, not in the sense that a strong Alliance movement was established in Ontario, for it was not, but in the sense that both the Brethren churches and the Conference churches being

established there possessed it at least to a degree. The Brethre
churches were more flexible on baptismal form in Ontario tha
anywhere else, and the Conference churches perceived themselves t
be not so many independent geographically determined units but
union (a "*Vereinigung*"), in Ontario for sure but also in Canada an
throughout North America. As their leader Jacob H. Janzen, soon t
be known throughout the continent, said:

> Every human being and every human corporation carries
> within itself an unmistakable urge to survive, and we immi-
> grants from Russia are no exception in our reluctance to sur-
> render our individuality (*unsere Eigenart*). We would like to
> join together in congregations and as such have the closest pos-
> sible association — but also join the conferences already in exis-
> tence here in order to build the kingdom of God hand in hand
> together with them.[39]

The "closest possible association," however, turned out to be ver
selective. Janzen did not have in mind an association with the Swi
or with the Brethren churches but rather with Conference church
elsewhere, including the General Conference of the Mennoni
Church of North America. And the Brethren churches felt the san
way. Thus, in all the Ontario communities where immigrants ha
settled and where worship services had begun jointly, the form
organization of congregations everywhere led to separate Conferen
churches and Brethren churches.

The first to organize were the Brethren on May 25, 1925.[40] Th
named their congregation the Molotschna Mennonite Brethre
Church. Kitchener was designated as the centre. Members include
persons of the Brethren as well as of the Alliance. The nan
"Molotschna" was very deliberately chosen. It so happened that
Russia the Molotschna Brethren had been more like the Alliance
sentiment. Molotschna was also reminiscent of the first Alliance, ar
thus Molotschna as a name was appropriately symbolic for embra
ing both groups. This meant, of course, that the newly organiz
Brethren church tolerated non-immersionist forms of baptism,
least when it came to accepting members already baptized. Th
crucial distinction from other Brethren churches would have to
resolved somehow, but for the time being that problem could be s
aside.

The new congregation had its affiliated groups, which were part of he Molotschna congregation in Kitchener, but which, for reasons of geography, also conducted some activities separately. For at least seven years there would be only one Ontario Brethren church with numerous affiliates, including Hespeler with 29 members, Kitchener with 144, Leamington with 50, New Hamburg with 37, and Vineland with 27.[41] The notion of a centre or mother congregation with numerous affiliates was not a new one. Historically, it had manifested itself in a number of ways but most often in congregations, where one ministry served a wider geographic area in which a single congregation with a single membership would none the less have numerous meeting places and perhaps even numerous semi-autonomous groups.

In Ontario, the Conference immigrants organized in June 1925 under the leadership of Jacob H. Janzen, a minister-teacher who was ordained as an elder to sanction fully his permanent leadership role. The first name chosen was The Mennonite Refugee Church in Ontario.[42] The refugee church embraced individuals and groups in whatever places immigrants were settling, such as Essex County, Hespeler, Kitchener, New Hamburg, Reesor, Vineland, and Waterloo, and Janzen was the *Reiseprediger*, or itinerant preacher, who ministered to them all. Very soon, the refugees did not want to be known as such any more, and so the name was changed to United Mennonite Church in Ontario.[43]

The formation of the Russlaender congregations effectively ended the formal interaction with the Swiss. Congregations emerged where there were no Swiss, but even where there was geographic proximity the cultural differences, familial relations, and love of individuality made separation inevitable. Yet all was not lost of that forceful and intimate coming together of the Swiss and the Russlaender. Seeds were sown, which for now lay dormant in the ground, quietly awaiting the day of germination and awakening.

In any event, the differences in Ontario between the Russlaender and the Swiss immediately became less pronounced because there was no ongoing testing of the relationship in formal interaction between the two communities. This was not the case in western Canada, where the immigrant and the indigenous communities could not avoid each other. While the differentiating features between the Russlaender and the Kanadier were fewer than between the Russlaender and the

Swiss, the tension between the former two groups actually increase
with time.

In Manitoba, the question of integration with the Kanadier cam
up most in the former reserve areas east and west of the Red Rive
and in communities adjacent to them. Both the Conference and th
Brethren churches recorded successes and failures when it came t
relating to congregations already in existence. In the Grunthal area
for instance, the Conference immigrants at first attended the Chor
titzer worship service. For a time it even seemed that they shoul
unite with them, for the immigrants were settling on the lands of th
Chortitzer emigrating to Paraguay, and the remnant needed rein
forcing. However, the Chortitzer aversion to four-part singing an
to free preaching in contrast to the traditional reading from a writte
sermon "in a monotonous tone of voice" soon made union unlikely.
Only about a dozen immigrants did become Chortitzer. [45]

Some Conference people were next drawn to the Holdema
services through a member who also happened to be the local agent c
the Intercontinental Land Company, and, while the requirements c
free preaching and four-part singing were met here, the insistence o
male members wearing beards and other such unaccustomed prac
tices made integration there impossible as well. [46]

The Brethren immigrants likewise "joined" the Kanadier close:
to their spiritual heritage, namely the Bruderthaler in Steinbach, bu
this liaison was of short duration, even though the cultural gap, as i
music or liturgy, was not as wide. The Bruderthaler had cultivate
four-part singing since their beginning a generation earlier and, lik
the Brethren, were characterized by an evangelistic style. [47] Bu
theological and liturgical affinity did not always overcome psychc
logical and cultural barriers, even when it came to relating Brethre
who were Russlaender and Brethren who were Kanadier. The differ
ent backgrounds caused "friction and misunderstanding" to aris
rather easily. [48]

In Manitoba, most of the new Brethren settlers had no choice bu
to found new congregations, because they settled where there wer
none, twelve of them between 1924 and 1930. [49] One of them was a
Arnaud, which very briefly was an Alliance church. The two existin
Brethren groups, Winnipeg and Winkler, however, became happ
homes for the Russlaender, the former because the city missionar
assisted immigrants with housing and employment, and the latte

because the immigrants arrived with such strength and leadership that their "many gifted and devoted ministers, leaders, teachers, and men qualified in practical affairs" soon assumed the dominant role in the congregation.[50]

Winkler, the home of the first permanent Brethren church in Canada,[51] became even more of a "mother church" for the Brethren than it had been before, because immigrant teachers led by one of the Russian church's most renowned Bible teachers, Abram H. Unruh, founded the Peniel Bible School.[52] Unruh personified the attributes of the old-time pedagogue for whom teaching was not just an occupation but the very reason for his being. He had taught at the Crimean Bible School until 1924, when he decided to emigrate to Canada, hopefully to establish another school there. His dreams were realized in October 1925 when Unruh started Bible classes in two rooms of a Winkler house. The student body totalled a modest six, but by Christmas the ranks had almost doubled to eleven.[53] Encouraging student increases in the following years justified the building of a large one-storey school building; by 1928, the enrolment had risen to 70.[54]

The Winkler school was not the only such centre founded with the coming of the immigrants, but it became one of the most influential in the training of ministers and Sunday school teachers.[55] Peniel's philosophy placed the accent on readying students for ministerial and other church work, while the Herbert Bible School, established by late Kanadier Brethren in Saskatchewan, placed the emphasis on preparation for missions.[56] Whatever the particular thrust of the schools in terms of training ministers, missionaries, or Sunday school workers, the curriculum offered studies in Bible doctrine, Old and New Testament exegeses, theology, church history, Mennonite history, and German grammar, literature, and music.

The school was popular also outside of Brethren circles. For a while it seemed that the Brethren would even co-operate in the venture with the Bergthaler. Bergthaler bishop Jakop Hoeppner actually donated the land for the Winkler school and publicly praised its good work.[57] Hoeppner's successor, David Schulz, who had taken classes at Peniel, felt that his church's support could continue, but only if the Bergthaler could add some of their own teachers to the Winkler staff.

This proposition apparently fell through, but this did not discour-

age the Bergthaler from co-operating with other Russlaender.
1929, a Bible school was established by the Bergthaler at Gretna
co-operation with the Blumenorter, a Conference congregati
whose Russlaender members had settled in the village homes
Kanadier leaving for Mexico. Together, the two church elders, J
Bueckert and David Schulz, recruited J.H. Enns, a Russlaen
minister-teacher to conduct the classes.[58] The school was initia
located in the upstairs reading room of Gretna's Mennonite Col
giate Institute and later transferred to Altona.[59]

In Manitoba, the Bergthaler represented the only Kanadier c
gregation, which fraternized a great deal with the Russlaender a
which did so at several levels. The co-operation with
Blumenorter in the founding of a Bible school has already b
noted. The Bergthaler made a serious attempt at bridge-buildi
partly because several of its members, including H.H. Ewert a
P.P. Epp, had played a leading role in the immigration and par
because of its charter membership in the Conference of Mennon
in Central Canada of which most of the Russlaender Confere
churches became members. In a number of places, as at Graysville
Russlaender joined existing or emerging Bergthaler congregatio
or they became the dominant element, as at Morden[61] wh
Russlaender J.M. Pauls and J.J. Wiens were elected minister a
deacon, respectively.[62]

Morden was unique in a number of ways. In Morden, the Sun
school was a joint effort of three groups: the German Lutherans, v
owned the building and used it for worship only once a month;
Bergthaler, who used it once a month; and the Brethren, who use
twice a month. Bergthaler and Brethren worked together in M
den's Alexander Hall until the 1930s, but, as happened in
communities where Conference and Brethren people co-operated a
worked together in time of need, they separated once they felt th
independent strength.

As in the case of the Brethren, so also with the Conference peop
the largest number of immigrant communities in Manitoba were
entirely new settlement areas where the question of relating
existing congregations could not come up.[63] To ensure that s
groups were served, whether organized as congregations or n
several elders and ministers were appointed *Reiseprediger* and gi
monthly allowances by the home mission board of the Gene

Conference of the Mennonite Church of North America. This happened without much delay, usually upon the recommendations of David Toews, who was chairman of the immigration board, as well as Canadian representative on that U.S.A.-based General Conference home mission board. Such appointments meant that uprooted and unsalaried elders, who had lost in Russia the economic base for their manifold ministries and who could regain such a base only by neglecting the ministry, had an income, however small it might be — the average monthly allowance was $50.[64] It also meant that the new settlements, especially the small ones, had the essential services of the ministry made available to them, at least occasionally.

Two of the most active Manitoba *Reiseprediger* were F.F. Enns, who became the elder of the Whitewater Mennonite Church, and J.P. Klassen, who became the elder of the Schoenwieser Mennonite Church. Together they served a large number of affiliated groups, as well as non-affiliated groups, until they became fully independent, something which occurred if and when these groups elected their own elders.[65] Although Enns and Klassen served somewhat overlapping territories — some groups actually experienced tensions because of divided preferences — Enns's primary responsibility was along the CPR line in southern Manitoba while Klassen, working first from Starbuck and then from Winnipeg, served groups in all directions from Winnipeg but mainly along the western rail lines extending to the Saskatchewan border.[66] At the peak, the Schoenwieser church and its elder served 37 groups.[67]

In the case of F.F. Enns, his appointment meant travelling to such distant settlements as Reesor in Ontario and Namaka in Alberta and to such nearby communities as Whitewater, Boissevain, Clearwater, Crystal City, Manitou, Mather, Ninga, and Rivers. He would serve with communion, with baptism, and, where the groups were ready, with ordinations of deacons and/or ministers.[68] After his first fourteen months as itinerant minister, he recorded in his notebook the following summary of his activity:

> Preached 192 times at 69 places
> Communion to 1267 souls at 16 places
> Baptism for 32 souls at 4 places
> Ordained 3 preachers and 1 deacon
> Attended at 3 elections — election of 5 ministers
>   and 1 bishop

Worked away from home 206 days
Visited 424 families at 69 places
Travelled 1596 miles by wagon and sleigh
Travelled 5832 miles by train
Travelled 27 miles in Ontario on foot
Four marriages
Gave medicines to 273 persons[69]

While such data was recorded, it was customarily not publicized. Publicity, it was believed, subtracted from the reward which would some day come to the loyal servant in heaven. But the secrecy also subtracted from the rewards on earth, because very few congregations were fully aware of their leaders' manifold ministries. Enns also withheld permission for others to have anything published "in the newspaper about my work" because "it goes against the grain to do so" if the groups themselves "have nothing to report."[70]

In due course, Enns and his wife left their married children at Lena and made their home in Whitewater, the centre of the largest of the immigrant groups in southwestern Manitoba. Thus, the groups he could conveniently include in the immediate geographic circuit came to be part of the larger multi-branch congregation called Whitewater Mennonite Church, named, as was frequently the custom, after the central locale of the congregation, which usually also was the residential home of the elder.

J.P. Klassen's congregation was named after Schoenwiese, the home village in Russia near Alexandrovsk, later Zaporozhje, from where he and the core of his congregation had come. Klassen was unique among immigrant ministers for his oratorical gifts, his ability to inspire and win people, and also his liberalism in many respects, arising in part from his emphasis on "the spirit of the Bible" as distinct from the dependence on the biblical letter.[71] Thus, he allowed, even encouraged, a rich social life for city young people, which included mixed folk games and the theatre. Otherwise, he avoided defining all the social prohibitions, including smoking, a frequent target for much preaching in both the Conference churches, where it was criticized but tolerated, and the Brethren churches, where it meant excommunication. Indeed, Klassen was known to "light up" in public following morning worship services.[72] He also went farther than anybody else in practising open communion, and when the German Lutheran members of his audience at Graysville chose to leave just before communion was served, he successfully invited them to stay:

> Good friends, whoever believes in Christ may come to the communion. If you think as I do, then I will serve you with great joy. You are our brothers and sisters.[73]

Between and among the well-defined territories of the various Russlaender congregations, Conference and/or Brethren, and Kanadier congregations were settlement groups that represented a mixture of people. Such groups would be served upon invitation by ministers from various sources. At Graysville, for instance, prior to the group's becoming an affiliate of the Bergthaler, the Schoenwieser, Brethren, Sommerfelder, Bergthaler, and others all worshipped together in a Presbyterian church building, which had become vacant owing to the 1925 union.[74] At Morris, the Schoenwieser were joined by people from the Brethren, the Bergthaler, and the Kleine Gemeinde, though only for a while.[75] And before the Schoenwieser had assumed the initiative, Morris had temporarily been an outpost of the Lichtenauer from St. Elizabeth.

Conference and Brethren people worshipped together in the early years of settlement in numerous places—at Vineland they even elected ministers together[76]—but eventual separation seemed to be the destiny of all such groups. Exceptions were in the rarest of cases where one group absorbed, replaced, or eclipsed the other, as for instance the Conference church at Winnipegosis[77] and the Brethren churches at Newton[78] and Gem.[79] Places where co-operation was followed by separation included Springstein,[80] Niverville,[81] North Kildonan,[82] Arnaud,[83] Steinbach,[84] and others. When separation came, often the only co-operative link remaining was in the context of burial societies.[85]

Saskatchewan, Alberta, British Columbia

More integration of the Russlaender into Kanadier congregations took place in Saskatchewan than in any other province,[86] and that for several reasons. The settlements in Saskatchewan, being more recent, were more scattered, thus touching more of the Russlaender areas than in Manitoba, where the two reserves and adjoining territory left much of Manitoba untouched until the Russlaender came. Furthermore, most Saskatchewan settlements of relevance to the Russlaender were settlements of the late Kanadier, that is, immigrants from the U.S.A., Prussia, and Russia in the years 1890 to 1920. Most of these late Kanadier congregations had already joined the two Canadian and North American conferences, to which the Russlaender would also relate. There was, in other words, a great deal of commonality between the late Kanadier and the Russlaender.

There was one important exception to this observation, namely in the Swift Current area. For at least a decade the Conference had sent itinerant ministers to serve scattered groups of early Kanadier. This activity was intensified when the emigration of the Reinlaender to Mexico left those who stayed behind without any spiritual care. A number of small groups thus became part of the Emmaus congregation, whose centre was Swift Current. The coming of the immigrants meant augmentation of both the centre and the affiliates.[87]

Another congregational meeting place of the early Kanadier and the Russlaender was formed where persons of both groups joined congregations of the late Kanadier, such as the Rosenorter in the Rosthern area. Numerous Russlaender of the Kirchengemeinde variety found their way into the Rosenorter church of which David Toews was the leader. But this development could not be taken for granted even where geographic proximity suggested such integration, as in the villages near Hague, where Russlaender were settling on land vacated by the emigrating Kanadier. It so happened that these new settlers were, for the most part, from Chortitza in Russia. A new congregation of such people (that is, from Chortitza) had organized at Hanley under the leadership of Johann J. Klassen. He was a strong and aggressive leader and soon his Nordheimer congregation had many affiliates. Indeed, so large did Klassen's field of activity become — 22 groups, some of which were as far away from Hanley as 150 miles — that his election as elder could be facilitated only by a series of local elections and the mailing of sealed envelopes to Rosthern, where they were counted by a pre-selected group of brethren.[88]

This then was the dilemma of immigrants settling in the Hague area. Geographically, they were closer to the Rosenorter congregation, which had meeting places in Hague and nearby villages. Culturally, they were closer to the Nordheimer, which represented their own kind from Russia. Most of the Rosenorter not only had arrived 35 years earlier, but had never been to Russia, having come directly from Prussia. None the less, most of the immigrants decided to join the Hague Rosenorter group. This move was partly due to the influence of D.H. Rempel, a minister in their midst, who had corresponded from Russia with David Toews and who keenly felt the need to express some solidarity with Toews. On one occasion, Toews had made known his disappointment that although the immigrants were "willing to receive the Canadian physical bread, they were not as ready to accept the spiritual."[89]

Thus, the Rosenorter became the most cosmopolitan of Mennonite congregational groups, partly because of the cosmopolitan David Toews and partly because the Rosenorter, having Prussian roots, did not cultivate the narrow allegiances and habits which were more characteristic of those from Russia, be they early Kanadier, late Kanadier, or Russlaender. Needless to say, those more open among the latter groups found the Rosenorter to be a congenial prairie church home.[90] If, on the one hand, the Rosenorter are credited with openness and tolerance, it must be said, on the other hand, that some others were not far behind. It was in the nature of widely scattered congregations like the Nordheimer — or like the Ebenfelder in the Herschel area or the Hoffnungsfelder in the Rabbit Lake area — to be accommodating of different views and styles.

The church chronicle (*Gemeinde-Chronick*) of the Ebenfelder church illustrates rather well the typical beginnings, development, and experiences of congregational life. Founded at Herschel on Easter Monday, April 13, 1925, the congregation's first 34 members were settlers at the Lamborn, Ramsey, and Meyers farms who had the mutual desire "to nurture a more active spiritual life."[91] The worship services were held at first in the main building of the Lamborn farm under the leadership of Elder Jacob B. Wiens and his brother, Gerhard B. Wiens, likewise a minister, both ordained in Russia. The chronicle of events tells the rest of the story:

18 March 1926: the death of the oldest member at age 69 followed by burial three days later.

24 May 1926: baptism of the first young people, 12 in all, after an extended period of instruction.

6 June 1926: the election by majority vote of two ministers, Kornelius Jacob Warkentin and Hermann Lenzmann, and one deacon, Heinrich Penner. Lenzmann, however, declined to accept.

6 July 1925: admittance to the membership of Conference of Mennonites in Central Canada.

22 – 29 August 1926: admittance to General Conference Mennonite Church of North America.

1 August 1927: start of construction of a new building with an $800 loan from the General Conference, interest free for two years and thereafter at four per cent.

1926 – 1930: incorporation into the Ebenfeld congregation of various settlement groups — including Truax with 12 members, Springwater with 8, Glidden with 16, and a trans-border group Provost (Alta.)-Marklin (Sask.), with 47 — and the separation in 1928 of the largest of these, across the border in Alberta, as a separate independent congregation for reasons of size and distance.

14 June 1936: congregational celebration for Jacob B. Wiens of 25 years as elder and 35 years in the university.

28 July 1936: twenty-fifth wedding anniversary of the Gerhard B. Wienses.

25 February 1937: death by his own hand of church member Kornelius Franz Funk.

4 July 1937: death by drowning of a youth Gerhard B. Wiens.

31 March 1939: death by poisoning of infant Mary Martens.

22 May 1939: death of Elder Jacob B. Wiens in Saskatoon City Hospital at age of 68.

Many of the Russlaender Brethren settling in Saskatchewan found their new congregational homes in Brethren churches already established, though "amalgamation of the Kanadier and Russlaender in a local church was not always easy."[92] In the Main Centre Mennonite Brethren Church, founded in 1904 by families from Manitoba, Russia, and the U.S.A., 78 immigrant members were received in the years 1924 to 1926, but in the next two years alone, 32 of these immigrants left, and in 1927 they founded a new congregation.[93] Thirteen other new Brethren groups emerged in Saskatchewan, with clusters around Herbert, where a Bible school already existed, and around Hepburn, where a Bible school then was founded.

One new immigrant congregation, the one at Watrous, identified itself as being of the Alliance, and immediately established a relationship with the other Bruderthaler congregations in Saskatchewan. There were two of these at Langham, the north and south wings of the congregation having formally divided in 1925 on the question of baptism.[94] A new one at Fairholme arose as the result of evangelistic work in a community which included a variety of Mennonites without a church home: Bergthaler, Bruderthaler, Brueder, and Sommerfelder.[95] These developments in Saskatchewan and similar growth in Alberta led the Bruderthaler to establish two Canadian districts, one for Manitoba and Saskatchewan, and one for Alberta, later also including British Columbia.[96]

The Bruderthaler centre in Alberta was the Lane Farm at Namaka, where the Alliance and Conference people worshipped together until the former built its own meeting house.[97] It was in Alberta where the Alliance established its strongest presence, though it did not endure, as will later be seen. The Namaka Alliance had several Alliance affiliates, including Gem, where the group referred to itself as the Free Evangelical Church.[98] The role of Namaka in nurturing Alliance groups at Gem, Linden, Munson, and Crowfoot was largely due to their leader, Aaron A. Toews, who had been the leading minister of the Alliance church in Lichtfelde, Molotschna.[99]

The Brethren church, which eventually integrated with itself all of the Alliance groups, had no congregation at all in Alberta until the immigrants arrived. Then its largest congregation was established at Coaldale, which became the strongest Alberta Mennonite centre, partly because the economy attracted so many immigrants and partly because of the leadership which people like B.B. Janz exerted. As time went on, Coaldale illustrated rather well how congregation-centredness helped develop a strong community and a sense of mission, as well as an excessive local patriotism for which Mennonite parochialism was well suited. A sense of special privilege, conse-quently a special calling and a special obligation, was part of the Coaldale experience and emphasized repeatedly throughout its early years, as the following sermon excerpt suggests:

> Coaldale has very special opportunities, more than any other congregation in Alberta and beyond: so many special visiting ministers, so many special meetings, including conferences, song festivals, youth festivals, ministerial courses, Bible and high schools, or Sunday school courses. . . . Coaldale is receiv-ing manifold blessings, and the Lord will expect much of Coaldale.[100]

The blessing was evident in the rapid growth of the Coaldale Brethren church. The congregation built the first meeting house

(32′×52′) with an annex (20′×32′) in 1929. Another addition (30′×30′) was constructed only three years later. A decade later all this was replaced by a "large sanctuary" (60′×104′) just in time to host the 30th annual Northern District Conference, which brought delegates and visitors from all over Canada and the U.S.A. who wanted "to see the 'Russlaender' and their church" in Coaldale. It was a great moment for the congregation, for at last its members felt they had been fully accepted. The Coaldale church "had come of age and stood equal in rank with the older 'churches.' "[101]

Coaldale, like many other Russlaender settlements, had a Conference church as well as a Brethren church. This duplication, so characteristic of the new settlements, happened also at Tofield, in the Peace River district, and at Namaka and Rosemary. At Rosemary and Tofield, the Conference and Brethren congregations were added to the Swiss groups that had already been in existence a quarter of a century or more. The Westheimer congregation at Rosemary was somewhat of a mother church for Conference groups in Alberta, for its elder served groups far and wide until they either dissolved or became independent. Only at Didsbury did the Conference Russlaender integrate with a congregation already in existence, namely the Bergthaler who had resettled from Manitoba at the turn of the century.[102]

The development of new churches in British Columbia paralleled to some extent the situation in Alberta in that there was one very strong congregation which overshadowed all the rest. The Coaldale of British Columbia was Yarrow where the Brethren churches expanded very rapidly after the beginning of settlement in 1928, though it must not be forgotten that there were other Mennonite beginnings in the West Coast province, however small. Since 1913, *Reiseprediger* had serviced a small Conference group at Renata in the Okanagan Valley.[103] At Vanderhoof in the B.C. interior, the Great War had produced a Brethren church settlement in 1918.[104]

These remote beginnings, however, were soon forgotten as the Mennonite discovery of the Fraser Valley led to a veritable settlement rush in the depression years. The Brethren moved to the West Coast earliest and strongest, paralleling somewhat the migrations of the American Brethren from the midwest to the west coast. Yarrow and other parts of the valley attracted leaders like J.A. Harder and C.C. Peters, who found that berry gardens and small dairies were more compatible with ministerial duties than the large mixed farms of the prairies. In Yarrow the Brethren swallowed up the Alliance, as in Alberta, and overshadowed the Conference churches, not only because the Brethren were established first but also because there were many defections from the Conference churches.

Yet, the Conference churches survived and remained a struggling minority in almost every settlement in the Fraser Valley, Greater Vancouver, and Vancouver Island, though not without a great deal of outside help. When Jacob H. Janzen came to British Columbia as an itinerant minister, he applied the same concept of a provincial United Mennonite church already operative in Ontario. Thus, all the Conference settlement groups were part of a single congregation, the parts of which drew strength and inspiration from each other. As a unit they joined the Canadian and General Conferences when the time came.

Congregational Life

Wherever they were founded, the new congregations met in homes, at first almost everywhere, in schoolhouses, in implement sheds, in barns, in haylofts, in grocery stores or lumber businesses, in community halls, and in the vacant buildings of various denominations. To give a few examples, the new congregations met in the vacant buildings of the Presbyterian church at Graysville and Whitewater, the United at Lena, the Lutheran at Starbuck, the Anglican at Oak Lake, and the Reformed in Winnipeg.[105] As soon as they could, the congregations put up simple buildings of their own. In the first decade, 47 congregations purchased or erected their own buildings at costs ranging from $200 to $6,000.[106] The effort required, and the sacrifices made, especially as the depression came, are indicated by the experience at Gem, where a structure measuring 32′×40′ was begun by the Brethren churches at an estimated cost of $400.[107] People contributed on the basis of farm produce: one dozen eggs brought 3 cents, one week's sale of cream 50 cents, one bushel of wheat 23 cents, and one fat two-year-old steer 24 dollars. This was supplemented by an appeal to 80 congregations, mostly in the U.S.A., which yielded the "exceedingly gratifying" results of $208.01. Such solicitation had been authorized by the 1924 and 1927 sessions of the General Conference of Mennonite Brethren Churches.[108]

The ingredients of congregational nurture, which typified many

Russlaender congregations, were those common also to other Mennonite churches. On Sundays and holidays, there always were preaching services. Special festival days in the Christian calendar were New Year's, Epiphany, Good Friday, Easter, Ascension Day, Pentecost, and Christmas. At Christmas, Easter, and Pentecost, there were normally two days of worship services. Once every fall, during or after the harvest, there was an all-day thanksgiving and mission festival.[109] Occasionally, there were prayer and Bible study meetings and annually, a two- or three-day Bible conference usually led by visiting ministers. Outside evangelists were invited to give evangelistic services three to five evenings a week every year.

The baptism festival was a high point in the life of every congregation, because it marked the formal induction, after a period of evangelism or catechetical training, of the young into the membership of the congregation. Becoming "a full-fledged member of a church through baptism" was experienced by those seeking it, usually in their late teens, as "an important and serious step." According to the memoirs of one, who had been baptized at age 19:

> I had joined the church of our Lord and all of its members were my brothers and sisters. . . . The venerable ministers of the church, the choristers with their strong voices, the [worshipping] congregation, . . . the mysterious communion service; all these left a lasting impression on me. All this spoke to me of God's great mercy, which seemed to reach out and give me inner peace.[110]

The festival of the Lord's supper, observed to commemorate the suffering and death of Christ as well as fellowship of the believers with each other and with Christ, was taken most seriously. The communion service was a time to get closer to God through Christ, because of His life, death, and resurrection, but also for church members to get closer to each other. It was a time for enmity and strife to end and for reconciliation to take place. To facilitate this a preparatory sermon, with admonitions towards that end, would be given usually a Sunday in advance. That would give everybody an opportunity to make things right with their neighbours. The communion service was viewed as the family feast of a congregation.

> Where is there a meal time on earth where rich and poor, those of high and low station, have such intimate fellowship?

> Everywhere there is separation and division, hate and envy of
> the various classes. But here the poor domestic sits next to the
> fashionable woman and the simple worker next to the learned.
> And both partake from the same dish. Therein lies a deep
> social significance.[111]

All believers, baptized and penitent, were expected to attend, and believers from other congregations were sometimes welcome too. The Conference churches tended to be most open in their communion practices, the Brethren churches most closed, and the Alliance churches held the moderate ground between the open and the closed systems. Careful records were kept both of the communion services themselves and of the number of participants, the latter being determined by calculating the number of thimble-size pieces of communion bread consumed.[112] Participation was viewed both as a holy obligation and a high privilege. Non-participation for whatever reason symbolized the breakdown of a relationship between the member and the congregation. Practices like foot-washing at communion services had not been uniformly practised in Russia and thus were recognized as an optional ordinance, especially in congregations where different traditions were represented.

The highest authority in the congregation, at least theoretically, was the brotherhood meeting (*Bruderschaft*), in which all the male members made the decisions important for the life of the congregation. The female members were gradually included in the franchise, beginning with such special occasions as the election of an elder or leading minister, minister, or deacon. These elected spiritual leaders met as a group and represented the spiritual authority of the congregation.[113] Paralleling the ministerial body, responsible for spiritual matters, was a lay body of about three members, a church council responsible for all the business matters of the congregation.[114] The operating expenses of a congregation were handled through freewill offerings or levies of one kind or another. In some congregations the annual levy was partly based on membership, at 50 cents per person, and partly on land ownership, at 75 cents per quarter section (or 160 acres).[115]

The most important duty of elders, ministers, and deacons was the spiritual nurture of the members, referred to as caring for the soul (*Seelsorge*).[116] *Seelsorge* had to do with the most important aspect of human existence, for to be damaged or to sustain the loss of one's soul was the greatest human loss of all. Thus the work of *Seelsorge* was fundamental in the nurture of a congregation. It was also very rewarding, because nothing enriched life as much as interpersonal relations. It was important, of course, to remember that every human being was an individual, and that not every individual needed the same kind of care or intervention in order to be right with God. It was also true that no person involved in *Seelsorge* was "sovereign or possessing the infallibility of a pope."[117] The motivation of all *Seelsorge* had to be love and compassion for the needy and the lost.[118]

The chorister was a common institution in most immigrant congregations. It was his duty to select hymns, announce them, and lead out in singing from his place in the pew or, in larger congregations, from up front, where he sat with ministers and deacons. The chorister was not a conductor, only a singer with a loud voice and enough musical sense to get a song and the congregation started on the right pitch. While the Russlaender were not opposed in principle to the use of pianos or other musical instruments, it was some time before many congregations could afford them. Unless, of course, the congregation was as fortunate as the one at Waterloo, which purchased not only an elegant Presbyterian sanctuary left vacant by the Union of 1925 but also a pipe organ to go with it.

An essential resource to the congregations were the denominational Conferences, which helped the congregations financially, with personnel, and through the provision of program materials. More importantly, they gave to the congregations a wider fellowship. Through the Conferences, also, the congregations were linked to the international work of missions and relief, either directly or indirectly through such mediating agencies as the Canadian Mennonite Board of Colonization and the Mennonite Central Committee. This connection was timely, because events unfolding elsewhere in the world, especially in the U.S.S.R., required of the congregations that they extend their normal, quite limited, borders to minister to the needs of the world and especially to Mennonite people elsewhere in distress. Thus, even as the Russlaender were settling into their parochial congregations to preserve their individuality, they were rudely reminded that their brothers and sisters in faraway Russia were struggling with their very survival.

TABLE 27[119]

MENNONITE CONGREGATIONS[1] IN CANADA

(including those in existence in 1920 and those established between 1920 and 1940)

A. ONTARIO

PLACE[2]	DATE[3]	NAME[4]	CONGREGATIONAL FAMILY[5]	CULTURAL IDENTITY[6]	MEMBERSHIP IN 1940[7]
Altona		See Stouffville			
Arkona	1868	Reformed M	RM	S	15
Aylmer	1900	Aylmer MBC	MBC	S	56
Ayr	1822	Detweiler M	OM	S	24
Baden	1824	Steinman Amish M	AM	S	550
	1840	Shantz M	OM	S	91
	1844	Hostetler's Reformed M	RM	S	New Hamburg
	1855	St. Agatha Amish M	AM	S	Steinman
	1913	Baden M	OM	S	M
Bloomingdale	1824	Bloomingdale M	OM	S	55
Bothwell	1874	Bethel M	OM	S	26
Breslau	1815	Cressman M	OM	S	170
	1882	Breslau MBC	MBC	S	51
Bright	1938	Bright Mission	OM	S	M
Cambridge		See Hespeler and Preston			
Colborne	1936	Prospect MBC	MBC	S	15
Collingwood	1897	Collingwood MBC	MBC	S	42
					Wellesley

TABLE 27 (continued)

MENNONITE CONGREGATIONS IN CANADA

A. ONTARIO (continued)

PLACE[2]	DATE[3]	NAME[4]	CONGREGATIONAL FAMILY[5]	CULTURAL IDENTITY[6]	MEMBERSHIP IN 1940[7]
Dunnville	1835	South Cayuga M	OM	S	20
	1889	South Cayuga M(1932)[8]	OOM	S	—
	1930	South Cayuga M(1940)	MWC	S	—
Elmira	1853	West Woolwich M	OOM	S	Waterloo
	1924	Elmira M	OM	S	160
	1939	Elmira M	MWC	S	125
Elmwood	1875	Elmwood MBC	MBC	S	48
Fisherville	1825	Rainham Reformed M	RM	S	10
Floradale	1889	Floradale M	OM	S	105
Gormley	1891	Gormley MBC	MBC	S	169
Hanover	1903	Hanover MBC	MBC	S	50
Harrow	1920s	Harrow United M	CM	R	Leamington
Hespeler	1829	Wanner M	OM	S	60
	1927	Hespeler MB	MB	R	27
	1927	Hespeler UM	CM	R	Waterloo
	1898	Hespeler MBC	MBC	S	69
Kitchener	1807	First M	OM	S	384
	1842	Weber M	OM	S	86
	1877	Bethany MBC	MBC	S	343

Place	Congregation	Year		S/R	Number
	Stirling M	1924	GC	S	400
	Kitchener MB	1925	MB	R	178
	See also Waterloo				
Leamington	Pelee Island United M (c. 1930)	1925	CM	R	—
	Essex County United M	1925	CM	R	573
	Leamington MB	1925	MB	R	115
	Richtige Bruedergemeinde(1939)	1938	MB	R	—
Listowel	Listowel MBC	1926	MBC	S	51
Lion's Head	Lion's Head MBC	1885	MBC	S	43
Mannheim	Latschar M	1839	OM	S	155
Markham	Wideman M	1803	OM	S	125
	Dickson's Hill MBC	1850s	MBC	S	35
	Cedar Grove M	1867	OM	S	26
	Markham MBC	1877	MBC	S	83
	Wideman M(1928)	1889	OOM	S	—
Markstay	Markstay Union Mission	1935	OM	S	M
Millbank	Amish M	1886	OOA	S	90
Milliken	Hagerman M	1932	OM	S	22
Milverton	Amish M	1891	OOA	S	85
New Dundee	Blenheim M	1839	OM	S	98
	Bethel MBC	1855	MBC	S	153
New Hamburg	Geiger M	1831	OM	S	77
	North Easthope RM	1844	RM	S	90
	Biehn M	1865	OM	S	88
	New Hamburg MB	1926	MB	R	29
	New Hamburg UM	1926	CM	R	Waterloo
Niagara-on-the-Lake	Niagara United M	1934	CM	R	141
Owen Sound	Calvary MBC	1899	MBC	S	70

TABLE 27 (continued)

MENNONITE CONGREGATIONS IN CANADA

PLACE[2]	DATE[3]	NAME[4]	CONGREGATIONAL FAMILY[5]	CULTURAL IDENTITY[6]	MEMBERSHIP IN 1940[7]
		A. ONTARIO (continued)			
Palmerston	1901	Wallace MBC	MBC	S	38
Petrolia	1920	Petrolia MBC	MBC	S	39
Pickering	1889	Reesor M(1932)	OOM	S	–
	1930	Reesor M	MWC	S	115
Poole	1903	Mornington Amish M	BA	S	160
	1874	Poole Amish M	AM	S	215
Port Colborne	1883	Reformed M	RM	S	50
Port Elgin	1868	Port Elgin MBC	MBC	S	33
Port Rowan	1926	Port Rowan United M	CM	R	20
	1926	Port Rowan MB	MB	R	51
Preston	1804	Hagey M	OM	S	94
Rainham	1930	Rainham M	MWC	S	20
		See also Selkirk			
Reesor	1925	Reesor United M	CM	R	60
Riedsville	1937	Riedsville Outreach	OM	C	M
St. Catharines	1899	St. Catharines MBC	MBC	S	40
St. Jacobs	1844	St. Jacobs M	OM	S	366
	1889	Conestoga M	OOM	S	Waterloo
St. Thomas	1897	Zion MBC	MBC	S	29

Place	Year	Congregation			Members
Selkirk	1836	Rainham M	OM	S	45
	1889	Rainham M(1932)	OOM	S	—
		See also Rainham			
Sherkston	1800s	Sherkston M(1931)	OM	S	—
	1835	Stevensville Reformed M	RM	S	50
	1889	Bertie M(1926)	OOM	S	—
Singhampton	1893	Shrigley MBC	MBC	S	25
	1885	Mt. Pleasant MBC	MBC	S	27
Spring Bay	1890	Salem MBC	MBC	S	47
Stayner	1881	Stayner MBC	MBC	S	73
	1890s	Sunnidale MBC	MBC	S	77
Stouffville	1852	Altona M(1889)	OM	S	—
	1872	Altona MBC	MBC	S	60
	1889	Altona M(1930)	OOM	S	—
	1903	Stouffville MBC	MBC	S	167
	1935	Glasgow M	OM	S	16
	1930	Altona M	MWC	S	Pickering
Stratford	1906	Stratford MBC	MBC	S	49
Tavistock	1837	East Zorra Amish M	AM	S	750
	1935	Cassel Amish M	AM	S	125
Toronto	1897	Banfield Memorial	MBC	S	99
	1899	Grace MBC	MBC	S	72
	1907	Danforth M	OM	S	36
		See also Scarborough			
Unionville	1858	Almira M	OM	S	24
	1889	Almira M(1932)	OOM	S	—
	1930	Almira M	MWC	S	Pickering
Vineland	1801	The First M	OM	S	80
	1881	Vineland MBC	MBC	S	130

TABLE 27 (continued)

MENNONITE CONGREGATIONS IN CANADA

PLACE[2]	DATE[3]	NAME[4]	CONGREGATIONAL FAMILY[5]	CULTURAL IDENTITY[6]	MEMBERSHIP IN 1940[7]
		A. ONTARIO (continued)			
	1889	Meyers M(1928)	OOM	S	—
	1927	Vineland MB	MB	R	156
	1927	Vineland United M	CM	R	208
	1934	Niagara MB	MB	R	249
Virgil					
Wallenstein	1901	South Peel M	OOM	S	Waterloo 70
	1917	David Martin M	DM	S	262
Waterloo	1837	Erb St. M	OM	S	850
	1889	Martin M	OOM	S	281
	1924	Waterloo-Kitchener United M	CM	R	150
	1939	Martin M	MWC	S	
		See also Kitchener			
Wellesley	1850	Kingwood Reformed M	RM	S	New Hamburg 420
	1859	Mapleview Amish M	AM	S	95
	1886	Wellesley Amish M	OOA	S	100
	1886	Mornington Amish M	OOA	S	190
	1911	Cedar Grove Amish M	BA	S	—
Windsor	1927	Windsor United M(1940)	CM	R	—
Woodbridge	1824	Schmitt M(1923)	OM	S	100
Zurich	1837	Zurich M	OM	S	

1848		Blake Amish M	AM	S	50	Waterloo
1889		Stanley M	OOM	S		Waterloo

B. MANITOBA

1926	Alexander	Griswold MB	MB	R	68	
1908	Altona	Bergthaler M	CM	EK	2735	
1918		Sommerfelder M	SM	EK	2500	
1927		Altona MB	MB	R	36	
1936		Rudnerweider M	Rud	EK	1211	
1935	Arden	Bergthaler M	CM	EK		Altona
1925	Arnaud	Arnaud EMB/MB[9]	EMB/MB	R	120	
1925		Arnaud M	CM	R	50	
1936	Bergfeld	Rudnerweider M	Rud	EK		Altona
1926	Birtle	Schoenwieser M(1930s)	CM	R	—	
1874	Blumenort(E)[10]	Kleine Gemeinde	KG	EK	811	
1923	Blumenort(W)[10]	Blumenorter M	CM	R	236	
1928	Boissevain	Boissevain MB	MB	R	58	
	Brooklands	See Winnipeg Schoenwieser				
1876	Chortitz(E)	Chortitz M	ChM	EK	1364	
1880s	Chortitz(W)	Reinlaender M(1920s)	ReM	EK	—	
1927	Crystal City	Whitewater M	CM	R		Whitewater
1926	Domain	Domain MB	MB	R	—	
1892	Edenburg/Halbstadt	Bergthaler M	CM	EK		Altona
1940	Eigenhof	Rudnerweider M	CM	EK		Altona
1930	Elie	Elie MB(1930s)	MB	R	—	
1925	Elm Creek	Elm Creek MB	MB	R	59	
1926	Foxwarren	Schoenwieser M(1930s)	CM	R	—	
1931	Gardenton	Schoenwieser M	CM	R		Winnipeg

TABLE 27 (continued)

MENNONITE CONGREGATIONS IN CANADA

B. MANITOBA (continued)

PLACE[2]	DATE[3]	NAME[4]	CONGREGATIONAL FAMILY[5]	CULTURAL IDENTITY[6]	MEMBERSHIP IN 1940[7]
Glencross	1936	Rudnerweider M	Rud	EK	Altona
Glenlea	1925	Schoenwieser M	CM	R	—
Gnadenthal	1923	Blumenorter M	CM	R	Blumenort(W)
	1929	Gnadenthal MB	MB	R	51
Graysville	1927	Schoenwieser M	CM	K/R	—
Griswold		See Alexander and Oak Lake			
Grossweide	1896	Grossweide MB	MB	R	88
	1890s	Sommerfelder M	SM	EK	Altona
Grunthal	1882	Chortitzer M	ChM	EK	Chortitz(E)
	1927	Elim M	CM	R	216
Halbstadt		See Edenburg/Halbstadt			
Headingly		See Pigeon Lake			
High Bluff	1924	Schoenwieser M	CM	R	Winnipeg
Holmfield	1928	Holmfield and Smith Hill MB	MB	R	55
Homewood	1938	Bergthaler M	CM	EK	Altona
Justice	1928	Brookdale MB	MB	R	34
Kirkella	1926	Schoenwieser M(1930s)	CM	R	—
Kirkfield Park		See Winnipeg Schoenwieser			
Kleefeld	1874	Kleine Gemeinde	KG	EK	Blumenort(E)

Place	Year	Congregation			
Kronsgart	1881	Holdemaner M	CGCM	EK	442
Kronsweide	1896	Kronsgart MB	MB	EK	56
Landmark	1890s	Sommerfelder M	SM	EK	Altona
	1920	Kleine Gemeinde	KG	EK	Blumenort(E)
LaSalle	1925	LaSalle MB	MB	R	42
Lena	1926	Whitewater M	CM	R	Whitewater
	1928	Lena MB	MB	R	Holmfield
Lindal	1935	Lindal MB Mission	MB	R	M
Lorette	1925	Schoenwieser M(1935)	CM	R	—
Lowe Farm	1892	Sommerfelder M	SM	EK	Altona
	1900	Bergthaler M	CM	EK	Altona
Manitou	1927	Manitou MB	MB	R	73
	1927	Whitewater M	CM	R	Whitewater
Manson	1926	Schoenwieser M(1930s)	CM	R	—
Marquette	1925	Marquette MB	MB	R	Winnipeg North End
Mather		See also Pigeon Lake			
		See Crystal City			
Mayfield	1940	Rudnerweider M	Rud	EK	Altona
McAuley	1926	Schoenwieser M(1930s)	CM	R	—
Meadows		See Pigeon Lake			
Melita	1932	Melita MB(1936)	MB	R	—
Morden	1928	Morden MB	MB	EK/R	90
Morris	1931	Bergthaler M	CM	R	Altona
	1920s	Lichtenauer M(1930s)	CM	R	—
	1938	Schoenwieser M	CM	EK	Winnipeg
New Bergthal	1937	Rudnerweider M	Rud	R	Altona
Newton Siding	1926	Newton MB	MB	R	93
Niverville	1926	Niverville MB	MB	R	89
	1926	Schoenwieser M	CM	R	—

TABLE 27 (continued)

MENNONITE CONGREGATIONS IN CANADA

B. MANITOBA (continued)

PLACE[2]	DATE[3]	NAME[4]	CONGREGATIONAL FAMILY[5]	CULTURAL IDENTITY[6]	MEMBERSHIP IN 1940[7]
North Kildonan	1936	Chortitzer M	Ch	EK	Chortitz(E) 175
	1928	North Kildonan MB	MB	R	Winnipeg
	1928	Schoenwieser M	CM	R	Winnipeg
Oak Lake	1927	Schoenwieser M	CM	R	Winnipeg
Osterwick	1920s	Sommerfelder M	SM	EK	Altona
Petersfield	1937	Schoenwieser M	CM	R	Winnipeg
Pigeon Lake	1925	Schoenwieser M(1939)[9]	CM	R	–
	1939	Schoenfelder M	CM	R	96
Plum Coulee	1897	Bergthaler M	CM	EK	Altona
	1917	Sommerfelder M	SM	EK	Altona
	1937	Rudnerweider M	Rud	EK	Altona
Prairie Rose		See Lorette			
Reinfeld	1936	Altkolonier M	OC	EK	390
Reinland	1870s	Reinlaender M(1920s)	ReM	EK	–
	1892	Sommerfelder M	SM	EK	Altona
	1923	Blumenorter M	CM	R	Blumenort(W)
	1937	Rudnerweider M	Rud	EK	Altona
Rivers	1929	Schoenwieser M(1939)	CM	R	–
	1939	Whitewater M	CM	R	Whitewater

Place	Year	Congregation			Location
Rosefarm	1937	Rudnerweider M	Rud	EK	Altona
Rose Isle	1920s	Sommerfelder M	SM	EK	Altona
Rosenbach	1920s	Sommerfelder M	SM	EK	Altona
Rosenfeld	1937	Bergthaler M	CM	EK	Altona
	1937	Rudnerweider M	Rud	EK	Altona
Rosengard	1930	Chortitz M	ChM	EK	Chortitz(E)
Rosenort (near Morris)	1874	Kleine Gemeinde	KG	EK	334
	1881	Holdemaner M	CGCM	EK	Kleefeld
Rosenort(W)	1880s	Reinlaender M(1920s)	ReM	EK	—
	1923	Blumenorter M	CM	R	Blumenort(W)
	1937	Altkolonier M	OC	EK	Reinfeld
Rudnerweide	1936	Rudnerweider M	Rud	EK	Altona
Ste. Anne	1890	Greenland Holdeman M	CGCM	EK	Kleefeld
	1920	Schoenwieser M(1932)	CM	R	—
St. Elizabeth	1920s	Lichtenauer M	CM	R	166
Schoenthal	1890s	Sommerfelder M	SM	EK	Altona
Silberfeld	1890s	Sommerfelder M	SM	EK	Altona
Sperling	1928	Sperling MB	MB	R	18
	1928	Schoenwieser M(1930s)	CM	R	—
Springstein	1924	Springstein MB	MB	R	Winnipeg North End
	1924	Schoenwieser M(1938)	CM	R	—
	1938	Springstein M	CM	R	85
Starbuck	1924	Schoenwieser M	CM	R	Winnipeg
Steinbach	1874	Kleine Gemeinde	KG	EK	Blumenort(E)
	1881	Holdemaner M	CGCM	EK	Kleefeld
	1897	Bruderthaler M	EMB	EK	274
	1923	Steinbach MB	MB	R	213
	1923	Schoenwieser M	CM	R	Winnipeg

TABLE 27 (continued)

MENNONITE CONGREGATIONS IN CANADA

PLACE[2]	DATE[3]	NAME[4]	CONGREGATIONAL FAMILY[5]	CULTURAL IDENTITY[6]	MEMBERSHIP IN 1940[7]
B. MANITOBA (continued)					
Stonewall	1925	Schoenwieser M	CM	R	Winnipeg
Stuartburn		See Gardenton			
Virden		See Oak Lake			
Waldheim	1890s	Sommerfelder M	SM	EK	Altona
Weidenfeld	1938	Chortitzer M	ChM	EK	Chortitz(E)
Westbourne		See High Bluff			
Whitewater	1925	Whitewater M	CM	R	427
Willen	1926	Schoenwieser M(1930s)	CM	R	—
Wingham	1920s	Blumenorter M	CM	R	Blumenort(W)
Winkler	1888	Winkler MB	MB	R	379
	1895	Bergthaler M	CM	EK	Altona
	1937	Rudnerweider M	Rud	EK	Altona
	1900s	Sommerfelder M	SM	EK	Altona
Winnipeg	1907	North End MB	MB	K/R	345
	1928	Schoenwieser (First)M	CM	R	692
	1936	South End MB	MB	R	126
	1938	Bethel M	CM	EK	60
		See also North Kildonan			
Winnipegosis	1931	Nordheimer M	CM	R	65

C. SASKATCHEWAN

Place	Year	Congregation			Number	District
Aberdeen	1902	Bergthaler (S)M	BM	EK		Rosthern
	1906	Aberdeen MB	MB	LK	109	
	1907	Rosenorter M	CM	EK/LK		Rosthern
Alsask	1910	Alsask MBC	MBC	S	43	
Arelee	1903	Arelee MB(1930s)	MB	LK	—	
Beaverdale	1931	Immanuel M	CM	K/R		Meadow Lake
Beaver Flat	1913	Bethania MB	MB	LK	79	
Beechy	1925	Friedensheim MB	MB	R	37	
Blumenhof	1906	Blumenort MB	MB	E/K	38	
Borden	1904	Borden MB	MB	LK	123	
Bornemouth	1927	Hoffnungsfeld M	CM	R		Rabbit Lake
Capasin	1931	Rosenorter M	CM	K/R	75	
Carrot River	1908	Bergthaler (S)M	BM	EK		Rosthern
	1926	Hoffnungsfeld M	CM	R	77	
	1926	Carrot River MB(?)	MB	R	—	
Compass	1933	Immanuel M	CM	K/R		Meadow Lake
	1938	Northern Evangelical	MB	K/R	20	
Dalmeny	1901	Ebenezer MB	MB	LK	230	
	1904	Dalmeny Bible	EMB	LK	500	
	1907	Neu Hoffnung MB	MB	LK	21	
Drake	1906	North Star M	CM	LK	286	
Duck Lake	1934	Horse Lake Rosenorter M	CM	K/R		Rosthern
Dundurn	1924	Nordheimer M	CM	R	319	
	1927	Nordheimer M	CM	R		Dundurn
Elbow	1927	Elbow MB	MB	R	11	
Erwood	1936	Hebron M	CM	R	74	
Eyebrow	1929	Eyebrow M	CM	R	59	
Fairholme	1927	Bruderthaler M(1930s)	EMB	K/R	—	

TABLE 27 (continued)

MENNONITE CONGREGATIONS IN CANADA

PLACE[2]	DATE[3]	NAME[4]	CONGREGATIONAL FAMILY[5]	CULTURAL IDENTITY[6]	MEMBERSHIP IN 1940[7]
C. SASKATCHEWAN (continued)					
Fiske	1925	Ebenfeld M	CM	R	Herschel
Fitzmaurice	1930s	Parkerview M	CM	K/R	30
Flowing Well	1907	Gnadenau MB	MB	LK	81
Foam Lake	1937	Foam Lake MB	MB	R	51
Fox Valley	1914	Fox Valley MB(1930s)	MB	LK	—
Frontier	1934	Eastbrook MB(1939)	MB	R	—
Garthland	1931	Rosenorter M	CM	K/R	Rosthern
Gilroy	1920s	Gilroy MB	MB	R	20
Glenbush	1927	Hoffnungsfelder M	CM	R	Rabbit Lake
	1928	Glenbush MB	MB	R	120
Glidden	1927	Ebenfeld M	CM	R	Herschel
Gouldtown	1926	Gouldtown M	CM	R	25
Great Deer	1912	Bethel M	CM	LK	140
Greenfarm	1913	Greenfarm MB	MB	LK	81
Guernsey	1905	Sharon M	OM	S	120
Gull Lake	1930	Kildron M	CM	R	25
Hague	1895	Reinlaender M(1920s)	ReM	EK	—
	1903	Rosenorter M	CM	LK	Rosthern
	1924	Hochfeld Rosenorter M	CM	R	Rosthern

Location	Year	Congregation			
Hawarden	1926	Neuanlage Rosenorter M	CM	R	Rosthern
	1930s	Altkolonier M	OC	EK	1200
	1940	Rudnerweider M	Rud	EK	Altona
	1940	Chortitz Rudnerweider M	Rud	EK	Altona
Hepburn	1928	Hawarden MB(c. 1936)	MB	R	—
	1910	Hepburn MB	MB	LK	305
Herbert	1905	Herbert M	CM	EK/LK/R	400
	1905	Herbert MB	MB	LK	223
Herschel	1925	Ebenfeld M	CM	R	279
Humboldt	1920s	Humboldt MB(1936)	MB	R	—
Jansen	1925	Jansen-Watson Group	CM	R	20
Kelstern	1907	Elim MB	MB	LK	75
Kerrobert	1928	Ebenfeld M	CM	R	Herschel
Kindersley	1927	Ebenfeld M	CM	R	Herschel
Laird	1898	Laird MB	MB	LK	100
	1910	Rosenorter M	CM	LK	Rosthern
	1910	Tiefengrund Rosenorter M	CM	LK	Rosthern
Langham	1900	Bethesda M	CM	LK	89
	1901	Emmanuel KMB	KMB	LK	Waldheim
	1902	Bruderthaler M	EMB	LK	Dalmeny
	1912	Zoar M	CM	LK	180
	1912	South Bruderthaler M	EMB	LK	Dalmeny
Lashburn	1936	Lashburn MB	MB	R	Maidstone
Lost River	1916	Bethany M	CM	EK	170
Maidstone	1926	Maidstone MB	MB	R	35
Main Centre	1904	MB of Main Centre	MB	LK/R	230
	1940	Capeland M	CM	LK	54
Mayfair	1928	Hoffnungsfeld M	CM	R	Rabbit Lake
	1936	Bethel M	CM	K/R	29

TABLE 27 (continued)

MENNONITE CONGREGATIONS IN CANADA

C. SASKATCHEWAN (continued)

PLACE[2]	DATE[3]	NAME[4]	CONGREGATIONAL FAMILY[5]	CULTURAL IDENTITY[6]	MEMBERSHIP IN 1940[7]
McMahon	1927	Reinfeld MB	MB	R	71
	1930	Emmaus M	CM	K/R	Swift Current
Meadow Lake	1930	Immanuel M	CM	K/R	118
Morse	1920s	Glen Kerr M	CM	R	20
Mullingar	1927	Mullingar MB	MB	R	41
Neville	1914	Pella Emmaus	CM	K	Swift Current
Osler	1928	Osler M	CM	R	50
Oxbow	1931	Oxbow MB(1933)	MB	R	—
Petaigan	1931	Hoffnungsfeld M	CM	R	96
Pierceland	1931	Immanuel M	CM	K/R	Meadow Lake
	1939	Pierceland MB	MB	R	25
Pleasant Point	1924	Nordheimer M	CM	R	Dundurn
Rabbit Lake	1926	Hoffnungsfeld M	CM	R	134
Rosthern	1891	Rosenorter M	CM	LK	1654
	1892	Eigenheim Rosenorter M(1928)	CM	LK	—
	1928	Eigenheim M	CM	LK	217
	1901	Bergthaler(S) M	BM	EK	906
Saskatoon	1932	First M	CM	R	147
	1937	Saskatoon MB	MB	R	136
Schoenfeld	1935	Emmaus M	CM	K/R	Swift Current

Place	Year	Congregation	Conf.	Dist.	No.	Town
Speedwell	1930s	Fairholme MB	MB	K/R	86	
Superb	1925	Ebenfeld M	CM	R	—	Herschel
Swift Current	1904	Reinlaender M(1920s)	ReM	EK	556	
	1904	Sommerfelder M	SM	EK	210	
	1914	Emmaus M	CM	E/K	27	
	1914	Swift Current MB	MB	E/K		Swift Current
Syke's Farm	1927	Emmaus M	CM	R	15	
Truax	1933	Ebenezer M	CM	R	18	
	1934	Truax MB	MB	R	25	
Turnhill	1901	Bruderfeld MB	MB	LK	250	
Waldheim	1899	Salem KMB	KMB	LK	122	
	1899	Brotherfield MB	MB	LK	186	
	1909	Zoar M	CM	LK	100	
	1918	Waldheim MB	MB	LK	—	
Warman	1932	Warman M(1939)	CM	EK	M	Rosthern
	1939	Warman MB	MB	EK	—	
Watrous	1903	Bergthaler(S) M	BM	EK		
	1927	Philadelphia EMB(1932)	EMB	R	112	
	1932	Watrous MB	MB	R	27	
	1932	Bethany M	CM	R		
Wingard	1935	Rosenorter M	CM	K/R	61	Rosthern
Woodrow	1909	Woodrow MB	MB	LK		
Wymark	1927	Emmaus M	CM	K/R		Swift Current

D. ALBERTA

Place	Year	Congregation	Conf.	Dist.	No.
Acadia Valley	1908	Acadia Valley M	OM	S	8
Bergen	1933	Bergen MBC	MBC	S	37
Berrymoor	1931	Berrymoor MBC	MBC	S	7
Bucks Creek	1935	Bucks Creek MBC	MBC	S	2

TABLE 27 (continued)

MENNONITE CONGREGATIONS IN CANADA

D. ALBERTA (continued)

PLACE[2]	DATE[3]	NAME[4]	CONGREGATIONAL FAMILY[5]	CULTURAL IDENTITY[6]	MEMBERSHIP IN 1940[7]
Carstairs	1901	West Zion M	OM	S	67
Castor	1906	Markham MBC	MBC	S	43
Chinook-Naco	1927	Neukirchener M	CM	R	31
Coaldale	1926	Coaldale MB	MB	R	494
Coaldale	1926	Coaldale M	CM	R	140
Condor	1933	Condor MBC	MBC	S	2
Countess	1927	Countess MB(1930s)	MB	R	—
Countess	1927	Countess M(1930s)	M	R	—
		See Rosemary Westheimer			
Cremona	1932	Cremona MBC	MBC	S	21
Crooked Creek	1929	Rosedale Holdemaner M	CGCM	EK	Linden
Crowfoot		See Namaka and Rosemary			
Didsbury	1894	Didsbury MBC	MBC	S	214
	1903	Bergthal M	CM	EK/R	126
Duchess	1916	Duchess M	OM	S	56
Galahad	1921	Gleichen MBC	MBC	S	21
Gem	1927	Gem EMB	EMB	R	61
Gem	1929	Gem MB	MB	R	154
Gem	1929	Gem M	CM	R	20
		See also Namaka			

Place	Year	Congregation			No.
Gimlet	1933	Gimlet MBC	MBC	S	16
Gore	1908	Gore MBC	MBC	S	23
Graindale	1915	Graindale MBC	MBC	S	21
Grande Prairie	1918	Bear Lake KMB(c.1930)	KMB	LK	—
	1927	Hoffnungsfeld M	CM	R	106
Grassy Lake	1928	Grassy Lake MB	MB	R	30
High River	1891	Mount View M	OM	S	57
Hoadley	1934	Hoadley MBC	MBC	S	11
Hussar		See Rosemary Westheimer			
James River	1925	James River MBC	MBC	S	9
Lacombe	1920s	Lacombe M	CM	R	25
		See also Rosemary Westheimer			
LaCrete	1936	LaCrete Altkolonier M	OC	EK	150
		Two meeting houses at Rosenort and Blumenort			
	1930s	LaCrete Bergthaler(S) M	BM	EK	50
La Glace	1927	La Glace MB	MB	R	73
Lindbrook	1928	Lindbrook MB	MB	R	58
Linden	1902	Holdemaner M	CGCM	EK/S	358
	1929	EMB of Linden	EMB	R	35
Lymburn	1927	Lymburn M(1930s)	CM	R	—
May City	1906	May City MBC	MBC	S	38
Mayton	1901	Mayton M(1920s)	OM	S	—
Munson		See Namaka			
Namaka	1927	Landskrone M(1937)	CM	R	—
	1927	Namaka EMB	EMB	R	60

The Namaka Allianz (EMB) group was somewhat of a "mother church" for EMB *Filiale* at Crowfoot, Gem, Linden (Swalwell), Munson, and Ryley, all of which disappeared (Crowfoot, Munson, Ryley) or merged with the MBs (Gem, Linden, Namaka) in the 1940s.

TABLE 27 (continued)

MENNONITE CONGREGATIONS IN CANADA

PLACE[2]	DATE[3]	NAME[4]	CONGREGATIONAL FAMILY[5]	CULTURAL IDENTITY[6]	MEMBERSHIP IN 1940[7]
		D. ALBERTA (continued)			
Pincher Creek	1928	Blumenthaler M	CM	R	47
Reist	1911	Clearwater M(c. 1930)	OM	S	—
Rosedale	1920s	Rosedale M(1930s)	CM	R	—
Rosemary	1930	Westheimer M	CM	R	312

Rosemary Westheimer was somewhat of a "mother church" in varying degrees for various groups, some of which dissolved as groups or settlements (Countess, Crowfoot, Seven Persons, Hussar), joined Rosemary (Namaka), or became independent (Gem, Lacombe, Tofield).

PLACE[2]	DATE[3]	NAME[4]	CONGREGATIONAL FAMILY[5]	CULTURAL IDENTITY[6]	MEMBERSHIP IN 1940[7]
Ryley	1930s	Rosemary MB(1930s)	MB	R	—
Seven Persons		See Namaka			
		See Rosemary Westheimer			
Stettler	1909	Stettler MBC	MBC	S	10
Sundre	1934	McDougall Flat MBC	MBC	S	13
Sunnyslope	1909	Sunnyslope MBC	MBC	S	17
Tofield	1910	Salem M	OM	S	231
	1929	Schoensee M	M	R	96
Vauxhall	1933	Vauxhall MB	MB	R	64
	1937	Vauxhall M	M	R	39
Youngstown	1910	Youngstown M(1930s)	OM	S	—

Mennonites from Russia embarking on the S.S. *Bruton* at Libau, Latvia, 1923.

Members of the new Stirling congregation in Kitchener excavating for a new meeting house in 1924.

Kanadier Mennonites leaving for Paraguay from Altona in 1926.

The Kitchener-Waterloo *Daily Record* announces the removal of the ban on Mennonite immigration in 1922.

ᴇ DAILY RECᴏ

KITCHENER-WATERLOO, FRIDAY, JUNE 9, 1922.

Mennonites Now Free To Come Into Canada

Order-in-Council passed by Union Government Forbidding Mennonite Immigration Into This Country Has Been Annulled By King Government As Result of Steps Taken By W. D. Euler M. P.

WAS INJUSTICE TO DESIRABLE PEOPLE

(Exclusive to Record.)

OTTAWA, June 9.—The order-in-council promulgated by the Union Government during the war restricting all Mennonite immigration into Canada has just been annulled by the Liberal government as a result of the efforts of W. D. Euler M. P., according to information received by Record's press gallery representative at Ottawa. The Mennonites are now as free to enter Canada as the adherents of any other faith. This announcement will be received with considerable pleasure by the thousands of Mennonites in Kitchener, Waterloo and the county.

MEMBERS OBJECTED

In 1919 the Union Government passed an order-in-council forbidding Mennonite immigration into Canada. This was done in spite of the vigorous protests of W. D. Euler M. P., I. E. Pedlow, M. P., of South Renfrew and others. The member for North Waterloo held that the regulation was unfair and offensive to many of the people of Waterloo county and elsewhere, the sons and daughters of its pioneers who are admittedly the most desirable citizens.

REMOVES DISCRIMINATION

As soon as the King government took office, the member for North Waterloo immediately took steps to have this objectionable regulation repealed. As a result the government has annulled the order-in-council which removes the discrimination against the Mennonite people. The objectionable regulation interfered with visits of American Mennonites with their Canadian relatives and friends. This particularly objectionable feature has been removed in the annulling of the order-in-council.

MENNONITES PLEASED

The announcement of the repeal of the order-in-council restricting Mennonite immigration into Canada will be received with a great deal of pleasure by the Mennonite people of North Waterloo, according to a statement made to the Record today by D. B. Betzner of this city, when informed by the Record of the annulling of the restrictions. The news, Mr. Betzner said, will be a matter of extreme satisfaction to the Mennonites of Canada.

TEA AND SUGAR PRICES ADVANC

Two Increases In Sugar Yester No Hope For Relief From Higher Prices This Year

The prices of two commodities soaring. Noted advances in the pr of tea and sugar have occurred wi the last few days. Tea prices gone up from 55 to 65 cents. S prices yesterday went up 50 cents advances occurring in one day, wholesale price is $6.93 a cwt. June 3 the price went up 10 cents

The Record learned from Ge Schell, grocer, today that there h hope for relief this year in the of either commodities. "Refiners

The first ditched road leading from the CNR tracks at Reesor in Northern Ontario to the new settlement there.

The wedding of Liese Wall and John Harder in Saskatoon in 1929.

Mennonite funeral procession in Manitoba in 1930.

The new meeting house of the Nordheimer built at Hanley in 1929.

Cartoon from the Toronto *Mail and Empire* illustrates the closing of the immigration door to Mennonites in November of 1929.

1931 baptism ceremony of the Kitchener Mennonite Brethren congregation.

e many others during the Depression, the destitute Abraham C. Fehr family from the
gue, Saskatchewan, area tried unsuccessfully to make a new beginning in the Peace
er country in 1934 and ended up heading for home again.

Young people, like these led by J. C. Fretz in 1938, went by the hundreds into various communities to teach community Bible schools.

Teachers J. B. Martin, S. F. Coffman, Oscar Burkholder, and C. F. Derstine (centre group in front row), surrounded here by cooks, maintenance staff, and students of the Ontario Mennonite Bible Institute in 1934, contributed much to the preserving of the culture and the keeping of the young people.

nnonites expressed their loyalty as citizens by paying tribute to King George VI and
een Elizabeth, seen here under the Peace Tower in Ottawa with Prime Minister
L. Mackenzie King, on the occasion of their visit in 1939.

David Toews.

B. B. Janz.

S. F. Coffman.

Jacob H. Janzen.

E. BRITISH COLUMBIA

Abbotsford	1939	North Abbotsford MB	MB	R	60
	1932	South Abbotsford MB	MB	R	255
	1936	Abbotsford M	CM	K/R	72
Agassiz	1932	Agassiz MB(1930s)	MB	R	—
Aldergrove	1934	United M. of Coghlan	CM	K/R	46
Black Creek	1934	Black Creek United M	CM	R	28
	1934	Black Creek MB	MB	R	45
New Westminster	1938	New Westminster M	CM	R/K	25
Oliver	1936	United M	CM	R/K	17
Renata	1907	Renata M	CM	K	10
Sardis	1929	First M	CM	R	36
	1930	Sardis MB	MB	R	149
Vancouver	1935	First United M	CM	R	60
	1936	Vancouver MB	MB	R	188
Vanderhoof	1918	Vanderhoof MB(c. 1920)	MB	LK	—
Yarrow	1928	Yarrow MB	MB	R	434
	1930s	Yarrow EMB(1930s)	EMB	R	—
	1938	United M	CM	R	42

Notes:

1 "Congregations" in the usage of this table includes also congregational units, meaning all the meeting places, if known, of a congregation. "Missions," as distinct from organized congregations with memberships, are identified with "M" in the membership column. Every effort has been made to make this table accurate and complete. Any errors should be reported, so that subsequent editions can be corrected.

TABLE 27 (continued)

MENNONITE CONGREGATIONS IN CANADA

2　"Place" has reference to post office, except in the case of some villages in former Mennonite reserve areas in Manitoba and Saskatchewan.

3　"Date" usually means the first date in the life of the group—in other words, the beginning of services. In some cases this date may coincide with the date of founding or organization or with the opening of the first building.

4　Every "Name" has been abbreviated to conserve space. The word "Church," a part of every name, unless replaced by a term like "Mission," is omitted. "M" stands for Mennonite, and other symbols appearing in this column are explained below. It should be pointed out that the emergence of congregations with symbols MWC, OC, and Rud is chronicled in Chapter 9 of this book.

5　The abbreviations used for "Congregational Family," meaning denomination, stand for the following, presented here in the order of their appearance (the reader is referred to the following parts of the book for further elaboration: Chapter 1, Chart 1, Table 9; Chapter 9, Chart 2; and Appendix 1):

RM　Reformed Mennonite Churches

MBC　Mennonite Brethren in Christ Conferences

OM　Mennonite Conference of Ontario and Alberta-Saskatchewan Mennonite Conference (now known as Mennonite Church Region I)

AM　Amish Mennonite Conference

CM　Conference of Mennonites in Canada

MB　Mennonite Brethren Churches in the Ontario and Northern (Western Canadian) District Conferences

MWC　Markham-Waterloo Mennonite Conference

OOM　Old Order Mennonite Churches

GC　General Conference Mennonite Church (the single usage in this table had only unofficial and informal meaning at this time)

OOA　Old Order Amish Churches

DM   David Martin Old Order Mennonite Church
BA   Beachy Amish Churches
EMB   Evangelical Mennonite Brethren Conference
SM   Sommerfelder Mennonite Churches
Rud   Rudnerweider Mennonite Church
KG   Kleine Gemeinden
ChM   Chortitzer Mennonite Church
ReM   Reinlaender Mennonite Churches
CGCM Church of God in Christ Mennonite
OC   Altkolonier (Old Colony) Mennonite Churches
BM   Bergthaler(S) Mennonite Churches
KMB   Krimmer Mennonite Brethren Conference

6   "Cultural Identity" symbols refer to concepts described in this chapter. "S" stands for congregations and missions originating in, or sponsored by, Mennonites of Swiss–South German origin and identity; the symbol "D" for Mennonites of Dutch–North German origin and identity is not used here, but the following are all subdivisions of "D": "K" — an inclusive term for Kanadier; "EK" — Early Kanadier; "LK" — Late Kanadier; "R" — Russlaender.

7   "Membership" does not include unbaptized children and young people and is given for 1940 or nearest date for which information is available. In a few cases, guestimates have been made. In most cases, the membership figure applies only to the particular entry. Sometimes, however, a composite figure is given for all the "units" in a particular congregational family. Related entries refer the reader back to the composite figure by giving the place and allowing the reader to check for the appropriate group symbol within the place category. Example: the membership of Hostetler's Reformed Mennonite Church is found under New Hamburg (Ont.), where it is included in North Easthope Reformed Mennonite Church.

8   Brackets and dates indicate dissolution.

9   Some congregations changed identity in terms of congregational family during this period. This is indicated in one of two ways: (1) through double symbols EMB/MB; or (2) by consecutive entries in which the date of "dissolution" in the first entry coincides with the date of "founding" in a subsequent entry.

10 (E) and (W) have reference to former East Reserve and West Reserve areas, respectively.

FOOTNOTES

1   Daniel Loewen, "Wert und Notwendigkeit der Gemein-dezugehoerigkeit," *Jahrbuch*, 1936, p. 59.
2   Herbert P. Enns and Jacob Fast, eds., *Jubilee Issue of the Waterloo-Kitchener United Mennonite Church* (Waterloo, Ont.: W-K United Mennonite Church, 1974), p. 9.
3   Erland Waltner, "Anabaptist Concept of the Church," *Mennonite Life* 5 (October 1950):40–43.
4   J. Winfield Fretz, "Mutual Aid Among Mennonites I," *Mennonite Quarterly Review* XIII (January 1939):58.
5   H.S. Bender, "Editorial," *Mennonite Quarterly Review* XVIII (January 1944):5.
6   Robert Friedman, "On Mennonite Historiography and on Individualism and Brotherhood," *Mennonite Quarterly Review* 18 (April 1944):121.
7   Based on "Statuten der Whitewater Mennoniten Gemeinde," in G.G. Neufeld, *Die Geschichte der Whitewater Mennoniten Gemeinde in Manitoba, Canada, 1925–1965* (n.p., 1967), pp. 160–61, which in turn were adapted from the constitution of the Schoenwieser church.
8   Galatians 6:2, RSV.
9   F.F. Enns, "Gemeindearbeiter," *Jahrbuch*, 1928, pp. 30–39.
10   *Ibid.*, p. 31.
11   Based on Table 29.
12   See Table 29 for examples. Exceptions were some bishop-oriented congregations in Russia and Canada where one membership and ministry covered several villages or districts and a number of meeting places.
13   Elder Peter Enns of St. Elizabeth in a report entitled "Our mode of living, or, how I have learned to know and love Mennonitism," quoted in Hank Unruh et al., *Of Days Gone By* (St. Elizabeth, Man.: St. Elizabeth Mennonite Community Centennial Reunion Committee, 1970), p. 99.
14   These observations are based largely on oral tradition transmitted to the author, as a descendant of the Russlaender and as a longtime resident among the Kanadier in southern Manitoba. See also E.K. Francis, *In Search of Utopia: The Mennonites of Manitoba* (Altona, Man.: D.W. Friesen & Sons, 1955), pp. 212–13. A further source on relations and comparisons is Hildegard Margo Martens, "The Relationship of Religions to Socio-Economic Divisions among the Mennonites of Dutch-Prussian-Russian Descent in Canada," (Ph.D. dissertation, University of Toronto, 1977). Of special interest is the suggestion by a Russlaender that the Kanadier had "*verhunzt*" (spoiled or murdered) the German language. See *Jahrbuch*, 1933, p. 44.

15   CGC, XV-30, J. Winfield Fretz, "Two Mennonite Cultures Meet," 1 June 1974.

16   Frank H. Epp, *Mennonite Exodus: The Rescue and Resettlement of the Russian Mennonites Since the Communist Revolution* (Altona, Man.: D.W. Friesen & Sons, 1962), p. 187.

17   CGC, XV-31.2, "1920-Immigration," Notes of Interview with Noah M. Bearinger, 30 July 1969.

18   Frank H. Epp, *Mennonite Exodus*, pp. 122, 328.

19   E.S. Hallman, "The Mennonite Immigration Movement into Canada," *Mennonite Year-Book and Directory*, 1927, p. 29.

20   *Ibid.*, p. 7.

21   Herbert P. Enns and Jacob Fast, p. 8.

22   G.G. Neufeld, p. 29.

23   Herbert P. Enns and Jacob Fast, p. 8.

24   There actually was some fraternization between the two groups. See, for example, "Verhandlungen der zehnten Noerdlichen Distrikt-Konferenz der Mennoniten Bruedergemeinde von Nord-Amerika, abgehalten in der Gemeinde zu Hepburn, Saskatchewan, vom 21. bis zum 25. Juni, 1919," reproduced in *Verhandlungen der 34. Bundes-Konferenz der Mennoniten Bruedergemeinde von Nord Amerika, 1919*, pp. 138–39.

25   David Adrian, ed., *Marvellous Are Thy Ways: A Brief History of the Rosemary Mennonite Church* (n.p., 1961), p. 4.

26   Franz J. Friesen quoted in *Gedenk und Dankfeier des 25-jaehrigen Bestehens der Coaldale Mennoniten Bruedergemeinde*, p. 39.

27   The *Allianzgemeinden* were a minority movement representing perhaps one per cent of the 100,000 Mennonites in Russia prior to the Great War (author's estimate), the *Bruedergemeinden* about 20 per cent (P.M. Friesen, *Alt-Evangelische Mennonitische Bruderschaft in Russland [1789–1910]* [Halbstadt: Radugu, 1911], p. 728), and the *Mennonitengemeinden* the rest. The influence of both Allianz and Brueder, however, far exceeded their number.

28   J.G. Rempel, *Fuenfzig Jahre Konferenzbestrebungen 1902–1952: Konferenz der Mennoniten in Canada*: 2 vols. (n.p., 1952).

29   Samuel Floyd Pannabecker, *Open Doors: A History of the General Conference Mennonite Church* (Newton, Kans.: Faith and Life Press, 1975), pp. 146–67.

30   J.A. Toews, *A History of the Mennonite Brethren Church: Pilgrims and Pioneers* (Fresno, Cal.: Board of Christian Literature, General Conference of Mennonite Brethren Churches, 1975), pp. 161–74.

31   H.F. Epp, "Evangelical Mennonite Brethren," *Mennonite Encyclopedia*, 2:262–64.

32   G.S. Rempel, ed., *A Historical Sketch of the Churches of the Evangelical Mennonite Brethren (1889–1939)* (n.p., 1939), pp. 5, 9–11, 17–20, 49–51.

33   H.F. Epp, p. 262.

34   Jacob P. Schultz, "Die E.M.B. Gemeinde zu Langham" in G.S. Rempel, p. 51.

35   For an assessment of relationships and attitudes between the two groups in Russia around the turn of the century, see P.M. Friesen, pp. 439–82, German edition.

36   Peter J. Klassen, "The Historiography of the Birth of the Mennonite Brethren Church," in Abraham Friesen, ed., *P.M. Friesen and His History: Understanding Mennonite Brethren Beginnings* (Fresno, Cal.: Center for Mennonite Brethren Studies, 1979), p. 124.

37   Franz Enns spoke about an "unholy war" on the question of baptism among Mennonites. See Franz Enns, "Die biblische Taufe," *Jahrbuch*, 1932, pp. 53–56.

38   Cornelius Krahn, "Evangelische Mennoniten-Gemeinden," *Mennonite Encyclopedia*, 2:268.

39   Jacob H. Janzen, "Siedlungsmoeglichkeiten in Ontario," *Der Bote* 2 (25 November 1925): 2.

40   I.H. Thiessen, ed., *Er Fuehret . . . Geschichte der Ontario MB Gemeinden, 1924–1957* (n.p., 1957), pp. 7–9.

41   *Ibid.*, pp. 10–13.

42   Herbert P. Enns and Jacob Fast, pp. 9–16.

43   *Ibid.*

44   David Wiens, "The History of the Elim Mennonite Church" (research paper, Canadian Mennonite Bible College, 1980), pp. 1–2.

45   Interview with Chortitzer Bishop H.K. Schellenberg, Steinbach, Manitoba, 18 April 1980.

46   *Ibid.*

47   Isaak Klassen, *Dem Herrn die Ehre* (Winnipeg, 1969), p. 54.

48   J.H. Lohrenz, *The Mennonite Brethren Church* (Hillsboro, Kans.: Mennonite Brethren Publishing House, 1950), p. 193. See also Peter Penner, "By Reason of Strength: Johann Warkentin, 1859–1948," *Mennonite Life* (December 1978):9.

49   J.A. Toews, p. 161.

50   *Ibid.*

51   Arnie Norman Neufeld, "The Origin and Early Growth of the Mennonite Brethren Church in Southern Manitoba" (M.A. thesis, Mennonite Brethren Bible Seminary, 1977).

52   See H.P. Toews, *A.H. Unruh, D.D., Lebensgeschichte* (Winnipeg: Christian Press, 1961), pp. 31–32.

53   See George David Pries, *A Place Called Peniel: Winkler Bible Institute, 1925–1975* (Altona, Man.: D.W. Friesen & Sons, 1975), p. 68.

54   *Ibid.*, p. 75.

55   Scores of church workers from many Mennonite groups attended this school.

56   J.A. Toews, p. 259.

57 Henry J. Gerbrandt, *Adventure in Faith:The Background in Europe and the Development in Canada of the Bergthaler Mennonite Church of Manitoba* (Altona, Man.: D.W. Friesen & Sons, 1970), p. 274. The author has based this conclusion on oral tradition.

58 *Ibid.*, p. 275.

59 Frank Isaac, *Elim 50th Anniversary, 1929-1979* (Winnipeg, 1979), pp. 1-11.

60 Isaak Klassen, p. 43.

61 Jake I. Pauls, "A History of the Morden Mennonite Bergthaler Church" (research paper, Canadian Mennonite Bible College, 1966), pp. 6-7.

62 *Ibid.*, pp. 7, 9, 11.

63 CGC, XV-31.2, Frank H. Epp, "Directory of Mennonite Congregations," in progress.

64 Frank H. Epp, *Mennonite Exodus*, pp. 312-14.

65 See, for example, Elim at Grunthal, in G.G. Neufeld, p. 13.

66 J.H. Enns, "Vorwart" in Isaak Klassen, pp. v-vi.

67 Isaak Klassen, p. 4.

68 G.G. Neufeld, pp. 6-7.

69 F.F. Enns, *Elder Enns* (Winnipeg: By the Author, 1979), p. 65.

70 Franz Enns to David Toews, 5 November 1927, reproduced in F.F. Enns, p. 62.

71 Isaak Klassen, p. 80 ff.

72 CGC, XV-31.2, "1920-Whitewater," Letter from a retired Manitoba elder to the author, 2 June 1980.

73 Isaak Klassen, pp. 42-43.

74 *Ibid.*, p. 43.

75 *Ibid.*, pp. 50-51.

76 *Fuenfundzwanzig Jahre: Vineland Vereinigte Mennonitengemeinde, 1936-61* (Vineland, Ont.: Vineland Vereinigte Mennoniten Gemeinde, 1967), pp. 5-6.

77 Heather Baerg, "History of the Nordheim Mennonite Church of Manitoba, Winnipegosis, 1931-1978" (research paper, Canadian Mennonite Bible College, 1978), p. 2.

78 CMBS, A.A. Dyck, Sr., "History of the Newton MB Church, July 1978."

79 J.P. Doerksen, ed., *Gem Mennonite Brethren Church, 1929-1979*, (n.p., 1979), pp. 10-11.

80 Isaak Klassen, p. 12.

81 Otto Loeppky, "Niverville Mennonite Church" (research paper, Canadian Mennonite Bible College, 1965), pp. 3-4.

82 *North Kildonan Mennonitengemeinde, 1935-1975* (Winnipeg: n.p., 1975), p. 4.

83 Hank Unruh, pp. 95-96.

84 Isaak Klassen, p. 55.

85 G.G. Neufeld, p. 112.

86 Frank H. Epp, "Directory of Mennonite Congregations."

87 Ernie Sawatsky, "The History of the Emmaus Mennonite Church of Swift Current and South" (research paper, Goshen College Biblical Seminary, c. 1961); Judy Epp, "Emmaus: Church of the Swift Current Reserve" (research paper, Canadian Mennonite Bible College, 1972).

88 Esther Patkau, *Nordheimer Mennonite Church of Saskatchewan, 1925-75* (Hanley, Sask.: Nordheim Mennonite Church, 1975), p. 2.

89 John D. Rempel, *A History of the Hague Mennonite Church, 1900-1975* (n.p., n.d.), pp. 19-20.

90 J.G. Rempel, *Die Rosenorter Gemeinde in Saskatchewan in Wort und Bild* (n.p., 1950), pp. 5-11, 21-22, 44, 70 ff.

91 CMCA, vol. 844, "Gemeinde-Chronik," Kirchenbuch der Ebenfelder Mennoniten Gemeinde, p. 1.

92 J.A. Toews, p. 163-64.

93 *The History of the Main Centre Mennonite Brethren Church, 1904-1979* (n.p., 1979), p. 7.

94 G.S. Rempel, p. 10.

95 *Ibid.*, pp. 22-23.

96 *Ibid.*, p. 8.

97 *Ibid.*, p. 15.

98 J.P. Doerksen, p. 17.

99 J.A. Toews, p. 166.

100 B.B. Janz, "Das Eben-Ezer der MB Gemeinde," in *Gedenk und Dankfeier des 25-jaehrigen Bestehens der Coaldale Mennoniten Bruedergemeinde*, p. 25.

101 *Fiftieth Anniversary of the Coaldale Mennonite Brethren Church, May 23, 1976* (n.p., 1976), pp. 7-8.

102 Jacob D. Harder, "Causes of Change in the Socio-Religious Structure of the Bergthal Mennonite Community" (research paper, Wayne State University, 1969).

103 J.G. Rempel, "Renata," *Mennonite Encyclopedia*, 4:300.

104 *Verhandlungen* (GC), 1919, p. 137. See also J.A. Toews, pp. 140, 308.

105 Isaak Klassen, pp. 4, 33, 42, 67; G.G. Neufeld, p. 156.

106 David Toews, "Hilfswerk und Immigration," *Der Allgemeine Kongress der Mennoniten gehalten in Amsterdam, Elpect, Witmarsum, 29. Juni bis 3. Juli 1936*, ed. Christian Neff (Karlsruhe: Heinrich Schneider, 1936), pp. 151-58.

107 J.P. Doerksen, p. 18.

108 A.E. Janzen and Herbert Giesbrecht, eds., *We Recommend... Recommendations and Resolutions of the General Conference of the Mennonite Brethren Churches* (Fresno, Cal.: Board of Christian Literature, General Conference of Mennonite Brethren Churches, 1978), pp. 21-22.

109 G.G. Neufeld, pp. 33–34.
110 Elder P.W. Enns, quoted in Hank Unruh, p. 99.
111 A.H. Harder, "Das heilige Abendmahl," *Jahrbuch*, 1933, pp. 23–26.
112 G.G. Neufeld, pp. 36–39.
113 *Ibid.*, pp. 43–44.
114 *Ibid.*, p. 59.
115 *Ibid.*, p. 109.
116 J.P. Klassen, "Seelsorge," *Jahrbuch*, 1928, pp. 24–29.
117 *Ibid.*, p. 24.
118 *Ibid.*, p. 28.
119 Frank H. Epp, "Directory of Mennonite Congregations," and related sources.

7. The International Connection

The great need of our brethren in Russia has brought all the Mennonites of the world closer together. Formerly we were strangers to each other and now we feel so close. One can sense this . . . in Germany, Holland, the United States of America and Canada — C.F. KLASSEN. [1]

THE SETTLING down in congregational communities and the resultant inward look was rudely disturbed in the fall of 1929 by two international crises, which shook not only the Mennonites but also much of the western world. The ruthless implementation by Joseph Stalin of his first Five-Year Plan[2] sent thousands of Mennonites and other German-speaking colonists fleeing to Moscow in a desperate attempt to escape to the West.[3] Their exodus, however, was at that very time held up because countries like Canada would not accept any more immigrants, no matter how destitute, because of the national anti-immigration mood, which was strongly reinforced by the international economic depression.

It is an irony of history that relatively good things often arise from adverse situations, and such was the case for the Mennonites in 1929. Responding to the plight of co-religionists in Russia, the world Mennonite community experienced a new international awareness and a new sense of peoplehood, which had formerly escaped them in their separated communities, nationally and denominationally. The

298

focus of this new spirit and outlook was provided by the emerging Mennonite world conference.[4] At last the far-flung and separated Mennonite churches had an international connection, which some leaders in Canada learned to appreciate the most.

The convening in Danzig in 1930 of a World Relief Conference (*Welt-Hilfs-Konferenz*) as a direct response to the latest emergency was actually the second of three such Russia-oriented gatherings of world Mennonite leaders.[5] A similar event in Switzerland five years earlier had been called to commemorate at its birthplace in Zurich the 400th anniversary of the founding in 1525 of the Mennonite movement.[6] But even then the tragic unravelling of the Mennonite community in Russia had already been a centre of concern, not least of all because the only delegate from Russia, Elder Jakob A. Rempel, had been turned back at the border by uneasy Swiss authorities, a rejection all the more painful because Rempel had previously been a theology student in Switzerland for six years.[7]

The critical times continued through the 1930s with enforced collectivization, repeated famines, the exile to Siberia of Mennonite *kulaks*, and the systematic destruction of Mennonite cultural and religious life. Thus, the third Mennonite world conference in 1936 likewise could not escape the Russian theme, even though that conference in Holland in 1936 was called to commemorate another 400th anniversary — Menno Simons's resignation from the Catholic priesthood in 1536 to become an Anabaptist minister.[8]

For Canadian Mennonite leaders, especially for David Toews, the international concern for the Mennonites in Russia and from Russia, repeatedly reinforced by the world conferences, was a most welcome undergirding of the efforts to help the uprooted people. Canada was given not only a much-needed hearing before the world Mennonite community but also a helping hand, as the various dimensions of the Russlaender burden — immigration, detention, settlement, payment of the transportation debt, preventing the deportation of dependants, and the relief of poverty at home and famine abroad — continued into the second decade.[9]

From Civil War to Collectivization

The earlier desperate circumstances of the Mennonites in Russia as a result of revolution and civil war had been alleviated to a very considerable extent by the mid-1920s. Foreign relief organizations played a most vital role in rehabilitation, according to the Soviet government, which awarded first and second place for the quality of their work and their overall achievement to the French Red Cross and to the Mennonite Central Committee (MCC), respectively.[10] The American Relief Administration under Herbert Hoover stood in fifth place.

Working out of the city of Zaporozhe, the MCC had fed up to 43,000 people a day at the peak of the need in July 1922 at a total cost of $600,000. The MCC also distributed $260,000 worth of clothing, provided 50 Fordson tractor-plough units as well as horses and seed grain, and dispensed medicine to doctors and hospitals. Additionally, an estimated 20,000 packages containing food and clothing were forwarded on behalf of individuals in North America to individuals in the U.S.S.R. via the American Relief Administration.[11]

Other factors contributing to the renewal were the emigration of the destitute to Canada, the New Economic Policy introduced by Lenin in 1921 as a temporary concession to private enterprise, and several Mennonite organizations established during this time to speed the process of reconstruction. The Union of Citizens of Dutch Ancestry, previously mentioned, worked for economic renewal in the Ukraine out of Kharkov, until 1926 under the leadership of B.B. Janz.[12] A similar organization, the All-Russian Mennonite Agricultural Society, working out of Moscow with Peter Froese and C.F. Klassen as leaders, was founded in 1923 and embraced some 6,000 Mennonite farms in 19 local organizations in Siberia, the Volga Region, Turkestan, and the Crimea, in other words all the Mennonite settlements outside the Ukraine. The Society achieved notable success in procuring and distributing seed grain, improving the breed of cattle, producing cheese, and setting up tractor stations and grain distribution centres.[13] The Society also published *Der Praktische Landwirt* (*The Practical Farmer*), a publication for agricultural and economic affairs, beginning in 1925.

That year also marked the initiation of *Unser Blatt* (*Our Paper*), a monthly periodical devoted to religious affairs and published at the behest of the January 1925 meeting in Moscow of the General Conference of Mennonite Congregations in Russia. This meeting of representatives of Mennonite congregations from all the regions of the Soviet Union turned out to be the very last. The harassment of teachers and ministers, the main groups constituting the delegate body, by the Soviet authorities made efforts on behalf of religious nurture increasingly precarious. Most of those attending the Moscow conference died in prison or exile in the 1930s.[14] These tragic developments were a reminder of the Martyrs' Synod at Augsburg in 1527, so called because most of the Anabaptist leaders attending met a martyr's fate soon after.[15]

After 1925, many of the efforts contributing to the renewal of the Mennonite communities or to the emigration of their members were coming to an end. Legal and political problems abounded. Passports, visas, and medical clearances were hard to obtain. In 1928, Canadian medical inspectors, admitted after once being excluded but restricted in their movements in the best of times, were once again banned from the U.S.S.R. altogether. More and more young men were denied exemptions from military service and, when they failed to comply, were imprisoned, placed in forced labour camps, or shot.[16] The Mennonite civic organizations also had many problems with the authorities. In 1926, the southern Kharkov-based Union was dissolved, and the publication of the *Landwirt* of the Moscow-based Society was suspended. The year 1928 saw the dissolution of the northern Society as well as the last issue of *Unser Blatt*.[17]

The termination of their own institutions was one problem confronting the Russian Mennonites, but another problem, much more serious, was coping with the new Soviet programs and institutions that were being thrust upon them. On October 1, 1928, the first Five-Year Plan was initiated as a second drive to achieve the full objectives of communism, temporarily suspended during the years of the New Economic Policy. This meant, above all, the collectivization of agriculture. Also associated with the Plan was a renewed attack on religion and on traditional education. This in turn required the disciplining of the recalcitrant leadership: ministers, teachers, and well-to-do farmers. All of these tended to be classed as *kulaks*, that five per cent of the population who were blamed for Russia's economic and social inequities but who were by no means equally responsible.

A standard definition of a *kulak* was never offered by the Party officials, but it quickly became apparent that many Mennonites were so defined. Once branded a *kulak*, one could expect expropriation of property, loss of voting privileges, imprisonment, and exile. The intention was to eliminate this class, and most often this meant their transfer to forced labour camps in distant parts of the Soviet Union.[18] Needless to say perhaps, being treated as undesirable elements and criminals was traumatic for the Mennonites. They had developed their own utopian communities as their best contribution to society as a whole; some had done their best to improve the life of the peasants, and now a century of pioneering and progress was treated negatively, even judgmentally, by the authorities. The numerous instances of false accusations levelled against the Mennonites and the persecutions, especially of their ministers and teachers, thoroughly confounded them. B.H. Unruh attempted to explain their dazed confusion:

> We cannot understand what sort of interest the state has in unprotected and defenceless people who themselves want to remain faithful to their way, to torture them to death with exceptional laws, with economic and political terror, with administrative banishment, and with the robbing of freedom. We cannot understand that the Moscow Government sends a whole group of our thoroughly innocent religious and sociable people into prison or into exile.[19]

The early phases of the collectivization program also featured massive grain requisitioning and exceptionally heavy taxation. Tax assessments in kind often bore little relation to the harvest actually produced by an individual farmer or by the collective. The taxes imposed upon the Slavgorod district, to cite one example, illustrated the depressing nature of the situation. Four villages harvested 25,000 poods of grain, yet were required to deliver 34,000 poods to the authorities.[20]

Any failure to fill assigned delivery quotas resulted in summary punishment. In order to meet the exacting demands, farmers were forced sometimes to purchase grain on the open market at vastly inflated prices, with money generated from the sale of their precious livestock and agricultural equipment. When even this amount of capital was insufficient to fill the quota, the authorities auctioned off remaining possessions and not infrequently deported family heads to the frozen north. A resident from Slavgorod described the impossible predicament:

> If he [the farmer] planted his seed grain, the tax on the crop
> yield was set at an exceptionally high rate. If he failed to seed
> his crop, he was branded as an enemy of the state, a status
> which deprived him of all political and legal rights of a full-
> fledged citizen of the land.[21]

Understandably, the Mennonites were becoming extremely rest-less. Little hope was held for any kind of tolerable future in Stalin's Russia. Some turned their backs on their beloved homeland and slipped across the border illegally into Persia or into China in the far east. Others liquidated their farms and, ignoring the midwinter temperatures, set out on the arduous train journey to Moscow. Their one desire was to get out of Russia and to join friends and relatives who were now in Canada. Thus began a series of events both happy and tragic, which saw a minority escape and a majority turned back, as by the end of 1929 the emigration gate of the east and immigration doors of the west were completely shut and the keys thereof, so to speak, thrown away.

These events included: the successful departure of several scores of families by August 30; the rush to Moscow of thousands in September and October and the further exodus of several hundred families until on October 30 Canada announced its refusal to accept them; feverish negotiations in Canada to obtain a reversal of that ruling, without the desired success; forceful removal from Moscow of the majority of refugees beginning in mid-November until Germany agreed to conditional acceptance; the transfer of those accepted to Brazil, Paraguay, and some to Canada over a period of years.

Seventy Mennonite families, all originating from points east of the Urals, had collected in Moscow by April 1929.[22] Theirs was a formidable and dangerous undertaking. At the risk of being classi-fied as subversives and of incurring the inevitable penalties, the would-be emigrants besieged the authorities with requests for per-mission to leave. They directed their appeals to the government, to top Party officials, and they also called at the German embassy.[23] Their early endeavours were not encouraging. As their departure was delayed, Mennonite organizations abroad and at home held out little hope for their success and urged them to return to their homes. Said one, severely criticizing a group of men departing for Moscow:

> I cannot understand how mature men can act in this way, leaving their nests with families in times such as these when one knows precisely that Moscow will not issue any passports.[24]

Those in Moscow, however, were determined, and their resolve held. They told themselves that at certain points in history people must risk all for the sake of the future. They were buoyed up by the news that the persistence of two families had paid off, and they were already in Germany.[25] Thereafter, the would-be emigrants troubled the officials and prayed to God as never before. "Whoever hadn't been stranded in Moscow," they later said, "hadn't learned to pray."[26] Suddenly, in midsummer the government relented, and the entire group was permitted to leave. On August 30, they departed by train in the direction of the western border.

News of the group's stunning success swept swiftly through the settlements. Hope surged that others would likewise be granted permission to leave; a mass panic-stricken flight to Moscow ensued. Families rushed to dispose of their households, often in such haste that they settled for a fraction of their real value. At first in single family units, later in groups of families, the Mennonites began to stream into Moscow. Unlike the officially sanctioned migration to Canada earlier in the decade, this flocking to Moscow enjoyed neither the benefits of a centralized organization nor foreign financial assistance. The rush to the capital was rather a spontaneous act on the part of people motivated solely by the slim prospect of leaving the country.

Most of the prospective emigrants came from the east, that is from beyond the Ural mountains. One elder writing in 1930 estimated that in one district 80 per cent of the people had left, or would have, had they not been forcibly restrained by the officials.[27] Not surprisingly, people from other regions in Russia were also infected by emigration fever. They came to Moscow from the Black Sea steppes, the Crimea, the northern Caucasus, Samara, Ufa, Orenburg, and Omsk. By the end of October, German officials in Moscow estimated the number of Mennonites and other German colonists assembled in the city to be 5,000. By mid-November, they claimed the total had swollen to 13,000. The would-be émigrés themselves believed the figure lay closer to 18,000.[28]

The unexpected deluge of refugees into the capital produced an acute housing shortage. Most clustered together in summer *dachas* or cottages, situated in the suburbs along the rivers up to fifteen miles outside of Moscow. The concentrated quarters created serious sanitation problems. Food remained a constant worry for many of the destitute migrants. However, their morale was sustained by the hope that eventually they would win their release. About 3,000 of the Mennonite transients were in possession of steamship tickets to North America, sent and guaranteed by relatives in Canada. These were useless, however, unless accompanied by an official exit visa issued by the government.

Accordingly, the refugees directed a persistent flurry of appeals to Party luminaries requesting permission to leave for Canada. Contacts were made with the central committees of Moscow, of the regional Russian republic, and of the U.S.S.R. Messages were sent to lower Party officials and even to Lenin's wife.[29] When these actions all failed to elicit any favourable response, the Mennonites turned their attention to the German embassy. This was extremely risky, since communication by Soviet citizens with foreign officials was generally interpreted by the police as counter-revolutionary activity.

The German consulate initially adopted a hands-off policy with respect to the refugees—everyone, that is, except the German agricultural attaché, Otto Auhagen.[30] Auhagen was deeply moved by the tragic circumstances. From early October on, he remained in daily contact with the refugees and publicly urged his government to intervene on their behalf. In Germany itself, B.H. Unruh presented the cause of the refugees to the government in Berlin. Both Unruh and Auhagen argued for a temporary admission of the refugees on the assumption that they could then be transferred to Canada. Their task was made easier by the favourable crystallization of public opinion. Under pressure, the German government broached the subject of resettlement with the U.S.S.R. and with success.

On October 19, Moscow agreed to the immediate movement of the refugees. The Soviet Union's sudden shift of mind probably reflected its fear of being driven even further into international isolation.[31] Those waiting were unaware of the negotiations and the official breakthrough. In the absence of any encouraging news, they continued to press their case before the Soviet authorities. Several hundred women relayed their anxious thoughts to the government via a petition. Later, a group of mothers with their children staged a mass demonstration in a waiting room adjacent to the office of Soviet President Kalinin.[32] In late October, a lengthy petition bearing three separate sheets of signatures was prepared and sent to each of six principal organs of the Soviet government. The statement concluded with the warning that, if exit passports were denied to the refugees, they would march as one down to Red Square and there await their death.[33]

Then came the extraordinary news that the people could leave. Jubilation flooded the congested dachas, though at first the colonists found it difficult to comprehend this incredible good fortune. In short order, the required eight refugee lists, each containing about 200 families, were prepared and submitted to the authorities.[34] The first assignment of refugees departed on October 27. Others were scheduled to follow shortly, since Moscow had made it plain that it wished to be rid of the burdensome Mennonites.

Canada Once Again Closed

But on October 30 all further movement ceased. On that day Canada announced that, for the present, it would not accept responsibility for any of the refugees destined for Germany, since it had thus far made no formal commitment to that effect. The other parties involved in the relocation of the refugees all had assumed that the earlier conditions favouring immigration still prevailed in Canada and that it was then just a matter of working things out. But this was no longer the case. Beginning already in 1927, stiff opposition to the entry of newcomers from southern and eastern Europe had been heard in Canada. This was true especially in the western provinces.[35] By 1929 the immigration door was completely closed.

The western plains had absorbed large numbers of agricultural settlers since the beginning of the century, and now many citizens and leaders believed that the region's settlement zones were saturated. Further immigration would tend to aggravate, rather than strengthen, the prairie's economic fortunes. Western labour organizations, along with the provincial governments, complained that the railways were bringing in unwanted immigrants who, besides aggravating the urban labour scene, proved impossible to assimilate.[36] As well, there were those who believed that the integrity and ideals of the British tradition were being eroded by the presence of non-English immigrants. The National Labour Council of Toronto, an affiliate of the All-Canadian Congress of Labour, was "absolutely opposed" to the admittance of the Mennonite refugees, as were such other groups and organizations as the Sons of England and the Native Sons of Canada.[37]

The federal government was sensitive to the western criticism. During the winter of 1928 – 29, the Department of Immigration and Colonization ordered the railways to reduce the immigration of continentals to one-third the number brought in the previous year.[38] Robert Forke, the Minister, responded further to the anti-immigration temper by holding conferences with the provinces in July 1929 in recognition of their demand for a greater voice in the formation of immigration policies. Under the provisions of the British North America Act, overall control of immigration lay with the federal government. But since immigration had an immediate bearing on economic, educational, and social conditions in a local area, the provinces maintained that they should be consulted on immigration matters. Following his consultations, Forke announced that henceforth the federal government would not act without first contacting the provinces.[39]

The Mennonites had learned from an incident earlier that summer that more immigrants would have difficulty entering Canada. The occasion was a request for the admission of about 170 refugees stranded in the Chinese city of Harbin, without passports, having left the Soviet Union illegally. Since they preferred to come to Canada, the Mennonite Immigration Aid in Winnipeg contacted Ottawa on their behalf and explained to the officials that in lieu of Soviet documents, the transients would carry a personal *Ausweiss*, or passport substitute, provided by the German representative in Harbin.[40] Mennonite officials of both the Aid and the Board also gave the standard guarantee that their organizations would supervise the maintenance and placement of each refugee, as well as assume the costs of maintaining in Canada any persons, dependent on others, who could not be admitted, or who, having been admitted, might subsequently be threatened with deportation.

The final decision of the government was handed down on August 22. The Department of Immigration announced that the Mennonites would not be admitted, since they possessed no valid passports and almost no money.[41] The deputy minister also doubted whether the Mennonites in Canada were in a position to accept further financial responsibilities, saddled as they were with the heavy obligations connected with the earlier movement of immigrants. Ultimately, the Harbin group went to Brazil, Paraguay, and the United States.

The developments in the U.S.S.R. during the fall prompted renewed attempts to change Canadian immigration policy. Pressure to accept the people in distress came also from non-Mennonite quarters. Ludwig Kempff, the Consul General of Germany assigned to Canada, told Department of Immigration officials on October 29 that his country held a special interest in the Moscow refugees, owing to their German ethnicity.[42] Kempff indicated that economic circumstances prevented Germany from accepting sole responsibility for their future. However, that country was prepared to accommodate the immigrants en route to Canada and to supply each of them with a personal *Ausweiss*. The latter was a guarantee that, in the event of rejection on medical grounds or deportation from Canada, Germany would accept any deportees.[43]

The League of Nations also demonstrated a keen interest in the refugee problem. In late October, Fridtjof Nansen, the high commissioner, cabled an urgent appeal asking Canada to offer a haven to the refugees.[44] The various transportation companies likewise urged the government to admit the refugees into Canada. As far as the railways were concerned, the reputation of the Mennonites in Canada was such that further transportation credits were offered. According to one official:

> I do not know of any other class of Central European settler
> that sticks to the land like the Mennonites do. Their reputation
> for honesty and industry has induced the Canadian Pacific
> Railway Company to advance in recent years, between one and
> two million dollars. . . . I doubt whether any other group of
> immigrants, British or foreign, has a reputation that would
> guarantee an equal amount of assistance.[45]

Towards the end of October, CPR representatives informed Canada that their company was ready to begin moving approximately one thousand families from Moscow to Canada at the rate of 500 persons every two weeks.[46]

The single missing piece needed to reactivate migration into Canada was official federal approval. To the dismay of the Mennonites and their supporters, Ottawa announced on October 30 that it did not consider itself to be under any obligation to assist the refugees. This, for the moment at least, was the government's official policy. Unofficially, and in marked contrast to the attitude of the western provinces, Ottawa expressed warm sympathy for the refugees and their cause and seemed genuinely anxious to help them.[47]

In November, the Department of Immigration, the CPR, the German consulate, and Board officials made concerted efforts to overcome prairie opposition to the proposed immigration, all with the tacit blessing of William Lyon Mackenzie King. At his request, the Prime Minister's associates kept him posted daily on the latest developments. On November 5, for instance, Robert Forke dispatched a telegram to King who was then on a pre-election speaking tour of the west.[48] Forke reported that his department was under great pressure to admit 1,000 families temporarily stationed outside Moscow and facing the real risk of deportation to Siberia. Forke conceded that the timing of the proposed movement was wrong, coming as it would at the onset of winter. None the less, and despite the impoverished conditions of the refugees, Forke was prepared to accept such families as could be properly absorbed by host farmers in Canada.[49]

The following day, David Toews approached King, then in Rosthern, with a similar proposal.[50] King's reply was carefully guarded. Any movement into the country depended on the willingness of the hosts to accommodate the newcomers and to provide firm guarantees that they would not become public charges. King avoided a direct personal commitment by deferring final decision to the Department of Immigration, which had obligated itself to discuss the matter first with those provinces most immediately involved.

King's cautious response to Toews's request was politically well advised, considering the disposition of Saskatchewan's outspoken premier, J.T.M. Anderson. The premier was unaccustomed to soft-pedal on any issue, including immigration. In fact, he had distinguished himself with his zealous crusading for the right of the

provinces to control the flow of immigrants into their territories.[51]
Ottawa correctly assumed that the key to the planned admission of the
Moscow refugees hinged largely on Saskatchewan's attitude.
Accordingly, that province was the first to be sounded out by
immigration officials.

Meanwhile, Germany and the League of Nations had informed
Canada that time was running out for those stranded in Moscow.
Hoping to respond positively to the renewed appeal, Forke dispatched a telegram to Premier Anderson on November 7, explaining
that Canada was being urged on humanitarian grounds to accept
about 1,000 displaced families and that refusal to accept the group
would result in their exile to Siberia and "inevitable starvation."[52]
Forke assured the premier that the Board and their hosts would
assume total responsibility for the welfare of the immigrants,
guaranteeing in particular that the newcomers would conform to
Canadian school regulations. It was a strange guarantee, because the
Russlaender already settled in Saskatchewan since 1923 had given no
occasion to doubt their interest in education.

Anderson summarized his initial position in a telegram sent to
Ottawa on November 8.[53] The Mennonites, he admitted, made
excellent citizens. However, the sagging employment situation
militated against further immigration. None the less, Anderson
provided some hope that, at a minimum, relatives of families already
established in the province would be admitted on the understanding
that they would not become public charges for a period of two years.
A final decision would be made following a meeting between the
Saskatchewan government and a delegation representing the Board.

The federal request was not opportune from Saskatchewan's point
of view. Times were difficult, unemployment was rising, and
government leaders had all they could handle to satisfy people already
in the country. Anderson said he wanted to decrease, rather than
increase, government spending. His concern that an influx of
refugees would aggravate the province's economic problems
emerged in his November 8 telegram to Ottawa. Would the federal
government, he asked, be prepared to assist Saskatchewan in relief
matters now being carried out among recent arrivals, which included
Mennonites?[54]

Another motive other than the economic one fuelled Anderson's
resolve to bar the Mennonites from his province. The premier was

an Orangeman of long standing, and he reflected that society's religious and racial prejudices.[55] Anderson also headed the provincial Conservatives, a party that generally subscribed to the view that non-British elements should be assimilated into the dominant Protestant and Anglo-Saxon culture as quickly as possible, or, alternatively, be kept out. The political leader articulated the sentiments of his party at a founding meeting of a branch of the Canadian Legion at Bienfait. To his audience he pledged:

> I will as long as I am premier of this province, be utterly
> opposed to and combat with all proper means any attempt to
> destroy the fundamental principles of our British
> citizenship.[56]

Popular Images and Public Opinion

One popular image held of the Mennonites in 1929 was that of a group of communally minded religious sectarians inclined to remain aloof from the usual economic and social enterprises. Many people still associated all Mennonites with Hutterites and Doukhobors on the basis of old images which had led to the 1919 immigration ban and with those Kanadier that had clashed with provinical governments over the issue of public schools. Uncritically, such people assumed that the newcomers would be like that, thus demonstrating that memories of a former day, no matter how distorted, or if correct no matter how irrelevant, are easily recalled if they happen to reinforce prejudice and serve the desired cause. A press release originating in Regina on November 5 reflected the distorted and outdated images:

> Mennonites are a problem. They are excellent farmers. But
> their insistent attitude toward Canadianization in general and
> Canadian school systems in particular make their assimilation
> difficult.[57]

The selective Mennonite resistance to the public schools was still living on in the public mind when another wave of negative publicity for the Mennonites of Saskatchewan arose from the so-called Friesen-Braun trials.[58] In those trials, which extended from 1925 to 1928 and resulted in a five-year prison sentence and deportation to

Russia for Braun in 1932, the Mennonites in general and officials of the Board, David Toews and A.A. Friesen in particular, were placed in a rather bad light.[59] The whole proceedings were grist for the mill for all those who were against immigration, certainly eastern European immigration, those who were against the Mennonites, those who were sure that the immigrants had very sharp operators or even Bolshevik sympathizers among them, those who were opposed to the Rosthern Board for whatever reason, those who liked to widen the gulf between Kanadier and Russlaender, and those who sided with either the Toewses or the Friesens in their ongoing quarrel. Henry P. Friesen, one of the principals, was the brother of Isaac P. Friesen, a ministerial colleague of David Toews, between whom there were a number of differences of opinion.[60]

The Friesen-Braun story began with the arrival of immigrant Isaac Braun from Halbstadt, Russia, in Rosthern in July 1924. Henry P. Friesen, a Kanadier farmer and businessman, tried to sell Braun some land. Negotiations were incomplete when in August Braun left Saskatchewan for Renata, B.C., from where he later wrote to Friesen demanding payment of $5,000, which he claimed Friesen had borrowed from him on August 29, 1924, at the Western Hotel in Saskatoon. Henry P. Friesen denied having made such a loan. Braun sued for the stated amount, and thus the protracted court proceedings began.[61] He won his case with the help of an I.O.U. bearing Friesen's signature and two witnesses, Jacob Friesen and Frank Hildebrandt, both youths who swore they had witnessed the transaction at the Western Hotel.

Later, the two youths gave sworn testimony that they had perjured themselves, that they had not been in Saskatoon on August 29, and that they had not seen Friesen or Braun on that day. Henry P. Friesen took the matter to court to have the earlier judgment against him set aside. At the same time, perjury or subornation of perjury charges were laid against Hildebrandt, Jacob Friesen, and Isaac Braun. Braun, somewhat surprisingly, retaliated by charging Henry Friesen with perjury. Henry P. Friesen won his case and the earlier judgment against him was set aside. Hildebrandt and Jacob Friesen were convicted and given suspended sentences. Braun's charge of perjury against Henry P. Friesen was dismissed. Braun, however, was convicted of subornation of perjury and sentenced to a five-year prison term.

Braun appealed his conviction and the appeal court judges ruled that his conviction had resulted from a mistrial and ordered a new trial. During this new trial Braun introduced new evidence, purportedly letters written by Henry P. Friesen in which Friesen acknowledged the $5,000 debt. Handwriting experts were called in and it was determined that the new evidence presented by Braun was fabricated. The crown then laid new charges against Braun and chose to proceed on the charge of fabrication of evidence rather than on the original charge of subornation of perjury. Braun was found guilty of fabrication of evidence on October 26, 1928, and sentenced to a five-year prison term, to be followed by deportation to the Soviet Union. In October 1933 Isaac Braun was deported, although his wife and two children were allowed to remain in Canada.[62]

The entire episode proved to be most embarrassing for Board officials, who were openly sympathetic with Braun, and for Russlaender generally, who at one point had furnished some $10,000 bail for Braun. One judge expressed the view "that the Mennonite Colonization Board was a fit subject for the careful attention of the authorities."[63] And as it is elsewhere written:

> The whole process produced much ill-will in the Rosenort
> church, in the Rosthern community, and in all of Canada. . . .
> the long, dark shadows cast by the Friesen-Braun trials were
> not easily dispelled.[64]

The effect of the public school issue and the Friesen-Braun trials was that any petitioning to allow new immigration had to include assurances that Mennonites would be "law-abiding" citizens.

Anderson exploited the distorted popular perceptions of the Mennonites.[65] In early November, he reported to the press that he knew of one instance in Saskatchewan where 60 children were without public school facilities.[66] The premier knew that not all Mennonites were opposed to public schools and that those now seeking admission were among them. But he also knew that approval of the proposed immigration would not sit well with an electorate who did not make those distinctions and to whom he had pledged the removal of "sectarianism" from the public school.

The premier quickly discovered that his negative response to the immigration department and to the Mennonites was politically advantageous. The public was kept well-informed on the course of developments, since the major newspapers regularly covered the exchanges between Ottawa and the provincial capitals.[67] The premier received support from various labour groups, the United Farmers, the Canadian Legion, the Orangemen, the Masons, and the Ku Klux Klan. Many of the protesters feared that the newcomers would take jobs from them or otherwise weaken the economy. Their alarm reflected popular prejudices as well as economic decline in the west.

The Klan had made its way into Saskatchewan in the mid-1920s. As an extremist, ultra-fundamentalist and pro-British organization it grew quickly, feeding on the prejudices that had been growing over the years. The federal government's immigration policy (especially that prior to the war) and the influx of many east European Catholics and other non-WASPs had alarmed much of the Anglo-Saxon Saskatchewan populace. Turning that alarm into racist prejudice was an educational policy and system, vigorously promoted in earlier days by Anderson, which "fostered the development of a society based on the one language" and which helped "to create an intolerance which would be amply demonstrated in the rapid inculcation of the Ku Klux Klan mentality in Saskatchewan people in the post-1927 period."[68] As one historian analysed the situation:

> The Klan provided hundreds with a vent for ingrained prejudices in the guise of safeguarding all that was admirable in British institutions, in Protestantism, and in the Canadian way of life.[69]

The Klan was an important factor in the 1929 election. There was no official link between the Klan and the Conservative Party, though many Conservatives were Klan members. However, the party made much political hay of the hysteria aroused by the Klan. In the words of William Calderwood:

> The Conservative party . . . adopted an attitude that was politically expedient by taking advantage of the emotionalism aroused by the Klan, by secretly obtaining the endorsation of the Klan leaders regarding certain planks in its platform, and by publicly remaining silent on the Klan issue. Obviously, the admission of Mennonites from Russia, though not Catholics, would have antagonized the very people who had so recently voted for the Conservatives.[70]

The negative public reaction against the proposed Mennonite migration was heard also in Alberta. J.E. Brownlee's United Farmers government was especially sensitive to the public climate, since an election campaign was then under way. The United Farmers movement was, to some extent at least, influenced by Norman F. Priestley, the United Church minister at Coaldale, who got involved in serious quarrels with the Mennonites and who was also very influential in the United Farmers of Alberta. Brownlee was advised that the Sedgewick local of the UFA was "utterly opposed" to bringing into Canada in general, and to Alberta in particular, "any of the band of Mennonites who are now stranded at some point in Russia or Germany."[71] A missive emanating from Rosedale was more explicit:

> Nothing can be gained by assuming further obligations of a people destined to reduce our standard of living, opposed to assimilation of our demands in social legislation, determined to adhere to their own ideas of total segregation.[72]

The burden of converting the indifferent, if not hostile, provincial governments to the Mennonite position fell upon David Toews. His was not an enviable task, but he pursued it, as he had all other causes on behalf of his people, with unflagging determination. After a personal appeal to federal immigration officials, at which time he was informed that the government was powerless to act without the consent of the provinces concerned, Toews returned west where, beginning on November 12, he conducted separate meetings with all three provincial governments.[73]

Manitoba was the first to respond formally to the Toews delegation, which also included G. Sawatzky of the CCA and R. G. Duncan of the CPR. The immigration department later assessed Manitoba's position as "reasonable and logical" alongside that of the other provinces. As it turned out, Manitoba's offer was the most generous one extended to the Mennonites. A maximum of 250 families were welcome to settle in the province with the understanding that they would receive care and shelter from the resident hosts.[74]

Toews next conferred with the Saskatchewan cabinet. He could not have been encouraged by the sceptical attitude displayed by Anderson. The premier questioned the veracity of reports describing the dire straits in which the Mennonite refugees found themselves and speculated that they owed their misfortune to their probable

refusal to comply with Soviet laws.[75] Anderson then denied that
Toews had the united support of all Canadian Mennonites on the
basis of a telegram received from a group in Dalmeny:

> We are not in favour of the immigration of Mennonites from
> Europe, and we cannot house any as we have plenty of our own
> Canadian Mennonites to help.[76]

Later that month Anderson again referred to the split in the Mennonite ranks, but this time he was challenged by a determined response.
Only one in 129 Saskatchewan farmers interviewed, he said, was
willing to assist the destitute colonists if brought to Canada.[77]

Saskatchewan Mennonites responded to Premier Anderson's scep-
ticism of group solidarity by showing rousing support for the Board's
immigration plan. A large November meeting held in Herbert,
attended by representatives of various local churches, unanimously
passed a motion committing themselves to the care of 250 refugees
until they would be able to help themselves.[78] For the time being at
least, their resolve made no difference at all to Anderson.

Anderson formally summarized his thoughts in a letter to David
Toews, which he also released to the press.[79] There could be no
admission of any refugees for several months, he said, and then
possibly only those with relatives willing to support them. He went
on to demand lists of established Mennonite farmers prepared to look
after incoming relatives as well as lists of refugees with full particulars as to their age, sex, and former occupation. The request could
only slow up the process, quite possibly its only intention, because
such information was obtained only with much effort and the passing
of precious time.

In Alberta the reception was kinder, but the end results were the
same.[80] Premier Brownlee readily extolled the virtues of the Mennonites in that province. The problem was that their petitioning
coincided with a provincial surplus of agricultural and industrial
labour and with a recent record of poor crops, at least in southern
Alberta. Brownlee explained that the farming opportunities should
be preserved for people already in Alberta, "many of whom, as a
result of complete crop failure, are in nearly as destitute a condition as
your people in Moscow."[81]

Brownlee also heard urgent pleas from the Mennonite Farmers
Association in the province, which offered the hospitality of 95

households,[82] from Alberta members on the Canadian Mennonite Board of Colonization,[83] and from the Mennonite Committee of Alberta.[84] The latter praised the freedom of Canada and peace enjoyed under the British flag and promised that the Mennonites would be good citizens, obey the laws, and in general assist in the welfare of the country. But the messages of the Alberta Council of the Canadian Legion,[85] the United Farmers of Alberta,[86] the United Mine Workers of Alberta,[87] the National Order of Canada,[88] and various Orange Lodges[89] were more representative of the general and popular feeling, which was very much opposed to immigration and which carried much more weight with the premier.

Ottawa kept up its pleading with the prairie provinces, the only ones considered by either the Mennonites or the federal government.[90] Immigration officials reminded the latter of the repeated warnings received from Germany of the certain banishment from Moscow of the Mennonites.[91] They also referred to Germany's offer to provide temporary care to the refugees until Canada could absorb them and to create a special fund to defray any deportation expenses that might subsequently arise. The news produced no softening on the part of Alberta and Saskatchewan. Even Manitoba reconsidered its original offer and informed Ottawa that it wished to defer the admission of the 250 families until spring when the critical period of unemployment would have passed.[92] Ottawa was reluctant to inflame public opinion and therefore ruled against accepting the refugees. On November 26, the government announced that no Mennonites would be admitted into the country during the winter, though there was some possibility of a limited movement in the spring.[93] Exaggerated press reports that 100,000 Mennonites could be knocking on Canada's doors didn't help the situation.[94]

The deference of the federal government to the provinces raised the fundamental question of jurisdiction over immigration policy. Both levels of government understood that the proceedings marked a departure from federal supremacy in the field of immigration. The trend continued. In March 1930, Ottawa conceded that henceforth all initiatives in immigration matters would come only from the provinces.[95] The Mennonites might have empathized with provincial positions, given their own historic provincialism and their fear of nationalism and imperialism, but the provinces had rarely sided with the Mennonites. As in education before, so in immigration now, Mennonites were the losers when the provinces chose to exercise their authority and the federal government could not or would not intervene.

The weak and mostly negative response of the governments appears to have been supported by public opinion, if it can be said that the press both reflected and determined the popular mood. The *Victoria Daily Times* bluntly stated that there was "no room in Canada for fanatics" and that "their unhappy relations with the authorities of Soviet Russia are not our concern."[96] The *Vancouver Daily Province* recognized that the Mennonite event in Moscow was "bad for the Bolshevist reputation" and hoped for "the interest and sympathy of the world" but did not see any relevance for Canada's immigration policy.[97] The *Manitoba Free Press*, fully aware that the Mennonites in Moscow were facing starvation and deportation to Siberia, editorialized on the "changing outlook" on immigration in Canada.[98] The *Regina Star* defended "constitutional rights conferred by the British North America Act to safeguard immigration into the province."[99] The Toronto *Globe*, commenting on the cruel shipments to distant Siberia, derided "Soviet cruelty deluxe" and hoped for a "world-wave of pity," but not a word was said about Canadian obligations.[100]

Among those who tried to correct the *Globe* on some of its biased or uninformed reporting were Swiss Mennonite leaders in Waterloo County. In some ways they were in the best position to do so because the Mennonite reputation as "good citizens" was "particularly true in Ontario."[101] C.F. Derstine was very critical of the *Globe*'s reflection of Premier Anderson's view on Mennonites and education.[102] To make a judgement about 100,000 Mennonites on the basis of a group near Swift Current, he said, was like characterizing all the Baptists on the basis of the "Hard Shelled Baptists," the Methodists by some "fanatical offshoots," and the Presbyterians by looking at the "blue stocking Presbyterians."

M.S. Hallman targeted the well-reported sentiments of the Native Sons of Canada, who claimed to reflect "the feelings of the Canadian people."[103] Placing himself in the line of "native sons" and of the United Empire Loyalists, Hallman asked what was to be done "with almost boundless spaces" if Canada's population was to be kept to less than 10 million and if entry was denied to an "agricultural people, proficient in the cultivation of the soil." Reflecting an amazingly good understanding of the Mennonite experience in

Russia, he suggested that Canada could not afford to be without a people who "have been tried and tested by fire, and are in deadly earnest to succeed again, having succeeded before." These Mennonites, he said, "are educated, cultured, musical, and would make altogether desirable citizens of Canada."

New Homelands for Some

The fateful story of the refugees occupied a prominent place in the German press, which reported their plight much more sympathetically than the Canadian papers.[104] Many Germans attributed their country's political and social position to communist agitation, and they demanded that the German *Volk* in Moscow not be abandoned to a freezing Siberian fate. The popular sympathy for the homeless led to a nation-wide fund appeal called *Brueder in Not* (Brothers in Distress), which attracted the support of the postal service, the banks, the railways, numerous charitable institutions, and even President Hindenburg.[105] The German cabinet was more cautious, at least for the time being, mainly on account of the country's staggering economic deficit, partly the result of war reparations. Its expressed hope was

> that other countries will regard this sudden and tragic exodus of Russian peasants as akin to such disasters as the sinking of the Titanic, the eruption of Vesuvius and the Japanese earthquake, when, irrespective of nationality, committees were constituted in numerous parts of the world to relieve the distress.[106]

Germany's energetic intervention on behalf of the desperate refugees contrasted sharply with Canada's indifference and negative verdict. Not surprisingly, the impact of Germany's benevolence on behalf of the refugees was profound. An earlier empathy for things German now turned into enthusiasm and even patriotism. Those receiving German beneficence, while the rest of the world ignored their plight, subsequently demonstrated an indiscriminate appreciation for anything connected with Germany, and this brought some of them into serious conflict with the non-German cultures in which they lived.[107]

Canada's intransigence led the Soviet government in mid-November to begin the forced removal of the refugees from the

Moscow environs. Within a week, all but 5,600 refugees had been cleared from their quarters.[108] One participant described the terrible ordeal of those being evicted:

> The trip from our living quarters to the railroad freight station was an experience in itself. Way up on top of their belongings crouched these poor, unfortunate victims, driven along in bitter cold weather. Their senses were so numbed they could not even cry. . . . They knew and realized now that they had no home; they had no protection; they had no shelter; they had no voice. . . . And now they were driven at breakneck speed into the night. . . into the dreadful, terrible, and seemingly endless and hopeless night.[109]

Families were separated, sometimes forever, as the Mennonites were returned to their former homes or shipped to new and unfamiliar localities. For days in the dead of winter they travelled in unheated boxcars that bore the deceiving words "settlers in transit." Blankets froze solid to the walls while the dazed travellers, pondering the consequences of their flight to Moscow, huddled together for warmth. Their desire had been a relatively simple one: only to leave the country. Now they were branded and treated as counter-revolutionaries. They paid dearly for their actions with their homes and possessions, their time, and sometimes their lives. Small wonder that they, and those who actually escaped from Russia, developed an enduring fear of, and loathing for, the Communist state.

The Soviet action prompted an adamant rejoinder from Germany. Attaché Auhagen informed Moscow officials that, should they continue to deport the refugees, diplomatic ties between the two countries would be severed. Auhagen's appeal was also directed to Germany in the new emergency and as a result the German cabinet ended its temporizing and agreed that state funds should be used to expedite the transfer to Germany of the refugee remnant.[110] All along, the position of the U.S.S.R. had been that the refugees could leave if they had a place to go.

Thus, on November 25, further transport of refugees to Germany was approved. Two days later, the Executive Committee of the Mennonite Central Committee, in session at Philadelphia, promised its "best efforts" and influence "to its fullest extent" for refugees so that they would not become a public burden in any way. The Committee also promised to bring together "leaders and representa-

TABLE 28[114]

PERSONS ACCOMMODATED IN GERMAN REFUGEE CAMPS
(1930)

RELIGIOUS AFFILIATION	NUMBER
Mennonite	3,885
Lutheran	1,260
Catholic	468
Baptist	51
Adventist	7
Total	5,671

tives of the different branches of our church in the United States" to enlist whole-hearted support.[111] Except for a minority now leaving Moscow, the intervention of the MCC was too late.

The remaining *dacha* residents learned of their imminent deliverance the following night. New passenger lists were prepared since many of the principals on the original lists were now missing, and passport fees were collected. Beginning on November 29 and continuing over a span of two weeks, nine crowded trains departed for the Latvian border. A final contingent of families was inexplicably denied their release and rerouted to an eastern exile.

The mood of the first group to arrive in Riga was a mixture of thankfulness and reflective sobriety. After a word of greeting from Latvia's German ambassador, the refugees attempted to sing a hymn. Choking and sobbing interrupted the singing. There were few dry eyes among the refugees, the German diplomats, the local German citizenry, the Latvian Red Cross workers, and others who were present. All of the emigrants were overwhelmed by the generosity shown to them.[112] In Latvia, the refugees were showered with gifts of clothing, food supplies, books, and sweets. Germany herself accorded them a hero's welcome replete with a decorated reception room, fir greenery, and garlands of flowers.

Three former military camps, situated at Hammerstein, Prenzlau, and Moelln, served as the temporary home of the refugees.[113] A total of 5,671 persons, of which 3,885 were Mennonites, passed through the camps during these months (Table 28). They were well cared for, charitable organizations providing them not only with the essentials of food and clothing but also with money, books, and even sewing machines. An American Mennonite observed:

> The attitude of the German nation and the government toward the refugees has been remarkable and too much cannot be said in praise of their generosity and services.[115]

Certain discomforts could not be avoided, however. Every person was subjected to a disinfection and quarantine process. An epidemic of measles among the children restricted all movement in and to the camps. Conditions were very crowded. In the barracks, families lived in rooms sometimes containing sometimes as many as four or five families. The most common complaint voiced by the refugees was that of boredom. Barbershops, basket-weaving, shoe repair services, and libraries afforded some distraction to the people, but many fretted at their general inactivity. They were impatient to proceed to the final destination where they could begin to rebuild their lives. The problem was where to go.

Canada, their preferred choice, remained closed to them. Even if the country had agreed at that time to accept a quota of immigrants, many would likely have been rejected for health reasons.[116] The ordeal in Moscow, where the people had subsisted in poorly heated summer cottages with inadequate food supplies, had left its mark upon them. Because Canada was closed, other possibilities had to be explored.

Mexico, Brazil, and Paraguay all received serious consideration. A small party, assisted by the U.S.-based Mennonite Colonization Board, established themselves in Mexico,[117] though only briefly. A larger group of just over 1,000 persons agreed to locate in the primeval forests of Brazil,[118] though most doubted the wisdom of their choice. Brazil's rugged terrain, together with its refusal to grant an absolute military exemption, presented obvious worries. However, great pressure was being applied to the Mennonites to vacate the German camps and thus several hundred families reluctantly agreed to settle in Brazil. The advance party left Germany on January 16, 1930, and was followed in the next months by the larger transport groups, all enjoying German help.[119]

Paraguay received the largest number of refugees. The active settlement assistance given by the Mennonite Central Committee, the presence in that country of other Mennonites recently arrived from Canada, and the privileges extended by the government to the settlers accounted for Paraguay's greater popularity. The first group of settlers left Germany for the Paraguayan Chaco in mid-March. Over 1,500 refugees eventually established themselves in the Fernheim Colony, located a short distance from Menno Colony, founded a few years earlier by the Chortitzer, Sommerfelder, and Bergthaler(S) from Canada, who now hosted and helped the newcomers.[120]

Mennonites in Canada clung to the hope that their country would absorb some of the refugees and expressed general disappointment at the cold indifference of the provinces. Efforts were continued to persuade the governments to act otherwise. Some individuals also did their best to have the Mennonites from Russia admitted. Abraham Funk from Carlton, Saskatchewan, for instance, made a pitch for the opening up of homestead lands in bushland areas owned by the Hudson's Bay Company and begged Canada's Minister of the Interior, Charles Stewart, to put together a delegation of Mennonite farmers, as well as government and railway officials, to examine the prospect.[121] Funk spoke from experience when he cited the potential of the bush country for Mennonite settlement. Having arrived from Danzig with a family of 10 children in 1903, he had with the aid of his sons in less than three decades brought 1,200 acres under cultivation on nine quarter sections, most of which had been cleared from bush in the so-called Parkland.[122]

And Joseph R. Tucker of Sub Rosa in Saskatchewan sent a map to support his offer to sell or lease enough land in the Sub Rosa district for a hundred or more Mennonite families, who were much to be preferred over other Europeans "of mongoloid or hybrid-mongol race under the tutelage of land speculative corporations." The appearance of such unpreferred settlers would "be hotly resented." But Mennonites were more than welcome. Tucker explained his generous offer to the Minister of Immigration:

> The leading men around Sub Rosa care nothing for religion
> and the Mennonites could profess any or none as they wished.
> Said Mennonites could practise any social customs they pleased
> at Sub Rosa as long as they kept the King's laws and turned
> over their rent-shares duly. They could suit themselves
> whether they sent their children to Sub Rosa school, if the pro-
> vincial government did not interfere in this particular.[123]

One proposal submitted to the Ontario government suggested that some of the refugees could be settled in the undeveloped north, meaning Reesor and other areas of the clay belt. Nothing came of the suggestion, even though it attracted the province's mild interest. Another petition sent to the governments in both Toronto and Ottawa in 1930 was more forcefully expressed. It requested that special immigration provisions be made for the persecuted fellow believers in Russia. The Mennonites justified their special appeal on the grounds that they "always believed that in Canada, the principles of humanity and Christian mercy outweighed economic and political consideration."[124]

The Conference of Mennonites in Central Canada, having heard David Toews's report on immigration and on the plight of the people in Russia, expressed "gratitude to the highly esteemed government" and expressed the confidence that "the new element of Mennonites" would "give an added impetus to agricultural growth and other lines of activity and in that way be a positive factor in the Canadian national life."[125] At the 1930 sessions, the David Toews report[126] was followed by a telegram to M.J. Kalinin, the Chairman of the Central Executive Committee, U.S.S.R., which requested that all those whose properties had been seized be allowed to emigrate and that individual cases of those imprisoned be examined objectively before the courts.[127]

The German government also exerted pressure on Canada to reverse its decision. Unless Canada accepted 500 Mennonite families, an urgent warning said, future relations between the two countries might be affected.[128] The message had a positive effect. The railways, for instance, which had been authorized to bring in 200 families each, were now encouraged to apply this allotment to the Mennonites in the German camps. The CNR explained that its quota had for the most part already been filled, but the CPR could, and did, agree to the request. On February 24, 1930, the first complement of 24 families set sail for Canada. Other groups followed in March and April, usually in small consignments, deliberately so as not to cause undue attention and disturb public opinion.

This minimal success was small comfort for the failure to achieve a much larger movement. David Toews had logged countless hours in his attempt to rescue all the refugees. His correspondence with the various levels of government was voluminous. When his written requests were dismissed, the elderly leader persisted in asking the authorities for personal interviews. "Any time and place," he assured them, "will be convenient for us."[129] A communication with the Prime Minister's office in early 1930 revealed that, while Ottawa's disposition was to co-operate more fully, its hands were tied by the intransigence of the western provinces. King confided by letter to Toews that his government would be prepared to go

> just as far as the Government of Saskatchewan were willing to have us go, but that it would not be in the public interest to adopt a different course with respect to Saskatchewan or any of the other provinces to which the refugees might hope to come.[130]

Toews did not give up. He presented a comprehensive report on Mennonite immigration activity past, present, and future to Saskatchewan's Royal Commission on Immigration and Settlement.[131] As he customarily went to the Mennonite press to plead his case with the Mennonite people, so also he went to the public press to plead the Mennonite case with the Canadian people. Soon after King's latest reply, David Toews wrote a lengthy letter to the *Saskatoon Star-Phoenix* "to correct some wrong impressions that have been created."[132] Mennonites, he said, were a religious denomination, not a nationality. Mennonites were greatly interested in education. Voluntarily they had established "something like one hundred public schools in the Province of Saskatchewan" and the conversation of the young people was such that they could have been "born of English-speaking parents."

Those opposing the public school, a small minority, had left the province so that "we are safe in saying that the public school is being taken advantage of by our people unanimously." But "in order to do justice to our conservative friends," he explained that they had in 1873 accepted "in good faith" the promises of the Dominion government concerning autonomy in educational matters, "not knowing that the Dominion government really had no jurisdiction over the school laws of the provinces." When compulsory education was enacted, they offered some passive resistance and then left for Mexico and Paraguay. They were a people of good character, honest and conscientious.

As to the Mennonite religion, it distinguished itself from other Protestant denominations in three respects: adult baptism, which put them in the good company of the Baptists; affirmation in the courts instead of swearing, but that was no reason for concern because false affirmations were punishable the same as perjury; and aversion to war or nonresistance, which also put them into the good company of generals who said "war is hell" and the Quakers, who are respected in England, the United States, and Canada. Such people, believing these things, severely persecuted in another country, were "modestly knocking at the door of Canada . . . to enjoy freedom of conscience and the fruits of their own labour . . . willing to assume their obligation as citizens." The Mennonites already in Canada were willing to guarantee that they would "not become public charges" and that they would "not aggravate the unemployment situation." If, then, the coming of these destitute people would not cost Canadians a single dollar, why did they not open wide the door? Toews invoked the evidence of history as he issued his passionate appeal:

> Has the British nation suffered by the coming of the Huguenots in 1685, have the Canadian people suffered by the coming of the British Empire Loyalists? Have the American people suffered by the coming of the Pilgrim Fathers? Even from a national point of view we know that they have gained.[133]

He promised:

> These people, if permitted to come to Canada, will be law-abiding, will send their children to school, will learn the English language, will cultivate lands that are now idle; they will become no public charges; they will lighten the burdens of the ratepayers by paying taxes themselves; they will help to produce wealth; they will not be clamoring for help or relief; they will be as good citizens as any class of immigrants that have ever been brought to Canada.[134]

Not all of those who desired to come to Canada could be accommodated within the 200-family allotment awarded to the CPR. Yet there were problems even in filling that quota. Admission depended on provincial approval, which in turn was dependent on proper sponsorship in the respective provinces. Therefore, the organizations busied themselves with arranging nominations for families related to Mennonites already established in Canada. Alberta was asked in the early summer to accept 38 sponsored families. Toews promised that the Board would do everything possible to settle them on homesteads in northern Alberta or possibly on CPR irrigation lands in southern

TABLE 29[138]

DISPERSION OF 1929 MOSCOW REFUGEES
(BY 1932)

COUNTRY	NUMBER
Argentina	6
Brazil	2,529
Canada	1,344
Europe	528
Mexico	4
Paraguay	1,572
U.S.A.	4
U.S.S.R.	c. 7,000-12,000
Total	c. 13,000-18,000

Alberta.[135] The guarantee had little effect. Alberta refused the appeal on the grounds that if the Mennonites were invited in, other groups and individuals would also apply for entry.

A similar list, nominating 127 families, was presented to the Saskatchewan government. At least 55 congregations from across the province had pledged their readiness to provide for one or more refugee families. Support for the undertaking was particularly strong in the Hepburn, Rosthern, Hague-Osler, Glenbush, Laird, and Herbert districts. Premier Anderson investigated some of the nominees and, in June, approved the entry of 27 families—100 families less than requested—totalling approximately 145 persons.[136] Owing to that year's federal election, even that small movement was deferred to the spring of 1931.

A greater degree of success was achieved in Manitoba. Early in May, that province authorized the admission of 118 families, conditional on the guarantee of their nominators to maintain them.[137] Because some of the nominated families had by this time proceeded on to South America, Toews asked that others be permitted to take their places. Manitoba vetoed any such substitution, and the actual number of families brought to the province was less than the figure originally agreed upon.

None the less, for some, the efforts paid off and by 1932 a total of 1,344 Moscow refugees had landed in Canada (see Table 29). Public antipathy to immigration in general, and to Mennonite immigration in particular, had prevented many more from coming and deflected them instead to South America. That several thousand had been safely plucked out of the Soviet Union was largely due to Germany's energetic involvement. Germany negotiated their release from Moscow, furnished them with transportation from Russia to Germany and later to the ocean ports, provided for their temporary maintenance in the camps, and donated an outfit of clothes and a small sum of money to the colonists destined for South America. Transportation to the southern hemisphere was also financed by Germany in the form of interest-free loans to be repaid in ten years.[139]

Germany's move to help them, when she herself was in great need and when all other countries desisted, deeply touched the refugees. In Brazil and Paraguay, two settlements were named Auhagen and Hindenburg, respectively, in appreciation of the work performed by the two German leaders. South America's youngest Mennonite communities retained intimate attachments with Germany in subsequent years. Not even the rise of fascism could destroy the association, since the German country, more so than its particular form of government, remained important. Germany also occupied a prominent place in the hearts of those who came to Canada. Their grateful sentiments were expressed in a statement of tribute and thanks directed to the German government shortly before the departure of one of the first groups to Canada. The testimony thanked the country for its good deeds and concluded, "May God bless the German Reich and its leaders for ever and ever."[140] There would be more such prayers before the 1930s were over.

International Mennonite Concern

For those remaining in the Soviet Union or for those nearly 1,000 who had fled across eastern borders, the problems were by no means over. The latter included nearly 200 persons who had crossed into Turkey, Persia, Afghanistan, India, or Western China.[141] An additional 700 or more left the settlements they had established in 1927 near the Amur River in the far east and fled 300 miles to the Chinese city of Harbin, which had already become an eastern refuge from collectivization.[142] Here they were led by Johann Isaak, a medical doctor who had been sent from Omsk by the Siberian Mennonites in

1920 to seek help from America but who had never gone farther than Harbin. Most of these people also hoped to be admitted to Canada, but all but a few ended up in Paraguay, 373 in 1932 and 184 in 1934, while 215 found refuge in the United States.[143]

The 100,000 Mennonites remaining in Russia faced successive waves of physical and psychological hardship. During 1929 and 1930 thousands of *kulaks*, including over 10,000 Mennonites, were exiled to distant places with or without their families. Working in northern forests, in eastern gold mines, or in new industrial and agricultural centres, they experienced severe winters, hard labour, spring floods, hunger, and disease, all of which took their toll in human life.[144]

For those not uprooted in Russia, there were other troubles. Crop failures, due to climatic conditions and the inefficiencies of the collectivized agriculture, brought to the Ukraine and the Caucasus in 1933 a famine greater than that of 1921. From Canada, David Toews continued his appeals for intervention and help. At one time, 15 leaders in meeting at Rosthern on behalf of the "Mennonite people of Canada and the United States" petitioned the Canadian representative at the League of Nations in Geneva "to fully open the way for relief work in Russia" because millions of people were dying of starvation.[145] Cultural and spiritual conditions reflected similar impoverishment. By the mid-1930s, most church buildings had been converted and were being used as clubhouses, theatres, granaries, or stables.[146]

The greatest tragedy was the loss of their leaders in the Great Purge. Initiated in 1934, the purge began with Stalin's cleansing of the Communist Party by imprisoning, exiling, or executing those suspected of disloyalty, including top Bolsheviks. It grew to embrace people from every level of Soviet society and eventually involved millions.[147] Hundreds of Mennonite men, indeed most of the leaders still remaining, were also sent into exile, this time to unknown destinations where they died alone and unheard.[148]

The western nations learned of the terrible fate of Mennonites and other peoples in the Soviet Union, but being preoccupied with the economic troubles of the time, they generally chose to ignore it. The three Mennonite world conferences, however, attested to the concern felt by the world-wide Mennonite community. This was particularly true of the 1930 conference, which was convened specifically for the purpose of considering relief action. Whatever conclusions there were to be drawn from the Russian experience about Mennonite innocence or guilt,[149] few people doubted that it was their duty to render whatever assistance they could to their suffering brethren. The manifold responses of the international Mennonite community were shared and reinforced at the world conferences.

For the decade-old Mennonite Central Committee in the U.S.A., the continuing Russian crisis meant a prolongation of its own life, and the expansion of activity to other areas of need for which, of course, there were precedents. Before the founding of the MCC in 1920, certain programs had been undertaken in Europe and in the Middle East which, together with the relief in Russia and in India, amounted to $2,500,000 and involved 80 workers.[150] Thus, while the Russian emergency precipitated the founding of the MCC, the concept of a wider ministry, extending not only to Mennonites but also to people in need anywhere, actually preceded that founding.

In the early 1930s the Mennonite Central Committee was again forwarding considerable amounts of relief to Russia, much of it through individual remittances via American Express and *Torgsin*, Russian stores where clothing and food could be purchased with American dollars. Used clothing was being sent to immigrants in Canada and Paraguay. The latter also received shipments of dried fruit, aid for a new hospital, for the high school, and for the co-operative in Fernheim, and allowances for destitute ministers. The refugees in China and other Asian countries were assisted, as were those in transit in Europe and Mexico.

The new immigrants in Brazil received aid not only from the German government but also from the Mennonites in Holland, who raised 100,000 guilders for those settlements alone and whose historic struggle for human rights and contribution to the relief of their destitute brethren in the faith was thus reinforced. Now the General Commission for Foreign Needs concentrated on helping people in transit, especially through the Bureau in Rotterdam, but also as far away as Persia.[151]

The German Mennonite Aid, founded in 1920 also in response to the Russian emergency, had delivered a variety of services to the Russian Mennonites, both those emigrating and those remaining in Russia. Included among its donations were 12,000 schoolbooks and 4,000 Bibles. The Aid had been discontinued in 1926, but beginning in 1929 the Germans once again gathered large quantities of clothing and amounts of money for the refugees from Russia. They were assisted by Mennonites in Switzerland, Poland, Alsace, and France.[152]

European aid had also gone to help resettle those immigrants who had been fortunate enough to enter Canada during the 1920s. Speaking to the 1936 world conference, David Toews acknowledged more than $18,000 received from Holland, Germany, France, and Poland to support immigrants detained in European camps for medical reasons. He also noted that for more than a decade about 15,000 pounds of clothing had been received annually from American Mennonites. Funds were also arriving from the United States to support ministers and to help build 40 churches for the immigrants.[153]

For Toews, it was most important that all the aid for the Russlaender not overlook the struggle in Canada.[154] He identified some of the burdensome responsibilities the Canadian Mennonite Board of Colonization had to deal with: a huge transportation debt, immigrants leaving the farms, mental patients and other dependants threatened with deportation if not cared for. But the main problem, he emphasized, remained the need in the Soviet Union. This was not surprising given the fact that 20,000 Russlaender in Canada had personally experienced the suffering of friends and relatives left behind. Toews summarized the problem as follows:

> After the emigration to Canada, also to Brazil and Paraguay, perhaps as many as 75,000 Mennonites remained in Russia. These have now been scattered throughout the Russian empire, and partly destroyed. It is questionable whether 50,000 are left. These have been silenced and are slowly going to their graves. The young people for the most part have been poisoned by the bolshevik system. . . . Over there they are longing for the time "when the Lord will redeem the prisoners of Zion." We too are longing for this time whenever we think of our brethren in Russia.[155]

Gratefully, Toews observed that the relief work for "our brethren in Russia" had brought together all the Mennonites of the world and he expressed the hope that there would be even more unity and joint action in the future.[156]

Relief action was one of the dominating themes at the world conferences and one of the forces working for unity, but there were also others. Information was shared about the history and state of Mennonite affairs in the different countries. Various theological themes were reviewed, and contemporary tasks, including missions and the nurture of young people, were outlined. The contributions of Menno Simons were assessed, and the origins of Anabaptism were recalled, as was appropriate especially at those world conferences, 1925 and 1936, which served as 400th anniversaries.

The rediscovery of common historical and theological roots was as essential, or more so, to an enduring international connection of the Mennonites as were relief programs. Thus, deep reflection on great historical events served the cause of commonality, while it also revealed some deep differences, which were already evident within the world Mennonite community. Yet, the discussions were felt to be so valuable for the rediscovery of history and the reaffirmation of identity that any divergences were tolerated, at least for the time being.

The heritage of faith itself received a positive review. Anabaptism, it was explained by Swiss representative Samuel Geiser, was not the result of cold calculation or fanaticism, as the work of Conrad Grebel, Felix Manz, and Georg Blaurock had been depicted in various church histories and by contemporary critics.[157] But rather, Anabaptism was, as the rich source materials amply documented, "a creative act of God," prompted by decadence in the church and the desire to form a fellowship of believers according to the precepts of early Christianity.[158] In Geiser's interpretation this meant emphasizing the inner experience of salvation, baptism upon confession of faith, the practice of separation from the world, the insistence on church discipline, the defence of complete religious freedom, the call to discipleship, and the rejection of the oath as well as of military service.[159]

Menno Simons, on the other hand, received a mixed review at the 1936 conference in Holland commemorating the 400th anniversary of his resignation from the priesthood. Dutch leader N. van der Zijpp noted that in many ways Mennonites in the Netherlands knew little about him, somewhat of an irony given the fact that Menno himself was Dutch. Very little had been said or written about him, the last Dutch edition of his works having appeared in 1681. As well, the Dutch believers had for many centuries referred to themselves as *Doopsgezinde*, meaning Anabaptists, rather than Mennonites.[160]

Van der Zijpp explained that part of the reason for this reluctance was that Menno Simons was not really the founder of Anabaptism: he did not leave behind him like other reformers a theological system.[161] He was also too indecisive to become "the head of the church." On the positive side, Menno did guarantee continuity at a time when Calvinism, Catholicism, the use of force, and fanaticism threatened the brotherhood. He was known for his uniting of word and deed, for striking the right balance between doctrine and ethics. Also, he would always be known for his piety.

The world conference reflections on the early movement and its leaders was followed by a close look at the historical development and contemporary expression of the church. The Swiss churches, it was reported, had suffered decline for many years owing to oppression from the state, consequent emigration, and the rural isolation of those who had stayed behind. However, a renewal had occurred early in the twentieth century with continuing positive results.[162]

In the Netherlands the General Society of Anabaptists, founded in 1811 as a voluntary association, had been reorganized in 1923–1924. The new society, it was hoped, would provide better support for the Amsterdam seminary, needy congregations, and foreign relief and would allow for more active participation in the ecumenical movement. The reorganization was also intended to strengthen the fellowship of 40,000 members, an increase from a low of 27,000 in 1800 following a steady decline from 160,000 a century earlier. The reasons for that decline were fragmentation, on the one hand, and the growth of wealth, on the other hand, which led to new modes of relating to the world, including mixed marriages, participation in government offices, and military service, all of which tended to make the church unimportant, if not unnecessary.[163]

The rest of European Mennonitism, apart from Russia, included 40 congregations in southern Germany, about half a dozen congregations in northern Germany, about 10 congregations in Danzig and nearby regions formerly known as Prussia, and 8 congregations in Poland. Altogether, these Mennonites numbered about 20,000.[164] France now embraced both French- and German-speaking congre-

TABLE 30[166]

SUMMARY OF FOREIGN MENNONITE MISSIONS
(*c.* 1930)

SPONSOR	AREA	MISSIONARIES	MEMBERS
Dutch Mennonites	Java	6	2,130
Old Mennonite	Argentina	17	565
General Conference	India	41	1,366
	East Africa	10	39
General Conference	America (Indians)	17	
Mennonite Church	India	31	3,190
	China	16	
Mennonite	America (Indians)		100
Brethren Church	India	} 33	{ 500
	China		1,000
Mennonite Brethren	Africa	} 21	–
in Christ	India		
Congo Inland	Belgian Congo	31	–
Mission			
Krimmer	Mongolia	6	–
Mennonites			
China Mennonite			
Mission Society	China	38	650

gations. The latter had previously been located within German borders, but with the transfer of Alsace-Lorraine after the First World War, they were now within France.[165]

None of the Latin American German-speaking congregations or, for that matter, mission congregations were as yet represented at any of the world conferences (1925 – 36). However, their pioneering did not go unremembered. Several presentations outlined the situations in South America, Africa, and Asia. In addition, there were letters of greeting from newly established churches in Brazil and Paraguay. From India, the most fruitful of the various Mennonite mission fields (see Table 30), came a message of identification with the suffering Russian brethren,[167] quite possibly because some of the refugees in Asia had found their way to the mission stations.[168] The work of the missionaries, at that time numbering over 260, most of them from the U.S.A., would change in due course the character of the Mennonite world conference and thoroughly diffuse its Dutch-German and Swiss-German ethnic bases. But the full extent of that diffusion could not yet be foreseen.

The ethnic continuity of the Mennonites, who had a European base, was clearly evident in the North American story as reported at the international meetings. Practically all, if not all, the congregations in both the U.S.A. and Canada were related to either the Swiss-South German or the Dutch-North German cultural families. The Dutch had been the first to arrive in America, a number of businessmen establishing themselves in New York in 1643, others in Delaware in 1663, and still others in Pennsylvania in 1683.[169] The majority of immigrants who laid the real foundations of Mennonite life in America were, however, the Swiss and the South Germans. They began to arrive in the United States in 1683, some of their descendants moving on to Canada a century later. Significant numbers of Dutch-German Mennonites from Russia settled in both the United States and Canada in the 1870s.

Mennonite faith and life in America was described as exceedingly varied owing to the many different groupings, but there was also a common character, marked by the rejection of modernism and the active support of, or empathy with, fundamentalism. The teachings of most churches included the full authority of the Bible, the necessity of personal salvation and the sanctified life, the role of the church as an agent free and independent of the state, the clear separation of church and state, and the doctrine of nonresistance. An aggressive denominationalism, strongly influenced by American Protestantism, manifested itself in Sunday schools, youth societies, Bible studies, prayer groups, revival meetings, men's and women's associations, mission societies, choirs, and Bible conferences. There were missionaries on three continents, many mission stations in America, eleven hospitals, five children's homes, nine homes for senior citizens, two deaconess institutions, as well as colleges, other schools, and publications of all kinds.[170]

Through the sharing of information, discussions on faith and theology, and joint relief action, the world conferences, not yet officially bearing that name, had united Mennonites from various groups and countries, at least symbolically so, for the first time in 400 years. This coming together was found to be so good, useful, and promising that further such gatherings were held in prospect. The common fellowship, the common faith, the common front, and joint action, it was believed, would contribute much to the survival of the parts as well as of the whole.

Meanwhile, it was more accurate to speak of the Mennonite reality in terms of parts rather than of the whole. The Mennonite World Conference had provided emotional and spiritual links, but it possessed as yet very little organizational strength, not even as an international umbrella. In Russia, the wholeness that had been there was slowly but most surely being decimated. And in Canada, David Toews could not yet count on all the Mennonites uniting to support what was for him the overriding cause of those years, the needs of the Russlaender in Russia, Latin America, and Canada. Parochialism, provincialism, and denominationalism were the stronger forces, which even the depression and the Mennonite sense of mutual aid could not overcome. In that way the Mennonites were no different from their opponents, the narrowly focused Premier Anderson of Saskatchewan and many other clannish Canadians.

FOOTNOTES

1   C.F. Klassen, "Die Lage der russischen Gemeinden seit 1920," in *Bericht ueber die Mennonitische Welt-Hilfs-Konferenz vom 31. August bis 3. September 1930*, ed. by D. Christian Neff (Karlsruhe: Heinrich Schneider, 1930), p. 57.

2   Robert Payne, *The Rise and Fall of Stalin* (New York: Simon & Schuster, 1965). See also Nicholas V. Riasanovsky, *A History of Russia* (New York: Oxford University Press, 1969), pp. 547–51.

3   H.J. Willms, ed., *At the Gates of Moscow or God's Gracious Aid Through A Most Difficult and Trying Period*, trans. by George G. Thielman (Yarrow, B.C.: Columbia Press, 1964), pp. 13–15.

4   Cornelius J. Dyck, "The History of the Mennonite World Conference," in *Mennonite World Handbook*, ed. by Paul N. Kraybill (Lombard, Ill.: Mennonite World Conference, 1978), pp. 1–9.

5   D. Christian Neff, *ibid.*, pp. 7–8.

6   *Bericht ueber die 400-Jaehrige Jubilaeumsfeier der Mennoniten oder Taufgesinnten vom 13. bis 15. Juni 1925 in Basel* (Karlsruhe: Heinrich Schneider, 1925).

7   See Cornelius J. Dyck, p. 2, and P.A. Rempel, "Auszuege aus Aeltesten J.A. Rempels Lebensgeschichte," in *Mennonitische Maer-*

tyrer, ed. by A.A. Toews (Winnipeg: The Author, 1949), pp. 34–46.

8 D. Christian Neff, ed., *Der Allgemeine Kongress der Mennoniten gehalten in Amsterdam, Elspeet, Witmarsum, 29. Juni bis 3. Juli 1936* (Karlsruhe: Heinrich Schneider, 1936), p. ii.

9 David Toews, "Hilfswerk und Immigration," in *Der Allgemeine Kongress*, ed. Neff, pp. 151–58. See also C.F. Klassen, p. 54.

10 H.S. Bender, "Hilfswerk der amerikanischen Mennoniten in Russland," in *Mennonitische Welt-Hilfs-Konferenz*, ed. by D. Christian Neff, pp. 59–64.

11 *Ibid.*, pp. 63–64.

12 John B. Toews, *Lost Fatherland: The Story of the Mennonite Emigration from Soviet Russia, 1921–1927* (Scottdale: Herald Press, 1967), pp. 76–79.

13 C.F. Klassen, pp. 52–53.

14 Frank H. Epp, *Mennonite Exodus: The Rescue and Resettlement of the Russian Mennonites Since the Communist Revolution* (Altona: D.W. Friesen & Sons, 1962), p. 223.

15 C. Henry Smith, *The Story of the Mennonites* (Newton, Kans.: Mennonite Publication Office, 1981), p. 21.

16 *Ibid.*, p. 330.

17 C.F. Klassen, pp. 54–57.

18 Frank H. Epp, *Mennonite Exodus*, pp. 229–30.

19 Benjamin H. Unruh, "The Mass Flight of the German Farmers from the Soviet Union, Their Basis, the Results in Russia and its Effects of Foreign Relief Work," in *Mennonite World Relief Conference at Danzig, 1930*, ed. Delbert L. Gratz (Akron, Pa.: 1946), p. 30.

20 Harvey L. Dyck, "Collectivization, Depression, and Immigration, 1929–1930: A Chance Interplay," in *Empire and Nations: Essays in Honour of Frederic H. Soward*, ed. by Harvey L. Dyck and H. Peter Krosby (Toronto: University of Toronto Press, 1969), pp. 144–59. A pood is a Russian unit of weight equal to about 36.11 pounds.

21 H.J. Willms, p. 12.

22 Walter Quiring, *Russlanddeutsche Suchen eine Heimat: Die Deutsche Einwanderung in den Paraguayischen Chaco* (Karlsruhe: Heinrich Schneider, 1938), p. 106.

23 Germany's role in the events is recounted by Harvey L. Dyck, *Weimar Germany and Soviet Russia, 1926–1933: A Study in Diplomatic Instability* (London: Chatto and Windus, 1966), pp. 162–80.

24 Quoted in Harvey L. Dyck, "Collectivization," p. 145.

25 H.J. Willms, p. 124.

26 *Ibid.*, p. 14.

27 John B. Toews, "The Mennonites and the Siberian Frontier," *Mennonite Quarterly Review* 47 (April 1973):83–101.

28 Harvey L. Dyck, *Weimar Germany*, p. 163. Estimates differ as to the exact number of refugees gathered in Moscow, though all agree

that Mennonites constituted a majority. David Toews referred to the movement as embracing 13,000 people of which 8,000 were Mennonites. PAC, Immigration Branch, RG. 76, Vol. 175, file 58764, part 12, David Toews to Gorden, 25 October 1930.

29   Harvey L. Dyck, "Collectivization," p. 147.
30   Walter Quiring, p. 110.
31   Harvey L. Dyck, *Weimar Germany*, p. 167.
32   H.J. Willms, p. 61.
33   *Ibid.*, pp. 61–62.
34   *Ibid.*, p. 64.
35   Howard Palmer, ed., *Immigration and the Rise of Multiculturalism* (Toronto: Copp Clark Publishing, 1975), pp. 55–58. See also "The Preference to British Immigrants," *Manitoba Free Press*, 15 November 1929, p. 17.
36   Harvey L. Dyck, "Collectivization," p. 151.
37   PAC, RG. 14, Vol. 214, file 178, pp. 68–71.
38   *Canadian Annual Review 1928–29*, pp. 159–60.
39   *Canadian Annual Review 1929–30*, p. 179.
40   PAC, Immigration Branch, RG. 76, Vol. 175, file 58764, part 11, A. Buhr to Deputy Minister of Immigration, 5 June 1919.
41   PAC, Immigration Branch, RG. 76, Vol. 175, file 58764, part 11, W.J. Egan to A. Buhr, 22 August 1929.
42   PAC, Immigration Branch, RG. 76, Vol. 175, file 58764, part 11, F.C. Blair to Robert Forke, 30 October 1929.
43   CGC, XV.31–2, "1920-Moscow(4)." This file contains "Deutsche Hilfsmassnahmen zugunsten der Auswanderung deutschstaemmiger Fluechtlinge ueberwiegend mennonitischen Glaubens aus der Sovjetunion und ihre Ansiedlung in ueberseeischen Gebieten, 1929–1932: 23 Dokumente aus dem Politischen Archive des Auswaertigen Amts der Bundesrepublik Deutschland." This collection of documents telling about the German response from 5 November 1929 was made public on the occasion of the 50th anniversary, July 1980, in Paraguay of Colony Fernheim, whose population base is Moscow refugees of 1929.
44   PAC, Immigration Branch, RG. 76, Vol. 175, file 58764, part 11, Memorandum for file prepared by F.C. Blair, 26 November 1919.
45   *Ibid.*
46   Frank H. Epp, *Mennonite Exodus*, p. 244.
47   As late as 9 November, Blair confided to Kempff that he believed the transportation of Mennonites from Moscow to Canada could commence in the next couple of weeks or thereabouts, though the movement might not be completed until spring. PAC, Immigration Branch, RG. 76, Vol. 175, file 58764, part 11.
48   PAC, Immigration Branch, RG. 76, Vol. 175, file 58764, part 11, Robert Forke to Mackenzie King, 5 November 1929.
49   "Mennonites Admission is Favourably Viewed by Federal Govern-

ment," Toronto *Globe* (9 November 1929); "Admission of Mennonites to Be Deliberated," Montreal *Gazette* (9 November 1929).

50 Frank H. Epp, *Mennonite Exodus*, p. 245. See also "Premier Discusses Mennonites' Case," *Manitoba Free Press* (5 November 1929); "Mennonite Refugees Cannot Be Allowed to Be Public Charge," Toronto *Globe* (7 November 1929).

51 Anderson knew of the Mennonites' desire to come to Canada. On 5 November, he released a statement to the press saying that his government should be consulted before any of the Mennonites settled in the province.

52 The telegram was reproduced in "Ask Saskatchewan to Take Mennonites," *Saskatoon Star-Phoenix*, 9 November 1929, p. 1. For a summary and chronology of events 7 November to 7 December see PAC, RG. 14, Vol. 214, file 178, pp. 26–58.

53 PAC, Immigration Branch, RG. 76, Vol. 175, file 58764, part 12, J.T.M. Anderson to Robert Forke, 8 November 1929. See also "Guarantee Asked They Will Not Be Public Charges" *Regina Daily Post* (9 November 1929).

54 PAC, Immigration Branch, RG. 76, Vol. 175, file 58764, part 12, J.T.M. Anderson to Robert Forke, 8 November 1929.

55 At an Orange meeting held in Regina several months after his election, Anderson affirmed that he had been an Orangeman for over 30 years. George Joseph Hoffman, "The Saskatchewan Provincial Election of 1934: Its Political, Economic and Social Background" (M.A. thesis, University of Saskatchewan, 1973), p. 185.

56 Quoted in *ibid.*, p. 48.

57 "Problems in West," Toronto *Globe*, 5 November 1929, p. 3. A similarly slanted article appeared several weeks later. "Few of Mennonites Likely to Emigrate," Toronto *Globe*, 20 November 1929, p. 5.

58 A compilation of newspaper reports is contained in George P. Friesen, *Fangs of Bolshevism: Friesen-Braun Trials in Saskatchewan, 1924–1929* (Saskatoon: Friesen, 1930).

59 *Ibid.* See also Frank H. Epp, *Mennonite Exodus*, pp. 214–17; Reports by RCMP, Saskatoon Detachment, "F" Division Prince Albert, 17 November 1926; CGC, XV-31.2, "1920-Friesen-Braun Trials."

60 See Frank H. Epp, *Mennonite Exodus*, pp. 216–17.

61 The major decisions of the Friesen-Braun trials are given in 2WWR 257, 2OSLR 512, 2DLR 1032, WWR Vol. 3, pp. 227–30, DLR, Vol. 23, pp. 205–8.

62 "Braun's Family Not to Be Deported," *Saskatchewan Valley News*, (19 October 1932).

63 RCMP, *op.cit.*, p. 4.

64 Frank H. Epp, *Mennonite Exodus*, pp. 216–17.

65 The federal government was not at all concerned about the attitude of

the Mennonite immigrants to education. F.C. Blair remarked: "Someone has very aptly described the difference between the 'Old Colony' and the 'New Colony' Mennonites by saying that the 'Old Colony' Mennonites could scarcely be got into school, and the 'New Colony' Mennonites can scarcely be kept out of it." PAC, Immigration Branch, RG. 76, Vol. 175, file 58764, part 12, F.C. Blair to Paul Viau, 31 March 1930.

66   "Premier Talks on Refugee Question," *Saskatoon Star-Phoenix*, 7 November 1929, p. 13.

67   Between 5 November and 3 December, the Toronto *Globe* carried 14 articles related to the Mennonite refugee question. Front-page mention was given to 8 articles. The *Manitoba Free Press* carried 11 Mennonite-related press releases between 4 and 29 November. Of these, 7 were presented on the first page.

68   Caroline Melis, "J.T.M. Anderson, Director of Education Among New Canadians and the Policy of the Department of Education: 1918-1923," *Saskatchewan History* 33 (Winter 1980):11.

69   Patrick Kyba, "Ballots and Burning Crosses—The Election of 1929," in *Politics in Saskatchewan*, ed. by Norman Ward and Duff Spafford (Don Mills: Longmans Canada, 1968), p. 101.

70   William Calderwood, "Pulpit, Press and Political Reactions to the Ku Klux Klan in Saskatchewan," in *The Twenties in Western Canada*, ed. by S.M. Trofimenkoff (Ottawa: National Museum of Man, History Division, 1972), p. 213.

71   PAA, Accession no. 69. 289/498, UFA Sedgewick local to J. E. Brownlee, 13 November 1929.

72   PAA, Accession no. 69. 289/498, V.M.W. of Rosedale local to J. E. Brownlee, 25 November 1929.

73   Frank H. Epp, *Mennonite Exodus*, p. 247.

74   PAC, Immigration Branch, RG. 76, Vol. 175, file 58764, part 11, R.A. Hoey to David Toews, 12 November 1929.

75   Frank H. Epp, *Mennonite Exodus*, pp. 247-48.

76   "Canadian Mennonites Protest Immigration of Their Compatriots," Toronto *Globe*, 15 November 1929, p. 1. The Mennonite Brethren Church regretted that some of its members had dispatched the telegram. The chairman of the semi-annual meeting of the Mennonite Brethren churches of the Rosthern District at Dalmeny critically explained that "the name of Christ had been shamed." The following resolution was unanimously adopted at the conclusion of the meeting: "We condemn with all our hearts the action of those who dispatched the telegram, as unchristian and declare that we as Mennonite Brethren churches of the Rosthern district have nothing in common with it." P.P. Nickel, "Ein Bedaurenswertes Telegram an Premier Anderson und unsere Stellung dazu," *Der Bote* 8 (21 January 1931):2-3.

77 "Mennonite Attitude Quoted by Mr. Anderson," Toronto *Globe*, 23 November 1929, p. 1.

78 C.C. Peters and H.A. Neufeld, "Eingabe der Herberter Mennoniten an den Premierminister, Hon. J.T.M. Anderson," *Der Bote* 6 (27 November 1929):3.

79 "Premier Replies Refugee Entry Is Conditional," *Calgary Albertan* (15 November 1929). He also wrote to the secretary of Mennonite Immigration Aid. PAC, Immigration Branch, RG. 76, Vol. 175, file 58764, part 11, J.T.M. Anderson to A. Buhr, 14 November 1929.

80 "Bishop Outlines Mennonite Plan for Settlement," *Edmonton Journal* (18 November 1929); "Alberta Will Probably Bar Russian Mennonite Families; Government Disapproves," *Edmonton Journal* (18 November 1929); "Mennonite Question May Go to League," Toronto *Globe*, 18 November 1929, p. 1.

81 PAC, Immigration Branch, RG. 76, Vol. 175, file 58764, part 11, J.E. Brownlee to David Toews, 19 November 1929.

82 PAA, Accession no. 69. 289/498, Extract of the Minutes, Mennonite Farmers Association, Coaldale, 21 November 1929.

83 *Ibid.*, B.B. Janz and A.W. Klassen to Hon. Mr. Brownlee, 27 November 1929.

84 *Ibid.*, B.B. Janz, J.B. Janz, and H. Kornelsen to Mr. Brownlee, 15 December 1929.

85 *Ibid.*, Telegram from Provincial Secretary, Canadian Legion to J.E. Brownlee, 15 November 1929.

86 *Ibid.*, Resolution of Rowley UFWA, Local 68, 21 November 1929.

87 *Ibid.*, Letter from J. Weir, President, United Mine Workers of Alberta, 25 November 1929.

88 *Ibid.*, Letter from A.J. Morris, National Scribe, National Order of Canada, 3 December 1929.

89 *Ibid.*, Letter from George Jenkins, Secretary, Belfast Orange Lodge, Mayerthorpe, 28 January 1930, and from W.L. Hall, Grand Secretary, The Loyal Orange Association, Calgary, 24 March 1930.

90 Frank H. Epp, *Mennonite Exodus*, pp. 248–50.

91 See CGC, XV-31.2, "1920-Moscow(4)," "Deutsche Massnahmen..." p. 15 ff.

92 PAC, Immigration Branch, RG. 76, Vol. 175, file 58764, part 11, R.A. Hoey to Robert Forke, 25 November 1929.

93 "Forke Bars Mennonites," *Saskatoon Star-Phoenix*, 26 November 1929, p. 1.

94 "Mennonites Seeking New Homes May Reach Big Total of 100,000," *Manitoba Free Press* (21 November 1929).

95 *Canadian Annual Review, 1929–30*, p. 185.

96 "No Use to Us," *Victoria Daily Times* 75 (15 November 1929).

97   "Moscow v. Mennonite," *Vancouver Daily Province* (13 January 1930).

98   "Admission of Mennonites," *Manitoba Free Press* (18 November 1929).

99   "New Light on the Mennonites," *Regina Star* (22 November 1929).

100   "Soviet Cruelty Deluxe," Toronto *Globe* (3 December 1929).

101   "Mennonite Request Is Being Considered," Toronto *Globe* (6 November 1929). In a report to the Consul General for Bolivia in Canada, F.C. Blair, the Acting Deputy Minister, Immigration, referred to the Swiss Mennonites of Ontario as "a fine hardy pioneering type of law-abiding people, who have made good citizens of this country." PAC, Immigration Branch, RG. 76, Vol. 175, file 58764, part 12, F.C. Blair to Paul Viau, 31 March 1930. In a letter to David Toews, Blair, referring to "my early days . . . in the County of Waterloo," says: "The reputation of Mennonites as law-abiding, industrious citizens, was such that I could not but be impressed with the desirability of such people." PAC, *op.cit.*, Blair to Toews, 1 March 1930. To Jacob H. Janzen, Blair wrote 28 October 1930: "My early life was spent in the County of Wellington and we were well-acquainted with Mennonite families and the successful settlement of Mennonite people in the adjacent County of Waterloo. Having had that experience it does not require any argument to convince me that Mennonites are a splendid, well-behaved, and industrious people." PAC, *ibid.*

102   "Mennonites and Schools," Toronto *Globe* (15 January 1930).

103   "The Mennonites," Toronto *Globe* (15 January 1930).

104   See Harvey L. Dyck, *Weimar Germany*, pp. 174–80.

105   President Hindenburg donated 200,000 marks ($50,000) from the funds at the president's personal disposal to a subscription of the German Red Cross and other charitable organizations. He made an earnest appeal for all Germans at home and abroad to contribute to the refugees' needs according to their means.

106   "Mennonite Problem Too Much for Berlin," Toronto *Globe*, 26 November 1929, p. 2.

107   See Chapter 12 and Frank H. Epp, "An Analysis of Germanism and National Socialism in the Immigrant Newspaper of a Canadian Minority Group, the Mennonites, in the 1930s" (Ph.D. dissertation, University of Minnesota, 1965).

108   Harvey L. Dyck, "Collectivization," p. 159.

109   H.J. Willms, p. 151. The story of one is included in Harvey L. Dyck, "Despair and Hope in Moscow: A Pillow, A Willow Trunk, and a Stiff-Backed Photograph," *Mennonite Life* 34 (September 1979):16–23.

110   Harvey L. Dyck, "Despair and Hope," p. 22.

111 PAC, Immigration Branch, RG. 76, Vol. 175, file 58764, part 12, P.C. Hiebert, Chairman, and Levi Mumaw, Secretary, "to whom it may concern," 27 November 1929.
112 H.J. Willms, pp. 92–96.
113 A description of the camps and their living conditions is found in Harold S. Bender, "Our Russian Refugee Brethren in Germany," *Gospel Herald* 23 (22 and 29 May 1930):170–71 and 190–91.
114 H.J. Willms, p. 102.
115 H.S. Bender, p. 171.
116 As with the earlier Russlaender immigrants, trachoma was the most common affliction affecting the travellers.
117 Joseph Winfield Fretz, *Pilgrims in Paraguay: The Story of Mennonite Colonization in South America* (Scottdale, Pa.: Herald Press, 1953), p. 37, f. 16.
118 Their experience is recounted in Peter Klassen, "The Mennonites of Brazil," *Mennonite Quarterly Review* 11 (April 1937):107–18.
119 The assistance given by Germany to the Mennonites in Brazil prompted one of their number to write, "The German government took the young colony under its wings in such a way and to such an extent that every writer of our history must recognize this wonderful service." *Ibid.*, p. 108.
120 Walter Quiring, "The Colonization of the German Mennonites from Russia in the Paraguayan Chaco," *Mennonite Quarterly Review* 8 (April 1934):67.
121 PAC, RG. 14, Vol. 214, file 178, Abraham Funk, Carlton, Sask., to the Hon. Chas. Stewart, Minister of the Interior, Ottawa, 6 January 1930.
122 *Ibid.*
123 PAC, RG. 14, Vol. 214, file 178. Joseph R. Tucker, Sub Rosa, Saskatchewan, to the Minister of Immigration, 27 January 1930.
124 PAC, Immigration Branch, RG. 76, Vol. 175, file 58764, part 12, "Memorandum to the Governments of Ontario and Canada Submitted for the United Mennonite churches in Ontario by the Bishop of the Same, Jacob H. Janzen," 15 September 1930.
125 *Jahrbuch*, 1929, p. 8.
126 David Toews, "Bericht an die Konferenz," *Jahrbuch*, 1930, pp. 65–73.
127 *Ibid.*, pp. 72–73.
128 PAC, Immigration Branch, RG. 76, Vol. 175, file 58764, part 12. Based on translation of code message by W.J. Egan, 28 November 1929.
129 Toews's tireless work prompted F.C. Blair to remark, "I am sure that Toews is sometimes at his wit's end to know what to do to help his people." PAC, Immigration Branch, RG. 76, Vol. 175, file 58764, part 12, F.C. Blair to J. Macalister, 19 April 1930. See

also David Toews, "Einwanderung nach Kanada von Herbst 1928 bis Jetzt," in *Mennonitische Welt-Hilfs-Konferenz*, ed. by Neff, pp. 94–99.

130   PAC, King Papers, MG. 26, J 1, Vol. 183, King to David Toews, 10 January 1930.

131   "Toews Gives Details of Colonization Plan to Bring Mennonites," *Saskatoon Star-Phoenix* (29 April 1930):3, 5.

132   CGC, XV-31.2, "1920-Moscow(3)," David Toews, "A Letter Regarding Mennonites which appeared in *Star Phoenix* early February 1930."

133   *Ibid.*, p. 3.

134   *Ibid.*, p. 4.

135   PAA, Accession no. 69. 289/498, David Toews to J.E. Brownlee, 26 July 1930.

136   PAC, Immigration Branch, RG. 76, Vol. 175, file 58764, part 12, J.T.M. Anderson to David Toews, 14 June 1930.

137   PAC, Immigration Branch, RG. 75, Vol. 175, file 58764, part 12, Albert Prefontaine to Charles Stewart, 2 May 1930.

138   Walter Quiring, p. 115.

139   Frank H. Epp, *Mennonite Exodus*, p. 258.

140   H.J. Willms, p. 112.

141   "Schicksale einer kleinen Gruppe Mennonitsche Fluechtlinge aus Russland in China," in A.A. Toews, pp. 35–38; David Toews, "Immigration und Nothilfe," in *Jahrbuch*, 1933, pp. 71–73.

142   For a first-hand account of this expedition, see Abram Friesen and Abram J. Loewen, *Die Flucht Ueber den Amur* (Steinbach, Man.: Echo-Verlag, 1946). See also Abram J. Loewen, *Immer Weiter Nach Osten Suedrussland, China, Kanada* (Winnipeg: CMBC Publications, 1981).

143   P.C. Hiebert, "Hilfswerk und Kolonization der Mennoniten seit 1930," in D. Christian Neff, *Der Allgemeine Kongress*, pp. 146–50. See also P.C. Hiebert, "Hilfeleistung," *Verhandlungen* (ND), 1932, pp. 30–31; and David Toews, "Immigration und Nothilfe," *Jahrbuch*, 1934, pp. 71–73.

144   Frank H. Epp, *Mennonite Exodus*, p. 265.

145   CMCA, XXII-A, Vol. 1178, File 107, David Toews *et al.* "to the Canadian Representative at the League of Nations," 7 December 1934.

146   *Ibid.*, pp. 266–67.

147   An excellent account of Russia during Stalin's terror-filled reign is given by Adam Bruno Ulam, *Stalin: The Man and His Era* (New York: Viking Press, 1973).

148   *Ibid.*, pp. 267–69.

149   Jacob Kroeker, the Russian Mennonite émigré who spoke at the 1925 world conference, claimed that the Russian tragedy was the judgement of God on Mennonite materialism. He said: "Our

fathers and brothers became wealthy in the steppes of Russia and succumbed to materialism to a frightening degree. And now that a shocking world judgement is affecting Russia especially, what has happened to the millions which were the possession not only of a few but of many? The judgements of God have caught up also with the materialistic Mennonites." "Festansprache," in *Bericht ueber die 400-Jaehrige Jubilaeums Feier*, pp. 33–34.

150   Harold S. Bender, "Hilfswerk der Amerikanischen Mennoniten in Ruszland," in *Mennonitische Welt-Hilfs-Konferenz*, ed. by D. Christian Neff, pp. 59–64.

151   W. Kuehler, "Helfende Bruderliebe in der Vergangenheit Seitens der Hollaendischen Bruderschaft," in *Mennonitische Welt-Hilfs-Konferenz*, ed. by D. Christian Neff, pp. 39–44; S.H.N. Gorter, "Hilfswerk der Hollaendischen Mennoniten," in Neff, pp. 65–66.

152   D. Christian Neff, "Hilfswerk der Deutschen Mennoniten," in *ibid.*, pp. 67–68.

153   David Toews, "Hilfswerk und Immigration," in *Der Allgemeine Kongress*, ed. by Neff, pp. 151–54.

154   *Ibid.*

155   *Ibid.*, pp. 157–58. Toews's estimate of 75,000 Mennonites in Russia was at least 25,000 too few.

156   *Ibid.*, p. 158.

157   Even the *New York Times*, commenting on the Mennonite flight to Moscow, identified them as "good revolutionists closely connected with the Anabaptists and through them with the Peasants' War of 1525." See editorial on Mennonites, *New York Times* (6 December 1929):26. Harold S. Bender, responding to the editorial, in a letter prominently published, pointed out that the *Times'* "conception of the Mennonites and Anabaptists is the traditional one based on the historiography of the enemies . . . now completely invalidated by modern scholarship." H.S. Bender on history of Mennonites, *New York Times* (11 December 1929):28.

158   Samuel Geiser, "Die Mennoniten der Schweiz und Frankreiches in Geschichte und Gegenwart," in *Der Allgemeine Kongress*, ed. by Neff, pp. 47–60.

159   *Ibid.*

160   N. van der Zijpp, "Die Bedeutung von Menno Simons Wirksamkeit fuer unsere Bruderschaft" in *ibid.*, pp. 26–33.

161   *Ibid.*, p. 27.

162   Samuel Geiser, pp. 58–61.

163   J. Yntema, "Die Taufgesinnten in den Niederlanden in Vergangenheit und Gegenwart," in *Der Allgemeine Kongress*, pp. 33–40.

164   D. Christian Neff, "Die Mennoniten in Deutschland, Danzig, und Polen in Vergangenheit und Gegenwart," in *ibid.*, pp. 40–47.

165   *Ibid.*, pp. 56–57.
166   Orie Miller, "Die Mission der Mennoniten," in *Der Allgemeine Kongress*, pp. 125–29.
167   D. Christian Neff, *Der Allgemeine Kongress*, pp. 21–22.
168   "Profile: Jacob J. Dick," *Mennonite Reporter* 10 (15 September 1980):11.
169   Harold S. Bender, "Die Mennoniten der Vereinigten Staaten in Amerika in Geschichte und Gegenwart," in *ibid.*, pp. 66–67.
170   *Ibid.*

8. Overcoming the Depression

Outstanding in the life of the Mennonite people is the practice of mutual aid in time of distress and loss. We have literally tried to do good to all men, but especially to those of the household of faith as the apostle enjoined — L.J. BURKHOLDER.[1]

Cooperation truly succeeds only when the people see in it a great social enterprise and are gripped by the desire for justice and the will to make the world a better place in which to live — J.J. SIEMENS.[2]

UNDIVIDED CANADIAN attention to the disaster facing the Mennonites in the Soviet Union was impossible in view of the calamitous onslaught in the 1930s of the world-wide economic depression. The international and national financial paralysis affected the Mennonites, particularly on the Canadian prairies, in diverse ways and brought forth a variety of responses to ensure survival. Old forms of co-operation and mutual aid were revived and strengthened, and some new forms were devised, partly to replace what had once been and partly to deal with the new circumstances. Mennonite individualism likewise manifested new vigour, as some resisted the dole both for themselves and for others, and as hundreds of families took to the road once again in search of a more promising land.

The thirties were a ten-year period like no other in Canadian history.[3] It was a very bad time for agriculture and business, and the number of workers unemployed exceeded one-tenth of the labour

347

force for almost every year of the decade. Any assessment of the disastrous meaning of the unemployment statistics must take into consideration that with few exceptions the unemployed were the sole breadwinners in their families and that they had no unemployment insurance or standing welfare programs to turn to. In 1933, unemployment actually rose to 20 per cent. Recovery from that apocalyptic year was slow and uneven and far from complete when the Second World War began.

For western, particularly Saskatchewan, farmers the depression was a crushing ordeal.[4] Everything seemed to go wrong at once. The weather was abnormal, and dust storms, rather than blizzards, swirled through village streets in midwinter. In summer, the fields baked and cracked under scorching, rainless skies. Blanket infestations of grasshoppers and caterpillars added to the rural miseries. Hostile natural forces were only part of the farmer's sorrows, because the market on which his livelihood depended experienced a catastrophic collapse. Prices offered for the cereal crops were appallingly low, and some households used their meagre harvests as a source of winter fuel.

The collapse of the wheat market, accompanying the stagnation of world trade and finance, was as central to the depression as the development of wheat for export had been to the Canadian economic boom prior to the Great War. After a temporary post-war slump in the wheat economy, the market had again picked up, and in 1928, the peak year of the 1920s, farm cash income from the sale of wheat was $451 million. Put in other terms, it represented 7.4 per cent of the GNP and 40 per cent of total farm income.[5] As in all previous decades, so in the 1920s wheat production had increased, 22 per cent in the first five years and 16 per cent in the last five.

The 1930s saw a complete reversal of that trend. In the first five years, production fell 26 per cent and in the second half of the decade another 15 per cent.[6] The drastic decline in wheat prices and the prices of all other farm produce exacerbated the situation. From the peak in 1928 to the ebb in 1933 agricultural income fell by almost 80 per cent.[7] One legend has it that a southern Manitoba farmer took his load of grain with horse-drawn wagon over 30 miles to Emerson, there to be offered 25 cents "for relieving him of the load."[8] And according to another chronicler:

In 1929 wheat sold for $1.13 a bushel, but by 1931 the price
had dropped to 29 cents per bushel and in 1932 farmers got
only 19 cents per bushel. Cattle prices also declined in the
same way and hogs sold for 1^{1}/2 cents per pound.[9]

History had taught the Mennonites to accept and adjust to adversity. While not all acknowledged suffering as a normal Christian or
human experience essential for the fulfilment of divine purpose or
even as a virtue to be sought, few believed that continuous prosperity
was a divine right or even a proper expectation. God would take care
of His children if they would do their share. While some accepted
relief, "even when the need was not so desperate," others felt "that
they had no right to take relief if they had any other way of helping
themselves."[10] Thus, the days of the depression were for the most
part not characterized by a lazy waiting for better times but by harder
work and the application of all those measures which the instinct of
survival suggested as pointing in the right direction. This included,
above all, belt-tightening and the reduction of whatever "luxuries"
had already been accepted.

One example of such adjustment lay in gasoline-powered transportation and farming. When the depression struck, tractors and cars
had in many places replaced horses for field work and transportation.
Because the economic crisis made cars unaffordable, they were
converted into wagons with rubber tires by removing the motor,
leaving the car body or replacing it with the box of a lumberwagon,
attaching a pole and a doubletree to it, and hitching horses to the
doubletree. Bennett buggies they were called, after R.B. Bennett,
who had the misfortune of being Canada's prime minister during
those fateful years, but whose ability to remain in good humour even
during difficult times represented a unique qualification for the
task.[11] A popular two-wheeler created from half a car frame was
named after J.T.M. Anderson, the Saskatchewan premier.

There were more Bennett buggies and Anderson carts in Saskatchewan than anywhere else, because that is where the depression hit the
hardest and continued the longest, bringing impoverishment and
dependence on emergency relief to tens of thousands. When the task
of relieving economic distress became too much for both the municipal and the provincial governments, the extra-governmental Sas-

katchewan Relief Commission was created to achieve a fair and equitable distribution of the relief available from all sources. Food was distributed, especially flour for bread, as well as clothing ranging from $2.50 worth per infant per year to $9.00 per adult with a maximum of $75 per family. Fuel, medical aid, and feed and fodder for livestock were also distributed and, in due course, seed grain to help farmers get started again.[12] The Relief Commission came to an end with the 1934 provincial election, but relief was needed and carried on by various branches of the provincial government throughout the 1930s and into the 1940s, as families and fields impoverished for so many successive years could not easily be rehabilitated. The reluctance with which most Mennonites needing relief accepted it is reflected in the memoirs of Ernest A. Jeschke:

> This [the 1937 crop year] brought us to the humiliating position where we stretched out our hands for "relief." Of course we were very reluctant to take that step, but we had six children all school age.[13]

By and large, the provincial governments were poorly equipped — philosophically, politically, structurally, and financially — to cope with the depression. After bailing out the wheat pools, which had paid the farmers more than the wheat was later worth, the governments of the prairie provinces were under great pressure to balance their budgets. In Saskatchewan, the Relief Commission was a limited operation and of limited duration.[14] In Manitoba, the Liberal-Progressive government of John Bracken was able to maintain relief and old age pensions only by imposing a two per cent tax on all wages and salaries.[15] In Alberta, the newly established Social Credit government neglected to implement its promise of a monthly 25-dollar dividend to all citizens.[16] In Ontario, the Liberal government of Mitchell Hepburn promised reform but much of its energy went into cutbacks and the balancing of budgets.[17] Most progressive in terms of public spending, both for relief and for job-creating works, was the Liberal government of Thomas Dufferin Pattullo in British Columbia.[18]

The distribution of direct relief "was supplemented by . . . church organizations, fraternities, welfare groups, and generous individuals."[19] In the first third of the depression decade alone, 577 carloads of fruit, vegetables, and clothing were donated by charitable people throughout Canada and shipped without cost by the railways. Among these carloads of donated produce, four filled with potatoes and other garden products were collected by the Mennonites of Waterloo County and distributed along with 42 bales of clothing in southern Saskatchewan communities.[20] Much clothing also arrived from the churches in the U.S.A., an average of 15,000 pounds a year. During one fall and winter, for example, one American shipment of 17,772 pounds of clothing was distributed among 646 families.[21] Such help was absolutely essential because distributors found children without stockings or shoes even in the coldest winter months.[22] From northern Saskatchewan came three carloads of potatoes. From Alberta five carloads of baled straw were sent to feed the cattle of Mennonite farmers in southern and central Saskatchewan, the parts hit hardest.[23]

Such concern had its origins in, and was undergirded by, the theology of the church, which stressed the moral obligation to do good to all people.[24] Though church-based mutual aid had a strong tradition in all Mennonite groups, the particular problems of the 1930s led to departures from particular practices. The Conference of Mennonites in Central Canada, for instance, resolved that its treasury for the poor should serve not only its own congregations, but also people in need who were not members anywhere.[25] Another example of deliberate extension beyond the borders was the sewing-circle movement, in the 1930s at its peak particularly in Ontario.[26] More formally known as the Women's Missionary Society, the movement excelled in sewing clothes for Toronto's "fresh air children," visiting the sick, providing home nursing services, comforting bereaved families, feeding the hungry, and gathering used garments for destitute people.

Mutual aid in all its forms was tried and tested, and, while institutional relief and collections in distant places made a great deal of difference, it was neighbourhood helpfulness and community solidarity which mattered most. Some of the care that neighbours had for each other in an earlier era was recalled and revived. In the Grunthal area, for instance, every farmer knew about "*Schmett Toews en Gruentol*" (Blacksmith Toews in Grunthal), because that was one place where farmers who had broken machinery and who were too poor to buy new implements could get some help. And the charges were according to the times. Schmett Toews expected no more than 50 cents for what had formerly been a ten-dollar job.[27]

Isolated Fields: Alberta

Good-neighbourliness, however, was not enough to keep Mennonites in place. They left the depressed wheat fields by the hundreds. And if they did not leave the fields, they left the wheat, as in southern Manitoba, where heavy dependence on grain now gave way to diversification.[28] In all the prairie provinces, there was scattered movement towards northern brushland areas, where the soil retained the moisture better, where agriculture always was and remained diversified, and where nature in the form of berries or wild animals provided some source of sustenance. The drought and the grasshopper plague in southern Saskatchewan resulted in a near-panic flight from the south to the north where there was more grass and feed and where there were better hopes of getting through the winter with cattle and family. Large tracts of land in the Meadow Lake area were being looked at in 1934 as possible areas of settlement.[29] But the more significant movements were from the grain farms of the prairies to the fruit orchards and the vegetable and tobacco farms of southern Ontario, and even more to the fruit and dairy farms of the British Columbia lower mainland.

In the 1930s, the Mennonite population in Canada increased by 22,818 — from 88,736 to 111,554 — resulting in increases in all the provinces, from Ontario to British Columbia. Even Saskatchewan gained more than 1,200. However, as a fraction of the total, Saskatchewan declined from 35.3 per cent to 29.2 per cent, while British Columbia, in quadrupling its Mennonite population, moved up from 1.2 per cent to 4.6 per cent of the total. What was equally significant was that the 1930s represented the beginning of a trend which continued in the 1940s, when the Saskatchewan fraction declined to 21 per cent and the British Columbia portion of the total moved up to 12 per cent.

For some, and this was true especially in the Hague-Osler area, the economic reasons for moving were reinforced by the impulses of religion and the search for cultural isolation which persisted in spite of the movements to Mexico and Paraguay in the 1920s. Those who stayed in Canada were leaderless and frustrated at first, but by 1930 the Reinlaender remnant had regrouped and renamed itself the

Altkolonier Mennonitengemeinde (Old Colony Mennonite Church), selected a new bishop, and begun confidently to build for the future.[30] However, the issue of isolation from society and of accepting the public school had not been fully resolved.

In the Mennonite community, as in society generally, no issue was ever solved for all time. New circumstances, or second thoughts about old circumstances, tended to produce a fresh division of opinion. There was, after all, no conservative faction so unanimous and cohesive that it could not ultimately give rise to some progressive thought, and there was no grouping of progressives that was not capable of some conservatism in the ranks. Indeed, each issue always had at least two sides to it, and whenever Mennonites insisted on turning one side or the other into rigid truth, they guaranteed the emergence, sooner or later, of another point of view. Thus, while the emigration had separated those who were in favour of leaving Canada and those who were against it, both those who left and those who stayed had second thoughts. In Latin America some people were thinking of coming back to Canada. And among the Altkolonier and Bergthaler(S) of the Hague-Osler area there were those who continued to fear absorption into the world, even though at an earlier time that fear had not been strong enough to cause the total uprooting that emigration required.

Should a greater isolation be possible within Canada, that would be another matter. The coming, and settlement in their midst, of the Russlaender started second thoughts precisely in that direction. On the one hand, the colonization agents working for the Russlaender had once again identified the vast Peace River district as a settlement possibility. On the other hand, the Russlaender represented a new threat. As far as some Bergthaler(S) and Altkolonier were concerned, a new element of worldliness, as they perceived it, had been added by the settlement of the Russlaender in their midst. It seems that the Kanadier were extremely disquieted by the presence of the immigrants, regarded by them as liberals who had not maintained intact the traditional values. A legal firm representing a group of Hague-Osler Old Colony people looking for land informed the Alberta authorities that

> the reason for their desire to move westward is that the new
> Mennonites who have come in from Russia since the war have
> proved a somewhat disturbing element, disturbing, at any
> rate, to their religious and home life idea.[31]

Inquiries regarding the possibility of settlement in the Peace River District were made late in the 1920s by a number of Kanadier groups with the help of J.J. Hildebrand of the Canadian National Settlement Association.[32] Despite several attempts to win education-related privileges for themselves, these groups failed to extract any special concessions from the Alberta government.[33] None the less, some families elected to move northward. They believed that a temporary reprieve from cultural intrusion was better than none at all and such a possibility existed in the northland.

The successive Alberta governments, both United Farmers and Social Credit, did not organize public schools where none existed or enforce compulsory school attendance legislation against the wishes of the local populace. In this, Alberta was quite different from Manitoba and Saskatchewan. There was in Alberta also less rigidity in curriculum-related matters. Private schools, like Prairie Bible Institute at Three Hills, could become fully accredited without reference to Shakespeare or "other worldly authors." In the English classes of PBI, only the writings of evangelical missionaries and preachers were used.[34]

In 1930, representatives of about 300 families at Hague-Osler and in southern Manitoba inspected lands along the Peace River, north of the town of Peace River. Special attention was given to an area in townships 97, 98, 101, immediately east of a small town called Carcajou. A certain Mr. Elias actually settled in Carcajou at the time and began to cut a road and await further settlers.[35] He was followed in 1932–33 by five other families from the Hague-Osler area. These pioneers praised the isolation of the northland and encouraged others to join them. But they also came to the early conclusion that the river valley flatlands of Carcajou, being too wet too long at the wrong time, were not the best choice.

Thus, in 1934 they moved farther north near the small trading post of Fort Vermilion on the east side of the Peace River. Others were on their way. In May of that year it was reported at the town of Peace River that four railroad cars of effects, including 25 head of cattle and horses, together with a large quantity of farm machinery, had arrived as a vanguard of a large movement to follow, and that over 300 quarter sections of land had been secured on long-term lease.

The first manifestation of the permanent settlement appeared at

Buffalo Head Prairie,[36] also known as Rosenort.[37] Then settlement expanded north about 40 miles to include the communities of La Crete, Blumenort,[38] and Rheinland, the latter nearest to Fort Vermilion.[39] While the numbers arriving were small,[40] the Kanadier movement once again opened up the Peace River District as a possible happy settlement option for others.

Among those selecting the northern wilderness as their new home were returnees from Mexico who were having second thoughts about their transfer to that country. In the fall of 1935, Bishops Isaak M. Dyck and Jacob Peters, with 13 ministers and 3 laymen, were consulting by mail with their former lawyers in Morden about a return to "the old beloved fatherland Canada."[41] Their schools had been closed since the month of June by the authorities and this caused them "more grief and suffering than the loss of our earthly goods" because "we find ourselves deceived in our expectations." Thirteen years of "hardships and molestations from the Mexican people" had been difficult to bear, but even more problematic was the establishment "of socialistic schools by law from which law the Mennonites are not exempted."

A wholesale return to Canada was being considered, perhaps to the Peace River District, but not unconditionally so. The guarantee of "our own private schools" and "complete exemption from any kind of military service" were the two main conditions of return set forth, in accordance with "the customs of the forefathers" which could not be sacrificed "without hurting our conscience." The desire to return to Canada, however, was unequivocally strong:

> . . . it would be our delight and joy to return to our old home, and no sacrifices, hardships, or labours would be too difficult for us to change the open and unsettled prairies of the far north with the blessings of Almighty God into fruitful cultivated fields. . . . And, because Canada has been to us and our ancestors a loving and well-meaning mother, who has had much patience and forbearance with the sins and transgressions of our people, so we would in the future seek the best of the state and the country.[42]

Bishop Jacob Abrams, along with three preachers and one deacon, addressed a petition directly to Ottawa and stated six conditions essential to the return of their group. They included administration of "our schools and churches ourselves with the use of German, our school and church language," the ownership of school and church property, the right to found a *Waisenamt* (an administration for the welfare of orphans), exemption from military service or any war services whatsoever, release from the oath and courts of justice, and —the paradox of the request probably escaped the petitioners—"the protection of the law for our property and also our life."[43] Such protection was normal in Canada but not, as the Mennonites had already many times discovered, in Mexico.

These and other petitioners[44] were given both favourable and unfavourable reports. They were told that the Militia Act allowed individuals to claim exemption from military service, that crown lands could no longer be reserved for colony settlements, that public homestead lands were administered by the provinces, and that there was no problem in readmitting Mennonites who were British subjects, being Canadian-born or naturalized. Because the immigrants to Mexico had retained their Canadian citizenship, there was no problem on that account. And children born in Mexico were also eligible for Canadian citizenship, though the parents rarely documented their choices in this respect. Officials warned that Mexican-born children would be examined at the port of entry and readmitted only if they were "in good mental and physical health and in possession of a passport."[45]

Meanwhile, efforts were also made in Mexico to clarify the status of the *Privilegium* in that country. The result was that the schools were reopened in January of 1936.[46] However, emigration sentiment did not end. Thoughts of returning to Canada from Mexico reached a high point in February of 1936, when throngs of Mexicans marched through the streets of Cuauhtemoc, demanding "expulsion of the clergy and establishment of socialistic education."[47] While their agitations were aimed as much at the Catholic clergy as at anybody else, the Mennonite bishops knew that their schools too could be affected.

There were other problems. Roving thieves were taking advantage of Mennonite nonresistance, breaking into the homes of the defenceless settlers, and in one instance killing two of them. Government agents told Mennonites to shoot the robbers, but Bishop Dyck insisted "that bearing arms is against our religion."[48] The Mennonites also refused to go to court and, in one situation, paid a colony *debt* a second time rather than resort to the law. There were, of *debts* course, Mexicans who appreciated the Mennonites. The victims of *apprec.* the Tampico flood and others benefited from their occasional exter- *charity* nal charity. They could be relied upon to keep their word, and the- *keep* businessmen of Cuauhtemoc knew best the source of their livelihood: *promise*

> Only the Mennonites can farm successfully here. There was *admired* no town here before they came. There will be none if they leave.[49]

A mass movement did not materialize, but scores of families did return to Canada, some of them to their former settlements and others to communities not too far away, as at MacGregor and Spencer in Manitoba. However, most of the returnees took up homesteads in the Fort Vermilion area until the world war brought the movement to a stop, at least for the time being.

In the 1930s, some Russlaender were taking another look at the Peace River area, primarily because of the social separation it offered. This was particularly true at Coaldale, where the tensions of the mid-1920s had not been fully resolved and were ready to flare up at any provocation. In April 1934, it was noted that "the Mennonites at Coaldale have been unsettled" because of the "bad feeling between the original settlers and the Mennonites" which continued to express itself mainly with respect to school matters. The Mennonite school population was about half of the total, yet Mennonite land holdings in terms of acreage were comparatively small, and thus the immigrants were believed not to be paying their share of the school taxes.

Aggravating the situation was the strong Mennonite presence on the school board. At one point, Mennonites had three members, in other words, the majority, and, "while their actions at that time were very careful and they did not offend any one, much capital was made of the situation."[50] Campaigning against their re-election, and particularly against their strongest member, Jacob B. Janz, a brother of B.B. Janz, was Norman Priestley, the local United Church minister.[51] Priestley was also vice-president of the United Farmers of Alberta during the 1930s, and in 1932 in Calgary he was elected secretary of the Co-operative Commonwealth Federation (a farmer-labour-socialist party). The following year he presented the Regina Manifesto to the founding convention of the CCF. Priestley stressed collectivist economic policies which could not be tolerant or respectful of minority interests and concerns. He could not allow individualism to stand in the way of collectivist policies supported by a progressive majority of the electorate. The majority, in yet another sense, was British, hence his nativism, which stood in the way of respecting cultural minorities.[52]

When one by one the Mennonites, including Jacob Janz, were ousted from the school board, "it annoyed him so much" that he and others thought that the Mennonites would have to leave Coaldale. Thus, they too were eyeing opportunities in the northland.[53] The Canada Colonization Association, however, discouraged any moves because of "all the difficulties you would have to be put up against in connection with the homestead lands." Besides:

> this antagonistic attitude will gradually disappear. It has done so in other cases and . . . patient effort and consistent citizenship . . . will cure the difficulties. . . . it will be much better for the Mennonite people of Coaldale to stay with it and overcome these prejudices than it would be for them to run away and practically bury themselves under backwoods conditions for a generation . . .[54]

Coaldale restlessness continued, however, but the people turned their eyes to southern British Columbia instead of northern Alberta.[55] Factionalism within the Coaldale Brethren Church helped that process along. As with Abraham and Lot in the Old Testament, a geographic separation was always one way for Mennonites to resolve their differences.

The northern frontier, where the winters were long and the growing season was extremely short, was difficult even for the hardiest of pioneers, such as the Kanadier always were. Once again, wells had to be dug by hand, wheat had to be ground for bread, and animal skins and sheep's wool had to be converted into footwear and garments. And markets had to be found for produce and the ways of river shipping had to be learned. Yet the rewards were sweet. The soil produced richly, up to 117 bushels of oats per acre. Weeds were scarce and so were pests such as potato bugs. But most important of all, the desired isolation from worldly influence and from the rigid enforcement of education laws had been found.

Greener Fields and Co-ops: B.C. and Ontario

The north was a refuge good enough to commend itself to other Mennonites, and in due course new settlements were also founded in north-central British Columbia, when at the end of the depression decade Mennonites were still on relief and economic prospects for them remained dim. The new communities in Cheslatta and Vanderhoof, though in part a consequence of the depression, were not established until the 1940s and therefore are best described in the context of that later period.

The new settlements of the Kanadier in northern Alberta and central British Columbia were the most significant new ones coming out of the depression. But they were not the only ones, inasmuch as individual families and groups of families pushed into brushland areas in Saskatchewan as well as Manitoba, as is indicated by the new congregational units established during this time. Other Kanadier and the Russlaender too were moving around as a result of the hard times, but for them other areas held a greater attraction than the north. The people at Coaldale eyed the Peace River District only in passing, and some Russlaender already there, as at Lymburn, were beginning to join the movement either to British Columbia or to Ontario. The same was true in the CPR brushlands in northern Saskatchewan, but no exodus was sufficiently complete to end the settlements or the congregations there.

The story was different at Reesor in northern Ontario, once the hope of all those who had visions of restoring, however partially, the Mennonite commonwealth. The end of Reesor did not come in the 1930s, but the beginning of the end could be foreseen in 1936 when Jacob C. Toews, one of the original pioneers and community leaders, left for Essex County in the south and thereby set in motion an exodus which saw 12 families leave in 1937 alone.[56]

In the early years of the depression, the Reesor settlers were not affected that much by the drought and the collapse of the wheat markets. Later, however, the orders for pulpwood declined, and a livelihood from the produce of the farms proved highly unlikely, partly because of the remoteness of the markets and partly because the government refused concessions on homestead lands, which would have allowed individual farmers to expand their acreages. The community was also wracked by internal dissension. Thus, when the "push" from Reesor was added to the "pull" of southern Ontario, the temptation to move to Essex County or the Niagara Peninsula became irresistible.[57]

Once Mennonites from the prairies had discovered the orchards of the Niagara Peninsula, they migrated in droves and set up new economic institutions. The Virgil community received its first settlers in 1935, but by the next decade, approximately 300 families made the area their home as parts of whole communities were transplanted.[58]

The migrations to Ontario and British Columbia led not only to the expansion of existing communities and the establishment of new ones but also to new experiments in economic co-operation, which arose not so much from the ideology of the co-operative movement as from very practical considerations. In the establishment of co-operatives, the Mennonites followed patterns already entrenched in Canada.[59] The co-op movement, both on the prairies and in Ontario, dated back to the late nineteenth century. In Ontario, co-op cheese factories, creameries, and mutual insurance companies were in vogue, whereas on the prairies the primary focus was on grain marketing. The twentieth century also saw the emergence of co-op livestock marketing organizations, poultry growers, and creameries. Creameries were organized among Mennonites in Manitoba before the Russlaender arrived.[60]

The ultimate objectives of the co-operative movement varied with the proponents. There were some who believed the co-ops would simply cure a fault in the free-enterprise system, namely the existence of and exploitation by monopolies. Others seemed to regard monopolies as an integral part of the capitalist system and wanted to see the co-ops replace private enterprise. Put another way, there were practical co-operators and there were doctrinaire co-operators. For most Mennonites—there were important exceptions, to be discussed later—the doctrinaire co-operators held little appeal. The Mennonites clearly preferred practical solutions to urgent local problems rather than grandiose schemes to replace the capitalist system.

The Russlaender, in their various communities, became part of the post-war expansion of the co-op movement, but it is important to note that they generally formed their own co-ops. The Mennonites of the 1930s were not yet ready to join the charitable organizations and co-operatives of their fellow Canadians. For several decades parallel institutions existed, owing partly to the WASPish nature of other organizations, partly to the clannishness of Mennonites themselves. And as long as they didn't need others for their own success, there was no great incentive to include them or to join them. A consumers' and producers' co-op established at Virgil enabled the fruit growers to market their produce at reasonable prices and to avoid excessive spoilage.[61] The co-op also served the community in a variety of other ways and ultimately became the foundation for a prosperous community credit union begun by Mennonites.[62]

Similar initiatives were undertaken in British Columbia.[63] A consumers' and fruit growers' co-operative was organized at Yarrow to operate a general store, a feed- and grain-buying business, and a berry-packing and -preserving plant.[64] Soon, over 2,000 barrels of raspberries, each containing 400 pounds, were being processed, trucked to Vancouver, then shipped by railway to eastern Canada and by boat to overseas markets.[65] The success of these ventures in turn prompted the founding of a credit union, a co-operative egg-grading and -marketing plant, a feed-mixing and -grinding mill, a creamery and cheese factory, and a jam factory.

During his visit to British Columbia, sociologist J. Winfield Fretz, on a Mennonite Central Committee assignment to study settlement- and community-building, identified at least eight different Mennonite co-operatives in the Fraser Valley. All of them were factors in the early stability and prosperity of the Fraser Valley settlements. According to pioneer Aaron A. Rempel, who had come to the valley from Russia via Mexico and Saskatchewan, "the use of co-operative techniques when starting a settlement is a 50 per cent guarantee of its success."[66]

The Co-op Movement in Manitoba

Co-ops were founded for very practical reasons, especially in the new settlements, but occasionally and particularly in southern Manitoba, the co-op ideology was also a motivating factor. The movement, which sprang up among the Kanadier in the West Reserve area, was a necessity borne of the depression, but it was also inspired by the international co-op philosophy, the work of the movement in Canada,[67] and the heritage of Mennonite mutual aid.[68]

Even the most productive Mennonite land areas experienced some of the worst features of the depression. Like many other westerners, the people here had been influenced in their policies by the post-war wheat boom. In their haste to capitalize on the soaring markets, few people bothered to assess the future consequences of a wholesale commitment to a single-crop economy, or the trend to consolidate large acreages under single owners. One of the first casualties claimed by the wheat bonanza was the old-time family farm. Diversity, and the accompanying self-sufficiency, had formerly characterized most farming operations. The shift to commercial wheat farms changed all this and mechanized farming, conducted on a large scale, divested the farmers of the time that was needed to maintain milk cows, hogs, chickens, and pasture crops. The sudden demise of the barnyard animal signified that farmers had taken a giant step towards reducing their own independence and had bound themselves to the whims and uncertainties of a market over which they had little control. The independence of the farmers was further impaired by their growing reliance on the petroleum industry.

The following statistics reveal in part the grim path along which agriculture was headed: of 1,240 farmers residing in the Rhineland Municipality, over half (626) were in danger of losing title to their holdings through foreclosures or bankruptcy; 455 households were so heavily in debt that they were obliged to turn over one-half of their annual crop to mortgage companies or other mortgage holders; the number of tenant farmers was growing daily, eventually leaving only 13 per cent of the farmers retaining clear title to their lands.[69]

It was against this distressing background of economic, and the accompanying social, attrition that a small group of concerned men met in Altona in January 1931. The participants, representing different villages, various occupations, and the different churches, all agreed that their once-prosperous area was in imminent danger of decline. Farming seemed to hold no future. For people who had been tied to the soil for generations, and who had come to regard farming as their divine calling, this was a troubling proposition to accept.

The consensus at the meeting was that a massive agricultural reorganization was necessitated by the situation. Specifically, the nccd was for greater farm diversity that would feature the introduction of new crops, better cultivation and tillage practices, and the return or improvement of livestock and poultry flocks. In order to better facilitate the contemplated reforms, the Rhineland Agricultural Society was organized.[70]

At the heart of this new initiative stood J.J. Siemens, whose economic and social contribution to southern Manitoba was reminiscent of the work of Johann Cornies in southern Russia a century earlier.[71] Born in 1896 in the Schoenthal district near Altona, he was destined to pioneer as his immigrant father before him had done, though in a different way. After graduating from the Mennonite Educational Institute in Altona and the Normal School in Winnipeg, he taught for ten years, taking up farming when his father retired.[72]

A strong believer in the psalmist's declaration that "the earth is the Lord's and the fulness thereof,"[73] Siemens advocated better stewardship of the soil and himself "experimented with many types of crops, sometimes using unorthodox methods of farming."[74] A public-spirited citizen, he was a man of great vision who established numerous co-ops, as well as the Rhineland Agricultural Society (RAS), which, as an educational force for economic co-operation, became the forerunner of the Western Co-operative College in Saskatoon.[75]

Since one of its principal functions was to educate, the RAS considered it vital to be closely allied with the provincial and federal departments of agriculture. Such policy would today seem commonplace and sensible. In 1931, however, the announcement was viewed by many as a bold break with the past. Mennonites were proud of their long tradition of self-reliance and their capacity to survive and prosper, using their own resources. The more reluctant Mennonites maintained that to solicit outside help was to admit to serious internal weaknesses and to invite unnecessary outside influence.

RAS officials, Siemens especially, objected to such reasoning. In his view it was outright folly to refuse proffered assistance that could well prove to be the farmers' salvation. While he appreciated and valued his heritage, Siemens realized the error of foolishly and stubbornly clinging to antiquated practices. He advised the Mennonites to observe and learn from the laws of nature, which were constantly altering the world around them, and from those who had insights to pass on:

> . . . we need to learn the techniques of farming but we need to learn first that techniques change. We must learn to keep abreast of our times, to keep our minds young, to experiment. We must learn how to learn, and let learning stop only when life stops.[76]

The RAS-sponsored programs soon produced results. Junior and adult agricultural clubs were organized, lectures, study sessions, films, essay contests, and tours to various experimental farms were offered, picnics and fairs were held. New crops such as corn, sugar beets, peas and other row vegetables, flax, potatoes, and sunflowers took hold on the land. Dairy herds were boosted, purebred hogs were introduced, and veterinarians were brought in. Other less tangible benefits accrued as increasing numbers of people became infected by the enthusiasm generated by the RAS. Troubles, if not always erased, were at least temporarily forgotten, as individuals worked together planning new programs or studying new techniques. Siemens was pleased with the regenerated agricultural spirit which saw new possibilities and prompted new initiatives:

> We began to feel that there were many things we could best do
> for ourselves. We had become community conscious and
> desirous of leaving the "Beaten Track."[77]

There were also those who recommended that the principles of collective organization could be extended to combat the most offensive features of private enterprise. It was said that the free-enterprise system, as originally designed, had taken a wrong turn and had evolved into a greedy monster. Ordinary citizens were left too much at the mercy of giant companies more interested in padding their already fat bank accounts than in serving the public fairly. A suggested corrective to such economic injustices was to place the distribution of goods more immediately within the control of the consumers.

Thus, the organization in 1931 of the unpretentious Rhineland Consumers Co-operative Ltd. marked the beginning of another movement which, complemented by the work of the RAS, would help to transform an impoverished district into the "Niagara" of Manitoba. Undaunted by the largely negative, mostly sceptical, and sometimes hostile reception of the co-op in the community, the original 67 members pledged themselves to the cause, along with a precious sum of $10 per member. The co-op's first order of business was to reduce the gas, fuel, and binder twine prices. A simple strategy was devised and the group purchased an existing oil station in Altona, then bought the needed products in bulk in Winnipeg. This led to substantial savings for the membership.[78]

Progress was slow but steady. The turning point for the Altona movement came in 1937. That year, the co-op returned to its members the first cash dividends. Sceptics now suddenly became believers as there was a rush to be included on the co-op's enrolment list. The gasoline co-op's proven ability to survive as a viable business effort, while rendering to its members real savings, produced a chain reaction. Other communities realized the value of the co-op system and requested help in establishing their own. A decade after the Altona venture came into being, there were 13 local co-ops in the West Reserve district offering a wide range of services to their members including retail stores, cheese factories, creameries, egg-grading stations, and machine repair shops.

The co-operative spirit arising from the depression also prompted the Mennonites to join the national and international credit union movement, and to found "people's banks" of their own, notably the Crosstown Credit Union in Winnipeg, whose membership was limited to Mennonites.[79] In such towns as Altona, Winkler, and Steinbach, the credit unions were led by Mennonites, who also represented the strongest membership base, but these community credit unions were open to all.

Siemens was naturally pleased with the financial successes of the co-ops, but for him financial viability was only part of the movement's significance. In his own words, "running a cheap store ⌊was⌋ not a great social aim; it ⌊had⌋ little social significance."[80] But as "a social enterprise" contributing to justice and a better world, the cheap co-op store had a special place. Co-ops reaffirmed the spirit of community and nurtured an appreciation for neighbours both far and near. For Siemens, the long-term consequences were clear:

> people working together in large groups for their mutual wel-
> fare, putting into practice the good principles of self-help,
> opposing exploitation in any sense cannot do other than have a
> beneficent effect on our society.[81]

Not everyone in the West Reserve area applauded the co-operatives or endorsed RAS policies. Some groups opposed them simply because they were new and unfamiliar. Merchants felt the co-ops presented a real danger to their own livelihood. Others reacted unfavourably to the socialist character of the co-ops and attempted to connect the movement with international communism. Labels of

"Red" were hurled at co-operators who were accused of transforming southern Manitoba into a "colony of Moscow."[82] Similar epithets were directed against Siemens, who was also variously denounced as a godless heretic and a foe of Christianity. Opposition to the co-ops came also from the Mennonite church leaders.

Much of the opposition undoubtedly arose from the further reduction of the church's sphere of influence. Historically, the introduction of municipal government, the disintegration of the villages, the opening up and ending of the reserves, the coming of the public school, and the intrusion of secular institutions generally had been hard to accept. Now the co-op movement represented further erosion of the place of the institutional church.

The leaders of the movement did not see themselves opposing the church. On the contrary, they believed themselves to be returning to some of the traditions of the community and mutual aid. They had no desire to usurp the church's authority or mission. They did not preach subversion, nor did they urge the overthrow of the existing political and religious order. They attempted to accommodate all persons within the ranks, regardless of their religious and political orientations, and advocated closer co-operation between individuals and groups for the benefit of them all.

On account of his high public profile and his image as a "man of the world," Siemens absorbed the brunt of the church's reaction. He was at home with the literary works of Shakespeare and Shaw, and he moved easily among people of high finance and industry. He read and recommended to others books written by religious liberals and socialists, and he crusaded on behalf of a new economic order. Siemens persevered in spite of the church's obstructions, though he was deeply scarred by the character assaults and insinuations directed his way.[83] Lesser men might have acquiesced to the dissenting pressure or have left the community. Not so Siemens. He maintained faith in his cause and his actions. Though he finally departed from the Bergthaler Church, he refused to forsake the people who had worked so tirelessly alongside him. His trust in the basic goodness of mankind preserved itself and was rewarded by the general, though gradual, acceptance of the RAS and the co-ops. Siemens confided that the satisfaction expressed to him by so many people compensated for the hurts administered by the movement's detractors. He took pride in the fact that the co-op success had not been achieved at public expense yet had returned to the community substantial economic and social dividends. After visiting communities across Canada, sociologist Fretz concluded:

> It is doubtful if any other community in the United States or Canada, whether Mennonite or non-Mennonite, has developed such a vigorous and thorough-going program of co-operatives as has Altona, Manitoba. There are many examples, but none of them have developed so many successful ventures in so short a time; and no other community is contemplating such far-reaching and permanent economic changes in the direction of co-operatives in the future.[84]

The Russlaender in the Winnipeg area also felt the need for co-operative endeavours in agriculture, but being more scattered in their communities, they met with less success. An initiating group of 19 persons from six communities in the Winnipeg area met on November 8, 1933, at Glenlea to discuss the formation of a Mennonite Agricultural Association, whose chief function would be to help Mennonites market their produce and also to purchase supplies co-operatively in order to keep in Mennonite hands those profits normally going to middlemen. While such an organization would have to begin working on a small scale, it should eventually attend to all agricultural needs, including such divergent directions as settlement and land purchases and representing Mennonite interests before the agricultural corporations. Something had to be done, it was felt, to compensate for the absence of a *geschlossene Ansiedlung* (closed settlement) and to help overcome the depression.[85] The Association, however, did not come into being because it lacked the driving force and leadership essential to its success.

Individualism and Secularization

The co-op movement had a much reduced appeal in the East Reserve area, although a co-op cheese factory operated successfully at Grunthal. During the depression, the agricultural advantages of that region, which had been in doubt since the earliest days of settlement, became obvious. Here mixed farming, having always been the rule, was now deeply entrenched and proving itself as the best means of "weathering the storm" of the depression. As the East Reserve enjoyed "a period of prosperity such as it had never experienced before" the population density rose, the number of farms increased, and farm income and farm value were significantly advanced. Even the smallest of farms, specializing in products such as poultry, potatoes, or berries,

> enabled many resourceful Mennonites to make a good living on notoriously poor soil by utilizing the supply of relatively cheap and efficient labour as well as the closeness to the Winnipeg market.[86]

The continuity during the depression of an agricultural tradition, already well established and whose time had now come, made the East Reserve area less in need of, and less susceptible to, reform movements and innovation. Consequently, the co-operative movement held less appeal.[87] The stronger individualism resulting from the much earlier break-up of the village system and its reinforcement by evangelical movements emphasizing individual salvation rather than communal responsibility led to an aggressive venture into capitalist enterprise, not least of all in the automobile trade.

Ironically, the automobile became king in that very locale where more than a generation earlier the first entrepreneurs had been excommunicated by the church because of their reaching for the car. Thus, reaction to the impossible demands by church leaders in an earlier day may have shaped, as much as any factor, the economic philosophy of the East Reserve's central trading centre.[88] The town of Steinbach in the northeast corner of the reserve, for instance, prospered more than most French or Ukrainian villages in the region, though Steinbach lacked what all others considered essential, namely a railway connection. A small but "significant commercial empire" was building up, based on "competitive enterprise and individual resourcefulness rather than on co-operative effort."[89] Steinbach boasted numerous industries already in the 1920s:

> a 100 bbl. flour mill, six stores, three large garages, blacksmith and tinsmith shops, a butcher business and cold storage plant, a creamery receiving station and pasteurizing plant, a cheese factory, two lumber yards and two sash and door factories, two implement businesses and two shoemakers, two barber shops, a watchmaker, a machine shop for repairing any-

thing from a set of harrows to a steam engine, a good restaurant – one of the best little hotels in the country, a doctor, a printing office and paper, and an electric light plant.[90]

Emphasizing individual initiative in the extreme, East Reserve people were "openly boasting" that they could get along without "economic crutches" like co-ops.[91] After all, it was individual farmers who had shaped East Reserve agriculture when the village system had proved unfeasible, and it was the "inventive genius," the "progressive" outlook, and the "top salesmanship" of its business-men that "blazed the trail of progress."[92] Relief was the very last resort for people in economic distress. The unemployed were given an axe and a pick and told by the municipality to "earn your warm meal a day" and thus learn that there was more to life than loafing, grumbling, and developing inferiority complexes.[93] As Francis has observed:

> Thrown without much mercy upon their own resourcefulness, they discovered many opportunities for rehabilitation, either by developing mechanical hobbies into gainful occupa-tions . . . or by cultivating small plots obtained on easy terms and netting satisfactory profits from small garden crops, such as berries and vegetables.[94]

Whereas in the West Reserve area economic stimulus and educa-tional direction came from the co-operative movement and the Rhineland Agricultural Society, in the East it was the Board of Trade, later known as the Chamber of Commerce, which "caught on strongly in the 1930s" and which sponsored short courses "on everything from bee-keeping to hog-raising" and which organized clubs and introduced high-grade livestock and poultry into the area.[95]

The East, however, was not entirely free from economic woes. One event, described by A.A. Friesen as "the greatest hoax or swindle in Mennonite history,"[96] was coincident with the depression, if not a consequence of it, and threw a dark shadow over the East Reserve area. That event was the 1934 foreclosure action against the Intercontinental Land Company by National Trust, one of the major holders of first (Class A) mortgage bonds, which financed the purchase in the 1920s by 300 Russlaender families of 40,000 acres of improved and equipped lands, sold to Intercontinental by the emigrating Kanadier.[97] In addition to the Class A landholders, there were 969 B-bonds, purchased for $113,000.[98]

The holders of these second mortgage bonds, earning seven per cent, were Mennonites and Amish in the U.S.A. and Ontario, whose involvement in this business venture came largely through the salesmanship of Alvin J. Miller, the former director of Mennonite relief in Russia, who was equipped with signed endorsements of the financial scheme from David Toews of the Board and also with the support of M.H. Kratz, a Mennonite lawyer from Philadelphia.

In the foreclosure action by National Trust — which could not be stopped, only delayed by the Board[99] — these B-bond holders were the losers, and the repercussions thereof were felt by the Board for years to come, for that is where the complaints were directed by those who once had given their trust. There were complaints such as the following, all of them in vain:

> My husband . . . died. Am left a widow . . . with $1100 debt at . . . bank. . . . Help me along by [getting me the] interest on the thousand dollars loaned to your people.[100]

Before leaving the subject of the economy of southern Manitoba, it must be noted that the depression marked the end of several of the community institutions transplanted from Russia to the reserves of Manitoba, by which the church had served — and controlled — much of the Mennonite society. These institutions were the *Waisenamt* in the West Reserve area and the *Brandschulze* (fire insurance).

The *Waisenamt* had originated in Prussia as a church institution established for the purpose of managing the property of orphans and widows. In time, its function as a financial institution had broadened to become a "bank," which received deposits for purposes of saving. Money was also loaned to alleviate economic need and to assist in the acquisition of farms. In the emigration of the 1870s, the *Waisenamt* not only facilitated the emigration of orphans and widows, the liquidation of their properties in Russia, and the transfer of their assets to a new country, but also rendered the same essential service for all the emigrants.[101]

Once the function of the *Waisenamt* had been expanded from its primary role as the protector of orphans and widows to a savings bank and multi-purpose financial institution, there was no easy backtracking. And it served well, at least for a while. The *Waisenamt* observed the established norms of "efficiency, honesty, and charity," and "debtors, creditors, and church officials co-operated in order to do justice to everybody concerned."[102] As one outside observer has written:

> . . . the letter of a contract was always interpreted in the spirit of Christian justice and charity. . . . the creditor . . . was morally bound to consider the welfare of a tardy debtor . . . to advise and to guide him in the management of his farm until he was able to repay his debts. . . . among the Manitoba Mennonites [there were no known] Shylocks and usurious money lenders. . . .[103]

In due course, however, the *Waisenamt* administrator in the West Reserve area, as well as government officials, had become uneasy about the fact that the institution was not incorporated under Canadian trust company laws. Contrary to the wishes of many church members, this incorporation had been pursued by the administrator and achieved early in 1907 with the result that the *Waisenamt* was split into two parts, one incorporated and operated by the Bergthaler church and the other unincorporated and operated by the Sommerfelder church.[104]

The incorporated Bergthaler *Waisenamt* was still under Bergthaler church control, but there was no provision limiting the business to Bergthaler members. On the contrary, the bylaws were rewritten to allow non-members (Sommerfelder, Altkolonier, Brethren, and others) to invest and vote but not to hold office. This was an ominous turn of events, as H. J. Gerbrandt has written:

> Although no one surmised the dark clouds that were already forming beyond the visible horizon, this move had negative implications. It barred from responsible office heavy capital investors who later caused so much grief.[105]

The activity of the Bergthaler *Waisenamt* increased markedly after incorporation. Soon the deposits exceeded one million dollars. And most of these monies were loaned and outstanding, lesser amounts against cosigned notes and greater amounts against mortgage notes.

The *Waisenamt* was continuing to operate in the new situation as it had always done, on the narrow interest margin of one per cent and with no reserves. As long as the withdrawals were few and small, the *Waisenamt* was safe. But withdrawals were bound to come. The emigration of the 1920s and the resulting withdrawals created a temporary emergency and represented forewarnings of what was to come. When the Wall Street stock market collapsed, depositors in the Mennonite *Waisenamt* panicked and began to withdraw their assets. The church, having authorized its elder to sign bank and mortgage company loans, signed its properties over to the *Waisenamt* as security against borrowings to make the withdrawals possible.

The assumption was that if only the people would be patient, the crisis would pass as new investors would replenish the treasury. Before this did or could happen, however, a non-Bergthaler depositor, unable to withdraw in 1931 his investment of nearly $20,000, filed suit. The courts issued an injunction naming Monarch Life Association as the executor and that was the end of the Bergthaler *Waisenamt*. A request two years later by the person filing suit that the Bergthaler *Waisenamt* be restored and not liquidated came too late. As the church's official historian has noted:

> There was nothing left to go back to . . . [and] the placing as
> collateral the deposits of widows and orphans to secure the
> monies of the rich investors and their losing everything, still
> casts a bad shadow over the testimony of the Bergthaler Men-
> nonite Church.[106]

The Bergthaler *Waisenamt* experience was not unique. Other financial institutions also collapsed at that time. Even so, Gerbrandt notes that while "greater sincerity" and goodwill could not have saved the *Waisenamt*, more financial and business expertise "beyond the limited Mennonite world" and a "healthy reserve of soundly-invested or frozen assets might have saved the institution."[107]

The Sommerfelder church continued to operate its unincorporated *Waisenamt*, according to its constitution.[108] In due course the Sommerfelder began to sense, as the Bergthaler had 15 years earlier, that incorporation was desirable, if not absolutely necessary, in view of the large amounts of money on deposit and on loan. Shortly after incorporation, amendments in the relevant statute gave the

Waisenamt the right "to receive money on deposit" and "to loan money on real, personal, and mixed securities."[109] By the mid 1920s, the investments totalled nearly $1,200,000.[110]

This "bank" was maintained until investor-panic early in the 1930s landed the Sommerfelder *Waisenamt* in the same predicament as that of the Bergthaler. Funds were withdrawn, yet loans could not be repaid as prices for farm products fell and land values themselves plummeted. Various measures were undertaken to prevent foreclosure, such as the sale of lands in lieu of bad debts, a two-dollar levy payable by every church member, reduction of the administrators' salaries, crediting every dollar of debt repaid with $1.25, and no interest on deposits for four years.[111]

The measures brought only short-term relief. A 1935 lawsuit against the *Waisenamt* revealed that the institution was insolvent, and, at the request of the *Waisenamt*, the Manitoba government appointed a permanent liquidator. The winding up of the Sommerfelder *Waisenamt* was more successful than the Bergthaler one, and in the end, creditors received a 50.5 per cent return on their money.[112] The records were burned thereafter,[113] but the judgement of history, recorded by Jake Peters, could not easily be avoided:

> When the *Waisenamt* changed its task from the protection of widows and orphans (regarded as a sacred duty) to being a co-operative bank (based on the laws of economics) it deserted those who needed the *Waisenamt* most, just before the depression when it would need them most.[114]

The judgements rendered after the closings could have been too harsh. After all, the money that was lost had been loaned to the most needy people. In fact, the problem was that more had been loaned to the needy than the *Waisenamt* could afford, given the fact that unlike the banks the *Waisenamt* had no double-indemnity banking and at least one purpose of incorporation had been to attract more investments precisely to enable a greater service. Thus, it is possible that the needy gained most from *Waisenamt* closings and that the less needy lost the most. That possibility, of course, does not remove the pain resulting from the loss of an historic and semi-sacred institution.

The *Waisenaemter* did not all collapse. There were several small ones in Saskatchewan, and others existed in Manitoba among the Old

Colony people and the Chortitzer.[115] The latter group made efforts in 1933 to strengthen its *Waisenamt* by updating and publicizing widely the provisions thereof.[116] The rules specified election of the administrator every four years with ratification by the church leaders. The rules of the *Waisenamt* provided for the proper care of orphans until the age of 21 and the just administration and ultimate distribution of any properties under the supervision and administration of the guardian or trustee, who himself had to answer to the *Waisenamt* and the leadership of the church.

Another traditional church-related mutual aid organization, which ended up as an incorporated commercial insurance company at the end of the 1930s, was *Die Mennonitische Brandtordnung* (Mennonite fire insurance). Founded in 1875 and based on Prussian and Russian precedents, the *Ordnung* became in 1940 the Red River Mennonite Mutual Insurance Company. Thus, an organization based on mutual aid and responsibility for one's brothers, symbolizing Mennonite separation from the world in its refusal to insure and rescue from fire such places as theatres and dance halls, became a business, allowing non-Mennonite membership, and determined, indeed obligated, to turn a profit.[117]

Resistance to Secularized Aid

While the "secularization" of Mennonite mutual aid organizations was proceeding among the Kanadier in western Canada, concerted efforts were made by the Swiss in eastern Canada to prevent or reverse that very process. The focus was the Mennonite Aid Union. The Union had come into being in 1866 with the approval of the Mennonite Conference of Ontario, which Conference reaffirmed its authority over it in 1932, precisely because membership and aid policies were in danger of becoming too broad.[118] As the Conference's historian noted:

> There has been a tendency on the part of some sons and sons-in-law, who are not members of the church to abuse their privilege and to consider the Union as a cheap insurance company.[119]

The original impetus for the organization was the desire for "a plan . . . which would be helpful in guiding the person in the amount which he should reasonably give in case of a brother suffering loss by fire."[120] The practice of mutual aid in "the household of faith" and among "all men" had been one of the "outstanding" characteristics of the Mennonite churches since their founding. Assistance was rendered without a "system to guide" those giving assistance "but each one followed his own conviction and judgement."[121]

This completely voluntary and rather informal method of recompense had become inadequate, in terms of both the methods employed and the amounts raised. As a consequence, there was a considerable temptation on the part of the brethren to insure their properties with commercial organizations, which were becoming a strong economic force, particularly in the Waterloo County area.[122] The Amish were sensing the same pressures, as is evident from the formation of their own Fire and Storm Aid Union at that time.[123] Their organization also required updating in the 1930s.[124]

In 1933, the Mennonite Aid Union of the Mennonite Conference of Ontario had about 1,350 members, whose total "risk" carried by the Union amounted to $7,500,000.[125] The affairs of the Union were managed on the basis of rules set forth in 27 bylaws. Administrative responsibility rested with an Executive Committee appointed by the Board of Directors. The Executive consisted of 30 church members from each church district in the Ontario and Alberta-Saskatchewan conferences.[126] The Executive set the annual levies on the basis of the losses for the previous year, and the directors collected the levies in their districts. Losses were paid at no more than two-thirds of actual cash value, and single risks on any one building were limited to $6,000 and an entire risk to $16,000, except if the Executive Committee ruled otherwise in particular cases.

All that was needed to become a member of the Union was a signature — later, church membership in good standing had to be certified — but continuous membership required at least every five years an outside valuation of the member's property, the prompt payment by January 1 of all rates levied, observance of all precautions against fire, and avoidance of insurance in both the Union and an insurance company without the consent of the Union's executive. Members "fully insured" in the Union lost their membership immediately if and when they applied for insurance in another company.[127]

The problems facing the Union were several. Regulations and administrative procedures needed updating to match the changing business affairs of the brethren, but even more important was the need to prevent the Union from becoming not the deliberate instrument of a Christian community to maintain brotherhood but the best way to get the cheapest insurance. The Conference, therefore, resolved that it could no longer admit "sons and sons-in-law of Mennonite church members, who themselves were not members, because this permitted undesirable characters" to "consider the Union as a cheap insurance company"[128] and to share the benefits of the Union.[129] Before the decade was over, the constitution of the Union was revised to require that all new applications for membership be accompanied by a signed certificate of good standing in the church.[130]

In other ways, however, the Union could not avoid adjusting to the demands of the times. At a special meeting of the Mennonite Conference of Ontario on June 20, 1935, a charter as a regular fire insurance company was approved for the Mennonite Aid Union upon the advice of the Inspector of Insurance for Ontario, who had ruled that a charter be secured unless the business was limited to members of the church. The latter had already become the policy of the Union, but even these members insisted on a charter because without it they could not obtain government loans for their farm operations. Such loans required fire insurance in a chartered company.[131]

The Mennonite Aid Union could not, however, be a comprehensive aid plan for the Mennonite congregation. To begin with, the purposes of the Aid were quite limited, even though losses caused by lightning, wind, and water were in due course added to those caused by fire.[132] Additionally, coverage was not universal in terms of membership. Some still looked upon the Union with suspicion and distrust or even as a "money-making scheme."[133] For these and other reasons, older forms of mutual aid continued to exist. Among the Old Order Mennonites the voluntary system was still the only way of responding to farm or family disasters. All that was needed for a barn to be rebuilt or a hospital bill to be paid was for the brethren to be informed of the need and the necessary manpower or funds would be donated.

The new problems of the 1930s, namely financial failings, including business and farm bankruptcies, were a strong reminder of the earlier tradition in which the brethren helped each other to carry their burdens, whatever they might be, in whatever way that seemed right and possible at the time. Such sharing required openness and frankness on the part of the brethren, which was unavoidable when very visible disasters caused by fire and storm struck or when the closeness of a community really made the hiding of even less visible troubles impossible. But the communities were no longer limited to intimate agricultural neighbourhoods, and financial problems had become much less visible. Noting all of these developments, the Conference tried in 1934 to restore, in the context of the depression and the new situation, this earlier sense of mutuality when it resolved as follows:

> Because of present-day economic conditions, resulting in many financial failures among our membership, be it resolved that we encourage our Bishops, Pastors, and Deacons to teach, to encourage and to caution our members in regard to all financial dealings, and to be perfectly open and frank with regard to inability to meet financial obligations. Romans 13:8, Luke 6:31, Romans 12:7.[134]

There is no specific data available concerning the number of failures, but the *Gospel Herald* noted editorially in 1935 that "hundreds of Mennonites" a few years ago "in easy circumstances" were "now either bankrupt or facing bankruptcy." Since these had been among "the most substantial givers," church activities were crippled for want of adequate financial support.[135]

In Ontario most of the "failings" had to do with "overextended farm operations," which, lacking adequate markets and income, could no longer maintain the debt burden.[136] Every congregation had "at least one or two or three" such cases, which resulted in "assignment sales." In such sales everything would be sold, and creditors would get "so many cents" on the dollar. Mennonites tried to avoid the courts, and this often meant that they were taken advantage of and "left holding the bag." Settlements made on an informal basis often involved "a referee" acceptable to both parties.[137] The inevitable consequence was the loss of farms, and the former "owners" working as hired hands or taking on factory jobs. Another consequence was a virtual end to the cordiality in economic relations that had formerly existed both among Mennonites and with their neighbours.

Business operations too were more and more carried on apart from the awareness of the brotherhood. The traditional fear of the business world was on the decline, even though the wish was "still generally expressed that we might continue a strictly rural people." A leading defender of business in the Old Mennonite church was Orie Miller, the young layman from Pennsylvania, who had entered Russia to help relieve famine in 1920. Acknowledging all the "pitfalls and temptations" and "the evils of the system" — such as ruthless competition, exploitation of human beings, and profit as the single standard of success — he noted that "individual Christians in the business world to-day are living witnesses" of what can be done "in mitigating the evils of the system" and in "using business and its rewards in positive service."[138] Thus, the church was not judgmental as once it had been but rather empathetic, though little could be done in concrete ways to help the businessmen in distress, except as poverty cases.

The provision for, and insurance of, human beings and their needs took on new meaning in the 1930s. The problems of the poor, the sick, and those who wanted to provide for their loved ones in the event of death or disability all came to the fore in a new way. Discussions in all of these matters were initiated by the Mennonite Conference of Ontario in 1932. At that time, the Conference was concerned about the "persistent inroads" into the church by secret societies and insurance companies who were offering systematic ways of providing "so that the needy may never be left in suspense and anxiety."[139] The end result of these discussions was the creation first of the Mennonite Welfare Board and later of the Mennonite Benefit Association.

The Mennonite Welfare Board of Ontario was organized in 1939 in order to centralize, under the deacon body of the Mennonite Conference of Ontario, the various charitable funds collected to help the poor so that they could be administered more equitably.[140] These funds were five in number and included the Conference Poor Fund, the Ministers' Aid Fund, the Waterloo County Deacons' Poor Fund, the Waterloo Township Poor and Church Building Fund, and the Emma McNally Estate Fund, all of which had arisen historically in response to specific needs. Besides planning for the care of senior citizens in a special home, the Board responded to the needs of those ministers and members presented for consideration by the congregational deacon.[141]

With regard to life insurance, the Conference asked Bishop Oscar Burkholder to make a study and to write clarifying articles concerning his findings.[142] After talking extensively to representatives of life insurance companies and reviewing the traditions and teachings of the church, Burkholder came to the conclusion that there were many "scriptural objections to life insurance," including: the care of the poor being the duty of the church; the immense holdings and extraordinary salaries found in insurance companies; discrimination against the poor and diseased; money, income, and wealth as standards of value and worth; the negative reflections on man's ability to manage his money and take care of his family, on God and his promises, and on charity as a Christian practice; the supplanting of faith and trust with cold reason and unsympathetic facts; and the unequal yoking of believers and unbelievers.[143]

Life insurance people, Burkholder said, belittled the work of the church, discouraged large families ("you can't expect a father and a mother who breed like rabbits to be entitled to insurance privileges"), paid back to policyholders only half of what they received and built skyscrapers and luxurious offices with the rest. He minced no words in assessing the role of the companies:

> . . . life insurance has become a huge octopus, draining the resources of millions of people, making them believe there is no material safety anywhere else, no possibilities of getting ahead in this life, but a gradual sinking into insignificance and despair for everyone who is not insured. Then rising to wonderful heights of sentiment and sympathy, their eloquence dripping with honeyed words of religion and human love they pose as the greatest benefactors the world has ever seen.[144]

As an alternative he suggested a permanent church fund, supported systematically and proportionately by every church member. He also encouraged the purchase of government annuities, rather than insurance company annuities, since the government was engaged in public service, while "the insurance companies conduct their business for profit."[145]

The Conference's position on life insurance — it was believed to be contrary to the principles of the church — meant that related schemes of protecting the present and providing for the future had also to be examined.[146] The result of such a special investigation led to the conclusion that "all questionable schemes of investment" should be avoided, but that government annuities were acceptable, as were mothers' allowances and old age pensions. None the less, needy widows and senior citizens were encouraged not to apply for government assistance before discussing their needs with deacons and ministers of the home congregation. If the congregation was unable to meet the need, the deacon should take it to the conference-wide welfare board before allowing the matter to come before government agencies.[147]

In the insurance field, a most vexing problem turned out to be that of liability insurance for car owners and drivers.[148] After wrestling with the issue for more than a decade, 1927–1940, the two conference executives from the Old Mennonites and the Amish Mennonites, and the respective aid union committees, came to the conclusion that such a plan was unavoidable in the context of the brotherhood.[149] The first stage of discussion dealt with its need and acceptability. The need was rather obvious and arose from "the present conditions of automobile traffic and risk, and the liabilities consequent upon these conditions."[150] The acceptability became clear when the special automobile liability committee placed auto insurance "in the same class of protection as that of the Aid Union in view of the fact that accidents occurred daily beyond the control of the operator."[151] But no sooner had a car aid plan become acceptable when it was found to be unfeasible, because the government regulations required a charter and starting capital and because the committee concluded that there were not enough church members and owners of cars who were sufficiently interested to make the plan workable in view of the fact that the rates would be higher than those of commercial companies.[152] It was much easier for Mennonites to accept church aid plans when they were cheaper than commercial plans.

Medical and Other Institutions

Further evidence of organized—and, after Burkholder, predictable —mutual aid activity was supplied by the creation in Ontario of the Mennonite Mutual Benefit Association "as the agency through which her membership will be provided with a systematic method of sharing, in a Christian way, the financial burdens of sickness, disability and death."[153] The fees were $10 per person between the ages of 18 and 65, plus an annual assessment. The benefits included hospitalization at $4 per day up to $120, surgery to a maximum of $150, disability of $3 per day to a maximum of $150, and a maximum death benefit of $500 reduced at the rate of $15 per year after the age of 35.[154]

In western Canada, the matter of medical and hospital insurance was accompanied by the actual hiring of doctors and/or the establishment of hospitals during the 1930s. In southern Manitoba, town churches and community leaders co-operated in the founding of hospital societies and the opening of hospitals, in 1930 in Steinbach, where they supplemented a care home for invalids,[155] and in 1936 in Altona and Winkler. Medical and hospital care was provided on the basis of family contracts costing about $18 per year.[156]

The Mennonite Hospital Concordia in Winnipeg came into being as a full-fledged hospital in 1930, following the organization of Society Concordia with 30 members from both the Conference and Brethren people.[157] The new institution, however, was preceded a few years by a maternity home established by alumni of the Halbstadt Commercial School, among them N.J. Neufeld, a medical doctor who had completed specialization in surgery in Austria and Germany and who had obtained Manitoba certification as a qualified doctor in 1926. Without him and, quite possibly, the support of a Kanadier doctor, Gerhard Hiebert, whom we have previously met as the president of the Mennonite Immigration Aid, Concordia would not have advanced as rapidly.[158] In the first eleven months of its operation, the hospital admitted 297 patients, of whom 113 were maternity patients, 114 surgical, 67 medical, and 3 with fractured bones.[159]

The incorporation of the Society under an act of the Manitoba legislature was followed by aggressive promotion to increase membership to 200 or more and by fund-raising in order to expand the facilities. The latter effort included the raffle of a $600 1931 Ford Tudor Sedan with net proceeds of $472.50 and a tour of U.S.A. churches by a delegation of the Society.[160] In 1934, the Society purchased for $21,250 the 40-year old Winnipeg Sanitarium. What was needed in addition to space, however, was the enabling of patients, as well as the hospital, to afford the required care, in other words a medical insurance plan.

A contract system was introduced whereby groups of insured

families, ten or more, were formed and a designated person was appointed to collect from each family a $12 annual levy, first to pay only for hospitalization but later, with a slight increase in fees, to cover medical costs as well. The contract system had wide appeal, and within a year about 400 families were signed up through 25 contracts. Revised from time to time, the system was in force until a generation later when a compulsory government hospital insurance plan replaced it, and, in the process, what had been the heart of the institution, namely the close involvement of the people on behalf of each other.

At Coaldale also a hospital was founded in 1934, preceded for several years by a medical plan and the services of a doctor through a newly formed health society.[161] The cost of medical care in the new country had shocked the immigrants into action. One immigrant girl, working as a domestic in Lethbridge for $20 a month, had been billed $40 for throat surgery and $20 for a week of hospital care, in other words a total of three months of salary for one week of medical care. One family, still living in a railroad car, fearing the cost, had declined to call a doctor to assist in the birth of a child, only to discover when the infant died 11 days later that a doctor had to certify the death — at a cost of ten dollars.

This reluctance to seek even urgent medical help led to the founding of the first immigrant medical group, namely the Coaldale Mennonite Health Society, which collected one dollar per family per month and acquired the free services, including surgery, of a Lethbridge doctor. The delivery of a child cost an extra $15. Membership grew rapidly from an initial 25 families to over 300. A further monthly fee of one dollar per family also guaranteed free hospital care by 1932. Soon the society was recruiting a German-speaking Mennonite doctor (1933) and establishing its own 12-bed hospital (1934).[162]

Following the Coaldale pattern, Mennonites in British Columbia organized the Bethesda Mennonite Health Society with over 100 families and individuals — members — agreeing to pay up to 10 dollars a year. The Society paid the doctor $85 a month, plus surgical fees of $27 for appendectomies and $50 for major operations.[163]

Burial aid societies of one form or another sprang up in almost every community, and these usually bridged the various church groups. At Whitewater, for example, a Burial Fund Society was founded in 1933 for both Conference and Brethren churches. The fees were 10 cents annually per person, and 10 dollars' support was paid in the case of a death.[164]

The depression would have been even more problematic for the Mennonite community had there been many other church institutions to finance, but such was not the case. In the local congregations there were no ministers to be salaried. The conferences placed no "levies" on the congregations, for their overhead was small and very few programs were mandatory. The fees that Mennonites were expected to pay were based on local covenants having to do with mutual aid societies. Besides that, the Russlaender faced some universal levies, including a five-cent-a-month-per-immigrant fee for the care of mental patients to prevent their deportation[165] and a 50-cent annual fee payable to the Canadian Mennonite Board of Colonization for the financing of its operations.[166]

The schools, of course, depended for their capital and operating needs on the constituency, but such educational institutions were few in number. On the prairies the church elementary schools had disappeared, and in Ontario they had not yet appeared. The Bible schools, basically on a winter schedule, were low-budget institutions, and the more costly Bible colleges of a later day had not yet been founded. Only the Gretna and Rosthern high schools, founded to help prepare teachers, were two institutions which really felt the depression, as can be illustrated from the life of the German-English Academy in Rosthern.[167]

The Academy had had a difficult financial struggle since it first opened its doors in 1905. Perennially in debt, there were years when the school's credit was stretched to such a limit that even the meagre teachers' salaries could not be paid. The year 1931 was another one like that, and when C.D. Penner, the principal, left to continue his university studies, with $455 or nearly one-third of his salary unpaid, he had to wait the better part of the 1930s until the institution's obligations to him were finally met.

The person chiefly responsible for the financial well-being of the Academy was its board chairman, David Toews, who at the same time was trying to liquidate an immense immigration debt. At the Academy, expenses were cut to the barest minimum, including several reductions of teachers' salaries, and every possible way of increasing revenue and resources was pursued, most of these yielding only small amounts, so that the whole effort became known as *Kleinarbeit* (the small effort). As it is written elsewhere:

> At Hochfeld near Hague the Kleinarbeit consisted of paying a few cents from each bushel of wheat harvested. In Saskatoon the working girls agreed to put away 15 cents a month for the school and thereby they contributed $75 in one year. Another example of Kleinarbeit was the printing of membership cards and selling them for 25 cents each.[168]

Students and teachers were sent out to raise funds. Greater pressure was brought to bear on student accounts in arrears. Donations were sought from well-to-do Mennonites in the U.S.A., with only marginal success. The German consulate provided books for the library and book grants. Youth programs were prepared and sold. In such ways "a dollar at a time the Academy was kept alive."[169] At the end of the 1937–38 school year all operating debts, including teachers' salaries, had been paid, and the treasury had $6.60 in it. The capital debt had been reduced to $12,500.[170]

One of the most vexing problems in the 1930s was the collection among the Russlaender of the outstanding *Reiseschuld* of the 1920s. At the beginning of 1931 this transportation debt, including principal and interest accumulated at six per cent, amounted to $1,040,727, more than half of the total credits advanced by then by the CPR, namely $1,924,727 on behalf of 13,354 of 20,201 immigrants who had been unable to pay their own way.[171]

This debt was an ominous burden, and when collections in 1930 amounted to less than the interest for the year, Board officials knew that they had a serious problem on their hands. That problem was due not only to the shortage of cash but also to the lack of willingness to pay.[172] The notion, widespread among the newcomers, that the CPR was profiting from the immigrants even without the payment of the *Reiseschuld* was supported in part by Col. J.S. Dennis's own arguments, previously cited (Chapter 5), and by the repeated willingness of the railway in the 1920s to overlook the legalities of the contracts and in the 1930s and 1940s to cancel several huge chunks of interest or debt, an amount eventually totalling more than one million dollars.[173]

Still the principal had to be collected, and for this purpose a full-time collector was put on the road, namely C.F. Klassen, who worked with the provincial immigrant committees and district representatives. Whatever the attitude of individual immigrants themselves, the leaders and all the officials of the Board considered the debt a holy obligation. Their influence was felt as congregations and conferences themselves emphasized the moral dimensions of the problem and called for disciplinary action against those able but unwilling to pay. For, and on behalf of, those unable to pay on account of death, sickness, depression, or other misfortune, the concepts of a general obligation, of solidarity and togetherness, came into play, meaning that in the end all immigrants were responsible for outstanding immigrant debts.[174]

Even so, when the 1930s drew to a close, a debt approaching three-quarters of a million dollars remained. There was no suggestion that the transportation debt be referred to the debt adjustment tribunals, created by special legislation in the 1930s to help people avoid declaring bankruptcy. Many Mennonites availed themselves of the provisions of the legislation to reduce their settlement debts, but adjustment of the transportation debt was not attempted. Why not isn't clear because the courts, in all probability, would have been more generous than the CPR.[175] Nearly another decade, further concessions from the CPR, a more prosperous wartime economy, and the motivation to help more Mennonite refugees, of which there would be tens of thousands, would be required before the collective debt would finally be retired.[176]

The *Reiseschuld* and other problems of the 1930s revealed that Mennonite solidarity and togetherness were really quite limited. Co-operatives, burial societies, medical associations, and mutual aid organizations were for the most part circumscribed by the local communities in which they existed. There wasn't a single problem or program which all the Mennonites in Canada, perhaps not even in a given province, were working at all together. Every universe of Mennonite activity was smaller than appeared desirable. David Toews, at least, was quite convinced that the Mennonite organizational structures were quite inadequate to meet the total needs of the Canadian community. This prompted an ambitious reorganization of inter-Mennonite structures, for which, however, the times also were not propitious.

FOOTNOTES

1   L.J. Burkholder, *A Brief History of the Mennonites in Ontario* (Markham, Ont.: Mennonite Conference of Ontario, 1935), p. 156.

2   CGC, XV-31.2, "1940 – J.J. Siemens," "Education in the Ideals of Cooperation," n.d.

3   A.E. Safarian, *The Canadian Economy in the Great Depression* (Toronto: McClelland & Stewart, 1971), p. 1.

4   James H. Gray, *The Winter Years: The Depression on the Prairies* (Toronto: Macmillan of Canada, 1966), and L.M. Grayson and Michael Bliss, eds., *The Wretched of Canada: Letters to R.B. Bennett, 1930 – 1935* (Toronto: University of Toronto Press, 1971).

5   A.E. Safarian, p. 40.

6   *Ibid.*, pp. 63 – 64.

7   *Ibid.*, pp. 194 – 96.

8   Walter Sawatsky, "History of the Evangelical Mennonite Mission Conference" (research paper, Goshen College, 1967), p. 11.

9   H.T. Klaassen, *The Birth and Growth of the Eigenheim Mennonite Church, 1892 – 1974* (n.p., 1974), p. 48. The 19-cent price for wheat was undoubtedly the price received by the farmer. Compare S.M. Lipset, *Agrarian Socialism: The Co-operative Commonwealth Federation in Saskatchewan* (Berkeley: University of California Press, 1950), p. 90.

10   H.T. Klaassen, p. 54.

11   *Ibid.*, p. 49.

12   Blair Neatby, "The Saskatchewan Relief Commission, 1931 – 34," in *Historical Essays on the Prairie Provinces*, ed. Donald Swainson (Toronto: McClelland & Stewart, 1970), pp. 274 – 82.

13   Ernest A. Jeschke, *Memoirs* (Goshen, Ind.: Marlin Jeschke, 1966), p. 171.

14   See Alma Lawton, "Urban Relief in Saskatchewan in the Depression" (M.A. thesis, University of Saskatchewan, 1970); Don Garfield Matheson, "The Saskatchewan Relief Commission, 1931 – 1934: A Study of the Administration of Rural Relief in Saskatchewan during the Early Years of the Depression" (M.A. thesis, University of Saskatchewan, 1975).

15   John Kendle, *John Bracken: A Political Biography* (Toronto: University of Toronto Press, 1979).

16   John A. Irving, *The Social Credit Movement in Alberta* (Toronto: University of Toronto Press, 1959).

17   Neil McKenty, "That Tory Hepburn," in *Profiles of a Province: Studies in the History of Ontario* (Toronto: Ontario Historical Society, 1967):137 – 41; *idem*, *Mitch Hepburn* (Toronto: McClelland and Stewart, 1967).

18 Margaret A. Ormsby, *British Columbia: A History* (Toronto: Macmillan of Canada, 1958).

19 *Ibid.*, p. 276.

20 CMCA, XXII-A-1, David Toews to Town of Herbert, 10 November 1933.

21 David Toews, "Something About Our Relief Work," *The Mennonite* 54 (7 February 1939):3. See also "Clothing for Canada," *Gospel Herald* 24 (19 November 1931):751; *Jahrbuch*, 1935, p. 80; *Jahrbuch*, 1938, p. 32; L.J. Burkholder, pp. 170–71.

22 David Toews, "Immigration und Nothilfe," *Jahrbuch*, 1934, p. 66.

23 Frank H. Epp, *Mennonite Exodus: The Rescue and Resettlement of the Russian Mennonites Since the Communist Revolution* (Altona, Man.: D.W. Friesen & Sons, 1962), p. 300.

24 "Relief Work," *Gospel Herald* 30 (21 October 1937):625–27.

25 *Jahrbuch*, 1931, p. 23.

26 "The Sewing Circles of Ontario," *Calendar of Appointments*, 1934, p. 34.

27 CGC, XV-31.2, "1930–Depression," P.A. Braun, Mt. Lehman, B.C., to The Editor, Derksen Printers, Steinbach, 8 January 1971.

28 E.K. Francis, "Mennonite Contributions to Canada's Middle West," *Mennonite Life* IV (April 1949):41.

29 David Toews, "Immigration und Nothilfe," *Jahrbuch*, 1934, pp. 68–69, 70.

30 CGC, XV-31.2, "1930–Old Colony," Paper by Abram Driedger, given at MCC (Canada) consultation, 13 May 1981.

31 PAA, 69.289/498, firm of Hudson, Ormond, Spice and Symington of Winnipeg to Premier Brownlee, 19 July 1928.

32 See, for example, CMCA, XXV-24, Vol. 674, "A Petition of the Mennonites Termed 'Sommerfelder Gemeinde' to the Dominion Government," *c.* 4 August 1926. See also PAA, Accession No. 69.289/498, Hand-written, unsigned letter to "Honorable Gentlemen" by a person or persons "Representing the Reinlaender Old Colony Mennonites Still Living in Canada."

33 The Alberta government categorically denied it had awarded any special education privileges to the Altkolonier or anyone else. The provincial Minister of Agriculture, writing to C.W. Reimer of Steinbach, Manitoba, on May 16 1927, declared that his government had "given no special privileges, in connection with this matter or any other, to anyone. The rights of all citizens are equal and their obligations as citizens are equal." PAA, 69.289/498.

34 Interview with T.D. Regehr, 3 July 1981.

35 GAI, 1743, Box 125, File 1222. C.A. Buchanan, CCA District Superintendent, Edmonton, "Memorandum to Winnipeg Office," 14 May 1934. See also "Mennonites Settling 300 Families on Land in Carcajou District," *Peace River Record* (11 May 1934):1.

36   When the Altkolonier settled in the Fort Vermilion district, the provincial government refused to permit the establishment of traditional village layouts. The Altkolonier were forced to acquire land in minimum parcels of quarter sections, the same as other homesteaders. The socio-religious structure of the Altkolonier settlements was thus dealt a devastating blow which had enormous repercussions, especially as other people moved in alongside them.

37   John A. Hostetler, "Pioneering in the Land of the Midnight Sun," *Mennonite Life* 3 (April 1948):7.

38   Edward W. Van Dyke, "Blumenort: A Study of Persistence in a Sect" (Ph.D. dissertation, University of Alberta, 1972), p. 31.

39   John A. Hostetler, p. 7.

40   *Ibid*. A 1948 figure says the Fort Vermilion settlement, as the total community became known, numbered no more than 377.

41   PAC, DMR, File 58764, Vol. 12, Isaak M. Dyck *et al.*, to "the Honourable Sirs" McLeod and D.C. Philip, Morden. While the letter is undated, it was received by the law firm in the middle of November 1935.

42   *Ibid*.

43   PAC, DMR, File 58764, Vol. 13, Jacob Abrams *et al.*, to Department of Immigration and Colonization, 21 October 1935.

44   On 21 May 1935, Cornelius D. Fehr and 12 other farmers in Blumenfeld near Cuauhtemoc wrote directly to "The Dominion Government" re: "Entering again in our good old home Maple Leaf Country." PAC, DMR, File 58764, Vol. 13.

45   PAC, DMR, File 58764, Vol. 13, F.C. Blair, Assistant Deputy Minister, Department of Immigration and Colonization, to Cornelius D. Fehr, Blumenfeld, Cuauhtemoc, Chihuahua, Mexico, 20 June 1935.

46   Harry Leonard Sawatzky, *They Sought a Country: Mennonite Colonization in Mexico* (Berkeley: University of California Press, 1971), pp. 148–59.

47   Marshall Hail, "Mexico's Picturesque Mennonites Flee Their Homes as Result of Disagreement on Education of Their Children," *Ottawa Evening Citizen*, 8 February 1936.

48   *Ibid*.

49   *Ibid*.

50   GAI, 1743, Box 125, File 1222, W.R. Dick, "Memorandum for Head Office," 19 April 1934.

51   CGC, XV-31.2, "1930–Coaldale," T.D. Regehr to Frank H. Epp, 18 August 1980.

52   *Ibid*. See also Walter D. Young, *The Anatomy of a Party: The National CCF, 1932–61* (Toronto: University of Toronto Press, 1969), pp. 42–44; Norman F. Priestley and Edward B. Swindlehurst, *Furrows, Faith and Fellowship* (Edmonton: Co-op Press, 1967).

53   GAI, 1743, Box 125, File 1222, W.R. Dick to Benjamin Janz, Coaldale, 18 April 1934.

54   *Ibid.*

55   *Fiftieth Anniversary of the Coaldale Mennonite Brethren Church, May 23, 1976*, 1976, p. 8.

56   Henry Paetkau, "A Struggle for Survival: The Russian Mennonite Immigrants in Ontario, 1924–1939" (M.A. thesis, University of Waterloo, 1977), pp. 54–55.

57   *Ibid.*, pp. 55–57.

58   J. Winfield Fretz, "Recent Mennonite Community Building in Canada," *Mennonite Quarterly Review* 18 (January 1944):9.

59   Ian MacPherson, *The Cooperative Movement on the Prairies, 1900–1955*, The Canadian Historical Association Booklets, No. 33, Ottawa, 1979.

60   *Ibid.*, p. 6.

61   J. Winfield Fretz, p. 9.

62   The Niagara Credit Union.

63   David Phillip Reimer, "The Mennonites of British Columbia" (research essay, University of British Columbia, 1946), pp. 43–48.

64   J. Winfield Fretz, pp. 16–17.

65   B.B. Wiens, "Pioneering in British Columbia," *Mennonite Life* 1 (July 1946):10.

66   In conversation with J. Winfield Fretz, 17 August 1943. For accounts of similar Russlaender co-operative ventures in other areas, cf. Ted Regehr, "Mennonite Change: The Rise and Decline of Mennonite Community Organizations at Coaldale, Alberta," *Mennonite Life* 32 (December 1977): 13–22; and "The Fruit and Vegetable Industry in Ontario," *Mennonite Life* 5 (October 1950): 24–26.

67   E.K. Francis, "Mennonite Contributions to Canada's Middle West," *Mennonite Life* 4 (July 1949), p. 41.

68   Ian MacPherson, *Each for All: A History of the Cooperative Movement in English Canada, 1900–1945* (Toronto: Macmillan of Canada, 1979). See pp. 59 and 114 for reference to Mennonite involvement in the co-ops already in the 1920s. A detailed account of the movement in southern Manitoba can be found in Robert Meyers, *Spirit of the Post Road: A Story of Self-Help Communities* (Altona: The Federation of Southern Manitoba Cooperatives, 1955).

69   Robert Meyers, pp. 11–12.

70   *Ibid.*, pp. 11–22. The elected officers for the Society during its first year were J.G. Neufeld, president; J.J. Siemens, vice-president; P.D. Reimer, secretary-treasurer.

71   David Schroeder and Menno Klassen in an interview with the author, 1 April 1972. See CGCA, XV-31.2, "1930–J.J. Siemens." The comparison applies if the focus is economic and community leadership, but not if ideologies are considered, because Siemens was

less capitalistic than Cornies and Cornies less socialistic than Siemens.

72   D.K. Friesen, "I Remember J.J. Siemens (1896–1963), a Steward of the Earth of the Lord," *The Canadian Mennonite* 14 (13 June 1967):48.

73   Psalm 24:1.

74   D.K. Friesen, p. 48.

75   Keith Dryden, "College for Cooperators," *The Western Producer Magazine* (December 1965):17,19.

76   CGC, XV-31.2, "1940–J.J. Siemens," "Report to Rhineland Trustee Association," n.d.

77   CGC, XV-31.2, "1950–J.J. Siemens," "Federation Annual Meeting, November 23, 1945."

78   Robert Meyers, pp. 34–47.

79   J.A. Kroeker, "The Crosstown Credit Union," *Mennonite Life* 4 (July 1949):32.

80   CGCA, XV-31.2, "1940–J.J. Siemens," "Education in the Ideals of Cooperation," n.d.

81   CGCA, XV-31.2, "1950–J.J. Siemens," "Your President's Message," n.d.

82   Robert Meyers, p. 29.

83   CGC, XV-31.2, "1940–J.J. Siemens," J.J. Siemens to Mary Loewen, n.d.

84   J. Winfield Fretz, "The Renaissance of a Rural Community," *Mennonite Life* 1 (January 1946):15–16.

85   CGC, XV-31.2, "1930–Agriculture," "Protokoll der Versammlung der Initiativgruppe zwecks Gruendung einer mennonitischen landwirtschaftlichen Genossenschaft, abgehalten am 8. November 1933 auf der Farm von Herrn Abram Rogalsky, Glenlea, Man." See also CMCA, Benjamin Ewert Papers.

86   CGC, XV-31.2, "1930–J.J. Siemens." E.K. Francis, *In Search of Utopia: The Mennonites in Manitoba* (Altona, Man.: D.W. Friesen & Sons, 1955), p. 225.

87   *Ibid.*, p. 225 ff., attributes the difference in attitude displayed to the co-op movement by the respective reserves in part to their divergent denominational backgrounds.

88   "The car dealers put Steinbach on the map" in *Reflections on Our Heritage: A History of Steinbach and the R.M. of Hanover from 1874*, ed. Abe Warkentin (Steinbach, Man.: Derksen Printers, 1971), pp. 106–11.

89   E.K. Francis, "Mennonite Contribution to Canada's Middle West," *Mennonite Life* 4 (April 1949), p. 41.

90   PAC, RG. 30, Vol. 5642, File 7500–1, Arthur H. Unruh, "Mennonites," a memorandum to F.J. Freer, Canadian National Railways, 3 January 1930.

91 E.K. Francis, p. 229.
92 Abe Warkentin, pp. 94–127, 182 ff.
93 E.K. Francis, p. 229.
94 *Ibid.*
95 Abe Warkentin, pp. 111–13.
96 CMCA, XXII-A-1, Vol. 1171, File 57, Letter from A.A. Friesen to S.M. Grubb, 29 November 1933.
97 Frank H. Epp, *Mennonite Exodus*, pp. 301–4.
98 *Ibid.* See also CMCA, XII-A-1, Vol. 1171, File 57, David Toews's correspondence with various B-bond holders.
99 David Toews, "Immigration und Nothilfe," *Jahrbuch*, 1934, p. 69.
100 CMCA, XXII-A-1, Vol. 1171, File 57, Letter from Mary W. Sensenig, Gordonville, Pa., to David Toews, 13 March 1933. See also Chas. F. Killins, Springs, Pa., to David Toews, 6 April 1933; Jacob Burkholder, Nappane, Ind., to Canadian Mennonite Board of Colonization, 24 July 1933.
101 E.K. Francis, pp. 53–54.
102 *Ibid.*, p. 54.
103 *Ibid.*, p. 133.
104 H.J. Gerbrandt, pp. 280–86.
105 *Ibid.*, p. 282.
106 *Ibid.*, p. 286.
107 *Ibid.*
108 *Waisenverordnung der Sommerfelder Mennoniten Gemeinde in der Provinz Manitoba, Canada* (Winnipeg, Man.: Nordwesten, 1913), p. 20.
109 Manitoba, Statutes, An Act to Amend An Act to Incorporate the "Sommerfelder Waisenamt," 1923, 4 George VI, Ch. 25.
110 CMCA, Vol. 1561, David Stoesz Papers, "Rechnungsbericht: The Sommerfelder Waisenamt."
111 Jake Peters, "A History of Manitoba Sommerfelder Mennonite Church Institutions, 1890–1940" (research paper, University of Manitoba, 1980), pp. 9–10.
112 CMCA, Sommerfelder Waisenamt Papers, XXII-J-3, Vol. 1007, Montreal Trust Report, 4 December 1950.
113 Jake Peters, p. 11, based on interview with Bishop J.A. Friesen.
114 *Ibid.*
115 H.S. Bender, "Waisenamt," *Mennonite Encyclopedia*, 4:870–72.
116 CGC, XV-31.2, "1930–Mutual Aid," "Teilungs-Verordnung der von der Molotschna aus Russland eingewanderten Menno-niten-Gemeinden in Manitoba," January 1933.
117 *Ibid.*, pp. 12–18. See also CMCA, Mennonite Mutual Fire Insurance Society Papers, XXII-J-2, Vol. 283, *Verfassung: Regeln und Vorschriften der Manitoba Mennonitische Verischerung, 1922*

(n.p., n.d.). For another look at Mennonite secularization, see C.A. Dawson, *Group Settlement: Ethnic Communities in Western Canada* (Toronto: Macmillan, 1936), pp. 137–71.

118   CGC, II-2.1.2.2.2, Mennonite Conference of Ontario, Secretary's Records, "The Authority of Conference over Decisions of the Mennonite Aid Union," n.d.

119   L.J. Burkholder, p. 157.

120   *Ibid.*, p. 156.

121   *Ibid.*

122   The Waterloo Mutual Fire Insurance Company, for instance, was formed in 1863. See Orland Gingerich, *The Amish of Canada* (Waterloo, Ont.: Conrad Press, 1972), p. 66.

123   *Ibid.*

124   CGC, XV-31.2, "1930 – Mutual Aid," "Rules and Regulations of the Amish Mennonite Fire and Storm Aid Union," 20 September 1938.

125   L.J. Burkholder, p. 157.

126   CGC, XV-31.2, "1930 – Mutual Aid," "Constitution of the Mennonite Aid Union," pp. 35 – 39.

127   *Ibid.*, p. 37.

128   L.J. Burkholder, p. 157.

129   Urias Snider, "Mennonite Aid Union," in *Calendar of Appointments of the Mennonite Church of Ontario, Centennial Issue: 1834 – 1934* (n.p., 1935), pp. 29 – 30.

130   CGC, XV-31.2, "1930 – Mutual Aid," "Constitution of the Mennonite Aid Union," adopted 11 January 1939.

131   CGC, II-2.1.2.2.2, Mennonite Conference of Ontario, Secretary's Records, "Special Meeting. . . 20 June 1935."

132   Urias Snider, p. 30.

133   Orland Gingerich, p. 66.

134   *Calendar of Appointments*, 1934 – 35, p. 19.

135   "The Financial Problem," *Gospel Herald* 27 (28 March 1935):1094.

136   Interview with Lorna Bergey, 7 October 1980. See CGC, XV-31.2, "1930 – Depression."

137   One such referee used in many cases was Gilbert Bergey. *Ibid.*

138   Orie O. Miller, "The Christian in Business," *Christian Monitor* (June 1930):169.

139   J.C. Fretz, "Mennonite Welfare Board," *Mennonite Encyclopedia*, 3:640.

140   *Calendar of Appointments*, 1934, p. 8.

141   CGC, XV-31.2, "1930 – Mutual Aid," "Report of Committee Appointed by Conference to Investigate Mutual Benefit Society" and "Revised Report of Committee . . . ," 2 June 1934. A lay committee to look into the matter of an old people's home was first appointed by the Mennonite Conference of Ontario in 1919. The

Braeside Home, the fruit of 24 years of discussion and work, was opened in 1943. See *Calendar(s) of Appointments*, 1919–20, p. [15], 1922–23, p. [14]; "Report of the Ninth Annual Meeting of the Mennonite Mission Board of Ontario," *Calendar of Appointments*, 1938.

142   Oscar Burkholder, "Life Insurance," *Gospel Herald* 23 (15 January 1931):908–9; "An Antidote to Life Insurance," *Gospel Herald* 24 (16 April 1931):73–75.
143   Oscar Burkholder, "Life Insurance," p. 908.
144   *Ibid.*, p. 909.
145   Oscar Burkholder, "An Antidote to Life Insurance," p. 75.
146   *Calendar of Appointments*, 1932–33, p. [25].
147   *Ibid.*
148   A committee was first appointed in 1927. See *Calendar of Appointments*, 1927–28, p. [16].
149   CGC, II-2.1.2.2.2, Mennonite Conference of Ontario, Secretary's Records, "Report of a Joint Meeting of the Mennonite and Amish Mennonite Conference Executive Committee, Aid Union Committee, and Automobile Aid Plan Committee held at the First Mennonite Church, Kitchener, November 1939."
150   *Calendar of Appointments*, 1927–28, p. [16].
151   *Calendar of Appointments*, 1930–31, p. [21].
152   *Ibid.*, and CGC, II-2.1.2.2.2, Mennonite Conference of Ontario, Secretary's Records, H.D. Groh to "Dear Christian Friends," 19 June 1940.
153   Oscar Burkholder, p. 75. See also "Mennonite Mutual Benefit Society," *Calendar of Appointments*, 1946–47, pp. 45–46. While the Society did not formally come into being until 1946 it can be reported here in the context of its beginnings in the 1930s.
154   *Calendar of Appointments*, 1946–47, pp. 45–46.
155   Abram Vogt, "Das 'Invalidenheim' in Steinbach, Manitoba," *Warte-Jahrbuch*, 1943, pp. 56–59.
156   J. Winfield Fretz, "Mutual Aid Among Mennonites, I," *Mennonite Quarterly Review* 13 (January 1939):53; "A First for the Area...The Altona and District Hospital," *Red River Valley Echo*, Centennial Supplement 30 (25 November 1970):16.
157   Abe Dueck, p. 1; H.J. Willms, "Concordia Hospital," *Warte-Jahrbuch*, 1943, pp. 45–48.
158   Two other doctors who made a contribution from the beginning were R.A. Claassen and H. Oelkers, a non-Mennonite. Magdeline Wiebe, an immigrant from Nebraska, was director of nursing for the first 10 years. Abe Dueck, pp. 5–7.
159   *Ibid.*, p. 6.
160   *Ibid.*, pp. 8–9.
161   Frank H. Epp, *Mennonite Exodus*, p. 309.
162   "Gesundheitspflege in Coaldale," in *Gedenk- und Dankfeier des 25*

jaehrigen Bestehens der Coaldale Mennoniten Bruedergemeinde am 27. Mai 1951 (n.p., 1951), pp. 72–75; "Das Coaldaler Mennonitische Hospital," *Warte-Jahrbuch*, 1943, p. 49.

163   CMCA, XXII-A-1, G.J. Derksen and A.J. Fast, "Report on Mennonite Settlements in B.C.," 9 October 1937. See also "Protokoll der Gruenderversammlung des Mennonitischen Gesundheitsvereins fuer B.C.," 26 May 1935.

164   G.G. Neufeld, *Die Geschichte der Whitewater Mennoniten Gemeinde in Manitoba, Canada, 1925–1965* (n.p., 1967), p. 171.

165   Frank H. Epp, *Mennonite Exodus*, p. 211.

166   *Ibid.*, p. 286.

167   Frank H. Epp, *Education with a Plus: The Story of Rosthern Junior College* (Waterloo, Ont.: Conrad Press, 1975), pp. 99–102.

168   *Ibid.*, p. 107.

169   *Ibid.*, p. 108.

170   *Ibid.*, pp. 114–15.

171   For a detailed treatment of the *Reiseschuld* problem, see "The Reduction of the Reiseschuld" and "The End of an Era" in Frank H. Epp, *Mennonite Exodus*, pp. 281–95, 335–48. Primary sources are CMCA, XXII-A-1, Vols. 1294–98.

172   See CMCA, XXII-A-1, Vol. 1309, Files 857–59, and Vol. 1313, File 875, correspondence from C.F. Klassen to David Toews, 23 November 1930 to 29 September 1933.

173   CMCA, XXII-A-1, C.F. Klassen, "Zur Reiseschuldfrage," *Protokoll der 14. Jahresversammlung der Organization der Mennoniten in Saskatchewan, abgehalten in Swift Current am 8. und 9. Juli, 1943*; see also J. Gerbrandt, "Die Taetigkeit der Canadian Mennonite Board of Colonization seit Anfang des Zweiten Weltkrieges," *Mennonitisches Jahrbuch* 61 (1956):3–4.

174   Frank H. Epp, *Mennonite Exodus*, p. 288.

175   Interview with T.D. Regehr, 3 July 1981.

176   J.J. Thiessen, B.B. Janz, J. Gerbrandt, "Die restlose Tilgung der Reiseschuld der seit 1923 nach Canada eingewanderten Mennoniten von Russland," *Der Bote* 23 (27 November 1946):1.

9. Federation and Fragmentation

*Hasn't the time come for us to look beyond pettiness and to reach
out to each other for the sake of a more brotherly, tolerant, and
effective working together so that we can view our institutions as
belonging to all the people . . . ? —* JOHANN G. REMPEL. [1]

THE ECONOMIC DEPRESSION revealed that the general
Mennonite community was too fragmented and the Mennonite organizations were too incomplete to deal with all the problems besetting the Mennonite people. This conclusion was strongest
in the Canadian Mennonite Board of Colonization, which was
wrestling not only with the monumental transportation debt but also
with various other needs of the immigrants. But everywhere where
there were concerns about such matters as education, culture, colonization, war and peace, and Russian relief, the question was asked why
a more united approach wasn't possible and whether it was really
necessary and desirable that the 18 different Mennonite congregational families all went their own way rather than increasing the
number of ways in which they attempted to do their work together.

In Canada and the U.S.A., there were two organizations that
represented a unified approach to the tasks at hand, namely the
Canadian Mennonite Board of Colonization and the Mennonite
Central Committee, but both were inter-church committees only,

395

created in the 1920s to attend to tasks assumed to be temporary. As Mennonite structures, they fell far short of the General Conference and the Congress that had existed in Russia. Indeed, the Board and the Central Committee were in danger of passing into history, their immediate goals, immigration from Russia and relief for Russia, having been accomplished. David Toews and his colleagues, however, thought otherwise. In their view, the inter-Mennonite task was not ending, it was just beginning.

Thus, in 1934 the leaders of the Canadian Mennonite Board of Colonization undertook a reorganization of that inter-Mennonite body in order to achieve greater co-operation or even task-oriented federations among Canadian Mennonites, in order to respond more adequately to the economic, educational, and cultural problems they faced. The reorganization, however, was less than successful because inter-Mennonite co-operation was a high priority with only a few leaders. The best that could be said for the effort was that it kept the Board alive and working at some unfinished tasks.

In their failure to achieve, or even to genuinely seek, any kind of wholeness, the Mennonites reflected the "immobilities of fragmentation" which, according to Louis Hortz, were common to new societies in the western world, torn from their former familiar moorings.[2] It was enough that much of the old security had been lost. Why compound the situation by creating new unknowns, such as would be represented by any closer moving together of the Mennonite parts? Thus, the Mennonites sought their identity and certainty, not in a single Mennonite entity, but rather in denominational units.

The time of increasing togetherness in the Canadian Mennonite family had not yet come. And it wasn't because there were no voices, whose calls to faithfulness transcended Mennonite denominationalism. One conference was told without equivocation that in God's heaven there would be "no Mennonites, no Methodists, no Presbyterians — indeed, no Protestants or Catholics. There [would only] be the children of God from all churches, races, cultures, languages, and gentiles."[3] The goal of all Christian churches, said one elder, should be unity, namely one flock and one shepherd. This did not mean that all denominations were bad; as deplorable as the many divisions were, some good sometimes came of them. Even so, most of the divisions wouldn't have happened — Lutheranism, Anabaptism, Mennonite Brethren, for instance — if the churches from which the new groups came had been as spiritual before the break as they were 10 years after.[4]

Jacob H. Janzen may have spoken tongue-in-cheek, but his famous characterization of the fragmented Mennonite family had in it more truth than most were prepared to admit. Of the 17 groups of Mennonites, he said, group 1 considers itself fundamental and groups 2 to 17 modernistic. Group 2 views group 1 as too traditional or backward and groups 3 to 17 as modernistic, and thus it is through all the 17 groups. Each group considers itself fundamental, those before as backward or traditionalistic and those following as modernistic, until, at the last, group 17 likewise views itself as fundamental, and groups 1 to 16 as traditionalist or even partly modernistic.[5] Janzen's count of 17 was short by one, and before the decade was finished, two more groups were formed, bringing the total to 20. It was not a good time to place one's hopes on Mennonite unity. Mennonites were not about to move closer together until they were forced to, as, for instance, by the exigencies of another world war.

There was no single reason for this state of affairs. Historic factors contributing to Mennonite fragmentation were still at work — the Anabaptist impulse to pursue smallness, the lack of a centralized authority, the migration into diverse settings, geographic distance, varying responses to environmental pressures, and schismatic leaders — but the growth and expansion of denominational structures, simultaneous with the reorganization of the Board, was a most important factor in the 1930s. As it was with the North-West (Alberta and Saskatchewan) Conference of the Mennonite Brethren in Christ, so it was with most Mennonite congregational families. Once in twenty years they stretched their hand towards Mennonite ecumenicity — they exchanged fraternal visitors with the Mennonite Brethren[6] — but thereafter, they concentrated on maintaining fellowship and unity within their own North American family.[7]

The obstacle to the development of a comprehensive and effective inter-Mennonite organization was not opposition to institutionalism as such. On the contrary, the fundamental role of organizations and institutions in the survival of Mennonite minority groups had already been widely recognized, especially in those sectors where land and the colony no longer served as a unifying factor. Some leaders were actually striving for "institutional completeness" though that modern sociological term was foreign to them.[8] Conference systems, educational institutions, and benefit organizations had all become part of both the Swiss and the Dutch Mennonite scenes prior to the arrival of the Russlaender. Their coming reinforced and escalated the trend towards institutionalism, because the Russlaender brought with them a tradition, which embraced "complex systems of institutions involving the economic, educational, political, and cultural aspects of life"[9] and which they were anxious to implement also in Canada.[10]

Denominationalism and Provincialism

The immediate problems requiring organized initiatives were adequate aid to the needy in Russia, the collection of the transportation debt, the settlement of those still, or again, without land, the sustenance of needy people otherwise threatened with deportation, health care for the sick and education for the young, some ongoing communication and organizational linkages, and the nurture of the Mennonite cultural life. Beyond these issues was the long-term survival of the Mennonite minority itself. In other words, the end of immigration was not ending the need for an inter-Mennonite board. On the contrary, the unfinished tasks and new tasks required not only continuity but also strengthening of the inter-Mennonite organizations.[11]

Strengthening was needed for a number of reasons and could happen in a number of ways. To begin with, the Board needed a new mandate from the constituency it presumably represented. The reader will recall that the origins of the Board in 1922 had been less than propitious. Had it not been for the dogged determination of a few individuals, the Canadian Mennonite Board of Colonization would then not have come into being and an immigration contract would probably not have been signed. As time went on, the Board's acceptability had increased and its activity had been more widely endorsed. And its chairman, so badly maligned in the early 1920s, was now a venerated senior statesman of the Mennonite people.

That happier state of affairs, however, was also part of the problem. If unquestioning opposition at an earlier time had made an autocratic approach to the task necessary for it to be accomplished at all, uncritical support a decade later made the autocratic manner readily possible. Official Board meetings had become a rarity for a variety of reasons. In other words, the Board was David Toews and David Toews was the Board, and this precisely was a cause for concern. Not because he wasn't competent and selfless — there probably was no one more able and willing — but because he was "now past 60, often tired and sometimes sickly."[12]

Additionally, David Toews was preoccupied with many things. Besides being leader of the Board and its relief and immigration tasks, he was bishop of the rapidly growing Rosenorter congregation, chairman of the board of the financially desperate German-English Academy, moderator of the Conference of Mennonites in Central Canada, and supervisor of home missions support being dispensed to immigrant bishops by the General Conference Mennonite Church from the U.S.A. A new look at the organization was necessary for it to survive beyond the life-span of David Toews. And no one made this point more strongly than he did himself.

Strengthening the inter-Mennonite organization was necessary further for the sake of integration and realignment of certain organizational elements already in existence. In addition to the Board, and alongside of it, were two other entities relevant to the overall task. The Mennonite Land Settlement Board, which had facilitated the settlement of thousands of immigrants, had confirmed the ongoing importance in Mennonite life of the settlement function. Yet, the settlement agency had become too much an arm, not of the Mennonites but of the CPR and its Canada Colonization Association. Besides, the Association was concerned with settling immigrants on CPR lands, when what was needed was a continuous program of colonization for all the Mennonites.

Meanwhile, the immigrants had developed effective local, provincial, and interprovincial organizations. These had grown from a small central Mennonite immigrant committee, established in the Rosthern locale in 1923, to a network of district representatives, which embraced all, or most, of the immigrant communities from Ontario to British Columbia. Most impressive of all were their annual provincial assemblies, where a wide range of problems — transportation debt, relief in Russia, settlement programs, farming methods, health care, welfare work, burial societies, cultural needs, and educational challenges — were discussed. The organizational genius of the Russlaender was properly expressed in the way the immigrants went about their work.

The Board and David Toews needed all of these, the organizational gifts, the energy and drive, the network of local and provincial
people, the sense of responsibility and closeness to the task represented by the Russlaender, and, last but not least, an overall sense of
purpose and unity. In his own words, "In the light of the big
problems facing our people, would that we would succeed more and
more to gather all our moral strength so that the good reputation of
our people, which they still have, not be lost."[13] Of all the problems,
the mammoth transportation debt was the most serious. According to
Toews:

> The problem of the transportation debt is becoming more dif-
> ficult all the time with disturbing effects on our various
> undertakings. . . . we believe that our whole Mennonite people
> will have to apply its strength and its total influence to solve
> the transportation debt problem, so that those who put their
> trust in us will not be disappointed.[14]

The burdens in Canada were amplified by the responsibility felt
by the Board and by David Toews towards the need in Russia. While
$63,000 had been forwarded in 1932, only $21,377 had been sent in
1933. The decline was attributed partly to the depression but also to
weariness and to the diffusion of the effort. Thus, Toews appealed
not only for unity, but also for loyalty: "It is our duty to be loyal to
our organizations."[15]

In planning and announcing the reorganization of the Board,
David Toews took into consideration the tasks to be carried out, the
people able to help with those tasks, and the three Mennonite bodies
who had been part of the Board continuously in the past.[16] He
proposed a new slate of 21 people, plus himself should his service still
be required. This no one debated. The wholehearted support which
he needed more of in the 1920s he now had. If the unquestioning
endorsement he now enjoyed could have been interchanged with the
watchful criticism of a decade earlier, both times might have been
better served, but it is a human fact that people often try to catch up
too late and in inappropriate ways on opportunities and obligations
previously missed. The three groups which had been part of the
Board in the 1920s — namely the Conference of Mennonites in
Central Canada, the Northern District of the Mennonite Brethren
Churches of North America, and the two Canadian sections of the

Old Mennonite Church, the Mennonite Conference of Ontario and the Alberta-Saskatchewan Mennonite Conference — now also participated in the reorganization.[17] A few years after reorganization, the Mennonite Brethren in Christ were also represented on the Board.[18] And the Kleine Gemeinde and the Holdemaner also showed some interest.[19] It seemed, almost, that the new Canadian Mennonite Board of Colonization could and would become a Mennonite Central Committee of Canada, in which an ever-expanding circle of Mennonite groups would be represented, and by which they would service the growing number of things that they would choose to do together.[20]

The renewal of the Canadian Mennonite Board of Colonization couldn't be delayed any longer, but in a number of ways David Toews couldn't have chosen a worse time to launch his inter-Mennonite venture.[21] Its success depended, first and foremost, on the close co-operation of the two, now the largest, Mennonite constituencies in Canada, namely the Conference of Mennonites in Central Canada and the Northern District of Mennonite Brethren Churches of North America.

The 1920s had brought them closer together through the coming of the Russlaender, but the 1930s were driving them farther apart, quite possibly because of the Russlaender. Togetherness had been the result of the experience in Russia and the subsequent migration.[22] Together the two Russlaender factions had faced the gathering storm, the revolution, Makhno, civil war, famine, and Soviet rule. Together they had established the General Conference of Mennonite Congregations in Russia, the Mennonite Congress, the Mennozentrum, and the two organizations for reconstruction in the Ukraine and Siberia. Together they had fed the hungry and housed the refugees. Together their leaders had gone to Moscow in 1925 to plan the future. Together many of those same leaders had been sent into Siberian exile.

Without regard to church affiliation, B. B. Janz working in Russia had helped members of both groups to emigrate. And without regard to church affiliation, David Toews working in Canada had helped members of both groups to immigrate. In Canada, members of the two groups had together founded the central immigrant committee and its provincial and local counterparts. Several hundred settlements had been jointly founded, and many of the first worship services in Canada had been joint services. In some places they had worshipped together for many months and years, or even, as in the case of Springstein, more than a decade.

Tribulations had brought them together and pioneering had kept them together, but not for long, quite possibly because they weren't ready yet to be together. Perhaps it was precisely the close proximity of the 1920s which had served to reveal the great difference between them with respect to religious style and outlook. And, simultaneous with the discovery that they really were not a part of each other, came the impact of the Canadian and North American conference structures on the respective Russlaender groups. Thus, B.B. Janz, who had every reason to have the relief moneys of the Mennonite Brethren sent to Russia via the Board and Rosthern — for all the immigrants the all-important inter-Mennonite centre in Canada — counselled instead that the Brethren congregations in Canada send their offerings via Hillsboro in the U.S.A., the administrative and educational centre of the Mennonite Brethren denomination.[23]

Mennonite Brethren integration of the immigrants, their leaders — B.B. Janz included — and their congregations into the General and Northern District conferences was rapid and complete. Russlaender Brethren soon knew where they belonged, and so impressive and attractive was the Mennonite Brethren sense of missionary purpose, the clarity of their doctrine, and the predictability of their church discipline that they not only won all of their own but absorbed, step by step, the Alliance churches and many individuals of the Conference churches. This happened particularly in British Columbia, where Brethren strength and Conference weakness was obvious from the earliest days of settlement. The Brethren were more numerous, had stronger leaders, and offered a more lively, committed, and simple religious experience.

And no sooner had a Conference leader like C. C. Peters moved from Herbert in the Saskatchewan dust bowl to the new land of promise in the Fraser Valley than he sensed where his future and his obligations lay. In 1929, the Conference of Mennonites in Central Canada, impressed with his leadership, had asked him to edit the annual report, which assignment he accepted.[24] Two years later, he submitted to rebaptism by immersion and became one of the preachers of the Yarrow Mennonite Brethren Church and of the struggling congregation at Agassiz.[25] At least in the west, his example was the beginning of a trend. Many Conference people sought rebaptism and membership in Brethren churches.[26] Trend or no trend, elsewhere in Canada too the forms of baptism, and all they symbolized, continued to be a point of sharp differentiation between the Brethren churches and the Conference churches, coexisting in the same communities and perhaps even in the same meeting houses.

The incorporation of Alliance and rebaptized Conference Mennonites into the Brethren family did not have the effect of moderating the Brethren position. On the contrary, it was often the newly won Brethren who were the most uncompromising and the most certain that baptism by immersion was the only way. Thus, John A. Toews, Sr., of Coaldale, who came out of the Alliance tradition, became so zealous in enforcing the MB baptismal standards that more tolerant communities like Linden referred to him as Batko Toews, Batko implying patriarchal authority and enforcement from the top.[27]

The form of baptism, of course, was not the only issue separating the two communities. The Brethren placed more emphasis on doctrinal purity and cataclysmic conversions.[28] The Conference Mennonites were more open and tolerant, their young people less regulated in their social life and more likely to participate in circle games and folk dancing involving members of both sexes, a practice regarded by many MBs as worldly and sinful.[29]

Baptism was an issue not only between the conferences but also within the conferences. In Ontario, for instance, the form of baptism became a point of contention within the Mennonite Brethren Conference. The reader will recall that the Ontario Brethren churches had established themselves with a more open and tolerant approach. Theirs was the spirit of Alliance, which allowed the Brethren to accept members baptized by either immersion or sprinkling. Gradually, the Ontario Conference of MB Churches, which, because of its more liberal attitudes on baptism and communion, had stood apart from any other Canadian or North American conference, was encouraged to take an interest in, and become involved with, the General Conference of Mennonite Brethren Churches in North America.[30] This happened partly through H.H. Janzen, Ontario's first moderator, who had a wide preaching ministry, and partly through Jacob Dick, who had left Russia via China and ended up staying in India as a Mennonite Brethren missionary, and whose reporting itinerary took him to Ontario, where he had relatives.

In 1936, the Ontario Conference expressed interest in "a common working together" especially in missions, on condition that "you dear brethren will not coerce us but allow us our position."[31] The General Conference welcomed this initiative, but felt obligated to set some limits to the relationship owing to the differences in doctrine and practice. These limits restricted the right to do missionary work to those baptized by immersion and they also prohibited delegates from Ontario speaking to, or voting on, issues related to doctrine and practice. It would, of course, be expected that the new members would support all General Conference causes with their gifts and their prayers, in spite of the restricted rights and privileges.

The lack of full participation in the General Conference had its problems, however, especially as the Alliance character of the Ontario Conference changed, owing to the influx of people from western Canada to whom the liberal ways were not familiar and not acceptable. They strengthened the hand of those Brethren church people in Ontario who had been uncomfortable all along with the Alliance position on baptism. As a result an internal division was threatened, between those who were inclined to be tolerant and those who insisted on the traditional Brethren position. At Leamington there actually was a brief split resulting in the formation of "the true [*die richtige*] Brethren church" alongside the Alliance-minded group. The new group joined the Northern District (meaning the Brethren in the four western provinces)[32] while the old group remained a part of the Ontario District.

To prevent such splintering, and for the sake of a more perfect unity, a petition for unrestricted acceptance in the General Conference was issued along with the promise that henceforth only baptism by immersion would be practised. At the same time, the hope was expressed that the General Conference would not exclude those members who heretofore had not been baptized in the river. The General Conference, meeting in Oklahoma in 1939, expressed readiness to receive with full membership privileges the churches in Ontario but only those persons who had been baptized by immersion.

At its subsequent annual meeting, the Ontario Conference gave its consent to the conditions, but then felt obligated to clarify its relationship to its non-immersed members, whom the General Conference had set aside. The Ontario Conference explained that such persons remained members of the local congregations and of the

TABLE 31[34]

BEGINNING DATES OF PROVINCIAL CONFERENCES

PROVINCE	MENNONITE BRETHREN	CONFERENCE MENNONITES
Alberta	1928	1929
British Columbia	1931	1936
Manitoba	1929	1937
Ontario	1932	1929
Saskatchewan	1946	1929

Ontario Conference and that they were entrusted with participation in all discussions and votes. They all were also eligible to preach, be deacons, teach Sunday school, and serve as delegates to the Ontario Conference. In matters pertaining to the General Conference, however, such members were asked to abstain from voting. Also, they could not be recommended as missionaries or elected as leaders of congregations, of congregational meetings, or of the Ontario Conference, or as delegates to the General Conference.[33]

Later, in the 1940s, the Ontario District Conference joined with the other MB churches in Canada, then constituting the so-called Northern District Conference, to form the Canadian District Conference of the Mennonite Brethren Churches of North America. Thereby, the Ontario Conference lost its status as a "district" conference conferred by the General Conference in 1939. The Ontario "District" identity was not completely lost, however, because the district conference became a provincial conference. The formation of provincial conferences also belongs to this period, for both the Mennonite Brethren and the Conference Mennonites.

The movement to form provincial conferences began in Alberta, with the Mennonite Brethren in 1928 and with the Conference Mennonites in 1929, the latter with a difference (Table 31). While all the MB provincial conferences included lay delegates from the beginning, the CM provincial conferences began as ministerial meetings attended by elders, ministers, and deacons only. The one exception was British Columbia, and gradually all CM provincial meetings evolved to include lay delegates. In Saskatchewan, a very active and program-oriented provincial youth organization was a form of influence, which had the effect of delaying the emergence of the Conference of Mennonites in Saskatchewan. The primary purpose of the provincial conferences was more immediate guidance and nurture of the congregations and their ministers.

Provincial denominationalism also had its effect on the inter-Mennonite structures. While the provincial conferences did not eliminate the provincial inter-Mennonite meetings of immigrants, they did have the effect of limiting the agenda and the significance of the latter. Without the denominational provincial conferences, the provincial inter-Mennonite conventions had the potential of becoming the most significant Mennonite structures, because in numbers they were large enough to be useful and in geographic area they embraced an area small enough to be functional. However, with the coming of the provincial conferences, they were relegated to a secondary, hence dispensable, status.

Denominationalism: CMs, MBs

The tendency to give priority to denominational structures and interests is well-illustrated in the three denominational groups most important for the success of the Board and inter-Mennonite structures generally. For all three groups the most important tasks of the church were denominational tasks, and since all three groups wrestled with internal difficulties, that is also where the issue of federation received its greatest emphasis, especially when the problems were viewed in the context of the North American conferences.

The Conference of Mennonites in Central Canada was by itself a federation and so was its North American counterpart, the General Conference Mennonite Church, which sought, unsuccessfully so, to include in its membership all the congregations in Canada which were a part of the Canadian Conference. And, as has in part already been illustrated, for the Mennonite Brethren in Canada the General Conference of Mennonite Brethren Churches in North America was their most significant Mennonite universe. The Northern (Canadian) District was not so much an autonomous conference as it was a district of the continental structure. Likewise, both Canadian district conferences — Ontario and Alberta-Saskatchewan — of the Old Mennonite General Conference were preoccupied with unity not in the

inter-Mennonite field but within their districts and within the Old
Mennonite denomination.

The Mennonite Conference of Ontario, for instance, illustrates
very well how difficult it was for some Mennonite groups to give
priority to inter-Mennonite structures on a national basis. The
Conference was distant, both in a geographical sense and in a cultural
sense, from the central concerns of the Board. The Conference was
happy to help in the immigration but making the Board and its
concerns very important was quite another matter. Thus, S.F.
Coffman, the Ontario Old Mennonite member on the Board,
attended hardly a meeting in the 1930s. "There has been no close
contact," he would say to his Conference, or "[I have] not attended
any of the meetings of the Board."[35] The reasons are not hard to find,
if one examines closely the life and work of S.F. Coffman. He was on
dozens of Old Mennonite committees and busy beyond understanding in that sphere alone.[36]

The nature of the group of which he was such an important
member casts further light on the situation. The Mennonite Conference of Ontario at that time consisted of 4 bishops, 28 ministers, and
23 deacons.[37] They met once or twice annually, and the executive
committee, of which Coffman was a member continuously from
1903, met monthly. Both the Conference and the Executive were
completely preoccupied with congregational and other internal
affairs: whom to ordain to the ministry, how to reconcile a minister
with his congregation and vice versa, whom to admit to communion,
how to maintain nonconformity and apartness from the world, and so
forth. In other words, the welfare of the congregations, as well as
right teaching and right practice, were paramount issues,[38] and not
how to move closer to other Mennonites, least of all to the strange
people from Russia.

Apart from maintaining internal solidarity, the Mennonite Conference of Ontario was concerned about relationships in three directions close to its own heritage and geography. Fraternal relations
were established and maintained with the faraway Alberta-
Saskatchewan Old Mennonite Conference through the sending and
receiving of fraternal delegates. And that was important, because the
small and scattered congregations in the west needed above all not to
be forgotten by the stronger communities in the east.[39] Steps were
also taken to implement the 1931 unity resolution of the parent Old

Mennonite General Conference, which asked the districts "to seek to carry out the recommendations which General Conference has made."[40] Given the fact that the Old Mennonite Conference of Ontario had preceded by 75 years the organization of the Old Mennonite General Conference, the authority of the latter over the former was a noteworthy development.[41]

The Ontario Conference also sought closer relations with the Ontario Amish Mennonite Conference through fraternal visitations and through membership on its mission board of Amish brethren to promote "fuller co-operation between these two bodies."[42] The two groups also planned their respective Sunday school conferences so that they would not conflict with each other. They also tried to make feasible a joint automobile insurance plan. Thus, it could not be said that the Old Mennonites weren't interested in Mennonite co-operation and unity. They just pursued inter-Mennonite relations closer to home.[43]

The Northern District of Mennonite Brethren Churches of North America was tied in even more, at least for the time being, to a continental system than was the Mennonite Conference of Ontario. The Northern District was a 1910 outgrowth of, and, at this stage at least, quite dependent on, the General Conference of Mennonite Brethren Churches of North America, which had been founded in 1879 following the immigration of that decade from Russia.[44] The Northern District was not yet a Canadian Conference, not in name, not in the sense of autonomy, and not in agenda. A portion of the agenda, city missions for example, included Minneapolis as much as Winnipeg.[45] Some of the most important programs—foreign missions, college-level education, and publications—were General Conference programs.

More importantly, the General Conference set the norms for all doctrinal and ethical teaching and did so with a deep sense of denominational responsibility and identity. The General as well as the Northern District sessions were closed to outsiders, except to some "persons who are close to us" and who could be admitted as "our guests" by permission.[46] And all submitted questions were revealed in advance to a committee of seven brethren so that they would be better able to provide answers in the discussions. Both the questions and the answers, as well as resolutions passed, were clear indications of the direction expected from the conferences by the congregations and of the willingness of the conferences to give such direction.[47]

The Northern District was in many ways a regional expression of the American-based General Conference of Mennonite Brethren churches. The Northern District sessions were a way of bringing, meaning promoting, General Conference MB concerns to the various regions. What the district conference did provide was opportunity for a closer-to-home scrutiny of mission funds—all the detail was annually reported and discussed—and their jurisdiction over certain regional programs like city missions, already mentioned, and home missions, the extent of which had vastly increased with the coming of immigrants.[48] Other Mennonite groups were viewed as a proper arena for MB home and city missions activity because "it is our duty not to leave the poor souls in the dark."[49]

Foreign missions, especially, were important, and no Mennonite mission field anywhere else in the world could report the satisfying results of the Mennonite Brethren in India. In a decade of bad news, Mennonite Brethren foreign missions were a bright spot for the church. In 1936 it was reported from the India field, which covered 7,000 square miles, 2,000 villages, and one million people, that there were 6,000 church members and 200 native workers. There were four hospitals, four middle schools, four boarding schools, and one Bible school.[50]

The Northern District's tie-in to the continental General Conference placed serious limitations on the nature and degree of cooperation with, and involvement in, the Canadian Mennonite Board of Colonization and related inter-Mennonite projects on the part of Canadian MB congregations. For the Northern District churches there were, for instance, two channels of relief for Russia, one via the Board in Rosthern and one via the General Conference Welfare Committee in Hillsboro, Kansas.[51] There was no report from Rosthern on the Northern District agenda without also a report from Hillsboro, though there sometimes were reports from Hillsboro without reports from Rosthern. Hillsboro always took precedence, partly because of the nature of the MB Conference and partly because the ultimate channel for the Hillsboro relief for Russia, namely the Mennonite Central Committee, was chaired by a prominent Mennonite Brethren leader, P.C. Hiebert.[52] David Toews, the chairman of the Canadian Mennonite Board of Colonization, was highly respected by the Mennonite Brethren — and the Russlaender among them knew that they owed their immigration to Canada largely to him, but denominational loyalty for the Mennonite Brethren pre-empted those sentiments.

The theological and structural nature of the Mennonite Brethren gave unusual strength to that denomination for what were perceived to be the fundamental tasks of the church, evangelism and missions, but that perception also dictated a weak response to inter-Mennonite co-operation and a limited commitment in 1934 to the reconstituted Board of Colonization. At the Northern District Conference of that year, the relief reports began with P.C. Hiebert and Hillsboro, followed by David Toews and Rosthern.[53] With respect to reorgani-zation of the Board, the Conference recognized the need to complete the liquidation of the transportation debt and for relief of needy immigrants, but no obligatory financial or other commitments were assumed. Moral support was necessary to bring the work to a blessed conclusion, and to that end the refusal to pay the transportation debt by any of its members was regarded "as a serious sin."[54]

The debt was taken seriously as a moral duty, but all other projects of the Board, and of the Mennonite people as a whole, were relegated to a secondary position, if not excluded altogether. This did not always happen with complete unanimity, and there were some exceptions. Before these can be reported, however, the place in inter-Mennonite affairs of the Conference of Mennonites in Central Canada must be more clearly identified.

Denominationalism: Conference Mennonites

The Conference of Mennonites in Canada had been founded in 1903 as a relatively loose association of like-minded Saskatchewan and Manitoba congregations. By 1920, seven congregations had become members, six in Saskatchewan and one in Manitoba. All of the Saskatchewan congregations and none of the Manitoba ones had become members of the General Conference.[55] This Canadian Con-ference membership was greatly increased as the Russlaender congregations joined the Conferences in the 1920s. The Conference saw itself as a resource to church workers in such matters as aids to sermon preparation[56] and to the congregations in such matters as home missons, the care of the poor, publication, and education.[57]

The Conference had made the Mennonite problem resulting from scattering and isolation,[58] as well as the congregational fragmentation resulting from ambition, factious spirit, disunity, and narrowness,[59] its overriding passions, and most of its Conference themes and programs all had to do with congregational survival and nurture. A monthly publication, *Der Mitarbeiter*, facilitated communication. The committee for home missions ensured that the small and scattered settlers, as well as urban dwellers, received occasional ministerial visits. The committee for the care of the poor supplemented, whenever necessary, congregational activity in this area. The program committee sought to design the annual programs in such a way as to make the Conference a congregational resource.[60]

In working for solidarity and unity,[61] the Conference had also committed itself to uphold the congregational principle and thus not to interfere or become involved in the internal affairs of a congregation if not requested to do so by such a congregation. The Conference was seen as a consultative, rather than a legislative, body, striving for unity not so much in external forms and customs but in a common love, faith, and hope, as well as in the common task.[62] The founding formula had been a good one, and at the 20th conference in Winkler, when eight congregations were already members, it was noted that no effort at uniting the congregations in a common task had been as successful as the Conference.[63]

The congregational principle was put to its most severe test by the issue of infant baptism and whether or not the Conference could accept or tolerate members, congregations that is, who themselves accepted or tolerated persons who had been baptized only as infants. No Mennonite congregation practised infant baptism, but there was enough intermarriage between Mennonites and others, Lutherans in particular, for a general problem to develop in this regard.

The matter came to a head in the Conference when the Eigenheim congregation near Rosthern and Russlaender congregations with such cases sought membership in the Conference. Understandably, there were some strong feelings on this matter, because the baptism of voluntary believers rather than infants had been one of the foundational principles of the whole Anabaptist movement. H.H.

Ewert, for instance, did not believe that so fundamental a matter could be decided by individual congregations alone. In *Der Mitarbeiter* he wrote, "A biblical tolerance can never demand of us that to please others we go against our own convictions."[64]

The Eigenheim congregation, it should be clarified, had been a member of the Conference since 1903 as a branch of the Rosenorter church. As the Rosenorter congregation and its numerous outposts had grown, however, the question of the Rosenorter remaining a single organization under a single elder inevitably arose. The workload of the elder, the unwieldiness of the system, the desire of some groups to be independent, rivalries among the ministers, and other such factors would cause the issue to surface. Normally, the elder would not be the first to suggest an independence movement among the branch, but in this case the matter of changing the system was raised publicly by the elder himself, David Toews, his reason being his own heavy workload.[65]

The "independence" movement took hold in Eigenheim, quite possibly because of the size of its membership, the strength of its leadership, the proximity to the mother-church, and interpersonal tensions.[66] The problem of Eigenheim was freely and openly discussed, and, by the end of the 1920s, it was agreed that Eigenheim should become an independent congregation with its own elder. Thus, the Eigenheim intention to "build ourselves as an independent church in co-existence with the mother church"[67] was legitimized and blessed. However, the change of status for Eigenheim required independent acceptance into the membership of the Conference, if that is what Eigenheim wanted.

That is what Eigenheim wanted and precisely at the time the issue of infant baptism was being hotly debated both in the Conference and at Eigenheim. The focus was on Herman Roth, who had grown up with the Moravians, who had married a Mennonite, and who wanted to join the congregation without rebaptism. Having debated the baptism issue occasionally over a period of two decades, the 1928 Conference at Rosthern decided in a "closed session of the delegates" to abide by its historic position and to accept "only members who have been baptized on the confession of faith."[68] Notwithstanding the Conference decision, the Eigenheim church agreed "to make concessions in a case like this one, where it affects a whole family. . . ." The congregational vote registered 85 per cent in favour of the action, and Roth was admitted without rebaptism.[69] In spite of this congregational action, clearly against a declared position of the Conference, the Conference accepted the Eigenheim congregation into its membership in 1929. The congregational principle had triumphed over conference legislation.

It wasn't always easy to observe the congregational principles because the principle of congregational autonomy and the spirit of liberality had two effects. The positive effect was that it made the Conference possible at all. The negative effect was that congregations, left on their own, were themselves fractured when some outside help could have moderated and mediated congregational conflicts. The Conference had its share of such conflicts. In Manitoba, especially at Oak Lake and Rivers, there was some shifting of loyalties between the Schoenwieser and Whitewater churches, both members of the Conference, as people expressed their preferences for either the more liberal ways of the Schoenwieser church or the conservative ways of Whitewater.[70] At Didsbury, there was a split over the question of baptism, one minister taking the immersionists with him.[71] At Morden, an outside evangelist ended up rebaptizing 13 Bergthaler persons and forming an independent congregation.[72] This loss was made up by the remnant of the nearby Herold congregation joining the Morden Bergthaler after Michael Klaassen, the Herold minister, died in 1934. The group had become too small to carry on alone. Klaassen, who like David Toews had been on "the great trek" in Russia in the early 1880s, had led his flock up from Oklahoma during the Great War.[73]

In spite of never-ending internal troubles, the Conference Mennonites showed new signs of vigour near the end of their third decade and the beginning of the fourth, partly due to the quantitative and qualitative strengthening provided by the Russlaender. The publication of annual reports was begun.[74] The constitution was printed for wide distribution.[75] A confession of faith was adopted.[76] And steps were taken to produce two of the materials most essential for the educational and liturgical life of the congregation: a new hymnbook and a catechism.[77] Financial support for church workers in newly organized congregations and church buildings was authorized if needed.[78]

The relationship of the Canadian Conference to the General Conference remained an ambiguous one, with the pendulum moving to and fro between greater and lesser identification. This is evident, for instance, in two conference name changes within a decade. In 1932, the Conference dropped "Central" as in "Central Canada" and at the same time added "General" to make the full name read "General Conference of Mennonites in Canada."[79] The dropping of "Central" reflected the inclusion of Ontario congregations in addition to those from the prairies and British Columbia, which joined as a body of United Mennonite Churches in 1937.[80] This name change reflected the idea, eventually unacceptable, that the Canadian Conference was, like district conferences in the U.S.A. (Pacific, Western, Northern, Central, Middle, and Eastern), a district of the General Conference, a notion which was gaining some credence in Canada.[81] In due course, the more traditional position, more to the liking of the Bergthaler as well as others, won out and the name "General" was dropped from the Canadian name in less than a decade.[82]

Co-operation Attempted and Failed

The Conference Mennonites, while concerned with problems of unity within the denomination, none the less were more open to a wider Mennonite identity and co-operation than were the other two conferences. To the Conference Mennonites the agenda of the Canadian Mennonite Board of Colonization was very important, as was the future of the two preparatory schools for Mennonite teachers at Gretna and Rosthern. While both schools had been cradled by conference-related constituencies, the Conference wanted them to enjoy general support and ownership among all Mennonites. The Mennonite Collegiate Institute at Gretna and the German-English Academy at Rosthern were basically boarding schools for high school students, but the purpose of their founding, namely to prepare bilingual teachers, equipped also to teach religious subjects in the public schools, had not been forgotten. Indeed, the notion that one went on to high school in order to become a teacher was still strong and was strengthened by the influx of the Russlaender, among whom were scores of teachers who needed Gretna or Rosthern to learn the English language in order to obtain Canadian certification.

The 1930 Conference envisioned the establishment of an inter-Mennonite and interprovincial commission responsible for the development and financing of the Mennonite educational institutions, meaning Gretna and Rosthern.[83] However, such a commission never came into being. The subsequent attempt to get all the Mennonite churches in Manitoba to assume responsibility for the school in Gretna also met with failure. This is somewhat surprising given the fact that the student population came in fairly proportionate numbers from the Brethren, the Bergthaler and other Conference churches, the Sommerfelder, the Rudnerweider, and the Kleine Gemeinde.[84] Most of the congregations were approached in 1930–31 on the basis of a 50-cent-per-member levy, but only $800 was raised in the first year. Contributors had been the Bergthaler, the Sommerfelder, most of the Russlaender Conference churches, one congregation of the Brethren, and one section of the Kleine Gemeinde.[85]

By 1932 a Manitoba School Conference had been established to support the school, but the Kanadier congregations were not a part of it.[86] And a few years later it was acknowledged that the Brethren churches were really not a part of it either, thus justifying transference of the support base from the intended inter-Mennonite School Conference to the newly formed denominational Conference of Mennonites in Manitoba.[87]

The withholding of support by the Mennonite Brethren to the extent that it was withheld was again largely due to their North American connection and the search for a unified program within the denominational context, one that met the need for the perpetuation of the denomination and its special doctrines. Thus, the Canadian Mennonite Brethren felt obligated to relate to, and support, Tabor College, the school at Hillsboro, Kansas, which was a college of the General Conference of Mennonite Brethren Churches of North America. Canadian Mennonite students were also going to Bethel College and to North Newton, Kansas, and to Bluffton College in Ohio, but these General Conference Mennonite schools were not denominational schools for General Conference people in the same structural sense that Tabor College was a school of the Mennonite Brethren of North America or that Goshen College was a school of the Old Mennonites of North America.

The cause of Tabor College — Bible school and academy as well as college — was forcefully presented to the Northern District in 1931.[88] The continued existence of the school was then in doubt, owing to an accumulated deficit in spite of spending cuts and a reduction in the faculty. Leaders expressed the view that "... this school may not be closed because then our church would suffer irreparable damage."[89] In 1932, Tabor College again had a deficit, but closing the school was unthinkable, because of the need in the land for fundamental Christian schools.[90]

The principal of the newly established Peniel Bible School at Winkler was the most vigorous proponent in Canada of the Tabor option, partly no doubt because the Winkler students could go on to Tabor, get academic credit for many of the subjects taken in Winkler, and graduate with a bachelor of theology degree within two years. And A.H. Unruh saw no reason why young people from Canada could not prepare for teaching by going to Winkler and Hillsboro as well as by choosing either Gretna or Rosthern.[91] However, the brethren did not all think alike, and repeatedly the support of Rosthern and Gretna was encouraged. In response to one such suggestion in 1933, the Northern District Conference resolved that the adequate training of teachers should receive more attention, but once again Tabor College headed the list of schools making a contribution towards that end.[92]

Gretna and Rosthern were included in the list but the more concrete steps of support, namely the taking of offerings, benefited Tabor College more than the other schools. Gradually, however, the sentiment for Gretna and Rosthern increased, not sufficiently to achieve unequivocal endorsement but sufficiently to ward off unequivocal opposition.[93] Indeed, when two brethren used unusually harsh words with respect to the Rosthern Academy, the Conference insisted on an apology as it condemned such "sharp, unwise judgements."[94] At the same time, the Conference's Committee for Schools gave a high rating to the Gretna and Rosthern schools as institutions to which one could "entrust the training of teachers for the public schools."[95] Even so, the longer-term trends separated the Brethren from both of these schools.

Unfortunately, at a time when the two schools most needed the full support of an inter-Mennonite constituency, they came to symbolize not only the widening gulf between Mennonite Brethren and Conference Mennonites but also between Russlaender and Kanadier. In the Gretna and Rosthern schools, the Russlaender students soon represented numerical majorities, and what was even more significant, both schools had Russlaender principals before the decade was out.[96]

This "takeover" of Mennonite institutions by the aggressive Russlaender could be observed on every hand. With Ewert's decease came also the death, a second death, of *Der Mitarbeiter*. Once a monthly Conference paper, *Der Mitarbeiter* had lost its status as such in 1925, allegedly for financial reasons.[97] Yet the Ewert brothers, H.H. as editor and Benjamin as business manager, though drawing no remuneration whatsoever for their work, doggedly continued the publication while they waited year after year for the Conference to pay the outstanding bills of 1925 still owing in 1930.[98] *Der Mitarbeiter*, probably one of the best-edited and most intellectually stimulating Mennonite perodicals of the day—every issue dealt with educational matters in some way—passed into history because the Conference, also dominated by immigrants, looked to *Der Bote*, founded by immigrants at Rosthern in 1924, as the semi-official Conference paper.[99] It was a sign of the times that the Bergthaler Church in Manitoba, basically a Kanadier group, then proceeded to establish its own *Bergthaler Gemeindeblatt*.[100]

Elsewhere, too, the literary dominance of the Russlaender became manifest. *Die Mennonitische Rundschau*, a weekly, which had moved from Scottdale to Winnipeg in 1923 because its German readership was now concentrated in the Manitoba Kanadier, also had a Russlaender editor.[101] And the *Steinbach Post*, begun in 1913 by Kanadier for the Kanadier, also fell into the hands of Russlaender publishers and editors.[102] Little wonder that the Kanadier felt and sometimes said that there were too many Russlaender around and that they tended to be somewhat bigmouthed.[103] It wasn't an easy time for those Kanadier who had made every effort to make the Russlaender feel welcome and to co-operate with them. And whenever the more liberal attitudes of the Russlaender with respect to nonresistance surfaced, Bishop David Schulz of the Bergthaler wondered whether he was in the right camp or not. But he continued to build bridges, as did his colleague J.N. Hoeppner, who admonished those who kept alive the differences and the tensions between Russlaender and Kanadier.

> I don't think this is so much the case among the church workers as among the individual members, where one can still

hear, "That is a Russlaender" with an emphasis that at times
does not evoke trust. Also there are warnings that the new
immigrants will arrange and run everything according to their
own style, and from the other side that they are being hindered
in coming into their own. It should not be that way. . . . [104]

Another test of inter-Mennonite co-operation was the proposal of
the Colonization Board's welfare committee that a *Nervenheilanstalt*
(mental hospital) be founded in western Canada.[105] The Board had
made itself responsible for all immigrant cases in the first five years
who were liable to be deported should they become public charges.[106]
In 1934, there was a total of nine patients in mental hospitals for
whom the Board was paying from 50 cents to one dollar per day,
depending on the province. There were other Mennonite patients in
such institutions — one count says 61 Russlaender alone in 1931[107] —
but having been in Canada for five years before becoming ill, they
were not in danger of deportation.[108]

A Mennonite mental hospital was seen as an economy measure, but
more importantly, as a health move. It was clear to the relatives and
to the ministers making pastoral calls that housing in alien institutions of those "sick with the nerves" tended to contribute to more ill
health rather than to healing. The founding of an all-Mennonite
mental hospital, however, was problematic from the beginning.
Admittedly, the times were tough, but the Welfare Committee of the
Board was suggesting that five cents a month per member was all that
was needed. A questionnaire sent to 200 congregations, however,
yielded only 46 positive returns and an income projection of only
$270 a month, insufficient to get the hospital started.[109] When the
Committee asked for voluntary offerings, only one-fifth of the
churches responded.[110] And when provincial field workers were
authorized to promote the cause and collect funds, the right persons
couldn't be found.[111] There was also disagreement on the best
structure for such an institution.[112]

Perhaps the greatest problem of all, underlying all others, was the
lack of enthusiasm for inter-Mennonite endeavours. Some Mennonite Brethren had already established a private institution near
Vineland in Ontario,[113] begging the question why there should be an
additional mental hospital, one owned by all the Mennonites. Additionally, the infighting between the Conference and the Brethren
camps in the Winnipeg-based Concordia Hospital Society had fur-

ther dampened interest for inter-Mennonite work, especially on the part of the Brethren. As that institution's historian has written:

> Those who were dissatisfied were clearly in the minority and the most outspoken critics were also members of the Menno- nite Brethren Church. . . . It became more and more obvious that the division between factions was taking place along denominational lines. . . . Attempts at reconciliation failed and this was reflected in the deep suspicion which prevailed between the two major Mennonite denominations. . . . [114]

Johann G. Rempel, one of the strongest believers in the proposed institution publicly lamented "the mutual distrust between the conferences":

> It is as if a dark shadow affects every project which is to belong to all the Mennonites, regardless of whether they are schools, hospitals, or other welfare institutions. Where in our commu- nities can we find breadth of heart . . . ![115]

For a variety of reasons, the settlement committee fared little better than the welfare committee. The problem of the "landless families" was a serious one, among both Kanadier and Russlaender, serious enough for the Conference of Mennonites to elect its own committee.[116] But the preference was to work at the land question in the inter-Mennonite context of the Board and its connection with the colonization branches of the CPR and the CNR.[117]

But even then, solutions didn't come easily because only home- steads in "wilderness lands" were recommended, as at Swan River in Manitoba, at Bredenbury, Foam Lake, and Swan Lake in Saskatche- wan, at Blue Ridge in Alberta, and on Vancouver Island in British Columbia. Even homesteads couldn't be established without cash and nowhere were there areas large enough for the Mennonites to form compact settlements — "there are everywhere many Ukrainians."[118] The biggest problem of all, however, was the lack of unity to move forward together on settlement questions. While people like C.F. Klassen felt that much could be gained from a network of local settlement committees working together with the Board, B.B. Janz in withdrawing from the Board's settlement committee felt that it could only function as an information service and that everything else had to be left to private initiative.[119]

The cultural affairs committee suggested a rather broad front of activity, including assistance to the Mennonite churches in Canada with respect to their religious, moral, and educational endeavours as through Sunday schools, *Jugendvereine*, libraries, Saturday schools, and summer schools. The committee saw itself providing instructional directives and arranging for appropriate courses.[120]

The ambitious plans were challenged and clipped, however, as once again the Mennonite denominationalists had their way. Religious training like Sunday schools was the business of the conferences and the churches, not of an inter-Mennonite organization like the Board, they said, and insisted that the respective spheres of activity be clearly delineated.[121] The cultural affairs committee could serve as the most economical source of German literature, as a protection against *Schundliteratur* (evil literature), and as a source of information about cultural affairs in the land.

In the end, the cultural affairs committee of the Board was a warehouse for literature, a warehouse provided by the returns of a 19-week fund solicitation in the U.S.A. by David Toews.[122] In due course, this project became a Canadian branch of the General Conference Mennonite Church bookstores.[123] But in 1938 it was still serving on a broad front, having in one year distributed 388 manuals for religious instruction, 787 manuals for German instruction, and 890 other books, including 500 copies of J.H. Janzen's *Bible Stories*.[124]

Virtually nothing of consequence could be structured as inter-Mennonite activity, though one important matter must not be overlooked. The representation of the Mennonites in Canada at the world conference in Amsterdam was arranged through the Board in consultation with leaders of the conferences. It was understood that David Toews and C.F. Klassen, the two delegates chosen, would represent not their conferences but all the Mennonites in Canada.[125] This happened in 1936, but only in 1936.

A breadth of heart among Mennonite people was a rarity indeed. Mennonite separatism and denominationalism in the 1930s manifested itself also in the emergence of two new Mennonite groups, one of them in the Dutch Mennonite community of southern Manitoba and one in the Swiss Mennonite community of southern Ontario. While there was no obvious connection between the two developments, relatively simultaneous, they resembled each other in that

CHART 2

MENNONITE GROUPS STARTED 1920–1940

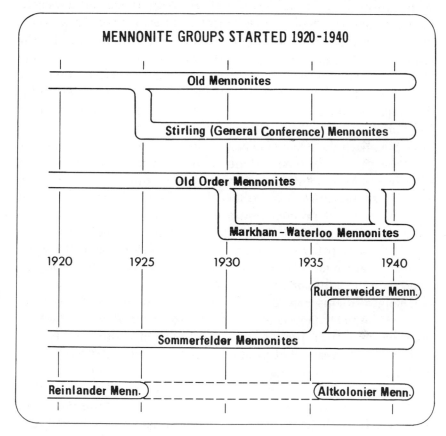

MENNONITE GROUPS STARTED 1920-1940

both were movements away from more conservative forms of Mennonitism. And, while both appeared to fracture particular Mennonite bodies, the divisions actually brought peace and unity as ways were found for different points of view to exist side by side in a more harmonious way in the respective communities. Fragmentation, rather than federation, revealed itself as the easier course of action.

Fragmentation in Southern Manitoba

The reshaping of Mennonite religious life in southern Manitoba actually involved a resurgence among the Kanadier groups of both conservative and progressive forces, in both the West and East Reserve areas. In the latter region, the Kleine Gemeinde was once again threatened by the Bruderthaler, the Mennonite urbanizers in the Steinbach area since the turn of the century. Always evangelistic, they were now adopting the name of Evangelical Mennonite Brethren. Having been constituted originally from Kleine Gemeinde dissenters and defectors, the new face renewed the appeal to a new generation of Kleine Gemeinde people. An effort had to be made, therefore, to make some accommodation without losing the basic orientation.

In Steinbach the Kleine Gemeinde, for instance, could no longer resist the ways already adopted much earlier by the Bruderthaler and still hope to keep their young people.[126] Very carefully, the Sunday school was introduced and then the Sunday school became an umbrella to bring in other traditionally questionable activities like choirs and other innovative youth activities. In due course, the publication of a paper was begun and the town church even changed the seating arrangement from the house church style to the cathedral style, with the pulpit on the platform at the far end.

Changes of this nature in the Kleine Gemeinde represented a paradox, however, and it became necessary therefore to pull things together again from time to time. This happened in 1937, for the first time in 31 years, when the bishops, ministers, and deacons got together to re-establish the normative religious teachings and practices of the Kleine Gemeinde.[127]

The set of rules and regulations then adopted forbade voluntary departure from the church to avoid church discipline, discouraged the use of musical instruments, including gramophones and radios, endorsed singing practices provided only the old hymnal was used and singing was only in unison, allowed high school education for only those young people "in whom the church would have the necessary confidence," encouraged more visiting of scattered families and groups, insisted on close examination of all applicants for membership, agreed not to make public "confessed secret sins which have nothing to do with public need," allowed the playing of ball and such entertainments to children but not to believers, recommended excommunication of erring members "after three unsuccessful admonitions," described "as unbecoming" the display of personal photographs on walls and furniture, opposed life insurance "definitely" but not "a protective church society," expected "a uniform headcovering for the sisters," cautioned against invitations to preachers of other denominations, labelled as indecent the "mixed bathing of males and females," provided for excommunication "after considerable patience and examination" in cases of premeditated avoidance of attending communion for a length of time, and suggested greater solemnity at wedding festivities, which were becoming bigger and noisier all the time.

Mennonite religious groupings in the West Reserve area at the time had grown to five in number.[128] Two represented to a very large extent the Russlaender influence. One of these, the Blumenorter congregation of the Conference variety, was hardly involved in the events here to be described, but it supplied a number of influential public school teachers to the area, notably J.D. Adrian of Reinfeld village.[129] The Brethren church of Winkler and its surrounding area was not purely of Russlaender vintage—converts among the Kanadier in the 1880s were the founders—yet through the Winkler Bible School and such village congregations as Gnadenthal, their particular evangelical form of church life had generated a certain amount of appeal beyond Brethren church borders.

The two strongest Kanadier groups were the Bergthaler and the Sommerfelder Mennonites, whose parting of the ways had come after 1890 over the issue of public schools in Mennonite communities and the support of a preparatory school for teachers being founded at Gretna at the time.[130] The differences, very significant at the time, had been reinforced through the years in the sense that a coming together of the two bodies was unthinkable. Both had their own network of congregations, often in the same localities, and both had their own bishops and ministerial infrastructures. The essential differences lay in their degree of resistance to the religious and economic cultures surrounding them and in their degree of accommodation. The Bergthaler had joined the Conference of Mennonites in Canada as a founding member, accepted the Sunday school, four-part singing, the *Jugendverein*, a freer style of preaching, and evening services.

The Sommerfelder had entertained none of these, and yet it could not be said that they were culturally immobile. After all, some Sommerfelder had been strong supporters of the Mennonite Educational Institute in Altona until it burned down in 1926, never to be rebuilt. After that, Sommerfelder students and offerings had also been sent to the MCI at Gretna, as we have already seen. Besides, the Sommerfelder in southern Manitoba had chosen not to join their more conservative Sommerfelder brethren in the resettlement to Paraguay and Mexico in the 1920s. Yet, their stance was a conservative one, which offered stronger resistance to outside influences, of which the incorporation of the *Waisenamt*, cited in the previous chapter, was one example.

The Sommerfelder elder since 1931 was Peter A. Toews, one of the most colourful bishops southern Manitoba had ever seen. He had begun his leadership career as chairman of the MEI school board and as a reeve of the Rural Municipality of Rhineland.[131] A progressive among conservatives, he promoted education and sought passage of a provincial bill that would have created a Mennonite school division, only to see the proposal defeated by Mennonites themselves. Then he became a Sommerfelder minister and a year later an elder.

It was not an easy time to be the leader of the Sommerfelder church, because that sizeable congregational family with about 5,000 members was torn in two directions. On the one hand, it was under the influence of progressivism, owing partly to the Bergthaler, Blumenorter, and Brethren around them, and partly to their own choices, particularly the one not to emigrate. Pulling and pushing in the other direction was a clear sense that the revivalistic style, increasingly characteristic of the so-called progressives, was a borrowed and superficial religious form. An additional pull in the conservative direction was the fact that much of the leaderless Reinlaender remnant in Manitoba had begun to move in the Sommerfelder direction. The liturgical styles of the two groups were similar. In both congregations the sermons were read and the same song book was used, though the Sommerfelder would tend more and more to sing those hymns which had the fewer verses.[132]

The Reinlaender church remnants in Manitoba and Saskatchewan had been struggling without a clear sense of direction ever since 75 per cent of their number — 3,340 out of 4,526 in Manitoba; about 5,180 out of 7,182 from the two reserves in Saskatchewan — with the three bishops had left for Mexico.[133] Thus, while the Sommerfelder were losing members to the Bergthaler because they were not progressive enough, they were gaining Reinlaender because they (the Sommerfelder) were conservative enough and close enough spacially and culturally to be attractive. The Sommerfelder bishop knew this and for that reason alone would have been foolish to innovate, though the failure to do so threatened the loss of more progressive-minded Sommerfelder, especially the young people.

In due course, the Reinlaender remnants had made up their mind not to allow the disintegration to proceed any further. A new organization, the Altkolonier Mennonitengemeinde (or Old Colony Mennonite Church), was struck, new membership registers were begun, because the old ones were now in Mexico, and new bishops were chosen in the Hague-Osler area of Saskatchewan and the West Reserve area of Manitoba. In the Swift Current area, the Reinlaender remnant had disintegrated to the point where reorganization was no longer possible, the people having either joined the Sommerfelder or mission outposts of other conferences or just drifted away.

As already indicated, the new bishop of the Altkolonier at Hague-Osler since 1930 was Johann Loeppky, ordained to that office by the neighbouring Bergthaler(S) bishop. In 1936, Loeppky came to Manitoba to ordain as bishop for that group of Altkolonier Jacob J. Froese, a man of unusual gifts and a prosperous farmer in the village of Reinfeld.[134] There was consultation with the parent body in Mexico before the reorganization, but the two groups "remained aloof from each other," partly because those who had stayed were considered by those who had left to have gone with the world, and partly because the Manitoba remnant welcomed with open arms those returning from Mexico, thus making easier the unwanted defections in Mexico.[135]

The establishment of the Altkolonier in southern Manitoba reduced the pressures on the Sommerfelder to be conservative enough to make themselves acceptable to the traditionalists, but this did not mean that the Sommerfelder were ready to accommodate other pressures and influences. On the contrary, those influences had become so strong and their carriers among them so radical that the breaking point was near. The new openness caused greater participation in the events of other Mennonite communions, the Bergthaler in particular, including such family events as funerals and weddings and church services, mornings and evenings on Sundays. Of special interest were *Jugendvereine*, missionary reports, and Bible-teaching services as well as evangelistic services. The participation in these events, however small and sporadic, brought new influences which indirectly affected more than just those who had the direct contact.[136]

Other sources of new influence were the public schools, the

teachers and the students themselves, now exposed to an English-language curriculum, including new books, new songs, new games, new ideas, and new attitudes. While the schools themselves did not represent the substance of the religious renewal that came, they helped to create a general climate for change and forward movement.[137] New forms of religious instruction became acceptable and eagerly sought after. Sunday schools for the teaching of Bible stories were introduced, and classes for the study of the catechism as well as the Bible itself attracted not only the young people but also the older folk. All of this produced much questioning, more searching, and the gathering of small groups who wanted more truth and also more fellowship around the common experience of truth.

In due course, such groups wanted additional nurture from outside speakers, and thus it happened that I.P. Friesen, a Saskatchewan evangelist with Manitoba roots, came from his home in Rosthern to his former village of Reinfeld, where close relatives helped to arrange a series of evangelistic meetings in the local schoolhouse with the co-operation of the aforementioned J.D. Adrian. Friesen had joined the migration to Saskatchewan in the 1890s as a Reinlaender, but he did not survive in that communion very long. For him, the frontier had meant not only the settlement of virgin lands, but the exploration of new life styles and acceptance for his children of the public school. Last but not least, the entry into the world of business had changed many things for him. As a lay preacher, he had developed a style so free that his poetic gifts sometimes resulted in spontaneous verse in the course of his pulpit presentations. Eventually, he published two volumes of his poems entitled *Im Dienste des Meisters*. His experience of the wider world made him a member of the General Conference Mennonite Church Missions Committee, and on his own he travelled to the Middle East, about which he had written in *Meine Reise nach Palastina*.[138]

Thus, Friesen offered to eager people fresh, and interesting, often emotional, presentations which were already known in revival-minded denominations as *Erweckungspredigten* (literally, sermons of awakening).[139] After several meetings in Reinfeld intended to awaken the people, Friesen invited decisions for the Lord. People responded. Word was spread abroad that something was happening in Reinfeld. The meetings extended from one week to two weeks and owing to lack of space were transferred after that time from Reinfeld to Winkler. There too the facilities were crowded, and thus there was a shift again after a few weeks from the smaller church of the Bergthaler to the larger meeting house of the Brethren. According to one chronicler:

> Brother Friesen preached and the people were converted. . . .
> Many found peace and testified concerning their experiences.
> From near and far people came to take part in the blessings.[140]

According to Isaac P.F. Friesen, a nephew of the evangelist and one of the participants, later a leading preacher in the movement, there was a spiritual movement such as Manitoba had not seen before.[141] Even the business community noticed and Sirluck, a merchant in Winkler, was said to have observed, "What Preacher Isaac P. Friesen has done here in Winkler, all the policemen together could not have done." Apparently, many citizens came to confess theft or to pay old debts.

Not all Sommerfelder and Altkolonier in southern Manitoba were caught up by the new movement. On the contrary, they felt called to resist the new styles, which in their opinion were not so much spiritual as they were sensational. The result was a great deal of disharmony in the organized Sommerfelder congregations where ministers and members were of a different mind. According to J.D. Adrian, the first historian of the phenomenon, "Discord and disagreements of all kinds appeared. These had to do also with the style and manner of work to be done for the members in the congregation."[142]

The new approach to the young people brought a ready response, but they in turn expected innovation on other fronts. The new life now required that the Sommerfelder church officially institute, or at least allow, Sunday schools, choir practices, *Jugendvereine*, and even evening services. If necessary, the Bible was invoked, as for instance the nighttime visit with Jesus of Nicodemus, as justification for the holding of evening services.[143] The way the Bible was being used became one of the most contentious issues in the ministerial meetings. The older brethren felt that the traditions of the church were solidly grounded on moral and biblical principles, but the younger brethren, touched by the revivalistic spirit and its fundamentalist-type reasoning, resorted to proof-texting to defend and advance their new styles.

The matter of evening meetings became the focal point of contention, and discussions for this purpose were held in five meeting houses: Grossweide, Kronsweide, Rudnerweide, Sommerfeld, and Waldheim, but positions had already hardened. Some had made up their minds in favour of evening services and some against. A meeting of the older ministers by themselves concluded that the one church could no longer contain the two points of view and that the cause of unity and harmony would be better served by a clear separation of the two positions and of the ministers and members who represented them. Consequently, they asked all the families to either stay with the older ministers or go with the group of the four young ministers, hoping, no doubt, that most of the people would stay with them.

The four younger ministers, one in particular, had had no intentions of founding a new church. They wanted only to renew the old one, but they felt their position had become untenable. P.S. Zacharias held out "until the elder accused him of just trying to be contentious and then his mind was made up too."[144] The four ministers resolved not to cultivate any enmity against the Sommerfelder elder or ministers so as to avoid any further falling out, and some communication was in fact maintained so that some time later some Sommerfelder ministers attended a Rudnerweider ministerial meeting to discuss matters of mutual concern. "Such working together," it was said at the time, "can bring us closer together."[145] However, the end result of the realignment was that 1,200 baptized members, with 1,600 unbaptized young people and children, decided to go with the younger ministers advocating revival and reform.[146]

The division of the Sommerfelder church into two groups was complete, except for the formal essentials, which included "organization," of which the most important elements were a membership list and the election of a bishop. According to tradition, a church required a bishop who was selected and ordained if at all possible in the presence of another bishop. There were three possibilities—P.A. Toews of the Sommerfelder, D. Schulz of the Bergthaler, or J.P. Bueckert of the Blumenorter. Bishop David Schulz was chosen. He agreed, and on January 8, 1937, W.H. Falk was elected and a month later, on February 4, ordained as bishop of the newly named Rudnerweider Mennonite Church, the name being derived from the village in which all of these events took place.

Most of the Rudnerweider innovations were in the context of the former tradition. There was no new doctrinal statement and some of the old practices, like baptism by pouring and the use of the catechism in preparation for baptism, were accepted. On the other hand, the Rudnerweider used non-fermented juice instead of wine at communion since "the tendency to excess among the ministers in the old traditions had been more than repulsive to the young 'ministers.' "[147] The instruction of the young took on a personal character. Candidates for baptism were visited personally by a minister, repeatedly if necessary, to give "counsel concerning the Christian life and . . . sex problems."[148] The Rudnerweider preaching style was extemporaneous without a manuscript written into a scribbler or notebook, as had been the tradition among the Sommerfelder.

The possibility of uniting with another group, rather than remaining a separate denomination, was considered. Overtures were made in two directions, the Bergthaler and the Kleine Gemeinde, but the former group could not guarantee the acceptance of the ministers as Bergthaler ministers and the latter group denied the visiting ministers, seated on the platform, the right to participate in communion.[149] Discussions were held and exploratory visits were made by Rudnerweider ministers with respect to joining the Manitoba Mennonite Conference or the Conference of Mennonites in Canada, but the ministers were not unanimous on the issue and so the matter was postponed year after year until it wasn't an issue any more.[150] The Rudnerweider agreed to support the MCI in 1940 and the Elim Bible School a year later.[151]

Fragmentation in Southern Ontario

Meanwhile, a movement for change was working itself out also among one branch of the Swiss Mennonites in Ontario, namely the Old Order Mennonites. The Old Order Mennonites, it will be remembered, were those Mennonites who in the late nineteenth century resisted not only the rapid acculturation allowed by the New Mennonites, but also the more moderate accommodation tolerated by the Old Mennonites. The resistance phenomenon at the time was general in both Ontario and several American states. The "Old Order" designation was never official but it became a popular, and as time went on, unavoidable, label to describe those who followed the "*alte Ordnung*" (old order), meaning the traditional style of life, including the religious and liturgical, the cultural and linguistic, and the economic and agricultural aspects of life.

The Old Order Mennonites had literally "frozen" their cultural norms and forms as they were at the time of the break with the Mennonite Conference of Ontario in 1889. The Old Mennonites had changed their religious language from German to English, had adopted the Sunday school, four-part singing, and other innovations, and had accepted some forms of modernization like the automobile and the telephone. But the Old Order Mennonites had successfully resisted all of these. They continued to be a rural people exclusively, to send their children to school at most through the eighth grade or age 14, whichever came first, and to elect only lay ministers, who served without any remuneration whatsoever. And, what was most pertinent for the tensions of the 1930s, they travelled by horse and buggy or by public transportation only. Any members who purchased an automobile or who installed a private telephone were not admitted to communion. They were said to be out of fellowship.

Not all of the believers could draw the line of their nonconformity to the world so precisely. Thus, some succumbed to these convenient methods of transportation and communication and, knowing that they were causing offence, stayed away from communion. Such abstinence from the ordinance was, of course, not a long-term solution to the problem. Eventually, the entire church would have to move in the direction of the dissidents or they would have to leave altogether and seek membership in a more tolerant congregation.

In the Waterloo area at least, only the latter option existed. As we have seen, it had happened already in the 1920s that Old Order people bought cars and/or installed telephones, stayed away from communion, and eventually joined another church. The rapid growth of the sister Floradale and St. Jacobs congregations during this time and the founding of the Old Mennonite congregation in Elmira were partly attributable to this movement. And it was partly the fear that the whole Old Order body would go in that direction that caused a smaller but even stricter Old Order group, the so-called David Martin group, to take its uncompromising stand. With the David Martin Old Order, deviations from the accepted norms meant not only the denial of communion but also the immediate forfeiture of membership, in other words, excommunication.

The Old Order Mennonites in Waterloo County were really not in immediate danger, because the majority held fast to the principle that nonconformity meant not having telephones and cars. The minority that felt otherwise, however, was never exhausted. Every year and, as we shall see, every decade saw additional people coming to the conclusion that buying into new ways of doing things was not necessarily a sign of pride or a moral succumbing to the world, but only a practical and convenient way of living one's life, as well as overcoming the "hypocrisy" of using other people's phones and driving in other people's cars.

One such person was Ananias Martin, a farmer just north of Waterloo, who was troubled by the fact that his neighbours, who had a telephone, were not allowed to take communion.[152] Yet, they of all people served all their neighbours best of all by receiving and transmitting messages for others and generally being the centre of a community communications network. The paradox of such ostracism also became Martin's experience. During the week he and his kind served the neighbours with their transportation and communication needs, but on communion Sunday they could not be part of the fellowship with those same people. After he bought a new Chevrolet car in 1929 — "with four-wheel brakes and back fenders" — his service to the community multiplied by the month, but he couldn't take communion. He, of course, also proved what the opposition feared most about the car, namely that it would become a connection with unwanted influences. The Ananias Martin family, like others in their situation, began to attend revival meetings and Sunday school elsewhere. By 1934, they had "stood apart" long enough and so the entire family joined the St. Jacobs Old Mennonite Church.

While the Old Mennonites were a convenient option for the Ananias Martins, this did not prove to be the case for others. By that time the cultural gap between the Old Order Mennonites and the Old Mennonites had widened further, making it increasingly difficult to make the move from one to the other all in one step. In the 1930s, Ananias Martin was the exception to the rule. There were few like him, who had already put himself on the voters' list during the war in order to vote against conscription and who was now ready to put a piano in his home for the musical education of his children. The implication of this action was greater even than he realized, because the piano in his house became, eventually, the cornerstone of a county-wide Mennonite choral group.[153]

Others, not at all inclined to modernize to that extent and looking around for other possibilities, discovered they could take communion with Mennonites at Markham, where the Old Order bishop and his entire church had followed a less rigid and conservative course since the 1920s. It must be pointed out that the Old Order Mennonites at that time were located, as they had been at the time of the division in 1889, not only in Waterloo (chiefly Woolwich Township) County, but also in York (chiefly Markham Township) and Haldimand counties.[154] The annual conferences of the Old Order were held alternately in these three districts.[155] It so happened that those in Woolwich were stricter about modernization than were all the others. As indicated, members there could be ostracized for installing a telephone or buying a car, and in fact in 1930 about 10 families were thus affected and knew not where to go, since the Old Mennonites were too modern even for them.

This was not the case in York and Haldimand, where a gradual acceptance of both the telephone and the car had occurred without the users being censured in any way. Indeed, for the sake of the young people, even the English language was already being used. In 1931, Woolwich Bishop Ezra L. Martin concluded that the difference between the Waterloo and the Markham Old Order groups was too great for them to continue working together.[156] Under the leadership of Bishop Levi Grove at Markham, supported by his ministers and deacons, the group of Old Order progressives now identified themselves as the Markham Conference, which assumed responsibility also for small remnants of Old Order members at Rainham and Cayuga in Haldimand County, a total of about 88 members.[157] This left a few Old Order families, not inclined to go along with the Markhamer, who "came to Woolwich for communion for the remainder of their lives."[158]

Through Bishop Grove the Markham Conference accepted into its fellowship the non-communicating Old Order members at Waterloo and an affiliation was also established with like-minded groups in Indiana, Ohio, and Pennsylvania, where there also had been a gradual, though sometimes not so gradual, shift away from tradition. As a matter of fact, in the same way that the Old Order identity was first established in the States, so the departure therefrom, in the form of moderate adjustments, occurred there first. Thus, in Indiana and Ohio, a break between the orthodox and the moderates had already come in 1907.[159] The former were called "horse-and-buggy" Mennonites and the latter "black-bumper" Mennonites. The "black-bumper" designation arose from the practice by the moderates of painting black all the chrome of the new cars, as a way of fighting pride or at least the appearance thereof, much chrome on cars apparently being a status symbol at the time.

It should not be assumed, however, that the Canadian Old Orders took all their cues from the U.S.A. On the contrary, one aspect of cultural adjustment on their part, namely a more stylish bonnet as headgear for the women, was never accepted among the American Old Orders because it was "too fancy." The bonnet, which was normative in Ontario, was simply the so-called "Queen Victoria bonnet," which had been copied from English and Scottish neighbours at a time when such cultural borrowing was not a sign of pride or indicative of any other sin.[160] Now it was an altogether appropriate style because the Old Orders were still living essentially in the Victorian age.

Bishop Levi Grove at Markham was also a step ahead of his "black-bumper" counterparts in the U.S.A., particularly in Pennsylvania, where he happened to be present "when the idea of a chromeless car was introduced." Not only was the car to be chromeless, but of the open, touring-automobile style, in other words, more like the black open buggy. Unacceptable were "late model cars, at that time referring to solid tops and glass windows."[161] Bishop Grove found himself in the embarrassing position of driving an unacceptable car, a closed car with windows and a solid top, unacceptable, that is, to the "black-bumper" (Weaverland Conference) people in Pennsylvania, whose fellowship and support he craved. According to Leonard Freeman:

> It is said that Bishop Levi Grove had to change autos to coincide with this decision. It has also been recalled that because touring cars were no longer manufactured auto dealers imported some from other states to Pennsylvania to fill the demand there among the Mennonites, and that touring cars became quite expensive so that by 1935, when Weaverland Conference decided to accept solidly closed cars, but only *out of style* models, these auto dealers were left with some very expensive cars on their lots, with no sale for them.[162]

The adjustment allowed Bishop Grove to be "in fellowship," meaning that he and his ministers were admissible to the pulpits of the Weaverland Conference and the Weaverland bishops and ministers were "in fellowship" with the Markham Conference. All of this was already happening when the formal break between Markham and Waterloo Old Order bishops came in 1931. The considerable geographic separation of the two groups made the ecclesiastic separation less painful, but pain there was none the less, because once again, Mennonite division meant the separation of some families.[163]

The formal 1931 "severance" gave to Waterloo families with automobiles—there were about 10 immediately—the option of taking communion and membership at Markham, and by the same token "horse-and-buggy" Mennonites still remaining at Markham could, and did, take communion in Woolwich. The traffic, however, was more in the other direction, and by 1939 the Markham Conference had 51 members in Woolwich.

Meanwhile, the Old Orders in Woolwich had selected by lot and ordained Jesse Bauman as bishop to assist Ezra Martin, who had been partly disabled by a farm accident and who was also showing his age. Jesse Bauman, however, had already distinguished himself as a nonconformist preacher, his style having partly been determined by the fact that Old Order young people were being attracted to another religious option, namely the evangelical gatherings of the Plymouth Brethren, sponsored from Guelph at Wallenstein and Hawkesville.[164] The *frema geisht* (strange spirit) of Bauman was troublesome, but Ezra Martin pacified critics of Bauman's preaching, giving the wise counsel "that the same ideas were preached by Jesse as the other ministers but a different wording was used."[165] When Ezra Martin died on March 22, 1939, leaving Bishop Jesse Bauman alone, the differences that had developed—"a row of automobiles, owned by non-communing members, was parked outside the fence at nearly every worship service"[166]—could no longer be reconciled. Three sessions of the ministerial meeting—Bishop Bauman, the ministers, and the deacons—produced no consensus.[167]

Bishop Bauman withdrew from the Old Order just in time "to serve as bishop and minister in the Waterloo area" for the Markhamers, who were in the process of forming their own congregation. Shortly after, in June, the Markham-Waterloo Conference came into being formally, as the Waterloo and Markham "black-bumper" groups recognized each other. Bauman's pilgrimage, however, had not yet come to an end. The Waterloo section of the Markham-

Waterloo Conference was not all of one mind. Two sets of motivations and expectations were present, inasmuch as two types of modernization were at work. Bauman and his followers from the Old Order wanted prayer meetings and Bible study and hoped to find those innovations in the Waterloo group of the newly established Markham-Waterloo Conference. But the group they were joining wanted cars and telephones. As the group's historian wrote:

> [one group] wanted more modern conveniences than the Old
> Order allowed, and one group wanted more spiritual activities
> than the Markham-Waterloo Conference had agreed to.[168]

Bishop Abraham Smith, successor in 1936 to the deceased Levi Grove, supported by other "black-bumper" ministers from Indiana, Ohio, and Pennsylvania, sided with the Markham tradition already established. Consequently, Jesse Bauman's position became untenable and before the end of the year Smith discharged Bauman, who proceeded with about 100 followers to take one more step. Fortunately for the Mennonites, the Bauman people did not form another new group, though some joined the Plymouth Brethren. Instead, most found a new home in the Elmira and St. Jacobs congregations of the Mennonite Conference of Ontario.[169]

Thereafter, the situation normalized for the Markham-Waterloo Conference, though a pattern of Mennonite ecclesiastical migration had now been established. And the Old Order couldn't have been entirely unhappy with the situation, because once more unity and harmony existed within the group. More importantly, a formula had been found for dealing in a non-disruptive way with every new group of nonconformists. The presence of two conservative bodies in the area, one less so than the other, provided a convenient and continuous release valve for dissenting members, the emergence of which was never-ending.

Since dissent had somewhere to go and the Old Order Mennonite community was now for all practical purposes limited to one geographic area, Waterloo County north and adjacent areas, it could build itself without disturbance and maintain its way of life without major interruptions in the years to come. And almost as if the presence of the Markhamer was welcomed, the Old Order readily agreed to share several of its meeting houses for use on alternate

Sundays, Martin's and Elmira immediately and North Woolwich a while later. One Sunday the "cars people" would meet and the next Sunday the "teams people" would meet.[170] Once again, division and separation had brought unity and peace.

The new conference grew rapidly in both areas. In Waterloo in 1940, about 300 persons attended communion. In that year, 43 young people were baptized, and three were ordained to the ministry. At Markham, "more young people were baptized . . . than they had ever experienced before, and . . . many young couples were married in the church."[171] Even people of non-Mennonite background were attracted, though not all stayed. Once inside, "they thought discipline was too strict and wanted more spiritual activity and freedom in dress and other restrictions, such as radio or record players."[172] But the liberalizers rarely all withdrew. Thus, the seeds were planted once again for tensions—and disintegration—in the years to come.

The Markhamer, while modernizing, definitely drew a line beyond which their own nonconformity did not permit them to go. Radios and musical instruments, for instance, were forbidden on the grounds that radio fostered frivolous thinking, undermined reverence, conditioned the personality for sensual living, reduced resistance to temptation, promoted a materialistic way of life, and instilled hatred towards certain classes and nations of people.[173]

Apart from the allowance of automobiles and telephones, the Markhamers were not much different from other Old Orders. Simplicity and modesty of life style remained a fundamental value, on Sundays and every day. The ministers continued to be chosen by lot from among the brethren, all or most of them farmers. The communion service remained central to the fellowship, and the inquiry service preceding it was still the time to process any conflicts and complaints. The young people of the Markhamer were encouraged not to seek their entertainment outside but to have their own gatherings for singing and games, harmless ones such as crokinole. Steady dating before there was any clear intention of marriage was discouraged. Fairs, shows, theatres, commercial transactions on Sundays, ornamentation on cars, life insurance, and other such practices of the world also were not tolerated.[174]

Thus it happened that new groups like the Markhamer and Rudnerweider confirmed and reinforced the essential nature of the

Canadian Mennonite reality, namely parochialism and denominationalism in the extreme, already so well-entrenched. Fragmentation, rather than federation, had the upper hand. In the context of
denominationalism, most leaders assumed they could best keep the
faith and the young people, and not, as David Toews felt, in a
substantial increase in inter-Mennonite activity and federation.

FOOTNOTES

1   Johann G. Rempel, "Bericht ueber die zu gruendende Ner-
    venheilanstalt," *Jahrbuch*, 1937, pp. 78–79.
2   Louis Hartz, *The Founding of New Societies: Studies in the History of
    the United States, Latin America, South Africa, Canada, and Australia*
    (New York: Harcourt, Brace & World, Inc., 1964), p. 3.
3   P.P. Tschetter, "Die Einheit der Kinder Gottes," *Jahrbuch*, 1935,
    p. 74.
4   J.B. Wiens, "Unser Verhalten andern Gemeinschaften gegenuber,"
    Jahrbuch, 1934, p. 33.
5   J.H. Janzen, "Modernismus—eine Gefahr fuer unsere Gemein-
    den," *Jahrbuch*, 1931, p. 62.
6   *Conference Journal* (NW), 1920, p. 14. The MBC also participated
    in Mennonite Mutual Fire Insurance in Alberta. *Conference Journal*
    (NW), 1939, p. 10.
7   In 1929, Presiding Elder A. Traub reported on his experiences at
    the Mennonite Brethren in Christ Conference at Albertown, Penn-
    sylvania: "So far as any aggressive forward movement was con-
    cerned, to our minds and from the standpoint of the smaller Confer-
    ences, there was nothing done. Unless General Conference changes
    its attitude, we may as well make up our minds that we shall have to
    continue to fight our own battles, solve our own problems and root or
    die." The suggestion from the North-West and Nebraska confer-
    ences that the Mennonite name be dropped was poorly received:
    ". . . others jumped onto it with both feet, evidently feeling that the
    poor ship would sink if its name was changed so the proposition was
    lost." *Conference Journal* (NW), 1929, pp. 14–15. See also *Confer-
    ence Journal* (NW), 1936, pp. 18–19.
8   Raymond Breton, "Institutional Completeness of Ethnic Communi-
    ties and the Personal Relations of Immigrants," *The American
    Journal of Sociology* 70:193–205; L. Driedger and G. Church,
    "Residential Segregation and Minorities," *Canadian Review of
    Sociology and Anthropology* 11:30–52.
9   Abe J. Dueck, *Concordia Hospital, 1928–1978* (Winnipeg: Men-
    nonite Hospital Society Concordia, 1978), p. 1.
10 A good example of this phenomenon is the Russlaender community
    of Coaldale. See Ted D. Regehr, "Mennonite Change: The Rise and

Decline of Mennonite Community Organizations at Coaldale, Alberta," *Mennonite Life* 32 (December 1977):13–22.

11   CMCA, XXII-A, Vol. 1389, File 1534, Minutes, Canadian Mennonite Board of Colonization, 14–15 November 1934.

12   Frank H. Epp, *Mennonite Exodus: The Rescue and Resettlement of the Russian Mennonites Since the Communist Revolution* (Altona: D. W. Friesen & Sons, Ltd., 1962), p. 297.

13   David Toews, "Immigration and Nothilfe," *Jahrbuch*, 1934, p. 75.

14   *Ibid.*, pp. 70–71.

15   *Ibid.*, p. 74.

16   David Toews, "Neuorganisation der Canadian Mennonite Board of Colonization," *Jahrbuch*, 1934, pp. 75–77.

17   The initial members were as follows: Conference of Mennonites in Canada: D.H. Epp, Rosthern; J.J. Dyck, Laird; J.J. Thiessen, Saskatoon; J.G. Rempel, Langham; J.J. Klassen, Dundurn; Jakob Gerbrandt, Drake; G.W. Sawatsky, Carman; J.P. Bueckert, Reinland; B.B. Wiens, Waterloo; Peter P. Epp, Morden; Peter J. Dyck, Starbuck; D.P. Enns, Rosthern; J.H. Janzen, Waterloo; Northern District of Mennonite Brethren Churches: B.B. Janz, Coaldale; P.P. Thiessen, Saradis; J.P. Wiebe, Herbert; Jakob Lepp, Dalmeny; C.F. Klassen, Winnipeg; C.A. De Fehr, Winnipeg; F.C. Thiessen, Winnipeg; Mennonite Conference of Ontario: S.F. Coffman; and the Alberta-Saskatchewan Mennonite Conference: Alvah S. Bowman.

18   *Jahrbuch*, 1936, p. 88.

19   CMCA, XXII-A, Vol. 1389, File 1534, Minutes, Canadian Mennonite Board of Colonization, 14–15 November 1934.

20   Mennonite Central Committee (Canada) did not come into being until 1963. At that time the relief, peace, immigration, and related elements of the Mennonites and Brethren in Christ were amalgamated into the one MCC (Canada) with a wide mandate and representatation. Its provincial counterparts brought together annually in representative assemblies all, or almost all, the Mennonite and Brethren in Christ congregations of the provinces. The proposed reorganization and CMBC, MLSB, and ZMIK foreshadowed much of this later development.

21   See references to the decline of the Board as an inter-Mennonite organization in Esther Ruth Epp, "The Origins of Mennonite Central Committee (Canada)," (M.A. thesis, University of Manitoba, 1980), pp. 29–30.

22   "Die Einheit der Kinder Gottes," *Unser Blatt* 1 (April 1926):141–42. The quote is a paraphrase of the editorial.

23   John A. Toews, *A History of the Mennonite Brethren Church* (Fresno, Cal.: Board of Christian Literature, General Conference of Mennonite Brethren Churches, 1975), p. 136.

24 *Jahrbuch*, 1929, p. 10. See also C.C. Peters, "Suendenbekenntnis," *Jahrbuch*, 1929, pp. 33–42.

25 CGC, XV-31.2, Abe Stobbe, "The Agassiz Settlement," February 1975.

26 The author, having lived in British Columbia, remembers this only too well. There was a period of about 15 years when the thing for "spiritual-minded" people to do was to join the Mennonite Brethren Church. This period began with the rebaptism of C.C. Peters in 1932 and crested about 1947 when Victor Adrian was baptized by the Brethren. The son of a prominent CM family, he became a prominent MB leader.

27 Based on T.D. Regehr. CGC, XV-31.2, "1930-Coaldale."

28 John A. Toews, pp. 369, 370.

29 Some Conference congregations also emphasized cataclysmic conversions and some Brethren were known for their tolerance in social matters, but the characterization of the two groups none the less applies in a general way.

30 I.H. Tiessen, ed., *Er Fuehret... Geschichte der Ontario M.B. Gemeinden, 1924–1957* (n.p., 1957), pp. 10–13.

31 *Ibid.*, p. 20.

32 *Verhandlungen* (ND), 1939, p. 37.

33 Protokoll (Ontario District Conference of M.B. Churches), 1940, p. 15.

34 Alberta, MB: CMBS, BA 100, "Register of Archival Materials Created by the Conference of the Mennonite Brethren Church of Alberta and Housed at the Center for Mennonite Brethren Studies, Fresno, California"; CM: David P. Neufeld, "Mennonite Conference of Alberta after Twenty-Five Years," *Mennonite Life* 9 (April 1954):57; British Columbia, MB: CMBS, BB 100, Protokoll, 21 June 1931; G.H. Suckau, "British Columbia Provincial Mennonite Brethren Conference," *Mennonite Encyclopedia* 1:431; CM: *Jahrbuch*, 1937, p. 12; Manitoba, MB: CMBS, BC 100, Protokoll, 14 June 1929; CM: Lawrence Klippenstein, ed. *In Quest of Brothers: A Yearbook Commemorating Twenty-Five Years of Life Together in the Conference of Mennonites in Manitoba, 1946–71* (Winnipeg: Conference of Mennonites in Manitoba, 1972), p. 3; Ontario, MB: CMBS, BD 100, "Protokoll der Bruderberatung der Vertreter der Mennoniten Bruedergemeinden in Ontario: von Hespeler, New Hamburg, Port Rowan, Vineland, Leamington (Essex) und Kitchener, Ontario am 31. January 1932"; CM: Johann Wichert, "Entstehung und Entwicklung der Vereinigten Mennoniten-Gemeinden in Ontario," in *Jahrbuch der Vereinigten Mennoniten Gemeinden in Ontario, Canada*, 1949 (Conference of United Mennonite Churches in Ontario, 1949), p. 15; Saskatchewan, MB: CMBS, BF 310, "Protokoll von der ersten Saskatchewan Provinzial

Konferenz der MB Gemeinde, abgehalten am 11. Juni 1946 zu Saskatoon, Saskatchewan." It is important to note that North and South Saskatchewan conferences had existed since *c.* 1899 and *c.* 1909, respectively, and that they continued to exist until *c.* 1964; CM: *Jahrbuch*, 1939, p. 75. Note also that the Alberta, Ontario, and Saskatchewan dates for Conference Mennonites represent the founding of provincial ministerial conferences, from which the delegate conferences evolved.

35 *Calendar of Appointments*, 1935, p. 16; S.F. Coffman, "The Mennonite Board of Colonization," *Calendar of Appointments*, 1938, n.p.; S.F. Coffman, "Immigration and Colonization Board," *Calendar of Appointments*, 1940, p. 21.

36 John S. Weber, *History of S.F. Coffman, 1872-1954: The Mennonite Churchman* (graduate research paper, University of Waterloo, 1975), pp. 156-70.

37 *Calendar of Appointments*, 1934, p. 27.

38 CGC, II-2.1.2.2.2, Mennonite Conference of Ontario, Secretary's Records; a close reading of the Conference and Executive Committee Minutes leaves this strong impression. See also *Calendar of Appointments*, 1927-28, p. [18].

39 E.S. Hallman, "Winnipeg the North-West," *Mennonite Year-Book and Directory*, 1924, pp. 16-17; C.F. Derstine, "A Five Thousand Mile Evangelistic Tour in the Canadian North-West," *Christian Monitor* 21 (November 1929):340-41; *Calendar of Appointments*, 1941-42, p. [11]; Oscar Burkholder, "The Churches in the Canadian North-West," *Mennonite Year-Book and Directory*, 1931, pp. 24-26.

40 CGC, II-2.1.2.2.2, Mennonite Conference of Ontario, Secretary's Records, Simon Gingerich, Secretary, Mennonite General Conference, to Gilbert Bergey, 6 October 1931.

41 The founding date of the Mennonite Conference of Ontario is *c.* 1820. Its *Calendar of Appointments* goes back only to 1834. The Mennonite General Conference was established in 1896. See *Calendar of Appointments*, 1941-42, p. [21].

42 *Calendar of Appointments*, 1926-27, p. [15]; CGC, II-2.1.2.2.2, Mennonite Conference of Ontario, Secretary's Records, Letter to Ontario A.M. Conference, 12 June 1934; C.F. Derstine, "The Canadian Field During 1928," *Mennonite Year-Book and Directory*, 1929, p. 21.

43 It should also be noted that the Conference had admitted the River Brethren into the Mennonite Aid Union (*Calendar of Appointments*, 1917, p. 15), but a similar request from the Mennonite Brethren in Christ was denied (*Calendar of Appointments*, 1920-21, p. [15]).

44 John A. Toews, *A History of the Mennonite Brethren Church* (Fresno, Cal.: Board of Christian Literature, General Conference of Mennonite Brethren Churches, 1975), pp. 195, 200-2.

45 John A. Toews, p. 198; see *Stadtmission* (city mission) reports in *Verhandlungen* (ND) in the 1930s for references to Minneapolis.
46 *Verhandlungen* (GC), 1921, p. 5; *Verhandlungen* (GC), 1927, pp. 66–69; *Verhandlungen* (GC), 1921, p. 54; *Verhandlungen* (GC), 1930, pp. 59–60.
47 *Verhandlungen* (GC), 1927, pp. 66–68.
48 See, for example, *Verhandlungen* (ND), 1931, pp. 14–30, 34–42, 44.
49 *Verhandlungen* (ND), 1933, p. 26. The reference here, in all probability, is to Old Colony Mennonites in the Saskatoon area, but the attitude expressed had a general application.
50 "Aeussere Mission," *Verhandlungen* (ND), 1936, pp. 16–17.
51 *Verhandlungen* (ND) 1933, pp. 10, 58–66. Even B.B. Janz, who understood better than any other MB the crucial role of the Board, represented the position that relief for Russia and China could be sent via Hillsboro, though he recognized the work of the Board in helping extremely needy cases in Canada. See "Hilfeleistung," *Verhandlungen* (ND), 1931, p. 42.
52 Note that David Toews was given a welcome hearing, but relief *actions* were directed via Hillsboro. See "Hilfeleistung," *Verhandlungen* (ND), 1935, pp. 39–47.
53 "Hilfswerk," *Verhandlungen* (ND), 1934, pp. 62–76.
54 *Verhandlungen* (ND), 1936, p. 79.
55 Samuel Floyd Pannabecker, *Open Doors: The History of the General Conference Mennonite Church* (Newton, Kansas: Faith and Life Press, 1975), p. 121.
56 Jakob Gerbrandt, "Was die Konferenz gewirkt hat und noch wirken sollte," *Jahrbuch*, 1932, p. 32.
57 P.A. Rempel, "Die Konferenz — ein Mittel zur Bewahrung unserer Gemeinden," *Jahrbuch*, 1932, pp. 45–48.
58 J.G. Rempel, *Fuenfzig Jahre Konferenzbestrebungen, 1902–1952*, p. 142.
59 *Ibid.*, p. 153.
60 These committees reported annually. See, for example, J.G. Rempel, p. 172.
61 *Ibid.*, pp. 24–25.
62 *Ibid.*
63 *Ibid.*, pp. 146–47.
64 *Ibid.*, pp. 194–95.
65 H.T. Klaassen, *Birth and Growth of the Eigenheim Mennonite Church, 1892–1974* (n.p., 1974), p. 43.
66 *Ibid.*, pp. 42–45.
67 *Ibid.*, p. 44.
68 H.T. Klaassen, pp. 46–47. See also J.G. Rempel, p. 209.
69 H.T. Klaassen, p. 47.
70 G.G. Neufeld, *Die Geschichte der Whitewater Mennoniten Gemeinde*

(Boissevain: The Author, 1967), p. 148 ff. Letter from a retired Manitoba elder to the author, June 1980. Isaak Klassen, p. 80 ff.

71 Helena M. Brown, *Bergthal Church: 1903 – 1978* (Didsbury, Alta.: Anniversary Committee, 1978), pp. 7, 10.

72 Jake I. Pauls, "History of Morden Bergthaler Mennonite Church" (research paper, Canadian Mennonite Bible College, 1966), pp. 18 – 20.

73 *Ibid.*, pp. 21 – 22.

74 The first issue was entitled *Konferenz-Bericht der 26. Konferenz der Mennoniten im mittleren Canada, Rosthern, Sask., den 2., 3. und 4. Juli 1928.*

75 "Konstitution der Konferenz der Mennoniten im mittleren Canada," *Jahrbuch*, 1931, pp. 3 – 4.

76 *Jahrbuch*, 1931, p. 7.

77 *Jahrbuch*, 1935, p. 21; *Jahrbuch*, 1937, pp. 82 – 83; *Jahrbuch*, 1938, pp. 27 – 28. See also S.F. Pannabecker, pp. 348 – 50.

78 *Jahrbuch*, 1929, pp. 8 – 9.

79 *Jahrbuch*, 1932, p. 18.

80 *Jahrbuch*, 1937, p. 12.

81 John G. Rempel easily integrated the two conferences in his own experience. He was longtime secretary of the Canadian conference and also a member of several committees in the General Conference (Peace and Gesangbuch, for instance). For him, the Canadian conference was a natural forum for reporting the latter.

82 *Jahrbuch*, 1940, pp. 15, 16.

83 *Jahrbuch*, 1930, p. 26.

84 D.D. Klassen, "Schulbericht von Manitoba," *Jahrbuch*, 1939, pp. 57 – 59. The 1938 – 39 statistics showed the following: Brueder 18; Conference Churches 20 (including Schoenwieser 6; Bergthaler 4; Blumenorter 3; Whitewater 3; Lichtenauer, Herold, Elim, and Misc. each 1); Sommerfelder 5; Rudnerweider and Kleine Gemeinde each 3; and Lutheran 1.

85 G.H. Peters, "Bericht ueber die Arbeit des von der Konferenz zu Winkler gewaehlten Komitees zwecks Vorbereitung der Gemeinden fuer die Uebernahme der mennonitischen Bildungsanstalten," *Jahrbuch*, 1931, pp. 47 – 49.

86 G.H. Peters, "Bericht des Schulkomitees von Manitoba fuer das Jahr 1931 – 32," *Jahrbuch*, 1932, p. 59.

87 J.H. Enns, "Ueber die Mennonitische Lehranstalt zu Gretna," *Jahrbuch*, 1936, p. 74.

88 "Schulsache," *Verhandlungen* (ND), 1931, pp. 31 – 34.

89 *Ibid.*, p. 33.

90 "Die Schulsache," *Verhandlungen* (ND), 1932, p. 48.

91 "Schulsache," *Verhandlungen* (ND), 1937, p. 19; *Verhandlungen* (ND), 1938, p. 22.

92 "Die Schulsache," *Verhandlungen* (ND), 1933, p. 76.

93   J.A. Toews, "Die Schulbestrebungen im Noerdlichen Distrikt der Mennoniten-Bruedergemeinden Canadas," *Verhandlungen* (ND), 1939, pp. 24–27.

94   "Regelung einer gewissen Angelegenheit," *Verhandlungen* (ND), 1941, pp. 56–57.

95   *Verhandlungen* (ND), 1941, pp. 15–17.

96   David D. Klassen, "Schulbericht von Manitoba," *Jahrbuch*, 1935, p. 78; "Bericht ueber die Rostherner Fortbildungschule," *Jahrbuch*, 1939, p. 55.

97   J.G. Rempel, p. 175.

98   *Jahrbuch*, 1930, p. 26.

99   *Jahrbuch*, 1935, p. 20. It was the gracious Benjamin Ewert who suggested that *Der Bote* become the official paper.

100   H.J. Gerbrandt, *Adventure in Faith: The Background in Europe and the Development in Canada of the Bergthaler Mennonite Church of Manitoba* (Altona, Man.: D.W. Friesen & Sons, Ltd., 1970), p. 117.

101   Frank H. Epp, "An Analysis of Germanism and National Socialism in the Immigrant Newspaper of a Canadian Minority Group, the Mennonites, in the 1930s" (Ph.D. dissertation, University of Minnesota, 1965), p. 309.

102   E. Derksen, "So wurde unsere Post: 50 Jahre Zeitungsgeschichte," *Die Post* L (31 December 1963):1–3.

103   See *Der mennonitische Immigranten-Bote* 5 (25 July 1928):1.

104   J.N. Hoeppner, "Wie steht es mit der Nachfolge Jesu in den Gemeinden?" *Jahrbuch*, 1936, p. 52.

105   *Jahrbuch*, 1936, p. 15; *Verhandlungen* (ND), 1937, pp. 61–65; *Jahrbuch*, 1937, p. 17. See also A.D., "Unsere werdende Nervenheilanstalt," *Warte-Jahrbuch*, 1943, pp. 50–55; Henrich Wiebe, "Ein Heim fuer harmlose Geisteskranke," *Warte-Jahrbuch*, 1943, pp. 55–56.

106   *Jahrbuch*, 1935, pp. 87–88.

107   Frank H. Epp, *Mennonite Exodus*, p. 309.

108   David Toews, "Immigration and Nothilfe," *Jahrbuch*, 1934, p. 67.

109   Johann G. Rempel, "Bericht ueber die zu gruendende Nervenheilanstalt," *Jahrbuch*, 1937, pp. 77–81.

110   "Unterstuetzung der Geisteskranken," *Verhandlungen* (ND), 1939, pp. 64–65.

111   *Jahrbuch*, 1939, p. 14. Some optimism in this regard was reported a year later. See *Jahrbuch*, 1940, pp. 41–42. Another year later, 1941, the Northern District encouraged "warm support" and an annual collection for the proposed institution. See "Nervenheilanstalt," *Verhandlungen* (ND), 1941, pp. 50–51.

112   *Jahrbuch*, 1936, p. 15; David Schulz, "Die Nervenheilanstalt," *Jahrbuch*, 1939, pp. 62–64.

113   John A. Toews, p. 173.
114   Abe J. Dueck, *Concordia Hospital, 1928–1978* (Winnipeg: Mennonite Hospital Society Concordia, 1978), pp. 13–15. The 1934 Northern District Conference did encourage the support of Concordia. See *Verhandlungen* (ND), 1934, p. 48.
115   Johann G. Rempel, pp. 77–81. It should be noted that the Northern District encouraged "warm support" and an annual collection for the project in 1941, but this encouragement did not have the strength of other authorized collections, as for instance, with respect to Tabor College. In other words, encouragement to hold a collection did not mean that a collection would be held. Besides, by 1941, other priorities had pushed this project far into the background.
116   *Jahrbuch*, 1928, p. 7.
117   CMCA, XXII-A, Vol. 1389, File 1534, Minutes, Canadian Mennonite Board of Colonization, 14–15 November 1934, pp. 1, 2.
118   *Ibid.*, p. 1.
119   *Ibid.*, p. 2.
120   CMCA, XXII-A, Vol. 1389, File 1534, Memorandum, "Kulturabteilung," presented to Canadian Mennonite Board of Colonization, 14 November 1934.
121   CMCA, XXII-A, Vol. 1389, File 1534, Minutes, Canadian Mennonite Board of Colonization, 14–15 November 1934, p. 3.
122   David Toews, "Bericht ueber die Publikationssache," *Jahrbuch*, 1937, pp. 90–91.
123   *Jahrbuch*, 1938, pp. 38, 41, 55.
124   *Jahrbuch*, 1938, p. 38.
125   *Jahrbuch*, 1936, p. 83.
126   P.J.B. Reimer, *The Sesquicentennial Jubilee: Evangelical Mennonite Conference, 1812–1962* (Steinbach: The Evangelical Mennonite Conference, 1962), p. 31 ff.
127   *Ibid.*, pp. 32–35.
128   For a review of religious developments arising from the immigration in the 1870s, see "The Church Struggle in Manitoba" in Frank H. Epp, *Mennonites in Canada, 1786–1920* (Toronto: Macmillan of Canada, 1974), pp. 283–300.
129   Gerhard Ens, "Johann D. Adrian," *Der Bote* 57 (17 December 1980):4.
130   Henry J. Gerbrandt, pp. 81, 91.
131   Henry J. Gerbrandt, "Wealth Is Rooted in People," *Mennonite Mirror* 1 (May 1972):11–12.
132   CGC, XV-31.2, "1930—Rudnerweide Mennonite Church," Isaac P. F. Friesen, "Kurzer Ueberblick ueber die Anfangsgeschichte der Evangelical Mennonite Mission Conference" (November 1979): 2.

133   Cornelius Krahn, "Old Colony Mennonites," *Mennonite Encyclopedia* 4:41.

134   The ordination sermon of Bishop Jacob Froese appears in Calvin Wall Redekop, *The Old Colony Mennonites: Dilemmas of Ethnic Minority Life* (Baltimore: The Johns Hopkins Press, 1969), pp. 253–56. See also CMCA vertical file for a paper on Jacob Froese.

135   Ron Sawatsky, "The History and Theology of the Old Colony Mennonites" (research paper, Conrad Grebel College, 1979), p. 39.

136   J.D. Adrian, *Die Entstehung der Rudnerweider Gemeinde* (Winnipeg: J.D. Adrian, 1958), pp. 8–9.

137   *Ibid.*

138   John G. Rempel, "Isaac P. Friesen," *Mennonite Encyclopedia* 2:405.

139   J.D. Adrian, p. 10.

140   *Ibid.*, p. 11.

141   Isaac P.F. Friesen, p. 3.

142   J.D. Adrian, p. 12.

143   Norman Friesen, "Revival Fires in Manitoba" (research paper, Mennonite Brethren Bible College, 1968), p. 13.

144   Walter Sawatsky, "History of the Evangelical Mennonite Mission Conference" (research paper, Goshen College, 1967), p. 8.

145   *Ibid.*, p. 9.

146   J.D. Adrian, pp. 14–15.

147   Frank Zacharias, quoted in Walter Sawatsky, p. 16.

148   Walter Sawatsky, p. 22.

149   *Ibid.*, p. 23.

150   *Ibid.*, p. 38.

151   *Ibid.*, p. 39.

152   Interview by the author with Ananias Martin, 18 April 1976.

153   Abner Martin, the founder of the Menno Singers in the 1950s, was the son of Ananias. Another choral group, called the Nightingale Choir, was led by Harold Schiedel.

154   L.J. Burkholder, *A Brief History of the Mennonites in Ontario* (Markham, Ont.: Mennonite Conference of Ontario, 1935), p. 199.

155   CGC, VIII-2.1, Isaac G. Martin, "The Story of Markham-Waterloo Mennonite Conference," p. 12.

156   *Ibid.*

157   Aden Frey, "The Markham-Waterloo Conference of Ontario" (research paper, Conrad Grebel College, 1972):4.

158   Isaac G. Martin, p. 12.

159   From notes by Leonard Freeman on Markham-Waterloo Conference. CGC, XV-31.2, "1930 — Waterloo-Markham."

160   Leonard Freeman, p. 4.

161   *Ibid.*, pp. 6–7.

162   *Ibid.*, p. 7.
163   *Ibid.*, p. 9.
164   Glenn Brubacher, "The Frema Geisht" (research paper, Eastern Mennonite College, n.d.), pp. 5 – 11; Allan G. Felstead, "A Socio-Historical Analysis of the Sectarian Divisions in the Mennonite Church of Waterloo County, 1849 – 1939" (M.A. thesis, University of Waterloo, 1978), p. 98.
165   Glenn Brubacher, p. 14; Leonard Freeman, p. 12.
166   *Ibid.*
167   Isaac G. Martin, p. 14.
168   Leonard Freeman, p. 13.
169   Glenn Brubacher, p. 18.
170   CGC, XV-31.2, "1930 — Waterloo-Markham," Lecture at CGC by Noah Martin, 16 March 1972.
171   Leonard Freeman, p. 11, 13.
172   *Ibid.*, p. 13.
173   Aden Frey, p. 11.
174   *Ibid.*, pp. 29 – 40.

10. Keeping the Young People

Who has the young people has the future — J.J. KLASSEN.[1]

The interest of the church in education lies in her interest in her young people — S.F. COFFMAN.[2]

MENNONITE SEPARATISM and denominationalism were at least partly rooted in the positive impulse towards self-preservation, through the winning and keeping of the young people. Without them, all the leaders knew, there was no continuity for the Mennonite way of life, no perpetuity for the congregational communities and their values. In the words of one elder, the best "ornament for the family, the church, and society" is a generation of young people pleasing to God.[3] And, while there was complete unanimity on the importance of every new generation in the Mennonite scheme of things, there was some divergence on how the loyalty of the young was to be won. Educational endeavours for children and young people, however, were general, and in the 1930s manifested especially with the Bible school movement.[4]

History revealed a wide spectrum of approaches to the winning of the young people. After the Great War, the Swiss in Canada and the U.S.A. knew that a rediscovery of, and a return to, the fundamentals of the faith was the highest priority. A large group of Kanadier was

447

convinced that escaping the nationalistic public schools of Canada was absolutely essential. The Russlaender knew that they had to flee communization in Russia. The Rudnerweider believed there was hope only in new experiences and styles of spirituality.[5] The Markhamer believed that the keeping of the young required just a slight adjustment to modernity. The Conference Mennonites needed a new catechism, a new hymnbook, and lots of education.[6] The Mennonite Brethren needed evangelism for every congregation, every year if possible, and a strict discipline. And so on.

The approaches to be taken varied with the leaders. H.H. Ewert of the Mennonite Collegiate Institute for over 40 years saw continuity only if the Mennonites produced a never-ending line of bilingual teachers, infused with religious values, for the public schools serving Mennonite children. A.H. Unruh believed the accent should be placed on Sunday school teachers and preachers who had four years of Bible school and maybe two years of Tabor College to make up a theology degree. Jacob R. Bender was convinced the time had come for the Amish to start preaching in English to the young people. Oscar Burkholder wanted the schools to teach pre-millennialism, the imminent end of the age, and nonconformity in this age as essential preparation for what was to come. J.J. Hildebrand and all "conservative" Mennonites wanted closed settlements. David Toews and all "progressive" Mennonites were convinced that adequate organizations and a full range of programs and institutions were essential. For him, the responsibilities of the Conference of which he was moderator were first of all to the children and the young people.[7]

The threatened loss of the young people was not a new phenomenon for the Mennonite churches, at least not for the Swiss, who had been in North America for over 200 years and in Canada over 100. The religious upheavals and realignments of the nineteenth century were in part a response to the decline in membership in Old Mennonite congregations.[8] In some cases, the loss was close to 50 per cent in the first generation and higher in succeeding generations.[9]

The Dutch Mennonites, who had arrived more recently from Russia in the 1870s and 1920s, and between those times in much smaller numbers also from the U.S.A. and Prussia, had thus far escaped serious losses, but the conditions in the past so conducive to the keeping of the young were giving way to new situations. The exclusive Mennonite colonies as self-sufficient economic, social, and religious units were gone forever. Settlement patterns in the 1920s and 1930s scattered both newcomers and old-timers ever so thinly across the five provinces.

There was hardly a conference where the needs of young people and children weren't discussed.[10] Elder Daniel Loewen in 1929 made the point that the greater scattering of the Mennonites and the greater involvement with, and influences from, the wider community had resulted in the loss of many young people.[11] Besides, those who were leaving were among the most talented. Ambition, vocational pursuits, and social contacts were largely responsible for the losses. Loewen wanted residential centres in the cities and schools that combined secular and sacred learning. J.N. Hoeppner, a Bergthaler educator, expressed the view in 1936 that the young people outside the church were becoming a bigger problem than the young people inside the church.[12] Factors contributing to the loss of the young people, it was explained, were jobs far away from home, "foreign" schools, external propaganda, the social events of the wider community, the language, and the conservative stance of the older people.[13]

Benjamin Ewert, an itinerant minister for the Conference of Mennonites in Canada, noted that there were anywhere up to 500 post offices where there were Mennonite settlers, but that many settlements had no Sunday school, no youth society, and some not even any preaching services.[14]

There were not only 500 post offices but at least 500 public schools, 500 general stores, 500 elevators and blacksmith shops, 500 implement and fuel dealers, in all of which the Mennonite frontier was touching the Canadian frontier and where Canadianization was most rapid and effective.[15] To be sure, Mennonites resisted anglicization as they had russification, but they soon learned to acknowledge that the cultural environment here was more congenial and much less threatening, if only the children wouldn't accept English as their conversational language quite so rapidly.[16]

Acknowledging this fact, David Toews regretted at least once that it had not been possible to found large and closed settlements for the Mennonites.[17] After all, the loss of young people was a rare occurrence in the days when the congregations existed in isolated communities. Perhaps Toews and others felt instinctively that the external frontier with its assimilationist impact, and the internal fragmentation, were really not in their favour and that gradual disintegration of

North American Mennonite society, later predicted by Walter Quiring, could already be under way.[18]

A co-operative and federal approach to most Mennonite problems having been rejected for the time being, and flights into further isolation no longer an easy option, the fragmented Mennonites accepted the methods of the frontier in order to ward off its dangers just a little longer. All or most of the institutions which now became important in the keeping of the young people were borrowed from the outside. As will be seen, these included the Sunday school and the first boys' and girls' clubs, the Christian endeavour, literary society, and other youth movements, music festivals and singing schools, and last but not least, the Bible schools, as well as a serious look at the professional and salaried ministry. Thus, the effort to keep the young people meant greater dependence on institutions to reinforce the Mennonite way of life.[19]

Children and Sunday Schools

None of the approaches to the keeping of the young people could overlook the emphasis on the home, the most fundamental of Mennonite institutions, and on the role of parents, especially the mothers. Children, said one church elder, had to be wanted by the parents, offspring they had prayed about to the Lord. And children should receive an education of the heart (*Herzensbildung*), which the parents alone could provide.[20] Education, he said, should consist of more than just "pounding knowledge into the heads of the young."[21] All the schools were emphasizing the acquisition of knowledge, but education (*Bildung*) of the heart was as important as knowledge (*Wissen*) for the head. The enlightenment of the head should not leave the heart empty. The best and the most successful means of guiding children and young people aright was the right example provided in the home.[22] Hence, the foremost contribution of the woman to the Mennonite society was as a mother who followed such biblical examples as Jochebeth the mother of Moses, Hanna the mother of Eli, Mary the mother of Jesus, and Lois the mother of Timothy.[23]

> Such mothers who themselves are children of God, and whose
> main concern it is to raise their children also as children of
> God, will do their greatest service to the congregation through

their children. Mothers are the natural educators of a people. No school and no church can replace them.[24]

One of the institutions already strong among some of the Swiss congregations in Ontario, notably the Old Mennonites and the New Mennonites, was the Sunday school, a most useful supplement to the training in the home. Although the first Sunday schools had been held in the 1840s, they were not quickly or universally accepted.[25] At that time, the Sunday school was supported by some and opposed by others because it pointed to a language transition, to innovative ideas and practices, and to the use of educational materials other than the Bible. Opinion on the matter remained divided in the church, until the 1889 separation of the Old Order Mennonites from the Old Mennonites ended the debate. The first Sunday school convention in the Old Mennonite Church in North America was held in Kitchener a year later, and in 1916 the Ontario Mennonite Sunday School Conference was organized with its own constitution, yet it was responsible to the parent body, the Old Mennonite Conference of Ontario.

The purpose of the organization was "to promote, unify, and safeguard our Sunday school interests."[26] All members of congregations, including those of "sister conferences of like faith," were members. An annual meeting, usually held on a weekend late in August or early in September, dealt with such themes as the Sunday school itself, young people's Bible meetings, mission work, and the Christian life. Typical topics were those in the 1920 program: the benefits of total abstinence, contending for the faith, how the Sunday school should affect the growth of the church, influences which the Sunday school should counteract, the superintendent's responsibility to the Sunday school, and the value of missionary education.[27]

While the Sunday schools themselves were quite limited in terms of the time devoted to them — at most an hour a week — their overall impact was diverse. By the mid-1930s, for instance, the Mennonite Conference of Ontario counted 29 such schools with an enrolment of nearly 4,000.[28] According to Oscar Burkholder, it was a movement of multiple influences, including the promotion of good literature through the establishment of libraries, the advancement of missions, and the acceptance of systematic giving.[29]

By that time, the neighbouring Amish Mennonite Sunday School

Conference, first established in 1922, had become a parallel institution, which co-operated with the Old Mennonite Sunday School Conferences by conducting their annual sessions on alternate Labour Day weekends.[30] As with the Old Mennonites, so also with the Amish Mennonites the Sunday school found its earliest acceptance as a German-language school.[31] Only later were lesson helps permitted, and only in the 1930s did the English language gain entrance. For at least a generation after its inception, the Amish Sunday School Conference was "the most popular and best attended meeting of the Amish in Ontario."[32] The greatest problem was to accommodate the crowds, and at times large tents were rented for this purpose.

The Sunday school provided the avenue for greater lay participation in the work of the church. Lay participants in turn demanded an innovative leadership, which then stood in sharp contrast to the ordained leaders, who tended to be more conservative, at least when performing their official duties. In the context of new institutions, however, even bishops allowed themselves more latitude than when they performed in their usual settings, in official roles, and in traditional functions. According to the Amish Mennonite historian O. Gingerich, "The Sunday School was the 'cutting edge' of the church beginning in the 1920s and continuing to the 1940s."[33] Through the Sunday school the evils of alcohol and tobacco were taught. Missions was another program that was stimulated by the Sunday school, as was the participation of the Amish of Ontario in the Old Mennonite General Conference.[34]

In the church conferences to which the Russlaender allied themselves, the Sunday school, already well established, became with their arrival the all-important vehicle for formally inculcating religious knowledge and values. The Russlaender felt keenly the loss of the day schools under their control in the colonies of Russia. What they could not lose was the special education those schools had represented. Three arenas were exploited to make up for the felt deficiencies of the public school. Wherever possible, the Russlaender influenced the recruitment of qualified Mennonite teachers so that extra classes in religion and language could supplement the required curriculum. Also wherever possible, half-day Saturday schools were instituted to teach primarily the language, but also religion and music. And alongside the Saturday schools were the Sunday schools, an institution nonexistent in Russia because religious training had been accomplished in the day schools.

In the Conference of Mennonites, the first comprehensive look at the Sunday school, undertaken in 1933, included a review of source materials and of Sunday school organization and administration.[35] The Conference that year adopted a resolution recommending the creation of a committee to prepare a unified Sunday school curriculum and to recommend appropriate Sunday school literature. Sunday school conventions, children's festivals, and meetings of Sunday school workers were commended, and the missions committee was encouraged to advance the Sunday school also in the small and scattered groups.

The recommendations were implemented immediately. In Saskatchewan, for instance, a convention attended by approximately 100 teachers was held in November of 1934 and followed by a short course in the summer of 1935, all of it geared to the implementation of the official curriculum.[36] This included texts for five age groups, six and under, seven to ten, eleven to fourteen, fifteen to seventeen, and adults.[37] Three of the Russlaender educators, P.A. Rempel, J.G. Rempel, and J.H. Janzen, were encouraged to produce supplementary curriculum materials, which all of them proceeded to do.

Among the Northern District Mennonite Brethren the Sunday school was on the front line of the struggle for the maintenance of the fundamentalist faith and the confirmation of the children in that faith. There it was reported, on the authority of the *Moody Monthly*, that the Sunday schools could be wrongly used to inculcate doubt rather than faith and that, in fact, there were in Canada already 1,700 Sunday schools "teaching not religion but promoting Communist propaganda."[38] The Sunday school also stood first in a wide array of church activities designed to evangelize the children and young people.[39] Perhaps nowhere else were the annual statistics of such activity recorded more carefully to reveal the progress or the lack of it from year to year than among the Mennonite Brethren.

Thus, in 1935, the Conference knew that of 57 reporting congregations, 56 had Sunday schools with 306 classes and 4,152 pupils, that, additionally, 45 had a *Jugendverein* (Christian Endeavour) with a total membership of 3,215, that 39 had choirs with 820 singers, that 32 congregations had conducted visits to every home with the help of evangelists, and that the average member gave $3.06 for home, city, and foreign missions and relief, and that the congregations altogether had 124 ministers, 72 deacons, and 103 co-workers.[40]

Here and there, Sunday school activity was supplemented by organizations which anticipated the Kindergarten and the boys' and girls' clubs of a later day. The first known Kindergarten schools were in Steinbach in 1923 and in North Kildonan in 1938.[41] The North-West Conference of the Mennonite Brethren in Christ created a "junior missionary band" as an auxiliary to the women's missionary circle. Members were encouraged to contribute five cents a month.[42] In Vineland, a young men's society (*Juenglingsverein*) for boys 13 to 17 was begun under the motto "Faithfulness to God, truthfulness before everybody, and a morally clean life."[43] Meetings were held weekly in the homes of participants with music and male choir activities and the introduction of such books as *What Every Boy Should Know* by Sylvanus Stall, a doctor of divinity. Sports, retreats, swimming, acrobatics, and overnight camp-outs were designed to help boys to become strong, healthy, and useful to mankind; to avoid that which harmed body and soul; to remain loyal, conscientious, and obedient at all times; and to become good citizens of Canada, while retaining and using the German language.

Youth Activity and Character Education

While the Sunday school movements were very similar in all the Mennonite groups, the only major difference being the times in which the English language was introduced, the churchly activities for young people were focused differently among the Swiss and the Dutch, though both wanted to counteract a situation in which young people had no place at all in the church until the day of baptism.[44] Among the former, the Young People's Bible Meeting (YPBM) was central in the 1930s, among the latter the *Jugendverein*.

The YPBMs grew out of the revivals in the 1890s and the concern already at that time "to engage the interests of the young people."[45] One answer that emerged lay in the introduction by the young people themselves of informal midweek meetings in homes through which "young people found a new contact with the church" and at which they had the opportunity to deliver messages of their own. After five years, the Conference leaders agreed that these "edification meetings" were harmless or useful enough to be held in the meeting houses. About another decade later, the Conference "lent encouragement" by appointing an organizer to extend the program into all communities, to prepare a systematic study of Bible books and topics, to organize an exchange of speakers in neighbouring communities, and also to allow occasional substitutions for Sunday morning preaching appointments. In due course, it was said that

> aside from Sunday School, no form of activity has commended itself so generally and so beneficially to our young people's spiritual development.[46]

So effective was the Young People's Bible Meeting movement in capturing the interest of the young that the Amish too accepted the idea.[47] It was Jacob R. Bender, the young minister in East Zorra at Tavistock, who initiated the activity among the Amish, who then also followed their Mennonite cousins in the sponsorship of weekend young people's institutes or conferences.[48] But the Amish too discovered that the YPBMs, like the Sunday school, were an educational medium that conveyed the message of innovation and a reinterpretation of the tradition.[49] It was important, therefore, to provide some guidance for these activities.

The standards and norms of the YPBM were set forth by the Old Mennonite General Conference and included: adequate organization to carry on the work, accurate records of duties performed, instructional programs for both "saved and unsaved," growth of the Christian character, scriptural social standards, more proficient and spiritual song services, greater activity in all lines of Christian service, fuller consecration to Christ, systematic and regular Bible study, and full co-operation with the church, the Sunday school, and the home.[50] Provincial help for such activities came from the Young People's Educational Committee, created by the Mennonite Conference of Ontario in 1938 by merging the young people's and educational problems committees.[51]

A popular form of youth activity, which was promoted in numerous Canadian Mennonite communities in the inter-war period, was the literary society, a community organization for the cultural, literary, and social development of the members.[52] A common feature of the European and American cultural scene in the nineteenth century, the literary societies entered Mennonite congregations via the colleges and academies, first in the United States and then in Canada. Their chief function was to satisfy cultural and recreational needs among the young at a time when they were forbidden to participate in activities of the world but weren't yet attracted by the religious offerings of the church.

As was the custom of the day, no literary society, and indeed few other organizations, existed without a constitution to set forth its purposes and procedures, its objects and rules.[53] The purposes of a literary society might include: the development of well-balanced character — mentally, morally, spiritually, and physically, the training of its members in the correct use and mode of thought and expression, or more specifically, the training of its members in public speaking, in the use of argument, parliamentary law, and song. A society was guided by a motto such as "master thyself" or "be thy real self, speak thy true thought, and strive for that which ennobles."

In addition to the usual offices of president, vice-president, secretary, and treasurer, there could also be an usher, an attorney, and a critic, all of which roles were well defined. Undoubtedly they reflected neglected needs in the community. The usher was responsible for appropriate physical arrangements for a meeting, including heating, lighting, and ventilation. The attorney was the expert in "parliamentary law," meaning *Robert's Rules of Order*, and on the constitution. It was the duty of the critic to criticize the general conduct of the meetings and the rendition of the programs, and to make any suggestions for the improvement of the society.

The activities of a literary society could include debates, drama, music, presentation of essays and poetry, as well as fun and games, including organized sports. The primary focus, however, was not on the social and recreational, at least not officially, but on the intellectual and educational. Since the literary society found its place in the Mennonite community as a stopgap between church activity, which was narrowly defined, and the offerings of the "world," which were frowned upon as inappropriate for Mennonite young people, if not actually off bounds to them, it was clear that the societies were treading on delicate ground. Most literary leaders did not want to cause trouble with the church, while responding to the needs and the interests of young people. Sometimes a specific clause in the constitution made the literary society subordinate to the wishes of the church, as follows:

> All organizations, memberships, and policies of the society
> shall be subject to the advice and correction of the church
> council.[54]

Various attempts were made within the societies themselves to reinforce the basic notion that the idealism of the literary societies was consonant with the goals of the church and helpful rather than detrimental.[55] The pursuit of ideals in everyday life, the building of character, the training and development of the talents of young people, all helped to "instill Christian principles and ideals" and thus "to serve a noble and useful purpose." But certain "dangers and tendencies" were also recognized. The "past record seems to prove," said one essayist defending the societies, "that unless there is competent church oversight, they degenerate into mere entertainment and foolishness."[56]

The prevention of degeneration, it was pointed out, lay in the first place with "suitable programs" which need not be limited to "religious material" but which could be "historical, practical, biographical, agricultural, musical, and inspirational." It was important that they "give a true conception of life" which the "world's entertainment" did not do. The literary societies were also counselled to promote "lofty social standards" and to "avoid all that is questionable." The maintenance of "a spiritual atmosphere in all exercises" was likewise important because "intellectual development" was "of value only when it is grounded in Christian religion." In all things, excellence was the watchword:

> Whatever we undertake we should try to do well. Aim to
> excel, not with a vain motive, but with a noble purpose to
> make good. In a literary society, the use of good English and
> choice of words should receive attention. In public speaking,
> by address, essay, reading, or debate, there are many faults
> and individual weak points to overcome. Notice should be
> taken of correct articulation, inflection, positive and general
> delivery. In music we should aim to have proper interpreta-
> tion of songs as well as good renditions.[57]

The societies did not always succeed in satisfying the church fathers. In the opinion of the latter, the societies had to curtail "the social and the entertaining" and emphasize "the truly literary endeavour" in accordance with the constitutions of the literary societies.[58] While literary societies opened the door to fun and games among the Old Mennonites, this was less the case among the Amish, where a freer social life had been part of the cultural tradition for years. The Amish literary societies, first introduced in East Zorra in 1934, were an intellectual supplement to a social pattern already in existence. As Gingerich has written:

> It must also be recognized that during this time traditional
> singings, parties, and dances continued among Amish young
> people. However, with more and more of the cultural barriers
> of language and dress removed, more young people partici-
> pated in non-Amish young people's activities. These included
> such things as community dances, movies, and sports.
> Although such activities were not sanctioned by the church,
> they were nonetheless practised.[59]

An event somewhat comparable to the founding of literary socie-ties among the young people was the emergence of reading circles among the women. Obviously designed to complement the physical and social activities of the sewing circles, the reading circles were designed as centres of dialogue and intellectual discussion. Their common ground was the missionary impulse. If, on the one hand, the sewing circles were determined to alleviate physical need through articles of clothing and offerings, then, on the other hand, the reading circles broadened the understanding and lifted the horizons. The Ontario reading circle constitution defined the purpose thus:

> In order to bring within reach the best literature, describing
> the actual conditions and problems and movements that are
> now going on in the mission field. . . .[60]

The reading circles or clubs, with a membership of 12 each, collected 60 cents per member annually, enough to buy 12 books at an average cost of 50 cents plus expenses. The clubs each had a librarian and together they had a general librarian through whom the purchase and circulation of books was co-ordinated. Such books were selected from a list of 72 dealing with various countries, religion, the Christian faith, and the missionary task. Included were J.S. Woods-worth's *Strangers Within Our Gates* and Sherk's *Pen Pictures of Early Pioneer Life in Upper Canada*.[61]

Literary societies also flourished among the Dutch. Indeed, the Russlaender brought that institution with them from Russia, where both German and Russian authors had been read with enthusiasm. These societies sometimes took on the characteristics of a seminar, with written reports or papers. When preparations for emigration were under way, the societies had turned to works of English literature, Shakespeare included.[62] Initially, many of their literary societies in Canada had no direct link with the churches or conferences. In some places, a voluntary and a church-sponsored literary society existed side by side — the one reading literary works and the other primarily devotional materials. As the churches gained more and more control, they radically changed and eventually destroyed the literary societies.[63]

Among the Dutch the one institution which had become universal in those Kanadier and Russlaender organizations with Sunday evening services was the *Jugendverein* (literally meaning youth society but also specifically referring to Sunday evening events; the North American Protestant parallel institution was the Christian Endeavour). The Endeavour or *Jugendverein* was not uniquely Mennonite in that it had a general Christian history similar to that of the Sunday school.

The purpose of the *Jugendverein* was also set forth in a constitution. It included the deepening and strengthening of the Christian-religious life of young people and the elevation of the cultural-social standard.[64] The means to accomplish this purpose were religious presentations, choir singing and music, educational lectures, literary readings and dramatizations, and the establishment of a library. The *Jugendverein* and the literary society resembled each other in that both were characterized by variety programs, the former held on Sunday evenings with more of a religious character and the latter on weekday evenings with more of a secular orientation.

All persons of both sexes, 40 years of age and under, persons not necessarily church members but leading "an unoffensive life," were viewed as active participants in the *Jugendverein* and qualified to vote on all important issues. Those over 40 were honorary members, qualified neither to vote nor to be voted in. The administration of the *Jugendverein* was by an elected committee of three, plus the ministers, who were "obligated" to participate in all substantial discussions.

Some *Jugendvereine* were more active and influential than others. At the Main Centre Mennonite Brethren Church, for instance, the *Jugendverein* gave hundreds of programs and all meetings were recorded in great detail.[65] Music had an important place and over the years "many solos, duets, trios, quartets, class sings, choir, family sings, and instrumental numbers were presented." Testimonies also were common and one time "so many shared in the testimony period that they ran out of time, so a motion was made to close the service and continue with testimonies in the following program." In Winnipeg, the Schoenwieser *Jugendverein* divided the young people into groups to assume responsibility for various undertakings like song festivals, oratories, drama, retreats, Sunday evening programs (nine every year), and social gatherings with debates, music, and games.[66] At Leamington, the young people met three Sundays a month. One Sunday was devoted to choral singing, a second to presentations on various themes, and a third to a variety of forms.[67]

The *Jugendverein* served many uses. It represented in most places the institution of greatest freedom for involvement. Innovation was not frowned upon. New talent was discovered. New projects like church libraries were undertaken. When Russlaender congregations of different denominations went their separate ways, it was often the *Jugendverein* that still brought them together once a month. Most important was the bridge-building between the generations.[68] The *Jugendverein* was the point where family and congregation came together, because the talent nights, which many *Jugendvereine* actually were, began in the family with music-making and mini-worship events.

Many families practised family devotions once or twice a day. These included a Scripture reading, prayer, and sometimes hymn-singing. Some families utilized the *Abreiszkalender*, a devotional calendar with detachable daily readings.[69] The involvement of family members in such activities carried over into the *Jugendverein* and vice versa. Many a Mennonite preacher, Sunday school teacher, or choir director was first stimulated in the context of the *Jugendverein* and family devotions.

The first makings of a young people's movement, run by the young people and for the young people, occurred in Saskatoon in 1938 when, for the first time, the triennial assembly of the General Conference Mennonite Church met in Canada.[70] At that time, it was recognized that the Christian Endeavour Societies (*Jugendvereine*) had outlived themselves in a certain sense. They were still useful as a church institution but not so much for keeping the young people, their interest and their loyalty. The average age and interest of *Jugendverein* participants were moving upward and were way beyond the teens. Now a constitution for a North American Young People's Union (YPU) was proposed with action thereon to follow three years later.

Inspired by the Saskatoon event, various Saskatchewan young people became impatient, and, before the continental YPU officially came into being, they were working on a youth organization for Saskatchewan, as a division of the YPU, and also on a Canadian Mennonite Youth Organization.[71] The new organization was necessary, said Heinrich Friesen, a Rosthern area youth leader, because of the young people who were staying and those who were leaving.[72] Those involved in choir, Sunday school, and the *Jugendverein* needed new ways of working. And something had to be done also about those who were going to the cities and either leaving the church altogether and going along with the world, or seeking a vigorous faith and spiritual life elsewhere because they couldn't find it among the Mennonites. The youth movement, said Peter Froese, a recent Rosthern Bible school graduate, needed a more aggressive promotion of musical activity, youth libraries, youth conferences, summer Bible schools, Bible courses, and above all, a youth publication to help young people to develop their character and to find their way in the world.[73]

The emphasis on character-building during this period in Mennonite history was not limited to the *Jugendvereine* and the literary societies. Perhaps nowhere did *Charakterbildung* have a sharper and more consistent focus than in the church-sponsored schools, as for instance at Gretna. There, G.H. Peters, the new principal, made the disciplined life, for the individual and the institution, both the cause and the effect of excellence in Christian education.[74] For him, character education for all young people, be they Christians or non-Christians, was the answer to juvenile delinquency and the undisciplined nature of young people generally, whose moral deviations and criminal offences filled the pages of the newspapers.

Good character, however, was not easily achieved, he explained. It was not just a matter of plucking ripe fruit from a tree. Many years of diligent effort were required to strengthen the will, to overcome temptation, and to become master of one's self. The pursuit of idealism was a lifelong task, even though good habits and good example were immensely useful in confirming a life marked by "the tendency to act on the basis of the Christian ethic."[75]

Character training included greater respect for parents and teachers, and for older and higher-ranking persons generally, because too many of the former customs were fading. Children and young people were becoming very rude. Not only did they involve themselves in adult conversations, but they took it upon themselves to interrupt and correct not only the guests but also their own parents. Even teachers were viewed by children as being on their own level. According to one minister's lament:

> But we are in a free America, where everybody is Pete, Jake, and John. This might be alright for the world, but we are Christians. . . no one will regret an education which leads to respect and honour. . .[76]

Music, Choirs, and Choristers

Another strong focus of youth activity was music, mostly vocal but, as time went on, including also the instrumental. While the Russlaender were not the pioneers of musical activity, their coming meant a vast acceleration of singing soon after their arrival. Four out of the five most outstanding leaders in the field, who made the big difference across Canada, were Russlaender: K.H. Neufeld, David H. Paetkau, F.C. Thiessen, and John Konrad, with Ben Horch, who was of the Mennonite Brethren with a Lutheran background.

Neither the Swiss Mennonites nor the first Dutch Mennonites in Canada, namely the Kanadier, had been a very fertile field for the cultivation of music. Both groups were in the beginning opposed to musical instruments, to four-part singing, and to special musical groups, including choirs, quartets, and the like. In the 1930s, this was still the case among the most conservative among them, namely the Old Order among the Swiss and the Old Colony among the Dutch.[77] In the west it was the late Kanadier who introduced musical innovations, with the encouragement of people like David Toews, who loved to quote a favourite German saying:

> When there is singing, feel free to settle down; people of ill will have nothing to sing about.[78]

The sense that musical activity was useful as an educational force was general. To the foremost promoters, among them H.H. Ewert in Manitoba and Aron Sawatsky in Saskatchewan, music was the right means of winning young people and of building character. While not a musically gifted man himself, Ewert believed that musical training was part of teacher education. He encouraged the development of choirs and introduced a triad of popular song books already being used by the Mennonites in Russia, namely *Heimat-klaenge*, *Frohe Botschaft*, and *Glaubensstimme*, available also as a *Dreiband* (three volumes in one).[79] It was among the Bergthaler and the Brethren where choirs were first formed, gospel songs first introduced, and the use of musical instruments first begun.[80]

In Saskatchewan, Aron Sawatsky, a 1903 immigrant from Russia, had amply prepared the ground before he moved to California in 1923, the year of the coming of the first Russlaender.[81] Under his leadership, a choir directors' association operated among the Mennonite Brethren from 1906 to 1923. The association published *Saenger-Bote*, a monthly magazine, which provided information on new hymnbooks and other musical events, and also reprints from German music periodicals. This fact came to the attention of the Canadian censor during the Great War, and publication ceased at the time, never again to be resumed.[82]

Few of the immigrants made as great an impact on the masses of young people as did K.H. Neufeld, "the flamboyant, theatrical... man from Winkler."[83] He became the "great 'popularizer' of lay choir singing throughout the whole of Canada."[84] No sooner had he arrived in Canada than he was organizing choirs and transforming the annual school festival at Gretna into a full-scale choral festival.[85] In 1932, he organized the southern Manitoba music festival competition, sponsored by his Winkler male-voice choir, which itself performed regularly on a Winnipeg radio station.[86] The biggest festival southern Manitoba had ever seen was the Ascension Day performance in 1938 by 450 singers before more than 4,000 people.[87]

His greatest contributions to the young people, however, were his regular cross-country tours to conduct workshops for conductors, to put together area-wide mass choirs, and to stage massive people's song fests. Mostly his work benefited the Conference Mennonites, whose musical activity was not as advanced as that of the Mennonite

Brethren.[88] Himself from the Brethren, Neufeld found the Conference Mennonites more open to his ways. According to one of Neufeld's contemporaries, his dramatic, often theatrical, approach to music and his casual references to opera and other worldly institutions were too much for his more pious brethren.[89] But the young people loved him, and the starved-for-musical-leadership Conference tolerated him.

Further musical help from the Mennonite Brethren for the Conference Mennonites came through F.C. Thiessen, whose first posting in Canada was at the German-English Academy.[90] While Neufeld had popularized the cantata, F.C. Thiessen defended "Kunst Musica" against considerable opposition and taught Mennonites to sing Handel's *Hallelujah Chorus*, Mendelssohn's oratorio *St. Paul*, and Andreas Romberg's *Das Lied von der Glocke*. All of that Thiessen had brought with him from Russia, where his last contribution had been to tell the ill-fated 1925 Conference of Mennonite leaders in Moscow that the congregations had to take up the musical mandate once carried by the schools. It was an appropriate message also for Canada:

> As long as we could cultivate sacred music in our schools we did not have to be concerned that our children would not make the musical heritage of our congregation their own. Now, when the wonderful chorales can no longer be practised in the schools, things are quite different. If the congregation does not now encourage the singing of the chorales in a special way, then we may be sure that the next generation will lose this treasure, and that would be unforgivable. What was until now the work and privilege of the teacher, has become the duty of the congregation.[91]

Thiessen's successor at the Academy, David H. Paetkau, strengthened what Thiessen had begun.[92] His Mendelssohn choir was known throughout Saskatchewan and Alberta for its performances of major choral works, and even more enduring were his collections of choral works, eventually published in a two-volume *Liederalbum*, which satisfied the needs of many Mennonite choirs as long as they retained the German language.[93]

In addition to Winkler and Rosthern, Winnipeg also excelled as a centre of musical activity, whose radius touched Mennonites from Ontario to British Columbia, largely owing to the work of Ben

Horch and John Konrad. The former of Lutheran parentage and the latter an immigrant, both were basically studio men, but they too directed workshops for conductors and also staged mass choirs. Among the Mennonite Brethren, Horch was the outstanding leader of courses (*Kurseleiter*).[94] Konrad, who became a famous violin teacher in charge of his own school of music, encouraged young people to take up the study of musical instruments. His instrumental ensemble founded in 1935 laid the foundation for the Mennonite Symphony Orchestra. A year later, he initiated the annual passion-day performance for at least two decades of Karl Loewe's *Das Suehnopfer des neuen Bundes*.

Among the Swiss, both Mennonite and Amish, the cultivation of music and song was not through instrumental ensembles or choir festivals but in the context of congregational singing and, at an even more popular and less formal level, in the so-called singing schools.[95] Singing in the congregation was viewed as a spiritual exercise, as a testimony to the praise and glory of God. Hence, singing as entertainment or as performance or as the expression of an art form was minimized and frowned upon, if not altogether forbidden. Consequently, there were no congregational choirs, smaller groups, or even soloists, and no pianos or organs; instead there were whole congregations singing a cappella under the direction of a chorister, for whom also enthusiastic singing was more important than artistic singing.[96] Male quartets, and other such groups, were also discouraged.

This emphasis on congregational singing exclusively was rooted in the Anabaptist principles of simplicity in worship and the priesthood of all believers. In the same way that the trained and supported ministry was resisted, so also there was opposition to selectivity of participation in the musical portion of congregational worship. As Harold S. Bender, in his generation the dean of North American Mennonite scholars, wrote:

> The emphasis upon the preaching of the Word and the
> response of the congregation, coupled with the priesthood of
> all believers as over against the special functioning of the
> priests and the clerical assistants, and the opposition to liturgy,
> particularly in Latin, resulted in a strong emphasis upon
> congregational singing and opposition to clerical or lay choirs
> in the regular worship, which has continued to the present
> day.[97]

The rejection of musical instruments as aids to worship was supported both from the Bible and from history.[98] "Jesus did not use, or sanction the use" and there was "no evidence that his apostles used instrumental music." Such biblical proof-texting was very selective, of course, and references to instruments in the Psalms and Revelations were conveniently ignored. After the days of the apostles, it was said, the church didn't use instruments in worship "for several hundred years" and "in all the ages since the days of the apostles the most pious men have opposed the use of instruments in worship." Among the men used as authorities were John Wesley and C.H. Spurgeon, two famous preachers who were quoted as saying:

> Wesley: I have no objection to instruments being in our chapels, provided they are neither heard nor seen.

> Spurgeon: We should like to see all the pipes of the organs in our nonconformist places of worship either ripped open or compactly filled with concrete. The human voice is so transcendently superior to all that winds or strings can accomplish that it is a shame to degrade its harmonies by association with blowing and scraping.[99]

The categorical disallowance of instruments meant, of course, that the congregations and their choristers had to work all the harder at the task of improving congregational singing so as to reduce the temptation to turn to instruments.[100] Choristers were encouraged to attend church schools, short-term Bible schools, and singing schools to supplement that which could be learned in the home and in the public schools.[101] The good work of the last "in training boys and girls in singing and in appreciation for good music" was recognized, but "the worship type of songs" were seldom touched. A new *Church Hymnal* with "a better grade of music" and songs that had "musical as well as poetical merit" was published as a further contribution to the winning of the young people without instruments in the church.[102]

There were variations, of course, in this tradition. In Old Order communities it was the minister who, in announcing and starting a hymn, would fill part of the function assumed by the choristers. And in New Order communities, like the Mennonite Brethren in Christ or Stirling Avenue Church, musical instruments and choirs were introduced not long after those groups separated from the Old Mennonites.[103]

Among the Old Mennonites and Amish Mennonites, the singing schools, as they came into use, pointed in the direction of greater musical sophistication. In some sense, they performed a function similar to the literary societies, for here was a striving for greater excellence and also a context for innovation.[104] In the singing schools the participants learned the rudiments of music as well as improved interpretation of the hymns.[105] The activity of the schools was enhanced by special publications, including John D. Brunk's *Educational Vocal Studies*, in use for many years.[106] The *Studies* included graded exercises for elementary sight-singing, a variety of religious and folk songs cited for young people's groups, as well as statements about the rudiments of music and voice culture. The sight-reading of the singing schools helped the congregation to sing in four parts and thus made a choir of the entire congregation.

The purpose of the singing schools was to improve good singing on earth in anticipation of "singing perfectly" the song of Moses and of the Lamb in heaven. The cultivation "of one of the richest of the divine endowments of man" was also seen as an antidote for the "light, sensational, spectacular, demoralizing if not sacrilegious music"[107] of "this jazz age."[108] Then also, it was important that "the Creator's highest mechanism of music," the human voice, not be supplanted by musical instruments. As D.H. Bender wrote in introducing the *Studies*:

> The only way to maintain the true chorus of the human voice, attuned to melody and expression, in our homes, in social life, in our educational institutions, and in our churches and missions, is to wisely encourage, carefully guard, intelligently foster and heartily support every rightful move made in the direction of the advancement of good singing.[109]

Bible Schools and Evangelism

An important institution for musical activity among both the Swiss and the Dutch at this time was the Bible school.[110] The Bible school movement among Canadian Mennonites did not begin in the 1930s, but no decade witnessed greater attention to that educational medium. Whereas schools founded in the 1920s and earlier had as their primary focus the training of ministers and other Christian workers, the emphasis in the 1930s appeared to be not only on

TABLE 32[111]

A CHRONOLOGY OF CANADIAN MENNONITE BIBLE SCHOOLS

DATE	PLACE	NAME	AFFILIATION
1907	Kitchener, Ont.	Ontario Mennonite Bible School[†]	OM
1913	Herbert, Sask.	Herbert Bible School[†]	MB
1913	Markham, Ont.	Winter Bible School	OM
1921	Didsbury, Alta.	Mountain View Bible School[†]	MBC
1925	Winkler, Man.	Peniel Bible School[†]	MB
1927	Hepburn, Sask.	Bethany Bible School[†]	MB
1928	Dalmeny, Sask.	Tabor Bible School	MB
1929	Gretna, Man.	Elim Bible School[†]	CM
1929	Coaldale, Alta.	Coaldale Bible School[†]	MB
1930	Winnipeg, Man.	Winnipeg Bible School	MB
1931	Yarrow, B.C.	Elim Bible School[†]	MB
1931	Steinbach, Man.	Steinbach Bible School[‡]	MB
1932	Glenbush, Sask.	Glenbush Bible School	MB
1932	Rosthern, Sask.	Rosthern Bible School[†]	CM
1932	Rosemary, Alta.	Rosemary Bible School	CM
1932	Tavistock, Ont.	Winter Bible School	AM
1933	La Glace, Alta.	La Glace Bible School	MB
1933	Gem, Alta.	Bethesda Bible Institute	MB
1933	New Hamburg, Ont.	Winter Bible School	AM
1934	Alberta	Winter Bible School	OM
1934	Winnipeg, Man.	Mennonite Bible School	CM
1934	Wembley, Alta.	Wembley Bible School	CM
1935	Springridge, Alta.	Springridge Bible School	CM
1935	Coaldale, Alta.	Mennonite Bible School[†]	CM
1936	Leamington, Ont.	Leamington Bible School	CM
1936	Vineland, Ont.	Vineland Bible School	CM
1936	Swift Current, Sask.	Swift Current Bible Institute[†]	CM
1936	Didsbury, Alta.	Menno Bible Institute[†]	CM
1937	St. Elizabeth, Man.	St. Elizabeth Bible School	CM
1938	Virgil, Ont.	M.B. Bible Institute	MB
1938	Sardis, B.C.	Greendale Bible School	MB
1939	Coghlan, B.C.	Bethel Bible Institute[†]	CM
1939	Countess, Alta.	Countess Bible School[†]	CM
1939	Drake, Sask.	Drake Bible School[†]	CM
1939	Sardis, B.C.	Mennonite Bible School[†]	CM
1939	Yarrow, B.C.	Mennonite Bible School[†]	CM
1940	Kitchener, Ont.	Emmanuel Bible College[†]	MBC

[†] Indicates schools still in existence in 1940.
[‡] The Steinbach school became an interdenominational school after a few years.

keeping the young people but also on keeping them grounded in the Mennonite faith and way of life. Nearly 30 new schools appeared during that decade, some, to be sure, for only brief periods of time (Table 32).

The movement was preceded and accompanied by a Bible school movement in Canada generally.[112] This movement, which peaked in the two decades after 1930, had its antecedents in a similar movement in the U.S.A. and such schools as the Moody Bible Institute and in a few Bible schools established in Canada prior to the 1930s, including Toronto Bible College in 1894.[113] Most of the Bible schools arose in the theological milieu of the fundamentalist controversy and were viewed as bastions of the faith not only in opposition to secular education but also over against those church colleges which combined biblical and theological education with the liberal arts, perhaps even with the natural sciences, and which were viewed as "hotbeds" of religious liberalism and modernism. It followed that the Bible schools left the arts and sciences alone.

In terms of appealing to young people, the schools capitalized on their idealism and their readiness to brave new frontiers, usually missionary frontiers, both domestic and foreign. The schools also opened the doors of educational opportunity for many who had dropped out before completing high school, or even elementary grades. The schools were small enough, safe enough, short enough in duration, and flexible enough in terms of entrance requirements to be rather desirable as well as affordable. And, in the words of W.E. Mann:

> Bible schools. . . offered rural youth a means of improving
> their social status. . . Bible colleges gave individuals with little
> schooling who were attracted to ministerial or missionary
> careers a chance to rise socially. . . . [114]

The many-sided attractions of the Bible schools and institutes did not go unnoticed by the Mennonite young people. As a matter of fact, it was the increasing drift of Mennonite young people to non-Mennonite schools that helped prompt the Mennonite effort. Indeed, the various Mennonite conferences were not only competing with non-Mennonite schools but also with each other. After all, the Bible schools were guardians not only of the faith in general but also of the peculiarities of faith and culture. Thus, the Conference Mennonites felt the need to found their own school at Didsbury after the Bergthaler congregation there had elected two additional ministers, both of whom had attended non-Conference schools, Jack Neufeld the Mountain View Bible College of the Mennonite Brethren in Christ, and Cornelius, his brother, the Herbert Bible School of the Mennonite Brethren.[115] And prior to that time, a Moody Bible Institute graduate and two other Mountain View Bible College graduates had served the congregation as ministers.[116]

The attendance of Mennonites at non-Mennonite or non-Conference schools was a general one. According to Mennonite Brethren historian J.B. Toews, hundreds of young people flocked to "English Bible institutes, some of them vanguards of fundamentalism."[117] In Ontario, enough Mennonite young people attended the Toronto Bible College at one point to cause the Mennonite Conference of Ontario to consider, and even to encourage, giving liberal financial support to the school.[118] In the west, the Prairie Bible Institute at Three Hills and the Prophetic Bible Institute at Calgary were special attractions.[119] The experience of the Ernest Jeschke family was typical. Three of six attended the Mennonite Brethren Bible School at Hepburn and the other three graduated from Briercrest Bible Institute, Prairie Bible Institute, and Millar Memorial Bible Institute.[120]

One ministers' conference noted with regret that "many young people from our communities go to Bible schools, which alienate them from our society."[121] There were cases of brethren coming back from educational institutions, having departed from that way which the conference and churches had recognized as the biblical way.[122]

The Mennonite Bible schools were useful in many ways. They were inexpensive and safe places to learn the English language sufficiently well to obtain employment or better-paying employment. They aided in character development, because the men and women of the Bible, who were steadfast in the faith, were good examples for the young people. The role of the Bible schools in preserving the heritage for the young people was also stressed.[123] They were alternatives to non-Mennonite Bible schools, but often only as imitations, as Toews has explained:

> . . . In response our own Bible institutes introduced major
> emphases on doctrine and apologetics. Resources for these
> courses were largely drawn from authors of evangelical funda-

mentalist orientations. In contrast to this emphasis there was little reference to the original . . . Anabaptist understanding of faith and life. . . . The curricula of our Bible schools provided only very limited emphasis on the understanding of our faith in distinction to that of American fundamentalism. . . . [124]

Of significance in the Bible school movement was not only that so many new ones were founded but also that some of the older ones reached new levels of maturity. This was particularly true of the oldest of the schools at Kitchener. The Ontario Mennonite Bible School was an outgrowth of the Bible Conferences begun in the 1890s and the one-week Bible Study Class established as an annual event in Berlin, 1907.[125] Gradually the time period was extended and the curriculum systematized until in 1918 the annual six-week session was designed to cover the entire Bible in six years. In 1929, the annual time was extended to three months and the cycle reduced to three years. In 1932, a constitution and bylaws were accepted. Enrolment reached 166 in 1932 and by the mid-1930s, 71 students had completed the full course.[126] A building program in 1936 was paid for through a special solicitation which extended to all the congregations of the Conference, to the Amish Mennonite Conference, and to the U.S.A.[127] Short-term Bible schools were also introduced in Amish Mennonite churches, first in East Zorra at Tavistock and then at Steinmans near New Hamburg.[128]

One of the most unique winter Bible schools was the one sponsored by the Alberta-Saskatchewan Old Mennonite Conference. It had no central location but travelled from congregation to congregation for 20 years.[129] The curriculum included doctrine and ethics, peace and evangelism and music, Bible studies and prophecy. Some students travelled with the school as it moved every three weeks, and thus could receive up to 15 weeks of study in one winter. The school made for doctrinal unity in the scattered congregations of the Conference and the inter-generational nature of the student body made for healthy adult-youth relationships.

A by-product of the Bible schools was the involvement of their students in various forms of mission activity. Most general was the summer Bible school movement, which saw hundreds of Bible school students fan out for two-week periods at a time to conduct daily Bible classes for children in rural areas of the provinces.[130] This program too was one adopted by the Mennonites from other denominations.[131] One Conference report counted 19 workers in 15 summer Bible schools and 49 children saved.[132] A variation on the theme was to use the vacation school to teach not only Bible studies but also the German language.[133] Here and there, the summer Bible schools led to permanent preaching outposts in so-called mission stations, or even in the establishment of new congregations, as for instance the one at Lindale in the Pembina Hills of Manitoba. Some 285 children had attended the summer Bible school and various German, Russian, Polish, and Irish people had been converted. Thirty persons were baptized and organized into an MB church.[134] In British Columbia, the Mennonite Brethren began the West Coast Children's Mission for this purpose in 1938.[135]

Another form of field work assigned to the Bible school students was the distribution of tracts or the selling of books. Three students of Winkler Bible School, for instance, entered 1,270 homes one summer to achieve the wider distribution of Bibles and Christian books.[136] In the west, many Mennonite young people became involved in the independent and nondenominational Western Tract Mission, whereas in the east, the Golden Rule Gospel Messengers were formed by a tract director appointed by the Mennonite Mission Board and tract representatives from each of the congregations.[137] A 15-minute gospel radio program was begun in Winnipeg in the fall of 1940.[138]

Increasingly, the winning and keeping of the young required an act of personal decision for both sociological and theological reasons. As the hold of the Mennonite society on its young people weakened with greater exposure to the outside world and more frequent societal interaction, the choices of the young people were not always predictable. Thus, new means were needed to bring about decisions favourable to the church when the young people arrived at significant crossroads. That means was evangelism, defined by L.J. Burkholder as follows:

> Evangelism, in the scriptural sense, is the act of going out
> after the lost ones and winning them to Christ. Instead of
> praying and waiting for the sinner to come, the church,
> through her servants becomes aggressive and employs special
> laborers to gather the wandering ones.[139]

Evangelism activity, of course, took on different forms. The New Mennonites, who in Ontario had pioneered not only Sunday school conventions but also church-sponsored young people's meetings, conducted two series of "camp meetings" each year in a pavilion built especially for that purpose.[140] One such camp meeting attended by 128 young people reported that 96 had been "serving the Lord prior to coming to camp," 18 had been "saved or reclaimed," 13 had been "saved or reclaimed and sanctified," 19 had been "sanctified," and many others had become "better established in God's service."[141]

In the Mennonite Conference of Ontario, a "Home Evangelist" was appointed to promote evangelism, engage evangelists, and co-ordinate their work.[142] A typical annual report of the Home Evangelist said that eight evangelists held meetings in 19 congregations, resulting in 100 converts, of which 84 were baptized. The results were encouraging but not entirely satisfactory. Four hundred and eighteen "unsaved persons in these communities remained outside the fold."[143] Recommendations for improving the situation included "less visitation with Christians and more intensive work among the lost," two weeks of meetings, and much more prayer.

Closely related to the work of the home evangelist was the activity of various mission committees. The rural committee, in a typical year, reported on work at eight locations.[144] At Baden, the Sunday school was discontinued "owing to lack of interest and workers." Seventeen young people "took their stand for Christ" at a series of meetings but the visitation work revealed that there were "many unsaved in the village of Baden." At Bothwell, two persons were "received into the church by water baptism, one of which was a French Catholic girl." At Bright, the workers were "greatly encouraged" by the baptism of "six souls," three of which united with the Mennonite Church and three with the United Church. At Glasgow, there were three baptisms, including an "aged man [who] has since gone home to glory." At Hagerman, some members had "withdrawn themselves" but there was "spiritual growth among the few who remain." At Markstay, "several thousand feet of lumber and some logs" were assembled for the building of a log church and donations were "within twenty dollars" of the total needed. At Roseville, the evangelistic meetings yielded "no confessions" but "the congregation was strengthened and encouraged to press on in spite of problems." At St. George, "a few carloads of interested ones" gathered at the Sims home once a month.

Among the Northern District Mennonite Brethren local and outside evangelists tried to cover all the congregations with evangelistic meetings once a year.[145] The Conference of Mennonites in Canada also had its evangelists, most commonly known as itinerant ministers. In one recorded six-month period, Benjamin Ewert, the foremost itinerant minister of the Conference, had travelled 4,000 miles, preached 120 times in 50 communities in Manitoba and Saskatchewan, served communion six times, baptized 12 persons, married three couples, and made hundreds of house visitations. Travel costs amounted to $76.25, of which all but $14.15 was covered by offerings.[146] He did this year in and year out in the 1920s and 1930s.

Evangelistic activity, of course, was another channel for innovation, another arena for borrowing from the outside, and much of the newness had its severe critics, who thought gimmickry and shallowness were making their entry. J.G. Rempel, the Rosthern Bible school teacher, for instance, was critical of all those fashions and fads designed to entice youth into the fold: slide projections and motion pictures, billboards and ads in the papers with exciting themes, sports facilities in churches, discussion sessions instead of worship services, and various other sensational techniques.[147]

Rempel did not object to adjustments and accommodations—after all the exemplary Paul became a Jew to the Jews and a Greek to the Greeks—but he could not see such methods as having the desired long-term effect or as being suited for "our situation and our people . . . [their] essence and character. . . ."[148] Techniques related to mass production inevitably led to shallowness. Fewer but deeper wells in the long run delivered more water than many shallow wells. Mennonites, therefore, should

> Treat the Word as a revealed mystery not just to awaken passing emotions but above all to achieve a lasting change of mind . . . deepen also the singing, the singing of the congregation as well as the choir, so that the content isn't sacrificed to the form and we become victims of superficiality.[149]

The movement of Mennonite young people to the cities was evident everywhere except in Toronto, where the reverse was true, at least in terms of Mennonite young people showing up at the Mennonite church.[150] There undoubtedly were hundreds in the city itself.[151] In cities like Winnipeg, Saskatoon, Calgary, and Vancouver, the focus of youth-related activity in the 1930s was in the girls' homes,

TABLE 33 [152]

HOMES FOR GIRLS
(ESTABLISHED BY CM AND MB CONFERENCES)

CITY	CM	MB
Winnipeg	1926	1925
Calgary	1945	1942
Saskatoon	1929	1930
Vancouver	1935	1931

which were established beginning in the 1920s in the major urban areas by the two large conferences (see Table 33). Run by a matron or houseparents, the homes served as places of temporary residence, as employment referral centres, and as centres of fellowship and worship for girls who had been attracted to the cities by the employment opportunities available to domestic servants. In all the cities where they were established they evolved sooner or later into city congregations. In Saskatoon, one such mission was led by J.J. Thiessen, an emerging leader in his own Conference. [153] The importance of these homes was illustrated by a report on the Maria-Martha Home for girls in Winnipeg, established in 1925:

> The Maria-Martha Home is a very important branch of our mission, the full meaning of which we would acknowledge if one day we should be without it. . . . Let us think for a moment, 250 of our precious young women, our daughters tossed by circumstances into the whirlpool of the big city, without this home. [154]

Marriage and Vocation

The homes also became counsellors to the parents and the home congregations concerning their young people. In 1940, the directors of the CM girls' homes jointly recommended that parents not send their daughters at too young an age, that they advise their daughters to visit the home and to attend Mennonite worship services, that they warn their girls about places of temptation in the city, and that mothers inform their daughters about sexual matters in good time. [155]

Of sex education, that is, overt, formal, and direct sex education, there was very little in most Mennonite homes and communities. Children growing up in large families and on farms well-stocked with animals of all kinds were hardly ignorant of what was essential to the continuity of life and the consummation of the attraction that males and females of all species had for each other. Even so, the need for some instruction and guidance was recognized, because the issues and problems of bad sex were ever-present in the lives of individuals and communities.[156] The dangers were many, and history provided much evidence of strong and prosperous societies declining because of sexual licence. Among Mennonites, the main issue was the purity of the young people, and in this regard two particular issues were raised publicly by Russlaender, namely venereal disease (*Geschlechtskrankheiten*) and masturbation (*Selbstbefleckung*).

Venereal disease had been a problem among the Mennonites in Russia, it was said, though the incidence of infection was relatively small compared to the population in general. However, the war, with its temptations and compulsions, had not left Mennonite communities and individuals, especially the thousands in the medical service, untouched. Life in the big cities, the many stops of the medical trains at the various stations, the population ratio favouring the women, and the absence of men—all represented temptations which overcame some young Mennonites as well. The percentage of infected young people in Russia was small, however, and in Canada even smaller. The many incidents of rape during the revolutionary and civil war years resulted in the venereal infection of a significant number of women.

Much more serious, especially among young men, was masturbation, a "secret sin" widely practised among Mennonites, it was said. In Russia, it had been possible for teachers of the upper elementary grades to provide enlightenment and warnings helpful to boys entering adolescence, but this had been possible because the sexes had been separated in these grades. In Canada, boys and girls were everywhere together, making sex education in schools more difficult, because the teacher would have difficulty establishing "the right tone" and finding "the right words." Some sex education had customarily been included in the catechism classes leading to baptism. At least one of the sessions would involve a special after-meeting with young men only, at which time they would be warned against this secret sin on the basis of Genesis 38:8 – 10, which records the Lord's displeasure over Onan who "spilled the semen on the ground."[157]

Masturbation was believed to be injurious to both the individual and society. Some Mennonites thought it inevitably led to insanity, lunatic asylums, suicide, death, and hell. Others were sceptical of this extreme view which, if true, would not leave enough "healthy people around to staff all the asylums." Masturbation, nevertheless, was thought to weaken the family if practised from generation to generation. It sapped energy essential to creativity. It reduced the desire to live, as well as the joy of faith.

The best means for curbing this evil and the temptation to indulge were perceived to be education and enlightenment, healthy social activities involving both boys and girls and including also adults, eating and drinking in moderation in order to reduce "unnecessary stimulation and day-dreaming." Strenuous work and exercise was also recommended because it produced a normal weariness, thus reducing sleeplessness and a long tossing to and fro in bed. Most important of all was purity of thought and clean conversation, which contributed to positive living and healthy action and became the foundation for a happy marriage.

In their warnings against masturbation, Mennonite leaders reflected the conventional and contemporary wisdom of society in both North America and Europe at the time. The aforementioned Stall book, introduced to teenagers at Vineland, was one of a popularly packaged series that circulated widely in Canada and somewhat secretly in Mennonite communities. Sylvanus Stall, a Lutheran minister, was a book publisher and for the most part author and editor of eight volumes in the best-selling series "Self and Sex," manuals that were published in Philadelphia and advertised in Canada as "pure books on avoided subjects" with "glowing commendations from prominent clergymen, medical experts, popular writers, and other public figures" and distributed, among others, by church agencies. These books, four for males and four for females, explained successively what boys and girls, young men and young women, young husbands and young wives, and men and women of 45 "ought to know."[158]

Generally, the books began by praising the powers and pleasures of sex, but then proceeded to deal with all its difficulties and problems. For the unmarried, "the most persistent and pernicious difficulty" of all was "the temptation to indulge in the habit of the secret vice, the solitary vice, self-pollution, self-abuse, onanism, or masturbation." Often innocently learned, masturbation led to declining health, eyes losing their lustre, skin becoming sallow, muscles turning flabby, backs plagued with pain and heads with dizziness. The appetite suffered, the entire body was wasted, and the mind, in extreme cases, fell victim to insanity.

Sexual intercourse outside of marriage was no substitute for masturbation because of the dangers of venereal disease. In any event, sexual excess was bad, even within the marriage relationship, and some degree of continence and discipline was always essential. Fortunately, nature provided that the natural aggressiveness of males was moderated by the sexual passiveness of women and after age 45 by the decline of desire and need on the part of both sexes.

Most marriage education happened shortly before the wedding. Parents and ministers would take their responsibilities seriously and counsel couples concerning the significance of their undertaking. The sanctity of marriage as an ordinance of God for procreation, fellowship, and the avoidance of sin was always emphasized.[159] Marriage partners were encouraged to love each other, to pray, to read the Word of God, to share joys and sorrows, and to train their children in the discipline and fear of the Lord. The women were also taught to be submissive and to obey. Both the engagement of a couple and the wedding day were family events, the latter involving the extended family, broadly defined, and most often also the entire community.

The traditional position concerning faith and marriage was that persons getting married should be of the same faith, baptized, and members of the same congregation.[160] But the times and conditions were changing, requiring exceptions to the former rules. According to elder P.H. Enns, Mennonites couldn't at one and the same time sanction new patterns of living and not accept the implications thereof.

> If we want to follow more strictly the rules of our fathers then
> we should also follow the way of the fathers and prevent those
> things which lead to undesired relationships, live more iso-
> lated, and not send our girls at 15 - 16 years of age in large

numbers into the cities there to work for people who hold different faiths, likewise not allow our boys to hire out to
strangers.[161]

Apart from the girls' homes, city mission work included evangelistic meetings, street meetings, hospital visits, home visitations,
Sunday school and other children's gatherings, *Jugendvereine*, young
men's and young women's meetings, prayer meetings and Bible
study, song and music activity, and tract distribution.[162] One of the
most far-reaching and courageous efforts to gather in the young
people was undertaken in Winnipeg in 1937 by Benjamin Ewert,
who had come to the conclusion that he couldn't in good conscience
travel the length and breadth of rural Saskatchewan as an itinerant
minister in search of lost Mennonites and at the same time neglect
those at his Winnipeg doorstep. His was a lonely initiative, because
the beginnings of the English-language Bethel mission for students
and young workers in the city was perceived by the rural church
leaders as encouraging anglicization and urbanization, both of which
they opposed.[163]

A resolute look at the youth problem also led to the conclusion that
the agricultural situation, the movement to the cities, and the
educational aspirations of the young people took them away from the
farm into other vocations. On the positive side, the entry into various
professions was seen as motivation for Christian service.[164] The new
options for young Mennonites were defended and encouraged by
some church leaders. Speaking about "Christianity and Vocations" at
a Conference session, J.J. Klassen concluded that the apostles had
worked with people in a great variety of occupations and none of
them had been asked to leave.[165]

> They were persuaded that every honourable work could be
> penetrated by the spirit of Christendom and that one could in
> every occupation help to build the kingdom of God. An occu-
> pation by itself is neither good nor bad, Christian nor unchris-
> tian but neutral. The bearer of a vocation, the human being,
> determines whether it will be a blessing or a curse.[166]

He made exceptions to the rule, of course. There were activities
excluded by Christianity, "the businesses of the night which thrive
only in the darkness," for instance.[167] Klassen established that no

occupation could be isolated from other aspects of life. All things belong together and are interlocked with each other to form an organic whole. As much as one may specialize, there is no detachment possible from the sum total of things. The farmer, for instance, is intimately tied to all manner of professionals, including the technologists, chemists, agronomists, and scientists generally. The farmer is also related to the doctor, the teacher, the businessman, and many others, because no one is excluded.

> Consequently it is impossible to differentiate between a more Christian or a more worldly vocation. Everything depends on what the human being puts into it. [168]

Daniel Loewen also felt that the acceptable professions for Mennonite young people shouldn't be listed too narrowly. After all, why shouldn't Mennonites be chemists and participate with God in the stewardship of resources also in that area, or businessmen, or doctors?[169] In other words, young people should not be pressured to follow the traditional way. It was more important that their individual interests and uniqueness be recognized.

There were those, of course, who continued their striving to keep the young people close to home. For J.J. Siemens, the socialist reformer of southern Manitoba, the issues of the day centred not only in a restored economy with the help of co-op philosophy and institutions, but also in the retention of the young people. He issued an open invitation to all people to enlist in an enterprise that transcended religious, racial, and international lines for the sake of all. Mennonites had customarily divided on the basis of their church affiliations. However, these divisions had broken down, and where the churches had failed to achieve harmony, the co-ops had succeeded in bringing new life and vision to the community. In Siemens's own words:

> We virtually became alive with the possibilities open to us in making farming a vocation full of interest and fascination. We became so occupied with the things we could do ourselves that we spent less time criticizing others. We talked a lot, held innumerable meetings in various districts, published a quarterly magazine with articles on farm practices, advice, and news of our fellow farmers. We kept the pot boiling and stirring. . . . We changed the pattern of our thinking as well as the

pattern of our farming along aggressive and progressive
paths. The young people were having visions and the old people began dreaming dreams. The future was ours to make it
what we desired it to be. [170]

Siemens regarded education as the key to developing a society
confident in itself yet respectful of the other cultures and creatures
with which it shared the planet. [171] Farmers had been conditioned to
view their profession as second-rate and socially inferior to city
employment, but Siemens believed that a well-rounded education at
home and at school could erase the stigma attached to farming and
instil in children a deep sense of dignity and pride in their family's
livelihood. [172] Here too he referred to the tremendous role that could
be played by parents and teachers. They could impart to children an
understanding and respect for nature that would guarantee that
generations yet unborn would inherit a world environmentally
sound. [173] Siemens also introduced literature that reinforced the
heritage. He saw to it that the Rhineland Agricultural Institute
sponsored courses in Bible, Ethics, and Mennonite history, [174] and
that the Rhineland Agricultural Society subsidized a Mennonite
historical project — the publication of P.J. Schaefer's three historical
booklets entitled *Woher? Wohin? Mennoniten!* [175]

Literature programs, specifically targeting the young people,
were another mark of the period for both the Swiss and the Dutch. In
Ontario, the Old Mennonites led the way in the production and
distribution of literature. They worked closely with the Mennonite
Publishing House at Scottdale. [176] In the mid-1930s, S.F. Coffman
and M.H. Shantz were members of the Board, the latter as vice-
president, while M.C. Cressman and Oscar Burkholder were
members of the Finance and Publishing committees, respectively.
S.F. Coffman and C.F. Derstine were non-resident editors. Lewis
S. Weber wrote a 122-page book *Ideals for Christian Youth* while he
was superintendent of the Toronto Mission. [177] C.F. Derstine wrote
some smaller works, including "Forty Principles in Bible and
Sunday School Study," "The Great Apostasy," and "The Last
Message of Jesus Christ." [178] Oscar Burkholder wrote "True Life
Stories" and "The Predicted Departure from the Faith." [179]

Book distribution centres arose in Kitchener with the founding of
the Golden Rule Bookstore, in Winnipeg at the Rundschau Publish-

ers, and in Rosthern under Board of Colonization auspices.[180] Special Conference committees were established to oversee literature preparation, and one reported in 1940 a list of 20 pamphlets for distribution, half of them in German and half in English, on such subjects as baptism, nonresistance, the oath, missions, eternal security, communism, Mennonite history, and Mennonite faith.[181]

Secondary and Post-Secondary Education

The educational problems committee of the Mennonite Conference of Ontario monitored and made recommendations concerning literature but also concerning high schools and colleges, generally. With respect to the high schools, it criticized the undue emphasis on sports and encouraged instead manual and agricultural training as well as other "useful and practical pursuits."[182] The trustees and ratepayers associations were commended for opposing cadet training in the schools.[183] The possibility of students taking one more year of high school locally, the so-called "fifth class," was noted with enthusiasm.[184] The Student Christian Fellowship movement in both high schools and colleges was perceived to be a good thing.[185] However, in spite of all these and other efforts to keep the high schools from danger, the Conference remained uneasy about the high school, and before the decade was out the school of the Brethren in Christ at Fort Erie was recommended "to all our high school students as a school affording safe Christian influence."[186]

Since Ontario Mennonite students attending college tended to go to Mennonite schools in the United States, which were not accredited in Ontario, successful efforts were made to obtain at least some academic credit for them. Both McMaster University and Waterloo College, the latter in affiliation with the University of Western Ontario, agreed to grant degrees to Goshen College graduates upon their completion of an additional academic year at the respective institutions.[187] The teaching content of Goshen College was also monitored by the Mennonite Conference of Ontario and one year the College was asked to represent pre-millennial views and nonconformity teachings to the students.[188]

Many young people attending colleges and universities moved out from their homes into the wider world. Some of the most gifted young people left the Mennonites not because they turned their backs on the faith but occasionally the better to express it in the wider arena.

A particular case was that of John K. Friesen, one of six brilliant sons and daughters of one of southern Manitoba's most concerned Mennonite leaders. A deacon in the Bergthaler church, D.W. Friesen was also Altona's postmaster and the proprietor since 1907 of a stationery and printing business. As an important wholesaler, he also got into the business of marketing books, especially Mennonite materials, the first copies of which always found their way into his own personal library. The best-read Canadian Mennonite of his day, he had become so impressed with his heritage that he wanted nothing more than to pass it on to his children and to have his children pass it on to others.[189] To one of his sons away from home at the Gretna boarding school he wrote:

> In all the hundreds of years of Mennonite history I know of no single case of a people receiving a greater blessing than we ourselves. Therefore, we have a debt and a duty . . . we are obligated to respond to our people and to participate in their endeavours, to unite ourselves with them . . . we are also obligated to our country . . . and the greatest of all obligations we have toward God.[190]

Human society, or "humanity in general, but our own people in particular," he told his boys, was facing a great future. It was important, therefore, to set the right goals, to avoid temptation, to look upon school as a time of preparation, and also to marry right. After all, with one's marriage, "one sets one's direction in life and often much more."[191] The elder Friesen was overjoyed when John, the second of his sons, but the first to enter university, became a teacher at the MCI and when he was elected a candidate for the ministry in the Bergthaler church. And he was equally saddened when, after completing a B.A. in history and music, the son sought a teaching position in a non-Mennonite area. Trying desperately to help his son find the right place, he advised him as late as the middle of July:

> I heard Steinbach still needs a teacher in the high school. If only you could serve among our own people. It is such a concern to me. I pray much about it.[192]

The Mennonite world, however, was too narrow for the idealistic young man. And what he wanted most in and from the Mennonite community—a strong youth movement and a positive promotion and wider application of the peace ideal—he found in the United Church of Canada. At last, he told his parents, he was exposed to a minister who was "an extraordinary thinker and speaker," whose sermons were thought out and well prepared.[193]

As a teacher of history and music at Hargrave first and then at Virden, he immersed himself in the local young people's society and through it in the Young People's Union of the United Church, becoming president of the Manitoba Conference in a few short years.[194] Along the way, he was also chairman of the Peace Commission of the Young People's Union of the United Church of Canada. Every context gave him an "outstanding opportunity to speak up for peace and nonresistance."[195] Acknowledging the militaristic attitudes of a community like Virden, he none the less insisted that his school choir sing two peace anthems "irrespective of opinions" at the Armistice Day ceremony.[196] In the local youth society he arranged a debate on Canada's preparation for war, and through the national executive he lent "full support to the anti-conscription movement" and to those who insisted that there "be sacrifice of profits if there is to be sacrifice of life."[197]

The college and university student became the new focus of the modernist-fundamentalist debate, this time in western Canada, as John Horsch continued his writing into the 1930s, using also the Russlaender paper, *Der Bote*, where his excellent German was appreciated.[198] In that paper, also, he met his literary and intellectual match in Jacob H. Janzen, who never shied away from controversy and who had his way of criticizing most points of view and who rarely saw either fundamentalism or modernism as black and white. Janzen's intellectual ability had been demonstrated at an early age in a variety of experiences.[199] He had become a school teacher at the young age of 16. His linguistic training in Russia already included Greek, Hebrew, English, and French, in addition to German and Russian. In Germany, he had studied at the ultra-conservative University of Greifswald and at the ultra-liberal university at Jena. His fields included theology, psychology, philosophy, and the sciences. Later, again a teacher, he had debated with the Soviets until they dismissed him. Janzen's antidote to modernism as a threat to the churches was not an incessant denunciation of modernism but rather the elimination of that which was "hollow and empty" in the life and faith of the churches. After all, modernism was a response, however erroneous, to a real need:

> I am bound to admit the conviction, that the danger of our churches lies in the defective lives of those who confess fundamentalism. . . ."[200]

Janzen's problem with the fundamentalists and with Horsch was their inclination to condemn "as modernists everyone who does not believe in their schemes even if they would believe in the whole Bible."[201] He further took issue with anti-intellectualism apparent in the fundamentalist movement. And the error of the modernists, he said, was their resort not to reason but rather to false reasoning and a general reluctance to accept as possible truth anything they themselves couldn't grasp with their minds.[202] Janzen's clear explanations were understood by the fewest of people.

For university students who had been exposed to the wider world of literature and science and of non-Mennonite culture, the Mennonite world suddenly became very narrow, much too narrow, in terms of religion, culture, and intellectual activity, generally. The experience of I. G. Neufeld was typical.[203] He had ended up at McMaster University in Hamilton in 1933–34. United States Immigration at Emerson, Manitoba, had refused his admission en route to Tabor College, his first choice as per the recommendation of A. H. Unruh, his principal and teacher at Winkler Bible Institute. His second choice was McMaster, because Unruh's missionary brother in India had met and praised John McNeil, the principal of the McMaster (Baptist) Divinity School and president of the World Baptist Union. If he, Neufeld, found McMaster "safe," Winkler would send some of its graduates there, Unruh had told him.

Following a year at McMaster, Neufeld crossed the country to the West Coast and was visiting relatives at Sardis. The leader of the *Jugendverein* happened to be a son-in-law of A. H. Unruh and that connection brought Neufeld an invitation to address the Sunday night service on "The Greatness of God in Nature." Neufeld was willing to speak but not on that subject, though in the end he consented. The young people were taken by what he had to say and a repeat invitation was given. Again Neufeld consented, on condition that the Wednesday night meeting be for young people only.

A day before the scheduled event, two ministers showed up in the barn where he was doing chores and told him that the church council had denied him the use of the church. A two-hour dialogue ensued, but the ministers would not change their minds. Although they could point out no error in his Sunday night presentation, they feared the influence of a university-educated man: "You have been one year in the University; you must be a modernist!" For preachers and a congregation whose continuous message for the young people was conversion and rebirth, any reference to astronomy, geology, and science generally, even when connected to the greatness of God in nature, was too much. As for Neufeld, those conversations about his alleged modernism followed him throughout his adult life. It had been said, people had heard, that I.G. was a modernist, and that was that!

At least in one Conference the leaders felt keenly that ministers of the congregations would require special and more advanced theological training than was offered by the existing Bible schools if the churches were to meet the needs of the educated young people. [204] One ambitious proposal called for elevation of at least one Bible school in every province to the level of the seminary. [205] Some even advocated an advanced general university education for the sake of better preparation for the ministry and better communication with educated young people. [206]

Ministers should have a good knowledge of the Bible but also a general education. On the paths of true knowledge were revealed many of the wonders of God, His greatness, and His might. Truth and atheistic tendencies, of course, were two different things, and it was for that reason that the minister should also be equipped in the science of nature so that the atheists didn't monopolize the field and mislead the young people. History as a discipline — both church and world history — was also most enlightening. Psychology likewise could be helpful in understanding the soul.

By the end of the decade, there was a general endorsement of the idea of a school for preachers which could evolve from one or more of the Bible schools already in existence. [207] Professional education, it was said, was essential for ministers just as much as for doctors, teachers, and lawyers. [208] The higher educational level of the members, as well as the dangers from unbelief, false cults, and materialism, made better education for the ministers necessary. [209]

TABLE 34[210]

MENNONITE POPULATION INCREASES
COMPARED TO SELECTED MEMBERSHIP INCREASES
(IN THE 1930S)

	1931	1941	% INCREASE
Total Mennonite Population	88,736	111,403	26
Old Mennonite Conference, Ontario	2,284	3,149	38
Mennonite Brethren in Christ, Ontario	1,927	2,294	19
Northern District of Mennonite Brethren Churches	4,186	6,732	61
Conference of Mennonites in Canada	8,911	12,471	40

Implementation was delayed, however, because of the times and other needs. The reader already knows how economic considerations determined many priorities in the 1930s.

As the 1930s came to a close, there was evidence that the effort to keep the young people was successful to a very considerable extent (see Table 34). Not only did selected Mennonite conferences show membership increases but for the main three groups these increases were in excess of the general increase in Mennonite population. In interpreting these figures, caution must be given that all of the three groups in question gained members from other Mennonite groups during this period. The Mennonite Brethren, for instance, completely absorbed the Alliance churches. The Old Mennonites received people from the Old Order churches and also from others. And the itinerant ministry of the Conference Mennonites to lonely outposts had also paid off.

How many of the gains could be credited to innovation in church programs and to institutional "borrowing" from the outside cannot be ascertained, but that conference-oriented Mennonites believed in the efficacy of those innovations there can be no doubt. However, those very innovations and borrowings meant greater Mennonite adjustment to society generally, and to fundamentalist religion in particular. This had the effect of changing not only the Mennonite theology but also the Mennonite culture, and such change was not the intention. The Mennonites wanted to keep not only the young people but also those aspects of culture believed to be essential to the historic faith.

FOOTNOTES

1   J.J. Klassen, "Bericht des Schulkomitees," *Jahrbuch*, 1931, p. 51.
2   S.F. Coffman, "Our Educational Interests," *Mennonite Year-Book and Directory*, 1930, p. 15.
3   Johannes Regier, "Was bedarf unsere Jugend?" *Jahrbuch*, 1928, p. 49.
4   The oldest of the schools, OMBS at Kitchener, completed a modest and much-needed building program in 1936. For the school's historic role, see Clare L. Martin, "An Evaluation of the Program of the Ontario Mennonite Bible School" (research paper, Goshen College Biblical Seminary, 1951).
5   The Rudnerweider placed the emphasis on the winning and teaching of the young people from the outset and met with considerable success, baptizing up to 100 in a single year. See Walter Sawatsky, "History of the Evangelical Mennonite Mission Conference" (research paper, Goshen College, 1967), pp. 15-16.
6   J.H. Enns, "Der Ausbau unserer Bibelschulen," *Jahrbuch*, 1935, p. 45, put it this way, "Our history and the history of other denominations shows very clearly that the spiritual life rose where the churches placed a great deal of emphasis on the schooling of the young generation and that it sank irretrievably where this was not the case."
7   *Jahrbuch*, 1939, p. 3.
8   William W. Dean, "John F. Funk and the Mennonite Awakening" (Ph.D. dissertation, University of Iowa, 1965), pp. 42-43. See also L.J. Heatwole, "The Mennonite Church — Her Past and Present Conditions Compared," *Mennonite Year-Book and Directory*, 1907, p. 14; J.S. Hartzler and Daniel Kauffman, *Mennonite Church History* (Scottdale, Pa.: Mennonite Book and Trust Society, 1905), p. 371; Douglas Millar, "Mennonites in the Melting Pot" (research paper, Conrad Grebel College, University of Waterloo, 1980), pp. 4-5.
9   Frank H. Epp, *Mennonites in Canada, 1786-1920* (Toronto: Macmillan of Canada, 1974), pp. 234-35.
10   Jakob Gerbrandt, "Was die Konferenz gewirket hat und weiter wirken sollte," *Jahrbuch*, 1932, pp. 41-44; see also D.A. Rempel,

    "Die Stellung der Jugend innerhalb der Gemeinde," *Jahrbuch*, 1931, pp. 37–47.
11 Daniel Loewen, "Unsere Aufgaben unserer Jugend gegenueber," *Jahrbuch*, 1929, p. 46.
12 J.N. Hoeppner, "Wie steht es mit der Nachfolge Jesu in den Gemeinden?" *Jahrbuch*, 1936, p. 56.
13 "Protokoll der Predigerversammlung," *Jahrbuch*, 1938, p. 5.
14 G.G. Epp, *et al.*, "Bericht von der Arbeit in der Inneren Mission...," *Jahrbuch*, 1934, pp. 61–62.
15 Frederick Jackson Turner, *Frontier and Section: Selected Essays* (Englewood Cliffs, N.J.: Prentice-Hall, Inc., 1961), p. 39.
16 See next chapter for the attempt to preserve the language.
17 David Toews, "Wie koennen wir dem Mangel an Predigern unter uns abhelfen?" *Jahrbuch*, 1929, p. 64.
18 Walter Quiring, "Zum Problem der innermennonitischen Abwanderung," *Mennonitisches Jahrbuch*, 1934, pp. 19–34.
19 Raymond Breton, "Institutional Completeness of Ethnic Communities and the Personal Relations of Immigrants," *The American Journal of Sociology* 70:193–205; L. Driedger and G. Church, "Residential Segregation and Institutional Completeness: A Comparison of Ethnic Minorities," *Canadian Review of Sociology and Anthropology* 11:30–52.
20 Johannes Regier, p. 49.
21 *Ibid.*
22 Jakob J. Nickel, "Die Ausuebung unseres Dienstes," *Jahrbuch*, 1939, p. 36.
23 J.J. Klassen, "Die Frau im Dienste der Gemeinde," *Jahrbuch*, 1939, pp. 39–43.
24 *Ibid.*, p. 40.
25 *Calendar of Appointments*, 1934, p. 29.
26 CGC, II-1.A.1, "Conference Programs, Reports, and Resolutions." See "Constitution of the Ontario Mennonite Sunday School Conference."
27 *Ibid.* From "Programme of a Sunday School Conference to be held in the Floradale Mennonite Church."
28 L.J. Burkholder, *A Brief History of the Mennonites in Ontario* (Markham, Ont.: Mennonite Conference of Ontario, 1935), p. 159.
29 Oscar Burkholder, "The Sunday School Movement and the Sunday School Conference," *Calendar of Appointments*, 1934, p. 29.
30 L.J. Burkholder, p. 160.
31 Orland Gingerich, *The Amish of Canada* (Waterloo, Ont.: Conrad Press, 1972), p. 69.
32 *Ibid.*, p. 94.
33 *Ibid.*, p. 93.
34 *Ibid.*, pp. 95–96.

35   J.N. Hoeppner, "Die geistlich-religioese Pflege unserer Kinder in der Sonntagschule," *Jahrbuch*, 1933, pp. 36–43. See also *Jahrbuch*, 1933, p. 11.

36   "Bericht des Sonntagschulkomitees in Saskatchewan," *Jahrbuch*, 1935, p. 80.

37   *Jahrbuch*, 1934, pp. 17–18.

38   *Verhandlungen* (ND), 1937, p. 19.

39   John A. Toews, quoting I.W. Redekopp, says that among the Brethren, Sunday schools were there "to evangelize, rather than to train children." The Brethren objected to a "memorized faith," an obvious reference to the catechetical instruction so common in the Kirchengemeinden. See Toews, *A History of the Mennonite Brethren Church*, pp. 216–17.

40   *Verhandlungen* (ND), 1936, pp. 52–53.

41   Arnold Dyck, "Der Kindergarten," *Warte-Jahrbuch*, 1943, pp. 14–20.

42   *Conference Journal* (NW), 1931, p. 15.

43   "Bericht des Vinelaender Juenglingsvereins: Wahrheit, Treue, Reinheit," *Jahrbuch*, 1939, pp. 52–53.

44   D.H. Rempel, "Die Stellung der Jugend innerhalb der Gemeinde," *Jahrbuch*, 1931, p. 38.

45   Joseph C. Fretz, "The Young People's Meeting Movement in Ontario, *Calendar of Appointments*, 1934, pp. 30–31.

46   *Ibid.*, p. 31.

47   Orland Gingerich, *The Amish of Canada* (Waterloo, Ont.: Conrad Press, 1972), p. 103.

48   *Ibid.*, pp. 124–25; *Calendar of Appointments*, 1931–32, p. 25.

49   This is effectively portrayed in the drama "The Quiet in the Land" by Anne Chislott, first presented at the Blythe Theatre in Ontario in the summer of 1981.

50   *Calendar of Appointments*, 1934, pp. 31–32.

51   "Conference Resolutions," *Calendar of Appointments*, 1938–39, p. [24]. See also *Calendar of Appointments*, 1938–39, p. [18].

52   Harold S. Bender, "Literary Societies," *Mennonite Encyclopedia* 3:353.

53   For sample constitutions, see CGC, Hist. Mss. 5.1, "A Literary Society Constitution."

54   *Ibid.*

55   George S. Good, "Christian Ideals for a Literary Society," *Christian Monitor* 24 (January 1932):4, 5.

56   CGC, Hist. Mss. 5.1, "Ideals for a Literary Society," n.a., n.d., pp. 2, 3.

57   *Ibid.*, pp. 3, 4, 5.

58   J.C. Fretz, "The Educational and Y.P.Problems Committee," *Calendar of Appointments*, 1940, pp. 21–22. See also "Conference Resolutions," *ibid.*, p. 24; CGC, II-2.1.2.2.2, Mennonite Confer-

ence of Ontario, Secretary's Records, H.D. Groh to "Dear Christian Friends," 20 July 1940.
59 Orland Gingerich, *The Amish of Canada* (Waterloo, Ont.: Conrad Press, 1972), p. 104.
60 CGC, Hist. Mss. 5.5, "The Ontario Reading Circle."
61 *Ibid.*
62 Based on T.D. Regehr, CGC, XV-31.2, "1930—Literary Societies."
63 *Ibid.*
64 G.G. Neufeld, *Die Geschichte der Whitewater Mennoniten Gemeinde* (The Author, 1967), p. 108.
65 *The History of the Main Centre Mennonite Brethren Church, 1904– 1979*, 1979, p. 10.
66 Isaac Klassen, *Dem Herrn die Ehre: Schoenwieser Mennoniten-Gemeinde von Manitoba, 1924–1968* (Winnipeg: First Mennonite Church, 1969), p. 77.
67 J.H. Enns, "Bericht uber Jugendvereinsbestrebungen in den Gemeinden unserer Konferenz," *Jahrbuch*, 1938, pp. 24–25.
68 B.B. Janz, "Das Eben-Ezer der MB Gemeinde," in *Gedenk und Dankfeier des 25. jaehrigen Bestehens der Coaldale Mennoniten Brueder Gemeinde*, p. 25.
69 G.S. Rempel, ed., *A Historical Sketch of the Churches of the Evangelical Mennonite Brethren (1889–1939)*, (n.p., 1939), p. 15.
70 Samuel Floyd Pannabecker, *Open Doors: The History of the General Conference Mennonite Church* (Newton, Kansas: Faith and Life Press, 1975), pp. 177–78, 374–75; *Jahrbuch*, 1940, pp. 52–61. It should be noted that the Mennonite Brethren in Christ appointed superintendents to organize young people's societies already in the 1920s. *Conference Journal* (O), 1923, p. 29; 1924, pp. 28–29; 1937, pp. 38–39.
71 "Statuten der provinzialen Jugendorganisation," *Jahrbuch*, 1940, pp. 60–61; see also p. 31; Homer Janzen, "Mennonite Youth Society of the Conference of Mennonites of Canada, Saskatchewan Division" (research paper, Canadian Mennonite Bible College, 1949).
72 Heinrich Friesen, "Wesen und Zweck der Jugendorganisation," *Jahrbuch*, 1940, pp. 52–55.
73 Peter J. Froese, "Praktische Betaetigung der Jugendbewegung," *Jahrbuch*, 1940, pp. 55–59.
74 His lessons on the subject were later published. See G.H. Peters, *Charakterbildung* (Winnipeg: The Author, 1955), for the second and revised edition.
75 *Ibid.*, p. 1. See also D.H. Rempel, "Die Stellung der Jugend innerhalb der Gemeinde," *Jahrbuch*, 1931, p. 40.
76 *Ibid.*, p. 51.
77 The German word is "Wo man singt, da lass dich ruhig nieder, boese

Menschen haben keine Lieder." See Peter Wesley Berg, "Choral Festivals and Choral Workshops Among the Mennonites of Manitoba and Saskatchewan, 1900–1960, with an Account of Early Developments in Russia" (Ph.D. dissertation, University of Washington, 1979), p. 50.

78 *Ibid.*, p. 61.
79 *Ibid.*, pp. 53–55.
80 *Ibid.*
81 *Ibid.*, pp. 67–83.
82 *Ibid.*, pp. 75–76.
83 *Ibid.*, p. 107.
84 Ben Horch quoted in Peter Wesley Berg, p. 112.
85 *Ibid.*, pp. 104–6.
86 *Mennonitische Rundschau* (6 July 1938), p. 7.
87 Berg, pp. 112–13.
88 Berg attributes.
89 *Ibid.*, pp. 111–12.
90 *Ibid.*, p. 97 ff.
91 Quoted in Berg, pp. 43–44.
92 *Ibid.*, p. 118 ff.
93 *Ibid.*, p. 121–22.
94 *Ibid.*, p. 122 ff. See also *Verhandlungen*, 1938, p. 29.
95 Walter E. Yoder, "Singing Schools," *Mennonite Encyclopedia* 4: 533–34. See also Cornelius Kran, "Musical Instruments," *Mennonite Encyclopedia* 3: 794–95; B.F.Hartzler, "Development of Music in the Mennonite Church," *Christian Monitor* (June 1929):185, 191.
96 John G. Rempel, "Chorister," *Mennonite Encyclopedia* 1: 565–66.
97 Harold S. Bender, "Choirs," *Mennonite Encyclopedia* 1: 563.
98 "The Voice of the Ages Against Instrumental Music in Worship," *Gospel Herald* (19 April 1934):77–78.
99 *Ibid.*, pp. 77–78.
100 Karl L. Massanari, "A Plea for the Choristers," *Gospel Herald* (10 June 1937):235; see also J.D. Hartzler, "Duties of the Chorister," *Gospel Herald* (2 September 1937):490–91.
101 J.D. Hartzler, p. 490.
102 B.F. Hartzler, p. 185.
103 *Ibid.*
104 Walter E. Yoder, *ibid.*
105 Harold S. Bender, "Music, Church," *Mennonite Encyclopedia* III:791–92.
106 John D. Brunk, *Educational Vocal Studies* (Scottdale: Mennonite Publishing House, 1912).
107 *Ibid.*, p. v.
108 Richard W.Lewis, "This Jazz Age," *Christian Monitor* (January 1929):30–32.

109   John D. Brunk, p. v.
110   J.H. "Mennonitische Bibelschulen in Canada," *Warte-Jahrbuch*, 1943, pp. 32–36.
111   The information in this table comes from diverse sources including *Mennonite Encyclopedia* (check under place names or institutional names); Frank H. Epp, *Mennonite Exodus*, p. 315; *Jahrbuch*, 1936, pp. 75–76; *Jahrbuch*, 1937, pp. 72–76; *Jahrbuch*, 1938, p. 21; *Jahrbuch*, 1939, pp. 59–62; *Jahrbuch*, 1940, pp. 47–49; *Verhandlungen* (ND), 1931, pp. 5–7; *Verhandlungen* (ND), 1932, pp. 50–51; *Verhandlungen* (ND), 1933, pp. 72–76; Orland Gingerich, *The Amish of Canada*, p. 99; L.J. Burkholder, *A Brief History of the Mennonites of Ontario*, pp. 166–67, 243.
112   Walter Sawatsky, "History of the Evangelical Mennonite Mission Conference" (research paper, Goshen College, 1967), p. 10.
113   Ben Harder, "The Bible Institute-College Movement in Canada," *Journal of Canadian Church Historical Society* 22 (April 1980):29–45.
114   W.E. Mann, *Sect, Cult and Church in Alberta* (Toronto: University of Toronto Press, 1955), p. 86.
115   Helena M. Brown, *Bergthal Church: 1903–1978* (Didsbury, Alta.: Anniversary Committee, 1978), p. 10.
116   *Ibid.*, pp. 7, 10.
117   J.B. Toews, "Influences on Mennonite Brethren Theology," a paper presented to Symposium sponsored by Center for Mennonite Brethren Studies in Canada, 21–22 November 1980, p. 3.
118   *Calendar of Appointments*, 1921–22, p. [17].
119   Gerhard I. Peters, *A History of the First Mennonite Church, Greendale, B.C.*, 1976, p. 46; G.S. Rempel, ed., *A Historical Sketch of the Churches of the Evangelical Mennonite Brethren* [1939], p. 16.
120   Ernest A. Jeschke, *Memoirs* (Goshen, Ind.: Marlin Jeschke, 1966), p. 175.
121   "Protokoll der Predigerkonferenz," *Jahrbuch*, 1939, p. 6.
122   J.A. Toews, "Die Schulbestrebungen im Noerdlichen Distrikt der Mennoniten-Bruedergemeinden Canadas," *Verhandlungen der 30. Noerdlichen Distrikt-Konferenz der Mennoniten-Bruedergemeinden von Nord-Amerika* (1939), pp. 24–26.
123   J.F. Redekop, "Die Gefahren unserer Gemeinden in der Jetztzeit," *Verhandlungen der 24. Noerdlichen Distrikt-Konferenz der Mennoniten-Bruedergemeinden von Nord-Amerika* (1933), p. 87.
124   J.B. Toews, *ibid.*, p. 4.
125   S.F. Coffman, "The Bible School," *Calendar of Appointments*, 1934, pp. 32–33.
126   L.J. Burkholder, *A Brief History of the Mennonites in Ontario* (Markham, Ont.: Mennonite Conference of Ontario, 1935), pp. 166–67.

127   CGC, II-2.1.2.2.2, Mennonite Conference of Ontario, Secretary's Records, 1936, "Report of Solicitation and Building Committee..."
128   Burkholder, p. 243.
129   CGC, XV-31.2, "1930—Bible Schools," Paul Voegtlin to Frank H. Epp, 23 September 1981.
130   "Bericht von den vereinigten Bibelschulen," *Verhandlungen* (ND), 1935, p. 48; *Jahrbuch*, 1940, pp. 37; CGC, II-1.A.1, "Conference Programs, Reports, and Resolutions"; C.F. Yake, "1937 Report of Summer Bible Schools in the Mennonite Church," *Mennonite Year-Book and Directory*, 1938, p. 30; CMBS, "Jubilee Celebration, Mennonite Brethren Church, La Glace, Alberta, 1928–1978," pp. 27–30.
131   W.E. Mann, p. 73.
132   *Conference Journal* (NW), 1934, p. 20.
133   *Jahrbuch*, 1938, p. 17.
134   J.B. Penner, "Innere Mission," *Verhandlungen*, 1936, p. 46.
135   CGC, XV-31.2, "1930—BC," H. Warkentin to John Krahn, 29 January 1955.
136   *Verhandlungen* (ND), 1937, p. 21. See also *Verhandlungen* (ND), 1936, p. 49.
137   Roy S. Koch, "Report of the Tract Director," *Calendar of Appointments*, 1946–47, p. 22.
138   *Verhandlungen* (ND), 1941, pp. 30–31.
139   L.J. Burkholder, *A Brief History of the Mennonites in Ontario* (Markham, Ont.: Mennonite Conference of Ontario, 1935), p. 161.
140   L.J. Burkholder, p. 196.
141   *Conference Journal* (O), 1938, pp. 29–30.
142   CGC, II-2.1.2.2.2, Mennonite Conference of Ontario, Secretary's Records, Jesse B. Martin, "Report, in part, of the Home Evangelist to Annual Conference," n.d.
143   *Calendar of Appointments*, 1934, p. 14.
144   Moses H. Roth, "Report of the Rural Mission Committee," *Calendar of Appointments*, 1940, pp. 13–14.
145   See, for example, *Verhandlungen* (ND), 1935, pp. 10–14.
146   G.G. Epp, "Bericht des Komitees fuer Inner Mission," *Jahrbuch*, 1933, p. 70.
147   Johann Rempel, "Wie koennte mehr Interesse...," *Jahrbuch*, 1930, pp. 45–47.
148   *Ibid.*, p. 46.
149   *Ibid.*, p. 47.
150   See *Calendar of Appointments*, 1937–38, p. [13], for summary of Toronto city mission activities.
151   Harold D. Groh reported in 1940 that "the general trend from the

city to the country which has been evident in recent years, has continued," in "Report of the Toronto Mission Superintendent," *Calendar of Appointments*, 1940, p. 11.

152   H.S. Bender, "Girls' Homes," *Mennonite Encyclopedia* 2: 521–22; J.J.Thiessen, "Bericht ueber die Maedchenheime," *Jahrbuch*, 1940, pp. 38–40; *Verhandlungen* (ND), 1933, p. 44; see also J.J. Thiessen in *Warte-Jahrbuch*, 1943, pp. 60–63, and "Das Maedchenheim in Vancouver, B.C.," *Warte-Jahrbuch*, 1943, pp. 63–65.

153   J.J. Thiessen, "Das mennonitische Maedchenheim in Saskatoon, 1931–1943," *Warte-Jahrbuch*, 1943, pp. 60–63.

154   "Entstehung und Entwicklung des Maria-Martha Heims," *Verhandlungen* (ND), 1933, pp. 30–38.

155   Thiessen, pp. 38–40.

156   Johann Rempel, "Beitrag zur sexuellen Frage," *Konferenz-Bericht der 26. Konferenz der Mennoniten im mittleren Kanada* (2–4 July 1928): pp. 17–23.

157   The entire passage reads as follows: "Then Judah said to Onan, 'Go in to your brother's wife, and perform the duty of a brother-in-law to her, and raise up offspring for your brother.' But Onan knew that the offspring would not be his; so when he went in to his brother's wife he spilled the semen on the ground, lest he should give offspring to his brother. And what he did was displeasing in the sight of the Lord, and he slew him also."

158   Michael Bliss, " 'Pure Books on Avoided Subjects': Pre-Freudian Sexual Ideas in Canada," *Historical Papers/Communications Historiques* (a selection from the papers presented at the 1970 Annual Meeting of the Canadian Historical Association held at Winnipeg), pp. 89–108.

159   See, for example, C.C. Peters, "Der Zerfall der Ehe . . . ," *Jahrbuch*, 1930, pp. 56–65.

160   *Ibid.*, pp. 31–34.

161   *Ibid.*, p. 33.

162   A.A. Kroeker, "Gesamtbericht der Stadtmissionsarbeit fuer das Jahr 1939 bis 1940," *Verhandlungen* (ND), 1941, pp. 32–33.

163   Harry B. Dyck, "The History and Development of the Bethel Mennonite Church" (research paper, Canadian Mennonite Bible College, 1965), pp. 5–9; *Jahrbuch*, 1939, p. 49.

164   A resolution passed in 1920 by the Mennonite Conference of Ontario on the subject of Bible instruction and secular education anticipated the changing times. See *Calendar of Appointments*, 1920–21, p. [15].

165   J.J. Klassen, "Christentum und Beruf," *Jahrbuch*, 1930, p. 38 ff.

166   *Ibid.*, p. 43.

167   *Ibid.*

168 *Ibid.*, p. 44.
169 Daniel Loewen, "Unsere Aufgaben unserer Jugend gegenueber," *Jahrbuch*, 1929, pp. 52–58.
170 J.J. Siemens, "Sunflower Rebuilds Community," *Mennonite Life* (July 1949): 28–29.
171 The international co-op movement repeatedly emphasized the importance of education as an instrument for enlightening and mobilizing the common people (cf. "Education, Coops Need of Mr. & Mrs. Canada," *Toronto Daily Star*, 6 December 1944). Siemens extended this argument even further in his promotion of co-ops as educational centres for social and non-violent evangelization.
172 CGC, XV-31.2, "1950 — J.J. Siemens," "Canadian Citizenship to Me as a Farmer Means. . . ," n.d.
173 *Ibid.*
174 Henry J. Gerbrandt, *Adventure in Faith: The Background in Europe and the Development in Canada of the Bergthaler Mennonite Church of Manitoba* (Altona, Man.: D.W. Friesen & Sons, 1970), p. 271.
175 CGC, XV-31.2, "1940 — J.J. Siemens," "Salute to Agriculture," n.d.
176 L.J. Burkholder, *A Brief History of the Mennonites in Ontario* (Markham, Ont.: Mennonite Conference of Ontario, 1935), p. 155.
177 *Ibid.*
178 *Ibid.*
179 *Ibid.*
180 Sue Steiner, "From Ewald's to Golden Rule to Provident: Bookselling Then and Now," *Mennonite Reporter* (12 November 1979), B1; *Mission News Bulletin* 15 (May 1938):1.
181 *Jahrbuch*, 1940, p. 42; see also *Jahrbuch*, 1939, p. 86.
182 *Calendar of Appointments*, 1931–32, p. [25].
183 *Ibid.*
184 *Calendar of Appointments*, 1933–34, p. [19].
185 *Calendar of Appointments*, 1934, p. 17.
186 J.C. Fretz, "The Educational and Young People's Problems Committee," *Calendar of Appointments*, 1940, p. 22. See also "Conference Resolutions," *ibid.*, p. 24.
187 *Calendar of Appointments*, 1931–32, p. [25]; *Calendar of Appointments*, 1933–34, p. 19; *Calendar of Appointments*, 1942–43, p. 21.
188 J.C. Fretz, "The Educational and Young People's Problems Committee," *Calendar of Appointments*, 1940, p. 22. See also "Conference Resolutions," *ibid.*, p. 24.
189 CGC, XV-31.2, "1930 — D.W. Friesen." This file contains correspondence from the 1930s of the father with his sons Dave, John, Ted, and Raymond.
190 *Ibid.*, D.W. Friesen, Altona, to Ted Friesen, MCI, Gretna, 29 May 1937.

191   *Ibid.*, D.W. Friesen to John K. Friesen, 9 November 1936.
192   *Ibid.*, D.W. Friesen, Altona, to John K. Friesen, Winnipeg, 14 July 1936.
193   *Ibid.*, John K. Friesen to "Eltern," 21 February 1937.
194   *Ibid.*, John K. Friesen, Virden, to "Folks at Home," 28 October 1939.
195   *Ibid.*, J.K. Friesen to "Liebe Eltern," 11 February 1940.
196   *Ibid.*, J.K. Friesen to "Folks at Home," 28 October 1939.
197   *Ibid.*, from "The Statement of the Executive of the National Young People's Union of the United Church of Canada," 1 January 1940.
198   For a bibliography and analysis, see Henry Paetkau, "The Fundamentalist-Modernist Controversy and the Defence of the Faith According to Horsch and Janzen" (research paper, Conrad Grebel College, University of Waterloo, 1976).
199   Henry Paetkau, "Jacob H. Janzen (1878–1950): A Man with a Mission to His People" (research paper, University of Waterloo, 1976).
200   J.H. Janzen, "Unsere Aufgaben angesichts des Vordringens des Modernismus," *Der Bote* 9 (4 May 1932): 1–2.
201   CGC, J.H. Janzen Collection, General Correspondence, J.H. Janzen, "The Modernist Fundamentalist Fear," 29 December 1933.
202   J.H. Janzen, "Modernismus—eine Gefahr fuer unsere Gemeinden," *Der Bote* 8 (21 October 1931):1–2.
203   CGC, XV-31.2, "1930—Youth," Letter from I.G. Neufeld to Frank H. Epp, 10 March 1981.
204   J.H. Enns, "Der Ausbau unserer Bibelschulen," *Jahrbuch*, 1935, pp. 45–46; J.P. Klassen, "Der Prediger in der Familie und im Gesellschaftsleben," and J.J. Thiessen, "Der Wert periodisch sich wierderholender Predigerkurse," *Jahrbuch*, 1931, pp. 8–15; J.H. Enns, "Mittel zur Foerderung des Predigers," *Jahrbuch*, 1936, pp. 29–30; J.P. Klassen, "Die Notwendigkeit einer deutschen Bibliothek mit besonderer Bereucksichtigung der Prediger," *Jahrbuch*, 1933, pp. 43–45; Isaak P. Klassen, "Ein Ratschlag fuer Bibliothekswesen," *Jahrbuch*, 1933, pp. 45–56.
205   J.G. Rempel, "Unsere Bibelschulen," *Jahrbuch*, 1939, p. 62.
206   Peter H. Dirks, "Die Ausruestung zum Predigtdienst," *Jahrbuch*, 1939, pp. 29–30.
207   *Jahrbuch*, 1938, p. 23.
208   Peter H. Dirks, "Die Ausruestung zum Predigtdienst," *Jahrbuch*, 1939, p. 30.
209   David Toews, "Ist es an der Zeit an die Gruendung einer Predigerschule zu denken?" *Jahrbuch*, 1937, pp. 36–40; see also *Jahrbuch*, 1937, p. 7.
210   Based on Census of Canada, *Calendar of Appointments*, *Conference Journal*, *Verhandlungen* (ND), and *Jahrbuch*, respectively.

II. Preserving the Culture

Loving, but drastic, action will be needed to save the doctrine [of separation and nonconformity] and its expressions within the brotherhood — OSCAR BURKHOLDER.[1]

We should be faithfully concerned about our mother tongue, to use it and to preserve it. We should be prepared to make big sacrifices, for this glorious heritage is for us a holy obligation — A.J. SCHELLENBERG.[2]

KEEPING THE YOUNG PEOPLE and preserving the culture, as has already been noted, were in constant tension with each other, but this did not mean that one had to be sacrificed to preserve the other. To be sure, they were, or appeared to be, in diametric opposition, whenever youth's impulse for change faced directly culture's respect for the status quo and whenever the inclination of the young to accept contemporary styles or to use the English language clashed with the determination of the older generation to preserve the old ways and the German language. Yet, the notion that Mennonite religion and culture was a total way of life, which it was good for the young to accept, was not easily set aside, and thus, more often than not, the concerns for youth and culture went hand in hand.

In the Mennonite situation, culture had at least two different but deeply interwoven meanings. On the one hand, Mennonite culture was the Mennonite way of life, firmly rooted in biblical religion, holistic in its theology, with a seven-day-a-week life-embracing ethic that called for a separation from the state and from the larger society.

498

It centred in the family and in the congregational community, both of which were viewed as images of the kingdom of God, both present and coming.

Culture also meant, or had come to mean, particular styles in which the Mennonite way of life appeared and without which it could not exist. Thus, for some Mennonites, culture above all meant agriculture and land-based communities. For others, for whom land had become less than absolutely essential, cultural priorities were focused on such factors as language. Then there were those for whom both land and the language had become secondary, and for them culture meant a particular nonconformed life style. Finally, for some Mennonites, none of the above were important as both religion and culture shifted to new arenas of experience and understanding.

Culture Interpreted and Explained

The efforts to preserve the culture were mostly focused internally, that is, within the Mennonite community, but bold attempts were also made to bring about an appreciation for, or at least accurate information about, the Mennonite way of life on the outside. The continuity of that way of life, it was recognized, required a much better public understanding. The Mennonites had devoted too little attention to defending and interpreting themselves, and thus, false reports in the media had done very considerable damage.

The negative publicity accompanying conscription in the Great War, the "nationalization" of the public schools, the emigrations to Latin America, the immigrations from Russia, the Friesen-Braun trials, and Canadian reluctance to admit Moscow refugees had taken their toll, and something had to be done to increase public acceptance and to strengthen Mennonite self-respect. To help prevent the "Mennonite problem" (*Mennonitenfrage*) from becoming acute again, the Conference of Mennonites in Central Canada in 1930 appointed a public relations committee (*Aufklaerungskomitee*).[3]

This initiative to bring about public enlightenment was an unprecedented undertaking, although individuals like David Toews and H.S. Bender had taken on the press from time to time. It was also unorthodox in the sense of the Mennonite assumption that misunderstanding, not unlike persecution, was one of the by-products of the faith and that its quiet endurance was one of the virtues of Christian life. Moreover, the best public relations for the Mennonites, it had always been assumed, were the Mennonite people themselves. As Johann G. Rempel, the spokesman for the committee, suggested:

> Our young people are studying at the universities, our girls working as domestics in the homes in large and small cities, the teachers from our people, our businessmen and farmers, in short — all [our people in the various] vocations, are involved consciously or unconsciously in negative or positive public relations [*Aufklaerungsarbeit*] for our people.[4]

Helpful literature was seen, however, as a useful supplement to a good reputation and the communications emanating therefrom. Therefore, the works of C. Henry Smith, the eminent Mennonite historian of the time, were strategically distributed.[5] *The Mennonites of America* and *The Coming of the Russian Mennonites*, however, were somewhat far removed from the contemporary situation in that the former concentrated on the Mennonites in the U.S.A. and the latter on the immigration of the nineteenth century.

One of the most useful tools of enlightenment, therefore, became a 1932 pamphlet *The Mennonites*, first presented as an address by H.H. Ewert before the Historical and Scientific Society of Manitoba. The monograph was published and distributed by the committee in both the English and the German language, the latter obviously for internal consumption. H.H. Ewert identified the Mennonites as a pioneer religious society, whose way of life was unique and worthy of perpetuation.[6] They were, he said, "the first to deny the authority of the state over the individual conscience, to take a positive stand against war, and to raise a protest against slavery."[7]

An event similar to Ewert's appearance to interpret the Mennonites before a regional historical society also happened in the east, when S.F. Coffman addressed the Waterloo Historical Society on "The Adventure of Faith."[8] Coffman listed Anabaptist leaders Grebel, Manz, and Menno among those religious adventurers who "set at liberty the conscience of men." They and their followers lived "a simple life, a pure life, and a peaceful life" and endured "hardship, suffering, persecution" like no others for their nonresistant faith. Everywhere they witnessed to their faith "in its three-fold form: liberty of conscience, separation of church and state, and obedience to the gospel of the prince of peace." While the pioneers gave "no inheritance of millions to their children," they bequeathed the treasures of character, of love for the Bible, and of peace for all mankind.

The historical sense communicated by Coffman several years later became a resolve on the part of the Mennonite Conference of Ontario to have its history preserved and recorded. The Old Mennonites were keenly aware that the New Mennonites had published their first history in 1920, albeit not solely for Ontario but for the whole denomination.[9] Lawrence J. Burkholder completed and published in 1936 the first book-length history of all the Mennonites of Ontario.[10] He viewed his people as a cultural force, "a strong resistance against the inroads" of evil forces such as "materialism, unbelief, and other forms of worldliness."[11]

Burkholder's review led him to be optimistic about "the outlook for the Mennonite Church" if only the various branches thereof could "celebrate a genuine spiritual union on a strictly scriptural basis."[12] A small beginning of "a few struggling settlers in the woods" had grown into a strong body of about 8,000 church members in about 60 regular preaching places. Several thousand children would undoubtedly grow up to "perpetuate the doctrine for which our forefathers died" and as far as the young people were concerned, "we are holding our own." About 1,700 had attended Bible school and other hundreds were taking part in other young people's functions.

> Generally, we are able to maintain our regular places of work. There has been very little retrenchment. New fields are being opened. The aggressive missionary spirit is gratifying. . . .[13]

The influential role of Mennonite religious culture in preserving and propagating certain values was noted also by Jacob H. Janzen. A prolific writer of interpretative articles for the Mennonite press as well as curricular materials for children—his *Tales of Mennonite History* was the first such English-language source produced in Canada—Janzen recognized that a full assessment of Mennonitism was not possible until more time had passed.[14] An epoch of church and world history, and not just a lifetime, were required to see a movement in its true perspectives. Judgements could not be made by the makers of history but by those who, in due course, analysed and wrote about it. Janzen did not subscribe to the view that Mennonites possessed the full and complete truth.

Yet, history had already made a judgement and, according to Janzen, it was a favourable one. Evidence thereof could be seen in the fact that many governments permitted the Mennonites to affirm rather than to swear and that even in Canada an almost limitless trust was extended to them as, for instance, in the business dealings of everyday life. All that was a heritage passed on from earlier generations of believers whose faith was a sound one. And faith's application in daily life is what counted:

> The world today knows very little or nothing about the special teachings of the Mennonites, but the strength and influence of their faith were known, and to the world that is all that mattered. [15]

For Janzen, the positive features of Mennonitism were represented by baptism upon confession of faith — he used the word adult baptism (*Grosstaufe*) — nonresistance, non-swearing of the oath, and the de-emphasis of ritualistic forms. Baptism upon confession of faith, he said, represented the struggle for a decisive and conscientious Christianity. Nonresistance was the symbol of the longing and the struggle for a world-embracing love which alone could save mankind. The non-swearing of the oath signified a higher loyalty and the struggle for truthfulness and veracity. And the lack of formalism was a sign that the peaks of Christian living were not to be sought in a highly developed ritual but rather in a fulfilled and sanctified daily life, in other words, in a practical Christianity.

The representative writings of persons like L.J. Burkholder, S.F. Coffman, H.H. Ewert, J.H. Janzen, and C. Henry Smith all reflected the deep conviction that the Anabaptist pioneers had rediscovered the true essence of the Christian faith, that this essence was contemporaneously represented, at least in theory, in the Mennonite way of life, and that its perpetuation deserved a special effort and required the help of certain factors, here identified as culture. Some preservative energies, of course, were concentrated on the past only, but even the two small archives that were established appeared because the record of the past was helpful for the future. Burkholder not only wrote the first book-length history of the Mennonites in Ontario, but along with that project began an archival collection, which, lacking any other appropriate placement, found its safekeeping in the Toronto archives of the Ontario government. The rationale for such record-keeping was that it would benefit the generations to follow. In the words of S.F. Coffman:

> We have lost a great deal of experience and have had many trials which otherwise might have been avoided had we the records of some of our brethren who have passed on without leaving us some guide by which to attain greater successes and avoid failures.[16]

The only other archives established at this time were in western Canada, where B.J. Schellenberg, a Russlaender, obtained token support ($25 a year) from the Conference of Mennonites in Canada to do something about preserving the Russian Mennonite heritage.[17] Russia was a precious homeland, and while it was gone forever it had to be remembered, said Schellenberg. Even the rich archives gathered by P.M. Friesen and others had been disturbed. It was desirable and necessary, therefore, to found an archives to restore and preserve as much as possible of that which had been lost.

> We left much behind. We were so blessed by earthly goods. We were rich in spiritual culture. Men full of spirit and life contributed to our development and many good schools we could call our own. Our settlements with their culture were like an oasis in the desert.[18]

Varieties of Separate Culture

Those who championed Mennonite religious culture generally believed that its expression and preservation required particular forms, moulds, or styles. Thus, culture was both an end and a means to an end; both substance and style; both wine and wineskins. However culture was defined, for most Mennonites it had, or had to have, a separatist quality about it. Long ago, the preservation of the Mennonite way of life had come to be associated with separation from the world. This remained true to a very considerable extent in the 1930s, though the particular focus of that separation varied among the different Mennonite groups. Basically there were three forms: geographic separatism, which tended to be the most extreme and the most inclusive of all other forms of separatism; social separatism, which took the nonconformity doctrine very seriously; and linguistic separatism, which in the 1930s translated itself into an unprecedented crusade to maintain the *Muttersprache* (mother tongue).

All three forms of separatism had been important to Mennonite immigrants coming into the country, and since geographic separation embraced them all, the lands of the German Land Company, the German Block of the Amish, and the East and West Reserves in Manitoba represented Mennonite culture in its most inclusive and concentrated form. As geographic separatism had become less and less possible, those to whom it was most important became the more insistent on that option. Among the Swiss, the Old Order Mennonites and the Old Order Amish represented the clearest examples of that position. Among the Dutch, the emigrants to Mexico and Paraguay had been the most unequivocal in this regard. As one sociologist wrote about that kind of Mennonite boundary maintenance:

> It is through the continuing efforts to maintain some semblance of geographical separation from the surrounding secular community, that the members of the church community reinforce their concept of cultural identity and maintain not only geographical boundaries but symbolic boundaries as well.[19]

Those Mennonites whose identity and survival were no longer linked to isolated parcels or colonies of land, or even to agriculture, but who none the less wanted to preserve the Mennonite ways, had to find other means to maintain the boundaries. For one sector of the Swiss Mennonite community this meant applying rather strict social nonconformity standards, in other words a distinctive life style. For one sector of the Dutch Mennonite community the German language was the all-important value not to be surrendered, lest all be lost. Like the land, so the nonconformed life style and the German language represented values in themselves, but they were also the actual and symbolic fences which kept the world out and Mennonite values intact.

Beyond the continuum of Mennonite cultural retentionists, for whom their religious way of life was incomplete without land and/or the nonconformed life style and/or the German language, were those Mennonites, one congregational family in particular, for whom all of these things had become unimportant or even a hindrance to the pursuit of the essentials. It wasn't that the Mennonite Brethren in Christ all left the farms or wore flashy clothing, but their explicit definition of religious faith and their implicit definition of culture had moved them rather far away from traditional Mennonite emphases.[20]

This was not surprising because their emergence in the nineteenth century had been a reaction to those who "clung tenaciously to the old traditions of the church."[21] The "New Mennonites," as they were popularly called, led in the introduction of the English language, four-part singing, and adjustment to change generally. That denomination became an example of how cultural change at one level tends to go hand in hand with changes at other levels. The Mennonite Brethren in Christ changed not only the styles, including the ministry, church government, and mode of baptism, but also the substance, as they became "so different from the various Mennonite groups in both doctrine and practice."[22] On the basis of the New Mennonite experience and his study of Mennonite assimilation, Paul Knowles concluded that to become a New Mennonite meant eventually to become a non-Mennonite.[23] It was the intuitive sense that a changing form produced, or was accompanied by, a change in religious essence that made other Mennonites zealous about culture maintenance. Upon observing the New Mennonites, the Old Mennonites and the Old Order Mennonites knew that the faith could be lost if they neglected the forms.

The New Mennonites continued to carry the name "Mennonite" and they saw themselves still within the nonresistant family of Christians, but their preachers rarely spoke on the subject and the borrowings from other traditions were extensive: from the Wesleyans, they accepted revivalism, a second work of grace, doctrines of holiness and the notion of complete sanctification, and new forms of church government; from the Pentecostals, the emphasis on the holy spirit, though never sufficiently to satisfy those who were really Pentecostal at heart; from the Calvinists, elements of predestination; and from the Darbyites, pre-millennialism.[24]

The new doctrines, the new spiritual styles, and the new ways of expressing the church life of the New Mennonites all had the effect of separating religion from its interwovenness with land and an economic order and with culture or a particular social order. The culture of the New Mennonites was the institutional church and the individual spirituality of the believer. No Mennonite group had advanced further down the road of finding one's religious identity in a

personalized salvation, a futurized millennium, and an institutionalized church than had the Mennonite Brethren in Christ. Of all the
conference-oriented Mennonites, they were the most conference-
centred. A wide array of activities were statistically accounted for
with the help of presiding elders, superintendents of various kinds,
and an almost endless list of committees.[25] In 1940, one Conference
of 25 congregations and 2,304 members had no fewer than 30
committees reporting to the annual meeting.[26]

The Conference wasn't really without culture, but rather
immersed totally in a new kind of denominational and institutional
culture. The New Mennonites were in many ways becoming non-
Mennonites, and given that fact, it should surprise no one that there
were calls for a complete erasure of the Mennonite identity. Such
requests were strongest from Alberta and Saskatchewan, where
public images of Mennonites and public linkages with Hutterites
and Doukhobors were felt as keen embarrassments and a hindrance to
missionary work. A resolution of the Canadian North-West District
Conference requested the church to "lay aside every weight" and
change its name:

> Whereas there are many thousands of Mennonites from for-
> eign countries already in Canada, and hundreds more are com-
> ing each year, who have but one thing in common with the
> MBC church, namely "non-resistance," and have many things
> which are quite objectionable, both to citizenship and spiritu-
> ality on account of which the name Mennonite has been
> brought into disrepute, thus becoming a great barrier and a
> positive hindrance to aggressive evangelism and church exten-
> sion in the Canadian Northwest.[27]

The eastern sector of the Mennonite Brethren in Christ church
was not quite as embarrassed by other Mennonites, hence not as
willing, at least not yet, to change the name. But the determination
with which other Mennonites defended the land, life style, and
language-related concepts of Mennonitism, was undoubtedly part of
the reason why the reaction to the culture was never-ending: not all
Mennonites were ready to go to Mexico or Fort Vermilion, back into
the nineteenth century, or to fall directly into the lap of those who
tended to equate German culture with religious culture.

The Old Mennonites of Ontario bore a resemblance to the New

Mennonites in the sense that they too evidenced many signs of acculturation. They had resisted many of the new ways about a generation longer, but the acceptance of the English language in preaching and worship, of four-part singing, of revivalism and the Sunday school, of more sophisticated conference structures, and of business and professions had come in due course. In other words, external forms and expressions had changed to a considerable extent.

The changes in theology and teaching now so characteristic of the New Mennonites, however, were less marked among the Old Mennonites. To be sure, doctrinal fundamentalism, as earlier described, had made deep inroads, but the emphasis on traditional Anabaptist fundamentals, especially the ethical teachings — nonresistance and nonconformity — had not been lost. On the contrary, the intense struggle for those fundamentals, begun afresh in the early 1920s, reached its peak in the 1930s and early 1940s as the Old Mennonites, and Amish along with them, sought to maintain those cultural borders, the crossing of which in their opinion imperilled the faith. Nonconformity was seen as the key to the maintenance of the borders.

The Nonconformed Life Style

The doctrine and practice of nonconformity to the world was established as the clear teaching of the scriptures and of the Mennonite heritage, as well as a principle of life.[28] One of the clearest explications of the doctrine came from the pen of Edward Yoder, who explained his position on the basis of both history and theology. From the historical perspective, it was the nonconformed minority on whom the advancement of certain ideals had always depended. The forward march of the kingdom of God was a slow and difficult one into terrain "every inch of which is bitterly contested by the forces of spiritual wickedness." Movement into the occupied terrain required "seemingly slow and patient effort. . . sowing, nurture, cultivation, [and] careful husbandry on someone's part." And that someone was the nonconformed minority, living and teaching neglected truths.

> Separation, a measure of isolation, or if we will, of noncon-
> formity to the prevailing environment, has been necessary for
> moral and spiritual culture in all ages.[29]

The philosophy of nonconformity was also behind the whole of the Old Testament history, Yoder explained. The life of Abraham and the Jewish nation represented "the principle of separation and of nonconformity" in biblical history. In order for that group of people to be a spiritual and moral blessing to the world, they had to be separated from their immediate surroundings, and they had to be schooled by special care and by a particular nurture. They needed to develop a tradition and "a national culture that embodied higher ideals of monotheism, of spiritual service and worship, of moral performance, than prevailed among mankind at large at that time."[30]

In the New Testament, Christ taught that his followers had to be separated from the world in their faith and life, even if this meant hostility, and that at the beginning of the church "there existed a compact and concentrated fellowship that marked them from the world and society at large." Much of this was changed after Emperor Constantine gave official recognition to the church. Christians lost their separateness, as they made alliances with the world "which became Christian in name, but in name only."[31] Thus, the line of demarcation between the church and the world was fatally obscured. However, nonconformity continued through small, separated groups including the medieval monastics, men and women who sought "a deeper spiritual culture." Other nonconformist groups were "Cathars, Novatians, Paulicians, Bogomils, Albigenses, Waldenses, Lollards, Anabaptists, Mennonites, Stundists . . . also Baptists, Independents and Assemblies of Brethren. . . ."[32]

In today's world a separated, nonconformed Christianity was necessary because there was no time when the "inevitable tension between his way of life, his divine gospel and the life of the surrounding world will cease to exist."[33] American society was a good example of the worldly spirit, the *Zeitgeist*, which had to be resisted. In America, conformity was "the social law" and everybody wore "the same sort of clothes, read the same sort of magazines, [belonged] to the same sort of social organizations."[34] The Puritan tradition was rapidly disappearing, as was evident in the "sabbath desecration, gambling, amusements both brutal and frivolous, the use of liquor . . . ," and, what was most problematic of all, the system of state education, which "emphasized the secular and material side of life," in many places to the exclusion of religious teaching.[35]

The general reduction of cultural tastes, intellectual standards, and morals "to the lowest denominator common to every citizen of the land" meant, of course, that the serious Christian church and the serious Christian had to offer resistance. And if the professed Christian church at large failed in this regard, then

> . . . let small groups heed the call to challenge the prevailing lukewarmness, indifferentism, worldliness, spiritual apathy of respectable society, by living a separated life, a Christlike life, a non-conformed life.[36]

Yoder was quick to recognize that nonconformity could be a negative phenomenon. No one should practise nonconformity "on merely unsocial or anti-social grounds." And conforming to a nonconformed group could also be misleading. One must, he said, "conform to Christ more than to even a non-conformed group."[37] Other writers also recognized that the teaching and practice of nonconformity could easily be abused or lead to undesirable consequences. This was evident throughout the Mennonite church, which was going through "a bewildering phase," resulting in many different interpretations "in different sections of the church."[38] There were two extremes, both of which should be avoided, according to one writer. One extreme view saw the essence of nonconformity only in "a uniform pattern of clothes prescribed by district conference." The other extreme view was devoid of specifics and expected only that Christians "live less extravagantly than non-Christians and have a genuine love for and practice of the simple life."[39]

Another problem was that nonconformity could lead to such extremes of isolation and insulation from the affairs of the world that some of the benefits of the world were denied.[40] Not only did a "self-chosen, restricted cultural status" mean the denial of such benefits but it also accounted for "the perpetual exodus of many of their most talented boys and girls."[41] And, equally important:

> It led inevitably to the deplorable error of renouncing as sinful the love of beauty in sound, color, and form.[42]

In the 1930s, however, Mennonite church leaders viewed insufficient nonconformity as a greater danger than excessive isolation. This fear was general among the Dutch, including both Russlaender and Kanadier groups, as well as among the Swiss Mennonites and Amish, but it found its most concrete and continuous expression among the Old Mennonites, throughout the 1930s. Especially from 1936 on, when the Old Mennonite General Conference meeting in Kitchener had nonconformity as its main theme, until early into the next decade was this the case. Then a special session of the Mennonite Conference of Ontario reconfirmed the nonconformist principle as well as its application in no uncertain terms. Once again — the reader must not forget the Ontario crises of the 1920s, which split Kitchener's historic first church on this very issue — nonconformity was the chief item of discussion not only at church conferences and in many congregations, but also in the papers of the denomination. The weekly *Gospel Herald* and the monthly *Christian Monitor* were full of nonconformist stories. Besides two major article series on "present-day issues" and "non-conformity" in the weekly *Herald*, there were editorials, letters, and reader contributions of all kinds. Generally speaking, all made the point that "the principle and call to separation runs through the Bible from beginning to end."[43]

The practice of separation and the pursuit of nonconformity was no longer a simple matter as it once had been. For the first two centuries of Mennonite existence in North America, isolation and insulation had been not only tolerated but also fostered by general social conditions. The rural existence, the compact communities, the frontier psychology, and the spirit of individualism all contributed to the segregation so much desired by the church. The use of the German language likewise contributed to a feeling of separateness.[44]

All the traditional barriers to conformity had vanished, and it was now a question of finding substitute symbols of, and standards for, separation. The most prominent symbol of nonconformity turned out to be dress. And this was not inappropriate, because the dress question was the first thing that was mentioned after the fall of man.[45] Both the Old and the New Testaments taught frequently against vain display, against immodest apparel, against costly array, and spoke in favour of modest apparel and clothing that was both serviceable and economical.[46]

It was easier to assert that Christian nonconformity required certain standards of dress than to determine in a way satisfactory to all what such standards should be. What, for instance, was meant by modesty of dress? Since fashions were constantly changing, guidelines good for all time couldn't easily be laid down. However, one could begin to establish some norm by rejecting the standards of the world and by applying some principles or tests to other options.[47] Three worldly standards were unacceptable without equivocation. They were: no apparel at all, meaning nudity; apparel insufficient or too flimsy, because God intended apparel for a covering and not for the advertising of the human form; and superfluous dress, meaning apparel for the purpose of ornamentation and display.[48]

It was too often the case, one writer complained, that the sisters and the brothers followed the fashion designers of the day.[49] "Colored neckties, fancy socks, stylish hats, and . . . other vanities," marked worldly men. Worldly women were those who "responded to the call of the world" when "the styles of the world called for full but short skirts" and who lengthened them only when "the fashion designers advertised a new trend." Even those "who wore a uniform garb" changed the design "from the full skirt to long, form-fitting skirt. . . ." All of which brought forth one preacher's lament:

> It is with shame that we must acknowledge that many Menno-
> nites today have a great deal more respect for fashion journals
> than they do for divine revelation . . . for the fashion designers
> than they have for faithful ministers. . . .[50]

All clothing, it was said, should pass the test of modesty and decency. Men should not appear shirtless while at work or "in public with open neck bands or sleeves rolled up, or short sleeves, as if they were coming from firing a furnace of molten metal."[51] For women, insufficient clothing and transparent clothing were out, and this included "bathing suits, low-necked dresses, short sleeves, sleeveless dresses, high skirts, flesh-colored stockings, [going] stockingless, waistless, tight skirts, sheer dress showing the form, diverse colors pointing out form. . . ."[52] Showmanship and display were roundly condemned. This included "all attempts at dressing up the hair for show," all ornaments or jewellery, meaning also wedding rings.[53] Christian people should be guided by the test of simplicity, which ruled against the use of "ribbons, ruffles, neckties, stick pins, elaborate tuckings, fancy workings, multiplied suits of variable fashion, costly materials, useless buttons, powders, paint, curled hair, etc., etc."[54]

Other tests of appropriate apparel included distinction of the sexes and church regulation. Obviously, men and women should be distinguishable by their clothing but beyond that "there should be sufficient uniformity among God's people to identify them in every phase of non-conformity as children of God."[55] Church members could not wear a soldier's uniform, a Boy Scout's uniform, the uniform of worldly organizations, or seasonal fads, but they should wear the uniform prescribed by the church. For the women this meant "the adopted form of devotional covering" and not substitutes like the loose veil, or hats, or caps, or worldly fashion bonnets, or fancy-textured bonnets.[56] For the men this meant the plain coat.[57]

Economy was a further test of the right thing to wear. The Christian should have a pattern that didn't have to be changed constantly with the changing styles of the world. The avoidance of coloured neckties and socks and fancy shirts, for instance, was an economy measure. Presumably, lower expenditures for clothing meant higher giving for the Lord. In one denomination, it was pointed out, the mission offering had dropped $65,000 a year when the dress question had been dropped.[58] A single set of clothes or a single kind of clothing represented economy but also democracy. In the words of editor Daniel Kauffman, one of the foremost nonconformity crusaders of the time:

> The Gospel of Christ nowhere upholds one standard of cloth-
> ing for ministers and another standard for laymen; one stan-
> dard for sisters and another for brethren; one standard to
> attend your own meeting and another standard when you
> attend other people's meetings; one standard when you are
> among your own people and another standard when you are
> among other people.[59]

Few issues on the annual agenda of the Mennonite Conference of Ontario brought forth resolutions so consistently in the 1930s as did the dress question. It was the problem which always pitted tradition-alists and modernizers against each other, with the former wanting the rules enforced and discipline applied at least at the time of communion.[60] This meant the denial of the bread and the cup for the disobedient.

In 1934, for instance, the Conference appointed all the bishops "to study the dress question and to apply the result of their study to all the congregations by way of example, practice and discipline."[61] A year later, they reported that "in the interests of Christian modesty and simplicity . . . we believe in the biblical teachings on the dress question (I Tim. 2:8 – 10, I Peter 3:1 – 7, Romans 12:2, Deut. 22:5, 1 John 2:15 – 17)."[62] Further, they concluded and recommended the following position: that the following of fashions, which change constantly, is deadly to the spiritual life; that the church cannot long imitate changing fashions without being led into following them entirely; that safety lies in breaking with changing fashions; that modesty and simplicity be insisted on; and that the "regulation garb" of the church be accepted as a practical solution to the problem.

For the carrying out of the above, the bishops recommended the preaching of biblical sermons on the dress problem frequently, appealing to the parents for co-operation, doing personal work by kindly and helpful appeals, calling in evangelists "who are effective on this problem," requesting the bishop of the district to preach at the church several evenings and make personal calls in the daytime, and requesting the assistance and co-operation of the ladies' aid. Further, the bishops suggested series of meetings in which the doctrines and disciplines were set forth, dress-related topics at the young people's institutes, and better counsel and examination of converts on this point before they were received into the fellowhip of the church. Loyal members were advised to encourage obedience to the principles. Then, if the desired result was not achieved, disciplinary action should be taken:

> . . . after proper work has been done with the offending
> member, that the same be visited, entreated to change, and,
> due time having elapsed, that the pastor notify the bishop in
> charge, and that scriptural action be taken, according to Matt.
> 18:17.

The 1935 position was difficult to enforce and a few years later the matter came up at the Conference again in the form of an inquiry as to eligibility for communion. Again the bishops were asked to study the question. Their reply revealed their impatience with the agitators on the dress issue and, in effect, told them to mind their own business. Reporting on behalf of the bishops, S. F. Coffman gave a seven-point set of principles for "governing the action of bishops and administering the ordinance of communion and in maintaining the proper order of fellowship with the church." Communion, he said, was administered "on the basis of individual confession of peace with God and the brotherhood, rather than on the basis of the judgment of others."[63] There were signs that some bishops were becoming quite reluctant to deny communion on the basis of improper dress. A year later, the Conference once again asked the bishops to be consistent in administering the policy on the bonnet:

> This conference advises and pleads for: unity of administration among bishops; such administration to be carried out as follows: 1) settlement of all old standing cases; 2) keeping all members up to date; 3) adhering, in such administration, to both biblical provisions and conference provisions, relative to all other problems, as well as the bonnet.[64]

The problem did not go away, but instead the considerable deviation from the standards of the church only increased and led the Conference to make further attempts "to solve this very vexing and oft-appearing problem."[65] In one year it dominated the Conference program at the regular and special sessions on three separate occasions. After special study sessions on the doctrine of separation in the Old and New Testaments and its relation to the doctrine of nonresistance, resolutions were adopted that influenced the Conference's "Constitution and Discipline" to be more conservatively directed. The plain bonnet was reaffirmed as "the approved headdress of our sisters," and "faithful compliance" was insisted upon.[66] Further:

> We maintain that our brethren and sisters should conform to the same principles of modest apparel with the purpose to witness to the Scriptural truth of simplicity and separation. We also believe that the wearing of the plain suit for the brethren and the cape dress for the sisters would consistently bear such testimony.[67]

Apparently, the resolution was necessary to avoid another split, this time in the conservative direction, "for the Mennonite Church in Ontario is very near the parting of the ways again." But everybody knew that the resolution alone wouldn't avoid it unless members were "loyal and obedient" and unless the bishops "deal with this problem in unity." It was a "now or never proposition" to save "the doctrine [of nonconformity] and its expressions within the brotherhood."[68]

A year later, support for the adopted position came also from the

Mennonite General Conference, which likewise had a special session on the nonconformity issue to bring bishops, district conferences, and congregations into line on the doctrine of nonconformity as "immodest and worldly attire (including hats for sisters), the wearing of jewellery (including wedding rings)" was made "a test of fellowship in communion" and, if persisted in, "a test of membership."[69]

The dress question was the most prominent but not the only nonconformity issue. Also important was the protection of the worship service from forms, rituals, and exercises that excited the sensibilities and pleased the flesh rather than moved the soul to deeper reverence of God.[70] To that end, "the use of musical instruments in public worship" was discouraged in order to "teach the superiority of congregational singing over that accompanied by musical instruments."[71] Entertainment did not belong in the church and Mennonites should not follow modern churches:

> Instead of scripture reading, preaching, singing of hymns, etc., there is the music of the pipe organ, the voices of chanting choruses or the opera type of solo, the reading of secular literature, movies, etc. —exercises that excite the sensibilities, are pleasing to the flesh rather than moving the soul to deeper reverence for God.[72]

Nonconformity also meant abstaining from worldly amusements such as "Sunday ball games, card games, fairs, play parties, dances, festivals, billiards, theatres, and summer resorts."[73] After all, John the Baptist lost his head at a birthday party "that included dancing, drunkenness, and an oath."[74] It meant total abstinence because "no total abstainer ever became a drunkard" and because no one wanted to be "under the influence of liquor when the Lord comes."[75] It meant staying away from movies, operas, dances, night clubs, and swimming pools, which places all were "feeders of lust and immorality . . . the means of wrecking countless young lives and others as they are led into sexual sins."[76]

Nonconformity also ruled out "life insurance for Christians."[77] God and "the fellowship of the saints" provided "all that life insurance offers without its objectionable features." Besides, life insurance was bad stewardship "because not one-half of the money paid in premiums by the policyholders is returned." It was also wrong to get something for a small investment and to place a money value upon a human life. Life insurance, said C.F. Derstine, was a species of gambling: it represented wealth gotten by vanity; it militated against labour and sacrifice; it undermined the law of frugality; it rejected trust in the Lord and help from relatives and the church; it violated Christian stewardship; it shut out the weak and the poor and the sick; it set aside the Lord's plan to aid the needy; and it fostered an independent spirit.[78]

Nonconformity meant not being "unequally yoked with unbelievers" or joining in "wrong affiliations."[79] Off limits were certain businesses because a Christian could enter business only to produce and distribute useful things.[80] The production and distribution of liquor and tobacco and the services of beauty parlours, movies, and billiard halls did not fall into this category. Nor did the making and selling of jewellery, powders, paints, lipsticks, and clothes of worldly design.

Nonconformity also meant non-membership in labour unions, because unionism resorted to violence and boycotts, which was anti-Christian, and because unionism destroyed personal freedom and individualism.[81] The "present day labor strikes" were offered as evidence and proof that nonresistant Christian people should hold themselves "aloof from every form of unionism, involving the unequal yoke with unbelievers."[82] The right of any man not to work, if in so doing he was not breaking a contract, was not questioned, "but violence resorted to by the labor organizations in an effort to prevent employers of labor to conduct their own business and to prevent non-union men from laboring cannot be defended." On unionism the Mennonite Conference of Ontario was unequivocal:

> In view of the intense activities of modern Unionism throughout the world, such as Bolshevism in Russia, and the CIO in North America . . . this conference wishes to reaffirm its position of non-affiliation [with] organizations that are both non-Christian and anti-Christian.[83]

Further, nonconformity meant not to be slothful in business. Misrepresentation in business transactions should be avoided and there should be no oppression or extortion. Having an abundance of capital was not a good enough reason for "living in luxury or extravagance." High-powered salesmanship was out, as was persuading a man to buy a new auto when he couldn't afford it. Get-rich-quick schemes, which had already made deep inroads among church members, were also warned against.

> Speculating in stocks and bonds, gambling on the Board of Trade, buying stock in oil wells, etc., etc., often truly are a source of great grief, and severe financial loss. As examples of real estate booms, we have cases in Florida, Texas, Montana, Canada, etc., where some of our well-meaning brethren have been victimized by unscrupulous promoters of real estate corporations.[84]

In a general way, the nonconformity emphasis of the Old Mennonites reflected the social ethic which most Mennonites in North America had claimed as their own at one time or another, with variations only in the specifics. Warnings against life insurance, the world of business, union membership, and worldly affiliation generally, and admonitions concerning immodest dress and indulgence in pleasure-related activities, were current in other Conferences, though nonconformity as a sustained crusade in this period in history most characterized the Old Mennonites.

Language and Values

There was, however, another crusade under way especially among the Russlaender, and this had to do with the preservation of the German language and ethnicity, and values related thereto. In the same way that the *Gospel Herald* and the *Christian Monitor* were overflowing with nonconformity concerns, so the papers serving the German-speaking Dutch Mennonites were characterized by admonitions concerning the German language and German identity. Chief among these was *Der Bote*, the weekly published at Rosthern by immigrants for the immigrants. But the *Mennonitische Rundschau*, published in Winnipeg, and the *Steinbach Post*, published in Steinbach, both of them edited by recent immigrants, were likewise vehicles of strong pro-German sentiments, though not written with the same intensity as could be found in *Der Bote*.[85] The *Post*'s readership consisted predominantly of Kanadier, who cared about things German but without Germany. The *Rundschau*'s readership was most cosmopolitan, inasmuch as it had subscribers in America, among the Kanadier, and also among the Russlaender.

It was the Russlaender, the most recent arrivals, for whom Germanism was a holy cause, partly because they were shocked to discover that their families could be anglicized in one generation and partly because they partook rather readily of the enthusiasm with which pan-Germanism filled the 1930s wherever there were German-speaking groups. The strong Germanism of the Russlaender had its roots partly in the ancestral Prussian home, partly in the Russian environment, and partly in the cultural relations between themselves and Germany prior to the Great War. Along with about one million other German-speaking Lutherans and Catholics in the Ukraine and Middle Volga regions, over 100,000 Mennonites in Russia had maintained an active interchange with the country and its institutions that had become their cultural mother. There were active intellectual-cultural relationships with Germany already before the Great War. In the words of one writer:

> In our schools we used German textbooks. German periodicals and books were found in every home. Mennonites pursued theological studies in Germany or Switzerland, received their vocational preparation in Germany, made holiday excursions to Germany, and went to Germany and Austria for medical treatment . . . [86]

It was in Prussia where the first major language transition of the Dutch Mennonites had been completed.[87] This happened well before the end of the eighteenth century, when immigrations to Russia began.[88] The Dutch language as an official church language was lost, but the related Low German dialect attained a greater significance as the social language of the Mennonites.[89] High German became the language of school and church and Low German took over as the language of the family, of the extended family, and in social and business communications, generally.

The Ukrainian and Russian environments enhanced the use of both German languages of the Mennonites because in that context languages and modes of living were clearly correlated. The Mennonites, along with the Lutherans and Catholics, showed little eagerness to adopt the Slavic styles, cultures, and languages of their adopted country. According to one Mennonite linguist, "the economical, intellectual, and ethical standards of the Russo-Ukrainian peasantry were low and seemed even lower to us."[90] The preservation and cultivation of the Mennonite languages, therefore, became synonymous with self-preservation.

This did not mean that the Ukrainian and Russian languages were completely ignored. On the contrary, a certain degree of russification of the schools had taken place in accordance with the will of the state. And some of those who went beyond the village schools learned the Russian language well and "gradually attained to a true vision of Russian culture, of the Russian mind, and of the Russian soul."[91] But this was less so for the Mennonite masses, who, while bilingual or even trilingual, knew instinctively what the respective languages symbolized. Russian and Ukrainian or a mixture of both were used with their labourers and Slavic neighbours. Official documents and business letters were usually in Russian, sometimes in German. Russian was the language of mental arithmetic and of the barnyard. Horses and sheep knew Russian better than German, and Mennonites, if and when they cursed, tended to do so in Russian, or Low German, a language also suited to irreverence. The language of religion was High German:

> We never prayed in Russian. All our religious services were
> conducted in High-German. In our Low-German homes
> grace at table was said in High-German, and even before we
> entered school we had learned a High-German bedtime prayer
> by heart.[92]

In Canada, the Russlaender became aware all too quickly that many of the protective boundaries for their way of life had vanished in the resettlement. Gone were the colony, the village, the community organization, and the schools on which they had depended so much. Little could be done about the Canadian scattering and the loss of the traditional defences. But it was still possible to maintain a linguistic and ethnic separateness, mostly by ensuring that the German language was taught and learned.

The retention of the German language was encouraged because it was the mother tongue, because it was so beautiful in its spoken and written forms, and because it was so rich, so expressive, so suited to every thought and emotion.[93] The cultivation of the mother tongue was true to natural law, hence divinely willed. Not to preserve it meant to forfeit one's roots and to cut oneself off from the cultural, intellectual, and spiritual treasures of a people. The assumptions of the American melting pot were said to be false, because assimilation did not produce a higher society, but rather an inferior one, monotonous and uninteresting, like a garden in which all the flowers were of one kind and one colour.

> What makes the rose so beautiful, the lily so alluring, the violet so refreshing, the hyacinth so gorgeous, and the gladiola so grand? Is it not because all are unique, each is different from the other, and each reflects some of the endless beauty and multiplicity of the creator? Is it not the same in the cultural sphere?[94]

The German language, said its most ardent promoters, was worthy to be preserved for its own sake, for the sake of the culture it represented, for the sake of the preservation of Mennonite ethnicity, and for the sake of the Mennonite faith. Faith could not be deepened, ethnic consciousness could not be strengthened, the fruits of German culture could not be experienced, and the historical heritage could not be appropriated without "the nurture and preservation of the German language."[95] Speaking on the theme of "German and Religion," one elder explained that the two appeared together in the Mennonite home, school, and church because they belonged together as carriers of cherished values. The German language should be preserved, he said, because it was the mother tongue, because two languages were better than one, because German was one of the most important languages of the world, and because Germany was experiencing a renewal which should give all Germans abroad a sense of pride. He wrote:

> Not only do a hundred million people speak this language as their mother tongue, but many strangers make an extraordinary effort to acquire facility in its use, because with the knowledge of the German tongue one can get along in most civilized countries. For this is the language of poets and philosophers![96]

German and religion were the two twin fountains of Mennonite faith.[97] They had become inseparable in the Mennonite school systems both in Russia and in western Canada, where russification and anglicization, respectively, had meant the isolation and close identification of the two most precious elements in the school curriculum.[98] Moreover, for hundreds of years, the German language had been the religious language of the Mennonite people and for this reason their spiritual growth was intimately tied up with the nurture of it. Loss of the language would mean a substantial loss of the Christian spirit[99] and of the Mennonite faith.[100] It was said:

> We German Mennonites are a religious society. Through the German language a significant stream of religious thought flows through our churches. . . . With the neglect of the German language this stream will cease and our church life will dry up. . . . [101]

Since language was an issue so fundamental to existence and fulfilment,[102] the long-term well-being of a people obviously depended on the preservation of the culture. This called for the cultivation of the German language in family, school, and church; in Sunday school, worship services, musical events, and youth programs; in Saturday schools, high schools, and Bible schools; and through the organization of libraries and societies for the nurture of the German language and literature.[103]

Many and varied were the ideas advanced in the interests of language preservation. Some Mennonites, for instance, expressed once again the traditional view that completely closed and isolated settlements were a must.[104] Others, much less demanding, felt that at least one German periodical in the home was essential.[105] In some communities, locally appointed statisticians kept accurate records of how many people read which papers.[106] The disallowance of the use of English at certain times and in certain places was essential to others.[107] Some felt that the path to successful preservation lay in the retention of the Gothic script, for even in this form lay some of the German essence.[108]

Of considerable prominence in promoting the language were the Canadian-German cultural groups, which in turn were aided by national German agencies. The German-Canadian organization encouraged local German schools and offered prizes to children for outstanding achievements.[109] Outstanding leaders in German-language education were given honourable mention. One of those receiving the silver medal was Professor H.H. Ewert.[110] German societies were organized in some predominantly Mennonite communities including the one at Hague, which was noted for its singing of

Canada's national anthem translated into German.[111] This society had sufficient influence to cause the teaching program in the church to revert back from the English language to German after a transition had already been made.

Teachers and schools had a special role in the nurture of both German and religion.[112] Among the schools serving the immigrants, the Bible schools were commended for their dual role in promoting German and religion. There, students could be trained as convinced German Mennonites.[113] Some insisted that the social language in the Bible schools be exclusively German.[114] A correspondent from the United States, where the language transition was already complete, lent his moral encouragement to the Mennonite school pattern. The nurture of the German language, he said, could stand in second place next to the Bible. Keeping the German language was a condition of life, because the loss of Germanism meant endangering spiritual treasures:

> Hold on to the German in your Bible schools. You'll never be sorry for the price you pay.[115]

Ethnicity and Racial Identity

German language and culture ultimately could not be separated from German ethnic or racial identity, and thus the 1930s also gave rise to an intense and multi-dimensional, though not especially profound, discussion on Mennonite origins and the nature of the Mennonite society. In some ways, the debate was a repeat of the *Hollaenderei* (an excessive emphasis on Dutch origins) in Russia in the Great War period, except now in Canada *Hollaenderei* did not have the upper hand. In Russia, the Mennonite escape from anti-German decrees affecting their property during the war lay in the reassertion of their Frisian origins. In the early Soviet period, the identification by the Mennonites of their citizenship organization as Dutch was also helpful. Now, however, and at least until the war broke out, the German connection was thought to be more advantageous.

The leading proponents of the German ethnic or racial connection were Benjamin Unruh and Walter Quiring, both Russlaender who were writing from Germany at the time. Among their people in Canada, Brazil, and Paraguay, they were opinion leaders, whose views were published without fail in *Der Bote*, well-received by the readers, and echoed by numerous other writers in Canada, though not by all, for there was much to criticize in what they said.

Benjamin H. Unruh had made his home in Germany towards the end of 1920 after completing a North American visit in search of a new home for the besieged Mennonites in Russia, being one of their four special commissioners to the west.[116] From his central European location, he continued to work as an ambassador-at-large and a spokesman for his people, officially recognized as such and financially supported from Canada by the Canadian Mennonite Board of Colonization.[117]

Unruh discussed at length and with an abundance of words the racial origins of the Russian Mennonites, a subject on which he conducted extensive research, culminating in his publication on the origins in the Dutch and German lowlands of the migrations eastward in the sixteenth, eighteenth, and nineteenth centuries.[118] His theories in the 1930s were expounded in three series of extended articles on "origins,"[119] on "fundamentals,"[120] and on "practical questions."[121] It was Unruh's conclusion that the Mennonites undoubtedly belonged to the Germanic races.[122] Many of the early refugees were Germanics who had fled to Prussia in the sixteenth century from the German and Dutch lowlands.[123] Besides, what was now known as the Netherlands belonged at the time to the Hapsburg empire, so that Menno Simons and Martin Luther both had the same emperor. The loss by the empire of both Switzerland and the Netherlands was not an organic separation from Germanic roots but simply poor politics.[124]

In addition to the Mennonites being Germanic in origin, the process of germanization had made them completely German. By 1750, or half a century before the emigration to Russia, Unruh maintained all ministers, with the exception of those in Danzig, had been preaching in German. Thus, the transition from Dutch to Low German, a development known already in the Dutch-German lowlands, and from Low German to High German, at least as far as the official language was concerned, had been completed in West Prussia.[125] And, disregarding completely the *Hollaenderei*, Unruh claimed that in Russia the Mennonites had become confirmed Germans, especially during the Great War and the revolution.[126]

Walter Quiring was also a native of Russia, who had made his home in Germany, first for studies and then for professional pursuits. Quiring graduated with his doctorate from Munich in 1927 and spent the next dozen years in education and cultural activities. The latter took him to the Americas on several occasions, resulting in the writing and publication of two books on the Russo-Germans in Latin America.[127] Both titles identified the Mennonites as ethnic or racial Germans, a basic premise in most of Quiring's writings in the 1930s.[128] When later he immigrated to Canada, he became editor of Der Bote, the paper in which his articles appeared.

Quiring's main concerns were to prove that the Mennonites were ethnic Germans, and that the Mennonites, therefore, should feel themselves a part of the great German people. For the purpose of the former argument he, like Unruh, made much of the fact that Mennonites had never been Dutch in the political sense,[129] that they had never really been acquainted with the Dutch language and literature,[130] and that, even if there was some ethnic Dutch residue in the Mennonites, the Dutch were but a branch of the Germanic race.[131] On the other hand, following the emigration from the Netherlands, the Mennonites in Prussia participated in the process of germanization, in both a cultural and a racial way, rather readily, so that good foundations were laid for the pure German development of the churches in Russia.[132] Hence the following conclusion:

> The Mennonites from Russia are Germans, German according to their blood, German according to their language, German according to their essence and customs, and most of them are German also in the innermost parts of their heart.[133]

Quiring's theories about Mennonite racial identification were supported not only by his interpretation of the Mennonite historical and sociological development, but also by the doctrine of the blood.[134] This doctrine was not a German invention, although the Germans were the first to make "the sensible demand" that the future be determined by this doctrine. Its basis was God's order in creation, by which humanity was organized into certain families according to blood types which should not be mixed.[135] That is why Germans could not marry Jews or Indians, for the blood types of the latter were different from the blood of the German race, as were also the blood types of the lion, the dog, and the frog, although admittedly the distances between them were of varying degrees.[136] Mixing, it was indicated, had disastrous racial, cultural, and spiritual consequences. To avoid such tragedy it was desirable and necessary to determine one's racial ancestry and to remain loyal to it.[137] German racial identity could be assumed or claimed as long as a link could be traced back to one generation born in Germany.[138] The ancestors, it was pointed out, continued to live on even in one drop of blood or in one cell of the brain.[139]

Cultural qualities, it was asserted also by others, were biologically determined and conditioned.[140] And if there was a biological base for cultural and racial identities, then obviously there was also theological support for this position, for what was found to be biologically true was in accordance with the order of God. Thus, cultural and racial Germanism found its rationale in a biological theory about human blood, which, in turn, became a theological doctrine of race. Both biology and theology taught that God had ordained the division of the human family into racial groups and that mixing these groups was degenerating, physically and also spiritually. The greater the distance between blood types the more harmful the effect of mixing the types. God made the white race and God made the black race but the mixed breeds came from the devil.[141]

If, then, the racial order was according to divine plan and purpose, it was of utmost importance that the racial identity of the Mennonite people be firmly established and properly claimed. This was no easy matter since at certain times in history the Mennonites had identified themselves as *Hollaender* (Dutchmen) and at other times as Germans. In the 1931 Canadian census, about 60 per cent of all Canadian Mennonites had given their race as Dutch, according to one correspondent.[142] Another claimed that the identification with the Dutch ran as high as 90 per cent.[143]

The actual figures for Dutch identification in 1931 were 42 per cent compared to 35 per cent for the German identification (see Table 35). These figures changed dramatically when Canada was once again at war with Germany. Fifty-eight per cent of Canadian Mennonites gave their racial origin as Dutch in 1941, whereas only 28 per cent claimed German origin.

Whatever the figures, *Hollaenderei* or identification with the Dutch had been a mistake, it was maintained. It had not helped the cause in Russia, or in Canada, or in Germany. Whenever the Mennonites had been in need, not the Dutch but the Germans had recognized their brethren of similar flesh and blood.[144] In this

TABLE 35

RACIAL IDENTIFICATION OF CANADIAN MENNONITES
IN THE CENSUS YEARS 1931, 1941

	1931		1941	
RACIAL ORIGIN	NUMBER	PER CENT	NUMBER	PER CENT
British	2,863	3.226	4,575	4.108
French	243	.274	891	.800
Austrian	452	.509	924	.830
Czechoslovakian	8	.009	24	.022
Finnish	1	.001	8	.007
German	34,687	39.090	31,465	28.250
Hungarian	2	.002	56	.050
Italian	18	.020	9	.008
Jewish	11	.012	4	.004
Dutch	37,555	42.322	64,934	58.300
Polish	134	.151	265	.238
Russian	12,084	13.618	7,204	6.468
Scandinavian	212	.239	203	.182
Ukrainian	385	.434	657	.590
Other European	36	.041	87	.078
Chinese	–	–	7	.006
Japanese	–	–	–	–
Other Asian	15	.017	9	.008
Indian or Eskimo	2	.002	–	–
Others	28	.032	58	.052
Total	88,736	100	111,380	100

assertion, too, there was historical inaccuracy, because of all the national Mennonite communities the Dutch had most distinguished themselves in the area of relief for their needy brethren over the longest period of time.

The identification of Mennonites as Germans and the primacy of ethnic, rather than religious, qualities[145] met with some opposition in the Russlaender communities. First of all, the critics argued that the germanization of the Mennonites had not proceeded nearly as easily, quickly, and completely as the Germanists suggested. For 200 years, the Mennonites of Prussia had maintained their contacts with Holland, as could be proved by correspondence filed in the archives of Amsterdam.[146] Even the church creeds brought from Prussia to Russia in a poor translation reflected the Dutch background.[147] Not only had germanization come recently and only partially, but there were many names reflecting non-Germanic elements—names of Czech, Dutch, French, Moravian, Polish, and Slavic origin—names like DeFehr, Delesky, Koslovsky, Ratzlaff, Rogalsky, Sawatsky, Selevsky, and Spenst.[148] And even if Mennonites were German Mennonites, it was made clear that they were not Mennonite Germans.[149]

Further evidence that Mennonites were more than a single race was provided by the international Mennonite conference held in Saskatchewan in 1938. The delegates and visitors came from all races and tongues and nations. The Dutch, the German, the Swiss, the American, and the Canadian cultures and races were represented, as were also the American Indian Mennonites. Under normal conditions, the Chinese and Hindu Mennonite Christians would also have been represented. All of these were Mennonites, Johann G. Rempel argued. At least, he added somewhat apologetically, they were Mennonites if the religious characteristic was the consideration.[150] The apologetic "ifs" and "buts" were not uncommon among those who wrote to question or counter strong pro-German expressions.

Other writers also objected vigorously to the idea that Mennonites were more of a *Volk* than a church. The focal point of Mennonite life, they said, was faith and religion.[151] Not the race but the spirit was the most important essence of the Mennonite people.[152] In Canada, the Mennonites were a religious fellowship. They might speak German but they were religious and their economic and political loyalties were to Canada.[153] Among them was Cornelius Krahn, who like Walter Quiring had come to Germany from Russia to complete doctoral studies, and who had then joined the faculty at Bethel College, where he proceeded to build up an archives and a historical library. He, too, was an opinion leader among the Russlaender, though less vocal than either Unruh or Quiring. He emphasized religion as a more fundamental principle of Mennonite historical development than culture.[154] Not blood but faith had brought the Mennonite forefathers together from all kinds of racial backgrounds.[155]

The contributions of Jacob H. Janzen, "teacher, preacher, elder, and author, a man of rare gifts and rich understanding,"[156] are of special interest because of his leadership in the immigrant community at various levels. As a literary man, Janzen expressed strong appreciation for German culture. "We are good Germans," he said, "because our culture is German and because we have learned to understand and appreciate best and most of all the beauty and depth of the German language and with it the depth of the German soul."[157] To Janzen, German virtue and character were the most valuable ingredients of the Mennonite ethnic and cultural heritage.[158] He issued urgent appeals to the immigrants to nurture the language, not only for the sake of the language but also for the sake of the total German cultural treasure.[159]

Janzen identified the immigrants as German ethnics[160] and as carriers of German culture and values,[161] but he also insisted that germanization had taken place only in Russia. The articles of faith brought along from Prussia, he said, had been only a very poor translation with strong Dutch overtones.[162] He also emphasized that Mennonites were first and foremost a religious society and not a *Volk*. The concept of a *Mennovolk*, he said, had first arisen in Russia and could not be viewed as fundamental or normative.[163]

In summing up the foregoing, it can be said that there were various degrees of, and motives for, the Germanism that was being promoted. Some germanizers were primarily lovers of the German language and its treasures and did not want to see something so valuable lost. Others, equally zealous, believed that bilingualism or trilingualism was better than unilingualism. Still others were certain that the maintenance of the German language was essential for the keeping of some distance from the world. Perhaps the vast majority had long ago become so habituated to the automatic twinning of religion and language, Mennonitism and Germanism, that their inclinations towards Germanism were as natural and predictable as was their love of land and learning.

The endorsement among the Russlaender of ethnic or racial Germanism was less universal, partly because of the uncertainty about origins and partly because of the primacy accorded to the religious and Christian nature of the Mennonite society. Jacob H. Janzen probably spoke for most of the Russlaender church leaders when he insisted that every religious soul needed a cultural body to carry it, and while he praised the attributes of German culture and ethnicity, he also insisted that all of this was secondary to the religious consideration. There was a more definite parting of the ways when ethnicity was dished up in the form of German racism or when, as will later be seen, the love of German culture and peoplehood was followed by a promotion of the German Reich and its political program.

The Dialects and Popular Culture

The cultural identities and borders of the Mennonites were determined not only by geography, nonconformity, High German philology, and ethnicity but also by two dialects, the contribution of which to Mennonite isolation and self-preservation may not be overlooked. The two were Pennsylvania German, spoken among the Swiss, and Low German, spoken among the Dutch. Both dialects served the function of popular social communication; both were better carriers of Mennonite humour than either High German or English; and both, but particularly Low German, gave rise to a special kind of Mennonite literature. Pennsylvania German culture, on the other hand, embraced cultural forms other than literature or language, such as Fraktur art and decorative painting.[164]

The Pennsylvania German language was living on despite predictions already in the nineteenth century that its death was imminent.[165] Also known as Pennsylvania Dutch, owing to a careless but understandable transliteration of Pennsylvania *Deutsch* (meaning German but sounding more like Dutch), Pennsylvania German was actually a shared language. It was common to a great number of people in Pennsylvania, who had brought a Germanic dialect with them, which in time had been adapted to the New World through the incorporation of new concepts and also convenient terms and usages from the English language. Catholic, Lutheran, and Mennonite immigrants to Upper Canada from Pennsylvania brought with them the same dialect, and when their distant cousins, like the Mennonite Amish, arrived directly from Europe, the community of those capable of using the dialect was enlarged.

Apart from the happy relationships with Catholics and Lutherans which the dialect helped to facilitate, Pennsylvania German was another source of isolation and insulation for the Mennonites.

Coupled with their rural and nonconformed life style and their nonresistant religious outlook, the dialect was a formidable contribution to boundary maintenance. Yet, it was not a sacred language in the sense that it could serve liturgical functions. Pennsylvania German expressions would find their way into sermons, but prayers, Bible readings, and official church acts could never be corrupted by Pennsylvania German.[166]

By contrast, the dialect helped to change a rather austere people, doleful in appearance, into one actually characterized in everyday life by a great deal of gaiety and laughter. The dialect itself is filled with humorous expressions. As one linguist, once an Ontario Old Order Mennonite, has written:

> A few years ago, my father, who is almost 76, followed my brother and me around the golf course. My father had never been on a golf course, but he was eager for the exercise, the outdoors, and the fellowship. We, of course, spoke the dialect and for the first time I discovered how humorous the game of golf could be. I listened closely to his many original descriptions and observations. I realized, perhaps more than ever, that the dialect can be very expressive and that it is filled with humorous words, idioms, and other linguistic constructions.[167]

The Low German dialect originated in the northern Dutch and German lowlands, whereas Pennsylvania German had southern German origins. While Low German or *Plattdeutsch*, like Pennsylvania German, was not exclusively a Mennonite language, at least in Canada as in southern Russia it was spoken almost exclusively by the Dutch Mennonites.[168] Kanadier used and cultivated it more readily than did the Russlaender. The latter had come to view Low German as a language too low and uncultured to pass on to their children. The new principal at the Gretna collegiate, for instance, conducted a virtual crusade against the use of Low German by the students, believing as he did that it was an obstacle to the mastery and preservation of High German.[169]

There were important exceptions to that rule and these, ironically, included Mennonite literary figures, whose works in the High German language were reputable in themselves. They were Jacob H. Janzen in Ontario and Arnold Dyck in Manitoba, who distinguished themselves not only as men of letters in their own right but also as promoters of the art on behalf of all Mennonite writers.[170] Dyck, in particular, produced a monthly magazine for the promotion of Mennonite literature and culture. The *Mennonitische Volkswarte* was bilingual in the sense of using both the High German and the Low German language, the latter particularly for short stories, poetry, and drama.

The paradox of two gifted Russlaender writers in High German turning to Low German was explained, however indirectly, by Jacob H. Janzen himself when he wrote about "the literature of the Russo-Canadian Mennonites" in 1935.[171] "Mennonitism had never been a fertile ground for belles-lettres," he said, pointing out that already three centuries previous "the most outstanding writer in Holland, Joost von den Vondel, felt impelled to leave the Mennonites (1645), so that his talents would not be hindered in their development."

This did not mean that Mennonites were unfavourable to all literature or to all good books. Some, like the writings of Menno Simons, were purchased — Janzen spoke tongue-in-cheek as he was wont to do — "to become dust-covered on the 'corner shelf.' " And Mennonites loved "good" stories, but Mennonitism itself "was regarded in certain respects as a 'terra sancta,' on which the jugglery of belles-lettres dared not appear . . . [writing] in this genre was simply sin." Janzen's observations were based on personal experience:

> . . . when I came to Canada and in my broken English tried to make plain to a Mennonite bishop that I was a "novelist" (that being the translation for "*Schriftsteller*" in my dictionary) he was much surprised. He then tried to make plain to me that novelists were fiction writers and that fiction was a lie. I surely would not want to represent myself to him as a professional liar.[172]

There were other writers in the community, in both Russia and Canada, Janzen went on to explain, who experienced a certain ostracism, if not in social terms then in economic terms — they just couldn't make a living. But Low German drama and stories were something else because they tended to be funny, and since they appeared in the non-official, non-religious language of the Mennonites, they did not come under quite the same judgement.[173] Thus, Janzen had experienced a breaking of the ice with his two Low German dramas, *De Bildung* and *Utwaundre*, through which he and all Russlaender discovered that they could treat serious themes like education and emigration humorously and in so doing even laugh at themselves.[174]

Arnold Dyck settled down in Steinbach, where he became editor of the *Steinbach Post* and where he continued what Janzen had begun but could not continue if only for the reason that his roles as bishop, leader, and writer of "official" literature took up all of his time. It was in the *Post* where Arnold Dyck tried out his beloved *Plautdietsch* on his mostly Kanadier readers. His *"Belauschte Gespraeche"* were unpretentious humorous conversations among typical Mennonite farmers.[175] In these writings, Dyck became one of the very few Russlaender who built bridges to the Kanadier and who earned the "right" to be the editor of their paper. When in 1936 he left the *Post* to devote himself full-time to the newly founded illustrated monthly *Warte*, not only did he publish short stories, poems, articles on Mennonite life and history, and first printings of historical documents but also "every little nook was filled with charming Low German nursery rhymes." The *Warte* was an ambitious undertaking and did not survive the depression as a monthly magazine, but Dyck constantly found new channels for his activity, including a remembrance of Russia in his fictional *Verloren in der Steppe* (Lost in the Steppes).

His real genius was established as a Low German stylist, for what he "accomplished with our Cinderella dialect is amazing."[176] The plain language of the plain Mennonite farmer he captured the best in his creation of two characters, Koop and Bua (Buhr), who came brilliantly alive in their travels in a Model T Ford in *Koop enn Bua op Reise*, including a trip to Toronto (*Koop enn Bua faore nao Toronto*). As far as his readers were concerned, Koop and Bua could have been on the road forever. His books were nearly all light in tone. In the words of Gerhard Wiens:

> His books are full of laughter of many kinds. There is pungent satire and fine irony, rollicking jocularity, farce and buffoonery with gusto and brilliant clowning, devastating caricature, roguish merriment, and sprightly whimsicality, and instance after instance of "Situationskomisk."[177]

Mennonites laughing at themselves has not been documented, apart from the likes of Janzen and Dyck, but that there was plenty of it in the social circles relatively distanced from the all-encompassing seriousness of the church of the martyrs can be attested to by anybody whose family memory goes back to the usage of either the Low German or the Pennyslvania German dialect. Gradually, the Mennonites learned to translate their humour into the English language with the dramatizations of such pioneering experiences as "the trail of the Conestoga." And Paul Hiebert, the Manitoba chemistry professor of Mennonite background, led the Dutch in this transition. His classroom doodlings in the 1930s were becoming *Sarah Binks*, a satire on literary criticism that one day would be a classic. The struggle for survival, however, circumscribed laughter for everybody in the years of depression and war, and particularly for Mennonites. They were very serious when they faced the world and the prospect of war.

FOOTNOTES

1 Editorial, "The Elmira Special Conference," *Church and Mission News* 8 (November 1943):4.

2 A.J. Schellenberg, "Die zweite Provinziale-Vertreterversammlung in Herbert, Saskatchewan, am 16. und 17. Juli 1930," *Der Bote* 7 (1 October 1930):3.

3 Johann Rempel, "Bericht des Aufklaerungskomitees," *Jahrbuch*, 1931, pp. 76–77.

4 *Ibid*.

5 Published in 1941, *The Story of the Mennonites*, a revised edition of an earlier work (1920), became the last of Smith's works. He died in 1948, at which time Harold S. Bender gave the following assessment: "Dr. Smith was unquestionably the greatest of the historians produced by the Mennonites of America and the peer of any of the European Mennonite historians. With his five major works written over a period of thirty-five years, he published more full-length historical works than any other Mennonite historian. His particular gift was that of synthesis of masses of material into well-written, interesting, integrated accounts. He was pre-eminently the general Mennonite historian who took the great sweep of our history in both Europe and America and put it into clear, easily read volumes that will remain standard works for years to come." See Robert Kreider, "Foreword," in C. Henry Smith, *Smith's Story of the Mennonites* (Newton, Kans.: Faith and Life Press, 1981).

6 H.H. Ewert, "The Mennonites" (a paper delivered before the membership of the Historical and Scientific Society of Manitoba, 1932).

7   *Ibid.*, pp. 6, 12.
8   S.F. Coffman, "The Adventure of Faith," *Mennonite Quarterly Review* 14 (1926):228–33. Coffman's presentation was given before Ewert's, but it was not as comprehensive in its scope nor was it as widely circulated.
9   J.A. Huffman, *History of the Mennonite Brethren in Christ Church* (New Carlisle, Ohio: The Bethel Publishing Company), 1920.
10   Lawrence J. Burkholder, *A Brief History of the Mennonites of Ontario* (Markham, Ont.: L.J. Burkholder, 1935), pp. 322 ff.
11   *Ibid.*, p. 321.
12   *Ibid.*, p. 320, Preface.
13   *Ibid.*, p. 320.
14   Jacob H. Janzen, "Warum bin ich Mennonit?" *Jahrbuch*, 1928, pp. 40–48.
15   *Ibid.*, p. 40
16   Quoted as a motto in John S. Weber, "History of S.F. Coffman (1872–1954)" (research paper, University of Waterloo, 1975). See introductory pages and also pp. 150–51.
17   *Jahrbuch*, 1933, p. 14; *Jahrbuch*, 1937, p. 21. See also B. Schellenberg, "Das mennonitische Archiv," *Mennonitische Volkswarte* 1 (January 1935):97–101.
18   B. Schellenberg, "Das mennonitische Archiv," *Jahrbuch*, 1933, pp. 78–83.
19   Allan G. Felstead, *A Socio-Historical Analysis of the Sectarian Divisions in the Mennonite Church of Waterloo County, 1849–1939* (M.A. thesis, University of Waterloo, 1978), p. 71.
20   Paul Knowles, "New Mennonite to Non-Mennonite: A Study in Assimilation" (research paper, University of Waterloo, 1979).
21   Everek R. Storms, *History of the United Missionary Church* (Elkhart, Ind.: Bethel Publishing Company, 1958), p. 31.
22   *Ibid.*
23   Paul Knowles, "New Mennonite to Non-Mennonite: A Study in Assimilation."
24   *Ibid.*, pp. 7–9, 11–12; J.A. Huffman, *History of the Mennonite Brethren in Christ Church* (New Carlisle, Ohio: The Bethel Publishing Company, 1920), pp. 145–48, 161–65; Everek R. Storms, *History of the United Missionary Church*, pp. 219–32.
25   *Journal*, 1940, pp. 1–59 illustrate this point rather well.
26   *Ibid.*
27   Everek R. Storms, p. 70.
28   John C. Wenger, "The History of Non-Conformity in the Mennonite Church," *Proceedings* of the third *Annual Conference on Mennonite Cultural Problems*, 1944, pp. 41–52.
29   Edward Yoder, "The Need for Nonconformity Today," *The Mennonite Quarterly Review* 11 (April 1937):131–41.

30   *Ibid.*, pp. 132 – 33.
31   *Ibid.*, pp. 133 – 34.
32   *Ibid.*, pp. 134 – 35.
33   *Ibid.*, p. 136.
34   *Ibid.*, p. 139.
35   *Ibid.*, p. 138.
36   *Ibid.*, pp. 139 – 40.
37   *Ibid.*, p. 141.
38   *Ibid.*, pp. 139, 141.
39   M.C. Lehman, "Bible Teaching on Non-Conformity: The Meaning of Non-Conformity as Implied by the Christian View of God, Man, and the World," *Gospel Herald* 32 (4 May 1939):98. See also T.E. Schrock, "Teachings in Our Non-Conformity Program," *Gospel Herald* 29 (5 November 1936):675 – 76.
40   Henry Stauffer, "The Mennonite Conscience and the World," *The Mennonite* 54 (12 September 1939):7 – 8.
41   *Ibid.*
42   *Ibid.*, p. 8.
43   Christian E. Charles, "Separation," *Gospel Herald* 29 (23 July 1936):375 – 76; "Facing the Drift," *Gospel Herald* 29 (26 November 1936):737.
44   Edward Yoder, p. 137.
45   "Old-fashioned Mennonitism: Christian Apparel," *Gospel Herald* 32 (28 September 1939):545.
46   *Ibid.*
47   J.R. Shank, "Bible Teaching on Non-Conformity: As Applied to Proper and Improper Clothing," *Gospel Herald* 32 (6 July 1939):274 – 75.
48   J.L. Stauffer, "Bible Teaching and Non-Conformity: As Applied to Proper and Improper Apparel," *Gospel Herald* 32 (29 June 1939):258 – 59.
49   *Ibid.*, p. 259.
50   *Ibid.*
51   *Ibid.*
52   J.R. Shank, p. 275.
53   J.L. Stauffer, p. 259.
54   J.R. Shank, p. 275.
55   J.L. Stauffer, p. 259.
56   J.R. Shank, pp. 274 – 75.
57   J.L. Stauffer, "Neglected, Rejected, and Forgotten Truths Relating to Christian Life and Conduct," *Gospel Herald* 28 (25 July 1935):371.
58   T.E. Schrock, pp. 675 – 76.
59   Daniel Kauffman, "Present-Day Issues: Maintaining Scriptural Adornment," *Gospel Herald* 27 (1 November 1934):662.

60   *Calendar of Appointments*, 1931–32, p. [26].
61   *Calendar of Appointments*, 1933–34, p. [24].
62   "Bishops' Report on the Dress Problem," *Calendar of Appointments*, 1934–35, pp. 18–19.
63   *Calendar of Appointments*, 1940–41, p. 23.
64   *Calendar of Appointments*, 1941–42, p. 10.
65   "The Elmira Special Conference," *Church and Mission News* 8 (November 1943):1, 4.
66   *Ibid.*, p. 1.
67   *Ibid.*, pp. 1, 4.
68   *Ibid.*, p. 4.
69   "Special Session of General Conference," *Church and Mission News* 9 (July 1944):1.
70   Paul Erb, "Bible Teaching and Non-Conformity: As Applied to Religious Life," *Gospel Herald* 32 (11 May 1939):130.
71   *Calendar of Appointments*, 1936–37, p. [14].
72   Milo Kauffman, "Present-Day Issues: Worship versus Entertainment," *Gospel Herald* 27 (31 January 1935):934.
73   D.A. Yoder, "Maintaining Our Testimony Against Worldly Amusements," *Gospel Herald* 27 (4 October 1934):565. See also *Calendar of Appointments*, 1936–37, p. [15].
74   J.L. Stauffer, "Neglected, Rejected, and Forgotten Truths Relating to Christian Life and Conduct," *Gospel Herald* 28 (25 July 1935):371.
75   David E. Plank, "Why Total Abstinence," *Gospel Herald* 27 (22 March 1934):1074–75.
76   John L. Horst, "Bible Teaching and Non-Conformity: As Applied to Social Life," *Gospel Herald* 32 (18 May 1939):147; *Calendar of Appointments*, 1937–38, p. 18.
77   J.L. Stauffer, "Neglected, Rejected, and Forgotten Truths Relating to Christian Life and Conduct," *Gospel Herald* 28 (25 July 1935):371. See also *Calendar of Appointments*, 1932–33, p. [25].
78   C.F. Derstine, "Present-Day Issues: The Life Insurance Question in the Light of the Word of God," *Gospel Herald* 27 (8 November 1934):693–94.
79   S.F. Coffman, "Maintaining Our Testimony Against Unequal Yokes," *Gospel Herald* 27 (18 October 1934):613–15; Oscar Burkholder, "Bible Teaching on Non-Conformity: As Applied to the Unequal Yoke with Unbelievers," *Gospel Herald* 32 (1 June 1939):178–79; see also *Calendar of Appointments*, 1935–36, p. [22].
80   Abner G. Yoder, "Bible Teaching and Non-Conformity: As Applied to Business Life," *Gospel Herald* 32 (25 May 1939):162–63.
81   J.L. Stauffer, "Neglected, Rejected, and Forgotten Truths Relating

to Christian Life and Conduct," *Gospel Herald* 28 (25 July 1935):371.

82 Editorial, *Gospel Herald* 27 (27 September 1934):549.

83 *Calendar of Appointments*, 1937–38, p. [19].

84 *Ibid.*, p. 162.

85 Frank H. Epp, "An Analysis of Germanism and National Socialism in the Immigrant Newspaper of a Canadian Minority Group, the Mennonites, in the 1930s" (Ph.D. dissertation, University of Minnesota, 1965). See especially pages 21–23 for identification and comparison of the roles of the three papers.

86 Anna Sudermann, "Zum Problem — Deutsche Sprache," *Der Bote* 38 (25 April 1961):3. See also Peter Klassen, "Die deutsche Sprache bei den Russlandmennoniten," *Der Bote* 37 (23 August 1960):3, 5; (also 30 August, 6 September, 13 September 1960).

87 Jacob A. Doerksen, "Transition from Dutch to German in West Prussia," *Mennonite Life* 22 (July 1967):107–9.

88 Gerhard Wiens, "Russian in Low German," *Mennonite Life* (April 1958):75.

89 Gerhard Wiens, "Mother Tongue Frustration," *Mennonite Life* (January 1954):32–33; J. John Friesen, "Romance of Low German," *Mennonite Life* (April 1947):22–23, 47.

90 Gerhard Wiens, p. 32.

91 *Ibid.*

92 *Ibid.*, p. 33.

93 CGC, XV-31.2, "1930 — Germany," "Der Wert der deutschen Sprache fuer uns," n.a., n.d.

94 *Ibid.*, p. 1.

95 A.J. Schellenberg, "Die zweite Provinziale-Vertreterversammlung in Herbert, Saskatchewan, am 16. und 17. Juli 30," *Der Bote* 7 (1 October 1930):3–4.

96 J.H. Enns, "Deutsch und Religion in Familien, Schule, und Gemeinde," *Jahrbuch*, 1933, pp. 30–36.

97 C.F. Klassen, "Der Weg der praktischen Hilfe," *Der Bote* 8 (18 February 1931):1.

98 Frank H. Epp, "An Analysis of Germanism . . . ," p. 39.

99 P.A. Rempel, "Warum wir die Gemeinschaftsschulen brauchen," *Der Bote* 9 (12 August 1931):2–3; Hermann Janzen, "Kettenbrief," *Der Bote* 14 (16 February 1938):5.

100 P.B. Krahn, "Was ist mir die deutsche Sprache?" *Der Bote* 14 (26 May 1937):2; P.A. Rempel, "Deutsche Lehrerkonferenz in Lowe Farm," *Der Bote* 14 (16 June 1937):6–7; J.J. Klassen, "Schulfragen," *Der Bote* 8 (4 February 1931):1.

101 D.P. Esau, "Was erwarten unsere Gemeinden von den Elementar- und Hochschulen in Religion und Deutsch," *Der Bote* 15 (15 June 1938):1–2.

102   Oskar Hamm, "Wie — ?" *Der Bote* 13 (8 January 1936):3.

103   J.D. Jantzen, "Die deutsche Sprache, ihre Erhaltung und Pflege," *Der Bote* 16 (2 August 1939): 1–2; A.J. Fast, "Unterstuetzt die deutschen Lehranstalten," *Der Bote* 8 (4 February 1931):3; D.P. Esau, "erziehungsfrage: Was erwarten unsere Gemeinden von den Elementar- und Hochschulen in Religion und Deutsch?" *Mennonitische Rundschau* 61 (22 June 1938):12–13; Maria Kornelsen, "Wie kann man in kleinen Kindern die Liebe zum Deutschen wecken und pflegen?" *Mennonitische Rundschau* 61 (5 January 1938):4–5.

104   Der Courier, "Geschlossene Siedlungen," *Der Bote* 8 (11 November 1931):3.

105   C.H. Friesen, "Haltet fest an der Muttersprache und wenn's nur im Dialekt ist," *Der Bote* 11 (10 October 1934):2.

106   Is. Is. Regehr, "Die Vertreterversammlung in Alberta," *Der Bote* 12 (18 September 1935):5.

107   A. Koop, "Bericht von Springridge und Glenwood," *Der Bote* 11 (1 March 1939):6.

108   Walter Quiring, "Deutsch oder lateinisch?" *Der Bote* 13 (22 July 1936):7; Wilhelm Brepohl, "Der Kampf um die deutsche Schrift und das Deutschtum im Ausland," *Der Bote* 13 (16 December 1936):5.

109   The author remembers such a contest in Manitoba *c.* 1938 and his own reward, two German books and the best fountain pen he ever possessed.

110   "Kundgebung des ersten deutschen Tages fuer Saskatchewan," *Der Bote* 7 (3 September 1930):2.

111   Ein Gast, "Hague," *Der Bote* 11 (18 April 1934):3.

112   J.C. Krause, "Die Vertreterversammlung in Rosthern," *Der Bote* 7 (22 January 1930):2–3; P.A. Rempel, "Die Organization mennonitischer Lehrerkonferenzen in Manitoba," *Der Bote* 7 (5 March 1930):3.

113   Jakob Toews, "Die Gemeindebibelschule ein Mittel zur Erhaltung unseres Mennonitentums und unseres Deutschtums," *Der Bote* 13 (22 April 1936):2.

114   A.J. Schellenberg, "Die zweite Provinziale-Vertreterversammlung in Herbert, Saskatchewan," *Der Bote* 7 (1 October 1930): 3–4; Ein Gast, "Briefe und Mitteilungen aus dem Leserkreise: Winnipeg, den 24. Maerz," *Der Bote* 9 (6 April 1932):2.

115   C.H. Friesen, "Die Pflege der Religion und das Deutschtums," *Der Bote* 16 (1 February 1939):1–2; see also G.H. Peters, "Und wieder unsere deutsche Sprache," *Steinbach Post* 24 (7 April 1937):2; G. Froese, "Pflicht der Eltern, dem Lehrer behilflich zu sein beim Unterricht in Religion und der Muttersprache," *Steinbach Post* 24 (16 June 1937):2.

116 Frank H. Epp, "An Analysis of Germanism...," pp. 44–46, 51–65.

117 *Ibid.*, pp. 231–39, 257–60.

118 B.H. Unruh, *Die niederlaendisch-niederdeutschen Hintergruende der mennonitischen Ostwanderungen im 16., 18., und 19. Jahrhundert* (Karlsruhe—Rüppurr, 1955).

119 B.H. Unruh, "Vorfragen zur wissenschaftlichen Klaerung der Herkunft des ruszlanddeutschen Mennonitentums," *Der Bote* 12 (22 May 1935):1, this being the first of 11 instalments ending 6 July 1938.

120 B.H. Unruh, "Grundsaetzliche Fragen," *Der Bote* 12 (17 July 1935):1–2, this being the first of 29 instalments ending 16 September 1936.

121 B.H. Unruh, "Praktische Fragen," *Der Bote* 13 (30 December 1936):1–2, this being the first of 26 instalments ending 23 March 1938.

122 B.H. Unruh, "Vorfragen zur wissenschaftlichen Klaerung der Herkunft des ruszlanddeutschen Mennonitentums," *Der Bote* 12 (29 May 1935):1–2.

123 B.H. Unruh, "Zur wissenschaftlichen Klaerung der Herkunft des ruszlanddeutschen Mennonitentums," *Der Bote* 15 (6 July 1938):5.

124 B.H. Unruh, "Vorfragen zur wissenschaftlichen Klaerung der Herkunft des ruszlanddeutschen Mennonitentums," *Der Bote* 12 (29 May 1935):1–2.

125 B.H. Unruh, "Praktische Fragen," *Der Bote* 14 (20 January 1937):1–2.

126 B.H. Unruh, "Praktische Fragen," *Der Bote* 14 (26 May 1937):1–2.

127 Walter Quiring, *Deutsche erschlieszen den Chaco* (Karlsruhe: Heinrich Schneider, 1936), and *Ruszlanddeutsche suchen eine Heimat* (Karlsruhe: Heinrich Schneider, 1938).

128 Walter Quiring, "Untern Indianern im Chaco," *Der Bote* 11 (4 April 1934):2.

129 Walter Quiring, "Unsere 'Hollaenderei'—ein geschichtlicher Irrtum?" *Der Bote* 12 (20 March 1935):1–2.

130 Walter Quiring, "Deutsche oder Hollaender?" *Der Bote* 12 (6 February 1935):1–2.

131 *Ibid.*

132 *Ibid.*

133 *Ibid.*

134 Walter Quiring, "Artfremdes Blut ist Gift," *Der Bote* 13 (15 April 1936):2–3.

135 *Ibid.*

136 *Ibid.*

137   Walter Quiring, "Volk ohne Heimat," *Der Bote* 11 (26 December 1934):1 – 3.

138   Walter Quiring, "Wir suchen unsere Ahnen," *Der Bote* 13 (19 August 1936):4.

139   Walter Quiring, "Ahnenkunde," *Der Bote* 12 (13 November 1935):4.

140   Jakob Thiessen, "Unsere Stellung zur deutschen Volksart und Sprache," *Der Bote* 13 (12 February 1936):3.

141   Walter Quiring, "Artfremdes Blut ist Gift," *Der Bote* 13 (15 April 1936):2 – 3.

142   Leser **#** 7, "Um ein treffendes Wort," *Der Bote* 13 (24 June 1936):4.

143   J.J. Dyck, "Ich wuensche zu dieser Angelegenheit die Tat," *Der Bote* 14 (17 March 1937):3 – 4.

144   Gerhard Toews, "Ich wuensche zu dieser Angelegenheit die Tat," *Der Bote* 14 (17 February 1937):2 – 3; Auslanddeutscher, "Unser Deutschtum," *Der Bote* 12 (2 January 1935):1 – 2; H. Wagner, "Die religioesen Motive der Bauernflucht," *Der Bote* 8 (8 January 1930):1 – 2.

145   Frank H. Epp, "An Analysis of Germanism . . . ," p. 112 ff.

146   Cornelius Krahn, "Mennonitisches Volkstum," *Der Bote* 12 (27 March 1935):1.

147   J.H. Janzen, "In Ruszland verdeuscht," *Der Bote* 12 (1 April 1935):3.

148   *Ibid.*; B.B. Janz, "Die Herkunft der Mennoniten Ruszlands, resp. der Mennonitengemeinden in Preuszen," *Der Bote* 11 (12 December 1934):1 – 2; Jakob Toews, "Mennonitischer Deutscher oder deutscher Mennonit?" *Der Bote* 13 (4 March 1936):3.

149   Jakob Toews, p. 3.

150   J.G. Rempel, "Aus allerlei Geschlecht und Zungen und Volk und Heiden," *Der Bote* 15 (14 September 1938):1 – 2.

151   C. Krahn, *loc.cit.*

152   J.H. Janzen, "Kirche und Staat," *Der Bote* 11 (6 June 1934):1.

153   *Ibid.*

154   *Ibid.*

155   C. Krahn, "400-jaehriger Irrtum," *Der Bote* 13 (15 January 1936):3.

156   N.N. Driedger, "Jacob H. Janzen," *Mennonite Encyclopedia* 3:95 – 96. See also Frank H. Epp, *Mennonite Exodus*, p. 314; and Arnold Dyck, "Jacob H. Janzen — Writer," *Mennonite Life* 6 (July 1951):33 – 37, 43.

157   J.H. Janzen, "Schwierigkeiten," *Der Bote* 12 (20 November 1935):2 – 3.

158   J.H. Janzen, "Der Auslanddeutsche als Deutscher," *Der Bote* 12 (29 May 1935):3; "Deutsch und Russisch," *Der Bote* 13 (12

August 1936):1-2; "Der deutsche Gedanke," *Der Bote* 16 (30 August 1939):1-2.

159   J.H. Janzen, "Deutsche Sache — Deutsche Sprache," *Der Bote* 14 (24 February 1937):1-2.

160   J.H. Janzen, "Die Geschichte vom toerichten Fiedelkasten," *Der Bote* 13 (8 July 1936):3.

161   J.H. Janzen, "Deutsches," *Der Bote* 13 (15 April 1936):3.

162   J.H. Janzen, "In Ruszland verdeutscht," *Der Bote* 13 (1 April 1936):3.

163   J.H. Janzen, "Kirche und Staat," *Der Bote* 11 (6 June 1934):1.

164   Nancy-Lou Gellermann Patterson, *Swiss-German and Dutch-German Traditional Art in the Waterloo Region, Ontario*, Canadian Centre for Folk Culture Studies, Mercury Series (Ottawa: National Museum of Man, 1979); Nancy-Lou Patterson, "Mennonite Folk Art of Waterloo County," *Ontario Historical Society* 60 (September 1968):81-100. See also Michael Bird and Terry Kobayashi, *A Splendid Harvest: Germanic Folk and Decorative Arts in Canada* (Toronto: Van Nostrand Reinhold Ltd., 1981).

165   Keith O. Anderson and Willard M. Martin, "Language Loyalty Among the Pennsylvania Germans: A Status Report on Old Order Mennonites in Pennsylvania and Ontario," *Germanica Americana*, 1976, p. 74; Allan M. Buehler, *The Pennsylvania German Dialect and the Autobiography of an Old Order Mennonite* (Cambridge, Ont.: The Author, 1977).

166   Keith O. Anderson and Willard M. Martin, *op. cit.*

167   CGC, XV-31.2, "1930 — Language," Willard Martin to Frank H. Epp, 9 June 1981.

168   Much has been written about the Low German dialect in recent years. See, for instance, J. John Friesen, "Romance of Low German," *Mennonite Life* 2 (April 1947):22-23, 47; Henry D. Dyck, "Language Dif-fer-en-tia-tion Among the Low German Mennonites of Manitoba," *Mennonite Life* 22 (July 1967):117-20; J. Thiessen, "The Low German of the Canadian Mennonites," *Mennonite Life* 22 (July 1967):110-16. Bibliographies of some Low German linguistic studies and some Low German literature are contained in *Mennonite Life* 22 (July 1967):116.

169   From the author's own experience.

170   Arnold Dyck, "Ein Geleitwort vom Herausgeher," *Mennonitische Volkswarte* 1 (January 1935):1-2; Jacob H. Janzen, "Die Belletristik der Canadischen Ruszlanddeutschen Mennoniten," *Warte-Jahrbuch* 1943, pp. 83-89.

171   Jacob H. Janzen, "The Literature of the Russo-Canadian Mennonites," *Mennonite Life* 1 (January 1946):22-25, 28. See also J. Thiessen, "Mennonite Literature in Canada," *Mennonite Mirror* 2 (November 1972):13-16; George K. Epp and Heinrich Wiebe,

eds., *Unter dem Nordlicht: Anthologie des deutschen Schrifttums in Canada* (Winnipeg, Man.: The Mennonite German Society of Canada, 1977), pp. ix-xxi, 290–92. This last work includes a "select bibliography of Canadian German Mennonite writing."

172   Jacob H. Janzen, p. 22.

173   See Gerhard Wiens, "Arnold Dyck at Seventy," *Mennonite Life* 14 (April 1959):81–82.

174   *Ibid.* Peter Paetkau, "Low German Drama Study," *Mennonite Life* 33 (December 1978):27–28.

175   Gerhard Wiens, p. 81.

176   Gerhard Wiens, p. 82.

177   *Ibid.* For other assessments of Arnold Dyck, see: Mary Regehr Dueck, "Arnold Dyck: Non-Conformist," *Mennonite Life* 30 (December 1975):20–24; Von Kurt Kauenhoven, "Arnold Dyck, ein Blick auf sein Schaffen," *Mennonite Life* 4 (April 1959):89–90, 95; N.J. Klassen, "Arnold Dyck: An Appreciation," *Mennonite Life* 26 (April 1971):59; Warren Kliewer, "Arnold Dyck as a Literary Artist," *Mennonite Life* 14 (April 1959):85–87; Hedwig Knoop, "Arnold Dyck — At the End of the Road," *Mennonite Life* 26 (April 1971):56–58; Elisabeth Peters, "The Popularity of Dyck's Writings," *Mennonite Life* 14 (April 1959):87–88; "A Tribute to Arnold Dyck," *Mennonite Life* 24 (January 1969):3–5; "Arnold Dyck — Our Last Visit," *Mennonite Life* 26 (April 1971):54–55; Elmer F. Suderman, "Arnold Dyck Explains the Origin of Low German," *Mennonite Life* 24 (January 1969):5–7; "The Comic Spirit of Arnold Dyck," *Mennonite Life* 24 (October 1969):169–70; Jack Thiessen, "Arnold Dyck — The Mennonite Artist," *Mennonite Life* 24 (April 1969):77–83; Gerhard Wiens, "Arnold Dyck in Translation," *Mennonite Mirror* 3 (March 1974):7–8.

12. Facing the World

The next war will be a total war in which all the resources of the nation will be harnessed to the supreme goal of winning a complete victory — H.S. BENDER.[1]

The Mennonite people should create a standing organization to negotiate with the government a service, which conscientious objectors could perform for their fatherland in time of war — H.H. EWERT.[2]

T HE PERSISTENT ATTEMPT to preserve values and communities with the help of geographic and cultural isolation from the world was largely due to a rather keen awareness of that world and particularly of the tensions in international affairs pointing to serious conflict. As a consequence, Mennonites contemplated the dangers of war, the avoidance of military service, a possible alternative to such service, and in general, the obligations of citizenship, even as they sought to keep their young people, to preserve their culture, and to develop their institutions.

In 1938, Mennonite leaders sent an adulatory and complimentary message to the British Prime Minister for his perceived role in heading off, for the time being at least, a second world war. The signing took place in Winnipeg on October 7 by 32 bishops and ministers from Manitoba congregations of the Conference Mennonites, from the Mennonite Brethren, and from the Chortitzer,

Holdemaner, Rudnerweider, Kleine Gemeinde, and Sommerfelder congregations.[3] Having sought the counsel and sanction of David Toews in Rosthern and Jacob H. Janzen in Waterloo, they were confident that their resolution spoke for all Mennonites, both in the east and in the west. This was perhaps an impulsive act,[4] but it meant that Mennonites were cognizant of the European confrontations and their possible effect on themselves as conscientious objectors to war.

The event was unique as a coming together of both Russlaender and Kanadier leaders of the various congregational families and also as an address on international diplomacy to an international leader. The unusual consensus could have been a consequence of several factors at work. For one, the world, including the Mennonite world, breathed a great sigh of relief when on September 30 the leaders of Britain, France, Germany, and Italy signed the Munich Agreement, by which Czechoslovakia was forced to give up to Germany the Sudetenland, equalling one-fifth of Czech territory, most of its industry, and three million people of German descent.

For a people to whom there was no greater sin than war, the diplomacy of Chamberlain was perceived as an extraordinary achievement. Where Mennonites viewed that Agreement through the eyes of empathy for Germany, which happened to be the case for some, or where they were anxious to affirm their British loyalties, as was also the case with some, Munich looked right and good. The signatories were grateful that a world-wide war had been successfully averted; they expressed admiration for the effective role of Chamberlain in bringing about "a bloodless peace for our empire and the world"; they voiced the hope "that the peace secured may be a lasting one" and that God's blessing would rest "upon His Excellency and the great Empire." Peacemakers, the message concluded, were called children of God.[5]

Thirty-two Mennonites had identified the right role in peacemaking for British leaders, but that did not mean that they had sorted out their own civic task, apart from keeping the Mennonite boys from going to war. The nature and direction of the Mennonite response to the state and to citizenship duties in the 1930s were determined by the original and traditional doctrine of separation both from the state and from society and by the historic and contemporary applications of that separation.

Separation and Involvement

The traditional separation from, and non-participation in, public life lived on in both the Swiss and the Dutch Mennonite communities, though modifications of the position were evident in both. Such changes or adaptations usually meant movement away from the traditional separation, but not away from separation itself. New forms of separation appeared to modify or replace the old forms. In all, at least five distinct forms of separation could be identified and, for want of better terms, will here be referred to as geographical separation, institutional separation, ethical separation, cultural/ national separation, and chronological or dispensational separation. All forms of separation could be, and were, modified in practice and sometimes one or more forms appeared in combination with others. The various separations in effect represented various perceptions of the kingdom of God. The three forms of separation most articulated in the 1930s were ethical separation, national separation, and "chronological" separation. The latter two appeared as pro-Germanism and dispensationalism.

The full-orbed Anabaptist ethic and the single-minded approach to life had very deep roots and lived on even after the Mennonite colonies were gone. The result was that some Mennonites tried not only to face the world but also to do so with the Anabaptist ethic or with the contemporary understanding of that ethic. There was, in other words, a new attempt to be in the world, the wider world, including economics and civics, and yet not be of the world in terms of its ethic and value system. This meant that Mennonites could accept the economic, social, and political orders of the day in the same way and to the same extent that they accepted the public school and then proceed to influence the direction of these orders in the same way that they had influenced the content of education. Articulators of this latter view included H.H. Ewert, whom we have already met as the champion of the enriched public schools, and Edward Yoder, whom we have already met as the champion of nonconformity as a way of changing society.

For H.H. Ewert, whose life mission was the creation of the best possible public schools in Mennonite areas, the issues of war and peace and the requirements of citizenship had not completely faded into the background with the end of the First World War. In his opinion, the implications of the war were that Mennonites needed not only an adequate educational philosophy but also an understanding of citizenship and a political strategy. As far as he was concerned, Mennonites had distinct duties to the state.[6] These duties were not new, for Christians had always been under obligation to seek the welfare of the society in which they lived.

Though an aging man, Ewert was in the forefront of involvement in public affairs, while seeking to advance the cause of peace. He recommended that Mennonites stage a festival to celebrate the diamond jubilee of the Dominion of Canada.[7] He debated writers in the public press who saw an inevitable relationship between education and militarism.[8] He criticized the Canadian Legion and the British Empire Service League for advocating restrictive immigration and the elimination of special privilege.[9] He attended a conference of 30 anti-war groups and was disturbed only by the high proportion of women (80 per cent), the lack of Christian motivation of same, and the advocacy of birth control to check population to reduce the chances of war.[10] He spoke favourably of the Gandhi movement in India, which was transforming a society through non-violent means, and unfavourably of the fact that Mennonites were content to seek personal privilege in society and then to retreat into their own world.[11]

The other leading advocate of what is here called ethical separation, meaning social and civic involvement based on an alternative ethic, was Edward Yoder, who, more than any other writer in the Swiss community, concerned himself with questions of Mennonite relations with, and responsibilities to, the state during this time.[12] A teacher at Goshen College, he was not part of the Canadian Mennonite story, except in the legitimate sense, previously alluded to, that Goshen College was an important source of theological and intellectual leadership for the Swiss Mennonites and the Amish in Canada and that much religious direction for them came from the Mennonite General Conference, its spokespersons, periodicals, and institutions. It can be said that Yoder and his colleagues laid the foundations for a 1937 statement on peace and war, church and state, Christianity and citizenship, later to be reported in greater detail, which was prepared by a committee of equal Canadian and American representation and which probably was the most influential statement of its time.

The state or any state, said Yoder, was not something mystical and idealistic or somehow "an entity in itself, some vague sort of super-being."[13] The state was people and it had no real existence apart from the people who composed it. The state was simply a community on a larger scale, a combination of peoples in a given geographic area "living and working together in certain ways."[14] Christians were members of the state in the same way that they were members of the ordinary human community "living in contact with neighbours and friends, exerting their influence among fellow men by example and testimony, and cooperating with them in a common civil life." At the same time, their "center of gravity" did not lie "in this plane of experience." Their ideals and principles of life were not drawn from the surrounding community, but strength and nourishment for their life came from some source outside the civil community.[15] This twofold relationship did not mean that the believer was a Dr. Jekyll and Mr. Hyde but rather a single integrated personality.

> He cannot live a part of his time "in the world" in one man-
> ner, and the remainder of his time "not of the world" in some
> other manner. He is a single person who lives all the time for
> God in the world, and all the time for God not of the world.[16]

The ethical separation, or involvement on the basis of an alternative value system, espoused by H.H. Ewert and Edward Yoder appeared to be the most likely position of the majority of Mennonites in Canada. Geographic isolation was receding but the ethical orientation to all of life lived on in the teaching of the church and in the lives of the people. Moreover, most Mennonites had not yet experienced the full impact of institutionalized religion and its tendency to isolate faith from daily life with its economic and political problems. The ongoing Mennonite involvement in, and obligations to, the larger society, in this case Canada, were being explored. The Conference of Mennonites in Canada, for instance, heard speakers encouraging responsible involvement in political affairs, including voting, though a conference resolution in 1934 cautioned the young people against those political movements which opposed the existing political order.[17]

Applying the values of the kingdom to everyday life and seeking the will of God on earth in accordance with Ewert-Yoder teaching was a difficult and demanding task. For this reason, convenient ways of escape had an intrinsic appeal. Separating preaching from politics, church from state, religion from business, and Sunday from Monday were constant temptations, and there were also other ways of escaping responsibility in one's own time and in one's own land. The former was provided by an eschatological school of thought known as dispensationalism and pre-millennialism and the latter by a political movement known as National Socialism. Both represented the transfer of loyalty to another age and to another country, respectively.

For and Against Germanism

The pro-Germanism formerly noted with reference to language and racial identification also had a political dimension with a most vocal minority among the Russlaender in the 1930s. Not all those Mennonites who were fond of the German language and not all those who were proud of German ethnicity had a love for the German Reich. All of the Swiss, most of the Kanadier, and perhaps also a goodly number of the Russlaender had no particular feelings for or against Germany, but enough Russlaender were, for a time at least, enamoured of Adolf Hitler and his new Germany that a brief but intense flirtation with National Socialism cannot be overlooked.[18]

The nurture and promotion of foreign loyalties or causes, be they right or wrong, by members of minority groups were not unique phenomena in Canadian history.[19] In fact, one of Canada's greatest worries in the Great War was religious and ethnic groups whose affinities to, and empathies with, alien states were well known. In the inter-war period, Canada had its share of communist and fascist sympathizers. And in western countries generally, generous immigration and refugee policies and unlimited political liberties produced an array of groups who were for or against communism, fascism, nationalism (for example, Ukrainian nationalism), and Zionism. Thus, Germany's National Socialism had followers in Canada other than Mennonites, whose ardour was checked for the most part before the world crossed the brink of the Second World War. Yet, so significant was the pro-Germanism among Mennonites, in Canada and elsewhere,[20] that the phenomenon, and the opposition to it, cannot remain unreported.[21]

Through the years, Germany had come to mean much for the

Mennonites in Russia and from Russia and this was reflected in much writing in the German Mennonite press in Canada, *Der Bote* in particular, and to a lesser extent *Die Mennonitische Rundschau*[22] and *Die Steinbach Post*.[23] The Germany of Bismarck and Wilhelm had nurtured a cultural relationship with German cultural minorities abroad which all German-speaking people in Russia had learned to appreciate. The Great War and German occupation of the Ukraine had not particularly enhanced that relationship, but the magnanimity of Germany with respect to the Moscow refugees revived deep and lasting emotions. Less than 6,000 of the estimated 13,000 believed to be at Moscow were able to leave Russia and enter transit camps in Germany en route to other destinations, but it was that country's generosity in the midst of her own poverty which made such a great impact on the hearts and minds of the Russlaender. All the latent affinity for the German culture and the German nation was brought to the fore. The remembrance of Dutch origins became muted and once again Germany was recognized as a fatherland.

Reporting in Canada on the second Mennonite world conference in Danzig in 1930, David Toews acknowledged that the greetings of German government officials had been of "special interest," for Germany showed such deep compassion for the Mennonites in Russia, China, Germany, Brazil, Paraguay, and Canada "or where else they might be."[24] It was the German government that really sacrificed itself on behalf of the refugees in spite of the Reich's own "rather difficult position." It was, therefore, quite natural that the Mennonite people should view Germany "as their fatherland" and remember "what Germany has done for our refugees."[25]

Others spoke with equal recognition and gratitude about Germany, her government, her social and economic organizations, and, last but not least, President Hindenburg.[26] His and Germany's acts of generosity were recalled when "thankless and ungrateful" criticism of Germany followed the emergence of Adolf Hitler.[27] Hindenburg's words on German unity, on loving the German fatherland not only on Sunday, and on appreciating it to the point of sacrifice were quoted and remembered.[28] After his death, grateful immigrants in Canada sent a wreath of flowers to decorate his grave.[29] While his passing was an intensely sad moment in the German community, his grave was also seen as the symbol of hope. One lay leader wrote:

> Even on this, and especially on this, grave we plant our hope.
> Hindenburg passed away, called of God, but before he died,
> he placed his hand of blessing on the head of Adolf Hitler.
> The blessing of a Hindenburg comes from above. In it there
> is strength.[30]

The appreciation for Germany increased with empathetic interpretations of her history and of her economic problems.[31] Through many years, foreign powers had either fought against the German states or fought out their quarrels on German soil, it was said, especially at times when Germany herself was inwardly divided and broken. These wars had all but destroyed the German spirit. The German soul, which was nigh dead as a consequence of the Napoleonic wars, had been revived in the Bismarckian era.[32] War came in 1914 when the imperial powers sought to curb Germany's commercial prowess, industrial growth, and economic power.[33] After the war, Germany was unduly burdened by heavy war reparation payments and by the war-guilt clause written into the Treaty of Versailles. That national humiliation was followed by internal political agitations of the Communists. All of this contributed to the miraculous and providential rise of Hitler.[34] When all efforts had failed to clean up the internal mess and to stand up against the powers, it was good to see a man take hold of all the problem areas of Germany and to proceed to solve them.[35] At last there was hope for a healthy Germany in the heart of Europe, a Germany which could become a blessing to all the nations of the world.[36] In the words of C.F. Klassen:

> We don't consider German people to be angels . . . but in spite
> of this we thank God, that at last a man has been found, who
> consolidated the national idea, who had courage to clean up the
> social democratic rottenness, the Communist insanity, and
> many Jewish machinations. . . [37]

The coming to power of Adolf Hitler in Germany was seen as a day of national rebirth. He was able to awaken powers long dormant, to initiate progress long hindered, to unify a nation long divided — almost as by the turning of his hand. A whole generation of shallow and depressed young people had been given a new soul, a new idealism, a new cause — the German nation.[38] The renewal that had come to Germany was not like the Russian Revolution, with all its ugliness. Rather, the German experience was a national uplifting, a springtime awakening, an internal rebirth.

One of the first achievements of the new regime was a domestic social clean-up, wrote Walter Quiring.[39] It was a big task to "take the manure out of the social-democratic-communistic barn," to do away with the corruption of administrators and judges, the treason, immorality, and thievery, which in the Jewish press were presented as virtues, to curb the immodest displays in the windows, the filth of the theatres, of the papers, and of drama and radio. However, the clean-up was undertaken, and, as with a steel broom, the whole country was swept and scraped, and all the foreign rabble was put in its place, it was reported. The clean-up began at the top and went right down to the bottom and affected administrators, policemen, schools, sports, art, theatre, the stage, film, the press, literature, organizations, the banking system, etc. In other words, in all areas of life there was a thorough and radical purging.

All the rubbish was being replaced with things that were honest, good, and true, reported Jacob H. Janzen along with Quiring and others. The great and forgotten German writers of the past were being resurrected from the dust to take the place of the Jewish writers and to give Germany a new literary face.[40] Now a Remarque could no longer sell hundreds of thousands of copies of his filthy book. On radio there was no longer any jazz music, but instead the wonderful creations of the German masters and the fresh and lively German folk songs were being played. Prospects were good that Germany would become well again, socially and morally, and that the old Prussian spirit of purity, honesty, sincerity, and uprightness would prevail again.[41]

The virtues, progress, and achievements of the new Germany were presented most comprehensively by a Canadian fundamentalist, a popular evangelist whose articles appeared in the Mennonite press.[42] In Germany there was security, said Oswald J. Smith. The people were optimistic and happy. All were working. All, old and young alike, loved Hitler. He recognized the values of recreation and encouraged the domestic life. Girls were not permitted to go to the university before they had spent six months in the home and learned how to keep house. And this was in harmony with the Christian emphasis. Immorality was curbed. Girls no longer painted their lips and cheeks, and how beautiful they looked. Papers no longer advertised birth-control methods, which before Hitler's time had been openly discussed by the young people. A great spiritual awakening was coming to Germany. A new, spiritually clean, and pure Germany was emerging.

The outstanding achievement of the Reich was halting the advance of Communism, internally as well as externally. Germany under Adolf Hitler was the one western nation that stood up bravely against the threat from the east.[43] And Mennonites could understand this best of all, because Russia now represented the image that was invoked to explain all the evils of the day, including atheism, modernism, immorality, and human exploitation.[44] While pure National Socialism probably was not the desired thing for Canada, it was clear that only a similar movement could save the American continent as well.[45] Since Communism endangered the Christian faith, resolute opposition to it could be considered the primary responsibility of the Mennonites in their foreign missionary undertakings.[46]

In his clear-cut stand against Communism, Hitler had proved himself a greater enemy of Communism than the church, and this also proved that the *Fuehrer* was sympathetic to Christianity. He and National Socialism based their policies on what was called "positive Christianity."[47] As a leader, Hitler was to be compared not so much with German political heroes like Bismarck but with religious leaders like Martin Luther.[48] In the words of B.H. Unruh:

> There are many Germans, very many National Socialists, who
> are believers at heart and who would never deny the Lord
> Jesus Christ. . . . This year I heard Hitler on the radio call
> upon his people to ask God for his grace. Many people are no
> longer inclined to take these words in their mouth. Our
> Fuehrer and Chancellor does not belong to this group.[49]

A defence of Hitler's Christianity required further explanation of what became known as the *Kirchenstreit*, or the quarrel between the church and the state.[50] The confrontation was explained away by Walter Quiring and others. The state, it was said, stood for a "positive Christianity," meaning a minimum emphasis on the word and a maximum emphasis on the deed, which, interpreted, meant love for the people and the fatherland. Further, Hitler had made religion respectable again and religious instruction had again become obligatory in the schools. The members of the *Reichstag* attended religious services before beginning the day's work.[51]

It was further explained that church and state were separated, meaning non-interference by the state in the internal affairs of the church, provided the church did not interfere in the affairs of state. This was the essence of the agreement made with the Vatican, and the same applied to the evangelical church.[52] The forced union of the 26 regional churches into one *Reichskirche* was a service not only to the nation but also to the church because centuries of fragmentation had harmed both. The government was concerned that all elements harmful to the German national consciousness be eliminated.[53] This meant that the various groups, including the Mennonites, had to place their statement of faith and their constitution before the government.[54]

The relationship of the Jews to the *Reich*, of course, was another matter. Not only were the Jews friendly to Communism but they were also the founding fathers of Communism. Karl Marx, the first Communist, was a Jew, his name having been Karl Mordechai.[55] The link between Judaism and Communism had been well documented, but those who had experienced the revolution in Russia did not require any documentation.[56] Jewish connections with Communism were given as one reason for suppressing them.[57] Another reason was their dominant position in German affairs and their determination to destroy the German people.[58] Their leadership in medicine, law, the press, and literature was due not primarily to intelligence but to a determined effort to seize power and to use Germany as the base for achieving the international Communist revolution.[59] Writers from within Germany were careful to point out that the maltreatment of Jews in Germany was highly exaggerated by the foreign Jewish-dominated press.[60] Once the half-truths and falsehoods of this press were exposed, things would be different in Germany too, because anti-Jewish action would then not be necessary.[61]

The foreign policy of Adolf Hitler, like the domestic policy, was designed to secure for Germany and her people their rightful place under the sun.[62] This meant political realism as well as the pursuit of peaceful international relations. The former required an uncompromising battle with Communism,[63] a resolute renunciation of the demands of the Treaty of Versailles,[64] the remilitarization of Germany "as in all other civilized nations on earth,"[65] and the bringing back into the German *Reich* of German peoples on the outside, as in Austria and the Sudetenland.[66] Recruits for the German army were sought among German nationals and German ethnics around the world. The German consul succeeded in placing his recruitment notices in *Der Bote*[67] and in *Die Mennonitische Rundschau*.[68]

The positive interpretation of German policies and the German leader was not universally accepted among the Russlaender Mennonites, though the opponents were certainly less vocal and fewer in number than the promoters. The first and deepest concern relating to the promotion of the German *Reich* grew out of the traditional Mennonite pacifist or nonresistance position. Although there were some who said it was the special duty of Mennonites, who knew Communism right down to its stone heart, to oppose it wherever and whenever possible and with whatever was necessary, there were also those who warned against any and all participation in, and sympathizing with, fascist movements. These were prepared to excuse the zealous participation of some young hotheads, but the wider sympathies in the constituency with the Brownshirts were inexcusable. After all, the sin against the nonresistant position in Russia, said one writer in referring to self-defence, had brought very bitter and undesirable consequences. The same had been true in other historical situations. Mennonites should not become guilty of the thirst for blood, which had made the nations of the world blind and insane.[69]

"Does Menno Simons come under the National Socialists?" asked B.B. Janz, as he attacked a wrong interpretation of that foremost Dutch Mennonite leader.[70] Being nonresistant, and being a follower of Menno Simons, he said, meant being nonresistant in every situation. National and racial ambitions, or even the need for self-defence, never justified the surrender of this position. In another article, Janz protested the excessive emphasis on German blood, Aryanism, and German books and stamps, which he said had only one object, namely "to tie us geographically to Germany."[71] Appreciation of the German language, he said, did not mean "adherence to German politics."

Generally speaking, the arguments used in defence of the nonresistant position were historical, theological, and practical. The Anabaptist pioneers of the Mennonite church were cited as evidence that it was possible to remain true and faithful even in persecution.[72]

The words of Jesus were quoted in a theological defence of nonresistance, and *Der Bote* published a series of articles answering in the negative the question "May Children of God Take Part in War?" After "proving" that the Old Testament wars were actually not God's will, but the people's choosing, the writer proceeded to show from New Testament scriptures that the higher loyalties of Christians to Christ should prevent them from participating in war. Some paragraphs from the church fathers and the early church history, as well as quotes from more contemporary leaders on the hellish nature of war, were further conclusive evidence that Christians were called to abstain.[73]

The religious argument was also used to challenge the politics of Germany in other areas. The cross of Christ could not give way to another cross, the swastika.[74] There was danger in overemphasizing family and blood ties. Had Jesus not warned the leaders of Israel to repent rather than to depend on having Abraham for a father? The important thing was not the pure race but the genuine faith.[75]

It was further pointed out that National Socialism had many shortcomings. Hitler was not without mistakes.[76] Germans, while they had their virtues, also had their vices. Germans had the capacity for selfishness, for crankiness and eccentricity, for flaming hate. Germans were bellicose and lacked consideration for others.[77] Germans, as fascists, preached a gospel of hate.[78] Germans, as National Socialists, were too much persuaded of the superiority of their own nation and race. As one teacher in Germany said, "The German young people have learned something in these times. They have learned to hate."[79]

This also meant that the Jews could not be blamed for the problems in Germany and the world. Admittedly, the Jewish people had abused the privilege of their chosenness, but the real reason they were feared so much was because of their ability. The Jews, it was said in their defence, combined the talents of both the Germans and Englishmen, could both research and theorize, and could also apply theory.[80] Another writer, the author of *The Russian Dance of Death*, sharply refuted all the talk about "*juedische Weltherrschaft*" (Jewish world domination) and about Jewish direction of the Communist revolution. Race had very little to do with it, he said. As a matter of fact, no race suffered as much from the Communist revolution as did the Jews.[81]

Mennonites who were international in their religious outlook had no reason to participate in a campaign against any one race, he continued. Mennonite ministers should condemn hate literature against the Jews in the same way that other filthy literature was attacked. *The Friends' Intelligencer* and *The Christian Century*, rather than Gerald B. Winrod's *The Defender*, were recommended as source materials for the Mennonite press.[82]

German-speaking Canadians were reminded that they owed their political loyalty to Canada and that Canada had remarkable achievements of her own. Canada had a friendly government and freedom to develop a religious and cultural life as one pleased. Canada also offered the rich values of English language and literature.[83] Besides, most of the Russian Mennonites in Canada had been saved from Communism not by Germany, but by Canada. One writer expressed alarm that every political gust of wind in Europe should bring such intense discussion and interest, when hardly any questions were asked about the country of one's own citizenship.

> Let us not make the mistake of nurturing to maturity a German beer patriotism and remaining strangers in our own country. Let us make Canada our real homeland. . . . Dear reader, if you have come into this country as an immigrant and if you have given vows to obedience before God and man, then become a citizen of this country also in your heart.[84]

The view that Mennonite citizenship obligations and national loyalties belonged in Canada prevailed in the end, as will later be seen more clearly. The older generation went out of its way to make public and official its appreciation of Canada and its fidelity to the crown. But the deep erstwhile empathy for Germany could not easily be set aside, and later, when Hitler occupied the Ukraine, some Russlaender cherished the hope of once again taking possession of the properties they had left behind. And the younger generation, undoubtedly reacting to a pacifism of the elders that was cloaked in pro-Germanism, went to war on the side of Britain in unexpectedly large numbers. But that story too must await a later unfolding.

The Nations and the Kingdom

Meanwhile, yet another school of thought, theologically verbalized but with political implications and affecting citizenship obligations,

swept through the Mennonite communities. An eschatology characterized by dispensationalism and pre-millennialism was not entirely
new. Both in North America and in Russia, Mennonites had been
exposed to the teachings of John Nelson Darby (d. 1882), an
outstanding leader of the Plymouth Brethren and a promoter of
dispensationalism. The earliest and strongest Mennonite carriers of
these ideas in Europe were the Mennonite Brethren and in North
America the Mennonite Brethren in Christ.

The leading proponent in the former group was Jacob W. Reimer, who frequently attended the Blankenburg Alliance Conference,
a centre in Germany for the propagation of dispensationalism.[85]
With his migration to Canada in the 1920s, the Dutch Mennonite
congregational families were exposed to dispensationalism and pre-
millennial teaching as never before. The Bible schools, almost
without exception, reinforced the itinerant educational role of J.W.
Reimer and his disciples. The curriculum and textbooks of the
schools were largely based on dispensationalist sources, and the
Scofield Reference Bible, heavily footnoted in dispensationalist
directions, was regarded as "equally inspired with the biblical
text."[86]

At least four important emphases followed from this interpretation
of Scripture and of history.[87] First of all, the saving of souls, as many
as possible, in preparation for the rapture was the most important
task of the church in the dispensation of grace. Least important were
the concerns about the kingdom on earth. All that would be taken
care of in a future dispensation. The Sermon on the Mount applied to
that future age, as did other ethical imperatives of the New Testament. Thus, every social ethic and every aspect of the social gospel
was minimized in favour of personal salvation.

Also flowing from dispensationalism was a concern for the Jewish
people, specifically their conversion. Expectations in this regard
were heightened by their movement to Palestine under the British
Mandate. Missions for the Jews sprang up in many places. Mennonite groups most preoccupied with dispensationalism were also most
interested in missions. The Mennonite Brethren regularly received
reports from Hugo Spitzer and his Jewish mission in Winnipeg.[88] In
Kitchener, the House of Friendship for people of all nations was
founded by the Old Mennonites, at least partly with the Jews in
mind.[89]

Perhaps no Mennonite group was taken in as much by dispensational and pre-millennial teaching as were the Mennonite Brethren, largely owing to the work of J.W. Reimer. According to the denomination's historian, "possibly no other theological system has influenced Mennonite Brethren theology...as much as dispensationalism."[90] Little wonder that the Brethren also had a great aversion for the social gospel and were careful to shun all who represented the socio-economic political implications of the gospel in the present age. Dispensationalism postponed all of that to another age.

The Conference of Mennonites in Canada was much less affected by dispensationalist thought, though the influence was strong enough for the issue to appear on several conference agendas. There was, however, no fear of challenging some of the dispensationalist assumptions, as was freely done by persons like Jacob H. Janzen in public presentations. J.H. Janzen, who had been asked to speak on the signs of the times, complained that he could not do this in terms of a system or systems because world history for him was not a chart with columns and paragraphs but an artistic production in which the colours often flowed into each other and the lines of demarcation and transition weren't always clear.[91] He rejected the manner in which the Bible was used to shape a system, namely by taking various Scripture passages out of context and fitting them to other passages likewise taken out of context, and in the process forgetting, neglecting, or relegating to an inferior position other passages equally important in God's revelation.

Dispensationalist thinking, along with fundamentalism and pre-millennialism, had made strong inroads in the Swiss Mennonite communities in the 1920s and became stronger yet in the 1930s. The Old Mennonite Conference of Ontario felt entirely at liberty to request Goshen College and the Mennonite Publishing House not to neglect "the pre-millennial view of prophecy," since the Conference was part of the constituency of those institutions and since the majority of the membership in the Conference accepted that view.[92]

It is also true, however, that the Old Mennonites did not leave some of their old teachings as they accepted some of the new ones. Along with fundamentalism there were the Anabaptist fundamentals and alongside dispensationalism there was Anabaptist ethics, nonconformity and nonresistance in particular. These, said the *Christian*

Monitor, were the two "great fundamentals of the Christian faith [which] must be defended at any cost,"[93] even while it also carried a yearlong series of articles on "the prophetic word."[94] The dual emphasis produced contradictions, especially in the *Monitor*, and no one articulated these better than C. F. Derstine.

Among Mennonite periodicals, the monthly *Christian Monitor* stood out as an attempt to comment in a regular and systematic way, from the perspective of the Christian faith, on important world happenings. Such events included the obvious power plays of the leading European states, but also the great changes coming to China,[95] the opening up of Africa,[96] the resistance movement building up in India,[97] the international implications of the Russian revolution,[98] and the real human need arising out of the Spanish Civil War.[99]

Responsibility for all of this rested with C.F. Derstine. When the Kitchener bishop laid down his task as editor of the *Monitor* in 1929, he became the World News Editor, whose assignment was to fill anywhere from one to four pages a month of the 32-page magazine with relevant material. The "Comments on World News" Section was subtitled "the voices of the age in the light of the voice of the ages." Almost every article was prefaced with a relevant — at least to the editor — scripture verse, which might or might not be referred to again in the material. From a variety of sources[100] the editor culled "the outstanding events of the day in church, educational, political, and social circles with an interpretation of the news in the light of the word of God."

Derstine's task and approach were characterized by a basic paradox and consequently filled with many contradictions, in which, in all probability, he mirrored the confusions and contradictions in significant sectors of the Mennonite community. At one and the same time, he and the *Monitor* editors were commenting on the problems of the world while minimizing Mennonite and Christian responsibility towards that world. As Mennonites, Derstine and the *Monitor* editors resolved "to remain aloof from politics" since they were committed to a platform of "separation from the world."[101] As evangelists and preachers, they insisted that the only remedy for the world's ailments was the gospel.[102] And as dispensationalists, they did not expect any improvement until the last dispensation and the millennial age was ushered in by Christ's second coming.[103] Thus, the immediate social and political responsibilities of Christians were left somewhat in limbo and many other issues were left unresolved.

Hence, the contradictions. Remaining "aloof from politics" was right and the official *Monitor* stance, but to remain silent in the face of "such giant evil forces [as] Communism" was wrong.[104] It was not for the church to introduce economic programs, but reforms such as those in Sweden could be welcomed.[105] It was good that "our testimony as a church against war is being effective" and that denominations like the Presbyterians — two million strong — wanted recognition in time of war for their conscientious objectors,[106] but the Federal Council of Churches, "a radical pacifist organization probably representing 20 million Protestants," was condemned. The reasons for the harsh judgement included its being listed by the Bureau of Naval Intelligence as subversive because of its "communist character or connections" along with 222 other organizations.[107]

The FCC was too "unorthodox, liberal, and unwise," yet its Social Creed for the Christian Churches was probably right because "the best way to defeat the atheism of Russia is to build a more human and righteous civilization ourselves."[108] Fundamentalism was in error because the peace principles of Christ required antagonism to war and because all Scripture, not just a 7-point creed, was fundamental and essential, yet the three-year program adopted by the World's Fundamentals Convention had in it much that was worthy.[109] All sinners needed saving and should be saved, so that there would be none "where murder may be lying dormant," but murderers themselves, especially Bruno Richard Hauptmann, the convicted kidnapper and murderer of the Lindbergh infant, should be executed.[110] The readers of the *Monitor* were discouraged from associating Gandhi's passive resistance with Bible nonresistance, and still it was said "the guns of the mightiest nations" were no match for "the boycott of the hapless Chinese [and] the passive resistance of India's millions."[111]

As evil as Communism was, there were some lessons to be learned about religion and about economics. In the first place, the whole situation in Russia was but "a natural reaction to the failure of the Russian Orthodox Church... a system that was dead, and preyed on the ignorance of the masses."[112] The Soviet insistence on economic communism was bad, very bad, but a sense of common ownership of the world's goods would surely be good since "looking out for number one" — Derstine was referring to trade barriers and high tariffs — "is the cause of the breakdown of civilization."[113] Besides, the world would have to choose "the communism of the New Testament which is Christian," in order to avoid "the Christless Communism of Russia."[114]

Mussolini, the Fascist leader of Italy, was somewhat of a problem, because he was viewed as "a protector from Vaticanism and Communism." And anybody who opposed both could not be far from Derstine's heart. Criticism of the Pope abounded in his columns,[115] and the Catholic Church itself was "the great whore" of revelation.[116] The Catholic Church had held "a powerful grip upon the nations of the world" but this grip was fast slipping, as in Fascist Italy, Republican Spain, and modern Mexico.[117] While Fascism was the enemy of Communism, as clearly illustrated in Germany, Italy, and Spain, it represented the rule of force by a minority.[118] Fascism, like Communism, exalted the state above the individual, the former in co-operation with capitalists, the latter in co-operation with the proletariat. Fascism was an opponent of other political bodies, of the free church, and of almost everybody. Besides, Fascism glorified war.[119]

Similarly, Adolf Hitler and Germany represented a dilemma. The *Fuehrer* and all Nazis were militant anti-communists and the guardians of certain values like the vigilantes of the West in America.[120]

> They are for the home. They are for marriage. They are for children. They are against sex-saturated moving pictures. They are for nationalism as against communism. They are for the peasant, and for putting back millions of people on to privately-owned farms, the re-establishment of a stout yeomanry. They are for an industrious, God-fearing body politic. They are for Christianity, through a vigorous ecclesiastical organization. . . . [121]

Hitler was given credit for resisting Communism in Germany, but why did he have to resort to Fascist tyranny, as was evident in the execution of nearly 70 men of his own party?[122] With Hitler assuming all the power, democracy in Germany was dead.[123] Hitler's *Mein Kampf* was a combination of terror, hatred, and racial prejudice, with hardly any humanitarian or moral spirit in it.[124]

The *Monitor* was not optimistic about Germany's future with Adolf Hitler as chancellor. She had chosen between two possible evils, Fascism and Communism.[125] The Germany of the day was not the Germany of the Reformation, because higher critics had emptied the churches and destroyed her spirituality. The courageous pastors of the confessional church were praised because "no group of men of science, no academy of teachers or of artists, no bar association, has risked concentration camp for scientific, academic or artistic ideals."[126]

In some areas, Derstine and his selected correspondents did not contradict themselves. They were certain that there was little else but evil in the world and that there was no salvation apart from that which individuals could experience in their hearts, that which Mennonites could retain by remaining separate from the world, and that which Christ would achieve upon his return. There were evil systems of thought, evil nations, evil leaders, evil deeds, and evil events, all of which pointed to chaos and revolution as the best the world could bring forth, the need for revival which was the task of the Christian church, and the return of the Lord to set everything right.[127] Referring to the sabre-rattling by Mussolini, to the rearmament program of France, and in general to the preparation for war, the *Monitor* commented:

> The world at large certainly has not been able to deal with the fundamental antagonisms of unregenerate life. This takes the power of the Gospel, which the masses still reject. However, all these conditions only make louder the footfalls of the coming of the Prince of Peace, the "Great Umpire," who will finally speak the last word to the nations, a word of judgment for their rule.[128]

For Derstine and the *Monitor*, the nations, be they fascist, marxist, or capitalist, were "ferocious beasts,"[129] all of whom would be judged by the Lord. Their constant grabbing for more land was wrong and Italy should have stayed out of Ethiopia.[130] Because of their evil ways, nations and empires and thrones were temporary. The dethronement of King Alfonso of Spain was another example of mighty thrones falling according to biblical prophecy. In the last 13 years alone, four powerful kingdoms had been overthrown: Austria, Germany, Russia, Spain, all a sign of the nearness of the return of the

King of Kings.[131] The *Monitor* viewed the daily happenings, the Russian nightmare, the Japanese invasion of Manchukuo, the antics of Hitler, the uprisings of grudging labour, and the crushing blows of conscienceless capital, as leading to "a final crash — a catastrophe unparalleled in the ages past."[132]

All that was happening in the world, inluding the realignment and power struggles in Europe and the migration of Jews to Palestine, were perceived to be the fulfilment of prophecy, leading to an imminent end of the present age, the return of the Lord, and the ushering in of the new age in which also the Jewish people would once again have a special role. This position made the *Monitor* a constant and consistent champion of the Jewish people, but it also assumed their conversion. Since the predestination and pre-millennialism of Derstine assumed a special role for the Jewish people, his contradictions disappeared when they became the focus of his commentary.

The Lord would punish nations "which take a jingo (warlike) attitude to the Jew."[133] The Jews had been oppressed too much and the Lord would judge the anti-Semitic spirit in both Germany and Italy. The way Germany was touching God's chosen people was unforgivable. Noting the measures being enacted by Hitler affecting negatively and seriously the Jewish merchants, the *Monitor* warned Germany:

> It has never paid any nation to misuse the Jew. Nations that kick this ancient and beloved people usually suffer seriously from stubbed toes. Hatred works like a boomerang. Germany, beware.[134]

God had a special place for the Jews because of their antiquity and their outliving of many empires, because of Abraham, who cast the world's longest shadow, because of Israel's custodianship of the Ten Commandments, because of their contribution to the Gentiles, because of the prophecies, because of the supreme personality emerging from the Jewish people, namely the Lord Jesus Christ, because of their contribution to the early church and the sacred writings, and because of their contribution to world knowledge and to science.

> The Lord's judgements have always fallen upon nations which touched Israel, the "apple of his eye." All the great nations that persecuted the Jews are but historical incidents, and the Jew

still lives on. . . . Truly, the Bible declares that the sufferings
of Israel are part of God's judgements upon them. This, however, does not give any nation or individual the divine permission to persecute the Jews.[135]

The *Monitor* observed that the Jews were being taunted, persecuted, and ostracized in many lands. In the U.S.A., 156 anti-
Semitic organizations had sprung up overnight.[136] The validity of
the Jewish Protocols was denied, and they were described as
forgeries.[137] Evidence that Jews were in any way determinative or
even influential with respect to Communism and Germany was
refuted.[138] As far as the relationship between Jews and Communists
in the U.S.A. was concerned, the exhaustive research of the American Hebrew Society had determined that in the New York area there
were only 2,000 out of 2 million Jews in the Communist Party and
the proportions weren't greater in cities like Philadelphia, Pittsburgh, and Chicago. No more than five of the 29 members of the
Central Committee of the Party in the U.S.A. were Jews, and only
about 30 out of 250 Party organizers were Jews.[139]

Christians should love and accept the Jews, refuse to persecute and
malign them, believe in the eternal purpose God had for the nation of
Israel, deny the lies being told about the Jewish people — Jewish
bankers did not control the world's finances — help them in their
hour of distress, explain that antagonism could bring about repent-
ance, and preach the gospel to both Jew and Gentile.[140] The Jew "is
cuddling closer to the Christian Church than any other group of
people," it was said, meaning that the opportunities for preaching the
gospel were increasing.[141] The apparent failure of political Zionism
in Palestine, its hopes "blasted through the antagonism of the
Arabs," clearly meant not that Jerusalem was out of focus as far as the
Jews were concerned but that their spiritual salvation was a higher
priority than their political entrenchment.[142]

Four Conferences on Peace and War

The concerns about world affairs, the threat of war, and civic
responsibility found their immediate and ultimate focus in the issue
of nonresistance, the avoidance of military service, and whether or
not there was an alternative. The discussions of militarism and
military service produced examples of all the separations previously

described. There were those who insisted on total exemption and non-involvement in accordance with the position of geographic separation[143] and there were those whose involvement on the basis of an alternative ethic produced calls for international disarmament, on the one hand, and an alternative service for Mennonite boys, on the other hand.[144] These two positions involved the majority of Mennonites. Minority positions were pacifism or militarism on the basis of empathy with Germany. A few Canadian Mennonites actually responded to foreign recruitment notices.[145] Others were affected by individualism and institutionalism to the extent that, whether or not persons became militarily involved, this was viewed as a personal decision beyond the discipline of the community of believers.[146] And there were those who insisted that disarmament could only happen in a future age.[147]

The discussions of these issues in the 1930s began in the separate congregational families but were then transferred to inter-Mennonite gatherings, where once again some differences between and among Russlaender and Kanadier and the Swiss became obvious. The discussions in four conference families are especially noteworthy: among the Swiss, the Old Mennonites and the Mennonite Brethren in Christ and among the Dutch, the Conference of Mennonites in Canada and the Northern District Mennonite Brethren Conference.

The Old Mennonites, for whom nonconformity and nonresistance were often the same issue and concern, kept alive their North America peace/military problems committees in the inter-war period. The task of these committees was to guide the church, including the conferences in Canada, in the peace witness.[148] The activities of these committees were varied. A petition bearing 20,000 signatures protesting a proposed program of universal military training was prepared in book form for mailing to Congress, but the joining of other movements that had been launched to find an alternative to war was discouraged.[149] Government officials were not only informed about the Mennonite position but urged to proceed with disarmament. The President of the United States, members of Congress, the 1930 London Naval Conference, and the 1932 Geneva Disarmament Conference all received communications encouraging stronger efforts for international peace and discouraging all movements that had an opposite tendency. The need for world disarmament was frequently stated in the *Monitor* as it noted with alarm the military build-up around the world.[150]

The Mennonite Conference of Ontario represented the Canadian side of the Old Mennonite peace position. S.F. Coffman, who had been the chief spokesman in the Great War, continued to press for true nonresistance, which neutralized or removed anger, antagonism, and hatred. He urged the avoidance of "aggressive" pacifist organizations like War-Resisters and the Anti-War League. Nonresistance negatively meant not suing at law and not resisting evil, and positively it meant turning the other cheek, going the second mile, and giving to him that asked.[151]

In the Conference itself, internal peace education and the external peace witness were both matters under discussion.[152] The position on peace of the Russlaender now in Ontario was also clarified upon the initiative of the Conference. Interviews with Bishop Jacob H. Janzen of the Conference Mennonites and with pastor Henry H. Janzen of the Mennonite Brethren had produced the conclusion that the Russlaender were opposed to participation in war, that "they, with us, believe in nonresistance upheld by love," that they desired help in clarifying that noncombatant service in Canada had a different status than had been the case in Russia, and that consultation and co-operation leading to united action in the event of war was desired by them.[153]

Three Canadians, working with three Americans as the Mennonite General Conference Peace Committee, prepared the "Statement of Position on Peace, War, and Military Service" which was accepted by the Mennonite General Conference at Turner, Oregon, in 1937 and by the Mennonite Conference of Ontario in 1938.[154] This so-called Turner Statement became a reference point also for other Mennonite groups, and was in all probability the most important Mennonite peace statement of the decade.[155]

The Turner Statement referred to other historic documents (Dordrecht of 1917, Germantown of 1725, Goshen of 1917, and Garden City of 1921), and there sought to apply "the main tenets of our peaceful and nonresistant faith" to present conditions.[156] This application forbade participation "in carnal warfare or conflict between classes, groups or individuals," the personal bearing of arms, service with "civilian organizations temporarily allied with the military" (such as the YMCA and the Red Cross), "the financing of war operations...in any form," "the manufacture of munitions and weapons," "military training in schools or colleges," and "any agitation, propaganda, or activity that tends to promote ill-will or hatred among nations...." This position ruled out government-administered alternative service, though the willingness "at all times to aid in the relief of those in distress or suffering," regardless of the danger and the cost, was emphasized. Should war come:

> we shall endeavour to continue to live a quiet and peaceable life in all godliness and honesty; avoid joining in the wartime hysteria of hatred, revenge and retaliation; manifest a weak and submissive spirit, being obedient unto the laws and regulations of the government in all things, except in such cases where the obedience to the government would cause us to violate the teachings of the Scriptures. . . . [157]

The New Mennonite Brethren in Christ were relatively silent on peace and military matters, but in 1938 the Ontario Conference appointed a committee to study the Old Mennonite statement. [158] The Committee found itself "in substantial agreement with this statement, though differing somewhat in a few details." It was decided, therefore, to prepare a statement—the word used was "Memorial" —based on the Turner Statement but with "such additions or other changes...as would make clear our MBC position." Subsequently, support for the Memorial was sought and secured from the Canadian North-West Conference of the Mennonite Brethren in Christ and from the Brethren in Christ Church (Tunkers) with whom the Mennonite Brethren in Christ formed a joint committee, to forward the message to Prime Minister W.L. Mackenzie King. The hope had been to have the message endorsed also by the Mennonite Conference of Ontario, and, while S.F. Coffman attended one of the joint meetings as an unofficial representative, he explained that the Turner Statement had already been forwarded to the Prime Minister by that Conference. [159]

Since the Mennonite Brethren in Christ would drop the Mennonite identity in less than a decade, it is of interest that the 1938 Memorial recognized commonality "with other present-day branches of the Mennonite church" with respect to the doctrines of peace and nonresistance as well as continuity with the historic Dordrecht Confession of Faith. [160] In regard to military service, the

MBC Memorial followed word for word the Turner Statement on carnal warfare or conflict between nations and classes, on the financing of war operations through voluntary loans and contributions, on the manufacture of munitions, on military training in schools and colleges, on propaganda producing ill will or hatred, and on wartime profiteering.[161] But, significantly, the Memorial omitted the Turner paragraph having to do with alternative service, namely:

> . . . consistency requires that we do not serve during war time under civil organizations temporarily allied with the military in the prosecution of the war, such as the YMCA, the Red Cross, and similar organizations which, under military orders, become part of the war system in effect, if not in method and spirit, however beneficial their peace-time activities may be.[162]

A subsequent report of the Committee to the Conference made clear that the omission was deliberate, but this did not mean that there was to be no co-operation with other Mennonite groups.[163] The Non-Resistant Relief Organization, founded during the Great War as an agency of all the Ontario Mennonite and Amish groups, and dormant since 1924, was reactivated in 1937, and the Mennonite Brethren in Christ resolved to forward their relief money through the NRRO.[164] That co-operation also helped prepare the way for participation in a new organization, the Conference of Historic Peace Churches and its Military Problems Committee, embracing also Quakers and Brethren in Christ (Tunkers).[165] The Conference restored the nineteenth-century alliance on matters of peace and nonresistance among the Mennonites, Quakers, and Tunkers which had existed since pioneer days.[166]

The two conferences of the Dutch Mennonites most conerned with issues of peace and war were the Conference of Mennonites in Canada and the Northern District Mennonite Brethren Conference. The former had the matter on its agenda at regular intervals during the inter-war period.[167] The Conference expressed willingness to explore with other Mennonite groups the possibility of an alternative service,[168] voiced concern about militarism in the schools,[169] insisted that new congregations joining the Conference hold to nonresistance,[170] encouraged the preparation and distribution of peace literature,[171] approved membership in the World Peace Union of Mennonites, whose headquarters was in the Netherlands,[172] requested research into the status of conscientious objectors in the military laws of the country,[173] and heard various position papers on nonresistance.[174]

The many articles about nonresistance in the periodicals, said J.J. Klassen, were a sign that the matter had become a problem among the Mennonites.[175] This he had difficulty understanding because 400 years of nonresistance had been part of the confession, and repeatedly the forefathers had sacrificed all their possessions in order to maintain what for them was a holy and precious conviction. And now there was a favourable climate for nonresistance in the universal anti-war movement, which was a continuing reaction to the Great War. Even the victors did not enjoy any good results. The war had been so terrible that many who had been part of it, including ordinary soldiers and the highest generals, were totally opposed to war. In many other Christian groups now, there was also a conscience about war, and even governments were denouncing war as a crime against humanity.

Responsibility, faithfulness, and loyalty were main themes of the 1937 Conference sessions, and they were also applied to the state.[176] Faithfulness to the state was seen to be the will of God, except in cases where the will of the state contradicted the will of God. For Mennonites, there were two areas of contradiction: participating in war and swearing of the oath. Otherwise, Mennonites were loyal citizens of the state, a special requirement at this time because "the spirit of disloyalty, disobedience, and revolution" was also at work in the west, especially through the press, making people unhappy and ungrateful and unmindful of the many things that come via the state, namely the promotion of the general welfare of its citizens.[177] Christians, and especially the Mennonite immigrants of the 1920s, could express their gratitude by engaging in a useful vocation, thus becoming an example to others, by not becoming a burden to the state and, indeed, by helping to carry the burdens of those needy persons who did not qualify for state aid, and by maintaining a moral and religious stance, especially with reference to educational matters.[178]

David Toews had written to Prime Minister King, Bishop S.F. Coffman, and four lawyers to clarify the situation with respect to Mennonite exemption from military service. The most definitive clarification received came from T. Magladery, the Deputy Minister of Immigration.[179] Magladery explained, first of all, that all the Mennonites were the same before the law and there was no difference whatsoever arising out of the various periods of immigration. Nor were orders-in-council determinative in this matter, he advised, because orders-in-council could only give or take away that which statutes gave or didn't give. The famous order-in-council of 1873, which granted exemptions specifically to the Russian Mennonites, was to give them assurance that they also were covered by the statutes. All exemption from military service, he explained, had been defined by statute since Confederation and was applicable to persons who, because of the teachings of their religion, were opposed to the bearing of arms. In brief:

> The only conclusion I can come to is that the Mennonites are as free now from military service as they have ever been. And if no changes are made in the militia act and if the confession of faith remains unchanged then they will be free from military service also in the future.[180]

In the Northern District Mennonite Brethren Conference, the issues of war and peace were placed on the agenda at Waldheim in 1934 by an unusual source. It so happened that there were in Saskatchewan several communities of Russian-speaking believers who had come under Mennonite influence before and/or after their migration from Russia. The Conference of Mennonites in Canada had such a connection[181] and the Mennonite Brethren were even more involved, evangelism among Russian people having been one of their special strengths.[182] In 1934, representatives of these people brought a resolution on the war question in language quite unusual for a Mennonite Brethren Conference.[183] The resolution asked that all wars be condemned because war did not resolve conflict, because it destroyed the moral foundations of society, because it left huge debts and many orphans, widows, cripples, and persons mentally ill, and because of the role in war played by capitalist industry and power-hungry diplomats.

The Conference declined to support the resolution because in its view its task was not "to proclaim anti-war resolutions into the wide world" but rather to deepen the peace conviction in the churches and to find a way to protect the consciences of the brothers in wartime.

The Conference also indicated that, while they would work together with all nonresistant bodies, they would have nothing to do with Quakers and other "popular movements which employ force."[184] With respect to the military question,[185] the Conference adopted a position on alternative service which included the medical corps:

> . . . as citizens we are duty-bound to our homeland to serve not only with taxes but with a service not contrary to our conscience. . . . we should be willing to do anything that serves the principle of life, even if this is tied up with problems. Cowardice or convenience or other considerations have no place in this matter. As disciples of Jesus Christ we cannot take a position against the medical corps. . . . if those healed are sent back to war and to their death, that is not our responsibility and it may not rest on our conscience.[186]

Needless to say, perhaps, the Russian brethren were never heard from again.

The alternative service and medical corps option was being promoted by the Brethren on the assumption that what was possible in Russia would also be desirable in Canada. But it was known already that Kanadier Mennonites didn't see things that way, so the Brethren decided that their own position should be interpreted on an inter-Mennonite committee by one of their own Kanadier.[187] The compromise was insufficient, because not all the Brethren were themselves satisfied with the Waldheim resolution. It was modified in 1937 to the effect that individual persons should not be coerced to go into the medical corps if they didn't want to and that understanding should be reached with the authorities so that medical corpsmen need not be armed and could be under civilian direction.[188]

Other positions were not modified. The Conference agreed to participate in all-Mennonite committees, provided they did not establish connections with social-political pacifist organizations. And peace literature could be distributed to the young people but not "the so-called pacifist writings [which] had a political basis and campaigned for a world peace which the Scriptures did not project" or other writings with a religious basis but with a radical approach to nonresistance. "One-sided pamphlets wouldn't be of help to our young people," said the Conference, only those writings which harmonized obedience towards the government with the love of one's neighbour and enemy.[189]

Mennonites, Militarism, and Their Majesties

The many-sided expressions of readiness to approach the problem of war and discussions with the government on an inter-Mennonite basis eventually led to such meetings, encouraged in part by events outside of Canada. In the U.S.A., meetings between Mennonites, Quakers, and the Church of the Brethren had begun in 1935 and were being held regularly under the auspices of a Continuation Committee.[190] And in 1936, Harold S. Bender, the chairman of the Old Mennonite General Conference Peace Problems Committee, was seeking the signatures of American Mennonite church leaders for the "Peace Manifesto," originating with some Mennonites in Holland and adopted at the third Mennonite World Conference in Amsterdam.[191]

Mennonites in Canada were not ready for a broad ecumenical approach among peace churches, except in Ontario, where Quakers, Tunkers, and Mennonites had a history of joint witness and action. However, a March 10, 1939, Chicago meeting of seven American Mennonite groups to prepare a plan for joint action became an acceptable model. David Toews, C.F. Klassen, and B.B. Janz attended the meeting, and proceeded to plan a similar gathering in Canada.[192]

The inter-Mennonite meeting of representatives to discuss problems related to military service was held at Winkler, Manitoba, on May 15, 1939.[193] Intended to be fully representative of all the Mennonites in Canada, seven congregational families of the Dutch heritage were present, and one from the Swiss heritage, namely the Old Mennonites. The former included the Conference Mennonites[194] and the Mennonite Brethren, both predominantly, though not exclusively, Russlaender, and the following Kanadier congregational families: Altkolonier, Bruderthaler (Evangelical Mennonite Brethren), Holdemaner (Church of God in Christ Mennonite), Kleine Gemeinde, and Rudnerweider. The Bergthaler, a leading Kanadier congregation in Manitoba, was also present and included in the Conference Mennonites. Not represented among the 230 registered participants were the Bergthaler(S), Chortitzer, and Sommerfelder.[195] The Hutterian Brethren, having been invited, were present.

The purpose of the meeting was explained by David Toews, who was then also elected to chair the day's proceedings, the recording of which was entrusted to C.F. Klassen and F.C. Thiessen, both of Winnipeg, both Russlaender, and both Brethren.[196] Toews identified the agenda of the day as follows: the possibility of "the outbreak of a disastrous war," the disunity of the Mennonites in the last war, and the desirability of "all Mennonite churches who esteem the principle of nonresistance to agree and proceed unitedly."[197] Knowing full well that no Mennonite group at the meeting would want to be coerced into a united position, Toews gave the Winkler event the status of an unofficial and informal meeting, the decisions of which could be official and binding only for those groups who chose to make them so.

Of greatest significance for the discussions of the day were the positions of the various congregational families to be taken in the event of war and the calling up of the young men, namely whether or not some alternative service instead of military service would be acceptable. It soon became clear that there was a sharp division of opinion on the question, and that it was the Russlaender, whose Russian history included alternative service in the forestry and medical corps, who were promoting a position favourable to an alternative service.

Helpful to those who were opposed was the Turner Statement and its chief interpreter, Harold S. Bender, who was present not only as the guest speaker of the day, but also as the representative of the Old Mennonites of Ontario, having been authorized in that capacity by S.F. Coffman. H.S. Bender "emphasized that the Old Mennonite churches are entirely opposed to any work in any organization which has anything to do with the conduct of the war, such as the medical corps or a war industry." Speaking for S.F. Coffman, Bender recommended "that if no service is requested none should be offered by the Mennonites in general."[198] Bender was supported in his stand by Bishop Schmidt of Guernsey, representing the Old Mennonites in Western Canada, by Bishop Jakob Froese of the Altkolonier, Rev. Jacob Wiebe of the Holdemaner, Rev. David Hofer of the Hutterian Brethren, Bishop William Falk of the Rudnerweider, and Rev. H.R. Reimer of the Kleine Gemeinde. Two groups expressed readiness "in case of need for an alternative service in the medical corps, thereby manifesting that the churches are willing to save life, but not to destroy it."[199] They were the Mennonite Brethren and the

Evangelical Mennonite Brethren (Bruderthaler), whose spokesmen, from Coaldale and Steinbach respectively, coincidentally bore the same name: Benjamin Janz.

Representatives of the Conference of Mennonites in Canada tended to speak in more general terms about adherence to the principle of nonresistance, but it was Jacob H. Janzen of Waterloo who stressed the need for a positive expression of one's citizenship, especially in Ontario, where the immigrants were highly suspect and where the meeting house at Virgil had been searched, unsuccessfully, for explosives alleged to be hidden there. Part of the Mennonite problem, it was recognized, was the excessive amount of German literature being brought into the communities, literature carrying propaganda for another state.

In the end, the meeting agreed to set forth those matters in a resolution on which there was full agreement.[200] They included a continued firm stand on the biblical principle of nonresistance "as received from the fathers," confession of failure to adhere to the principle consistently, a sense of urgency to much more fully teach the doctrines of nonresistance to the young people, gratitude for freedom of religion and conscience, and willingness "to remain loyal to our Canada."

The latter was further elaborated on in a special address to their majesties for which there was unanimous consent. The meeting also agreed to the formation of a continuing committee consisting of three persons from the three leading conferences: David Toews, B.B. Janz, and S.F. Coffman, to which others could be added. And, finally, a unanimous request was addressed to the editors of *Rundschau* and *Bote* "to refrain from printing any news or articles contrary to our principles." There was no need to specify what was meant because it was clear that writers in both papers had carried their pro-Germanism far enough to suggest disloyalty to Canada and a discarding of nonresistance.

Harold S. Bender was impressed with the strength and unanimity of nonresistance convictions expressed, but for him and others enthusiastic about the outcome it was premature relief. The differences on an alternative service were deeper than most were ready to admit. Most ominous for the future also was the exclusion of any one of the Kanadier bishops or churches—David Toews and the Rosenorter hardly spoke for them—from the continuing committee.

The Mennonites had come together to record the things on which they agreed. Very soon those things on which they did not agree, which disagreements they did not record, would matter the most, at least when it came to forming a united Mennonite front as the war clouds gathered ever thicker.

As the horizons darkened, the Mennonites became even more aware not only that they were not united and that they had not adequately prepared their young people but also that they had given both them and Canadian society a mixed message. Basically, they were concerned about doing the will of God and advancing His kingdom, but they had postponed it into another age, transferred it to another country, or limited it to their colonies and their conferences. The time had come, following the cues of H. H. Ewert and Edward Yoder, to take society very seriously, not to withdraw from it, but to be involved on the basis of, and separated from it in terms of, an alternative ethic and value system.

The first, most obvious step was to accept that they were Canadian, to express appreciation for that fact, and to do so both by acknowledging those placed in authority and by rendering service to others. In the latter category were the reactivation of the Non-Resistant Relief Organization in Ontario, already noted, and in the West the raising of funds for the Red Cross Society.[201] And in terms of ethnic identification, people like C.F. Klassen, who had once praised Hitler, were beginning to say that Mennonites were Dutch, not German.[202] David Toews went to the public media to explain that Mennonites might be German in a cultural sense but not in a political sense,[203] and later, B.B. Janz gave to the Lethbridge paper an article denying National Socialism on his part.[204]

B.B. Janz, like David Toews, had made it his special assignment to give the public a better understanding of Mennonites. Perhaps it was the ongoing experience with anti-Mennonite agitators in Coaldale, but Janz had early come to the conclusion that flirtation with Germany was wrong and that some service in wartime would be right. He also used every public occasion possible to praise Canada and its leaders. One such event was a visit to the Mennonites at Coaldale of Colonel J.S. Dennis and Sir Edward Beatty, the president of the CPR, who was referred to by a Calgary newspaper as Coaldale's "sugar daddy."[205] Both were profusely thanked by Janz and David Toews, who offered their loyalty to Canada.[206] The event was good for the Mennonites, inasmuch as the *Lethbridge Herald* observed editorially:

> The Mennonites are a God-fearing, hard-working people who left Russia with a curse in their ears, and as Bishop Toews said Sunday, were received in Canada in the spirit of St. John. . . . There is a lesson in the Mennonite ceremony of Sunday for many of us who are apt to regard much too lightly these days the freedom which is ours here in Canada.[207]

Another occasion for mutual admiration by Mennonites and Canadian leaders was the 1939 session in Coaldale of the Northern District Conference. Acknowledging the presence of Senator W. Buchanan from Ottawa and W.H. Fairfield, the superintendent of the Dominion Experimental Farm at Lethbridge, B.B. Janz praised the "full freedom to establish ourselves economically and spiritually." There was no country in the world where "the people enjoy such religious liberty as we do here in Canada."[208] J.F. Redekop of Main Centre likewise affirmed the desire of Mennonites to be good citizens:

> . . . we would like to be citizens of the British Commonwealth of Nations, which pledge their loyalty to and pray for their country and their Government and endeavour to perform their duties and obligations in every respect as far as they are in accordance with the Scriptures and with their Christian conscience.[209]

The best opportunity of all for expressing loyalty and obligation was the unprecedented visit to Canada in 1939 of King George VI and Queen Elizabeth. The response to that visit had more Mennonite unity and integrity in it than some other public relations events, for positive feelings about the British monarchy dated back to that time in the late seventeenth century when William and Mary took up the cause of the dissenters and generous portions of religious liberty became one of the general characteristics of the British Empire.[210] It was partly the trust in the monarchy and British laws that had brought the Swiss from the U.S.A. and the Amish from Europe to Ontario,[211] and, later, the Mennonites from Russia to Manitoba.[212] At this point in history, the most conservative of the Kanadier would likely have at least one portrait of the King in their homes,[213] and it was one imperial symbol which was not out of bounds in their schools. And, at the other end of the Mennonite continuum, the New Mennonites were known not only for their enthusiasm for George VI but also for their message to Edward VIII upon his assumption of power, assuring him of "our loyalty" and prayer "always for God's blessing on Him, His Government, and His subjects, and for peace and prosperity in all his realm."[214] Nothing was said when a short while later he abdicated to marry a person he loved but who was unacceptable as a queen.[215]

The Winkler message to "George VI, King of Canada" conveyed the "deepest devotion and unwavering loyalty" of the 80,000 Canadian Mennonites both "to yourself and the Government of which you are the head."[216] Reviewing the history of Mennonite migrations, the message acknowledged that "in this Dominion" the Mennonites had found "a haven of rest, freedom, and security after having been severely oppressed at different times and in different countries... because of their faith." The Canadian government had "by and large kept the promises made" and the Mennonites had been allowed "to live their lives according to the dictates of their conscience," to follow their occupations "as they pleased," and to enjoy the fruits of their labour "without any molestation or interference."

Dressed up in the best calligraphy the Mennonites could provide,[217] the sentiments thus expressed in western Canada were echoed in eastern Canada. It so happened that the dates of the annual session of the Mennonite Conference of Ontario coincided with the visit of Their Majesties to Kitchener-Waterloo. But the opening of the session was delayed until the royal train left the cities. The Conference engaged in special prayer for Their Majesties' safety and in the singing of "God Save the King."[218] A message sent after the King's and Queen's departure thanked the Prime Minister for their visit to Canada and reminded him that the Mennonites had "entrusted the safeguarding of these [religious] liberties to the British Crown."[219]

These positive expressions were reinforced in the *Monitor*, where strong words of praise for the monarchy and the monarch found repeated outlet.[220] If C.F. Derstine was generally negative about the nations and their leaders, he was effusive about Great Britain. He attributed the "ovation" and "thrilling reception" received by Their Majesties to the fact that "here is one nation that God has used through the ages, which still stands—and stands for something."[221]

Great Britain was admired for the immensity of its territory, for laying "the foundation of political and religious liberty for the world," for "one of the finest systems of law in the world," for its attitude towards Christianity, and for its present King and Queen, whose "home life appeals to the nations."[222] Derstine considered that the Munich Agreement had halted "the four grim, deadly horsemen"[223] and that British statesmanship deserved its fair share of praise because "the world may have been saved a bath in blood."[224]

The world was not saved a bloodbath. World War II broke out in September of 1939, and Canada was immediately drawn into it. Though the mobilization of manpower and conscription were delayed for a time, the beginning of another world-wide conflagration marked a turning point not only in world and Canadian history but also in Mennonite history. For the present, it was clear that the Mennonites had to focus on new and unaccustomed ways of exercising their faith and citizenship. They could not escape into a future kingdom or to a foreign country. A retreat into their geographic enclaves or conference institutions was also not a way out. They were facing the world, and they needed to decide on the ethic which would guide them at the crossroads.

FOOTNOTES

1   Harold S. Bender, "Church and State in Mennonite History," *Mennonite Quarterly Review* 13 (April 1939):103. The original says "totalitarian war" but the probable meaning is "total war."

2   H.H. Ewert, "Welche Aufgaben haben wir jetzt nach dem Kriege unserm Lande gegenueber?" *Der Mitarbeiter* 13 (February 1920):9–11, 16; (April 1920):31.

3   Signatories were the following: Benjamin Ewert as chairman and J.G. Toews as secretary; from Conference congregations: D.D. Klassen, John F. Nickel, Jacob J. Loewen, Wm. S. Buhr, David Schulz, J.N. Hoeppner, J.J. Siemens (Bergthaler); P.A. Rempel, John P. Bueckert, J.H. Klassen, J.P. Klassen (Blumenorter); J.H. Enns, Jacob Paukratz (Schoenwieser); Brethren congregations: Jacob Epp, J.W. Reimer, A.A. Regier, C.N. Hiebert, F.F. Isaak, H.S. Voth; others: P.S. Wiebe (Chortitzer); J.T. Wiebe (Holdemaner); P.W. Friesen, H.R. Dyck, P.P. Reimer, P.J.B. Reimer, D.P. Friesen, H.R. Reimer (Kleine Gemeinde); W.H. Falk (Rudnerweider); Peter A. Toews (Sommerfelder); B.P. Janz (Bruderthaler).

4   Benjamin Ewert and Julius G. Toews, "Eine wichtige Ver-
     sammlung," *Der Bote* 15 (26 October 1938):3 – 4. See also CGC,
     XV-31.2, "1930 — Chamberlain," Benjamin Ewert, et al., "To the
     Right Honourable Neville Chamberlain, Prime Minister of Great
     Britain, London, England," 10 October 1938.

5   Benjamin Ewert, et al., *ibid.*

6   H.H. Ewert, *op.cit.*

7   H.H. Ewert, "Zur diamanten Jubilaeumsfeier der Dominion von
     Canada," *Der Mitarbeiter* 20 (May 1927):6.

8   H.H. Ewert, "Sind die Mennoniten Canadas auf dem Wege Mili-
     taristen zu werden?" *Der Mitarbeiter* 20 (June 1927):6 – 7.

9   [H.H. Ewert,] "Das Zunehmen der Unduldsamkeit und Engher-
     zigkeit in unseren nordamerikanischen Laendern," *Der Mitarbeiter*
     21 (April 1928):6 – 7.

10   H.H. Ewert, "Eine Versammlung der Friedensfreunde in Winni-
     peg," *Der Mitarbeiter* 22 (May 1929):6 – 7.

11   [H.H. Ewert,] "Gewaltlosigkeit," *Der Mitarbeiter* 23 (November
     1930):4 – 5.

12   Yoder published the following articles in the *Mennonite Quarterly
     Review* in the 1930s: "The Christian's Attitude Toward Participa-
     tion in War Activities," 9 (January 1935):5 – 19; "The Need for
     Non-Conformity Today," 11 (April 1937):131 – 41; "Christianity
     and the State," 11 (July 1937):171 – 95; "The Obligation of the
     Christian to the State and Community — 'Render to Caesar,' " 13
     (April 1939):104 – 22. See also Harold S. Bender, "Church and
     State in Mennonite History," *Mennonite Quarterly Review* 13 (April
     1939):83 – 103; Guy F. Hershberger authored the following in the
     MQR in the 1930s: "Is Alternative Service Desirable and Possible?"
     9 (January 1935):20 – 36; "Some Religious Pacifists of the Nine-
     teenth Century," 10 (January 1936):73 – 86; "The Pennsylvania
     Quaker Experiment in Politics, 1682 – 1756," 10 (October
     1936):187 – 221; "Nonresistance and Industrial Conflict," 13
     (April 1939):135 – 54; *Can Christians Fight?* (Scottdale, Pa.: Men-
     nonite Publishing House) was published in 1940. His comprehen-
     sive treatment *War, Peace and Nonresistance* (Scottdale, Pa.) did not
     appear until 1944; Melvin Gingerich, "The Menace of Propaganda
     and How to Meet It," *Mennonite Quarterly Review* 13 (April
     1939):123 – 34.

13   Edward Yoder, "The Obligation of the Christian to the State and
     Community — 'Render to Caesar.' " 13 (April 1939):106.

14   *Ibid.*, p. 107.

15   *Ibid.*, p. 108.

16   *Ibid.*, pp. 108 – 9.

17   H.H. Ewert, "Welche Aufgaben haben wir jetzt nach dem Kriege
     unserm Lande gegenueber?" *Der Mitarbeiter* 13 (February
     1920):9 – 11, 16; (April 1920):31; D.J. Loewen, "Welche Stellung

nehmen wir dem Staate gegenueber?" *Jahrbuch*, 1934, pp. 55–60; *Jahrbuch*, 1934, p. 20; H.J. Gerbrandt, *Adventure in Faith* (Altona, Man.: D.W. Friesen & Sons, 1972), p. 317.

18   E.K. Francis, *In Search of Utopia* (Altona: D.W. Friesen & Sons, Ltd., 1975), pp. 233–34.

19   Lita-Rose Betcherman, *The Swastika and the Maple Leaf: Fascist Movements in Canada in the Thirties* (Toronto: Fitzhenry and Whiteside, 1975); Watson Kirkconnell, *Canada, Europe, and Hitler* (Toronto: Oxford University Press, 1939); Watson Kirkconnell, "The European-Canadians in Their Press," *The Canadian Historical Association*, 1940, pp. 85–92; Sam Steiner, "Kitchener Germans and National Socialism" (research paper, Conrad Grebel College, University of Waterloo, 1973); Jonathan F. Wagner, "Transferred Crisis: German Volkish Thought Among Russian Mennonite Immigrants to Western Canada," *Canadian Review of Studies in Nationalism* 1 (Fall 1973):202–20; Jonathan F. Wagner, *Brothers Beyond the Sea: National Socialism in Canada* (Waterloo, Ont.: Wilfrid Laurier Press, 1980).

20   James C. Juhnke, *A People of Two Kingdoms: The Political Acculturation of the Kansas Mennonites* (Newton, Kans.: Faith and Life Press, 1975), pp. 137–43; Theo Glueck, "Mennoniten im Dritten Reich —und heute," *Mennonitische Blaetter* 5 (June 1978):84–85; "Adolf Hitler von deutscher Seite betrachtet," *Bethel College Monthly* 29 (April 1934):13–17; "And Thou Too, Brutus," *The Mennonite* 52 (22 June 1937):3; John C. Wenger, "German Mennonites," *Gospel Herald* 30 (11 November 1937):706–7; Gerhard Ratzlaff, "An Historical-Political Study of the Mennonites in Paraguay" (M.A. thesis, University of Fresno, 1974).

21   This subject is treated extensively in, and what follows is largely borrowed from, an unpublished work by the author, namely, "An Analysis of Germanism and National Socialism in the Immigrant Newspaper of a Canadian Minority Group, the Mennonites, in the 1930s" (Ph.D. dissertation, University of Minnesota, 1965).

22   Examples of materials in *Rundschau* are the following: "Reichkanzler Adolf Hitler Rede," *Mennonitische Rundschau* 56 (8 March 1933):14; "Das grosse Sterben," *Mennonitische Rundschau* 56 (24 May 1933):1 ff.; "Die Nationalsozialisten," *Mennonitische Rundschau* 56 (7 June 1933):13; "Zeitspiegel," *Mennonitische Rundschau* 58 (9 January 1935):12; Ein Mitglied, "Deutscher Bund, Ortsgruppe Kitchener-Waterloo," *Mennonitische Rundschau* 58 (23 January 1935):12; J. Goebbels, "Jeder der ihn wirklich kennt..." *Mennonitische Rundschau* 56 (22 March 1935):12; "Begegnung mit Hitler," *Mennonitische Rundschau* 59 (29 April 1936):10; Dr. Weber, "Die Losung: Gutes Deutsch," *Mennonitische Rundschau* 59 (8 July 1936):9; "Tag der Nationalen Erhebung," *Mennonitische Rundschau* 61 (2 February 1938):3, 10; Hein-

rich H. Schroeder, "Was heiszt voelkisch?" *Mennonitische Rundschau* 61 (2 February 1938):12–13; Heinrich H. Schroeder, "Was heiszt voelkische Kultur," *Mennonitische Rundschau* 61 (23 February 1938):12–13; C. DeFehr, "Meine Reiseeindruecke," *Mennonitische Rundschau* 61 (25 May 1938):10; "Zum 11. Deutschen Tag fuer Manitoba," *Mennonitische Rundschau* 61 (6 July 1938):13. See also Lothar Fromm, "Nazistische Einfluesze in mennonitischen Zeitshriften" (research paper, Mennonite Biblical Seminary, Elkhart, Indiana, 1961).

23   Examples of relevant materials in *Post* are the following from the year 1933: "Die Hintergruende der Hetzpropaganda," *Die Post* 20 (27 April 1933):1–2; "Die Hitlerregierung in Christlicher Beleuchtung," *Die Post* 20 (8 June 1933):3; "Editor-Spalte," *Die Post* 20 (3 August 1933):3; "Zum mennonitischen Problem," *Die Post* 20 (3 August 1933):4–5; "Die Rede Hitlers," *Die Post* 20 (25 May 1933):1; "Kampf gegen den Bolshevismus," *Die Post* 20 (17 August 1933):2–3; "Kanadische Nationalisten halten meeting in Winkler," *Die Post* 20 (December 1933):1.

24   David Toews, "Reise und Konferenzbericht," *Der Bote* 7 (5 November 1930):1–2.

25   *Ibid.*

26   D. Enns, "Aus dem Fluechtlingslager," *Der Bote* 7 (9 July 1930):1; Deutsche Allgemeine Zeitung, "Jahreswende bei den Auswanderern," *Der Bote* 7 (22 January 1930):1–2.

27   B.H. Unruh, "Zur Aufklaerung," *Der Bote* 11 (25 April 1934):3.

28   "Hindenburg sieht vertrauensvoll in die Zunkunft," *Der Bote* 10 (25 January 1933):4.

29   C.A. DeFehr, "Unsere Winnipeger," *Der Bote* 12 (13 February 1935):3.

30   *Ibid.*

31   A.J. Fast, "Was geht in Deutschland vor?" *Der Bote* 10 (17 May 1933):5–6, (24 May 1933):4.

32   *Ibid.*

33   *Ibid.*

34   Amerika-Herold, "Die Hitlerpartei und was sie Deutschland bringen mag," *Der Bote* 9 (11 May 1932):4.

35   "Die Anstrebung einer politischen Konzentration in Deutschland," *Der Bote* 7 (21 May 1930):3–4; Deutsche Allgemeine Zeitung, "Buecher fuer den Unterricht," *Der Bote* 10 (24 May 1933):4.

36   A.J. Fast, *op.cit.*

37   C.F. Klassen, "Gegen die geistlose Judenhetze," *Der Bote* 10 (19 April 1933):2.

38   Eugen Kuehnemann, "Das neue Deutschland," *Der Bote* 10 (15 November 1933):2–3.

39   Walter Quiring, "Im fremden Schlepptau," *Der Bote* 11 (5 September 1934):3.

40   J.H. Janzen, "Deutschland's Erwachen," *Der Bote* 10 (3 May 1933): 4; Walter Quiring, "Woche des deutschen Buches," *Der Bote* 8 (11 December 1935):1-2.

41   J.H. Janzen, "Deutschland's Erwachen," *Der Bote* 10 (3 May 1933):4. See also N.J. Neufeld, "Als Kanada-Deutscher in Deutschland," *Der Bote* 13 (12 February 1936):2-3; "In Deutschland," *Der Bote* 13 (13 May 1936):3.

42   Oswald J. Smith, "Mein Besuch in Deutschland," *Der Bote* 13 (28 October 1936):3.

43   Deutsche Allgemeine Zeitung, "Unsere Meinung," *Der Bote* 7 (30 April 1930):3; "Deutsche Arbeitsgemeinschaft, Saskatchewan," *Der Bote* 15 (9 March 1938):6; M.Q., "Bin ich Nationalsozialist? Bewahre." *Der Bote* 15 (7 December 1938):3; H. Goerz, "Arden Manitoba," *Der Bote* 16 (22 February 1939):5; H. Goebbels, "Kommunismus ohne Maske," *Der Bote* 12 (4 December 1935):5; G. Toews, "Was ein Laie so aus dem politischen Teich fischt," *Der Bote* 15 (9 March 1938):4; B.H. Unruh, "Straeflich-Leichtsinnig," *Der Bote* 16 (8 March 1939): 1-2; Ein pro-Nazi, "Kritisches beurteilen oder kritiklose Aufnahme?" *Der Bote* 11 (4 April 1934):2.

44   See, for example, J.H. Janzen, "Gebt acht auf die Zeichen der Zeit," *Jahrbuch*, 1933, p. 66; *Jahrbuch*, 1930, p. 44; *Jahrbuch*, 1931, pp. 54, 65.

45   G.G. Schmidt, "Die andere Seite," *Der Bote* 16 (8 February 1939):2.

46   Christlicher Bundesbote, "Der Kirchenstreit in Deutschland," *Der Bote* 11 (2 May 1934): 3; m., "Unsere Aufgabe," *Der Bote* 14 (17 February 1937):1-2.

47   T.J., "Unsere Pflicht," *Der Bote* 14 (14 April 1937):4-5; Fritz Kliewer, "Schwierigkeiten," *Der Bote* 13 (22 January 1936): 203; P. Schulz, "Etwas ueber 'Das Verhaeltnis der Nationalsozialisten Partei zur Kirche' im deutschen Reiche," *Der Bote* 11 (28 February 1934):3; Julius Heinrichs, "Bewahre uns vor . . . ," *Der Bote* 16 (22 February 1939):4.

48   Eugen Kuehnemann, "Das neue Deutschland," *Der Bote* 10 (15 November 1933):2.

49   B.H. Unruh, "Um die deutsche Sache," *Der Bote* 14 (10 February 1937), 2.

50   Water Quiring, "Der Kirchenstreit in Deutschland," *Der Bote* 11 (13 June 1934):1; Muenchener Zeitung, "Um die Einheit des Volkes," *Der Bote* 11 (20 June 1934):4; Walter Quiring, "Warum schlaegst Du deinen Naechsten?" *Der Bote* 11 (31 October 1934):2-3; "Um den deutschen Kirchenstreit," *Der Bote* 12 (23 October 1935):1-2; H.H. Schroeder, "Aus dem neuen Deutschland," *Der Bote* 12 (27 March 1935):5; Fritz Kliewer, "Schwierigkeiten," *Der Bote* 13 (22 January 1936):2-3.

51   P. Schulz, "Etwas ueber 'Das Verhaeltnis der Nationalsozialistischen Partei zur Kirche' im deutschen Reiche," *Der Bote* 11 (28 February 1934):3.

52   Walter Quiring, "Der Kirchenstreit in Deutschland," *Der Bote* 11 (13 June 1934): 1; Walter Quiring, "Um den deutschen Kirchenstreit,"*Der Bote* 12 (23 October 1935):1–2; P. Schulz, *op.cit.*, p. 3.

53   "Die Glaubensbewegung in Deutschland," *Der Bote* 11 (9 May 1934):4.

54   "Die Mennoniten in Deutschland in Verlegenheit," *Der Bote* 11 (14 February 1934):2.

55   H. Goebbels, "Kommunismus ohne Maske," *Der Bote* 12 (13 June 1935):4.

56   Walter Quiring, "Judentum und Weltpolitik," *Der Bote* 11 (20 June 1934): 5; C.F. Klassen, "Gegen die geistlose Judenhetze," *Der Bote* 10 (19 April 1933): 2; D.H. Epp, "Gegen die geistlose Judenhetze," *Der Bote* 10 (12 April 1933):3; A. Reimer, "Gegen die geistlose Judenhetze," *Der Bote* 10 (26 April 1933):2–3; "Ruszland-Briefe," *Der Bote* 12 (23 October 1935):2.

57   C.F. Klassen, "Gegen die geistlose Judenhetze," *Der Bote* 10 (19 April 1933):2; "Neue Verordnungen fuer Eheschlieszungen im deutschen Reiche," *Der Bote* 13 (25 December 1935):4.

58   G. Hege, "Wie ich Deutschland wiedersah," *Der Bote* 12 (13 March 1935):2; H.H. Schroeder, "Einiges ueber unseren Vierjahrplan," *Der Bote* 14 (28 April 1937):5; A. Kroeker, "Eine gewissenlose Hetze," *Der Bote* 16 (5 April 1939):4.

59   Eugen Kuehnemann, "Das neue Deutschland," *Der Bote* 10 (15 November 1933):2–3.

60   C.F. Klassen, "Gegen die geistlose Judenhetze," *Der Bote* 10 (19 April 1933):2; A. Reimer, "Gegen die geistlose Judenhetze," *Der Bote* 10 (26 April 1933):2–3; "Greuelpropaganda im Ausland," *Der Bote* 10 (26 April 1933):3; A. Kroeker, "Waffen der Gerechtigkeit," *Der Bote* 16 (15 March 1939):1.

61   "Greuelpropaganda im Ausland," *Der Bote* 10 (26 April 1933):3.

62   H.H. Schroeder, "Die Aussenpolitik des Dritten Reiches," *Der Bote* 12 (18 September 1935):4.

63   B. Wiens, "Bericht des Vertreters des Zentralen Mennonitischen Immigrantenkomitees," *Der Bote* 9 (7 December 1932):5–6; J.P. Classen, "Gedanken ueber Gemeindebau," *Der Bote* 16 (10 May 1939):1–2.

64   G. Toews, "Was ein Laie so aus dem politischen Teich fischt," *Der Bote* 11 (19 December 1934):4; 14 (10 February 1937):4–5; 15 (15 June 1938):4–5; Adolf Hitler, "Hitler's Rede vor dem Reichstag," *Der Bote* 14 (10 February 1937):4.

65   H. Seelheim, "Bekanntmachung," *Der Bote* 13 (18 March 1936):5.

66   Karl Goetz, "Karl Goetz schreibt," *Der Bote* 16 (25 January

1939):5; G. Toews, "Was der Laie so aus dem politischen Teich fischt," *Der Bote* 16 (5 April 1939):50 – 56.

67   Dr. Granow, "Die Erfassung der dienstpflichtigen deutschen Staatsangehoerigen," *Der Bote* 14 (23 June 1937):4 – 5; Deutsches General-Konsulat, "Ueber die Erfassung der dienstflichtigen deutschen Staatsangehoerigen," *Der Bote* 14 (23 June 1937):4 – 5; Deutsches General-Konsulat, "Ueber die Erfassung der wehrpflichtigen deutschen Staatsangehoerigen und ueber die Einstellung von Freiwilligen," *Der Bote* 16 (14 June 1939):4 – 5.

68   "Ueber die Erfassung der wehrpflichtigen deutschen Staatsange-hoerigen und ueber die Einstellung von Freiwilligen," *Mennonitische Rundschau* 61 (11 May 1938):7.

69   Auch Einer, "Wehrlosigkeit auf Kruecken," *Der Bote* 11 (22 August 1934):2; Ein Leser, "Um hohen Preis," *Der Bote* 11 (27 June 1934):2; J.B. Wiens, "Wehrlosigkeit?" *Der Bote* 11 (3 October 1934):2.

70   B.B. Janz, "Kommt Menno Simons unter die Nationalsozialisten?" *Der Bote* 11 (26 December 1934):1.

71   Frank H. Epp, *Mennonite Exodus*, p. 325.

72   J.H. Janzen, "Zur Wehrlosigkeitsfrage," *Der Bote* 15 (1 June 1938):2.

73   Theodore H. Epp, "Duerfen Kinder Gottes sich am Kriege beteiligen?" *Der Bote* 14 (28 July – 24 November 1937):1 – 5.

74   J.B. Epp, "Und es wird gepredigt werden in aller Welt. . .," *Der Bote* 11 (21 March 1934):1; Jak. Thiessen, "Offener Brief an Dr. W. Quiring," *Der Bote* 11 (10 October 1934):2 – 3.

75   Heinrich J. Klassen, "Aus der Stille," *Der Bote* 14 (31 March 1937):3; C. Krahn, "400-jaehriger Irrtum," *Der Bote* 13 (15 January 1936):3; J.G. Rempel, "Aus allerlei Geschlecht und Zungen und Volk und Heiden," *Der Bote* 15 (14 September 1938):1 – 2.

76   Ein pro-Nazi, "Kritisches beurteilen oder kritiklose Aufnahme," *Der Bote* 11 (4 April 1934):2.

77   J.H. Janzen, "Deutsch und Russisch," *Der Bote* 13 (12 August 1936):1 – 2.

78   A.K., "Wie man ueber Ruszland und Deutschland urteilt," *Der Bote* 15 (29 June 1938):1 – 2.

79   Ein Leser, "Kampf oder Friedhofsruhe," *Der Bote* 11 (5 December 1934):2 – 3.

80   J.H. Janzen, "Der deutsche Gedanke," *Der Bote* 16 (30 August 1939):1 – 2.

81   Dederich Navall, "Gegen die geistlose Judenhetze," *Der Bote* 10 (12 April 1933):3.

82   *Ibid.*

83   H. Goerz, "Arden, Manitoba," *Der Bote* 16 (22 February 1939):5.

84   Ein Schulmeister, "Sind wir dem Namen oder dem Herzen nach

Buerger Kanadas geworden?" *Der Bote* 10 (20 December 1933):1–2.

85   John A. Toews, *A History of the Mennonite Brethren Church*, pp. 375–79.

86   *Ibid.*, p. 378.

87   See *Prophecy Conference: Report of Conference Held at Elkhart, Indiana 3–5 April 1952* (Scottdale, Pa.: Mennonite Publishing House, 1953), especially John R. Mumaw, "Dispensationalism and the Postponement Theory," pp. 78–86.

88   *Verhandlungen* (ND), 1932, p. 24; 1933, p. 11; 1936, p. 33.

89   *Church and Mission News* 5 (March 1940):1. See also *Calendar of Appointments*, 1934, p. 20.

90   John A. Toews, p. 377.

91   J.H. Janzen, "Gebt acht auf die Zeichen der Zeit," *Jahrbuch*, 1933, pp. 59–68. See also J.G. Rempel, "Endzeit der Welt," *Jahrbuch*, 1935, pp. 46–65.

92   *Calendar of Appointments*, 1940, p. 24.

93   "Some Present-Day Issues," *Christian Monitor* 27 (June 1935):169.

94   John Thut, "The Prophetic Word," a series of articles in the *Christian Monitor* 26, including "The Need of Prophetic Study," (January 1934):9–10; "The World Systems," (February 1934):42–43; "The World System Analyzed," (March 1934):74–76; "The Mission and Destiny of Israel," (April 1934):107–8; "The Mission and Destiny of the Church," (May 1934):138–39; "The Personality of Christ," (June 1934):171–73; "Signs of the Times," (July 1934):203–4; "Signs of the Times —Continued," (August, 1934):235–36; "The Reign of the Antichrist," (September 1934):266–67; "The Great Tribulation," (October 1934):300–1; "The Coming of the Son of Man," (November 1934):332–33; "The Coming of the Son of Man—Concluded," (December 1934):363–64.

95   Paul H. Bartel, "China—A Land in Transition," *Christian Monitor* 23 (July 1931):205–6.

96   I.E. Burkhart, "The Call of Africa," *Christian Monitor* 21 (September 1929):269–73.

97   "India—Gandhi—Nonresistance," *Christian Monitor* 24 (November 1932):348.

98   Harold S. Bender, "A Flying Trip Through Russia," *Christian Monitor* 22 (March 1930):80–81; (April 1930):114–15.

99   Levi C. Hartzler, "Spain and Its Present Needs for Relief of War Sufferers," *Christian Monitor* 29 (August 1937):227–28; "Spanish Relief," *ibid.*, p. 233.

100   Identification of sources was often missing and rarely precise or complete, but *The Pathfinder*, *New Outlook*, *Missionary News* were some of the papers from which clippings originated.

101   "The Evil Fruits of Communism and the Spectre of Communism

on the American Horizon," *Christian Monitor* 30 (March 1938):94.

102   C.F. Derstine, "World Evangelization," *Christian Monitor* 24 (September 1932):276–77; "Efforts for World Peace," 22 (February 1930):41; "Blessed Are the Peacemakers," *Christian Monitor* 25 (June 1933):168–69; "Bible Standards and Our Present Social System," *Christian Monitor* 23 (October 1931):317.

103   CGC, Hist. Mss. 1–58, Box 16, Clayton F. Derstine Collection, C.F. Derstine, "Prophet Sermon," Delivered at the Belmont Tent Meetings held at Elkhart, Indiana during the summer, 1940; "Jesus is Coming," *Christian Monitor* 23 (January 1931):41.

104   "The Evil Fruits of Communism and the Spectre of Communism on the American Horizon," *Christian Monitor* 30 (March 1938):94.

105   John Horsch, "Communism and the Attitude of the Defenders of the Social Gospel Toward It," *Christian Monitor* 29 (February 1937):37–38.

106   "The Crying Need for the Return of the Prince of Peace," *Christian Monitor* 24 (September 1932):285.

107   "The Federal Council of Churches of America," *Christian Monitor* 31 (February 1939):62–63.

108   "The Proposed Protestant Social Creed," *Christian Monitor* 25 (February 1933):63.

109   "Fundamentalists Adopt Three-Year Program," *Christian Monitor* 22 (September 1930):285.

110   "Kidnapping—the Hauptmann Trial—Capital Punishment," *Christian Monitor* 27 (March 1935):94–95.

111   "India—Gandhi—Nonresistance," *Christian Monitor* 24 (November 1932): 348; "Disarm or Disappear," *Christian Monitor* 24 (March 1932):95.

112   "The Land of the Soviets in the Limelight," *Christian Monitor* 22 (March 1930):94.

113   "The Imperial Economic Conference at Ottawa," *Christian Monitor* 24 (September 1932):284.

114   "Christian or Christless Communism," *Christian Monitor* 23 (August 1931):253–54.

115   "Mussolini a Protector from Vaticanism and Communism," *Christian Monitor* 26 (March 1934):93–94; "The World Listens to the Pope of Rome," *Christian Monitor* 23 (April 1931):125; "The Pope's Invitation to Return to the Roman Fold," *Christian Monitor* 24 (March 1932):95; "Is the Pope Secretly Backing Mussolini?" *Christian Monitor* 28 (February 1936):62.

116   "The Religious Conflict in Mexico," *Christian Monitor* 27 (September 1935):286.

117   "The Pope and the Blackshirts of Italy," *Christian Monitor* 23 (August 1931):253–54.

118   "Fascism—Friend or Foe—Which?" *Christian Monitor* 25 (October 1933):318.

119   "The Fascists Roar," *Christian Monitor* 28 (March 1936):95.

120   "Impressions of the Nazi Regime and Its Effect on the Churches," *Christian Monitor* 26 (January 1934):30–31.

121   *Ibid.*

122   "Hitler—Whence and Whither? Chancellor and President. 'Fuehrer.' " *Christian Monitor* 26 (September 1934):285–86.

123   "Hitler Starts Life Job as German Caesar," *Christian Monitor* 26 (October 1934):318.

124   "Hitler's Triumphant Entry Into His Native Austria," *Christian Monitor* 30 (April 1938):126–27.

125   "The German Venture Into Unknown Land," *Christian Monitor* 25 (March 1933):94.

126   "German Church Cause Lost?" *Christian Monitor* 29 (May 1937):159.

127   "Shall Communists Rule America?" *Christian Monitor* 28 (May 1936):158–59.

128   "Saber Rattling by Mussolini," *Christian Monitor* 23 (January 1931):26.

129   "Babylon, Media-Persia, Greece, Rome, and Succeeding Gentile Nations," *Christian Monitor* 32 (August 1940) 254–55.

130   "The Italo-Ethiopian Land Grab," *Christian Monitor* 27 (November 1935):350–51.

131   "The Tumbling Thrones—Exit King Alfonso," *Christian Monitor* 23 (June 1931):190.

132   "The Stormy Night Amid the Nations of the World," *Christian Monitor* 25 (May 1933):158.

133   "Jehovah's Judgements on Jew Jingo Nations," *Christian Monitor* 31 (January 1939):30.

134   "Hitler with His Hands on the Jew," *Christian Monitor* 25 (May 1933):159.

135   *Ibid.*

136   "A Glimpse at the World-Wide Growth of Anti-Semitism," *Christian Monitor* 26 (July 1934):222–23.

137   "World Jewry Today—and the Protocols," *Christian Monitor* 27 (February 1935):62–63.

138   "Clearing the Atmosphere of Anti-Jewish Slander," *Christian Monitor* 28 (April 1936):126.

139   "Anti-Semitism a Dangerous Boomerang," *Christian Monitor* 27 (May 1935):158.

140   "The Christian Attitude in the Rising Tide of Anti-Semitism," *Christian Monitor* 31 (September 1939):286–87.

141   "The Jews' Awakening from their Age-Long Sleep," *Christian Monitor* 32 (July 1940):223.

142   "The Hour for Jewish Evangelism Has Struck," *Christian Moni-*

tor 22 (January 1930):17; "A Palestine Rabbi Finds Christ," *Christian Monitor* 32 (January 1940):30 – 31.

143   This stance was strongest among early Kanadier groups and some of the Swiss, as will later be seen.

144   Calls for disarmament were heard most from within the Swiss community (see especially the *Monitor*), but it was the Russlaender who spoke most about an alternative service.

145   Frank H. Epp, *Mennonite Exodus*, p. 324.

146   This turned out to be true most about the Mennonite Brethren in Christ, who though they adopted a relatively strong nonresistance position, through lack of preaching and lack of discipline, left the matter to individuals. Interview with E.R. Storms, 5 August 1981.

147   John H. Mosemann, "The League of Nations," *Gospel Herald* 29 (23 July 1936):376.

148   Guy F. Herschberger, "The Committee on Peace and Social Concerns (of the Mennonite Church) and Its Predecessors" (A summary review of the witness of the Mennonite Church to other Christians, to the State, and to Society, with respect to peace and the social implications of the Gospel, 1915 – 1966).

149   *Ibid.*, pp. 2 – 6.

150   "The World Back on the War Road," *Christian Monitor* 28 (May 1936):159; "The Churches and Conscientious Objectors," *Christian Monitor* 26 (March 1934):94 – 95; C.F. Derstine, "The Dark Side, and the Brightest Side of the War and Peace Problems in the World," *Christian Monitor* 26 (February 1934):58 – 59; John Horsch, "The Lesson of the World War," a review of *Preachers Present Arms* by Ray H. Abrams, *Christian Monitor* 26 (February 1934):37 – 39; C.F. Derstine, "The Universal Inquiry Into the Legitimacy of War," *Christian Monitor* 26 (July 1934):221 – 22; C.F. Derstine, "The Gathering War Clouds of Europe," *Christian Monitor* 31 (May 1939):158 – 59; "The Coming Disarmament Conference," *Christian Monitor* 22 (January 1930):16; "The Prophet David's Advice to the Nations," *Christian Monitor* 22 (February 1930):62; "The Costly and Bloody Business of War – Under Consideration at the London Conference," *Christian Monitor* 22 (March 1930):94; "The War Question and the Coming Disarmament Conference," *Christian Monitor* 24 (January 1932):30; "The Holocaust of the Past War, and the Nightmare of the Next," *Christian Monitor* 23 (May 1931):158.

151   S.F. Coffman, "Positive Non-Resistance," *Mennonite Yearbook and Directory*, 1938, pp. 26 – 30, 96. Another differentiation between nonresistance and pacifism was that made by John E. Lapp, who suggested that pacifism was a popular movement in the world and represented opposition to those wars which were not waged for righteous causes. Nonresistance was a way of Christian

living with respect to all human situations and all wars. John E. Lapp, "Non-resistance," *Mennonite Yearbook and Directory*, 1940, pp. 27–30.

152 *Calendar of Appointments*, 1934, p. 19; *Calendar of Appointments*, 1935–36, p. [22]; *Calendar of Appointments*, 1939–40, p. [11].

153 *Calendar of Appointments*, 1939–40, p. [20].

154 Guy F. Hershberger, p. 10; J.B. Martin, "The Peace Committee," *Calendar of Appointments*, 1937–38, pp. [15–16]; J.B. Martin, "Report of the Peace Committee," *Calendar of Appointments*, 1938–39, p. [18].

155 See Urbane Peachey, ed., *Mennonite Statement on Peace and Social Concerns, 1900–1978* (Akron, Pa.: Mennonite Central Committee U.S. Peace Section, 1980). A similar compilation is being prepared by Mennonite Central Committee (Canada), Winnipeg, Manitoba.

156 "Peace, War, and Military Service" (A Statement of the Position of the Mennonite Church: Resolution Adopted by the Mennonite General Conference at Turner, Oregon, August, 1937), in Conference Minutes, pp. 123–26; see also Urbane Peachey, pp. 168–70; David P. Reimer, pp. 31–37.

157 *Ibid.*, p. 35.

158 "Report of the Committee to the Prime Minister of the Dominion of Canada a Brief Stating Our Position as a Non-Resistant Church," *Conference Journal*, 1939, pp. 38–39.

159 *Ibid.*, p. 39.

160 CGC, XV-31.2, "Memorial: A Statement of the Position of the Mennonite Brethren in Christ Church as Regards Peace, War, and Military Service" (Drawn up by a Committee appointed by the Ontario Annual Conference of the Mennonite Brethren in Christ Church, meeting 21–25 September 1938, at Gormley, Ontario).

161 *Ibid.*, pp. 6–7.

162 Urbane Peachey, p. 169.

163 "Report of the Peace Problems Committee," *Conference Journal*, 1940, p. 29.

164 Esther Ruth Epp, "The Origins of Mennonite Central Committee (Canada)" (M.A. thesis, University of Manitoba, 1980), pp. 30–40; *Conference Journal*, p. 29.

165 "Report of the Peace Problems Committee," *Conference Journal*, 1940, pp. 27–32.

166 Frank H. Epp, *Mennonites in Canada, 1786–1920*, pp. 93–111.

167 See J.G. Rempel, *Fuenfzig Jahre Konferenzbestrebungen 1902–1952* (n.p., 1952), pp. 129–30, 133–34, 165, 264–65, 284, 289.

168 *Der Mitarbeiter* 13 (February 1920), p. 14.

169 *Der Mitarbeiter* 14 (August 1921), p. 65.

170 *Der Mitarbeiter* 18 (July 1925), p. 50.

171   J.G. Rempel, "Bericht ueber Friedensbestrebungen," *Jahrbuch*, 1934, pp. 84–85; Johann G. Rempel, "Bericht ueber Friedensbestrebungen," *Jahrbuch*, 1935, p. 84.

172   *Jahrbuch*, 1935, p. 22; *Jahrbuch*, 1936, p. 17. See also reference to International Mennonite Peace Committee in Guy F. Herschberger, p. 9.

173   *Jahrbuch*, 1934, p. 20.

174   J.J. Klassen, "Die biblische Begruendung der Wehrlosigkeit," *Jahrbuch*, 1935, pp. 65–70. See also H.H.Ewert, "Welche Aufgaben haben wir jetzt nach dem Kriege unserm Lande gegenueber?" *Der Mitarbeiter* 13 (February 1920), pp. 9–11, 16; 13 (April 1920), p. 34.

175   J.J. Klassen, "Die biblische Begruendung der Wehrlosigkeit und ihre Durchfuehrung in Leben," *Jahrbuch*, 1935, pp. 65–70.

176   Jakob Nickel, "Unsere Treue dem Staate gegenueber," *Jahrbuch*, 1937, pp. 46–50.

177   *Ibid.*

178   *Ibid.*, pp. 48–49.

179   David Toews, "Wehrfreiheit der Mennoniten in Canada," *Jahrbuch*, 1935, pp. 81–82. The four lawyers were J.E. Doerr, Regina; W.A. Tucker, Rosthern; P.J. Hooge, Rosthern; and A. Buhr, Winnipeg.

180   *Ibid.*

181   In 1929 Herman Fast, a former teacher at the German-English Academy and then a mission worker at Perdue, Saskatchewan, extended greetings from Russian Christians and the delegates gave a standing response. *Jahrbuch*, 1929, p. 5.

182   John A. Toews, *A History of the Mennonite Brethren Church*, pp. 98, 196, 286, 316.

183   "Wehrfrage," *Verhandlungen* (ND), 1934, pp. 76–77.

184   *Ibid.*, p. 77. See also B.B. Janz, "Bericht des Komitees in Bezug auf Wehrlosigkeit," *Verhandlungen* (ND), 1935, pp. 49–55; *Verhandlungen* (ND), 1936, p. 80.

185   "Wehrfrage," *Verhandlungen* (ND), 1936, pp. 79–81.

186   *Ibid.*, p. 80.

187   See also B.B. Janz, "Bericht des Komitees in Bezug auf Wehrlosigkeit," *Verhandlungen* (ND), 1935, pp. 49–55.

188   "Wehrfrage," *Verhandlungen* (ND), 1939, pp. 61–63.

189   "Wehrfrage," *Verhandlungen* (ND), 1937, pp. 60–61.

190   Guy F. Herschberger, pp. 7–10.

191   *Ibid.*; Frank H. Epp, *Mennonite Exodus*, pp. 326–27.

192   Frank H. Epp, pp. 326–27.

193   David P. Reimer, comp., *Experiences of the Mennonites of Canada during the Second World War, 1939–1945* (Altona: Committee of Directors, *c.* 1947), pp. 37–56.

194   Both the German and the English editions identify this group as

General Conference (Allgemeine Konferenz), but, as has been previously pointed out, not all Conference congregations in Canada, notably the Bergthaler, were members of the General Conference, though they were members of the Conference of Mennonites in Canada.

195 *Ibid.*, p. 37. Reasons for non-attendance aren't given. It is probable that not all were invited, since Reimer says that nine of ten invited congregational families were present.

196 The record, referred to as "Report of a Discussion," is contained in *ibid.*, pp. 37 – 56.

197 *Ibid.*, pp. 37 – 38.

198 *Ibid.*, pp. 43 – 44.

199 *Ibid.*, p. 41.

200 *Ibid.*, p. 51.

201 "Red Cross Activities among Mennonites," *Morden Times* (29 November 1939):1; "Red Cross Activities at Winkler," *Morden Times* (19 June 1940):1.

202 Frank H. Epp, *Mennonite Exodus*, p. 325. A statement to that effect was given to the RCMP in 1940, but Klassen had changed his emphasis before that.

203 Letters to *Saskatoon Star-Phoenix* (29 April 1939), (13 June 1939).

204 "Canadian Mennonites Loyal to New Fatherland Leader Coaldale Colony Declares," *Lethbridge Herald* (1 June 1940):14. This article first appeared in Mennonite weeklies in January 1939.

205 Ted D. Regehr, "Mennonite Change: The Rise and Decline of Mennonite Community Organizations at Coaldale, Alta.," *Mennonite Life* (December 1977):13 – 22; "Sir Edward Beatty and Col. J.S. Dennis Receive Presentations from Mennonites of Coaldale," *Lethbridge Herald* (20 September 1937):1, 3.

206 "Happy Welcome Tendered Sir Edward Beatty at Coaldale; Mennonite Colony's Tribute," *Lethbridge Herald* (22 September 1937).

207 "Not Soulless," *Lethbridge Herald* (21 September 1937).

208 *Verhandlungen* (ND), 1939, p. 6.

209 *Ibid.*, p. 7.

210 Frank H. Epp, *Mennonites in Canada, 1786 – 1920*, p. 37.

211 *Ibid.*, pp. 54, 81, 98. See also *Calendar of Appointments*, 1939 – 40, pp. [7, 25 – 27].

212 Gerhard Wiebe, *Causes and History of the Emigration of the Mennonites from Russia to Canada*. Translated by Helen Janzen (Winnipeg: Manitoba Mennonite Historical Society, 1981), p. 34.

213 H.J. Gerbrandt, p. 313.

214 *Conference Journal*, 1936, p. 10.

215 According to a review of subsequent issues of *Conference Journal*.

216 David P. Reimer, *op.cit.*, pp. 54 – 56.

217 David Toews, "Die Hilfsarbeit," *Jahrbuch*, 1939, p. 69. A copy of the text is in CMCA, XXII-A, Vol. 1178, File 107, David Toews

on behalf of the Mennonites in Canada "To His Most Gracious Majesty George VI, King of Canada," May 1939.

218   "The King and Queen Leave American Shores," *Christian Monitor* 31 (July 1939):223. Another record says S.F. Coffman led an Ontario Conference delegation to the train depot to greet the royal family. After a brief public ceremony, he led the audience in singing "God Save the King." *John S. Weber*, p. 159, based on an interview with Coffman children.

219   *Calendar of Appointments*, 1939–40, pp. [7, 25–27].

220   "George V, King for Twenty-Five Years," *Christian Monitor* 27 (June 1935):190; "The Far-Flung Empire Greeted by the King," *Christian Monitor* 28 (February 1936):63; "The Passing of King George V," *Christian Monitor* 28 (March 1936):94; "The Coronation and Protestant England," *Christian Monitor* 29 (May 1937):157–58.

221   "The Coming of the King and Queen of the British Empire to Canada and the United States," *Christian Monitor* 31 (June 1939):190–91.

222   *Ibid.*

223   Revelation 6:2–8.

224   "The Four Grim Deadly Horsemen Halted in Europe," *Christian Monitor* 30 (November 1938):353–54.

Epilogue

TWENTY YEARS of history is too short a time-span on which to base any great or firm conclusions, and yet this Canadian story of the manifold Mennonite struggle for survival in the inter-war period cannot be ended without further summation and analysis. For the Mennonites, this was a time of considerable desperation, of diverse responses to the problems encountered, of strong determination to overcome those problems, and of nagging doubts about the outcome, all of which took on new dimensions when the world once again exploded with the sounds of battle.

The period began with great uncertainties. Some Mennonites doubted whether either Canada or Russia could remain a homeland for them and whether they could survive in those countries. Others wondered whether or not they had already lost or were rapidly losing the fundamental features of their faith and whether or not they could be sustained as a separate people with an alternative life style. During this period, there were major crises which raised the question of survival, but by 1939 it was clear that the Mennonites in Canada had survived. Their numbers had doubled and hundreds of their communities were firmly established (see Appendix 2).

The Second World War brought renewed tension between Mennonites and their national homeland, but at least until that time the Canadian development generally was increasingly congenial to the Mennonite experience. The racial and religious prejudices which had kept the Mennonites out in 1919 and again in 1929 had largely vanished by 1939 and with some exceptions been replaced by more complete information, understanding, and respect.

The Mennonites were no longer alone in questioning the validity of war, its objectives, and its methods. French Canadians also resisted war propaganda, the war effort itself, and conscription in particular. Under Prime Minister King, Canada insisted on its own national destiny and on shaping its own foreign policy, apart from European considerations and British desires. Like Mennonites, King applauded statesmen who took diplomatic risks for peace and, far from nurturing a jingoistic patriotism, he infused Canada with a great reluctance to go to war and to mobilize its young men for battle.

Other emerging features of the Canadian society favoured the Mennonite situation. Dissent, for instance, no longer came only from strange and poorly understood religious minority groups but also from more popular social-protest movements and from a wide range of new political parties. Canadian economic shifts from agriculture to industry and from the country to the city coincided with greater Mennonite readiness to urbanize. The lifting of trade barriers and the wider opening of the borders to the United States were also appropriate for the Mennonites and their numerous continental connections. And the shift of power from the provinces to the federal government, along with the growing sense of a federal responsibility for the welfare of all the people in all the regions, could be appreciated by those Mennonites whose greatest enemy had been not the federal establishment but certain provincial politicians and governments. The occasion of Their Majesties' visit to Canada in 1939 helped the Mennonites to assess their situation, to discover that all or most of the earlier uncertainties had been overcome, and to express renewed appreciation for their homeland in which they had not only survived but in which they were beginning to thrive.

The struggle itself, of course, could not be forgotten, primarily because it had not yet come to an end. An epilogue to this book is not complete without another look at those events and responses which in a few short years made so much momentous and fascinating history, both for the religious minority group under study and for the national society of which they were a part.

Mennonite migrations during this time were not all like the panic-filled flight to Moscow, and yet, the movements from Canada to Latin America and to Canada from Russia were treks of great urgency. Even the resettling within Canada in places more isolated and culturally more secure or in places more urban and vocationally more promising were conditioned by a deeply felt necessity. The non-physical migrations, such as the reaching for strange ideologies and the broad acceptance of non-traditional institutions, likewise happened because there seemed to be no other way. Having come to the conclusion that Canadian public schools would mislead their children, or that the Soviet system would destroy their religious and economic culture, or that modernism in all its forms would under-mine the faith, the Mennonites made desperate moves away from the perceived dangers towards the nearest promises of security.

The multiplicity of Mennonite responses to the problems they faced was due to a number of factors. Desperation was one of them. A sense of emergency is rarely accompanied by the wisdom of fore-thought or deliberate reflection about the outcome. When on a ship which appears to be sinking, one runs to the nearest lifeboats and worries later about their safety and destination. Mennonite pluralism was another factor. As the foregoing record makes clear, the Menno-nite people were actually many peoples, at least twenty in terms of their organizations, more in terms of their viewpoints. Social forces were another factor. When a social tradition or an ideological synthesis no longer holds and needs to be altered and perhaps displaced, suggestions for change are usually not singular but plural. As it was in the Protestant Reformation, so it was in the Mennonite evolution; the separation syndrome knew no end!

In the 1920s and the 1930s, Canadian Mennonites responded in many different ways to the dangers they perceived in the changing national and international situations. Those unhappy with Canada chose either to stay or not to stay. Those who left did so voluntarily or under religious duress. Some left proudly and judgmentally, insist-ing that they were right and everybody else was wrong. Some left sadly, humbly, and reluctantly, though convinced that the future welfare of their children required that some of the elders act bravely and sacrificially. Those leaving chose not one but two destinations in

Latin America, Mexico in the Northern Hemisphere and Paraguay in the Southern Hemisphere. Those who chose Mexico founded not one but three colonies and bought land for a fourth. Those who chose Paraguay established not one but two congregational families in a single colony. Those resettling assumed either that they would interact with their new neighbours or that they would do everything possible to avoid the indigenous populations. Some began their new life where they left off, insisting on the status quo within their system; others tried to inject new dynamism into the old system. Some quickly endeared themselves to the authorities and enlarged the Mennonite welcome, while others disappointed those who had granted them a *Privilegium*, thereby narrowing the entrance for others also in need of that space.

Those who stayed in Canada likewise were of many minds. Some were all in favour of finding a new isolation, but in Canada, not in a foreign country. Some of the geographic isolationists insisted on private schools, while others were ready to accept "public" schools, provided those schools were theirs, run by their trustees. Others were certain that the only reasonable course of action was to fully accept the public schools. Those who did so without reservation were either indifferent or careless or they were deliberately accepting a wider citizenship and identity. Perhaps they were even secularizing. Some accepted the public schools, believing they could meet Mennonite needs if only the Mennonite trustees did their duty and if they hired Mennonite teachers who were adequately trained. A very deliberate injection of Mennonite values into public institutions was the approach of some who believed that complete isolation was not possible and perhaps not even desirable. They believed that special education for their children was the best way to strengthen them as they moved out into the world.

Those who believed that evangelism was the answer to outside danger concentrated their efforts not on non-church institutions but on non-churched individuals. For them, Mennonite problems could be resolved by the winning of Mennonite young people as well as outside converts. Some believed in missions among the neighbours close to home so that ethnic barriers would be crossed and, erroneously, for this period at least, that Mennonite numbers would be thereby increased; others preferred missions overseas, some to maintain vitality in the domestic community through foreign activity, others to protect the ethnic integrity of the domestic community by having its converts far enough away to avoid facing the problems of Mennonite parochialism at home.

Most Mennonites feared modernism, but modernism meant different things to different people. For some, it meant modern styles, which in turn could mean many things: fancy buggies and harnesses, or flashy cars, or fancy, many-coloured clothing, or jewellery. Modernity could also mean attending public fairs, circuses, and theatres. Or it could mean fancy ideas. Those resisting ideological modernism reached for its opposite, namely fundamentalism, but not all to the same extent or with the same enthusiasm. For some, fundamentalism simply meant getting back to Mennonite fundamentals. For others, it meant the tenets of the fundamentalist movement. For still others, it was a mixture of the two. Some fundamentalists emphasized dispensationalism, some did not; some dispensationalists were pre-millennialists, some were not. Some who embraced fundamentalism lost their social ethic. Some Mennonite fundamentalists continued to believe in the importance of the Sermon on the Mount and, to that extent, in the social gospel.

Those who entered Canada from Russia also were variously motivated. Some were simply escaping an impossible situation. Some really viewed Canada as a land of great promise. Some were poor and completely dependent. Some were able to pay their own way. Some believed the best future in Canada lay in the cities, some on the land. Those who wanted land had different ideas about what land types and areas were most desirable. The greatest differentiation was between those who preferred the isolation of homestead lands even in the wilderness and those who felt best about lands already developed, even if this meant scattering and the loss of compact communities.

In terms of their cultural and religious orientation, those arriving from Russia were likewise not one of a kind. For some, Mennonite ethnicity and culture were all-important, for others less so. Some were eager to learn English, some clung to German with great zeal. Others were fanatic about High German, even to the point of disparaging Low German, on the one hand, and exalting all things German, including the *Reich* and its politics, on the other hand. Some were ready to use every religious institution, including Sunday schools and Bible schools, for the propagation of German; others were content to let the home and the Saturday school take care of linguistic training. Some didn't care enough to make any efforts to preserve the language.

The religious emphases and styles of the newcomers were many as well. At the one end of the continuum was a great dependence on evangelism and revivalism to achieve cataclysmic emotional conversions followed by an immersionist baptism. At the other end of the continuum was a disparagement of emotional religion and instead a dependence on the chorale instead of the gospel song, on education and a more gradualist approach to the Christian life, and on sprinkling or pouring as a more meaningful and reverent approach to baptism. In between were many variations of, and permutations on, the above themes. At the centre stood those who simply wanted spirituality and true religion without the legalism of rigid ordinances, strict liturgical styles, or inflexible modes of communication.

Nonresistance, the foremost common denominator of all Mennonites, also elicited a spectrum of approaches. At the one end were those who claimed the total traditional exemption from military service based on Mennonite identity certified by the ministry. At the other end were those reaching for some recognized, non-embarrassing, national service, if necessary with a uniform, as long as it did not involve the personal shedding of blood by Mennonite boys. In between were gradations of the non-involvement or involvement approaches. Most Mennonites represented combinations of what being a good Mennonite and also a good citizen were perceived to mean.

The kaleidoscopic response to the problems encountered, and the institutional incarnations of these responses, suggest that the Mennonite religious minority was actually many religious minorities engaged in many struggles. Readers can be excused for coming to that conclusion as a way of making sense of Mennonite confusion. In part, they are right. None the less, the common theological heritage of Anabaptism, common historical experiences especially with reference to land and the state, and a common social orientation or separation of one form or another or of one degree or another, justify the integrated inclusion of all Mennonite groups into this single story. They belong together not only because the Mennonite identity was carried by all but also, and primarily, because the common nomenclature signified some underlying similarities, no matter how far the Mennonite groups were spread on certain issues. And no matter how great the fragmentation and how prevalent the syndrome of sectarianism, there was some structural federation, however limited, with potential for the increase of co-operation as the war threat increased.

The inclusion and integration of a Mennonite diversity as great as this volume reveals inevitably highlights ambiguities and contradictions. However, these can easily be exaggerated if one forgets that ambiguity and contradiction are human phenomena common to all national, religious, or ethnic groups. During this period, Canada too was full of diversity and full of confusion and paradox. In a more particular sense, ambiguity and contradiction are characteristics of minority groups, partly because of the inner microcosmic reality, which knows of many smaller worlds within the larger worlds, and partly because of the external perceptions or the microscopic reality, which is enamoured of, and which exaggerates, the parts rather than the whole, the eccentricities rather than the normalities.

The relationship of the parts to the Mennonite whole carries an inherent contradiction also from the perspective of survival strategy. At one and the same time, the parts were the greatest threat to Mennonite survival and also the greatest prospect of Mennonite survival. On the face of things, the smaller the islands the more they were endangered by the roaring sea. And yet, precisely because they were islands, the various Mennonite groups knew exactly where the dangers lurked, how to cope with them, for how long and at how great a price.

From this perspective the determination and, in a sense, invincibility of the various Mennonite groups is amazing. They actually believed that they could remove themselves to the dry plateaus of Mexico or to the green hell of Paraguay and survive. They actually believed that they could define alternative life styles and maintain them against all odds. They actually believed that they could leave behind a compact Mennonite system in Russia and scatter in all directions in an expansive Canada and still maintain what was dearest to them. They actually believed that nonresistance could be maintained even though no one else around them shared their faith. And as they believed, they set out to achieve.

All they needed to do was to call on God and to do their share. And doing their part meant a willingness to make any sacrifice, to exchange better land for worse land, and to pay for new programs and institutions even in the depression. What they demanded of themselves, they also asked of their young people, who, quite possibly, were asked to pay the highest price of all, nonconformity and the resultant social ostracism by their peers, for the sake of the faith of the fathers. Clearly, values were often more important than material and social success.

At the end of the 1930s, the Mennonites had survived and were surviving. The visible continuity of the Mennonite communities, congregations, and conferences was obvious. The loyalty of the young people was impressive, in terms of both the quantity and the quality of their responses. Within and across the five main provinces in which they were now scattered, the Mennonites were tied together by informal networks and formal organizations, which contributed both to identity and to solidarity. The culture was being preserved. The faith was being taught. And every new generation was being challenged.

The doubts about continuity were not so much based on a Mennonite decline, which wasn't evident, as they were occasioned by those forces which threatened to weaken the culture and dilute the faith. The Mennonites knew instinctively that the all-pervasive influences of public education, economic forces largely outside of their control, social attitudes, political policies, and religious influences were inevitably shaping their destiny to the extent that they themselves were too weak to offset these forces. However, there were dangers even beyond those which were perceived at the time.

Historical hindsight, at least, suggests that significant chinks in the theological and cultural armour of the Mennonites were appearing, pointing to a possible disintegration of the historic Anabaptist faith and Mennonite religious culture at the core. In a variety of ways, that core, which envisioned the kingdom of God on earth, was threatened, because Mennonites were limiting, and in the process emasculating or short-circuiting, that kingdom. Such limitations included deliberate geographic and cultural segregation of the kingdom, thus withholding it from any application to the larger world; the identification of the kingdom with, and its circumvention by, religious institutions and Mennonite conferences, thus effectively removing it from the social, economic, and political spheres of life;

the reduction of the kingdom to an individual experience of salvation with its resulting irrelevance to society; the postponement of the kingdom and its ethical imperatives to a future dispensation; and the equating of the kingdom with nationalisms, either domestic or distant.

By limiting the scope and the quality of the kingdom, the Mennonites were really opening wide the floodgates of those worldly kingdoms they dreaded the most and whose waters rushed in to fill the voids that were being created in the theology and culture of their own people. So it seemed. It was too early to assess the situation with any finality. But that the end of traditional separation, with its special life-encompassing value system, and an alternative *Weltanschauung* (world view), was in sight, and that a transition of some kind was under way, there could be no doubt. Only the future could tell how far the Mennonites would go down the roads in the directions they were already choosing.

APPENDIX 1

SUMMARY OF CANADIAN MENNONITE GROUPS IN 1940

NO.	POPULAR NAMES	FORMAL NAMES	RELATED AMERICAN/ NORTH AMERICAN BODY
		A. Swiss Mennonite Groups	
1.	Old Mennonites, OMs	Mennonite Conference of Ontario Alta.-Sask. Mennonite Conference	Mennonite General Conference
2.	Reformed Mennonites, Herrites	Reformed Mennonite Church	Reformed Mennonite Church
3.	New Mennonites	Mennonite Brethren in Christ, Ontario and North-West Districts	Mennonite Brethren in Christ Conference
4.	Old Order Mennonites, Wislerites, Horse-and-Buggy Mennonites	Mennonite Churches	Mennonite Churches
5.	David Martin Old Order Mennonites, Newborns	Mennonite Church	N/A
6.	Markhamer, Cars People, Black Bumper Mennonites	Markham-Waterloo Mennonite Conference	Weaverland Mennonite Conference
		B. Swiss Amish Mennonite Groups	
7.	Church Amish	Amish Mennonite Conference	Mennonite General Conference
8.	Old Order Amish, House Amish, Holmsers	Amish Mennonite Churches	Amish Churches
9.	Beachy Amish	Nafziger & Cedar Grove Amish Mennonite Churches	Beachy Amish
		C. Dutch Mennonite Groups	
10.	Conference Mennonites, Kirchengemeinden	Conference of Mennonites in Canada	General Conference Mennonite Church

APPENDIX 1 (continued)

SUMMARY OF CANADIAN MENNONITE GROUPS IN 1940

NO.	POPULAR NAMES	FORMAL NAMES	RELATED AMERICAN/ NORTH AMERICAN BODY
11.	Brethren, Brueder, MBs	Northern and Ontario Districts, Mennonite Brethren Churches	General Conference of Mennonite Brethren Churches
12.	Kleen-gemeenta (Low German for Kleine Gemeinde)	Kleine Gemeinde	N/A
13.	Chortitzer	Chortitzer Mennonite Church	N/A
14.	Altkolonier, Old Colony	Old Colony Mennonite Churches	N/A
15.	Sommerfelder	Sommerfelder Mennonite Churches	N/A
16.	Bergthaler	Bergthaler Mennonite Churches in Saskatchewan	N/A
17.	Rudnerweider	Rudnerweide Mennonite Church	N/A
18.	Krimmer, KMBs	Krimmer Mennonite Brethren Churches	Krimmer Mennonite Brethren Conference
19.	Bruderthaler, EMBs	Evangelical Mennonite Brethren Churches	Evangelical Mennonite Brethren Conference

D. Dutch-Swiss Mennonite Groups

NO.	POPULAR NAMES	FORMAL NAMES	RELATED AMERICAN/ NORTH AMERICAN BODY
20.	Holdemaner	Church of God in Christ Mennonite	Church of God in Christ Mennonite

APPENDIX 2

MENNONITE POPULATION IN CANADA
BY PROVINCES AND CENSUS DIVISIONS
IN THE YEARS 1921, 1931, & 1941

PROVINCES Census Divisions	1921	1931	1941
PRINCE EDWARD ISLAND	3	2	—
NOVA SCOTIA	2	1	3
NEW BRUNSWICK	4	—	5
QUEBEC	6	8	80
YUKON AND NWT	1	—	4
ONTARIO	13,645	17,661	22,219
Algoma	2	1	3
Brant	15	1	25
Bruce	363	304	360
Carleton	3	—	14
Cochrane	Formed in 1931	223	110
Dufferin	44	28	44
Dundas	1	—	—
Durham	—	—	—
Elgin	107	111	139
Essex	2	829	1,157
Frontenac	1	7	4
Glengarry	—	—	—
Grenville	1	—	—
Grey	241	248	340
Haldimand	170	212	156
Haliburton	—	—	3
Halton	13	1	21
Hastings	11	—	—
Huron	223	213	309
Kenora	—	5	67
Kent	9	43	88
Lambton	71	74	117
Lanark	—	—	—
Leeds	3	7	—
Lennox-Addington	—	—	—

APPENDIX 2 (continued)

MENNONITE POPULATION IN CANADA
BY PROVINCES AND CENSUS DIVISIONS
IN THE YEARS 1921, 1931, & 1941

PROVINCES Census Divisions	1921	1931	1941
ONTARIO (Continued)			
Lincoln	329	653	2,277
Manitoulin	65	99	185
Middlesex	18	20	39
Muskoka	6	3	13
Nipissing	—	—	1
Norfolk	12	140	223
Northumberland	5	—	30
Ontario	189	238	240
Oxford	699	769	847
Parry Sound	1	11	15
Peel	2	5	19
Perth	1,335	1,691	2,060
Peterborough	5	—	2
Prescott	—	—	—
Prince Edward	1	—	—
Rainy River	—	—	9
Renfrew	1	—	1
Russell	—	—	—
Simcoe	417	449	470
Stormont	—	—	—
Sudbury	1	2	46
Thunder Bay	3	1	53
Timiskaming	1	—	5
Victoria	—	—	17
Waterloo	7,130	8,752	9,398
Welland	422	340	389
Wellington	508	668	894
Wentworth	16	51	97
York	1,199	1,462	1,932
MANITOBA	21,295	30,352	39,336
Division # 1	3,815	5,727	8,798
Division # 2	16,343	17,902	20,927
Division # 3	28	942	844
Division # 4	—	598	457
Division # 5	5	159	744

APPENDIX 2 (continued)

MENNONITE POPULATION IN CANADA
BY PROVINCES AND CENSUS DIVISIONS
IN THE YEARS 1921, 1931, & 1941

PROVINCES Census Divisions	1921	1931	1941
MANITOBA (Continued)			
Division # 6	940	3,658	5,193
Division # 7	15	124	233
Division # 8	1	366	291
Division # 9	12	290	702
Division #10	1	126	555
Division #11	1	273	166
Division #12	3	21	80
Division #13	14	85	230
Division #14	30	17	30
Division #15	—	—	51
Division #16	87	64	35
SASKATCHEWAN	20,544	31,338	32,511
Division # 1	57	208	35
Division # 2	24	208	180
Division # 3	163	258	333
Division # 4	744	721	670
Division # 5	17	111	48
Division # 6	43	138	115
Division # 7	4,564	6,328	5,340
Division # 8	1,616	1,903	1,839
Division # 9	39	86	494
Division #10	126	323	371
Division #11	909	2,974	2,970
Division #12	1,165	1,822	1,782
Division #13	51	258	187
Division #14	605	876	2,338
Division #15	10,188	12,708	11,868
Division #16	212	1,992	2,812
Division #17	13	421	964
Division #18	8	3	165
ALBERTA	3,125	8,289	12,097
Division # 1	10	276	894
Division # 2	888	2,713	3,788
Division # 3	59	436	1,080

APPENDIX 2 (continued)

MENNONITE POPULATION IN CANADA
BY PROVINCES AND CENSUS DIVISIONS
IN THE YEARS 1921, 1931, & 1941

PROVINCES Census Divisions	1921	1931	1941
ALBERTA (Continued)			
Division # 4	122	161	256
Division # 5	176	609	203
Division # 6	1,330	2,503	3,155
Division # 7	119	297	225
Division # 8	38	130	191
Division # 9	14	20	133
Division #10	180	203	372
Division #11	89	155	392
Division #12	—	4	20
Division #13	9	9	4
Division #14	—	22	22
Division #15	1	113	234
Division #16	90	630	690
Division #17	—	8	438
BRITISH **COLUMBIA**	172	1,085	5,105
Division # 1	Divisions	3	15
Division # 2	not	87	121
Division # 3	applicable	47	114
Division # 4	in 1921	923	4,321
Division # 5		6	235
Division # 6		1	15
Division # 7		—	6
Division # 8		—	250
Division # 9		1	4
Division #10		17	24
TOTALS	58,797	88,736	111,360

Bibliography

A. REFERENCE WORKS

BENDER, HAROLD S., and SMITH, C. HENRY, eds. *The Mennonite Encyclopedia: A Comprehensive Reference Work on the Anabaptist-Mennonite Movement.* 4 vols. Hillsboro, Kans.: Mennonite Brethren Publishing House; Newton, Kans.: Mennonite Publication Office; Scottdale, Pa.: Mennonite Publishing House, 1955–1959.

Calendar of Appointments . . . and Reports of the Annual Conference and Mennonite Mission Board of Ontario, 1932–40.

Conference Journal, Proceedings of the Ontario Conference of Mennonite Brethren in Christ, published by Order of the Conference, 1920–1940.

Conference Journal of the Canadian North West Conference of the Mennonite Brethren in Christ Church, 1920–1940 (with variations in the title).

HILDEBRAND, J.J. *Hildebrand's Zeittafel: Chronologische Zeittafel: 1500 Daten Historischer Ereignisse und Geschehnisse aus der Zeit der Geschichte der Mennoniten Westeuropas, Russlands und Amerikas.* Winnipeg: By the Author, 1945.

Jahrbuch, Die Konferenz der Mennoniten in Kanada, 1928–40 (with variations in the title). Referred to as *Jahrbuch*.

Kalender fuer die Versammlungen der Mennoniten-Gemeinden in Ontario, Annual, 1836– .

KRAYBILL, PAUL N., ed. *Mennonite World Handbook*. Lombard, Ill.: Mennonite World Conference, 1978.

Mennonite Year-Book and Directory. Scottdale: Pa.: Mennonite Publishing House, Annual, 1905–40.

SMUCKER, DONOVAN E., ed. *The Sociology of Canadian Mennonites, Hutterites and Amish: A Bibliography with Annotations*. Waterloo: Wilfrid Laurier University Press, 1977.

SPRINGER, NELSON P., and KLASSEN, A.J. *Mennonite Bibliography, 1631–1961*. 2 vols. Scottdale, Pa.: Herald Press, 1977.

URQUHART, M.C., and BUCKLEY, K.A.H., eds. *Historical Statistics of Canada*. Toronto: Macmillan of Canada, 1965.

Verhandlungen der Noerdlichen Distrikt-Konferenz der Mennoniten-Bruedergemeinden von Nord-Amerika. Referred to as *Verhandlungen* (ND).

Verhandlungen . . . 1910–1940. Hillsboro, Kans.: MB Publishing House (includes both General Conference (GC) and Northern District (ND) sections or editions).

B. BOOKS

1. General Books

ALLEN, RICHARD. *The Social Passion: Religion and Social Reform in Canada, 1914–1928*. Toronto: University of Toronto Press, 1971.

ANDERSON, J.T.M. *The Education of the New-Canadian*. Toronto: J.M. Dent & Sons, 1918.

AVERY, DONALD. *"Dangerous Foreigners": European Immigrant Workers and Labour Radicalism in Canada, 1896–1932*. Toronto: McClelland & Stewart, 1979.

BECK, J. MURRAY. *Pendulum of Power: Canada's Federal Elections*. Toronto: Prentice-Hall, 1968.

BERCUSON, DAVID JAY. *Confrontation at Winnipeg: Labour, Industrial Relations, and the General Strike*. Montreal and London: McGill-Queen's University Press, 1974.

BETCHERMAN, LITA-ROSE. *The Swastika and the Maple Leaf: Fascist Movements in Canada in the Thirties*. Toronto: Fitzhenry & Whiteside, 1975.

BREBNER, J. BARTLET. *Canada: A Modern History*. Ann Arbor: University of Michigan Press, 1960.

BRIDGMAN, WELLINGTON. *Breaking Prairie Sod*. Toronto: Musson Book Co., 1920.

BROWN, ROBERT CRAIG, and RAMSAY COOK. *Canada, 1896–1921: A Nation Transformed*. Toronto: McClelland & Stewart, 1974.

CARELESS, J.M.S. *Canada: A Story of Challenge.* Toronto: Macmillan of Canada, 1963.

CLARK, LOVELL, ed. *The Manitoba School Question: Majority Rule or Minority Rights.* Toronto: Copp Clark, 1968.

COAD, F. ROY. *A History of the Brethren Movement: Its Origins, its Worldwide Development and its Significance for the Present Day.* Grand Rapids: Wm. B. Eerdmans, 1968.

COOK, RAMSAY. *The Politics of John W. Dafoe and the Free Press.* Toronto: University of Toronto Press, 1963.

The Co-operative Movement in the Americas. Montreal: International Labour Office, 1943.

CREIGHTON, DONALD. *Dominion of the North: A History of Canada.* Toronto: Macmillan of Canada, 1957.

DARNELL, REGNA, ed. *Linguistic Diversity in Canadian Society.* Edmonton: Linguistic Research, 1971.

DAWSON, R. MACGREGOR, and H. BLAIR NEATBY. *William Lyon Mackenzie King: A Political Biography.* 3 vols. Toronto: University of Toronto Press, 1958–1976.

DREYFUS, A.E., ed. *City Villages: The Co-operative Quest.* Toronto: New Press, 1973.

DYCK, HARVEY LEONARD. *Weimar Germany and Soviet Russia, 1926–1933: A Study in Diplomatic Instability.* London: Chatto & Windus, 1966.

ENGLAND, ROBERT. *The Colonization of Western Canada.* London: P.S. King & Son, 1936.

————. *The Central European Immigrant in Canada.* Toronto: Macmillan of Canada, 1929.

FEST, JOACHIM C. *Hitler.* New York: Vintage Books, 1975.

FOGHT, HAROLD J. *A Survey of Education in the Province of Saskatchewan.* Regina: King's Printer, 1918.

FOWKE, VERNON C. *The National Policy and the Wheat Economy.* Toronto: University of Toronto Press, 1957.

FRANCIS, R.D., and H. VANDERVOORT. *The Dirty Thirties in Prairie Canada.* B.C. Geographical Series. Vancouver: Fantalus Research Ltd., 1980.

FURNISS, NORMAN F. *The Fundamentalist Controversy, 1918–1931.* Hamden, Conn.: Archon Books, 1963.

GIBBON, JOHN MURRAY. *Canadian Mosaic: The Making of a Northern Nation.* London: J.M. Dent & Sons, 1938.

GIESINGER, ADAM. *From Catherine to Khrushchev: The Story of Russia's Germans.* Winnipeg: By the Author, 1974.

GRANATSTEIN, J.L., and J.M. HITSMAN. *Broken Promises: A History of Conscription in Canada.* Toronto: Oxford University Press, 1977.

GRANT, JOHN WEBSTER. *The Church in the Canadian Era.* Toronto: McGraw-Hill Ryerson, 1972.

————. *The Canadian Experience of Church Union.* Richmond, Va.: John Knox Press, 1967.

GRAY, JAMES H. *The Winter Years: The Depression on the Prairies.* Toronto: Macmillan of Canada, 1966.

GRAYSON, L.M., and MICHAEL BLISS, eds. *The Wretched of Canada: Letters to R.B. Bennett, 1930–1935.* Toronto: University of Toronto Press, 1971.

HARKNESS, ROSS. *Atkinson of the Star.* Toronto: University of Toronto Press, 1963.

HARTZ, LOUIS. *The Founding of New Societies: Studies in the History of the United States, Latin America, South Africa, Canada, and Australia.* New York: Harcourt, Brace & World, Inc., 1964.

HEDGES, JAMES B. *Building the Canadian West: The Land and Colonization Policies of the Canadian Pacific Railway.* New York: Macmillan of Canada, 1939.

HOFSTAEDTER, RICHARD C. *Social Darwinism in American Thought.* Boston: Beacon Press, 1955.

HORN, MICHIEL. *The Dirty Thirties: Canadians in the Great Depression.* Toronto: Copp Clark Publishing Company, 1972.

KENDLE, JOHN. *John Bracken: A Political Biography.* Toronto: University of Toronto Press, 1979.

KOVACS, MARTIN, ed. *Ethnic Canadians: Culture and Education.* Regina: Canadian Plains Research Centre, 1978.

LEWIS, M.M. *Language in Society.* New York: Social Sciences Publishers, 1948.

LIPSET, SEYMOUR MARTIN. *Agrarian Socialism: The Co-operative Commonwealth Federation in Saskatchewan.* Berkeley: University of California Press, 1971.

LOVERIDGE, D.M. *A Historical Directory of Manitoba Newspapers, 1859–1978.* Winnipeg: University of Manitoba Press, 1980.

Lowe Farm: 75th Anniversary. Altona, Man.: Lowe Farm Chamber of Commerce, n.d.

MACGREGOR, JAMES G. *North-west of Sixteen.* Rutland, Vt.: Charles E. Tuttle Co., 1968.

———. *A History of Alberta.* Edmonton: Hurtig, 1972.

MACKINTOSH, W.A. *The Economic Background of Dominion-Provincial Relations.* Toronto: McClelland & Stewart, 1964.

———. and W.L.G. JOERG, gen. eds. *Canadian Frontiers of Settlement.* 9 vols. Toronto: Macmillan of Canada, 1934–1940. Vol. 1: *Prairie Settlement: The Geographical Setting*, by W.A. Mackintosh. Vol. 6: *The Settlement of the Peace River Country: A Study of a Pioneer Area*, by C.A. Dawson. Vol. 7: *Group Settlement: Ethnic Communities in Western Canada*, by C.A. Dawson. Vol. 8: *Pioneering in the Prairie Provinces: The Social Side of the Settlement Process*, by C.A. Dawson and Eva R. Younge.

MACPHERSON, IAN. *Each for All: A History of the Co-operative Movement in English Canada, 1900–1945.* Toronto: Macmillan of Canada, 1979.

———. *The Cooperative Movement on the Prairies, 1900–1955.* The Canadian Historical Association Booklets, No. 33, Ottawa, 1979.

MANN, W.E. *Sect, Cult and Church in Alberta.* Toronto: University of Toronto Press, 1955.

MARUNCHUK, MICHAEL H. *The Ukrainian Canadians: A History.* Winnipeg and Ottawa: Ukrainian Free Academy of Sciences, 1970.

MASTERS, D.C. *The Winnipeg General Strike.* Toronto: University of Toronto Press, 1950.

MCNEILL, WILLIAM H. *Plagues and Peoples.* Garden City, N.Y.: Doubleday, 1976.

MEYERS, ROBERT. *Spirit of the Post Road: A Story of Self-Help Communities.* Altona, Man.: The Federation of Southern Manitoba Co-operatives, 1955.

MORTON, W.L. *Manitoba: A History.* 2nd ed., reprint with additions. Toronto: University of Toronto Press, 1970.

NEATBY, H. BLAIR. *The Politics of Chaos: Canada in the Thirties.* Toronto: Macmillan of Canada, 1972.

O'LEARY, GRATTAN. *Recollections of People, Press and Politics.* Toronto: Macmillan of Canada, 1977.

OLIVER, EDMUND H. *The Country School in Non-English-Speaking Communities in Saskatchewan.* Regina: Saskatchewan Public Education League, 1915.

ORMSBY, MARGARET A. *British Columbia: A History.* Toronto: Macmillan of Canada, 1958.

PALMER, HOWARD, ed. *Immigration and the Rise of Multiculturalism.* Toronto: Copp Clark, 1975.

———. *Land of the Second Chance: A History of Ethnic Groups in Southern Alberta.* Lethbridge, Alta.: Lethbridge Herald, 1972.

PAYNE, ROBERT. *The Rise and Fall of Stalin.* New York: Simon & Schuster, 1965.

PENTON, M. JAMES. *Jehovah's Witnesses in Canada: Champions of Freedom of Speech and Worship.* Toronto: Macmillan of Canada, 1976.

PETERS, VICTOR. *Nestor Makhno: The Life of an Anarchist.* Winnipeg: Echo Books, 1970.

PICK, FRANZ, and RENE SEDILLOT. *All the Monies of the World.* New York: Pick Publishing, 1971.

PICKERSGILL, J.W., and D.F. FORSTER. *The Mackenzie King Record.* 4 vols. Toronto: University of Toronto Press, 1960–1978.

PRIESTLEY, NORMAN F., and EDWARD B. SWINDLEHURST. *Furrows, Faith and Fellowship.* Edmonton: Co-op Press, 1967.

RASPORICH, A.W., and H.C. KLASSEN, eds. *Prairie Perspective 2: Selected Papers of the Western Canadian Studies Conferences, 1970, 1971.* Toronto: Holt, Rinehart, & Winston of Canada, 1973.

RIASANOVSKY, NICHOLAS V. *A History of Russia.* New York: Oxford University Press, 1969.

RUTH, ROY H. *Educational Echoes: A History of Education of the Icelandic-Canadians in Manitoba.* Winnipeg: n.p., 1964.

RYAN, JOHN. *The Agricultural Economy of Manitoba Hutterite Colonies.* Toronto: McClelland & Stewart, 1977.

SAFARIAN, A.E. *The Canadian Economy in the Great Depression.* Toronto: McClelland & Stewart, 1970.

SANDEEN, ERNEST R. *The Origins of Fundamentalism: Toward a Historical Perspective.* Philadelphia: Fortress Press, 1968.

SILCOX, CLARIS EDWIN. *Church Union in Canada: Its Causes and Consequences.* New York: Institute of Social and Religious Research, 1933.

SISSONS, C.B. *Bi-lingual Schools in Canada.* Toronto: J.M. Dent & Sons, 1917.

————. *Church and State in Canadian Education: An Historical Study.* Toronto: Ryerson Press, 1959.

SKELTON, OSCAR DOUGLAS. *Life and Letters of Sir Wilfrid Laurier.* Introduction by David M.L. Farr. Toronto: McClelland & Stewart, 1965.

STACEY, C.P. *Arms, Men and Governments: The War Policies of Canada, 1939–1945.* Ottawa: Queen's Printer for Minister of National Defence, 1970.

SUTHERLAND, NEIL. *Children in English-Canadian Society: Framing the Twentieth-Century Consensus.* Toronto: University of Toronto Press, 1976.

SWAINSON, DONALD. *Historical Essays on the Prairie Provinces.* Toronto: McClelland & Stewart, 1970.

THOMPSON, JOHN HERD. *The Harvests of War: The Prairie West, 1914–1918.* Toronto: McClelland & Stewart, 1978.

ULAM, ADAM BRUNO. *Stalin: The Man and His Era.* New York: Viking Press, 1973.

WALSH, H.H. *The Christian Church in Canada.* Toronto: Ryerson Press, 1956.

WEIR, GEORGE M. *The Separate School Question in Canada.* Toronto: Ryerson Press, 1934.

WOODSWORTH, JAMES S. *Strangers Within Our Gates.* Frederick Clarke Stephenson, 1909; reprint ed., Toronto: University of Toronto Press, 1972.

YOUNG, WALTER D. *The Anatomy of a Party: The National CCF, 1932–61.* Toronto: University of Toronto Press, 1969.

2. Mennonite and Related Books

ADRIAN, DAVID, ed. *Marvelous Are Thy Ways: A Brief History of the Rosemary Mennonite Church.* n.p., 1961.

ADRIAN, J.D. *Die Entstehung der Rudnerweider Gemeinde.* Winnipeg: J.D. Adrian, 1958.

ARNEL, RUTH. *A Time for Change, 1948–1973.* Nairn Mennonite Church, 1973.

BAUMAN, SALOME. *150 Years First Mennonite Church.* n.p., n.d.

BEHRENDS, ERNST. *Der Steppenhengst.* Bodensee: Hohenstaufen Verlag, 1969.

BELK, FRED RICHARD. *The Great Trek of the Russian Mennonites to Central Asia, 1880-1884*. Scottdale, Pa.: Herald Press, 1976.

BENDER, D.H., comp. *Mennonite Church Polity: A Statement of Practices in Church Government*. Scottdale, Pa.: Mennonite Publishing House, 1944.

BENDER, HAROLD S., ed. *John Horsch Memorial Papers*. Scottdale, Pa.: Mennonite Publishing House, 1947.

BENDER, URIE A. *Four Earthen Vessels: Biographical Profiles of Oscar Burkholder, Samuel F. Coffman, Clayton F. Derstine, and Jesse B. Martin*. Scottdale, Pa.: Herald Press, 1982.

BENDER, WILBUR J. *Nonresistance in Colonial Pennsylvania*. Scottdale, Pa.: Herald Press, 1949.

Bericht ueber die 400 Jaehrige Jubilaeumsfeier der Mennoniten oder Taufgesinnten vom 13. bis 15. Juni 1925 in Basel. Karlsruhe: Bibelheim Thomashof, 1925.

BIRD, MICHAEL, and TERRY KOBAYASHI. *A Splendid Harvest: Germanic Folk and Decorative Arts in Canada*. Toronto: Van Nostrand Reinhold Ltd., 1981.

BIRD, MICHAEL S. *Ontario Fraktur: A Pennsylvania-German Folk Tradition in Early Canada*. Toronto: M.F. Feheley Publishers Limited, 1977.

BLUFFTON COLLEGE FACULTY. *An Adventure in Faith, 1900-1950*. n.p., 1950.

BOLDT, LEONARD C. *Fortieth Anniversary: Osler Mennonite Church, 1928-1968*. n.p., 1968.

BREDNICH, ROLF WILH. *Mennonite Folklife and Folklore: A Preliminary Report*. Ottawa, Canada: National Museums of Canada, 1977.

BROWN, HELENA M. *Bergthal Church: 1903-1978*. Didsbury, Alta.: Anniversary Committee, 1978.

BUEHLER, ALLAN M. *The Pennsylvania German Dialect and the Autobiography of an Old Order Mennonite*. Cambridge, Ontario: The Author, 1977.

BURKHOLDER, L.J. *A Brief History of the Mennonites in Ontario*. Markham, Ont.: Mennonite Conference of Ontario, 1935.

BURKHOLDER, OSCAR. *The Predicted Departure from the Faith*. Scottdale, Pa.: Mennonite Publishing House, 1930.

_____ . *Cressman Mennonite Church*. n.p., 1955.

_____ . *True Life Stories*. Scottdale, Pa.: Mennonite Publishing House, 1929.

BURKHOLDER, OSCAR, S.F. COFFMAN, and GILBERT BERGEY, comps. *Resolutions: Ontario Mennonite Conference, 1847-1928*. n.p., 1929.

Calendar of Appointments of the Mennonite Church of Ontario, Centennial Issue: 1834-1934, n.p., 1935.

COFFMAN, S.F., ed. *Mennonite Church Polity: A Statement of Practices in Church Government*. Scottdale, Pa.: Mennonite Publishing House, 1944.

COOPER, CHARLOTTE SLOAN. *The Mennonite People.* Saskatoon, Sask.: The College of Education, 1978.

CORRELL, ERNEST A. *Das Schweizerische Taeufermennonitentum.* Tuebingen: J.C.B. Mohr, 1925.

Diamond Jubilee of Mennonite Brethren Church, 1908–1968: Arelee, Saskatchewan. n.p., 1968.

DICK, C.L., ed. *The Mennonite Conference of Alberta: A History of its Churches and Institutions.* Edmonton, Alberta: The Mennonite Conference of Alberta, 1981.

Die Mennoniten Gemeinden in der Gretna-Altona Umgebung in Manitoba. n.p., 1963.

DOERKSEN, J.H. *Geschichte und Wichtige Dokumente der Mennoniten von Russland, Canada, Paraguay und Mexico.* n.p., 1923.

DOERKSEN, J.P., ed. *[Gem] Mennonite Brethren Church, 1929–1979.* Gem, Alta.: Gem Mennonite Brethren Church, 1979.

DRIEDGER, N.N. *The Leamington United Mennonite Church: Establishment and Development, 1925–1972.* n.p., 1972.

DUECK, ABE J. *Concordia Hospital: 1928–1978.* Winnipeg: Mennonite Hospital Society Concordia, 1978.

DUECK, PETER G., BENNO SCHROEDER, and J.L. BRAUN, eds. *75th Anniversary, Lowe Farm Bergthaler Mennonite Church 1905–1980.* Lowe Farm, Manitoba, 1980.

DYCK, ANNA REIMER. *Anna: From the Caucasus to Canada.* Hillsboro, Kansas: Mennonite Brethren Publishing House, 1979.

DYCK, CORNELIUS J. *An Introduction to Mennonite History.* Scottdale, Pa.: Herald Press, 1981.

⸺. *A Legacy of Faith.* Newton, Kans.: Faith and Life Press, 1962.

⸺, ed. *The Mennonite Central Committee Story.* Scottdale, Pa.: Herald Press, 1980.

DYCK, ISAAK M. *Die Auswanderung der Reinlaender Mennoniten Gemeinde von Canada nach Mexico.* Forward by Heinrich Dyck. Cuauhtemoc, Mexico: Imprenta Colonial, 1970.

DYCK, J.P. *Das 25-Jaehrige Jubilaeum der Springsteiner Mennoniten-Gemeinde, 1938–1963.* n.p., 1963.

DYCK, JOHN H., and ALVIN P. SCHELLENBERG, eds. *First Mennonite Church, Queen Street and Fifth Avenue, Saskatoon, Saskatchewan.* n.p., 1973.

DYCK, JOHN P., ed. *Troubles and Triumphs, 1914–1924.* Springstein, Manitoba, 1981.

ECHOES, 39–64: *The Conference of United Mennonite Churches of British Columbia.* n.p., 1964.

EHRT, A. *Das Mennonitentum in Russland.* Berlin, 1932.

Elim Gemeinde, 1927–1972. Grunthal, Man.: Elim Church, *c.* 1972.

Elmwood Mennonite Brethren Church: Pictorial History, 1970. n.p., 1970.

ENNS, F.F. *Elder Enns.* Winnipeg: By the Author, 1979.

ENNS, HERBERT, and JAKOB FAST, eds. *Jubilee Issue of the Waterloo*

Kitchener United Mennonite Church, 1924 – 1974. Waterloo, Ont.: K-W United Mennonite Church, 1974.

ENNS, JOHN H. *The Story of the Mennonite Settlement of Reesor, Ontario.* Reesor, Ontario: The Author, 1973.

EPP, D.H. *Die Chortitzer Mennoniten: Versuch einer Darstellung des Entwickelungsganges Derselben.* Odessa: By the Author, 1889.

EPP, FRANK H. *Mennonite Exodus: The Rescue and Resettlement of the Russian Mennonites Since the Communist Revolution.* Altona, Man.: D.W. Friesen & Sons for the Canadian Mennonite Relief and Immigration Council, 1962.

_____. *Mennonites in Canada, 1786 – 1920: The History of a Separate People.* Toronto: Macmillan of Canada, 1974.

_____. *Education with a Plus: The Story of Rosthern Junior College.* Waterloo, Ont.: Conrad Press, 1975.

EPP, GEORGE K., ed. *Unter dem Nordlicht: Anthology of German Mennonite Writing in Canada.* Winnipeg, Manitoba: Mennonite German Society of Canada, 1977.

ERB, PAUL. *Orie O. Miller: The Story of a Man and an Era.* Scottdale, Pa.: Herald Press, 1969.

ESTEP, WILLIAM R. *The Anabaptist Story.* Revised edition. Grand Rapids: William B. Eerdmans, 1975.

FAST, HEINOLD. *Die Vereinigung der Deutschen Mennonitengemeinden, 1886 – 1961.* Weierhof: Vereinigung der Deutschen Mennonitengemeinden, 1961.

FAST, KARL, ed. *Fiftieth Anniversary of the Mennonite Settlement in North Kildonan.* Winnipeg: Anniversary Book Committee of the Mennonite Churches, 1978.

Fiftieth Anniversary of the Coaldale Mennonite Brethren Church, May 23, 1976. n.p., 1976.

FLINT, JOANNE. *The Mennonite Canadians.* Toronto: Van Nostrand Reinhold, 1980.

Fortieth Anniversary: Mennonite Brethren Church: Vineland, Ontario. n.p., 1972.

FRANCIS, E.K. *In Search of Utopia: The Mennonites of Manitoba.* Altona, Man.: D.W. Friesen & Sons, 1955.

FRETZ, J. WINFIELD. *Mennonite Colonization in Mexico: An Introduction.* Akron, Pa.: Mennonite Central Committee, 1945.

_____. *Pilgrims in Paraguay: The Story of Mennonite Colonization in the Paraguayan Chaco.* Scottdale, Pa.: Herald Press, 1953.

FRIESEN, ABRAHAM, ed. *P.M. Friesen & His History: Understanding Mennonite Brethren Beginnings.* No. 2: Perspectives on Mennonite Life and Thought. Fresno, Cal.: Center for Mennonite Brethren Studies, Mennonite Brethren Biblical Seminary, 1979.

FRIESEN, ABRAM, and ABRAM J. LOEWEN. *Die Flucht ueber den Amur.* Steinbach, Man.: Echo-Verlag, 1946.

FRIESEN, GEORGE P. *Fangs of Bolshevism: Friesen-Braun Trials in Saskatchewan, 1924–29*. Saskatoon: Friesen, 1930.

FRIESEN, H.F. *Fiftieth Anniversary, Morden Mennonite Brethren Church: Historical Report*. n.p., 1969.

FRIESEN, MARTIN W., ed. *Kanadische Mennoniten Bezwingen eine Wildnis: 50 Jahre Kolonie Menno, Chaco, Paraguay, 1927–1977*. Loma Plata: Verwaltung der Kolonie Menno, 1977.

FRIESEN, P.M. *Alt-Evangelische Mennonitische Bruederschaft in Russland (1789–1910)*. Halbstadt, Taurien, Russia: Raduga, 1911.

――――. *The Mennonite Brotherhood in Russia (1789–1910)*. Translated from the German. Fresno, Cal.: Board of Christian Literature, General Conference of Mennonite Brethren Churches, 1978.

FRIESEN, WILLIAM, and JOHN L. BRAUN, eds. *Lowe Farm 75 Anniversary*. Lowe Farm, Manitoba, 1976.

FROESE, FR., ed. *Fuenfundzwanzig Jaehriges Jubilaeum der Steinbach Mennoniten Gemeinde, 1968*. n.p., 1968.

From His Fullness: A Brief Survey of the History of the Vineland Mennonite Brethren Church. n.p., 1962.

Fuenfundzwanzig Jahre: Vineland Mennoniten Gemeinde, 1936–61. n.p., n.d., CGCL.

Fuenfzige Jubilaeum der beiden Ebenezer Gemeinden in Saskatchewan, Canada, 9. bis 11. Juni 1939. n.p., 1939.

GATES, HELEN KOLB; JOHN FUNK KOLB; J. CLEMENS KOLB; CONSTANCE KOLB SYKES. *Bless the Lord O My Soul: A Biography of Bishop John Fretz Funk, 1835–1930*. Edited by J.C. Wenger. Scottdale, Pa.: Herald Press, 1964.

Gedenk- und Dankfeier des 25-jaehrigen Bestehens der Coaldale Mennoniten Brueder Gemeinde am 27. Mai 1951. n.p., 1951.

Gedenkfeier der Mennonitischen Einwanderung in Manitoba, Canada. Steinbach, Man.: Festkomitee der Mennonitischen Ostreserve, 1949.

GERBRANDT, H.J. *Adventure in Faith: The Background in Europe and the Development in Canada of the Bergthaler Mennonite Church of Manitoba*. Altona, Man.: D.W. Friesen & Sons for the Bergthaler Mennonite Church of Manitoba, 1970.

GINGERICH, MELVIN. *Mennonite Attire Through Four Centuries*. Breinigsville, Pa.: Pennsylvania German Society, 1970.

GINGERICH, ORLAND. *The Amish of Canada*. Waterloo, Ont.: Conrad Press, 1972.

GINGRICH, NEWTON. *History of the Ontario Mennonite Bible School and Ontario Mennonite Bible Institute*. n.p., n.d.

GOERZEN, JAKOB WARKENTIN. *Low German in Canada: A Study of "Plautdietsch" as Spoken by Mennonite Immigrants from Russia*. Edmonton: By the Author, 1970.

Golden Jubilee of the Mennonite Brethren Church of Hepburn, Saskatchewan, Canada: 1910–1960. n.p., 1960.

GRATZ, DELBERT L., ed. *Mennonite World Relief Conference at Danzig, 1930.* Translated by Paul Schmidt. n.p., 1946.

Grunthal History, 1874–1974. n.p., 1974.

GUENTHER, F.D. *Meine Inneren und Aeusseren Erlebnisse in Mexico und Canada.* Inwood, Man.: By the Author, 1957.

HACK, H. *Die Kolonisation der Mennoniten im Paraguayischen Chaco.* Amsterdam: Koenigliches Tropeninstitut, n.d.

HAMM, H.H. *Sixty Years of Progress, 1884–1944, Diamond Jubilee.* Altona, Man.: Rural Municipality of Rhineland, 1944.

HARDER, DAVID. *Schule und Gemeinschaft: Erinnerungen des Dorfschullehrers.* Gretna, Man.: Mimeographed by Jacob Rempel, 1969.

HARDER, JACOB, and HANS DUERKSEN. *Fernheim 1930–1980.* Kolonie Fernheim, Paraguay, 1980.

HARDER, LELAND. *Steinbach and Its Churches.* Elkhart, Ind.: Mennonite Biblical Seminary, 1970.

HARDER, PETER R., ed. *Arnaud Through the Years.* n.p., 1974.

HARTZLER, J.S. *Mennonites in the World War or Nonresistance Under Test.* Scottdale, Pa.: Mennonite Publishing House, 1921.

HARTZLER, J.S., and DANIEL KAUFFMAN. *Mennonite Church History.* Scottdale, Pa.: Mennonite Book and Tract Society, 1905.

He Leadeth: History of the Ontario Mennonite Brethren Churches, 1924–1957. n.p., n.d.

HERSCHBERGER, GUY F., ed. *The Recovery of the Anabaptist Vision.* Scottdale, Pa.: Herald Press, 1957.

––––––. *War, Peace, and Nonresistance.* Scottdale, Pa.: Mennonite Publishing House, 1944.

HIEBERT, CLARENCE. *The Holdeman People: The Church of God in Christ Mennonite, 1859–1969.* South Pasadena, Cal.: William Carey Library, 1973.

HIEBERT, P.C., and ORIE O. MILLER, eds. *Feeding the Hungry: Russia Famine 1919–1925.* Scottdale, Pa.: Mennonite Central Committee, 1929.

Histories of the Congregations of the Church of God in Christ Mennonite. Ste. Anne, Man.: Gospel Publishers, 1975.

The History of the Main Centre Mennonite Brethren Church, 1904–1979. n.p., 1979.

HOFER, D.M. *Die Hungersnot in Russland und Unsere Reise um die Welt.* Chicago: KMB Publishing House, 1924.

HORSCH, JOHN. *Modern Religious Liberalism.* Scottdale, Pa.: Fundamental Truth Depot, 1920.

––––––. *Mennonites in Europe.* Scottdale, Pa.: Mennonite Publishing House, 1950.

––––––. *The Mennonite Church and Modernism.* Scottdale, Pa.: Mennonite Publishing House, 1924.

––––––. *Die Biblische Lehre von der Wehrlosigkeit.* Scottdale, Pa.: Mennonite Publishing House, 1920.

HORST, ISAAC. *Up the Conestogo*. Mount Forest, Ont.: The Author, 1979.

HOSTETTLER, JOHN A. *God Uses Ink: The Heritage and Mission of the Mennonite Publishing House After Fifty Years*. Scottdale, Pa.: Herald Press, 1958.

HUFFMAN, J.A. *History of the Mennonite Brethren in Christ Church*. New Carlisle, Ohio.: The Bethel Publishing Co., 1920.

HUNSBERGER, ALBERT I. *Nineteen Nineteen*. Kitchener: Ainsworth Press, 1979.

ISAAC, FRANK K. *Elim 50th Anniversary: 1929 – 1979*. Winnipeg: Conference of Mennonites in Manitoba, 1979.

JANZEN, A.E., and HERBERT GIESBRECHT, eds. *We Recommend...Recommendations and Resolutions of the General Conference of the Mennonite Brethren Churches*. Fresno, Cal.: Board of Christian Literature, General Conference of Mennonite Brethren Churches, 1978.

JANZEN, JAKOB H. *David Toews: Vorsitzender der Kolonisationsbehoerde der Mennoniten in Canada*. Rosthern, Sask.: D.H. Epp, 1939.

JESCHKE, ERNEST A. *Memoirs*. Goshen, Ind.: Marlin Jeschke, 1966.

JUHNKE, JAMES C. *A People of Two Kingdoms: The Political Acculturation of the Kansas Mennonites*. Newton, Kans.: Faith & Life Press, 1975.

KAUFFMAN, DANIEL, ed. *Bible Doctrine*. Scottdale, Pa.: Mennonite Publishing House, 1914.

————. *Fifty Years in the Mennonite Church, 1890 – 1940*. Scottdale, Pa.: Mennonite Publishing House, 1941.

KEENEY, WILLIAM ECHARD. *The Development of Dutch Anabaptist Thought and Practice from 1539 – 1564*. Nieuwkoop: B. de Graaf, 1968.

KLAASSEN, H.T. *Birth and Growth of the Eigenheim Mennonite Church, 1892 – 1974*. n.p., [1974].

KLAASSEN, WALTER. *Anabaptism: Neither Catholic Nor Protestant*. Waterloo, Ont.: Conrad Press, 1973.

KLASSEN, A.J., ed. *The Bible School Story (1913 – 1963)*. Clearbrook, B.C., Canadian Board of Education, 1963.

KLASSEN, ISAAK. *Dem Herrn die Ehre: Schonwieser Mennoniten Gemeinde von Manitoba 1924 – 1968*. n.p., 1969.

KLIPPENSTEIN, LAWRENCE, ed. *In Quest of Brothers: A Yearbook Commemorating Twenty-Five Years of Life Together in the Conference of Mennonites in Manitoba, 1946 – 71*. Winnipeg: Conference of Mennonites in Manitoba, 1972.

KLIPPENSTEIN, LAWRENCE, and JULIUS G. TOEWS, eds. *Mennonite Memories: Settling in Western Canada*. Winnipeg: Centennial Publications, 1977.

KOESTLER, ARTHUR. *Darkness at Noon*. Translated by Daphne Hardy. New York: Modern Library, 1941.

KRAHN, CORNELIUS. *Dutch Anabaptism: Origin, Spread, Life and Thought (1450 – 1600)*. The Hague: Martinus Nijhoff, 1968.

KROEKER, ABRAHAM. *My Flight from Russia*. Scottdale, Pa.: Herald Press, 1932.

LICHDI, DIETHER GOTZ. *Mennoniten im Dritten Reich: Dokumentation und Deutung.* Weierhof, West Germany, 1978.

LITTELL, FRANKLIN. *The Anabaptist View of the Church.* Boston: Star King Press, 1958.

LOEPPKY, JOHAN M. *Ein Reisebericht von Canada nach Mexico im Jahre 1921.* n.p., n.d.

LOEWEN, ABRAM J. *Immer Weiter Nach Osten: Suedrussland, China, Kanada.* Winnipeg: CMBC Publications, 1981.

LOHRENZ, GERHARD. *The Fateful Years: 1913 – 1923.* Winnipeg, Manitoba, 1978.

_____ . *Heritage Remembered: A Pictorial Survey of Mennonites in Prussia and Russia.* Winnipeg: CMBC Publications, 1977.

_____ . *Mia oder Ueber den Amur in die Freiheit.* Winnipeg, Manitoba: DeFehr Foundation, Inc., 1981.

_____ . *The Odyssey of the Bergen Family.* Winnipeg, Manitoba, 1978.

_____ . *Storm Tossed: The Personal Story of a Canadian Mennonite from Russia.* Winnipeg: Christian Press, 1976.

Mennonite Brethren Church, Winkler, Manitoba, 1888 – 1963. n.p., (1963).

MUSSER, DANIEL. *The Reformed Mennonite Church: Its Rise, Progress, with its Principles and Doctrines.* Lancaster, Pa.: Elias Barr & Co., 1873.

NEFF, CHRISTIAN, ed. *Bericht ueber die Mennonitische Welt-Hilfs-Konferenz vom 31. August bis 3. September 1930.* Karlsruhe: Heinrich Schneider, 1930.

_____ , ed. *Der Allgemeine Kongress der Mennoniten gehalten in Amsterdam, Elspeet, Witmarsum, 29. Juni bis 3. Juli 1936.* Karlsruhe: Heinrich Schneider, 1936.

NEUDORF, J.J. *Osterwick, 1812 – 1943.* Winkler: n.p., 1974.

NEUFELD, DIETRICH. *A Russian Dance of Death: Revolution and Civil War in the Ukraine.* Translated and edited by Al Reimer. Winnipeg: Hyperion Press for the Mennonite Literary Society and the University of Winnipeg, 1977.

NEUFELD, G.G. *Die Geschichte der Whitewater Mennoniten Gemeinde in Manitoba, Canada, 1925 – 1965.* n.p., 1967.

Niagara United Mennonite Church History: Eben-Ezer 25 Jahre, 1938 – 1963. n.p., n.d.

NICKEL, JOHANN J. *Thy Kingdom Come: The Diary of Johann J. Nickel of Rosenhof, 1918 – 1919.* Translated by John P. Nickel. Saskatoon: By the Author, 1978.

Nordheimer Mennonite Church of Saskatchewan, 1925 – 1975. Saskatoon: n.p., 1975.

North Kildonan Mennonitengemeinde, 1935 – 1975. n.p., 1975.

Old and New Furrows: The Story of Rosthern. Rosthern, Sask.: Rosthern Historical Society, 1977.

OMBS Clarion. Kitchener, Ont.: n.p., 1939.

PAAR, JOAN, ed. *Manitoba Stories.* Winnipeg, Manitoba: Queenston House Publishing, 1981.

PANNABECKER, SAMUEL FLOYD. *Open Doors: The History of the General Conference Mennonite Church.* Newton, Kans.: Faith and Life Press, 1975.

PATTERSON, NANCY-LOU. *Swiss-German and Dutch-German Mennonite Traditional Art in the Wrterloo Region.* Canadian Centre for Folk Culture Studies, Mercury Series. Ottawa: National Museum of Man, 1979.

PENNER, GERHARD. *Mennoniten dienen in der Roten Armee.* Winnipeg, Manitoba, 1975.

PENNER, HORST. *Die Ost- und Westpreussischen Mennoniten in Ihrem Religiosen und Sozialen Leben in Ihren Kulturellen und Wirtschaftlichen Leistungen.* Weierhof: Mennonitischer Geschichtsverein, 1978.

PETERS, G.H. *Characterbildung.* Winnipeg: The Author, 1955.

PETERS, GERHARD I. *A History of the First Mennonite Church, Greendale, B.C.* n.p., 1976.

PETERS, HENRY, ed. *Nordheimer Mennonite Church of Saskatchewan, 1925-1975.* Hanley, Sask., 1975.

PETERS, KLAAS. *Die Bergthaler Mennoniten und deren Auswanderung aus Russland und Einwanderung in Manitoba.* Hillsboro, Kans.: Mennonite Brethren Publishing House, [1922].

PETERS, VICTOR. *Nestor Makhno: The Life of an Anarchist.* Winnipeg: Echo Books, 1970.

PETKAU, IRENE FRIESEN, ed. *Just When We Were: The Story of the Conference of Mennonites in Canada.* Winnipeg, Manitoba: The History Archives Committee of Mennonites in Canada, 1978.

PETKAU, IRENE FRIESEN, and PETER PETKAU. *Blumenfeld: Where Land and People Meet.* Blumenfeld, Manitoba, 1981.

POETTCKER, HENRY, and RUDY A. REGEHR , eds. *Call to Faithfulness: Essays in Canadian Mennonite Studies.* Winnipeg: Canadian Mennonite Bible College, 1972.

PRIES, GEORGE DAVID. *A Place Called Peniel: Winkler Bible Institute, 1925-1975.* Altona, Man.: D.W. Friesen & Sons, 1975.

QUIRING, WALTER. *Deutsche Erschliessen den Chaco.* Karlsruhe: Heinrich Schneider, 1936.

————. *Russlanddeutsche suchen eine Heimat: Die Deutsche Einwanderung in den Paraguayischen Chaco.* Karlsruhe: Heinrich Schneider, 1938.

RATZLAFF, GERHARD, ed. *Geschichte der Mennoniten Brueder Gemeinde in Paraguay.* Asuncion, Paraguay: Instituto Biblico Asuncion, 1977.

REDEKOP, CALVIN WALL. *The Old Colony Mennonites: Dilemmas of Ethnic Minority Life.* Baltimore: Johns Hopkins Press, 1969.

REIMER, DAVID P., ed. *Experiences of the Mennonites of Canada During the Second World War, 1939-1945.* n.p., n.d.

REIMER, P.J.B., ed. *The Sesquicentennial Jubilee: Evangelical Mennonite Conference, 1812–1962.* Steinbach, Man.: Evangelical Mennonite Conference, 1962.

REIMER, PETER. *Wir Waren mit Dabei: Errinnerungen eines alten Kommunisten.* Alma Ata, Kasachstan, Verlag Kasachstan, 1977.

REMPEL, G.S. *A Historical Sketch of the Churches of the Evangelical Mennonite Brethren.* n.p., 1939.

REMPEL, HANS, ed. and comp. *Waffen der Wehrlosen: Ersatzdienst der Mennoniten in der UdSSR.* Winnipeg, Manitoba: CMBC Publications, 600 Shaftesbury Blvd., 1980.

REMPEL, J.G. *Fuenfzig Jahre Konferenzbestrebungen, 1902–1952.* 2 vols. n.p., [1952].

_____. *Die Rosenorter Gemeinde in Saskatchewan in Wort und Bild.* Rosthern, Sask.: D.H. Epp, 1950.

REMPEL, JOHN D. *A History of the Hague Mennonite Church, 1900–1975.* Hague, Sask.: Hague Mennonite Church, 1975.

REMPEL, OLGA. *Einer von Vielen.* Winnipeg, Manitoba: CMBC Publications, 1979.

RIMLAND, INGRID. *The Wanderers: The Saga of Three Women Who Survived.* St. Louis, Missouri: Concordia Publishing House, 1977.

RITTENHOUSE, WILLIAM. *Vineland Cemetery.* n.p., 1922.

RUTH, JOHN L. *Mennonite Identity and Literary Art.* Scottdale, Pa.: Herald Press, 1978.

SAUDER, DOROTHY. *Trail's End — The Oxbow: History of the Bloomington Church.* n.p., 1972.

SAWATZKY, HARRY LEONARD. *They Sought A Country: Mennonite Colonization in Mexico.* Berkeley: University of California Press, 1971.

SCHAEFER, PAUL J. *Heinrich Ewert: Lehrer, Erzieher und Prediger der Mennoniten: Zuege aus seinem Leben und Wirken.* Gretna, ·Man.: Manitoba Jugendorganisation der Mennoniten-Konferenz von Canada,1945.

_____. *Woher? Wohin? Mennoniten! Vol. 3: Die Mennoniten in Canada.* Altona, Man.: Mennonite Agricultural Advisory Committee, 1946.

SCHELLENBERG, DAVE. *. . . to the Glory of God: Steinbach Evangelical Mennonite Church.* n.p., 1975.

SCHMIEDEHAUS, WALTER. *Ein Feste Burg Ist Unser Gott: Der Wanderweg eines Christlichen Siedlervolkes.* Cuauhtemoc, Mexico: G.J. Rempel, 1948.

SCHREIBER, WILLIAM I. *The Fate of the Prussian Mennonites.* Goettingen: Goettingen Research Committee, 1955.

SCHROEDER, GERHARD P. *Miracles of Grace and Judgement.* Lodi, Cal.: By the Author, 1974.

SCHROEDER, WILLIAM. *The Bergthal Colony.* Winnipeg: CMBC Publications, 1974.

SHANK, J.W., et al. *The Gospel Under the Southern Cross.* Scottdale, Pa.: Mennonite Publishing House, 1943.

SIEMENS, JACOB. *Chronik der Schoenfelder Gemeinde von 1925 bis 1968.* n.p., 1968.

SIMONS, MENNO. *The Complete Writings of Menno Simons, c. 1496 – 1561.* Edited by J.C. Wenger. Translated by Leonard Verduin. Scottdale, Pa.: Herald Press, 1956.

SKWAROK, J. *The Ukrainian Settlers in Canada and Their Schools.* Edmonton: n.p., 1958.

SMITH, C. HENRY. *The Coming of the Russian Mennonites: An Episode in the Settling of the Last Frontier, 1874 – 1884.* Berne, Ind.: Mennonite Book Concern, 1927.

――――. *The Story of the Mennonites.* Berne, Ind.: Mennonite Book Concern, 1941.

――――. *The Story of the Mennonites.* 5th ed., rev. and enlarged by Cornelius Krahn. Newton, Kans.: Faith and Life Press, 1981.

SMITH, C. HENRY, and E.I. HIRSCHLER. *The Story of Bluffton College.* Bluffton, Ohio: Bluffton College, 1925.

SNYDER, MABEL. *25th Anniversary of the Hawkesville Mennonite Church.* n.p., 1974.

SNYDER, PETER ETRIL, and A.K. HERRFORT. *Mennonite Country.* St. Jacobs, Ont.: Sand Hill Books, Inc., 1980.

STAUFFER, EZRA. *History of the Alberta-Saskatchewan Mennonite Conference.* Ryley, Alta.: Alberta-Saskatchewan Conference, 1960.

STAYER, JAMES M. *Anabaptists and the Sword.* Lawrence, Kans.: Coronado Press, 1972.

STORMS, EVEREK R. *History of the United Missionary Church.* Elkhart, Ind.: Bethel Publishing Company, 1958.

The Story of the Mennonite Brethren of St. Catharines (Scott St. M.B. Church), 1943 – 1968. n.p., 1968.

SUDERMANN, LEONHARD. *From Russia to America: In Search of Freedom.* Translated by Elmer F. Sudermann. Steinbach, Man.: Derksen Printers, 1974.

SWALM, E.J. *Nonresistance Under Test: A Compilation of Experiences of Conscientious Objectors as Encountered in Two World Wars.* Nappanee, Ind.: E.V. Publishing House, 1949.

TEIGROB, DAVID. *What Mean These Stones? Mennonite Brethren Church, Port Rowan, 1927 – 1977.* Port Rowan: The Congregation, 1977.

TIESSEN, I.H., ed. *Er Fuehret. . . . : Geschichte der Ontario M.B. Gemeinden, 1924 – 1957.* n.p., 1957.

TIESSEN, PAUL, ed. *People Apart: Portrait of a Mennonite World in Waterloo County, Ont.* St. Jacobs, Ont.: Sand Hill Books, Inc., 1977.

TIESSEN, PAUL, and JOHN D. REMPEL, eds. *Forever Summer, Forever Sunday: Peter Gerhard Rempel's Photographs of Mennonites in Russia, 1890 – 1917.* St. Jacobs, Ont.: Sand Hill Books, Inc., 1981.

TILITZKY, JAKE, compiler. *Churches in Profile: Conference of Mennonites in British Columbia.* Clearbrook, B.C., 1978.

TOEWS, A.A., ed. *Mennonitische Maertyrer*. Winnipeg: The Christian Press, 1949.

TOEWS, A.P. *The Coming of the Mennonite Church to Manitoba*. Rosenort, Man.: n.p., 1973.

TOEWS, H.P. *A.H. Unruh, D.D., Lebensgeschichte*. Winnipeg: Christian Press, 1961.

TOEWS, JOHN A. *A History of the Mennonite Brethren Church: Pilgrims and Pioneers*. Edited by A.J. Klassen. Fresno, Cal.: Board of Christian Literature, General Conference of Mennonite Brethren Churches, 1975.

_____ . *Alternative Service in Canada During World War II*. Winnipeg: Publication Committee of the Canadian Conference of the Mennonite Brethren Church, 1959.

_____ . *People of the Way: Selected Essays and Addresses*. Edited by Abe J. Dueck, Herbert Giesbrecht, and Allen R. Guenther. Winnipeg, Manitoba: Historical Committee, Canadian Conference of Mennonite Brethren Churches, 1981.

TOEWS, JOHN B. *Lost Fatherland: The Story of the Mennonite Emigration from Soviet Russia, 1921–1927*. Scottdale, Pa.: Herald Press, 1967.

_____ , ed. *Selected Documents: The Mennonites in Russia from 1917 to 1930*. Winnipeg: Christian Press, 1975.

_____ . *With Courage to Spare: The Life of B.B. Janz (1877–1964)*. Hillsboro, Kans.: Board of Christian Literature, General Conference of Mennonite Brethren Churches, 1978.

The Torchbearer: The Coaldale Bible School Jubilee Yearbook, 1929–1954.

Twenty-fifth Anniversary: Niagara United Mennonite Church, 1938–1963. n.p., 1963.

UNRUH, BENJAMIN HEINRICH. *Fuegung und Fuehrung im Mennonitischen Welthilfswerk, 1920–1933*. Karlsruhe: Heinrich Schneider, 1966.

UNRUH, HANK, et al. *Of Days Gone By: History of the St. Elizabeth District*. St. Elizabeth, Man.: St. Elizabeth Mennonite Community Centennial Reunion Committee, 1970.

UNRUH, JOHN D. *In the Name of Christ: A History of the Mennonite Central Committee and its Service, 1920–1951*. Scottdale, Pa.: Herald Press, 1952.

Vereinigte Mennonite Gemeinden in Ontario. n.p., 1956.

VON ROSENBACH, MARIA. *Family Kaleidoscope: From Russia to Canada*. Vancouver, B.C., 1977.

Waisenverordnung der Sommerfelder Mennoniten Gemeinde in der Provinz Manitoba, Canada. Winnipeg, Man.: Nordwesten, 1913.

WARKENTIN, ABE. *Reflections on our Heritage: A History of Steinbach and the R.M. of Hanover from 1874*. Steinbach, Man.: Derksen Printers, 1971.

WARKENTIN, MARY, and ROSE ANNE RAHN, eds. *The Story of Renata*. Renata, B.C., 1965.

WENGER, JOHN CHRISTIAN. *The Doctrines of the Mennonites*. Scottdale, Pa.: Mennonite Publishing House, 1950.

————. *The Mennonite Church in America*. Scottdale, Pa.: Herald Press, 1966.

————, ed. *The Complete Writings of Menno Simons*. Translated by Leonard Verduin. Scottdale, Pa.: Herald Press, 1956.

WIEBE, GERHARD. *Ursachen und Geschichte der Auswanderungen der Mennoniten aus Russland nach Amerika*. Winnipeg: Nordwesten, n.d.; reprint ed., Cuauhtemoc, Mexico, 1962.

WIEBE, JOHANN. *Die Auswanderung von Russland nach Kanada, 1875*. Cuauhtemoc, Mexico: Campo 6^1/$_2$ Press, 1972.

WIENS, A.K., and GERTRUDE WIENS. *Shadowed by the Great Wall: The Story of Krimmer Mennonite Brethren Missions in Inner Mongolia (1922 - 49)*. Hillsboro, Kans.: Board of Christian Literature, General Conference of Mennonite Brethren Churches, 1979.

WIENS, HENRY J. *The Mennonite Brethren Churches of North America: An Illustrated Survey*. Hillsboro, Kans.: Mennonite Brethren Publishing House, 1954.

WIENS, PETER, ed. *50 Jahre Kolonie Fernheim*. Kolonie Fernheim, Paraguay, 1980.

WILLMS, H.J., ed. *At the Gates of Moscow or God's Gracious Aid Through a Most Difficult and Trying Period*. Translated by George G. Thielman. Yarrow, B.C.: Committee of Mennonite Refugees from the Soviet Union, 1964.

————. *Die Sued-Abbotsford Ansiedlung, Abbotsford, B.C.: Historischer Bericht*. n.p., 1955.

WITMER, LESLIE D. *Pioneers of Christendom in Waterloo County, 1800 - 1967: History of the Hagey-Preston Mennonite Church*. n.p., 1967.

YODER, SANFORD CALVIN. *For Conscience Sake: A Study of Mennonite Migrations Resulting from the World War*. Scottdale, Pa.: Herald Press, 1945.

ZACHARIAS, PETER D. *Reinland, An Experience in Community*. Altona, Man.: Reinland Centennial Committee, 1976.

C. UNPUBLISHED THESES AND DISSERTATIONS

1. M.A. Theses

BERGEN, JOHN JACOB. "A Historical Study of Education in the Municipality of Rhineland." M.Ed. thesis, University of Manitoba, 1959.

DRIEDGER, LEO. "A Sect in Modern Society: A Case Study of the Old Colony Mennonites of Saskatchewan." M.A. thesis, University of Chicago, 1955.

EPP, ESTHER RUTH. "The Origins of Mennonite Central Committee (Canada)." M.A. thesis, University of Manitoba, 1980.

FELSTEAD, ALLAN G. "A Socio-Historical Analysis of the Sectarian Divisions in the Mennonite Church of Waterloo County, 1849-1939." M.A. thesis, University of Waterloo, 1978.

FRANSEN, DAVID. "Canadian Mennonites and Conscientious Objection in World War II." M.A. thesis, University of Waterloo, 1977.

FRIESEN, ABRAHAM. "Emigration in Mennonite History with Special Reference to the Conservative Mennonite Emigration from Canada to Mexico and South America after World War One." M.A. thesis, University of Manitoba, 1960.

FRIESEN, I.I. "The Mennonites of Western Canada, with Special Reference to Education." M. Ed. thesis, University of Saskatchewan, 1934.

FRIESEN, RICHARD JOHN. "Old Colony Mennonite Settlements in Saskatchewan: A Study in Settlement Change." M.A. thesis, University of Alberta, 1975.

HOFFMAN, GEORGE JOSEPH. "The Saskatchewan Provincial Election of 1934: Its Political, Economic, and Social Background." M.A. thesis, University of Saskatchewan, 1973.

KRAHN, JOHN JACOB. "A History of Mennonites in British Columbia." M.A. thesis, University of British Columbia, 1955.

LAWTON, ALMA. "Urban Relief in Saskatchewan in the Depression." M.A. thesis, University of Saskatchewan, 1970.

MATHESON, DON GARFIELD. "The Saskatchewan Relief Commission, 1931-1934: A Study of the Administration of Rural Relief in Saskatchewan during the Early Years of the Depression." M.A. thesis, University of Saskatchewan, 1974.

NEUFELD, ARNIE NORMAN. "The Origin and Early Growth of the Mennonite Brethren Church in Southern Manitoba." M.A. thesis, Mennonite Brethren Biblical Seminary, 1977.

PAETKAU, HENRY. "A Struggle for Survival: The Russian Mennonite Immigrants in Ontario, 1924-1939." M.A. thesis, University of Waterloo, 1977.

PALMER, HOWARD. "Response to Foreign Immigration: Nativism and Ethnic Tolerance in Alberta, 1880-1920." M.A. thesis, University of Alberta, 1971.

RATZLAFF, GERHARD. "An Historical-Political Study of the Mennonites in Paraguay." M.A. thesis, University of Fresno, California, 1974.

SAWATSKY, ARON. "The Mennonites of Alberta and Their Assimilation." M.A. thesis, University of Alberta, 1964.

SAWATSKY, RODNEY. "The Influence of Fundamentalism on Mennonite Nonresistance, 1908-44." M.A. thesis, University of Minnesota, 1973.

TISCHLER, KURT. *The German Canadians in Saskatchewan with Particular Reference to the Language Problem, 1900-1930.* M.A. thesis, University of Saskatchewan, 1978.

VAN DYKE, EDWARD W. "Blumenort: A Study of Persistence in a Sect." M.A. thesis, University of Alberta, 1972.

WIEBE, GEORGE DAVID. "The Hymnody of the Conference of Mennonites in Canada." M.A. thesis, University of Southern California,
1962.
WILLOWS, ANDREW. "A History of the Mennonites, Particularly in
Manitoba." M.A. thesis, University of Manitoba, 1924.

2. Ph.D. Dissertations

APPAVOO, MUTHIAH DAVID. "Religion and Family Among the Markham Mennonites." Ph.D. dissertation, York University, 1978.
AVERY, DONALD H. "Canadian Immigration Policy and the Alien Ques-
tion, 1869–1919: The Anglo-Canadian Perspective." Ph.D. disserta-
tion, University of Western Ontario, 1973.
BERG, WESLEY PETER. "Choral Festivals and Choral Workshops Among
the Mennonites of Manitoba and Saskatchewan, 1900–1960, with an
Account of Early Developments in Russia." Ph.D. dissertation, Uni-
versity of Washington, 1979.
DEAN, WILLIAM WARD. "John Funk and the Mennonite Awakening."
Ph.D. dissertation, State University of Iowa, 1965.
ELLIS, WALTER E. "Galboa to Ichabod: Social & Economic Factors in the
Fundamentalist-Modernist Schisms Among Canadian Baptists, 1894–
1934." Ph.D. dissertation, Pittsburgh Theological Seminary, 1975.
ENS, ADOLF. "Mennonite Relations with Governments: Western Canada,
1870–1925." Ph.D. dissertation, University of Ottawa, 1979.
EPP, FRANK H. "An Analysis of Germanism and National Socialism in the
Immigrant Newspaper of a Canadian Minority Group, the Mennonites,
in the 1930s." Ph.D. dissertation, University of Minnesota, 1965.
FRIESEN, G.A. "The Development of a Western Regional Consciousness,
1896–1921." Ph.D. dissertation, University of Toronto, 1975.
GORZEN, J.W. "Low German in Canada, a Study of 'Plautdietsch' as
Spoken by Mennonite Immigrants from Russia." Ph.D. dissertation,
University of Toronto, 1952.
HAMM, PETER. "Continuity and Change Among Canadian Mennonite
Brethren, 1925–1975: A Study of Socialization and Secularization in
Sectarianism." Ph.D. dissertation, McMaster University, 1978.
JANZEN, WILLIAM. "The Limits of Liberty in Canada: The Experience of
the Mennonites, Hutterites, and Doukhobors." Ph.D. dissertation,
Carleton University, 1981.
LEHN, WALTER. "Rosenthal Low German, Synchronic and Diachronic
Phonology." Ph.D. dissertation, Cornell University, 1957.
MARTENS, HILDEGARD MARGO. "The Relationship of Religious to
Socio-Economic Divisions Among the Mennonites of Dutch-Prussian-
Russian Descent in Canada." Ph.D. dissertation, University of
Toronto, 1977.
REMPEL, DAVID G. "The Mennonite Colonies in New Russia: A Study of

Their Settlement and Economic Development from 1789–1914."
Ph.D. dissertation, Stanford University, 1933.

SAWATSKY, RODNEY. "History and Ideology: American Mennonite
Identity Definition Through History." Ph.D. dissertation, Princeton
University, 1977.

THIELMAN, GEORGE G. "The Canadian Mennonites: A Study of an
Ethnic Group in Relation to the State and Community with Emphasis on
Factors Contributing to Success or Failure of its Adjustment to Canadian
Ways of Living." Ph.D. dissertation, Western Reserve University,
1955.

UNGER, WALTER. "The Niagara Bible Conference." Ph.D. dissertation,
Simon Fraser University, 1982.

URRY, JAMES. "The Closed and the Open: Social and Religious Change
Amongst the Mennonites of Russia (1789–1889)." Ph.D. dissertation,
Oxford University, 1978.

VAN DYKE, EDWARD W. "Blumenort: A Study of Persistence in a Sect."
Ph.D. dissertation, University of Alberta, 1972.

WARKENTIN, JOHN H. "The Mennonite Settlements of Southern Manitoba." Ph.D. dissertation, University of Toronto, 1960.

D. ARCHIVAL SOURCES

1.   British Columbia Archives (BCA),
      Parliament Buildings,
      Victoria, British Columbia,
      Canada.
      V8V 1X4

2.   Centre for Mennonite Brethren Studies in Canada (CMBS),
      77 Henderson Highway,
      Winnipeg, Manitoba,
      Canada.
      R2L 1L1

3.   Conference of Mennonites in Canada Archives (CMCA),
      600 Shaftesbury Blvd.,
      Winnipeg, Manitoba,
      Canada.
      R3P 0M4

4.   Conrad Grebel College Library and Archives (CGC),
      University of Waterloo,
      Waterloo, Ontario,
      Canada.
      N2L 3G6

5. Glenbow-Alberta Institute (GAI),
   9th Avenue and 1st S.E.,
   Calgary, Alberta,
   Canada.
   T2G 0P3

6. Historical Library and Archives,
   Eastern Mennonite College,
   Harrisburg, Va., 22801,
   U.S.A.

7. National Archives and Records Services (NARS),
   Washington, D.C., 20408,
   U.S.A.

8. Provincial Archives of Alberta (PAA),
   12845 102nd Avenue,
   Edmonton, Alberta,
   Canada.
   T5N 0M6

9. Public Archives of Canada (PAC),
   395 Wellington Street,
   Ottawa, Ontario,
   Canada.
   K1A 0N3

Index